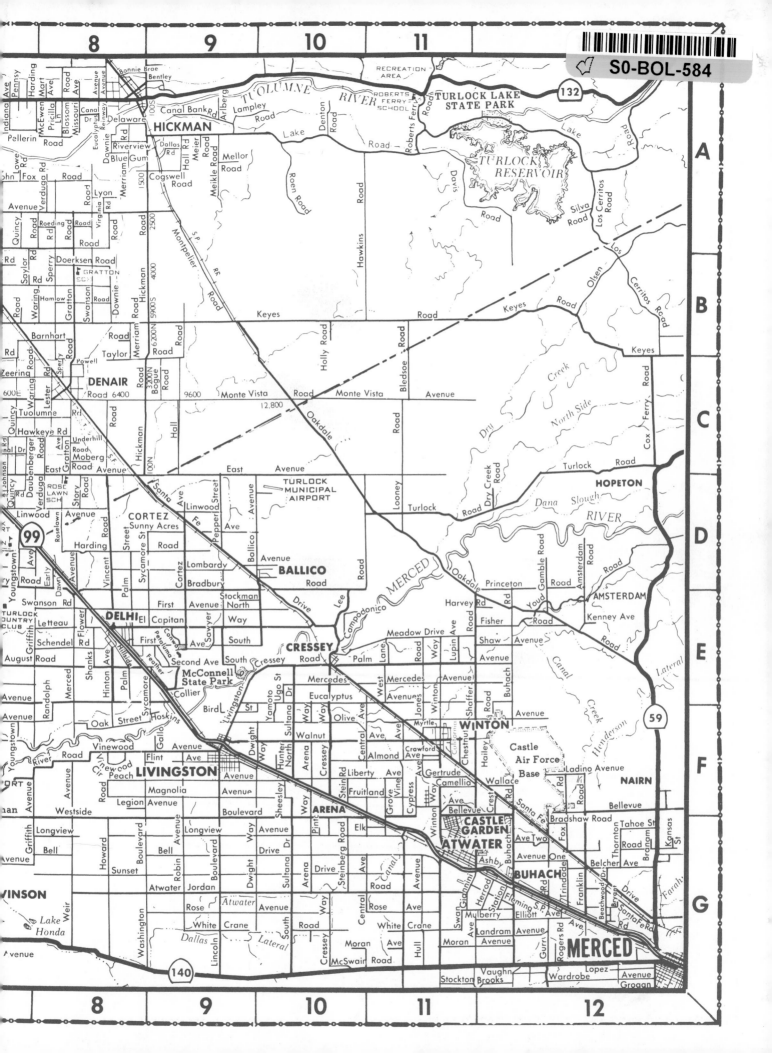

STREAMS IN A THIRSTY LAND

A History of the Turlock Region

LIST OF CO-AUTHORS

Listed below are those individuals who have made substantial contributions to the actual literary form of the work.

Helen Hohenthal, Principal Author

Marjorie Brooks	Tony Kocolas
Douglas Boehme	Doran Kopp
Christine Chance	Carolyn Larson
Chrissie Collins	Helen Manha Miguel
Joe Debely	Roy V. Meikle
Ramon Desagun	Carl W. Muller
Thomas E. Durbin	Victoria Yonan Nevils
Fleming E. Haas	Esther Noda
Margaret Harmon	Ernestine Rojas
Jacqueline Harris	Henry T. Schendel
William Hurd	Margaret Sturtevant
Sarah Sergis Jackson	Mernell Thompson
Geraldine Johnson	Stanley T. Wilson

John E. Caswell, Editor
Original Drawings by Viola Siebe Sonntag

STREAMS IN A THIRSTY LAND

A History of the Turlock Region

By

Helen Alma Hohenthal

And Others

John Edwards Caswell, Editor

Original Drawings by Viola Siebe Sonntag

CITY OF TURLOCK
TURLOCK, CALIFORNIA
1972

ISBN 0-9600622-1-1

LC Card No. 72-91045

Third printing, 1982

Order from Turlock Centennial Foundation
P.O. Box 1694, Turlock, CA 95380

Designed by Peter and Hester Greene
Los Altos, CA 94022

Printed by Peninsula Lithograph Co.
Menlo Park, CA 94025, U.S.A.

Typeset by Editorial Associates
Los Altos, CA 94022

Cover color photography by
Manuel Dias
Modesto, CA 95355

DEDICATED TO

The Pioneer Men And Women
Who Made The Desert Blossom

CONTENTS

Helen Hohenthal, 1962

Biographical Note

Helen Alma Hohenthal, the principal author of this volume, taught history at Turlock High School from 1922 until her retirement in 1962. Early in her teaching career she began work on the master of arts degree at the University of California. Her mentor, the distinguished historian Herbert Eugene Bolton, suggested that she write "A History of the Turlock District." With characteristic diligence and thoroughness, she interviewed old-timers, corresponded with others, searched the files of early newspapers, and turned out a thesis of some 300 pages.

In succeeding years townspeople used her manuscript repeatedly for information on the community. It was particularly useful at the semi-centennials of the Turlock Irrigation District in 1937 and of Turlock's incorporation in 1958.

For long Miss Hohenthal dreamed of bringing the manuscript up to date and having members of different nationality groups tell their stories. This has been achieved at a most appropriate time, Turlock's Centennial Year, when over two hundred individuals, families, and organizations became patrons of the Centennial Pageant and the Centennial History. Many of the individuals had been among Miss Hohenthal's six thousand pupils.

No one of the co-authors has been more diligent in searching out and checking data, no one has had a surer eye for the illuminating story, no one has displayed more affection for all elements in the community than Miss Hohenthal.

Miss Hohenthal was born in Bishop, California. Her father followed John Denair to Turlock in 1907 and bought a tract of forty acres which is now bounded by Berkeley and Johnson, Canal and Marshall Streets. She attended in turn Turlock Grammar School, Hawthorne, Lowell, and Turlock High Schools. In 1917 Miss Hohenthal enrolled in the University of California, graduating in 1921. Her teaching career at Turlock High School began in 1922. For some years she headed both the Social Science and Audio-Visual Departments.

Miss Hohenthal's many years in the community, her wide acquaintance, her training in historical research, and her interest in people have all contributed to the richness of this volume. Turlock is fortunate in having found its historian in Helen Hohenthal.

John E. Caswell, Editor

PATRONS

The following individuals and organizations, by their contributions, have assured the publication of this volume and have financed the Turlock Centennial Pageant presented on 1 and 2 June 1972.

Mr. and Mrs. Carroll E. Adams
Mr. and Mrs. Clarence N. Ahlem
Dr. Judith Ahlem (Mrs. Walter Nilson)
Mr. and Mrs. Wm. R. Ahlem
Mr. and Mrs. E. LaVern Allen
Allen's Home Furnishings
Mr. and Mrs. William E. Allen
Mr. and Mrs. W. Howard Allred
American Legion, Rex Ish Post 88
Dr. Rex D. Anderson
Mr. and Mrs. George J. Arakelian
Mrs. John H. Arakelian
Mrs. A. A. Austerland
Mr. and Mrs. Jerry Baddell
Dr. and Mrs. Lyle A. Baker
Mr. and Mrs. Charles E. Bakke
Mr. and Mrs. Clarence Balisha
Mr. and Mrs. Louis W. Bates
Mrs. Idalene Garnett Batterman
Hazel Berg
In Memory of M. M. Berg
   Mrs. Selma C. Berg and Hazel Berg
Mrs. Selma C. Berg
Bethel Temple
Mr. and Mrs. A. T. Bettencourt
Beulah Covenant Church
Mr. and Mrs. Boies M. Bevans
Mr. and Mrs. Jess Charles Blaker
Dr. Gordon and Mary Lou Bonander
H. Emory and Dorothy G. Bonander
Dr. and Mrs. Marvin P. Brain
Mr. and Mrs. Ralph W. Bridges
Mr. and Mrs. Calvin E. Bright

In Memory of Mrs. Maud H. Britton
   Kathleen Britton
Dr. and Mrs. Joseph E. Bruggman
Dr. and Mrs. John E. Caswell
Dr. and Mrs. Harry D. Channing
Mr. Enoch L. Christoffersen
Mayor and Mrs. Enoch S. Christoffersen
Mr. and Mrs. Holger D. Christoffersen
Mr. and Mrs. Richard Clauss
Mr. and Mrs. Robert R. Coffin, Jr.
Dr. and Mrs. Marion C. Collins
Mr. and Mrs. Walter F. Commons
Mr. and Mrs. J. Hilary Cook
Mr. and Mrs. Jeremy C. Cook
Councilman and Mrs. Darryl E. Crow
Mrs. A. G. Crowell
Mr. and Mrs. A. Verne Crowell
Mr. and Mrs. Gerard J. Crowley
Mr. and Mrs. Chester W. Dahlstrom
Mr. and Mrs. Pershing F. Dahlstrom
Mr. and Mrs. Roy M. Day
Sheldon and Paulyne Decker
Mr. and Mrs. Kelam Divanian
Deet Eichel Volkswagen, Turlock
Doo Brothers
Mr. and Mrs. Leon V. Etnyre
Mr. and Mrs. Wm. R. Fernandes
Mr. and Mrs. Anthony R. Ferreira
Mrs. Francis Fiorini
Free Methodist Church
Mrs. Ruth Hale Gandolfo
Mr. and Mrs. R. Burton Gartin
Dr. and Mrs. Carl Gatlin

Mr. and Mrs. Ernie T. Gemperle
Mr. Paul F. Gibson
Mr. Donald and Mrs. Belle Goldstein
Mr. and Mrs. Guy Gong
Mr. and Mrs. Roger L. Gregg
Mr. and Mrs. Lin H. Griffith
Mr. and Mrs. David M. Gustafson
Mr. and Mrs. Charles C. Hammer
Mr. and Mrs. Wm. (Bill) Hammond
Mr. and Mrs. Dean M. Hanson
Mr. and Mrs. John S. Hardin
Mr. and Mrs. Forrest R. Harkins
Mr. and Mrs. Merle Harmon
Dr. and Mrs. Robert J. Harris
Mr. Robert V. Hendrickson
Mrs. R. J. Hill
Mr. and Mrs. C. E. Hillberg
Mr. and Mrs. Oscar C. Holt
Mr. and Mrs. James G. Hughes
Mr. and Mrs. Edward H. Hutz
Mr. and Mrs. Buddy T. Iwata
Mr. and Mrs. Lamar Jackson
Mr. and Mrs. E. L. Jacobson
Mr. and Mrs. Lowell E. Jessen
Mr. and Mrs. Donald E. Johnson
Dr. and Mrs. Everett H. Johnson
Mr. and Mrs. Lester W. Johnson
Mrs. Fred Johnston
In Memory of Dr. Albert Julien
   Gertrude Julien
Mrs. Mabel Bothun Julien
Dr. and Mrs. Robert K. Julien
Dr. and Mrs. Ronald L. Julien
Mr. and Mrs. George Kapor
Mr. and Mrs. Leroy H. Kennedy
In Memory of Mr. and Mrs. Andrew Larson
   Evelyn and Harold Larson
Mr. and Mrs. Elmer E. Larson
Mr. and Mrs. Verne M. Larson
Mr. and Mrs. Harvey B. Lazar
Mr. and Mrs. E. B. Leduc
Dr. and Mrs. Joseph David Lee
Mrs. August Lindblom
Mr. Harold Lindblom
Kermit and Thora Lindblom
Dr. and Mrs. E. R. Lindsay
Mr. and Mrs. Wallace N. Lindskoog
Mr. and Mrs. Jack Linn
Mr. and Mrs. Harold W. Logsdon
Sam T. Maddox
Mr. and Mrs. M. T. Manha
Mr. and Mrs. Harold F. Markley
Violet M. Mayo

Mr. and Mrs. R. V. Meikle
Mr. and Mrs. Frank S. Mendonsa
Mr. and Mrs. Lee Metzger
Mr. Laurence L. Miller, Sr.
Dr. and Mrs. Donald Walter Moline
Mr. and Mrs. Kenneth A. Monteith
Mr. and Mrs. Gilbert E. Moody
Mr. and Mrs. Shawn Moosekian
Mr. and Mrs. Carl W. Muller
Mr. and Mrs. L. H. McDaniel
Mr. and Mrs. W. Frank McNeff
Mr. and Mrs. Ken Nelson
Mr. and Mrs. Morris K. Nelson
Oliver K. K. and Ruth Nelson
Mayor Protem and Mrs. Joel Nikolauson
Mr. and Mrs. William M. Noda
Mr. and Mrs. Quaile R. Norton
Mr. and Mrs. George H. Nunes
Mr. and Mrs. Gordon D. Olson
Dr. and Mrs. Sidney J. Olson
Mrs. John Franklin Osborn
Pacific Telephone
Mr. and Mrs. John S. Pallios
Mr. and Mrs. John William Palmer
Patterson Frozen Foods, Inc.
Patton Music Co.–L. G. Atherton,
   W. R. Patton
County Supervisor and Mrs. Joash E. Paul
Mr. and Mrs. Philip Paul, Jr.
Mr. and Mrs. Carl R. Peterson
Councilman and Mrs. Dale Pinkney
John H. Pitman
Clarence Pool Family
E. M. and Winifred Raney
Mrs. Stephanie Marie Reach
Mr. and Mrs. Arnold M. Richard
Geoffrey Riches
Madelon Riches
Margaret Gertrude Riches
Ben A. and Mamie L. Roth
Sacred Heart Parish
Mr. and Mrs. Louis J. Santos
Mr. and Mrs. James W. B. Shade
Mr. and Mrs. Arthur M. Silva
Mr. and Mrs. Charles L. Smith
Smith Chevrolet Co.
Mr. and Mrs. Donald J. Smith
Mrs. James H. Smith
Mr. and Mrs. Bernell E. Snider
Mr. and Mrs. Thornton Snider
In Memory of Ed. Soderquist
   Mrs. Ed. Soderquist
Mr. and Mrs. Emanuel J. Soderstrom

Mr. and Mrs. Sam F. Soderstrom
John J. Souza and Zelda A. Souza
Dr. and Mrs. Alfred J. Speckens
Mr. and Mrs. M. Kirk Sperry
Mr. and Mrs. Harold E. Springer
Stop N Save
Mr. and Mrs. Rudolph A. Strunk
Mr. and Mrs. Lester L. Sutherland
Mr. and Mrs. Elwood W. Swanson
Mr. and Mrs. John A. Swenson
Les and Gladys Talkington
Mrs. Lloyd W. Terrell
Mr. and Mrs. W. O. Thompson, Jr.
Mr. and Mrs. LaMonte F. Thornburg
Mr. and Mrs. Andy R. Thorsen
Mr. and Mrs. Rodney J. B. Thorsen
Reynold and Mae Tillner
Dr. and Mrs. V. Stanley Todd
Mr. and Mrs. Everett L. Tomlinson, Sr.
The Torosian Family

Marillyn and Irene Triplett
Turlock Garden Club
Turlock Medical Clinic
V. F. W. Post No. 5059
Mr. Tony J. Volk
Mr. and Mrs. J. Rankin Wallace
Mr. and Mrs. John H. Ward
Dr. and Mrs. Hugh DeVere Washburn
Mrs. Fern B. Wassum/D.B.A. Jake Wassum Ranch
Mr. and Mrs. Roy E. Weaver
Mr. and Mrs. David E. Weise
Mr. and Mrs. Henry J. Weiss
Mr. and Mrs. Charles N. Whitmore
Mr. and Mrs. Stanley T. Wilson
Woods Furniture
Ernie and Sachi Yotsuya
Mr. and Mrs. Gerald T. Yotsuya
Mrs. Esther Youngdale
In Memory of Frank J. Youngdale

ACKNOWLEDGEMENTS

The authors and editor thankfully acknowledge the work of scores of individuals, many of them living, some of them long since dead, who have made this book possible. Such a person was Howard Whipple, whose picture collection and interview notes made in the early 1920s finally came to rest in the Turlock Public Library. Around 1930 Aunt Abby Fulkerth and other pioneers contributed their reminiscenses to Helen Hohenthal. Esther Hall Crowell's knowledge of the Swedish settlement was shared with Geraldine Johnson and Carolyn Larson. Individuals who have contributed research are recognized in the introductory notes to the appropriate chapters. In the footnotes and select list of sources we have sought to recognize all interviewees and others who have supplied substantial amounts of information. The record is less than perfect; the authors have checked scores of facts by telephone calls to friends and acquaintances. To these and others not otherwise acknowledged, we extend our gratitude.

Special thanks are due the co-authors, particularly Carolyn Larson, who gave Miss Hohenthal personal assistance, as well as contributing the chapter on the Swedes. The excellent drawings are the work of Viola Siebe Sonntag, who also served as a consultant in selecting and arranging photographs. Darlene Freeman, instructor in Business at Modesto Junior College, offered her professional skills in typing copy during the summer of 1971; she continued her services during the press of the school year. Alberta Caswell gamely came to the editor's aid, contributing not only her typing skill but also her precise knowledge of grammar and sense of style.

Steve Browning and Jack Claes are responsible for the high quality copying of old photographs. A number of the modern photographs were also taken by Steve Browning. With many older photographs we have not been able to determine the original photographer. We have sought to acknowledge each individual contributor of photographs. Where no contributor is listed, the reader may assume that they have come from one of two principal institutional sources: the Turlock Public Library or the *Turlock Daily Journal.*

The assistance of a number of institutions and their staffs is gratefully acknowledged: the Turlock Public Library, the Turlock Irrigation District, the Chamber of Commerce, the Turlock City Government, the Stanislaus State College Library, and the Stanislaus County Agricultural Extension Service.

The expenses of publication of the Centennial History and of production of the Centennial Pageant have been underwritten by the Patrons whose names are listed earlier in the volume. The authors and all persons who purchase or read this volume are in their debt.

The Turlock Centennial Committee, chaired by Gerard J. Crowley, loyally supported the production of this history as a permanent memorial of Turlock's Centennial Year.

Any moneys realized from sale of the book beyond actual costs, by contract between the principal authors and the City of Turlock, are to be turned over to the non-profit Turlock Centennial Foundation. The Foundation will use income from its endowment to encourage the study of California history and culture in its broadest sense through the awarding of scholarships, prizes, and grants-in-aid. The Foundation is also authorized to accept gifts and bequests, to be administered for the purpose stated.

Materials assembled in the course of writing the volume will be deposited in the Archives of the Stanislaus State College Library for use by responsible researchers. It is hoped that this example will stimulate others to offer manuscripts, correspondence, key records of local governments and business firms, society minutes, memoirs, files of periodicals pertaining to California local history, and similar materials to the Archives for the use of future scholars.

Community cooperation in preparation of the present volume has been outstanding. For this the authors and editor are deeply grateful.

In making our manuscript fit our means, we have had to omit almost half the photographs copied or taken for the volume and several topics which we originally intended to cover. To those individuals who kindly supplied photographs and material we were not able to include, we express our sincere appreciation and regrets.

PREFACE

This is the story of an agricultural region in the heart of the great Central Valley of California, of the principal town within that region, and of the smaller communities surrounding it. We witness the coming of the railroad and the decline of river transportation. We see the growth of wheat ranching in the 1870s and its decay in the 1890s. Next we follow the organization, legal battles, and construction of one of the first two public irrigation districts in California. After water is available, farmers shift to intensive farming: dairying, melons, fruits, and nuts. New groups come in, many of them immigrants: Swedish, Portuguese, Mexican, Assyrian, and Japanese. We see them battling drought, sandstorms, and jack rabbits, and gradually learning which crops are profitable. We see the school children digging a well, the townspeople collecting money for an "opera house," the farm families gathering for barn dances.

The book is also an account of the varied aspects of American life: work and play, religion and entertainment, business and politics, education and medicine. We believe that it has more than local significance, both as a story of the development of agriculture in a key region of California and as a reflection of town life in rural America.

First and foremost, however, we have sought to preserve for future generations of Turlock youth the story of how it was "in the olden days." In doing so, we have come to appreciate more than ever the courage, vision, and endurance of the pioneers who turned a wasteland into a garden and left their descendants the priceless heritage of their own fortitude.

This volume should be thought of as the first, rather than the last word on the history of the Turlock region. We hope that it will stimulate others to research on the area, and on other parts of California as well.

Helen Hohenthal
John E. Caswell

Turlock, California
May 10, 1972

Yokuts Indians' dwellings.

Chapter I

From Discovery to Settlement

Helen Hohenthal and Thomas E. Durbin

The Turlock region lies in the heart of the great Central Valley of California, which is drained by the Sacramento River flowing from the north and the San Joaquin River flowing from the south. Once hot, sandy and inhospitable, a century of labor has transformed it into a land of orchards and vineyards, grainfields and pastures, shady streets and emerald lawns.

The region is bounded on the east by the foothills of the Sierra Nevadas; on a clear winter's day the snow–covered crest of Half Dome in Yosemite Valley can be seen from almost anywhere in the region. On its southern border is the Merced River, whose sparkling waters leap down their gorge from Yosemite. The Tuolumne River, principal tributary of the San Joaquin and source of San Francisco's water supply, forms the northern boundary, while the San Joaquin itself sets off the region from the west side of the Valley.

The history of the Turlock region begins with the exploration of the northern San Joaquin Valley by the Spaniards. Early in the fall of 1806 a little caravan of horseback riders slowly picked its way across Pacheco Pass, eastward bound from the nine–year–old Mission San Juan Bautista. The leader of the party, Lieutenant Gabriel Moraga, had been assigned the task of finding suitable locations for future mission sites in the great interior valley. The route he chose led him across the "west side," past extensive tule swamps,[1] and from the vicinity of Chowchilla to Mariposa Creek and north to the vicinity of the Calaveras River.

Moraga found none of the beauty and color which marked the same scene in the spring of the year. Before the white man began cultivating the soil, early fall found the valley, especially the west side, bare and fruitless after a thorough baking during the long, hot and rainless summer characteristic of the San Joaquin.

Moraga recommended that a mission and a presidio be established on the Merced River. In the next few years Moraga was repeatedly in the valley.[2] His recommendation for the establishment of a mission was not acted upon, and the Indians remained undisturbed in their possession of the San Joaquin Valley until American and British trappers became interested in its economic wealth and opportunities.

Then the Indians' disappearance was so rapid that, by 1840, few remained in the entire northern valley area.[3]

A brief study of the life of these people and of the whites' attitudes toward them will give one a key to the causes of their vanishing. The Indians who dwelt in the Turlock region were of the Yokuts people, the most widespread and probably the largest group of California Indians. Their territory covered most of the San Joaquin Valley. To the east of them in the Sierras and to the north were the Miwok, whose language, like that of the Yokuts, belonged to the broad Penutian family.[4]

The whites who settled in the area in post–Civil War years spoke very derisively of both the Miwok and Yokuts peoples of the northern San Joaquin. They may indeed have observed the Wallalshumnes or, more properly, the Tawalimni Yokuts near Turlock when L. C. Branch wrote,

> The California Indian is anything but an easy subject for civilization. Knowledge he has none: his religion and morals are of the crudest form, while, all in all, he is the most degraded of mortals. He lives without labor and exists for naught save his ease and pleasure.[5]

The Indians lived in rancherias or villages located along the rivers. At one time these rancherias were numerous, each one containing from fifty to one hundred dwellings. Each dwelling, called "ho" if of tule or thatch, "samish" if of bark, housed a separate family. The chief's dwelling was usually the largest and was located in the center of the group. Another important and centrally located structure was the "mosh," the Yokuts' term for the men's sweat house. In the center of each structure a fire was built. All the structures were round and set over pits from one to three feet in depth, typically twelve to fifteen feet in diameter and furnished with grass mats, rabbit–skin blankets, stone utensils, including mortars and pestles for grinding acorns, and basketry containers for food storage.

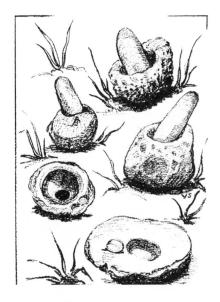

Indian mortars collected by Marie Trent.

Mortars in rock ledge by river.

The chief foods of the Indians were acorns, pine nuts, roots, grass seeds, berries, grasshoppers and fish. The streams of the valley furnished them with good fish which were caught by both spearing and netting. For winter use fish were dried in the sun and stored.[6] One white observer thus described their gathering of vitamin–rich spring greens: "In February and March they live on grass and herbage; clover and wild pea vine are among their best kinds of pasturage. I have seen hundreds of them grazing together in a meadow, like so many cattle."[7] Actually, the Yokuts were specialized food collectors, with a far more perfect knowledge of the total plant and animal food resources than the white observers who thought them to have been "grazing" indiscriminately.

Indian women gathering grasses and seeds.

During the periods of drought, which were frequently felt in this valley, the Indians suffered from famines. The droughts prevented the maturing of grass seeds and the wild animals, in search of food, shifted to other regions.

At various seasons, however, the Indians would go forth and hunt deer, antelope, puma, black bear and the fierce grizzly. Antelope and deer were often separated from their herds or bands and driven into enclosed areas where they were slain. Rabbit drives were also held in which large numbers of those animals were slain and skinned and consumed at once.[8]

For many years after the occupation of the country by the Spaniards, the Indians would desert their rancherias and, lying in ambush, would resist the small groups of Mexicans sent against them from the presidios for the recovery of mission deserters and stolen stock. Upon this last mentioned practice hinges the story of the naming of Stanislaus County.

A neophyte, Estanislao, escaped from Mission San José. He killed mission stock and persuaded other Indians to run away. The government sent out military expeditions against him; but Estanislao, fortified in a thick wood on the Laquismas River (now called Stanislaus), succeeded in repelling the expeditions of both Lieutenant José Antonio Sanchez and Lieutenant (later General) Mariano G. Vallejo in the spring of 1829. Following his victory, the name Stanislaus was applied to the river and later to the county.[9]

Many are the reasons given for the disappearance of the Indians from this valley, but no one reason alone can explain the phenomenon.

Most of the Indian population was wiped out in the spring and summer of 1832, when a pestilence swept over the valley. Until recently it was thought to have been a smallpox epidemic, but according to Frank F. Latta, a tireless researcher on the Yokuts, it was probably measles. The Indians, by their sweat house treatment of the disease, were themselves largely responsible for its disastrous results.

Col. John J. Warner of Los Angeles, who made a trip through the valley in 1832, returning south in 1833, stated that in 1832 there were dead and dying Indians the entire length of the valley, a most pitiful sight; in 1833, he saw not more than eight live Indians from Sacramento to the San Joaquin sloughs, but skulls and skeletons were everywhere in evidence.[10]

The Indian population could hardly have recovered in the sixteen years between the epidemic and the beginning of the Gold Rush. Now the Indians, unable to adapt to the whites' methods of agriculture, found their food supplies gone as the whites slaughtered the game, herded sheep and cattle over the wild grass fields which had yielded the important grasses and seeds needed in the Indian diet, and generally changed the entire environment of the valley. So the Indian villages along the river bottoms were again abandoned and the people returned to the mountains, from which, according to their traditions, the Great Spirit had in anger driven them in the distant past.[11]

The Indian's life was considered of little value by the whites. Upon the slightest pretext, raids were made upon his village. Rarely was the question raised as to the justice of an Indian's death. Leading valley newspapers, such as the *San Joaquin Valley Argus,* frequently carried stories of terrible punishments meted out to Indians for offenses, many of them minor, against the white man's regulations. A horse stolen from a settler would often result in the destruction of an entire village to which a culprit had fled.

Later an attempt was made by the Government of the United States to save the Indians through appointment of a Commission to negotiate treaties of peace and friendship with the various tribes of the Sacramento and San Joaquin Valleys. This Commission, of which three humane men, Redick McKee, George W. Barbour, and Dr. Oliver Wozencraft, were members, finally did negotiate a treaty with six bands of Indians in the vicinity of the Tuolumne and Merced Rivers, numbering possibly a thousand individuals. The treaty was ignored by the settlers, failed of ratification by the Senate, and was buried in the archives for years.

Dr. Wozencraft, in begging the settlers to desist from wholesale killing of the Indians by such expeditions as those of Savage and Burney in 1851, said:

> There is no 'farther west' to which the whites can now push the aborigines. It will either be extermination or domestication. Nothing else is possible. Their very imbecility, poverty, and degradation should, with enlightened and liberal white men entitle them to commiseration and long forbearance.[12]

The provisions of the unratified treaty with the Indians would have substituted for the old plan of paying money annuities,

> Temporary supplies of beef and flour, breeding stock, agricultural implements, seeds, schools, blacksmiths, carpenter substations, etc., to be supported among them for five years, and as much longer as the government may direct.

Twelve parcels of land were to be appropriated "to the use of these tribes and guaranteed to them forever. . ." One of these was "Between the Tuolumne and Merced rivers, about twelve miles east and west by ten or eleven miles north and south, generally hilly and gravelly, some good spots."[13] The area thus defined includes the present eastern half of the Turlock region. As it was below the mining region and seemingly too dry for agriculture, the apparently worthless area was assigned to the Indians. Little did the treaty makers realize that it would be considered valuable agricultural land a century later.

Three Indian reservations were to be established in and immediately adjacent to Stanislaus County (according to its final boundaries) as a result of the treaty of 1851. One was at Knight's Ferry, where G. W. Dent, brother-in-law of U. S. Grant, was Indian agent. Another was across the river from Merced Falls, where George Belt was appointed agent by the Indian Commissioners. The third was set up in the Turlock region, south of the Tuolumne and several miles downstream from Dickenson's Ferry (say, three to four miles west of the Roberts Ferry bridge). Here the Co-co-noon, Apang-as-se, Aplache, and A-wal-ache bands of Yokuts were reported to have gathered, and W. J. Howard, a partner in Belt and Company, set up a store. According to a map of January 1852, 450 Indians had been gathered there.[14] They must have departed rapidly, as at Merced Falls, for a report later in 1852 states that there were but 270 Indians in Stanislaus County, and of that number all but twenty were living in or near Knight's Ferry.[15] There was no Indian opposition to face when American settlers began to preempt the land.

Although the Spanish and Mexicans made no use of the Turlock region, American trappers and traders—the colorful "mountain men"—are known to have been in the area as early as 1826. They were the first to blaze a trail from the American frontier to California, and were the first to bring to the attention of the world the economic opportunities in the San Joaquin Valley.

Jedediah Strong Smith, whom Robert Glass Cleland calls "the true pathfinder of the Sierras," was the first American to have led a party of trappers into the San Joaquin Valley.[16] Smith had just become the senior partner in the fur trading firm of Smith, Jackson and Sublette when he set out to open up new territory west of Salt Lake. One idea behind the expedition was to discover a suitable port in the Oregon Country, then held jointly by the United States and Great Britain.[17] Why he then swung southwest is obscure. Did he want to give the Hudson's Bay Company parties a wide berth? Noting that the Mexican settlements were within thirty miles of the coast, did he expect to trap the streams flowing out of the Sierras without arousing the Mexican authorities?

After a difficult crossing of the Great Basin and the Mohave Desert, Smith led his exhausted party into Mission San Gabriel in mid–November 1826, and was well received by the padres. Ordered out of the province by Governor José Maria de Echeandia, Smith started eastward, then swung northwest, crossed the mountains and entered the San Joaquin Valley. Smith wrote General William Clark, Superintendent of Indian Affairs, that he had traveled "three hundred miles. . .through a country somewhat fertile, in which there was a great many Indians, mostly naked and destitute of arms, with the exception of a few bows and arrows. . .their manner of living is on fish, roots, acorns and grass." On reaching a river that H. C. Dale identifies as the Stanislaus, Smith "found a few beaver, and elk, deer, and antelope in abundance."[18]

Beaver drew the mountain men to the San Joaquin.

Needing to meet his partners at the annual rendezvous, Smith and his whole party started up the American River to cross the Sierras with 1500 pounds of beaver skins. Failing in his attempt, he wended his way back to the Stanislaus and crossed the Sierras with two men and some pack animals. Again he barely survived the desert crossing to the rendezvous at Cache Valley, northeast of Salt Lake.

Recruiting a fresh party, Smith set out southwestward a second time, only to have ten of his men killed by the Mohaves and to be forced once more to seek aid of the Mexican padres.

Smith, with his fellow–survivors, set forth from Mission San Gabriel, crossed or skirted the Turlock region a second time, and rejoined his companions of 1826 where they had been camped on the banks of the Stanislaus.

Smith's two trips marked the beginning of a new age in California. Said Dale Morgan, "Just as Jedediah's appearance in the Snake Country two years before had announced to the British the American oncoming, so now his bursting on the California scene announced to Mexican authority the disintegration of a historic barrier."[19] No longer would deserts and Sierras keep the Americans out.

American and British trappers heard of Smith's reports and headed for California's Central Valley. Ewing Young of Tennessee set out for California in 1829 at the head of a company of forty American, French, and Canadian trappers, including young Christopher "Kit" Carson. They entered the San Joaquin Valley through Tejon Pass. Before going far, they came across some Hudson's Bay Company trappers under Peter Skene Ogden. These two parties "trapped side by side" down the San Joaquin and north to the Sacramento.[20] The presence of the Hudson's Bay trappers in California was part of a strategic plan to trap bare an area between their posts in the Oregon Country and the American trappers' bases in the Rockies. Jedediah Smith's appearing at Fort Vancouver with three other survivors after the rest of his party had been massacred on the Umpqua River had alerted the "Bay's" officers to the incursions of the Americans from the south as well as from the east.

Young was again on the Kings and San Joaquin Rivers in 1832, with another party. Among his fourteen men was a brother of Kit Carson.

In 1833 Joseph Reddeford Walker, leading a group of trappers in the service of Captain Benjamin L. W. Bonneville, set out from the Great Salt Lake region for California. The party crossed the Sierras, striking the headwaters of the Tuolumne River. After many days of difficult traveling they came in sight of the San Joaquin Valley. As they descended into it they found deer and bear in great abundance. They followed the Merced River down to the San Joaquin, on which they trapped for beaver.[21]

By this time a number of mountain men had found their way into California. They were a rough element, disturbing to the Mexican authorities, good horsemen and better rifle shots, in a day when few Californians had as much as a musket. In 1846 a number of them would be Bear Flaggers.

Only a few names and landmarks remain to remind us of the two decades when fur trapping flourished in the San Joaquin Valley. One such name, perhaps, is Beaver Dam, a few miles east of Turlock.

Two United States Government expeditions made the San Joaquin known to the American people through their reports. The Wilkes Expedition reached California in 1841. A boat trip was made up the San Joaquin in October. Reports of the summer's heat impressed the explorers. "The temperatures of Buena Ventura's summers are oppressive, the thermometer ranging, it is said, higher than within the torrid zone, and the heat continuing without cessation."[22]

The second United States exploring expedition to enter the San Joaquin Valley was that of John Charles Frémont, who in 1842, on orders from the Secretary of War, set out to explore the region from the Rockies to the Pacific. Leaving eastern Oregon, he entered what is now western Nevada. There he divided his party, leading one section over Carson Pass, and sending Joseph R. Walker, Bonneville's former subordinate, to enter the valley through what is now known as Walker Pass. Upon reaching the valley, Frémont wrote in his diary that the fields were ablaze with the colors of the wild flowers. Green pastures and scattered groves existed in great numbers.[23]

By the mid-1840s beaver trapping largely ceased because the animals were no longer numerous enough to make it profitable; the bands of elk and deer were being replaced by herds of wild cattle and horses. The Indians were retreating to the Sierras, while immigrant trains were crawling over the mountains and deserts, westward bound to California, and the weak Mexican government was making efforts to keep the Americans out, rightly fearing the loss of California, as it had lost Texas.

The opening wedge had been driven for permanent American settlement in the San Joaquin Valley. Among the earliest settlers in the vicinity of Turlock were Joseph Griffith and William Hawkins, reputedly members of Colonel Ashley's outfit (but not in Smith's party), who after many years of wandering, returned to the valley and settled along the Merced River in 1852.[24] The opportunities and riches of the San Joaquin Valley were to be temporarily neglected for an easier road to wealth. Hardly a year passed, however, before people began to migrate from the creeks of the Mother Lode and the chills of San Francisco to the great interior valley, locating along her rivers. A brief four years passed until settlers along the Tuolumne were demanding a separate county, and Stanislaus was created in 1854. Among the settlements in the county was a small English colony on the south bank of the Tuolumne River, and there the modern history of the Turlock region properly begins.

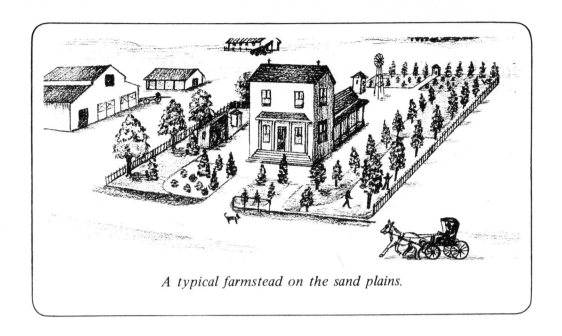

A typical farmstead on the sand plains.

Chapter II

Pioneers and Pioneer Days

Helen Hohenthal

The first settlers in the Turlock region located along the banks of the Tuolumne and San Joaquin Rivers, which form its northern and western boundaries. These waterways furnished them the cheapest and quickest means of transportation; their river–bottom lands gave promise of a plentiful supply of green pasturage, and their trees furnished sufficient timber for temporary dwellings. Here the pioneers found ideal conditions for a location. Nature once more beckoned with an opportunity for free and easy living and those of pioneering instincts responded.

The gold rush days were directly responsible for the settlement of this region. Down from the mining districts came a few who saw greater possibilities of wealth in furnishing the miners with food supplies than in mining. Traders studied the rivers to find how far up into the mining areas they were navigable; stockmen found in the plains wild oats and other grasses on which to fatten cattle for market.[1]

No authentic records are available to show the exact time when the first of these men located here, but it was before 1850.[2] The first of whom we have record was Mr. J. W. Laird. He located in 1846 on the south side of the Tuolumne River. There his herds of wild cattle could roam at will, restricted only by the natural river boundaries.[3] By 1850 Laird and his partners, Dick Riddle and George Smith, had built up a profitable business in raising stock for the market at the mines. At that time beeves sold for six ounces of gold and calves for three ounces. One of the partners, Dick Riddle, used to say that that was a pretty good price, at least for the cattle escaping from the butcher and resold several times.[4]

That a real settlement existed is indicated by the fact that in 1853 Mr. Laird established a private school for about twelve children, including his own and George Smith's. The Laird property was limited finally to several sections of land between the south bank of the Tuolumne and the east bank of the San Joaquin. It was not until after the land was in demand for agriculture that these first settlers found it necessary to buy their range.

The next settler of whom there is record was William K. Wallis. Mr. Wallis, an Englishman,[5] came from his home in Wisconsin by way of Panama to make his fortune in the gold mines. He mined around in Tuolumne County for a while but was not satisfied with his earnings. Hearing of the San Joaquin

Valley as a stock-raising territory, he investigated and decided to locate there, which he did in 1853. He stayed a short while, then placing everything in charge of his partner, went East. Returning in 1861, he found a large herd built up. Just at the time the partners were ready to sell and live off the interest on the proceeds, two unforeseen disasters, the flood of 1862 and the drought of 1864, destroyed three-fourths of the stock. In spite of this Wallis was able to sell some of his share for enough to buy a 1160-acre ranch along the San Joaquin.

Before 1860 three more men moved down from the mines to stock ranches in the vicinity. John Vivian, an Englishman, in 1854 moved to the plains, established a home on the east bank of the San Joaquin, and entered the stock-raising business. Later he bought 4090 acres of land at that place, but only 220 were ever used for grain production. In 1857 two others, John Vincent Davies[6] and John Carpenter,[7] joined them. Davies located along the Tuolumne east of the Laird claims, and Carpenter next to the Vivian claim on the San Joaquin. John Carpenter had crossed the plains in the gold rush days of 1850. He mined for a while with his partner, John Vincent Davies, then engaged in the blacksmith business in Stockton. He returned to the mines and in 1857 moved to the valley. He described this locality at that time as a vast stock range. Homes were located along the rivers exclusively. For forty miles to the east of the San Joaquin River there wasn't a house.[8]

J. H. Carpenter. Courtesy of Vernon Thornburg.

Benjamin Sanders. Courtesy of Vernon Thornburg.

The rest of the English settlers came in the 1860s, with the one exception of Benjamin Sanders who came in 1877. They were Matthew Moyle in 1861, T. K. Wallis in 1865, Thomas Wallace in 1864, and Joe Vincent, the year of whose arrival is not known.[9]

It was while on his way to visit his brother's stock ranch in April 1863, that T. K. Wallis received his first introduction to herds of wild cattle. When he arrived in Stockton, he was informed that no steamer would leave for the San Joaquin River settlements for two weeks. With no stage or team at hand he decided to make the trip across the country on foot. This was a very dangerous undertaking as the grass on knolls was high enough to hide a herd from view until a person was upon it and had no way of escape. The rest of the story is best related in his own words:

> There were no houses on the plains and wild cattle roamed over them at freedom in vast numbers. When travelling between the Stanislaus and Tuolumne Rivers, I saw a band of wild cattle coming toward me, shaking their heads. I immediately fell to the ground and crawled on my hands and knees for a long distance until they had lost sight of me. I afterwards learned that they were infuriated by being caught and branded, and would have killed me had they caught me.[10]

Wallis assisted his brother at branding and working among the cattle for three months; then he left for the mines. At that time these cattle were not even herded. They took care of themselves just as any wild animals do. Once a year, following the Spanish custom, the bands of cattle were rounded up and branded. This process was very dangerous, but the "rodeoing," or branding, was the period of excitement and celebration. Branding was regulated by a settlers' law. No man took his neighbor's stock; should he do so he would be forced to return to that neighbor four times as many as he took.[11]

Cattle raising was not very profitable except during the early days when the miners paid high prices for beef. The lack of profit was due to weather conditions and shipping conditions. A dry season would mean reduction of the herd through starvation. Driving the cattle overland to the market meant a great reduction in their weight before reaching the market.

When cattle were first brought in on the lower plains, elk, antelope, and deer were still plentiful to the east of them.[12] As these herds increased they pushed the animals native to the soil out entirely. Besides the herds of wild cattle, there were thousands of wild horses, mustangs, eating the grass. Sometimes people would try to capture these horses, but not often.[13] They were of little value except for their hides and hoofs and to capture them was a dangerous undertaking. As the roaming herds increased, the grasses no longer were given an opportunity to ripen and reseed the fields. Then the stockmen introduced sheep and pastured the other stock in the mountains or on fields to the south. The flocks of C. C. Baker numbered into the hundreds of thousands as did those of J. W. Mitchell and others.[14] All over the plain, trampled already by thousands of cattle and horses, the sheep now could be seen. One change was made, however. Herders were required to look after them, and so now at regular intervals herders' tents dotted the horizon.

The period 1862 to 1865 marks the transitional stage from stock-raising to farming. Several conditions combined at this time to usher in the new era. The first of these was the famous flood of 1862. Swollen by winter rains, the rivers rose so high that they not only overflowed into the natural river bottom lands, but they also spread out over the low lands until the whole region was flooded. When the waters first began to rise the people drove their herds up into the high lands; but often the water rose so rapidly that herds in safety at sundown were lost by morning. Even after the waters receded the troubles of the stockmen continued. Mrs. M. H. Kittrelle recalled that "thousands of cattle coming back too soon to their old feeding grounds, bogged all over the valley; men patrolled the plains with ropes and shovels digging out the helpless creatures, and shooting all they could not save."[15]

Mark Moyle pointed out to the author the fissure formed by the force of the water. The river at this point is perhaps thirty feet below the top of the banks—a proof that on the Tuolumne irrigation and river shipping could not be carried on at the same time.

From among the stock spared by the flood the drought of 1864 took its toll. There could be no greater tragedy in the stock-raising game than to be forced to look on, powerless to help, while whole herds were being lost through starvation. The profits of many years were wiped out in a few months. Recovery from this blow was a slow process, but the lesson which it taught the stockmen was well learned. They began to supplement the natural grass growth with planted grain.

Another cause of the passing of the stock range was that among the sheep which had gradually replaced the cattle on the plains, a disease broke out which left sheep dying everywhere.[16]

The stockmen had discouraged agriculture whenever it was proposed because it would mean the end of free range for their cattle. One man, whose property was located along the north bank of the Tuolumne, in 1853 sowed a small field of barley. Since it was against the interests of the stockmen he didn't repeat the experiment, but instead talked discouragingly about the use of the soil for farming purposes.[17]

Ten years later settlers moved into the Paradise section and inside of four years made Stanislaus County the greatest grain-producing county in the State of California. By 1868 Stanislaus was producing nearly two and one-half million bushels of wheat a year. Paradise was in the present Modesto region just north of the Tuolumne River and west of the later intersection of Paradise and Carpenter roads. Among the large grain producers at the time were: Timothy Paige of Stockton, who had 4000 acres; John Mitchell, who had nearly 5000; Cressey Brothers, with 2500; Dr. Ashe with 1800; and Mr. N. W.

Longhorns were common until the '70s.

Wells with about 1500 acres. The latter was the man who had experimented with barley growing in 1853. Paige, Mitchell, and Ashe at that time held large acreages in the present Turlock region.[18]

Robert Dallas, another pioneer, who had herded sheep for L. M. Hickman in early days, describes the raising of grain as an "experiment by a few bold adventurous settlers who were tired of the worry of stock raising."[19] One of the first to raise grain was a Mr. Wakefield, who harvested his crop by turning his cattle in on it.[20]

The "experiment" successful, settlers pushed in upon the plains and the stockmen who had not already done so were forced to buy their lands in order to save them from the newcomers. The plow was applied to the virgin soil, trampled on by thousands of animals until it appeared an unattractive wasteland, overrun by weeds which even the sheep refused. Fences, unused during the days of free range, now appeared to confine the stock to pasturage on the poorer soils. The temporary stage of stock raising was over. The wild cattle and horses had given way to sheep; sheep had given way to grain.

With the coming of the railroad the final chapter of the story was written. The raw-boned, long-horned Spanish stock was replaced by better breeds. If the new breeds were perhaps not as sturdy, the provision of sure food and railroad transportation to market made that quality no longer necessary. In noting the passing of the open range, the *Stanislaus County News* of 1871 said, "The vaquero, the branding iron, and the rawhide lariat will soon be relics of a barbarous past."[21]

Migration onto the plains was both from the northern and the southern mines, although those coming in from the south were in many cases here for a short while only, and did not leave their mark upon the history of the region. A Snelling newspaper editor interpreted their migration from the mines to the valley as an indication "that the wealth of California is to be developed with plow and not pick and shovel."[22]

Town development in the Turlock region followed the lines of transportation. In the days of river boat transportation towns developed along the banks of the San Joaquin and Tuolumne Rivers. With the appearance of the railroad and the decline of river navigation, the river communities were deserted and the railroad towns developed.

Most of the river towns were built either on the north side of the Tuolumne or the west side of the San Joaquin. While they were the towns at which the people of the Turlock region traded and shipped their goods, they were not located within the region's boundaries. Only three communities were found within the region before 1871. They were Adamsville, Westport, and the original Empire.

Adamsville was founded by Dr. Adams of Sonora, who later sold his interests there and moved back to Sonora.[23] At what date the town was established is not known but it was probably 1850. It was located on the bank of the Tuolumne, just across from Paradise City, approximately six miles west of the present Modesto Bridge.[24] Like all river towns in the valley, Adamsville hoped to become a great shipping center, and for a time it was important, due to its location on the river route to the mines. When the county was organized in 1854, Adamsville had the honor of being chosen the first county seat. Its glory was short–lived, for in the next few months public opinion changed again and Empire became the county seat. L. C. Branch believed that money was used unsparingly to influence public opinion. While Adamsville was the county seat, officials made use of what accommodations the little town had to offer. Court was held in a little frame building which looked much like a small edition of a cheaply constructed barn.

Several buildings were constructed there, but no trace of them remains today. The largest building was an old two-story hotel, used by Captain Humphrey Jones's family as a residence after the river boat captain had purchased the land and buildings from Dr. Adams. The presence of the hotel indicated the importance of the town as a trading center.

The stories woven about the history of the town before 1855 are representative of all frontier places, especially those that came into existence during the gold rush days. The hangman's noose in the old oak tree and the stories of the wandering ghost of the murdered duelist, George Worth, indicate that, true to the frontier code, human life was not valued highly.

During the floods of 1861–1862 Adamsville, being located on a high bank, was the only place not flooded. It was a place of refuge for the settlers in all the area between the San Joaquin and the south bank of the Tuolumne. For a while the river was one mile wide at Adamsville.

When the first settlers moved onto the plains to the south, Adamsville was one of three possible shipping points for them. The Paradise ferry, operating across the river to Paradise City, carried many loads of Turlock grain to the Paradise mills and warehouses. After 1870 Adamsville became a "ghost" town and today nothing remains to show that it was once a prosperous place.

Westport was just a small community center located at the crossing of Keyes and Carpenter roads. Today, none of the old buildings exist. It was located some distance from the San Joaquin River, but really at the most accessible point for the English colonists.

As early as 1861 Methodist services had been held in the J. V. Davies home and a congregation organized. Later, worship was held in the community schoolhouse. The English colonists had thus made Westport a religious center even before the congregation, numbering less than thirty members, built the Primitive Methodist Church at the northwest corner of the intersection in 1880.[25] Westport was just a crossroads, and at no time could have been called a town.

Land Acquisition in the Turlock Region

The first settlers in the Turlock region were fortunate in having no Mexican land grants engrossing large parts of the area, while later comers were equally fortunate in having no railway land grants forcing them into the hands of a monopoly. The early residents, however, had to wait several years before they were able to obtain legal titles of any sort from the federal or state governments. Meanwhile they "squatted" on the land, confident that United States land laws would be extended to California.

Extension of the Preemption Act to California in March 1853 did not immediately affect this area. This act permitted people who had been in the state prior to a specified date to claim 160 acres of federal land as a gift. The first claim applying to the Turlock region in the Stanislaus County Preemption Book is dated 27 July 1854.

Meanwhile the Legislature of 1852 provided for sale of land under the federal Swamp and Overflow Lands Act of 1850, which donated such lands to the State. Under this act a person could purchase up to 160 acres for $1 an acre in cash, or pay off over five years, and by proving that he had put in money to reclaim the land, receive a refund up to the amount of his payments.[26] First to file on overflow lands in this region was Jacob Harvey Gardenhire, who on 9 November 1855 claimed 80 acres just downstream from Dickenson's Ferry on the Tuolumne.[27]

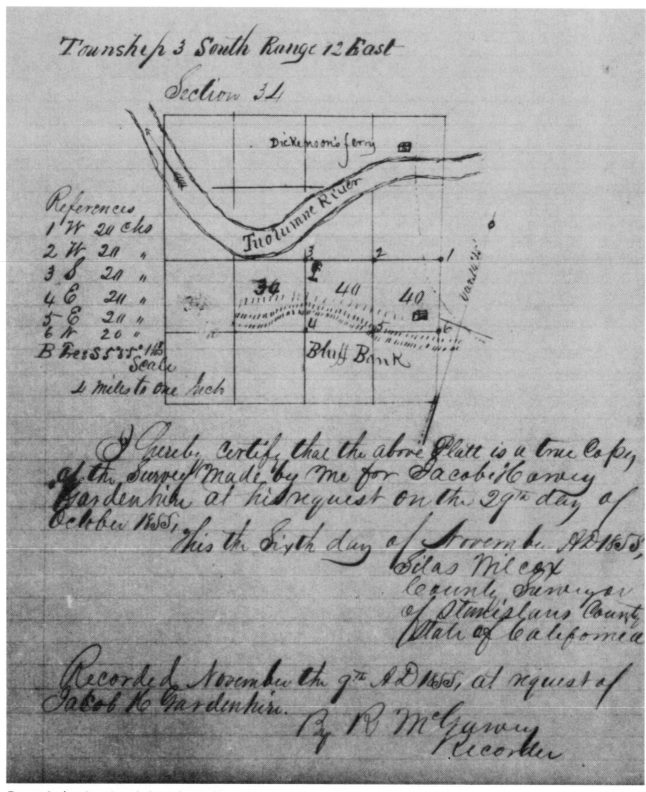

Recorder's sketch of first land claimed under Swamp and Overflow Act.
Courtesy Stanislaus County Recorder.

When a Federal Land Office opened a new tract for sale, the lands were first put up for auction. Parcels not sold could be purchased for $1.25 an acre, and most land in the Turlock region probably went for the minimum price.

There were several ways of purchasing federal lands without paying full price. Mexican War veterans (and later other veterans) were given Military Bounty Warrants entitling them to land from the public domain in proportion to their length of service. Many veterans preferred to sell their warrants at a discount rather than seek new land in the West. Much land in the Turlock district was paid for in military warrants between 1857 and 1867. Similarly, Agricultural College Scrip was issued to the states to finance the establishment of land grant colleges. This was sold by some states for as little as 65 cents an acre.[28]

The Homestead Act of 1862 functioned much like the Preemption Act, giving a settler 160 acres free in return for building a cabin and doing a minimum of development. A number of homesteads were taken up in the region, but they represented a minor fraction of the area.

John W. Mitchell, the founder of Turlock, began heavy land purchases in the region in the summer of 1867. A real wave of speculation hit the area a year later, when it became known that the Central Pacific planned to build a railroad to Visalia. Among the large investors were L. M. Hickman; Colonel Daniel Whitmore; G. W. Kidd, a banker of Stockton; and W. S. Chapman, a well known California land speculator. Much of the land was paid for in Agricultural College Scrip.[29]

By the end of 1868, most of the land in the Turlock area had been alienated from the public domain. The large holdings made possible the application of large machines to wheat farming and helped Stanislaus in a few short years to become one of the leading wheat counties of the nation.

Farmers Hotel stable with Stephen Crane house and outbuildings.

Chapter III

Settlement Spreads to the Sand Plains

Helen Hohenthal

The abundant crop of 1866 in the Paradise section sent many of its grain farmers southward across the Tuolumne into the present Turlock region.[1] Dr. Richard P. Ashe, one of these, in the fall of 1866 located east of the present site of Keyes. In the spring of 1867 he summer–fallowed a part of his 2720 acres and erected a house and barn. That winter he put the whole in grain. The summer–fallowed ground produced sixty bushels of barley per acre and from the rest he secured a fine wheat crop. In 1868 he put up granaries and the rest of the buildings necessary on a large grain ranch.[2]

Two other prosperous Paradise farmers, John W. Mitchell and Timothy Paige, soon followed in Ashe's footsteps. Mitchell's extensive holdings stretched from the Ashe property at Keyes to Atwater in Merced County.[3] Timothy Paige located southwest of the Mitchell and Ashe properties. On the land which he had formerly used for sheep ranges, Mitchell now raised bumper grain crops.[4]

In the fall of 1867 three other families moved into the district: Colonel Daniel Whitmore and his family, his friend C. P. Warner, and Warner's son-in-law, John Service. Whitmore and Warner had crossed the plains together in 1854. Whitmore had a ranch near Stockton, while Warner had located near Auburn. Service had crossed the plains as a lad of twenty in 1859. He and Warner's daughter, Julia, were married in July 1867. Shortly after that, Whitmore invited the Warners to join him on new land south of the Tuolumne, for he had grown tired of farming the heavy peat soil around Stockton. Warner and Service took land in partnership. The three families settled on and near the present site of Ceres. Their first homes were small frame houses, which were later supplanted by substantial homes.[5]

Of the three pioneers, Daniel Whitmore took up the largest amount of land, still possessing over 9000 acres in 1880. This he rented out to tenants in sections ranging from 800 to 1000 acres. His permanent home was located in the town of Ceres which he founded in 1870. The Warners soon returned to Auburn because of his health. The Services combined the occupation of farming with that of storekeeping, establishing a store in Ceres. They raised a typical pioneer's family, consisting of eight boys and three girls.

To the south and west of the Ceres settlement, another group as early as 1867 was making plans for farming. The first person is not known but both Edward McCabe, the leader of the Irish Colony in the district, and William L. Fulkerth came about the same time in 1868. Mrs. Fulkerth, known to the community best by her title of "Aunt Abby," described very vividly the pioneers' first impressions of the district. She said that the owners had been trying to get people to settle here but they would leave after one look. "Not even a chicken could live here," they said. Mr. Fulkerth came first and bought a section of land from the government. Then he shipped lumber from Stockton on a river boat to Crows Landing, from which they hauled it by team across the open fields. When the house was completed except for the doors and windows, Mr. Fulkerth brought "Aunt Abby" down from Stockton. She described her arrival and subsequent experiences:

> From the river boat at Crows Landing they hauled me across to my new home on a mattress. I was seriously ill with consumption but I loved this place from the first time I saw it and I knew I would get well. Over the open fields we drove through tall weeds until we suddenly came upon our place. It was the only home to be seen. I stayed in bed for six months after I arrived but I did get well. One time I was very sick and I needed a woman to care for me. The men tried to think of some one, and finally they recalled seeing one around a sheepherder's tent many miles away. Only my little niece was with me and she was hardly more than a baby but someone had to find that woman, so they hitched up a horse, it was very wild, and telling her in what general direction to go, gave her the reins. She found the place and brought back Mrs. Allen, Stonewall Allen's mother, who took care of me. It was a miracle that the little girl could make the trip in safety and a still greater miracle that she found Mrs. Allen. The Allens had been trying to make a home out of a shack and tent on Mitchell property. Besides the Allens the other two early families were the McCabes and Hessions. McCabe moved a house over from Tuolumne City and old Mike Hession. . .and his wife said they would build a house and they did.[6]

In the next decade many more pioneer families joined those already mentioned. A boom in land sales began in 1867 and 1868, but the date of purchase had no necessary relationship to the time of settlement. Some of the river settlers had been on the land close to twenty years before they found it necessary to purchase their ranges. Others purchased land, but did not move on immediately. Still others bought as a speculation, with no intention of settling. The following table gives the dates of arrival of some of the prominent early families on the plains, and an idea of the area where they settled.

Prominent Early Plains Settlers[7]

*Asterisks indicate families whose arrival date is uncertain.

YEAR	FAMILY	LOCATION
1867	Daniel Whitmore	Ceres
	C. P. Warner	Ceres
	John Service	Ceres
	T. Harp*	Ceres
1868	James Kehoe	Irish Colony, NW of Turlock
	Henry Osborn[8]	W of Turlock
1869	W. L. Fulkerth	Irish Colony
	Richard Whitmore	Ceres
	George Tully*	Ceres
	L. M. Hickman	Hickman (in area for a decade)

Prominent Early Plains Settlers (Continued)

YEAR	FAMILY	LOCATION
1869	John Dallas*	Hickman
	Robert Dallas*	Hickman
	Levi Jones	?
1870	Willis Bledsoe	NE of Turlock, about 12 miles
	Asa Fulkerth	Irish Colony
	Tom Fulkerth	Irish Colony
1871	S. H. Crane[8]	E of Turlock
	J. G. Annear	Ceres
1872	E. V. Cogswell	Hickman
	Michael Joyce	Irish Colony
1874	Henry S. Geer[8]	NE of Turlock
1875	Daniel Casey	Irish Colony
1878	I. W. Updike	Irish Colony
1879	W. H. Thornburg	E of Hill's Ferry

Some of the newcomers took up government land first, then later bought from private owners enough to satisfy themselves. Others just rented the land from such men as Mitchell and Whitmore in about 1000-acre pieces. Mitchell would advance the expenses for seed, feed for the teams, and so forth, for half of the crop at harvest time. All over his vast holdings he built substantial homes for his tenants: the typical two-story frame houses of that day. One of the best known of these was the old white house at the present site of Delhi, the only thing that really marked the existence of the station. In early days Mitchell also had a frame warehouse there from which to ship his grain.

As long as the price of grain remained high it was more profitable to rent out or farm the land than to sell it. The crop prospects around Turlock attracted city capital as a good investment and so, like the Ashe and Ryer purchases of an earlier date, land now exchanged ownership in very large amounts. The earliest large sale on record at this time was the sale by Mitchell of 61,000 acres to two large speculators, A J. Pope and J. O. Earl of San Francisco.[9]

Some men came into the district with a little capital and while prices were good they appeared to be well-to-do. With the failure of the grain crops in the 1880s many lost their holdings and admitted their failure. Such a man was J. J. Crossley who once owned most of the present Youngstown colony.[10] Others came with almost nothing and became wealthy by their labor and foresight. The outstanding example of this type was George Tully. His original capital was a bunch of mules. With these he plowed land for men who had purchased it with Civil War script; in return they traded or paid him one section of land for every one he plowed for them. When he died he left an estate of about three thousand acres and a great deal of money, $10,000 of which was found sewed up in the lining of his clothing.[11]

By 1870 grain raising was no longer an experiment. The "golden age" had been ushered in by a bountiful harvest from over 60,000 acres in 1868 and the next few years saw the rest of the land in the region under cultivation. It was not until thirty years later that the people emerged from this grain growing era. Their history, therefore, can only be given with the story of grain production constantly in the foreground.

The farmers' year began with the fall rains. Should the dry season be prolonged into the early fall, great anxiety was felt. No rain meant no crop, and no crop brought in its train the horrors of mortgages, failure, hard times, and perhaps even the loss of the property itself. One writer referred to those autumn days before the rains as "gloomy days of drought."[12]

As soon as the rains were sufficient to permit plowing, on every farm the gang plows were brought out to turn the soil for seeding. Each plow in the gang plow cut a furrow one foot wide and from three to six inches deep. While most of the farmers used a span of horses for each plow in the gang, some were able to operate a six–gang plow with only eight horses. At first the surface of the soil was barely scratched, the plow often going no deeper than three inches. A five-gang plow handled about eight acres a day, at a cost for large acreages of from forty cents to a dollar per acre. A harrow and seeder followed the plow. The amount of seed sown varied, but it averaged about one and one-half bushels to the acre.[13] In a good season during the early years, a typical crop would run about fifteen bushels per acre, a return of ten for one.

The seed once in, the farmer rested until the harvesting season, although sometimes the hauling in of the old crop was not completed until after the new one was sown. Some of these farmers said that they were always busy. No valley newspaper went to press during the growing season without detailed accounts of the rains, the drought, and the appearance of the growing fields. Fortunes were made and lost by a few inches more or less of rain. Sometimes glowing predictions of bumper crops filled the paper. Again, late in the growing season, when rains no longer could help, came reports which spelled tragedy for many. Take for example the dry year of 1870.

> 6 May 1870. "Yield of grain exceedingly light. . .at most not over half a crop. . .due to lack of rain. Crops look sickly."

> 13 May 1870. "The drought has reduced the crop in Stanislaus County from four and a half million bushels to two and a half million. . .the population of 5000 people has suffered a loss of two to three million dollars in income."

> 20 May 1870. "Unusual good spot of grain half way between the Merced and Tuolumne rivers. . .rest shows the effect of drought."

> 27 May 1870. "New demands for irrigation as the result of drought."[14]

Preparations for the harvesting season started about the first of June, as soon as the grain was headed and turning yellow. Only a few farmers owned threshing machines; among them were the Fulkerth brothers, Levi Carter, John Fox, and somewhat later a group of five which included John Service. Machines were overhauled and improvements made in preparation for the intensive activity of the weeks of harvesting. Rye and barley were the first grains ready to be threshed; wheat required longer to ripen.

Under the oldest method, a reaper was pushed from behind by eight to twenty-four horses, depend–ing on the width of the swath to be cut. It was then collected and bound into sheaves by a binder, and delivered to the thresher.

The header soon replaced the reaper in the San Joaquin Valley. The driver rode upon the tongue of the machine with his eyes upon the grain and his hand on a lever by which he raised or lowered the scythe, thus securing the heads of grain and little of the stalk. An endless belt carried the heads up a slanting gangway and dumped them into the "header wagon." The latter had a box on the bed very low on the side next to the reaper, and very high on the opposite side; it was driven close alongside the reaper, one man doing the driving and another, by means of a fork, pushing the heads away as the gangway of the reaper threw them into the wagon. As soon as a wagon was full it was driven away to the thresher. There, two men with forks pitched the wheat upon a platform six or eight feet high, while four others fed it to the separator. At the far end of the machine clouds of threshed straw and chaff fell to the ground, soon to be dragged away by a twelve-foot horse-drawn wooden shovel. At the side, protected by a canvas awning from the dust and chaff, a man filled sacks from the steady stream of newly threshed grain while another man sewed up the ends of the sacks and carried them out to a pile.

The power of the thresher was provided by what appeared to be an old-fashioned locomotive, but which was in reality a steam engine upon wheels. In the front of it stood the engineer, who fed the engine either with wood or waste straw.[15] Under the fire box a large tank of water caught the sparks and burning straws as they dropped. A tight-box water wagon supplied the water, which when made into steam caused a large driving wheel to revolve rapidly. This wheel was connected with the separator, some thirty feet away, by means of a long belt. As long as waste straw was used the cost of harvesting was not high, but it was slow.[16] In 1868 Mitchell estimated that it would take him two months to thresh 5000 acres by steam power.[17]

Threshing machine. Here a steam engine furnished the power.
From L. C. Branch, History of Stanislaus County, 1881.

In 1878 one of Tom Young's threshing machines, run by an Enright engine, threshed 1618 sacks of grain in one day on the Henry Osborn place near Turlock. Since the grain was already stacked in four stacks this required that the machine had to be moved (at one time a mile) and set three times. The longest run was three hours and twenty minutes, in which time 664 sacks were threshed. The whole run was nine hours and forty-five minutes. The machine was managed by J. T. Thompson of Modesto, considered at that time one of the state's best machinists.[18]

That year, 1878, was a happy one in the farmer's calendar, because a very heavy crop followed a slender one in the previous drought. As early as July four machines were working in the fields immediately surrounding the town of Turlock. In fact, as late as September of that year newspapers claimed that the number of threshing machines was insufficient to handle the crop.[19] The cost of threshing the grain was estimated to be eight cents a bushel, including board and room for the men, that year. The average yield was twenty to twenty-five bushels per acre (twelve to fifteen sacks). A still heavier tax on the farmer's profits was that of sack costs. In 1872 sacks cost twenty-two cents apiece, when wheat was selling for $1.32 a hundred-pound sack.[20]

The combined harvester came into use about 1880.[21] By this method the harvester cut, threshed, and sacked the wheat as it went over the field. The machines were drawn by twenty-four to thirty-two horses or mules and cut swaths sixteen to thirty feet wide. They could harvest forty or more acres in a day, and were especially valuable to farmers possessing several thousand acres in a single field. Some of these "patches" were so large that the machines could only go around the field four or five times from sunrise to sunset.

L. C. Branch in describing the first harvesters said,

> We were astonished at the sight, and looked long in wonder and amazement at a combined header and thresher. Twenty-four horses were pushing this immense machine over the ground, and as it passed along dropped sacks filled with wheat.

View of "combine." Courtesy of George Sperry.

It is worth a long journey to see this wonderful machine, with its twenty-four horses trained like circus animals, and all moving at the command of the man 'at the wheel' who guides the header by a tiller attached to a wheel at the end of the tongue, which acts as a rudder for this 'agricultural ship.' While watching its operations the writer wonders if on his next trip that way he would not also see the grist-mill attached and the machine throwing off sacks of flour.[22]

When the combines first appeared, they had serious flaws which the farmers tried to correct. In 1886 H. F. Geer of Turlock proudly announced that he had fixed his Houser Combined Harvester so that it would always produce clean grain regardless of the weed seeds present.[23]

From field to field the harvesters pushed their way; no roads or fences interrupted a short cut to the next job and so, like the modern war tanks, they moved slowly but surely on their way.

A harvesting crew presented an interesting study in itself. Gathering its members from the homes of the farmers and from the wandering workers of the valley, a crew contained representatives of every type and class and almost every race. The mass were seasonal workers, many of whom returned year after year to thresh for the same farmer.

The harvester's day started at 3:30 a.m. and frequently lasted until 9 p.m. For such hours he was paid $2.00 or thereabouts a day during the season.[24] Should he be hired during the winter months, wages would be $1.00 a day.[25] Mr. Moyle said, "At first you felt pretty sore but after a while the hard work built up your muscles and by the end of the season you were in excellent condition."

Accidents were numerous during the harvest season. Each week the papers carried stories of arms and feet horribly crushed as they were accidentally caught in the revolving cylinders. The county hospital was crowded beyond capacity at this time.[26] Many of the tragedies could be attributed to carelessness and indifference, but it must be admitted that no pains were taken to make the machinery accident-proof. Insurance of workers was an idea not yet born; every man had to take upon his own shoulders the responsibility for his well-being.[27]

Before 1878, the crews were fed in the farm homes. The women as well as the men were drawn into the labor of harvest. The kitchens in the old homes frequently were constructed so that long tables and benches could be arranged at which the crew was served. The women worked upon a cooperative basis, all helping at the place where the crew happened to be. A harvesting crew was a hungry bunch, never too tired to eat of the home-cooked foods which these women heaped upon the table.

In 1878 some kind husband thought up the idea of a cook wagon to accompany the harvester.[28] So great was its popularity that even today the idea is in use. The cook wagon was a kitchen on wheels; at one end a range was located, and down the length of the wagon was a long center table at which the meals were served. The whole was screened, so no flies worried the diners. It was the rule of the camp never to stint on meals—no matter how hearty the appetite, plenty was provided.[29]

During the week there was little time for relaxation except in the form of sleep. The men slept out in the open, laying their blankets on a straw stack, as comfortable to the tired worker as the softest mattress in the world. Saturday was pay-day, the finest day in the week. At this time banks did not exist in the rural regions, so cash was used instead of checks. The money was brought out to camp in a sack and distributed among the men. No cases are known of a robbery occurring during the procedure. Men were careless in handling money, trusting one another much more than they do today. Col. Wood repeated a story concerning One-arm Hughson and his money. He went to the Tynan Hotel in Modesto one night and rented a room. Once in it, he threw a sack of $20 gold pieces under the bed and slept soundly that night. The sack, it was said, contained $8,000.[30]

Quarrels in camp were frequent, some ending in tragedy. Men were very handy with knives and guns, and when liquor was present the danger was increased. It took little to provoke a quarrel when all concerned were too tired or too drunk to think.

An interesting case is recorded involving two workers on the Pope ranch east of Turlock. In a scuffle which came as the result of an argument, one laborer stabbed another. The assailant escaped while other workers were taking care of the victim. He struck out across the country to the north, heading for the Tuolumne River. A posse took up the chase, but while they were beating the brush in one section of the river bottom, the man eluded them, and thinking he was safe, he became bolder and appeared in a small open space just as the sheriff who had been separated from the posse entered it from the other side. Possessing no gun, the culprit was easily captured.

Men were willing to work on harvester crews, but the manager of a harvester crew often had difficulty in rounding up his crew Sunday evening or Monday morning. Sometimes he would be forced to get an entirely new crew due to "overcelebration" on the part of the previous one. Monday was a real "blue Monday" and "broke" Monday for most of the men. With long periods of unemployment followed by back-breaking work for a few months it is easy to understand why saloons and gambling dens flourished as they did, and why Turlock at one time in her history had as many saloons and bars as she did private homes.[31]

Saturday evening and Sunday meant not only rest or recreation; they also stood for the weekly cleanup of both the worker and his clothes. A few of the workers sent their washing in to the Chinese laundry; the rest would make some attempt at rinsing them out, or simply would wear their clothes until they were beyond redemption and then destroy them. Colonel Wood, who himself worked with the harvesting crew, said the men would do their own washing after a fashion on Sundays, then on Monday morning they would hit their clothes against a wagon wheel to knock out the dust.

The luxury of a steam bath was theirs, too. After work was over on Saturday night, while the steam was being blown off from the boiler, the entire crew would take a bath in the exhaust steam.[32]

One of the greatest hazards facing the farmer was the possibility of fire, not only before harvesting but even after the grain was in the warehouse. A grain fire once started was difficult to put out. All people watched for signs of smoke and reported them immediately. A man coming in from Hill's Ferry one afternoon discovered a fire in John Osborn's field. Twenty acres were burned over before it could be put out.[33]

Children were early taught the meaning of fire. Mrs. Thomas Menzies related a story of her own experience with a fire. In those days the sandy roads were strawed to permit the heavily loaded grain wagons to pass over them. "I can remember one hot day when Father and Mother were gone I discovered the straw in the road on fire. I knew if it were left to burn, the dry grass would carry it to the grain fields on both sides of the road and many acres of grain would be destroyed. So I frantically threw sand on it until it was partially smothered, then carried bucket after bucket of water from our pump until it was out."[34] Old settlers said that fires were often set.

Self-reliant Bertha Lander (Mrs. Thomas Menzies)
saved the grain fields from fire.

As soon as the threshing was over, and sometimes even sooner, **hauling the grain to the river piers** and warehouses commenced. During the time when the people had a choice of either shipping by water or hauling overland to Stockton, all efforts were bent on getting it in as soon as possible, for with the fall of the water level river shipping stopped.

All day long, lumbering grain wagons with a trailer or two behind could be seen hauling the grain over the straw-covered roads to the nearest shipping point. Drawn by six to ten horses, these old clumsy wagons creaked and groaned under their loads as they moved over the fields to one of the few main roads. The trip to Stockton with one load took several days; from the more distant ranches east of Turlock the minimum time for the round trip was three days.

Teams had to be cared for on the way, so every logical stopping place became also a roadhouse at which "refreshments" were served to the drivers. The drivers prided themselves on managing their teams with a single line, or jerkline, and their extensive and profane vocabularies, without which, according to them, no team could be handled.

Later such men as L. M. Hickman, with their very extensive ranches, would advertise for six, eight, and ten-horse teams to haul grain to Ceres and Turlock. In order to reach Turlock on time, the teamsters on nearby ranches were up and off with their loads by three o'clock in the morning. Only one trip a day was made, for by noon there were so many wagons standing in line waiting for their turn to be unloaded that the lines extended sometimes outside of the town itself. With some wagons carrying six to nine tons, an idea can be gained of the amount of grain produced in the immediate neighborhood of Turlock. One time a man counted six hundred mules and horses in Turlock on a single day, all engaged in the hauling business.[35]

Accidents during the hauling season were as numerous as during the threshing days. Riding on a load of grain sacks was not as simple as it might appear. Two examples will illustrate this point. On 11 August 1878, Dr. Thomas E. Tynan, while driving from his ranch to Ceres with a load of grain sacks, was thrown from the wagon and his right arm was broken. He mounted his wagon, drove on to Ceres and unloaded, then on to Modesto where his arm was set. A week later the same paper recorded the following:

> Mr. John Ireland, a rancher residing about eight miles from Turlock, met with a terrible accident Monday. He was hauling grain from his ranch to Turlock, when three miles from his home, with a load of sixty sacks, the weight of the grain forced the end board out, precipitating Mr. Ireland, who was sitting on the grain, to the ground. Both wheels passed over his hands and feet, breaking nearly all the bones. His head also was injured. He has a large family dependent on his industry for support.[36]

With the grain hauling once over, the little towns settled down to their usual routine of business. The two most important shipping and warehousing centers at that time were Ceres and Turlock. In Turlock the warehouses of H. S. Crane, J. W. Mitchell, Charles Dallas, Hall and Russell, and the Grange Company were lined up along the track. In these the farmers stored their grain and then shipped it out during the winter and spring when grain prices were higher. During the hauling season in good years a steady stream of railroad cars carried the grain away as fast as they could be loaded. In 1878 three trains a day of forty cars each were not enough to carry the grain out of the valley. The cars loaded for Stockton on one day came back empty the next.

By August warehouses were filled to the roof and shipment was only limited by the number of cars available at the railroad stations. Everywhere warehousemen competed for the use of the empty cars, even as today in the summer and fall, shippers compete for the use of refrigerator cars for eastern shipment of perishable fruits. According to Sam Strauss, in the summer and fall of 1880 grain was hauled so rapidly to the warehouses in Turlock that they were filled to capacity. The rest was stacked in a long and broad pile extending along Front Street almost from Main to Crane, some two hundred and fifty feet. Over the pile the shippers constructed a shed. Not only were the railroads taxed to the limit, but in the river towns likewise, grain could not be shipped as rapidly as it was brought in.[37] Mark Moyle recalled seeing grain stacked on the Grayson piers and beyond them for the distance of half a mile, although on some days the boats would take away as much as 24,000 sacks. Mr. Moyle had also seen as much as 700 tons on a barge at a time, an exceedingly large load.[38]

Hills Ferry on the San Joaquin, 1880. A trail led to Turlock. From Branch's History.

For a time after the Central Pacific line was constructed, trade with Stockton took a set-back. Many preferred shipping directly to San Francisco, which accounts for the attempts of Stockton shippers to regain trade by such advertisements as the following:

> The Central Pacific Railroad charges $1.15 per ton less to carry wheat from all stations on the line of their road to Stockton than to San Francisco, and by boat the Stockton Transportation Company carries wheat to San Francisco by water for as low as $0.75 a ton; never higher than $1.00. Our facilities are such that all wheat can be disposed of, to first hands or to English houses direct for one per cent commission. The Stockton Transportation Company is operating (and mostly owned by the Stockton Warehouse Company) in connection with the **Warehouse Company**. There is a side track of the C. P. R. R. here, too, and wheat

can be transferred from cars to either the warehouse or steamer without extra charge.

In bidding for the farmers' business this warehouse company also advertised that it lent money at 10 percent on wheat stored in its warehouse, the interest to be compounded only semi–annually. Storage charges on the grain were $1.00 per ton for the season. The capacity of this warehouse was 24,000 tons.[39]

Besides the grain shipped to Stockton and San Francisco, a considerable amount was used by the Paradise Flour Mill. The Paradise Mill turned out a high grade of flour and in the '70s a great deal of the wheat from this district was hauled to it. T. C. McCumber, who operated the Paradise ferry, reported in August 1878 that as many as sixteen teams were making the round trip to the mill daily.[40] Big teams drawing the wagons were charged 25 cents for the first span and 10 cents for each additional span.[41] The Paradise Mills were the pride of the valley. Had they been located in any town on the railroad line they might have continued in operation for decades. Men worked against time in the old days, too, and prided themselves on new records attained. Mark Moyle told the following story. "In the '80s Tom Young's threshing machine cut and threshed the wheat in the morning; it was hauled to the Paradise Mills where Knoles ground it, and for dinner that noon, they served biscuits made from this flour."[42]

As a person watched the tons and tons of grain shipped out of the valley each year he would come to the conclusion that the farmers here were operating an agricultural gold mine. For a good season that was true, but dry, unprofitable seasons were also numerous. The farmers were gamblers in grain and by the law of averages, if they remained with the game long enough, succeeded only in making an ordinary living. Exceptions to this rule existed, however. George Tully is an example of the men who started with nothing, and a few years later were wealthy.

Only large farms with small initial cost make a living possible. For example in 1880 the price was very high, $2.25 per hundred pounds. Average crop estimates were from ten to fifteen bushels an acre, or 600 to 900 pounds. A very good income per acre was $20.00 gross. One of the old timers said that his father "sometimes" made a living on land that supported twenty families in 1935. Yet incomes of $2000 to $20,000 were not unusual.

Horses at the watering trough.

The farm homes were situated far apart, sometimes miles, depending upon the number of acres in the ranch. Here and there in the great fields of grain these homes dotted the horizon. In between, depending on the season, the ground was covered with waving fields of green grain, pleasant to the eye, or heat-reflecting fields of yellow, ripened crops, or, after the harvest, stubble fields little less hot than the full grain itself. In the 1870s there were no fences and no trees around the houses to break the monotony of the picture. All summers were hotter than in the irrigated areas of today. Mrs. W. R. Service told the story, verified by others, of seeing a jack rabbit that had come from miles away in order to rest in the shade of a fence post. When the summer temperatures registered so high, the men were too busy with harvesting to have time to think about it and the women remained indoors, unless the home was fortunate enough to possess a shady yard.

The houses, too, presented a distinct contrast to the bungalow types of a half-century later. Most of them were large and two-story but they were designed for use and comfort rather than appearance. The main part of the house was two stories high and then, as if it were an afterthought, a lean-to porch was attached to the front and a large kitchen to the back, with another lean-to porch, or porches, depending on the width of the original building. These were frame houses, many of which were poorly constructed. They had no hard foundations. The upper story was not always finished, being left in one room as a bunking place for the boys and hired men. Beneath the house was the dug-out cellar in which were stored the canned fruits, the butter, the pans of milk, and the other articles of food which needed protection from the heat.

At first a great deal of the furniture was handmade and benches took the place of chairs. Later, however, a few bumper crops provided the wherewithal to purchase better furniture, and manufactured articles gradually replaced the homemade ones. No picture of an early home is complete without its coal oil lamps, all-over carpets, stuffy and gay colored draperies, "flashy" wall paper, the family album, the large wood-burning kitchen range, and sometimes an organ in the parlor. The kitchen was the most "lived-in" room in the whole house. In it the meals were served, and during the winter months its large range made it the most attractive room in which to while away the long evening hours.

Later, in the 1880s and 1890s, the windmill came into general use and people had water enough to care for trees and plants. Homes became surrounded by family orchards and vineyards. The orange trees in front of the Whitmore home in Ceres are an example of what was often done to beautify the place. Some of these old orchards still exist, bearing bountiful crops of fruit. Shrubs, cut and trained in rather fantastic designs, surrounded the houses. "Aunt Abby" Fulkerth said she had beautiful flowers, too.

For each house there usually were several barns, tool sheds, and machine shops. These were white-washed and could be seen for a long distance. Some of the old barns were still in use 80 years later. Each ranch, too, had a large number of horses, perhaps twenty or more, besides a few cattle, sheep, and a good variety of poultry.

While the large grain fields separated the people, the determination of the settlers to overcome their handicap of distance brought about a closer and fuller community life and neighborly understanding than people possess today.

Early-day schoolroom.

Chapter IV

School Life "In the Olden Days"

Helen Hohenthal

The school has always been an important focus of American community life, and in this respect the Turlock region was no exception. In 1853 John W. Laird provided funds for a teacher's salary and for a small schoolhouse. This private school was located on Laird's land near the mouth of the Tuolumne River. The first teacher in the school and in Stanislaus County was James Sylvester (alias Murphy), a native of Ireland. He was credited with "wonderful powers of computation." The pupils in the first class were Elvira, Mary and J. M. Laird; William Greene, who came down from Tuolumne, forty-five miles away; and Joel, John, and George Smith.[1]

It was not until 1864 that a public school district, Adamsville, was organized within the boundaries of the Turlock region.[2] By 1880 there were five district schools: Davis and Westport, both organized in 1869 but united in 1870; Fairview, 1870; Laird, a part of Adamsville, 1877; and Union School (date unknown). The teachers' salaries range from $60 to $80 a month, and the length of the term varied from seven to ten months.[3]

Fairview was the only school in the county at the time with a ten-month term. The Fairview School was first located where the present Turlock cemetery is, but it was moved into Turlock in 1872 to the 400 block of East Main Street. While it was called the Fairview District, the school went by the name of Washington and later the district changed its name to the Turlock District. It was this school which the children of the Irish colony and of the Turlock settlement attended.[4] The studies, the pranks, the experiences of those children were representative of those of other schools of the same period.

The old Washington School, a one-room building, was about thirty-five feet wide and sixty feet long—just a plain, whitewashed frame building.[5] When the school was first moved to East Main the pupils assisted in planting the trees and digging the school well.[6] The china-locust trees they planted were the first trees planted in Turlock, and were over sixty years old when removed. The open well which the boys dug was the type then in general use in the district. Although it was lined with boards, skunks, rats, rabbits, and other animals as well as millions of insects managed to commit suicide in it. The well was cleaned out frequently but that did not free it of dangerous germs. Horace Crane recalled that sometimes a bar of soap would be dropped down "accidentally," and while the guilty boys had to pump out the new "flavor," it was not much worse than the old. The children used tin cups, passing them around from friend to friend. It is little wonder that epidemics closed the school frequently.[7]

The school seats and desks were homemade at first. They were double seaters, a little higher than the present school desks. Being of soft wood, they yielded easily to the carving instincts of the boys, and were so whittled and covered with initials, double hearts, and other designs that of necessity they were soon relegated to the wood pile and new ones took their place.

The teacher's desk was upon a platform in the front of the room. Also on this platform in later years was the school organ purchased through funds raised at socials and dances.

Outside in the schoolyard there was neither play equipment nor sheds to shelter the horses which the children drove or rode to school. Consequently the horses were unhitched in the morning and tied to the wagons during school hours. A favorite trick of the younger pupils was to hide the harness, change the wheels of the buggies, or throw away the bolts and other small essentials on a wagon or buggy.

From the superior height of the platform the teacher would look down on his class of ninety or a hundred, ranging in ages from five to twenty-five years. A slight indication of tittering among the occupants of the smaller seats brought the old fashioned "dinner bell" into action. In the old school held in the Grange Hall (Jeffer's Hall) on Front Street there were four rows of seats and desks, two up against the outside walls and two down the center.

Neither the curriculum nor the method of instruction would have conformed with those in later use.[8] Then, it was a question of "mass production" and not individual supervision. There were no "grades" in the school. The students went by readers; they were in the First Reader, the Second Reader, etc. When they finished the Sixth Reader they were through. The subjects taught included reading, writing, arithmetic, grammar, geography, spelling, and history. The pupils bought their own books but they didn't cost much: about a dollar for the geography, the biggest book, and 25 cents for the speller.[9] They were either sold to someone else at the beginning of the new school term or passed down to a younger brother or sister.

In the school days of Horace Crane, Ed Osborn, and others of the same age, they had no examinations, not even county "exams," at the end of the term, and no report cards. The county superintendent was supposed to visit the school once a year, but that was sometimes forgotten. The visit was made toward the end of the year; he was expected to take the pupils forward and examine them, but it was pretty much of a farce because the pupil could always turn to a part of the book in which he had been drilled many months before, even last year's book perhaps. This annual visit was a source of irritation to the superintendent, to the teacher, and to the pupils alike.

Until the '80s men teachers were the only ones capable of holding the attention of the students. Mr. Crane said they changed teachers every two weeks at first. Finally one managed to stay longer.

The first teachers boarded out among the families represented in the school. Each family kept the teacher a few weeks at a time. The teacher was hired as much, or more, for his disciplinary powers, than for his actual knowledge. The daily schedule of classes was very monotonous and dry, but the "school spirit" of the pupils managed to keep things so lively that the teacher only hoped for rest after the day's work was over. Just before lunch each day, the pupils "spelled down." The whole school, big and little, was lined up in two rows. Before they were dismissed each child was given a number to indicate his position in line for the next day.[10]

The first thing after lunch was the copy lesson for twenty minutes. This was the quietest time in the whole day and yet even these few minutes of silence were often broken by a general nose-blowing epidemic, one of the few tricks for which the teacher could prescribe no punishment.

Friday was speech day. Many of the boys ditched regularly as no attendance record was kept. Others who refused to give speeches were given until Monday to prepare one, but by that time the teacher had other worries and so the speech was forgotten.

The first teacher remembered by Mr. Crane was a Mr. Wright. Changing teachers frequently left with the pupils only a chance memory of some peculiarity or special form of punishment by which to distinguish the teacher. When a new teacher arrived the pupils studied him carefully to find his weak points. Once they were discovered, it was only a matter of a few weeks before the man would depart for other places, leaving to his successor the hope of not exposing his weaknesses.

The first teacher to stay any length of time was a Mr. McCall. He started in with a club as big as a wagon spoke, but he kept order. One day Jack Ireland and Bill Lewis visited the school and tried to break up his class discipline. He stood for it for a while, then, armed with his club, he went down to where they were seated, yanked them out of the seat, and showed them the door. They went. Later he caught lung fever (pneumonia) and had to quit anyway.

W. B. Howard, another teacher, was a very nervous man. He chewed tobacco and had spittoons placed at convenient spots in the room. He would walk up one aisle and down the other. The pupils could irritate him but he still stayed with the job. At last Johnnie Ward provided them all with snuff from his father's store. They sneezed at the same time. That was the last straw for Howard so he left.

Palmer, a later teacher, was seen stopping in at Ward & Gidding's store on his way to school, to purchase a rawhide horsewhip. Before that he had been content with cutting switches from the locust trees on the school grounds. News of his purchase preceded him and a hasty conference was called by the boys. It was decided that there was a state law against the use of the rawhide in the schoolroom, so the whole group was to "rush" him as soon as he tried to use it. When he did use it on John Crane, only Horace Crane rushed forward to save him. The tussle which followed witnessed the use of uppercuts and rawhide licks, but the whip was no longer used in the classroom.

*Here the school children
quenched their thirst.*

Each teacher had his favorite mode of punishment. One preferred making a boy sit with a girl. Davies used a small but powerful hickory stick. Walter Scott cut locust tree limbs or made the boys stand on one foot. If the other foot touched the floor he hit it. This was a real punishment because most boys went barefooted part of the year. Sawing wood for the school supply or staying in after school were frequent punishments but easily avoided.

School days were periods in which the teacher and the pupils matched wits to see which was boss for the day. Tricks on teachers and on each other were daily indulged in by the pupils. These boys and girls took great pains to provide original tricks and only resorted to the usual tack and pin ones when immediate action was required. Digging mud pits in front of the school door, and covering the trap nicely to avoid suspicion on the part of the victim (this actually was done and earned a forced half-holiday for the pupils); stringing tin cans under the building in such a way that the strings could be operated from the inside of the room on the opposite side from where the noise was produced; imprisoning noisy blow-flies in holes bored into the desk top; all these were to irritate the teacher only. One trick against his fellow-pupils temporarily stopped Johnnie Ward's activities—but also nearly stopped the school. Johnnie could get by "with murder" almost because his father was a school trustee.[11] Having access to his father's drugstore supplies, he secured some croton oil and dipped cheap candy in it. The next day he put a few pieces on each desk. No deaths resulted but one of the Osborn boys nearly died and Loren Fulkerth (Judge Fulkerth) was sick for weeks.

Col. John R. Kelso, a southerner from Texas, who taught this school in the '70s, stands out in the minds of the old-timers as a teacher particularly well-liked and efficient. He stayed in Turlock for three years. He was tall, slim, and dignified, with a gray moustache. In dress he was truly southern, always wearing a broad-brimmed hat and a coat with long tails. He talked with a southern accent and was described as an "infidel." It was he who wrote poetry to mark the death of little children. He was teaching at the time the diphtheria epidemic took victims from many homes. From one home alone, that of Asa Fulkerth, it took three little boys within a month.[12] Kelso wrote a long, six-stanza poem in commemoration of them and a part of it is given here because it is so representative of the type of poetry found in nearly every weekly paper of that day.

OUR LITTLE BOYS

I

Our little boys have left us! alas! that they should go;
Should leave our home so desolate, our hearts so crushed with woe.
Oh! why should Death relentless, have marked them for his prey,
And borne them in his icy arms, from our fond hearts away.

IV

Our little boys have left us! how lone! how very lone!
The brightest days how dreary now! the hours how long they've grown.
We see their books and playthings, the clothes that late they wore,
And think with agony untold they'll use these things no more.

V

Our little boys have left us! but we will not complain,
For well we know they're happy now, forever free from pain;
We know that they are angels bright, and taste immortal joys,
We know that in the 'Better Land,' they're still our sweet boys.

When the schools were first organized, they vied with one another in publishing long lists of "honor" students. Mr. Crane said that since no reports were made out, and no examinations were given, these "honors" could not have represented class work. The only excuse which he could offer was that of "halfway decent behavior." There were names on these lists, however, of boys and girls who later became worthy citizens of the community and some of them Mr. Crane pointed out as being very bright in school work.[13]

No organized play took up the recess time. The only game played was tom-ball, the forerunner of our present day baseball.

The story of no school is complete without mention of its school bully. In the '70s Lee West held that position in the Turlock school. He was not large, but he could lick everyone and forced others to admit authorship for the bad things which he did.

In 1880 the school was moved into the Granger Hall on Front Street north of the old Turlock Hotel. It was a two-story building built by the Turlock Grange on Joe Joyce's property. School was held in the first story through 1884, and dances and public meetings were held in the second story. By 1885 the school had been moved to a new building on West Main, at the site later occupied by the Hawthorne School. The land was given to the district by John W. Mitchell with the understanding that if the school should be removed from there, the property would revert to his estate.[14]

When the school was moved to this site, another teacher was added to the staff. Miss Eva Entwistle, later Mrs. A. G. Chatom, assisted Mr. R. E. Murtha, the principal. The school was then conducted in two rooms and the presence of a woman teacher indicated a change in the school atmosphere.[15] Final examinations were given by the principal. Since funds would not permit terms that were very long, school closed in May, and then for the next month Mr. Murtha conducted a private summer school.

Turlock Grammar School, predecessor of Hawthorne School. Courtesy of Mrs. Clara Lundahl.

"The whole family attended the dances, which lasted until dawn."

Chapter V

Community Life and Society During the Grain Era

Helen Hohenthal

Community life presented interesting contrasts in the period when grain was king. By its production and harvesting schedules, grain set the pattern for work and leisure for all the people.

Schools were the first meeting houses built, so there was a close connection between the school and community life. Often town meetings were held in the schoolhouse.

The greatest gathering of the year was the annual Christmas tree program, also held in the school. Before Christmas a collection was taken up, and with it each child was provided with a bag of candy and an orange. Expensive presents were out of the question. One year when the rainstorms prevented the men from getting a tree down near the river, they made one.

> They ripped boards to long narrow strips and nailed them to an upright post. The women covered this "tree" with cotton and "diamond dust" and strung yards of popcorn for it. In those days everyone brought their presents to put on the tree, and, when all done it was as pretty a tree as one could wish to see.[1]

The winter months witnessed many other forms of indoor entertainment. Socials and dances rather than cards attracted the people. These were attended by young and old alike. The holiday season seemed a favorite time in which to gather. Frequent references to these events appeared in the newspapers. In one paper the following large notice was found:

> Grand Christmas Ball at Turlock, Wednesday evening, Dec. 25, 1878. Place: Jeffer's Hall. Tickets, $2.50. Committee of Arrangements: H. C. Russell, J. D. Jeffers, C. F. Lander, G. Cline. Committee of Invitation: J. M. Allen, C. Hummeltenberg. [Names for other towns are not given here.] Reception Committee: J. L. Brown, H. H. Bates, C. Coulthard. Best of music. The tickets include the supper.

In commenting on the above notice the paper stated:

> It's useless to promise those who attend a good time, as it is well known that Turlock folks get entertainments up in first-class style.[2]

Again at a later date, the account of a dance given by Thomas Gaddis in the Union Hall on Thanksgiving eve reports that the prize for the waltz, a beautiful album, was awarded to Miss Sophia Masterson and George Hummeltenberg. Supper was served at the Turlock Hotel.[3]

The same paper carried a notice of another social affair which reflects the country humor of the time.

> The boys are requested by Levi Jones to bring their own [portable] hitching posts when they come to the exhibition Christmas tree and dance in the Union School House on Dec. 21. The money raised will be used to pay for a school organ.[4]

The late '80s saw many of these benefit socials. In 1886 the dime social was a means of raising money for church building funds. The first of these was given Thanksgiving evening 1886 in Mitchell's Hall. At that time $32.00 was raised, but not all of it came from the dime admission fee. A raisin cake, made by Mrs. S. H. Crane, Horace Crane's mother, sold for $16.00.[5]

The present given to Mr. Henry Osborn on his sixtieth birthday would be of great historical value, could it be found today. It was an autograph album containing the names of those present at the birthday party. Those names probably included nearly all prominently connected with the early history of the Turlock district.[6]

Both local talent and out-of-town companies provided plays for evening entertainments, which were neither regular nor frequent. Local talent plays always drew a crowd, and it is difficult to say whether these plays were good or bad. The writer has never seen a write-up of any local talent performance which unfavorably criticized any of the cast. On 16 April 1886, local talent presented *The Last Loaf* to a large audience. Among the members of the cast were: John Osborn, Anna Legalle, Lily Mitchell, and E. B. Osborn.

Apparently pleased with their success, they presented another play on 3 July of the same year. This oft-produced play, *Ten Nights in a Barroom*, was most appropriate for a community which still had almost as many saloons as the total number of all other businesses. The play was presented at the schoolhouse; and the special drawing features of the evening, according to the notices, were "music by Stanley" and "painted scenery."[7]

Unlike the amateurs, professional talent was spared no criticism. The following item under Turlock News in the *Modesto Herald* for 17 October 1878 is the most biting comment a reporter could offer.

> Our little town can now vie with many of larger size as to the quantity of shows. The less said of quality, the better, a large portion being emphatically termed "bilks." The Houseman troupe gave a social dance at Jeffer's Hall last Saturday evening. Quite a number enjoyed themselves. The music was excellent.

And again in the same year, in a detailed account of a professional *Uncle Tom's Cabin* entertainment given in Turlock, not one member of the cast escaped criticism.

> The leading light of the play was Emma Grant, a colored lady. In plantation songs and dances, she has but few equals, but her voice is not suited to sentimental singing.

"Little Willettie, a bright, talented, six-year old who played the part of Eva" and, who in the course of the program sang, "Father, dear Father, Come Home," likewise displeased the audience. Quite a contrast to the support given a minstrel performance presented by the "Turlock Jollities" for the benefit of the cemetery fund![8]

There was one form of professional entertainment that never failed to please. Wherever it went it was given a royal welcome, no matter how poor the program. Once a year the circus came to town. The event was one of great joy to the whole population. Before the railroads went through, it travelled from place to place in wagons. The circus ground in Turlock was the vacant lot on Center Street opposite "Aunt Abby" Fulkerth's home. From many years of use for the same purpose the ground was gradually hollowed out. For years afterward these "circus spots" showed on the lot.

The people in the river settlements had their circus grounds, too. One was located on the north side of the Tuolumne River, near the Tuolumne City ferry. The Montgomery-Queen Circus was the first one attended by Horace Crane. A few facts in connection with this circus long remained vivid in his mind. One was Molly Brown, the bareback rider, jumping through the hoops; another was the sale of the ten-cent song books, which contained, among other songs, the long-time favorite, "Silver Threads Among the Gold."

Another circus was the Bailey Circus. The circus had a regular traveling schedule just like trains, but once this Bailey Circus was delayed. All day the boys and girls waited, straining their eyes to get the first glimpse of the wagons. Some of the boys perched themselves on the roof of the old Farmers' Hotel in order to have a vantage point, but morning passed and no circus appeared. Noon and afternoon and still no sign of the wagons. A few went home for rest and food—but not many of the boys. At last night came and at least one tired little boy decided that there would be no circus, so he went home and to bed. The morning news which greeted him was that the circus arrived at 11:00 p.m., put on its show for those present, and left before morning for its next stop. The circus with its wild animals, its clowns, its freaks, and its pink lemonade never lost its hold on the hearts of the youth of the land.

Fairs and Fourth of July celebrations were regular events. In early days the fairs were held at Tuolumne City and later at Modesto. The fair that most attracted the people, however, was the Stockton Fair. The long three-day drive did not prevent people from attending. Betting was high at the horse racing. The Fulkerth brothers raised racehorses with considerable profit.

Horse races were often held on other occasions than fair time. The favorite race course from 1872 to 1877 was on East Road, now called East Avenue. "By the fall of 1878 a round track for horse races was established (by the Murphy ranch). There they had big races for a week or ten days in which they used imported horses."[9] The east terminal of this race track was at the three-mile house, which was a rest stop for teamsters and teams coming from grain fields several miles farther east of Turlock. Here new horses were tried out or trained before being entered in regular races, but many times bets were laid on these races, too.

Blacksmith shop.

A sport that was very popular in early days was foot racing, combined, of course, with the ever present betting. Just when this sport ceased to be popular is not known, but in all probability it died out at the end of the grain era. The following advertisement would look queer should it appear on a sports page of today.

> The following races will take place at Turlock, October 30 and 31: Quarter-mile dash, free for all, purse $40.00; Six-hundred yards dash, free for all, purse $60.00.

An entrance fee of $10.00 will be added to the above. At the conclusion of the second day's racing, there will be a glass-ball shooting match for all who wish to participate.[10]

Professional runners would come into a town, hang around the bars and stores for a while, and direct conversation in such a way that they would be asked about running. At other times these professionals would deliberately announce themselves and would invite local backing by trying out before a crowd on some roadway.

One time a poorly dressed, hump-shouldered fellow started hanging around the saloons in Turlock. After a week or so he was tried out and matched against the town favorite, Stoney (Stonewall Jackson) Allen. The match was a running race, fifty yards for $50.00 a side. It was held near the brick kiln and was advertised as "S. J. Allen of Turlock against Hurd, the 'unknown'." Just before 5:30 p.m., the time set for the race, Hurd went up to his hotel room, reappearing in a short time in pink tights. Instead of a humpback, he was a well built man. The side bets on the race were heavy. In the race Allen kept looking behind him to see how the other fellow was coming. Hurd was accused of "throwing" the race. Pistols were drawn, and in the fracas that followed Hurd was hit over the head by someone who thought he did not run his best. Finally the race was declared a draw, and all bets were called off. Hurd was given his share of the money and left town.[11]

In the field of athletic entertainment we find baseball games as early as 1886. These, too, were accompanied by the lure of a prize as the following item indicates. "The Ceres Lone Stars and the Turlock Lightfoots matched for a baseball game for a $50.00 purse." These were town teams, not school teams. Among Turlock's favorites again appeared the name of Ed Osborn.[12]

Croquet was the favorite outdoor sport for the women. Most of the wealthier homes had their own croquet ground or course laid out on the lawn. It is not known whether bets were ever laid by the womenfolks on these rather quiet games, but the game was not always played in strict conformity with the rules. From a man, the report comes that sometimes the fair young maids would walk over the balls and move them to a more advantageous point by means of their long skirts.

The rivers and river bottom lands furnished the people with many forms of amusement. Picnicking at Stevenson's and Fox's Grove, boating, swimming, and fishing, all afforded many hours of clean pleasure. Wild blackberry picking along the river bottoms, too, was very popular. It was a dangerous activity, however, because the season often occurred while the rivers were still swollen from the effects of the spring freshets. Wild grapes were found in great abundance in the fall of the year and, while too sour for eating, the housewives prized the jelly made from them. The vines of the wild grapes made wonderful swings for the young folks during picnicking times.

Hunting was a sport only when the hunters were after bear and deer. For this game they usually went to the Coast Range instead of the Sierra Nevadas.[13] In the floor of the valley jack rabbits, squirrels, and coyotes were plentiful. The country was full of jack rabbit hunters, such as Stoney Allen. They were paid $1.25 a dozen for those shipped to San Francisco. A good hunter could easily get a hundred a day. Rabbit drives were not popular in this district until after 1900.

Geese were so plentiful they would follow the plows around. People never bothered to shoot them except for an occasional few to eat.[14] A sport, if it could be called such, was that of capturing pelicans. During the high waters or rainy seasons, fish collected in certain depressions in the river bottoms. These spots were covered with a willow undergrowth. The pelicans would go in after the fish, and when they tried to get out, they were so heavily loaded down with fish that they could not get away. The young boys would then catch them, slit their throats and remove the fish.[15]

The most popular amusement for the people, young and old alike, was the barn dance. In the spring and early summer the people gathered for the socials and dancing in the granaries or barn lofts. The whole family attended the dances, which lasted until dawn. The farmers took turns in holding these gatherings in their barns, and people drove long distances in lumbering wagons or fancy surreys to attend.

The favorite dances of the day were the square, the polka, the schottische, and the ever popular waltz. The music was furnished by local bands or fiddlers, whichever happened to be handy. Over the musicians' platform were posted such notices as "Don't hurt the players, they're doing the best they can," but the whole atmosphere was that of friendship and wholesome enjoyment. Often the young folks brought their own refreshments, consisting of sandwiches, cookies, etc. In those days drinking was confined to the saloon or similar places. No man thought of drinking at a dance, and no decent woman would smoke or drink. The rules of society were very few and simple, but they were not broken without drawing severe penalties upon the violator.

The first Turlock Band was organized in 1881. Each player paid $1.25 a week to hire a leader. The first leader, D. C. Smith, was an expert player himself. The next leader was a little Frenchman by the name of Pauncelette. He, too, was a fine leader. In Fresno one year the band missed winning first prize in the Band Tournament only because it lacked one musical instrument the judges thought necessary. This band played at many dances, but the greatest event of the year for it was the annual La Grange May Day Celebration. The band was paid $150.00 for its services for the day, including the afternoon concert and evening dance.

The day before the celebration, the members left in their own band wagon. This was drawn by six horses. It had seats on the side and a place for the drum on the back. The gay band wagon loaded with its blue-uniformed[16] members must have been a very attractive sight.[17]

The first night the band put on its own dance in the old adobe jail. Its own party had accompanied it from Turlock. The dance lasted all night. The next day was devoted to the La Grange festival and picnic; the all-night dance followed, refreshments being served at midnight. The third day was the homecoming—with a wagonload of sleepy men trying to take turns at driving the team home. Later the band was reorganized under the leadership of Ernest Siem.

Very few of the old-timers took vacations. Those who did went to the seacoast. Yosemite was known but generally ignored by the people. A few did make the trip into the valley, going up by way of Hornitos and over Mt. Bullion to Mariposa. The trip was made by horseback or by wagon and required several weeks to complete, going and coming. Only one farmer in the district is known to have taken a vacation in the Sierras. He was Harry Clark, who spent two weeks every summer fishing at the Kennedy Lakes.

When the crops were harvested, the farmers paid their bills at the general merchandise stores. These bills were allowed to run for a year or longer, depending on how often the crops failed. With their debts cleared, some of the farmers and harvest hands celebrated the event by drinking and gambling. Drunken men could be found everywhere, especially in the straw-covered streets, suffering from the effects of too many visits to the counter behind swinging doors.

Except during the harvesting season, crimes were not very numerous, although a few terrible murders were committed.

Gambling by professionals against the ever hopeful farmers and businessmen lasted throughout the year, but was especially heavy during the harvest season. Stories are told of men gambling all day or all night, leaving their horses hitched to the racks unattended. As acts of mercy, these horses were sometimes turned loose and allowed to find their own way home.

At one time Jim Van Dorn and another professional gambler played cards in the Turlock Hotel with revolvers on the table. The agreement was that the first one caught cheating would be shot. No shooting!

Sam Strauss said that in the evening the gamblers would call for a 150-pound box of crackers, a great many new decks of cards, and start in. In the course of the night thousands of dollars would be stacked on the tables. By morning the money would usually be in the possession of the professionals, the drunken and disappointed losers on their way home, and the saloonkeeper sweeping out the torn decks of cards and other refuse of the night's playing. The next night the scene would be repeated.

On Sundays when they were not busy, hundreds of harvest hands would mill up and down the streets looking for excitement, which they found. Of Turlock, Will H. Osborn told Howard Whipple that "for the first two years after the town was built, it was not safe for a woman to appear on the streets during the harvesting season. Threshing crews on weekends were so thick you could hardly get through."[18]

Gambling at harvest time.

Tragedy mingled with pleasure in the daily experiences of the people. Those living along the rivers faced the annual possibility of losing all their stock and property and even their lives during the floods in the spring. The greatest flood affecting this district was that of 1862, already referred to.

To the people on the plains, as well as along the rivers, the open well was a cause of illness and death. Year after year, before the bored well was used, epidemics swept over the valley. Typhoid, diphtheria, scarlet fever, malaria, and many other diseases were present. Proper medical attention was impossible with only a doctor or two for the whole county.[19] The mortality rate was especially high among children, and it seemed as if the people had large families in order to assure themselves of the survival of a few. Consumption, the white plague, took a heavy toll of human life.

Diphtheria was the dreaded disease during the period 1876-1879. Rev. Mr. E. B. Winning wrote, "The terrible scourge of diphtheria took place during our stay. I cannot remember how many cases in all but I do remember of their saying there were seventy-eight at one time. Many died during this scourge. Father and mother were going almost day and night, helping with the nursing, etc. Seventy-eight cases in Modesto now would be alarming but seventy-eight cases then meant one or more in almost every home."[20]

Malaria was prevalent along the Merced River to such an extent that whites could not live there. Every family that tried to lost several children and had to move out to save the rest. The Chinese who lived there were less affected by it, and so on the choicest lands along the river they raised fruits and vegetables for the people on the plains. These they brought in daily in their Chinese peddle wagons. The vegetables were cheap, too! People wondered why the Chinese were not bothered with malaria. Some said it was a particular kind of Chinese lettuce they used, and some that a Chinaman didn't get sick.

Smallpox came in the 1880s. While it was more greatly feared than the other diseases, it was not so serious in its effects. As a precaution against further spreading it, guards were placed at the entrances to Turlock. One of the old-timers said that the town was roped off and business for a time came to a standstill. Carbolic acid was about the only commodity sold for a while.

The disease was brought to town by a Negro hostler. He was found in the barroom of the Fountain Hotel, moaning and delirious. The men sent over to Captain Ward's store for pills, and the Negro took the whole box. No one would take care of him, so he was put in a pest house near the Tuolumne River. Food was brought to him. He escaped from the building and was drowned in the river.

During the epidemic, hotels refused to take in people because the disease was bad in other places. One night a man came into town but he was not offered a place to sleep. He looked perfectly well and insisted he had not come in contact with the disease. D. D. Bonnett felt sorry for him and allowed him to spend the night in one of his sheds. The next day the stranger went on to the next farmer's place. Smallpox broke out at the Bonnetts' and every other place he stopped.[21]

Not all the communities could afford churches, but they were not deprived of church services. The Westport church was the first built in the area.[22] Ceres had no church as late as 1880, and the first Turlock church was constructed in 1889. But as early as 1873 Baptist services were held in a Whitmore store building in Ceres with Rev. Mr. Ely Reese as the first preacher. Other preachers occasionally held services for the people.

In 1876 Rev. Mr. E. A. Winning was installed in Modesto as a circuit preacher for almost the whole county. His son, Rev. Mr. E. B. Winning, described his father's work. "He was pastor in Modesto and surroundings from 1873 to 1879. I say surroundings, for he preached not only in Modesto but in Ceres, Turlock, Westport, Burneyville, etc.; Modesto in the morning and evening and at the other points on Sunday afternoon. The drive to Westport was a hard afternoon—thirteen miles, as I remember, but the sand was deep and the team of mustangs, in summer time was dripping with sweat."

Winning was well remembered by the Turlockers. At that time the church services were held in the schoolhouse.[23] Mrs. R. R. Lander, who often entertained the preachers, spoke frequently of him. It was he who preached the funeral services for Richard Whitmore, a pioneer of the Ceres district.

In 1886 the people of Turlock decided to have a church building. Dime socials and dances were the means of raising part of the funds necessary for construction. The women of the community formed a sister society to aid in this work. The people were largely Methodists and Congregationalists, with a few scattered members from other churches. Mr. S. R. Crane donated the land. The last $300.00 was given by a Congregational Church Board in the East with the understanding that the new church would be Congregational.[24] The church was completed and dedicated on 10 March 1889. Rev. Dr. Warren conducted the dedication services and Rev. Mr. L. N. Barber was the first pastor.[25] The history of the church was brief. In "Aunt Abby's" words, "It lasted only three months. We had a fine preacher and two converts. They quarreled over sweeping the church and paying the pastor. Boys broke up the meetings."

The Methodists, who had failed to support the first church, then constructed one of their own on the corner of West Main and Lander Avenue. It, too, failed. Many years later the Brethren Church bought the Congregational Church building from Horace Crane, who had bought it at tax sale. He turned it over to the Brethren members for the price of the tax bill he paid.[26] In turn, the Methodist Church was sold for taxes, but when the Swedes came in 1902 they bought it for the price of the tax bill and it was once more in use.[27]

The Catholic Church was established in Turlock in 1888. The Irish were united in its support, so it was a success. The first priests, like Rev. Mr. Winning, were holding services in many places, so mass was said about once a month. Catechism classes were held each Sunday. The first circuit priests were Fathers McGuire, Smith, Maddon, and Giles. The money for construction of the church was donated largely by the Kehoe, McCabe, Casey, and other Irish families.[28]

Besides the churches, lodges and clubs were organized. As early as 1878 the Fairview Lodge of the Order of Good Templars, was flourishing in Turlock. Mrs. S. V. Porter, its secretary, reported its membership at fifty. "There were several inducements offered to the members to insure attendance, among which was the establishment of a bi-monthly newspaper, to which all members were allowed to contribute, and at stated meetings the paper was read aloud, and the contributions criticized."[29]

In 1885 the Knights of Pythias Lodge was organized with eighty-five members from the town and surrounding neighborhood.[30]

The following year witnessed the organization of the "Anti-Chinese League of Turlock." It had a printed constitution and bylaws and a hundred members. Its chief purpose was to drive out the Chinese laborers, and the first step toward this was to secure the aid of hotels in boycotting them.[31]

In 1889 Miss S. C. Burnett, a State Women's Christian Temperance Union organizer, spoke in Turlock. She had hoped to organize a branch, but no records of such an organization have been found.[32]

The Turlock and Ceres Granges, centers of farm social life, existed for many years. Only farmers and farmers' wives were allowed membership. The leaders of the Turlock Grange, organized on 6 June 1873, were the Cranes, the Fulkerths, and the C. C. Wrights. These Granges were very active on the question of irrigation and were influential in opposing what they considered undesirable irrigation plans.

By 1895 the soil no longer responded to summer-fallowing. Drought often robbed the people of what little crop the earth could produce. Land which Mitchell had earlier refused to sell for $45.00 an acre now was a drug on the market at $10.00. The farmers went from wheat to barley and oats; from these crops to the least profitable of grains but the most easily grown, rye.

W. D. Adams, who farmed to rye in the '90s, in a few well chosen statements showed the hardships in the dying grain era.

> Two sacks of rye was more than an average crop. Wouldn't expect more. Didn't plow every year, but would cultivate each year with rolling cultivator—went a whole year without sight of money—sold hogs for $.02-3/4 a pound—never had hay—fed wheat and rye straw—gave horses away to get rid of them.[33]

The temporary wealth of a single crop was fast disappearing, and the people were in the midst of another transitional period—one which finally carried them over into the twentieth century of irrigated lands, diversified crops, and permanent agriculture. With all its fame, its wealth, and its appeal to the gambling instincts of man, the era of the grain-covered plains, like those of the cattle range and trapping, was only a stepping stone to the real "golden age" of the region.

Combined harvester on the Sperry Ranch. Courtesy of George Sperry.

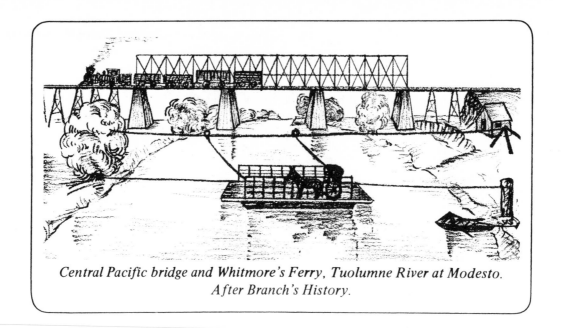

Central Pacific bridge and Whitmore's Ferry, Tuolumne River at Modesto.
After Branch's History.

Chapter VI

Road and River Transportation

Helen Hohenthal

Before 1870, pioneer travelers to or from the Turlock district had a choice of three modes of transportation: horseback, stage or wagon, and steamboat—none of which offered any great degree of speed, comfort, or convenience. How important a part transportation plays in the history of any section is indicated by the fact that it was one of the first problems claiming the attention of the newly organized California State Legislature. In 1850 that body passed a law, commonly referred to as the "Roads Act." By it county committees were created, consisting of the county surveyor and two others, to investigate and report on the road situation in their respective counties. The road supervisor was ordered to prepare a list of all persons resident in his road district and to indicate every person liable for road work. The supervisor provided the tools. While the people were entitled to credit on their road tax for this work, they had to work or provide a substitute.

The first county road report which concerned this district was one on the proposed road from Graysonville (Grayson) to Sonora.[1] The report recommended its construction with the following comments:

> A part of the permanent road would probably be submerged three or four feet during the high water season on the San Joaquin. . .there would be no difficulty in constructing the permanent road from Grayson to Tuolumne City, a distance of four miles, but on the eight-mile stretch from there to the Dry Creek crossing a two hundred-foot bridge was necessary across Dry Creek; from there on, through Crescent City and Empire City, to Sonora, the road would be on high ridges affording little difficulty.

While this road served the people of the Turlock district, no part of it was located within its boundaries.[2] At that early date the greater part of the population lived on the west bank of the San Joaquin River or on the north bank of the Tuolumne.

Over this road the first express and mail routes serving the district were established. In 1850 the Marvin Express made a regular trip from San Francisco to the southern mines, stopping, among other places, at Tuolumne City, Empire City, and Indian Ranche Ferry (Claxton and Horr). The prices Marvin charged for mail service were almost prohibitive:

> $2.00 for each letter when we pay postage, $1.50 when postage is prepaid, $1.00 for a drop letter, $0.25 for newspapers, $0.50 for each letter at San Francisco, and $0.30 for mailing each newspaper.[3]

Through the efforts of Marvin a new post road from Stockton to the mouth of the Merced River was established in 1854. There were post offices located at French Camp south of Stockton, at Empire City (J. G. Marvin, Postmaster), at Tuolumne City on the Tuolumne River, at Grayson, and at Hill's Ferry on the San Joaquin. This was a decided improvement, for settlers in the Turlock region could now get mail at four post offices.

On the first route established from Stockton to Mariposa, the first post office was at Horr's Ferry on the Tuolumne River, a distance of fifty miles. From there to Quartzburg, forty miles away, there was no post office, although there were settlers. The soldiers at Fort Miller on the San Joaquin sent an express twice a month to Stockton, and people in Tulare County had to go to Stockton or Mariposa to mail or receive letters.

Stages, too, followed this route but not more frequently than twice a month. The road led through fields where herds of wild cattle grazed. Even by 1860 the road was not very distinct, especially the section of it across the open plain. No regular stage lines went through the Turlock district, due to the lack of improved roads.[4] The stages to nearby points were usually six-horse mud wagons. The drivers considered it quite a feat to manage the six lines and crack the long whip over the lead horses' heads at the same time. A trip on one of these stages is described by a pioneer, Mr. J. S. Bishop of Crows Landing.

> In order to reach my sister's place I had to go from Lathrop to my destination near Hill's Ferry by way of stage. This trip was taken in 1876. The stage was the old-fashioned type; the driver sat on the outside seat and the passengers were packed on the inside. At Lathrop I was packed in the back seat with two others. At first all seemed well, but uncomfortable, due to the lack of space. Then I noticed that my seat mates were making funny signs but no sounds. The more signs they made, the more nervous I became. I thought they were either drunk or crazy. At last we reached Grayson, where we stopped for dinner. I asked the driver to change my seat—and when I explained my reason, he laughed and informed me that they were harmless deaf and dumb mutes. Well—they were the first I had ever seen. I got off the stage about two miles from the present Crows Landing Bridge and walked down to the ferry.[5]

These stages were large enough to carry six or eight passengers, but not very comfortably. Mail was carried underneath the driver's seat. The "strong box" was at times carried up by the driver; in other stages it was bolted to the floor in the middle section of the carriage. The boxes, about eighteen inches long, twelve wide, and ten deep, were ironbound wooden boxes with iron padlocks.[6] They were locked or sealed by the station agents, the driver having nothing to do with it. In this box money, jewelry, etc., were sent in special wrappers.[7]

Stage robberies were frequent. One that occurred in June 1886 was on the same route described by Mr. Bishop. The *Stanislaus County Weekly News* described it as follows:

> On last Saturday morning while the Hill's Ferry and Banta stage was only about one and one-half miles from Banta, a knight of the road—short, thickset, with a mask on his face—stepped out into the road and using a Spencer rifle muzzle as a persuader, induced the driver to hand over the strong box of the Wells Fargo and Co. Express. The driver stopped and hurriedly handed down the box while the two passengers were busy keeping their hair from assuming a pompadore.

Celerity coach or "mud wagon."

Concord-type coach.

The bandit then ordered the stage to move on. About a hundred yards ahead the driver stopped and watched the bandit open the box with hammer and chisel. The box was bare. With a yell the bandit dropped his tools and started on a run through the woods to the river.[8]

Only one stage line is known to have operated for a short time in the vicinity of Turlock, for the railroad, coming in 1871, eliminated need for through stage service. That one stage line served the people of the Snelling-Hopeton-Turlock road.[9]

Across the three rivers which formed the boundaries of the region many ferries took the place of bridges until the 1890s. They were operated as a rule by the farmer on whose property they were located. Someone was in charge at all times, day and night, to accommodate the public. These ferries were described by one old-timer as "barges operated by pulleys." The large wire cables and ropes by which they were held in place and operated were high enough to allow the steamboats to get by without interference. The ferries were of various sizes, according to what the traffic demanded. The ferry at the Crows Landing bridge site was only large enough to carry a couple of rigs, and was not built for grain wagons. Others were large enough to accommodate two six-mule teams and wagons.[10]

The ferry prices seem to have varied. One person recalled the price for two horses, round trip, as 25¢, another as 50¢ (providing the return trip was made the same day there was no extra charge). A third said the price was 25¢, but for big teams the charges were 25¢ for the first span and 10¢ for each additional span of horses.[11]

One of the first ferries was across the Tuolumne at Tuolumne City. Dr. William M. Ryer, a wealthy doctor from San Francisco, established the ferry as early as 1850. During the period of Mexican emigration from the Sonora mines his ferry was the one used by all, and by charging for ferriage at the rate "of $1.00 per head, more for animals," he made $5000.00 in a short while.[12]

Dan Baldwin, who ran the Whitmore Ferry just west of the railroad bridge across the Tuolumne at Modesto, was one man whom all his customers remembered. Rev. E. B. Winning said, "He was a great talker. . .sometimes he would get the ferry in the middle of the stream and then stop so as to have his say before the passengers got away."[13] One time when "Aunt Abby" Fulkerth was being ferried across, Baldwin forgot to put up the guards, and the frisky team she was driving almost went into the river. Such an incident did happen at Durham's Ferry in 1878 when L. A. Richards' horses drowned and the ferry owners paid him $350 for his loss.[14]

Mrs. Stephen Crane said John Mitchell used to ferry all harvesting machines across the Merced River at McSwain's Ferry. Each time it took a whole day to complete the transfer. Later McSwain's Bridge was built there.

One of the busiest ferries was at Paradise City until the flour mills were shut down. T. C. McCumber, who ran this ferry, had faith in the power of advertising and when, during the quiet months of winter, his business was slow, he placed the following "ad" in the newspapers:

> The undersigned, proprietors of the Paradise Ferry across the Tuolumne, desire to call the attention of the travelling public to the fact that our boat has been recently thoroughly repaired by a competent mechanic, and is now in better condition than ever before. Cable and tackle are in the best possible condition. We have just completed a high water grade over the low ground on the north side of the river, which will enable passengers to reach our ferry, at any stage of the water, with ease and safety. The boat will run day and night when traffic requires it. No pains will be spared by the undersigned to accommodate the public and a share of patronage is solicited. (Signed) T. C. McCumber.[15]

During the summer months as many as sixteen large grain wagons and teams passed over this ferry daily, besides the regular business.

The Crows Landing Ferry went across just south of the old bridge which was still in use when the writer visited the spot in 1930. The bridge tender, Mr. J. S. Bishop, pointed out the path in the river bottom just below his house, over which the people and buggies passed on their way to the ferry. Across the way on the opposite side still stood the old oak tree to which both river boats and ferry tied up. When Mr. Bishop first arrived at that place in 1876, the man in charge of the ferry was a Mr. Eastin. The ferry was kept over on the far side and anyone desiring transportation had to call the ferryboat man.[16]

This ferry remained in use until the Crows Landing drawbridge was constructed in 1887.[17] Mr. Bishop's father was installed as bridge tender when the bridge was first built. It was his duty to open the bridge when the steamers wanted to get by. Mr. Bishop himself was in charge of the bridge in 1930, but since the bridge was no longer opened his duties were few. One by one, bridges were constructed across the San Joaquin and its tributaries until by 1900 most of the ferries had disappeared.

Had it not been for the river steamers, agricultural development of this valley would have waited until the appearance of the railroad, but as early as 1850 steamers were making regular trips up the Tuolumne and San Joaquin Rivers. A few years later they went up the Merced River, too.

In 1850 Mr. N. Wells saw the possibility of developing a trading center at Tuolumne City. He went to San Francisco and made arrangements with a steamship company to run the *Georgia* up to Tuolumne City. The company agreed to make the one trial trip for the consideration of $6000.00. That was a big price to pay, but Wells felt that it was worth it. After that the *Georgia* made regular trips up the Tuolumne until the water was too low for navigation.[18] Beginning in 1852 the two steamers *Georgina* and *Maunsell White* made regular trips to Empire City as long as the population was sufficient to provide business.[19]

For twenty years the steamers were the only cheap means of transportation available to the plains dwellers, and for over thirty years, to the "west siders." For this reason the first towns or settlements were along the rivers and the first lands taken up by settlers were those nearest the river. Here some of the poorest land in the district was included.

The steamboats were first put into use to accommodate the miners in Tuolumne County. Their supplies would be shipped by boat to the highest navigable point, and from there by pack mule into the heart of the mining area. These river steamboats were smaller than the freighters used on the Sacramento River in the 1900s. The upper deck was used by the pilot and the few passengers. On the lower deck the cargo was stored for the trip.

During the era of the cattle range the boats were used to transport the stock to the nearest market, but it was not until the grain era that the steamboat came into its own. The steamboat days of the 1860s and 1870s on these rivers were as worthy of the efforts of some California "Mark Twain" as were the river boat days on the Mississippi. For many months of the year the regular traders went quietly up and down the rivers; then with the first grain harvested, the real shipping season began. The towns on the

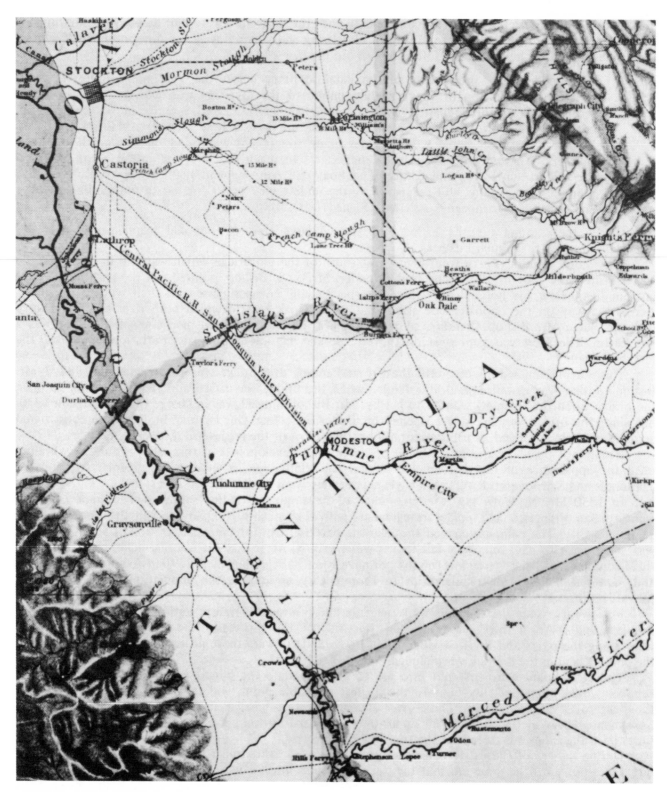

Routes in the Turlock region, 1873. State Soil Survey of California, J. D. Whitney, State Geologist. Courtesy of Turlock Irrigation District.

river seemed suddenly alive with people and teams rushing from place to place. All was noise, excitement and confusion as the loading of the grain on the boats proceeded, a welcome relief from the monotony of the other months. Crews in charge of the warehouses or piers were on hand day and night to meet the boats as they whistled their approach to the town. With the boat once made fast to the bank or pier, loading started immediately. No time could be wasted as the high waters lasted for only a short while during the harvesting season. With the boat and its trailing barge loaded to capacity, the perspiring crew was allowed to rest for a time as the boat backed out into the river channel and started on its return trip to Stockton. With the chucking and splashing sounds of the side paddles, and an occasional shrill whistle to warn other boats of its approach as it rounded a sharp curve in the river, the boat soon disappeared from view.

On all grain not shipped during high water the owner had to pay storage and wait until winter to get any returns from his crop. The size of a good crop can be estimated by the fact that although two or more boats took away loads of grain each day, during the rush of the season the grain would be piled up for a distance of half a mile on the Grayson pier and beyond it. The river steamers were a boon to the wheat ranchers, for the trip to Stockton from the Turlock region required three days by team, and the driver's expenses and ferry tolls were high. By steamboat, Mark Moyle said, the trip from Tuolumne City to Stockton took twenty-four hours. From other points equidistant from Stockton, however, estimates of as low as twelve hours were given.

The boats did not run on regular schedules. Sometimes two or three boats would stop at a pier in the course of a day. The farmers along the river constructed their own piers wherever possible, as did the colonial farmers in old Virginia. There were many landing places such as Carpenter's Landing and Mahoney's Landing. These were often nothing more than a pier extending out a short distance over the edge of the bank.[20] From the pier or bank of the river, a plank runway was thrown across to the boat and held in place. Mr. J. S. Bishop amusingly described his first impression of a pier.

> When I reached the river bank I noticed a sort of little platform projecting out into the water from the south-east side of the bank. Since it had been raining in northern California I concluded that the rains had washed away the bridge. While I was figuring out what to do a man called to me from the other side and asked if I wanted to get across. I said, 'yes', so he brought the ferry across for me. On the way over I said, 'I see the June water raise has washed the bridge out.' The ferryman laughed and explained that what I thought was the end of the bridge was in reality the pier at which the river boats landed.[21]

The transportation costs were not high. They varied somewhat according to the distance, but were not over $1.00 a ton to Stockton.[22] A single trip would net the owner of the boat and barge a neat little income when the barges were capable of carrying from 200 to 700 tons at a time.

During the harvesting season the farmers watched eagerly the reports of the water levels in the rivers and their rates of fall, just as they watched the rainfall figures during the winter and spring. The following is typical of notices or news items found in the papers:

> The San Joaquin is falling rapidly; navigation on the upper river will close soon. Every effort is being made to get the grain out before the river gets too low for boating. Last Sunday at Durham's Ferry [Grayson Ferry] it fell fourteen inches and the average has been five to six inches every twenty-four hours. It is estimated that at least one third of the crop will remain when navigation stops. Then the cost of transportation by teams will destroy the profits. Some of the steamers already find it difficult to come down with their loads. The grain owners realize this and the rivers are lined with Stockton, San Francisco, and Sacramento steamers. These steamers have the right-of-way at all times and greatly interfere with the ferries.[23]

A Stockton man waited at Durham's Ferry on the San Joaquin for one and one-half hours before he could cross on account of the steady stream of boats passing up and down. At this time it was estimated that navigation would close in ten days.

Steamboat and barge.

The shipping season was not without its accidents. Most of these were due to carelessness. For example:

> Last Tuesday a steamboat hand, James Wellington, on board the steamer "Ellen," loading at Grayson, stepped into a coil in the slack of the line. The steamer drifted out and tightened up the line suddenly, crushing the man's leg terribly. He was taken to the County Hospital in a wagon where it is expected that the leg will have to be amputated.[24]

In order to avoid accidents, each spring boats went through to dredge out the river and clear it of snags and other dangerous material. In spite of this, boats were frequently caught on sand bars or snags. Often heavily loaded barges would get stranded during a rapid fall of the river water level. One case of a too adventurous boat nearly being lost was that of the *A. C. Freed*, snagged in the Merced River. It required the aid of two other boats before it was finally pulled free.[25] During the spring floods of 1862[26] one of the river steamers, Capt. Humphrey Jones' *Alta*, piloted by Capt. J. F. Ward, steamed across the country from Ward's Ferry to Adamsville over the great lake formed by the flood waters of the San Joaquin and Tuolumne.[27]

The San Joaquin was navigable at all times as far up as Crows Landing by steamers drawing five feet of water. During the June freshets, J. S. Bishop said, boats went up the river as far as Firebaugh, a distance of one hundred and sixty-two miles above Crows Landing. In high water times a boat drawing fifteen inches could ascend to Fresno City, one hundred and fifty miles further.[28]

There were many steamers plying up and down these rivers. In 1878 Captain Yates, who owned and operated the *Ellen*, published a list of steamers operating on the San Joaquin and their owners. Besides his own vessel, he listed

> The "Constance" and "Pioneer" owned by Nelson and Anderson, the "Ceres" and "Harriet" owned by Cornwall, Peters and Company, the "Caroline" owned by the Hooper Bros., and the "Alice" owned by Capt. McNeal. Besides the two barges, "Rosalind" and "Paterson" with a capacity of 1000 tons, there were other barges ranging down to two tons.[29]

Many other vessels operated up and down the river, including the *Clara Crow* and the *J. D. Peters*, but perhaps not in that particular year.

The current in the San Joaquin was very strong. In fact one steamer captain said that if it were not for the many twists and curves breaking the force of the current, no boat could ascend it.

Many interesting stories have been told regarding the personalities of some of the river boat captains. On the whole they were a rather jolly group. They managed their crews in much the same way the crews of seagoing vessels are handled, and apparently the use of profanity was an essential and important part of their effectiveness. Of the earlier captains, Humphrey Jones stands out above the rest. Marlow Hinton was one of the best known of the later captains whose boats went up the Tuolumne. The most amusing story related about these concerned an unnamed captain, who, while the women were on the upper deck to admire or to watch him, always managed the wheel of the boat, but with the women gone, the job would be assigned to some member of the crew.[30]

Before the steamboats left the river trade, bridges had been constructed to take the place of ferries and a bridge tender in charge was required to open the drawbridge to allow the boats to get by.

There were several factors causing the disappearance of the river steamer. As early as 1869 people recognized the fact that the rivers were rapidly becoming unnavigable. A few irrigation projects under way on the west side indicated in the 1870s that the steamboat was doomed.[31] The railroads also contributed to the extinction of the San Joaquin River boats.

The sight of the attractive river steamers loaded with lumber and other products on the outward-bound voyage to the grain-land towns and loaded with grain on the return trip to Stockton was only a memory after 1890. Over the same sandy, straw-covered roads on which the lumbering, creaking, long grain wagons of the plains and foothill settlers had hauled their loads to the river warehouses, the river-land farmers were now hauling their grain **to the railroad** centers on the plains.

Grain awaiting the steamboat.

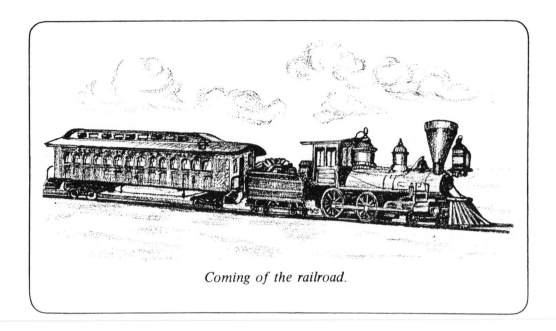

Coming of the railroad.

Chapter VII

The Railroad Transforms Transportation

Helen Hohenthal

The United States Government very early became interested in the construction of transcontinental railroad lines connecting the Pacific with the Atlantic. In 1853-54 five teams of U.S. Army engineers under the direction of Secretary of War Jefferson Davis explored as many routes from the Mississippi to the Pacific Ocean to find the most practicable line for a railroad. Sectional rivalry stalemated any bill authorizing construction of a railroad until Southern representatives had withdrawn from Congress at the beginning of the Civil War. In 1862 the Pacific Railway Act was passed, making extensive grants and loans available to the Central Pacific and Union Pacific Railroads for transcontinental railroad construction. Only when the last spike had been driven on the transcontinental line did the officers of the Central Pacific turn to building a road down the great San Joaquin Valley.[1]

By 1867 the era of the cattle range in the San Joaquin was over and the ranchers required a new means of getting their large wheat crops to the markets. As the population pushed from San Joaquin County to Stanislaus County and on south, the cost of shipping to the Stockton market became more and more prohibitive.

In 1867, the same year that the first plains settlers moved into the Turlock region, the valley newspapers began their campaign for railroads and canals. The *Stockton Independent* for April 18, 1867, said that there would be no progress in Merced, Stanislaus, or Mariposa Counties until both irrigation and railroads were established. It estimated at the time that these would treble the valuation of land, which was then not selling for more than $2.50 per acre. By 1869 the question of river navigation became so serious that even the river towns were demanding some relief. Stockton was indifferent to the situation. Several railroad projects were under way but none of them extended down into the heart of the valley. In 1863 the California State Legislature had authorized the counties to aid the Stockton and Copperopolis Railroad Company in constructing its line to the Copperopolis mining district. This idea of county aid to the railroads now suggested the possibility of constructing the line by not just aid, but actual local ownership.[2] Stockton was confident that she would be the terminal for any great railroad line anyway, so she did not push the matter, much to the disgust of the interior towns.

Leading economists and many high officials so thoroughly recognized the pressing need for railroads that they were even willing to back a "local aid" bill. At the time the bill permitting county aid to a valley railroad was pending in the State Legislature, J. Ross Browne said that a railroad line to Stanislaus County, the greatest grain-growing locality in the United States, would not only increase production and save one-fifth of the costs of transportation to markets, but it would also encourage the building of branch lines.[3]

At the same time that Stockton shippers were considering the construction of a Stockton-Visalia line, the Southern Pacific and Central Pacific were consolidating their forces preparatory to the completion of a network of railroad branches on the Pacific coast.[4] The main line was to be constructed down through the San Joaquin Valley. The valley was a desolate looking place, yet the railroad men foresaw possibilities of great development. When the route was first suggested, "Stanford and Hopkins with their engineers, rode over the upper section of the valley on horseback and camped out. For miles and miles they rode without seeing any signs of habitation except an occasional sheepherder's cabin."[5]

The construction of the San Joaquin Valley line was started on 31 December 1869, at Lathrop, and was extended to the Stanislaus River by the first part of 1870.[6] Then construction was discontinued until the railroads were consolidated in August 1870. Construction started once more in September of that year, and proceeded rapidly down the valley to Goshen, which it reached by the summer of 1872.[7]

There were no land grants or government loans to aid in the construction costs of the line north of Goshen. Landowners along the way made extensive grants of land to the railroad for its right-of-way. John W. Mitchell of Turlock, who owned the land over which the road passed from Keyes to Merced, granted them the right-of-way *gratis.*[8]

The surveys for the line south of Lathrop to Tipton were made by Assistant Engineer Slade, while nearly all the construction work was done under the supervision of Engineer Lott D. Norton. How much local aid the Central Pacific expected is a question. Dr. Stuart Daggett in his *Chapters on the History of the Southern Pacific* stated that it was the policy of the Company to start its railroad track and survey the line near a small town. Then representatives of the Company would approach the citizens of that town with the proposition that unless its citizens gave the railroad money, the town would be passed by and would die. Paradise, on the Tuolumne, was cited as an example of where this was done. None of the early settlers recall any statement made to this effect, and for the most part agreed with Mr. H. S. Crane, who said, "The Southern Pacific (Central Pacific at that time) did not solicit bribes from the people or towns as a reward for constructing the line through their lands."[9]

Just why the line did not go through Paradise is not known, but R. E. Kelly, manager of the development and colonization department of the Southern Pacific, stated, "When construction of the present Southern Pacific line was started south from Lathrop, the main objective was Los Angeles and the route taken was the one considered most practicable. At that time there were no towns of any size anywhere in the valley and the line of the railroad was kept away from the San Joaquin River to avoid conflict with the water transportation and to better aid in the development of the country not served with any means of transportation other than wagon roads."[10]

The construction of the railroad, once started, proceeded rapidly. It took the crew about six months to complete the line across the Turlock region, from the Tuolumne River to the Merced River. On 16 June 1871, the railroad bridge across the Tuolumne was rapidly approaching completion and by 6 October 1871, the rails had been laid as far as the Merced River. Twelve carloads of timber had been sent south for the construction of the bridge across the Merced.[11]

The construction work was all done by hand labor, the Central Pacific employing none but Chinese for ordinary work. No horses were used, even when a great deal of digging was required such as north of the Merced River. The Chinese used wheelbarrows for moving dirt and materials. When the Irish gang boss thought that the wheelbarrows were not full enough, he would send them back for more before they could unload. Since the Chinese could not talk English these Irish bosses worked out a very effective system of sign language and "cuss" words to direct the job. White labor was used in the timber construction of the bridges.

Chinese building the railroad.

The Chinese formed a company of their own whereby goods were bought wholesale and then later handed out to individual members. Chinese laborers were paid $26.00 a month and had to board themselves, but all supplies were bought from the railroad stores.

They lived in little tents located along the line of construction. Since these tents were just large enough to sleep in, all cooking had to be done outside the tents. Big kettles were provided for this purpose. In them they boiled their rice and cubed pork together. The Chinese scoured the country for the fattest pigs obtainable. What a novel sight these workers must have presented, squatting around the big black pot, eating pork and rice with their native dining service—chopsticks—and sipping tea from small cups. This very plain meal was followed by the opium pipe. As the hot sun disappeared in the west, one by one the "pig-tailed" Chinese left the chattering group in front of the tents and retired to enjoy the "producer of wonderful dreams."[12]

The materials for construction were brought to the places needed by means of handcars or an engine on the part of the track already constructed. The first track laid was of very light rails laid on split redwood ties. However, these rails were replaced later by rails of heavier and stronger materials.

When the first train ran through the district there were no towns along the line. Ceres consisted of a few houses and was a flagging station only. The first flagging station for Turlock was at Henderson's Crossing, one mile south of the present station, at the place better known today as the Golf Road Crossing. There were no buildings there and baggage dumped out on the ground sometimes landed in a mud hole. Therefore, a short while later the flagging station was moved up to a sandy spot, one mile farther north, the site where the first Turlock depot was built a year later.[13]

The first trains passing over the road were freight trains and emigrant trains. The latter were a combination of freight and emigrant passenger cars.[14]

Besides the freight, express, and emigrant cars there was one other which made regular trips down the valley on the railroad's pay day, called the pay day car. There were no banks, so this car was a necessity. The railroad used the same kind of strong boxes used by the Wells Fargo Express in earlier days. The men would enter the car at one side, and after receiving their pay would leave from the other side.

The second railroad line to pierce the Turlock region was that known as the East Southern Pacific.[15] This branch line passed through the northeast corner of the region. As early as 1869 a Stockton and Visalia Railroad Company was organized and constructed a line as far south as Oakdale by October 1871. The Central Pacific leased this line in 1874. The connecting link between Oakdale and Merced was built twenty years later by the Stockton and Tulare Railroad Company, the line being opened to traffic early in the year 1891. As the Stockton and Tulare Company had been consolidated with the Southern Pacific in 1888, the line as completed was a Southern Pacific line.[16]

Competing with the Southern Pacific for the trade of the valley, the San Francisco and San Joaquin Valley Company was organized in 1895 to construct a line to the southern part of the San Joaquin Valley. The construction of this line was under the leadership of a group of San Francisco capitalists including the sugar baron, Claus Spreckels. The men secured the right-of-way by purchase or gifts.[17] It was considered by the people of the valley as an enterprise backed by the Santa Fe. It was thus no surprise when in 1901, the Atchison, Topeka, and Santa Fe Company took over the control of the line.[18]

The last line to enter the Turlock district was the Tidewater Southern Railroad, now a branch of the Western Pacific. The line was constructed to Hilmar in 1918. A few years later, at the peak of the melon industry, a short branch was completed to Turlock.

Thus in less than forty years from the time the first railroad line went through the district there were four railroads serving the people. When Stanford and his associates made the survey for the first line, the lands of the valley were used for pasturage or grain raising. The valley was described as "An absolutely raw country that could promise no volume of traffic for years to come." Seven years later, however, the crops were so immense that the newspapers estimated the capacity of the railroad would be taxed for months to come, even though "three daily trains of forty cars each were in service."[19]

The railroad was a great aid to the farmers; it saved both time and money. In 1878 wheat was leaving Turlock in carload lots, some cars carrying as much as twenty-four tons, the cars returning the following day from Stockton for another load. During the summer months both flatcars and boxcars were used as there was no danger from rain.

The profit to the farmer was greater because the railroad cut down his costs of transportation, eliminated unnecessary waste in riverbank warehouses, and allowed him to hold over his crop until the higher winter prices. However, he shared this profit with the railroad company, for as early as 1878 the Union Pacific and Central Pacific started the practice of "pooling the traffic" and entered into business agreements whereby the freight rates from New York to San Francisco were doubled in cost to the shipper. As competition for the trade decreased, Professor Daggett has shown that rates from Lathrop south into the valley were greatly increased without justification.[20] The costs for passenger traffic were not excessive, the trip from Turlock to Modesto and return being $1.50.[21]

Today a network of concrete or blacktop state and county highways serves the farmers in the district where in 1880 a road was "the shortest distance between the place you are and the place you wish to be." A person desiring to go to Ceres or Modesto from his home near Turlock would strike out across the grainfields in a beeline to his destination. For years afterward these "roads" could be recognized by the fact that the grain was not as good there as on the rest of the ground. Some farmers objected to these cross-county roads so much that they resorted to various tricks to keep them off of their land. One man fenced his land; another dug a ditch three feet deep and three feet wide around his whole section.

The railroads which drove out the stages, wagons, and boats in the '80s are today being faced with the problem of competition with their successors, the private autos, buses, airplanes, and trucks. A bus service, with buses leaving in both directions every few hours, cut down passenger traffic on the trains, to say nothing about the number of people who used their private cars. A steady stream of trucks leaving the valley during the fruit season took thousands of dollars of trade from the railroad. By 1960, however, Turlockers had to go to Modesto to board many of the express buses. Passenger service on the Southern Pacific was finally eliminated in 1971 after a hundred years of operation.

Two factors were necessary to develop this region, the railroad and irrigation. Neither of these two could have done it alone. The water was necessary to produce the crops, and without transportation the value and size of the crops would have been limited by the amount of local consumption. The demands for both a railroad and irrigation were first voiced at the same time, but there were three railroad lines serving the district before the canals brought water to the worn-out grain fields. The dream Stanford, Huntington, and others had of cultivated fields and orchards made possible by the coming of the railroad became a reality only after irrigation appeared.

Warehouse of John W. Mitchell at Turlock. From Branch's History.

Chapter VIII

Early Turlock, 1871-1900

Helen Hohenthal

Turlock's location, like that of Ceres, was determined by its suitability for shipping grain from nearby ranches on the new Central Pacific Railroad line. The original siding was placed a mile south of the permanent site, but the ground was uneven and held water. Turlock was founded by John William Mitchell in 1871. Mitchell had run large flocks of sheep in the vicinity and in the Paradise City area north of the Tuolumne River for years before towns or even settlers had appeared upon those plains. After having engaged in land speculation for a time around Lodi, Mitchell began buying up land until he had some 100,000 acres beginning near Keyes Switch on the railroad and stretching twenty-five miles south to the vicinity of Atwater.

An affable and kindly man, he was known to the youngsters of Turlock as "Uncle Johnnie." One of those "nephews," Loren Fulkerth, later described him as "rather fleshy, smooth faced," with "a kindly disposition, bright eyes," and a sociable nature.

Mitchell farmed his thousands of acres through the tenant system. In most cases he did not furnish teams. If he did, he got a much larger percentage of the crop. But he did furnish a section of land, more or less, house, barns and sheds for equipment, implements, windmill and tank, and both stock feed and credit to carry the renter until the first crop was harvested.[1] Mitchell had a string of warehouses along the railroad, moving from one to another of them. He took a fatherly interest in all the affairs of Turlock and was always a leader in programs which would improve the economic or social conditions of the region.

A few scattered settlers were living northwest of Turlock when it was established, and some of them moved promptly into town. The first postmaster, Clark Lander, proposed the name of Turlock to the postal authorities on the suggestion of his brother, the second postmaster, H. W. Lander. In view of the lively discussions which have surrounded the naming of the town, the following letter from Henry Lander to his sister, Florence Lander Porter, is quoted in full. The name "Turlock" is unusual and distinctive, regardless of its origin.

*John W. Mitchell,
founder of Turlock.*

Prattville, Sept. 24th, 1908

Sister Florence:

Yours of Aug. 25th duly received making inquiries to the naming Turlock. I was the main one in getting the Post Office at the Old Crane Ranch. Mitchell's name was never sent in by Brother Clark. Clark picked on the name "Sierra" and sent it to Washington and the Department said it would not do as it would cause confusion with Sierra County and to send another name and avoid sending any person's name if possible. I had been reading about some people that lived on a bay called Turlock Bay. It was some where on the Coast of England or Scotland (I forget which) and I told Clark to send "Turlock" as there was not another post office of the name in the United States and it was accepted of course.

When they put the Railroad through the officials wanted to honor J. W. Mitchell (as he had given the right-of-way) and they called it Mitchell Station. But Mitchell said, "No, let it be called after the post office, Turlock." And when he went to shipping grain he called it "Turlock" and wrote it "Turlock" and notified the officials to call it "Turlock."

I think the first thing that was started was the Old Mitchell Warehouse. Scantling laid on the ground and filled in level between them and then 1x12 boards nailed on them. The first freight was unloaded on the old Mitchell platform and then 4x4 redwood scantling set in the ground to make the building. I was one of the first that drove nails in Turlock.

The next building started was the old Jim Allen Hotel.[2] Then Giddings and Ward moved their store from the River and then Clark moved the Post Office in the back end of the store and kept it there until I built him a small building.

Your Brother

H. W. Lander

At exactly what time the name "Turlock" was first applied is not known, but its first appearance in print in a valley newspaper was in the *Stanislaus County News* for 12 May 1871. The same paper carried the first description of the new town on 22 December.

Another new town has been laid out within this County, on the Southern Pacific lines south of this place [Modesto]. We hear lots have already been sold and a switch, depot, and telegraph are to be established. The new town will be known as Turlock and is situated on Mr. Mitchell's land. The firm of Giddings and Ward will move to there from Empire City.[3]

In Turlock, as in other towns, early settlers included men and women who moved to the valley from mining areas. Among these were several of a party of Frenchmen who came here from Sonora. In this group were Peter and Bernard Le Cussan and Joe Blanc. In the winter of 1872 Joe Blanc and Bernard Le Cussan cut wood in the Merced River bottoms for Mitchell to sell to the farmers.[4]

In the town was a saloon run by "Dad" Purdy. James Allen hauled an old hotel from another dying town, Westport, and soon was advertising in the valley papers that good lodging and home-cooked meals awaited the visitor at the Turlock Hotel.[5] Not only that, but a livery stable would take care of his teams, and a bar in the hotel his desire for liquid refreshments. The Fulkerth brothers set up a blacksmith shop and wagon-making shop on the southeast corner of East Main and Center Streets.[6] Within a short time another blacksmith shop was put up on the southeast corner of East Main and Center Streets. This was the Donovan shop. During that year Mitchell built a large warehouse east of the railroad on Olive Street. So six months after the railroad was put through, the town of Turlock was ready for business, with its two blacksmith shops, one hotel, one general merchandise store,[7] a saloon, a warehouse, and a livery stable. The railroad was at the same time erecting a temporary depot and section gang houses.[8]

The post office was established in 1870. At that time the postmaster, Clark Lander, brought the mail from Empire or Paradise City not more often than twice a week, receiving for this service one dollar a month. The first post office was in the Stephen Porter home about a mile north of Turlock. It was later moved to the back of the Giddings and Ward store, which was opened for business in January 1872. There was no regular time for getting the mail. Often men making the trip to Modesto or these other two towns would take the mail bag along and drop it at Porter's or Lander's home on their way back.

Mr. and Mrs. S. V. Porter (Florence Lander) at left, about 1889. Whipple Collection, Turlock Public Library.

The Porters rented 600 acres of Mitchell land in 1868. Stephen Porter also worked for John Mitchell, plowing up his prairie land for grain crops several years before Turlock was established. In addition to the Porters, there were three families on Mitchell land in the Turlock town area. The Henry A. Osborns were a mile to the east of the future town. The Allens were a mile to the west, and the Warners to the northeast about where Geer and Monte Vista Roads intersect in 1971.[9]

Dwellings in Turlock were not as numerous as business houses during the first year. Captain J. F. Ward moved a house from Empire City, a typical small one-story, five-room frame dwelling,[10] and Giddings and Shrimple each built a new house. The Giddings home was on Center near Crane Avenue. The reason for the few dwellings is that most of the people, including some of the businessmen, such as the Fulkerths, lived on nearby farms.

Inquiry as to whether the town was laid out according to a plan or just grew brought the answer that the town survey started at a post in front of Donovan's blacksmith shop at the "southeast" corner of Center and East Main Streets.[11] The older part of Turlock, like many San Joaquin Valley towns, is laid out parallel and at right angles to the railroad track. "North" according to convention is the direction the train goes when headed toward Sacramento, although it may be more nearly west than north. The newer part is laid out on a true north-south, east-west grid based on the U.S. survey.

Great hopes were held for the future development of the little town. One paper predicted that it would command the trade of Snelling, Hopeton, Merced Falls, Coulterville, and share in the Yosemite trade.[12] But these towns themselves were declining as gold mining waned and people moved away to the new towns on the railroad. The grain ranches stretching far east of Montpellier, pouring hundreds of wagonloads of grain into Turlock during the harvest season, contributed more to her prosperity. The local purchases of the large grain ranches were modest, which accounts for the fact that ten years after it was founded Turlock was described as a town of about fifteen dwellings, many saloons, two stores, five grain warehouses, a couple of hotels, a butcher shop, and a Chinatown. The census of 1880 listed 192 inhabitants, but many of these were living in hotels or boarding houses and most were probably transient laborers.[13]

The Giddings and Ward general store carried some drugs and patent medicines, and there was a barbershop in one of the saloons. In addition to James Allen's Turlock Hotel, there was now the Farmers' Hotel.

Harry C. Russell moved the Farmers' Hotel to Turlock from Ward's Ferry. Russell ran the hotel for some time before selling it to Charles Hummeltenberg. Russell's warehouse was across Front Street facing the hotel, which occupied the southeast corner of Front and Crane Avenue. The hotel's livery stable was on the corner of Crane and Center.

The hotel was an attractive and popular place. Downstairs there were a bar, game room, kitchen, and dining room; upstairs, close to twenty rooms.

Well prepared meals cost fifty cents at Hummeltenberg's in the early years of its operation. Later the price was dropped to twenty-five cents, but the quality did not change.[14]

Before the end of the first decade, another blacksmith shop was added to the list of business establishments. Donovan opened a big shop on Front Street in the same block as the Farmers' Hotel, while continuing to operate the one on Main. It was a story and a half, painted white, with a white picket fence and a few locust trees. The owner was very proud of his shop.

A Chinatown, large in proportion to the size of Turlock then, was located along south First Street. Chinese worked on the railroad and about 100 were employed as cooks, laundrymen, and farm laborers. Their "boss" was Yanikee. He also was their storekeeper and the supervisor of their living quarters— small shacks.[15]

The 1880s saw a rapid development within the town, although the surrounding country was not as productive as it had been in the '70s; and many farmers, hit by a series of crop failures, were already hopelessly in debt.

Charles Lander had a small store on the southeast corner of present-time First and West Main Streets. When John Mitchell built the Fountain Hotel, the roof of the Lander store was removed and the store absorbed by the new construction. It was called the Fountain Hotel because there was a fountain in the center of the inner court. Construction was done a piece at a time, and finally the three-storied hotel was completed.

Every room had a marble washstand and running water. Brass faucet fixtures added to the beauty of the basin. The building plumbing included one-and-a-half-inch lead pipes. Water for the building was pumped by windmills and stored in three big wooden tanks on the south end of the building.

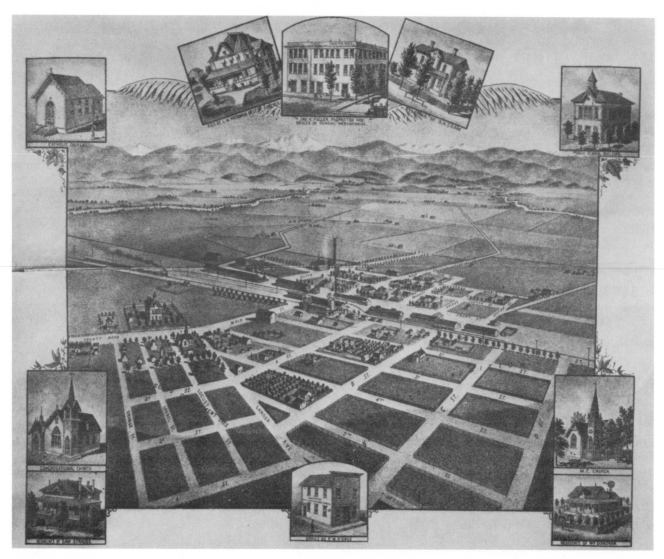

Turlock, 1888. Idealized aerial perspective. From TDJ, 11 Feb. 1910.

The hotel never showed profits and stood idle for a long time. Young looters robbed it—knocked off the brass faucets and sold the brass. Mrs. John Clipper said her parents, Mr. and Mrs. J. L. Brown, ran the hotel for a time and she thought it was a beautiful place.

After completion of the building, J. E. Fuller bought out Lander's store. Then Henry A. Osborn bought out Fuller, but the latter continued as hotel manager.

By 1886 the Fountain Hotel was doing business under the direction of J. E. Fuller, who then had an ice and coal house built along the railroad opposite the hotel. The hotel was in bad condition when Horace Crane, administrator of the Mitchell estate, had it torn down about 1901.[16]

The Lander Tin Shop on the corner of Broadway and West Main was the beginning of the west side development, beyond which were grainfields. The Chatom slaughterhouse, located at about East Main Street and Canal Drive, marked the other extremity of the business section.

Progress of the town was shown when the four general stores of Worth and Waters, C. F. Lander, J. E. Fuller, and Dave Elkins added a good supply of fresh fruits and vegetables to the staples usually carried.[17]

Fountain Hotel.

By the 1880s a pile of "junk" began to collect around the Mitchell Warehouse—abandoned prairie schooners that had carried their owners across the plains. Mitchell seemed to fall heir to things nobody wanted. These schooners were described as "wagons with beds eighteen feet long, six to seven feet deep, wheels seven feet or more high and with two to two and a half inch tires, canvas tops and wooden sides. They were finally sold for junk."[18]

Hoboes rated in this grain-growing area as potential laborers in the harvest season. In his Turlock warehouse John Mitchell had a woman cook who ran "the Beanery" just for hoboes. This woman did nothing else but cook beans and bread free of charge for the hoboes. E. L. Fine told Whipple that there was an old hobo lodging house three-quarters of a mile out on West Main Street. The constable used to arrest the hoboes in the morning and fine them up to $2.00 per head, then turn them loose, and later go back and get them again.

Mitchell had some old buildings to the east of his Olive Street warehouse, including a barn with a big hayloft. Constable Jim Parker and Deputy George Spires used to go down to the Mitchell barns and arrest hoboes. They were allowed $1.00 to $2.00 per head. When Mitchell found out about it, he put up a big signboard and painted on it a statement to the effect that no officer was allowed to arrest anyone sleeping in the barn. Thereafter he let anyone sleep there who wanted to.[19]

Mitchell did not drink or treat in drinks. He called Front Street "Barbary Coast" or "Cannibal Street," but the rule of the community was that anyone hungry was to be fed. The saloonkeepers added, "If you are busted, you get a drink for nothing." Sometimes there were 100 to 150 men lying around waiting for work, so many free drinks were passed out.[20]

While many gambled and drank to excess, there were few who were vicious or criminally minded, and few who did not meet their financial commitments if they had the money to do so.

Pete Johnson, who claimed that he was the first Swede in Turlock, having come in 1873, kept $500.00 or more in his monkey wrench box in the back of the wagon without ever having any of it stolen. When Purdy wanted money to build a saloon on the northeast corner of Center and East Main Streets, he borrowed $800.00 of Pete and paid it back in six months. Purdy named his location Hog Corner because hogs ran loose in the little town and wallowed in the mud around his water trough. This Purdy saloon was also called "no place."

Jails were only for temporary holding of drunks or others. All cases were handled in Modesto. At first the town used a handy boxcar to hold the accused. The only reason a jail was built was that the Southern Pacific would not allow the use of boxcars as jails any longer. So Turlock built a jail about 1890—a small one about 12' x 12' with bars over the windows. It was located approximately in the center of the 1971 parking lot south of Coey's Shoe Store on First Street. The writer as a child remembers it as a mysterious small red building, standing alone, probably empty most of the time.

West Main Street in the 1880s.

Old-timers said that Bill Dalton, leader of one of the famous outlaw gangs, tended bar in the Turlock Hotel for a time. Another bad one, W. D. Howell, ran a store in the late 1880s on Hog Corner. He was a member of a gang of counterfeiters and passed his counterfeit gold here and in Stockton, where he was finally caught.[21]

Sonntag and Evans, train robbers, had a livery stable at Modesto. Sam Strauss said they used to bring drummers with their samples to Turlock stores. When the stable burned, some thought the fire was set by the owners to kill their Negro stable boy, who may have known too much. After a train hold-up, their trail was picked up at Ceres. A detective from San Francisco, Len Harris, was wounded and died soon after.[22]

Front Street around 1890.

In 1886 statewide agitation against the Chinese resulted in the formation of the Anti-Chinese League of Turlock. Chinatown, which consisted of a number of shacks located on First Street opposite the American Railway Express Company's building, was no longer on undesirable land. A fire in Chinatown hastened the departure of the Chinese to a new location on Center Street and East Avenue. Of the fire, "Aunt Abby" Fulkerth said, "Old Purdy, the saloonkeeper, wanted to get rid of Chinatown. He pretended to help put out the Chinatown fire but handed watercans full of coal oil. Others were setting fire to the Chinese beds. The Chinamen caught on to what was happening and cried, 'Gadammy, Gadammy!' "

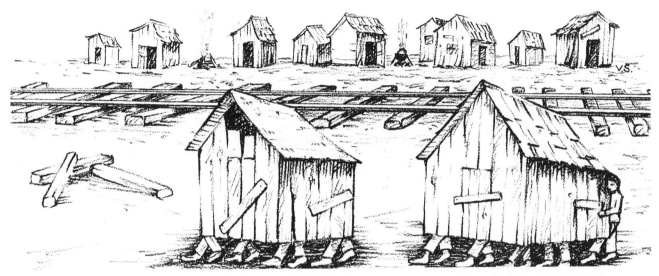

Chinatown on the move.

The Chinese were ordered to move and were given permission to settle on the north side of East Avenue between the present Alpha and Minaret Streets. In moving they knocked the floors out of the remaining shacks, then lifted them on their shoulders and walked them to the new destination. Here they reestablished their wash houses and raised new gardens. In the back yard of every Chinese house was a pen for a few chickens and pigs.

The end of the Chinese colony was told by Horace Crane. One by one the Chinese either died or moved away, leaving their empty shacks. At last only one Chinaman remained. He was a very old man. One night his house caught fire and he was burned to death. The next day a coroner's jury was held in the old Fountain Hotel barroom, Bentley acting as foreman. The jury, after much deliberation, concluded that the Chinaman had met his death by burning up. The next question was what to do with him. His total estate consisted of two pigs, about 30-pounders, that had escaped the fire. Finally a professional gambler, Cochrane by name, said he would bury him for the two pigs, and his offer was accepted. He went over to the store, secured a 150-pound cracker box, and put the Chinaman in it.

The Chinese had their own burial grounds located north of town. When the Chinese colony of Turlock died out, Chinese from other places came, dug up the bodies, and shipped them back to China for burial.

The population increase in the late 1880s, though small, stretched the meagre resources of the community. No houses were available for rent. To some, the situation suggested a profitable business in the building and renting of houses.[23]

This period saw the appearance of the first churches in the town. They were the Congregational Church located on the corner of Center and Olive, the Methodist Church on the corner of Lander and West Main, and the Catholic Church on South Broadway. Only one of these, the Catholic Church, remained in use any length of time.[24]

Turlock had several early newspapers, printed in the '80s and '90s. Some time between 1886 and 1889 E. W. Pierce, railroad agent and postmaster, published the *Turlock Pioneer*. Its contents consisted of news items of Turlock, but his remarks were often so slurring and sarcastic that the paper was shortlived.[25] Horace and Stephen Crane took over the post office job when Pierce was ousted. The post office was located in the Max Strauss store.

The Cranes got tired of the job and placed Carlos De Seda, a very bright and popular young man, in charge. He was also telegraph and express agent. De Seda is given credit for putting out the second paper in Turlock. It was called the *Item* and consisted of two sheets a little larger than an ordinary sheet of business paper. Copies were made by means of a hectograph. In his paper he covered local items of interest and pinned the paper on doors of homes and businesses. Besides owning a Turlock paper, De Seda wrote up local news for the *Modesto Herald*. His column heading was "Razzle Dazzle."[26]

Mr. and Mrs. Stephen Crane and three sons in front of their home.
Whipple Collection, Turlock Public Library.

A third paper, the *Turlock Times,* was published in 1892 by D. James Foley. While smaller than the *Turlock Pioneer,* it contained just as many local news items. Foley's *Turlock Times* was four pages, four columns to a page. The page was ten by fifteen inches. Foley used a Gordon Press and printed one page at a time. His first shop was next to Reilly's blacksmith shop on Main, which he had bought from Donovan. Then he moved to the south end of the Fountain Hotel. After the 1893 fire, he moved to Modesto and sold the paper. From Modesto he moved to Yosemite Valley and became a photographer. His *Turlock Times* was jokingly called the "cobweb."

Turlock in the early 1890s was described as a fairly prosperous busy town, consisting of three hotels, one restaurant, three general merchandise stores,[27] one drug store, one tin shop, one boot and shoe shop, three livery stables, two blacksmith shops, a butcher shop, five warehouses, and sixteen saloons.[28]

Occasionally before 1900 doctors came to practice in Turlock, but little information about them is recorded. With the sand plains homes far apart, pioneers depended on patent medicines or homemade remedies for medication, and the services of friends or family members for nursing care. There were no hospitals in the area south of Modesto. If the sick person was a man, the men took care of him; if a woman, the women nursed her.

The general stores carried patent medicines and a plentiful supply of whiskey and carbolic acid. People could only guess as to the cause of many illnesses. Horace Crane said white people could not

Wheat wagons coming in from Montpellier area. Courtesy of T. W. Randolph.

live along the rivers, but the Chinese could. Perhaps the Chinese habit of drinking hot tea instead of cold water was the reason.

The three doctors mentioned very briefly by interviewees were probably representative of the profession in small towns. In 1880 a Charles Phipps, popular cornet player in the town band, was called "Dr. Phipps." He did not have an office, but he did the "human doctoring" in emergencies. Usually Dr. Evans of Modesto handled the rest.[29]

Thomas Gaddis said that for a time in the late 1880s Turlock boasted of having both a doctor and a druggist. Dr. J. A. Young was that doctor. He lived next to the tank of the old China House on Front Street, north of the location of the old Granger Hall. Dr. Young's brother-in-law, William (Tom) Smith, had a drug store in which he sold more whiskey than drugs. People bought whiskey by the gallon at the drug store because they thought it was of better quality.[30]

When the Farmers Hotel burned, they moved the bar outside and kept serving drinks.

A third doctor was an Irishman, Dr. Purdon. He had invented a mechanical device that worked by wrist action movements. The *San Francisco Examiner* sent a woman writer, Ella Wheeler Wilcox, down to interview Purdon. She told him she was surprised to find a man of his ability in a town composed of seven trees and a couple of box cars. His reply was that the only reason he was here was his health.[31]

Destitute families were given three or four months' provisions as soon as the need was known.

By the end of 1889, Turlock had unused church buildings but did hold Sunday School classes in the Fountain Hotel Lodge Hall or the Gaddis Hall. In fact, many of the children attended the Methodist Sunday School classes Sunday morning and Congregational Church classes in the afternoon. As soon as the Congregational classes were over, they would take the shortest route to Washington Hall where the Turlock Band was playing.

For those who believed in baptism by immersion, services were held at the old reservoir a mile south of town. This reservoir was used also for swimming lessons until the irrigation canals were in operation.

There were no banks in Turlock until 1905, but many Turlock citizens did business with banks in San Francisco, Modesto, or Sacramento. Pay cars came to small towns on regular schedules. Otherwise, the general stores performed certain banking services for their customers.

Little paper money circulated; gold and silver coins were the money media. There were no pennies in circulation. Mitchell used postage stamps for amounts below five cents because he insisted on exact amounts of change.

Fraternal organizations came with the early development of the town. Captain Ward organized the first lodge, the Sons of Temperance. It held its meetings in the waiting room of the depot. Other groups included the Knights of Pythias, the Ancient Order of United Workmen, the Independent Order of Good Templars, and the Turlock Grange, a farmers' organization.

The failure of the grain crops in some dry years already had its effect on the town, for it was not able always to boast of profitable business.

On the night of 3 October 1893 a disastrous fire wiped out the main part of the business section on Front Street from Crane (Market Street) to East Main. The fire started in the back of Pat McGraw's saloon on Front Street. Mrs. J. L. Brown, whose home was on the corner of A Street and First Street, was an eyewitness to the blaze. She said Mr. Brown was just returning from the Knights of Pythias Lodge at 10:00 P.M. when it happened. There was no fire-fighting apparatus. Men worked with water-soaked sacks and buckets to save the Davis Warehouse across the street and the Turlock Hotel. The big saloon at the corner of Front and East Main burned the longest—until after midnight.

After the fire Sam Strauss opened a small store in Fred Geer's barn on Center Street. He remained there for a couple of years until his supply warehouse was emptied. Then he returned to San Francisco. Gus Gerlach was the only one who rebuilt his place of business. His saloon was the only building in the block for a long time.

One saloon owner had been in business for just a month before the fire. He had no insurance. However, he started another saloon in Granger Hall, but the town was dead and there was no business. He finally lost his mind and killed himself with coal oil. An inquest was held in Granger's Hall. The coroner waited for the verdict, but the jury said it had to dispose of his liquor. After they drank all the booze, they brought in the verdict. The deceased man's estate consisted of one watch.

After the fire, many farmers did their trading in places like Modesto or Stockton.

In 1894 the Farmers' Hotel and Mrs. Martin's boarding house next to it burned, increasing the devastation.

Another major cause of the failure of Turlock to stage a comeback was the construction of the two railroad lines east of Turlock. When east side wheat ranchers started hauling their grain to the "East Southern Pacific" at Hickman and Montpellier, Turlock lost a good share of its former trade.

Even after 1900, big burnt-over spots were visible. Turlock was a sorry sight, with her cheap shacks; her closed churches; her occasional stretches of wooden sidewalks, often with loose boards; her hitching bars in front of every building; her sandy, dirty, and strawed streets or mudholes, depending on the season. The town was not rebuilt until after 1902, when the Swedes and the Portuguese began to settle in Turlock.

Irrigation canals were carried across ravines on wooden trestles which were later replaced by earthfills.

Chapter IX

Creation of the Turlock Irrigation District

Helen Hohenthal

Just as they found that the railroad was necessary to supplement the carrying power of the wagons and river boats, so now the people were convinced that irrigation was required for the continued productivity of their valley ranches.[1] Irrigation in the Central Valley was not a new idea, but no scheme had yet been presented which would satisfy the demands of the people living in the present Turlock and Modesto Irrigation Districts. Elsewhere in the state, irrigation companies seem to have been formed more for the purpose of speculation in land and water rights than for increased farm productivity and profit. Such speculative schemes had not inveigled the farmers of this area, even though in periods of great drought they had lost almost enough to pay for such a system.

The people had faith in the soil and its response to irrigation. They waited only for a law which would allow them to proceed without becoming involved in the court cases and dissatisfactions of previous systems. Weighing the relative values of these earlier organizations, the farmers gradually formulated opinions as to what would be satisfactory, and from among their own citizens picked one who could draft a correct law. On 28 May 1886, Vital E. Bangs, a Modestan but a member of the Ceres Grange, in an address to his Grange, summarized what he considered should be the demands of the farmers.[2] He said,

> That the farmers should demand a change in the state constitution and laws so that; first, there could be no more unlimited appropriation of water for speculative purposes; second, that the almost universal doctrine of the civil law, as regards water rights, should be asserted; and third, a new water code for equal distribution of water and water rights, under strict regulations, with no chance of monopoly, should be drawn up.

It is rather interesting to note here that the Ceres and Turlock Granges were the only active Granges in this section of the valley. They were both located within the boundaries of the present Turlock Irrigation District, and by their frequent joint meetings and resolutions indicated that they were in accord on this vital question of irrigation.

In the fall of 1886, the Ceres Grange passed a resolution against the policies favored by members of an irrigation convention held in San Francisco. The Ceres Grange wanted the law changed so as to allow the County Board of Supervisors to pass judgment upon all the acts and books of an irrigation company.[3]

As an answer to the demands of the progressive leaders of the county, C. C. Wright,[4] a young attorney from Modesto, was elected to the State Assembly, and by the spring of 1887 had drafted the law bearing his name, and which later gained for him the title of "the father of irrigation districts." This act has been used as the basis for all similar legislation throughout the United States.[5]

It has been the good fortune of the Turlock and Modesto Districts to have had, since the inception of the Irrigation Act, many men of wisdom and foresight to direct and advise them. Not least among them was the author of this Act. C. C. Wright, having been closely associated with the people of these districts, first as a La Grange school teacher, then later as District Attorney,[6] knew that the crying need of the worn out grain lands was irrigation. Before attempting to draft the law, however, he consulted many lawyers[7]—and apparently engineers—of experience. The result was a law, which if not perfect in every detail, was at least one which lent itself to constructive revision as conditions required.[8]

According to C. E. Grunsky, the first Engineer for the Modesto Irrigation District and Assistant State Engineer under William Hammond Hall, the Wright Irrigation Law was based in a large part upon the draft of an irrigation district law prepared by William Hammond Hall, State Engineer of California, a draft published in 1886.[9]

The Wright Act, which was approved 7 March 1887, provided "for the organization and government of irrigation districts and. . .for the acquisition of water and other property and for the distribution of water thereby for irrigation purposes." It is described as an attempt to give "highest legal sanction to the permanent union of land and water, but at the same time to recognize every other existing right and equity."

C. C. Wright, author of the Irrigation Districts Act.

Wright, in referring to his election, stated: "I was elected for the express purpose of advocating some measure providing for municipal control of water for irrigation."[10]

Wright patterned the water district government on that of California counties, with an elected board and powers to assess and collect money in a manner with which all were familiar. All land in the district was to be taxed, the property being assessed at its full cash value.

The farmers of many districts rushed into organization without knowing what it was all about. The law as first drafted was not restrictive enough to save these unwise farmers who, regardless of whether the conditions of their soil, water source or resources would warrant it, organized and then, when failure occurred, blamed the Wright Act. This Act was intended to provide the legal machinery for those who had the necessary materials—not to act as a genie, producing something out of nothing. The speculative character of some of these districts was criticized by the man who saved the Turlock District, Judge James A. Waymire. The writer believes that Mr. Wright, in drafting his law, had in mind the two areas, the Turlock and Modesto Districts, where almost ideal conditions prevailed. Mr. Wright watched the operation of the law very closely in the early years of its existence and was one of the first to suggest changes.[11]

With the legal machinery provided for them, it did not take the farmers and businessmen of the Turlock district long to act. Only three months (7 March to 6 June 1887) elapsed between the time the Wright Act was approved by the State Legislature and the Turlock Irrigation District was declared "duly organized."

The process of organization under the Wright Act is described in a report on the Turlock Irrigation District by the Irrigation District Bond Commission.

A petition for organization was presented to the Stanislaus County Board of Supervisors, signed by a majority of the landowners whose property would be affected by the proposed irrigation project. The board then fixed a date for the election of district officers, which was held accordingly in each division of the district on 28 May 1887. On 6 June 1887, the County Board of Supervisors met again, this time to pass judgment upon the election returns.[12] It declared that the election had been regularly held according to the provisions of the law, and that the officers were regularly elected. Finally, it fixed the boundaries for the district and declared it "duly organized as the Turlock Irrigation District."[13]

The original territory in this district, according to government reports, amounted to 176,210 acres of land. This land, generally speaking, included almost all irrigable land between the Tuolumne and Merced Rivers, from the foothills on the east to the San Joaquin River on the west.

The next few steps of the story will best be related through references to the minutes of the meetings of that first Irrigation District board.

In the rooms of the Stanislaus County Board of Supervisors, the newly elected members of the Turlock District Board gathered for their first meeting on 15 June 1887. We find in this little group men who were accustomed to assuming leadership in new undertakings: W. L. Fulkerth, who in 1863 came to California via the covered wagon route, and who was one of the first settlers in this district; E. V. Cogswell, a pioneer grain farmer of the Waterford region; R. M. Williams, a farmer of the Keyes neighborhood; J. T. Dunn, who not only served as a director, but who in later days spent his own time and money to help it survive when litigations and financial difficulties almost forced the District to "give up the ghost"; and E. B. Clark, who was a progressive farmer of the Hilmar section.

Upon the shoulders of these men rested great responsibilities. They were the pivot upon which was balanced the success or failure of this significant undertaking.

As we meet them gathered in the board rooms in Modesto, we wonder what their thoughts are for the moment. We have no records of the conversation that passed between them; no records except the minutes of the meeting to show whether they had made a study of the problems of irrigation prior to the meeting; no records describing them as they sat around the table at that first board meeting. Yet that meeting was the opening scene in the great drama of successful irrigation district organization.

E. B. Clark was elected president of the Board, and R. M. Williams was appointed secretary *pro tem.* Clark was appointed a committee of one to investigate the status of water rights, while W. L. Fulkerth and E. V Cogswell were appointed to study the irrigation systems already built in the area to the south and to recommend a man for the post of surveyor and engineer. Next day the Board voted to locate the offices of the District at Turlock.[14] District Assessor J. W. Davis and Collector A. N. Crow presented their bonds and certificates of election. P. J. Hazen was selected as attorney for the District.

Thus we see the directors had set in motion some of the necessary machinery for irrigation development. Even the first meeting was not devoted solely to the routine of organization. These men meant business. They divided the work of investigation, so that each would have some definite responsibility.

The twenty-seventh of June 1887 found the directors back in board conferences again. Reports were in order. Director E. B. Clark, "the committee appointed to look after the water rights of the

District," reported that he had located a water right for two hundred and twenty-five thousand inches about forty feet above a place on the Tuolumne River known as Wheaton's Dam; also one about forty feet below, and another about a quarter of a mile above, each for the same amount as the first.

The committee on engineering had gone to Fresno. It reported on the management and cost of the different canals which they visited, and the standing of the different engineers who had done work there.

At this time a committee composed of Fulkerth and Clark "was appointed to consult with the State Engineer." The latter agreed to meet with the Board at any time, the only charges being his actual traveling expenses.

By 7 July 1887 the directors had chosen Mr. George Manuel of Fresno as engineer for the District, for which services he was paid a salary of $200 a month.[15] Manuel had been consulted several times previously by people in this region in regard to establishing irrigation systems here, so he was fairly well acquainted with the existing conditions.[16] Before coming to Turlock he had been chief engineer of the Fresno Canal and Irrigation Company which operated a canal on the north side of Kings River near Fresno.[17]

In the minutes for 25 July 1887, the Board ordered that its members "go to La Grange with the engineers for the purpose of inspecting the site for a dam and also the route selected for a canal."

Two months later, on 16 September 1887, Engineer Manuel reported to the Board that "his estimated cost of the canal, with the necessary distributing ditches, bridges, dam, and other necessary expenses was $467,544.62."[18]

Mr. Manuel's plans from the first were based on the assumption that the Turlock diversion of water would be from the Wheaton Dam site.

Knowing the danger of being bound by too low an estimate of financial needs, the Board called for an election to authorize the issuance of $600,000 in bonds, and set the election for 8 October 1887. No tangle of legal terms, or of "saids" and "therefores," can hide the importance of this step. The Board was about to ask the people to burden themselves and their lands with indebtedness in order to insure against certain failure in the future. The board members were confident that the people, who voted for organization in the ratio of four persons in favor to every one against, would now stand behind their chosen directors.

Long meetings those early board conferences must have been! That particular day's business was wound up with the appointment of two very important committees. Williams was appointed a committee of one, to go to La Grange for the purpose of filing water rights, while Clark, Fulkerth and Cogswell, together with Engineer Manuel, were assigned the duty of consulting with a similar committee from the Modesto District "in regard to building a dam across the Tuolumne, to be used by both districts."

On 12 October 1887 the results of the election were examined. The directors found that out of the 188 votes cast in the District only 12 opposed the bonds. Since the only changes in the District's five divisions have been for the most part additions of land, which would not alter the originally established boundaries, it is interesting to note the way in which the people voted.[19] In Division No. 1, which includes the Denair and Hickman areas, the vote was 17 votes for, none against; in Division No. 2, which includes Hughson, Ceres, and Keyes, the vote was 36 for, 2 against; in Division No. 3, which includes land southwest of Modesto, 47 for, 5 against; in Division No. 4, which includes Turlock, 70 for, 4 against; and in Division No. 5, which includes all TID land in Merced County, such as Hilmar, Irwin, and Delhi, 6 for and 1 against.

The Board decided to issue for its first sale $50,000[20] of Turlock Irrigation District bonds. Sealed bids for these bonds were received, and on 7 November 1887 these bids were opened and it was found that Robert McHenry had bid $45,000 for the bonds.[21] While these bonds were sold in November 1887, it was not until 1890 that any contracts were let for construction.[22] According to the *Modesto Evening News* of 13 December 1888, McHenry's bid was the only one received by the Turlock Irrigation Board in November 1887. His bid stated that he would take them for reselling only.

In their meeting of 16 February 1888 the TID Board decided not to commence surveying the canal until the State Supreme Court should rule on the legality of the Wright Act. It was necessary to test the constitutionality of the law before capital would consider the bonds for investment. So on 17 November 1887, ten days after receiving the McHenry bid, a friendly suit was commenced in the State Supreme Court for that purpose. The Turlock Irrigation District sued the Secretary of the Board, R. M. Williams. It was hoped that by pre-testing the Wright Act before any action involving expenditures of tax or bond money, the District would avoid costly litigations and work stoppages later. The decision was handed down on 31 May 1888, and upheld the Wright Act in all respects mentioned: constitutionality, the public nature of irrigation districts, powers of assessments and condemnation. The test case in the California Supreme Court, however, did not bar action through the federal courts.[23]

The only further comment on this case to be found in the minutes of the Turlock District Board, was that on the records for 20 December 1887, Mr. Williams, Secretary of the Board, and the one who started this friendly action, was allowed "expenses while attending Supreme Court on December 6, 1887."

As soon as the Court pronounced the Wright Act lawful in the Williams case, directors Clark and Cogswell, together with P. J. Hazen, the District's attorney, and George Manuel, its engineer, went to San Francisco "to attend to the printing and if necessary the transfer of the $50,000 of bonds already sold to Robert McHenry."

While waiting for the resale of the McHenry bonds and the printing of all of them, the District decided to levy a tax for the purpose of paying the salaries of officers and employees. The money needed was $12,466.30 and the tax rate adopted was $0.425 on each $100 valuation.

These taxes were voted by the Board on 18 September 1888 and by the end of the year the tax money began to come in. To J. W. Mitchell goes the honor of being the first to pay his taxes; on 8 December he handed A. N. Crow, the Collector, the sum of $1581.00. He was the largest landowner in the district, and many of the "dry farmers" had hoped that he would resist the payment of his taxes.[24] By Christmas time, Crow reported, all taxpayers having large land holdings had paid up.[25]

There were a few protests against the assessed valuation levied on property. The Turlock Irrigation District Board, acting as an Equalization Board, passed upon these cases and in nearly all cases found that the landowner was correct in his protest. For instance, D. D. Bonnett, one of these farmers, said that the cash valuation of his land was but $15.00 per acre so the Board reduced his assessment to that.[26]

Meanwhile the Board had offered $550,000 of bonds for sale. These were the rest of the original $600,000. L. M. Hickman, a large landowner northeast of Denair, was the highest bidder for the bonds, his bid being 90 percent of their face value, but only on condition that he could resell them.[27]

Attorney P. J. Hazen of the Turlock Irrigation District,[28] who had been in San Francisco for some time trying to sell the District's bonds, caused great rejoicing in Turlock when on 8 December 1888 he sent the following telegram to the Directors, "Contract of sale of the bonds of T. I. D., fully executed."

To all newspapers this appeared to be a very significant fact. Bonds of other districts could not be sold until those of the first district organized under the Wright Act were disposed of. The *San Francisco Daily Alta California* recommended that these bonds be put up for popular subscription so that they "would interest more people in the stability of the law and the success and permanence of irrigation." The *Alta* opined of the bonds, "Investment good, interest fair, and security first-class."[29]

The *Modesto Daily Evening News* gave this particular news considerable space. It stated:

> The contract was signed and the first payment deposited in the bank to the credit of the representatives of the district, at 6 o'clock p.m. December 10, 1888.[30] This date is worthy of remembrance by all who have the prosperity of Stanislaus County and our glorious state at heart. It marks the end of the probationary period of the Wright Irrigation Law. Its vital principle is that which secures to every land owner his just proportion of water used for irrigation.—The success of a system which does this is no longer a problem but a living fact. The funds for construction being secured nothing now remains but to use them in such a way as will best secure irrigation, and Turlock District with her 176,000 acres of land will be the garden spot of California.

First to organize under the new law, first to vote bonds for construction, first to test the validity of the law, Turlock District is now first to sell her bonds for coin. This result has not been attained without long and earnest struggles by her directors. They have not only done this without money, but they in many cases gave of their own time, labor, and money.

The bonds just sold had been offered to all capitalists, even some who resided in Europe. None felt that they could afford the risk and so the District had been turned down again and again.[31] On 18 December Hickman appeared before the Turlock District Board and notified them that he had sold $500,000 of the bonds, for which he bid at 90% of their face value. He agreed to pay to the District all he received from the sale of bonds beyond the 90% and expenses of sale.

On 4 June 1888, the committee appointed to look after the sale of district bonds in San Francisco was also ordered to see Col. Wheaton and the Hydraulic Mining Company about the right-of-way for the canal across their lands at La Grange. On 1 March this committee reported to the Board that little difficulty was encountered in securing a right-of-way.

The District had followed Engineer Manuel's suggestion of constructing a dam at La Grange and had filed claims on water rights there. On 5 January 1889 the District, through its president and secretary, posted notices claiming 225,000 inches of water "at a place where Wheaton's Dam crosses the river" and 225,000 inches "at a point of rock about 150 feet north of the La Grange Hydraulic Mining Company's house situated about one-fourth of a mile above Wheaton's Dam."[32]

The oldest right to divert water from the Tuolumne River in the vicinity of La Grange Dam was owned by the Franklin Water Company organized 30 November 1854. On 17 November 1855, their rights were transferred to Reedy Dye and Company. The dam which this firm erected at about a cost of $15,000 for flour milling purposes was destroyed by a flood on 24 December 1867. John Reedy bought out his partners' rights in 1868 and then turned them over to Michael Kelly. Kelly sold to J. M. Thompson, Charles Elliott, and M. A. Wheaton in 1871.

In 1871 this Company, with a capital of $50,000, started construction of an extensive dam in the river immediately above the town of La Grange. It stated that the water was to be used for milling, mining, and irrigation purposes. The Wheaton Dam was near La Grange, while the ditch commenced about eighteen miles farther up at a place called Indian Bar (two miles above Don Pedro's Bar). About 850 men were working on the construction of this ditch.

In 1871 Wheaton became sole owner,[33] and on 11 June and 15 August 1890 he conveyed his water rights to the Modesto and Turlock Districts jointly.

Following up the suggestion offered as early as September 1887 that Turlock and Modesto jointly construct the La Grange Dam, the two districts entered into an agreement on 8 August 1890 whereby such construction was to be a joint undertaking.

Mr. C. E. Grunsky[34] said that originally the two districts made separate plans and estimates for the construction of the irrigation systems. His plans, which suggested the use of the Tuolumne River as a source of Modesto District water supply, did not meet with great favor. It was not until Modesto eliminated some of her high lands near Oakdale by a change of boundary that she decided to join with Turlock in the La Grange project. Since this idea of joint operation had been discussed from the time of organization, no one person could be given full credit for originating the idea.

The division of water rights according to the contract gives Turlock 68.46% of the total.[35] The contract reads:

> All water diverted by means of said dam shall be divided and distributed between said districts in proportion to the number of acres in the respective districts.
>
> It is further understood and agreed that in case either district shall acquire any additional water rights, privileges or rights in stored water above said dam, the other district shall have the privilege of sharing in such property by paying therefore within sixty days after written notice of the intention to purchase, or the acquisition of such property, its proportional part of the cost and the expense thereof, said

cost and the water so acquired to be divided in proportion to the number of acres embraced in the respective districts.[36]

This policy, by which Modesto was to take water from the Tuolumne River instead of the Stanislaus, was suggested by William Hammond Hall, State Engineer, as early as 1880. In his State Engineer's *Report* of that year we read:

> It is found that the Tuolumne. . .has a comparatively narrow district of land adjacent to it on each side, between it and the Stanislaus on the north, and the Merced on the south so that the lands which can be watered by it on both sides, are no more than its share; thus the Stanislaus waters should all go out northward, and the Merced waters all go out to the south, leaving the districts between to the Tuolumne, to be taken out on both sides.[37]

The first construction done in the creation of the Turlock Irrigation system was the building of the La Grange Dam. This structure is located at the site of the old Wheaton Dam, about a mile and a half above the town of La Grange.[38]

The dam was completed in 1893 at a cost of $543,164, Turlock and Modesto sharing equally in payment of this cost.[39]

The dam at La Grange backs up the water in the narrow gorge of the Tuolumne River, forming the La Grange Reservoir. The latter is about two and one-half miles in length, varying in width along the upper stretch of two miles, from forty to three hundred feet. The dam was built to a height that would allow the canals to be supplied with water.

Luther Wagoner, Engineer for the Modesto Irrigation District, was the person who was given credit for doing most of the La Grange dam designing, while E. H. Barton, Engineer for the Turlock District, supervised its construction.[40] The two Districts had agreed that the engineers of each District should submit their plans or designs for the construction of La Grange Dam. The one whose plan was adopted should be construction engineer.

> The designs as prepared were submitted to Col. George H. Mendell of the Engineer Corps of the U.S. Army. Col. Mendell submitted a modified design using the Wagoner design as his basis. Meanwhile, however, Mr. Wagoner has resigned as engineer of the Modesto District and Mr. Barton was placed in charge of the erection of the dam.[41]

The main Turlock diversion canal leads from the dam at La Grange. Diversion is made at the east end of the dam through a tunnel. The canal leading through from the tunnel has a capacity of 2,000 second feet. Starting at an elevation of more than one hundred feet above the bed of the river, the line of the canal necessarily crosses branch canyons and ravines, entering the river at a considerable height above the bed. When constructed, the canal was carried across these depressions by means of wooden flumes. By 1913 these flumes were replaced with earthfills, carrying the concrete-lined canal across depressions.[42]

The main Turlock diversion canal flows along the south bank of the Tuolumne for about seven miles to Turlock Lake, formerly called Owen Reservoir. Then the Main Supply Canal, with a capacity of 1600 second feet, diverts near the west end of Turlock Lake and carries water to the northeast edge of the Turlock District a few miles east of Hickman. At this point the Ceres Main Canal takes off, flows west on the highland above the Tuolumne channel, and then south through the center of the Turlock Irrigation District. The Turlock Main Canal diverts at the same gate as the Ceres Main, flows south for about ten miles, and then the main laterals divert at intervals of two and three miles, running west to the San Joaquin River.

The Highline Canal diverts from the Main Supply Canal a few miles east of Hickman, flows south near the eastern boundary of the District for about eighteen miles to the Merced River, then west to supply Delhi and Hilmar.

After eight decades, the Turlock District owned and operated 193 miles of concrete-lined canals and underground pipes.[43] Looking back to the early years, it is difficult to visualize the long period of disappointments, litigation, and interruptions of construction.

Since the La Grange Reservoir was not intended for storage, the Districts had to find storage reservoir sites farther down in the foothills. In 1912 the Turlock District had two reservoir sites surveyed, both in the foothills about ten miles below La Grange. The Owen Reservoir was decided upon. At this place a series of earthfill dams, several of which are now faced with concrete, hold back the water which spreads over five sections of land in the foothills.

In 1889 the plans of canals and works filed by Engineer Manuel were approved, and a survey of the works above the district line was ordered. The little town of La Grange reported that it was "livelier than usual at present owing to the presence in our midst of the surveying party laying out the route of the proposed Turlock canal. A full corps of engineers are busily engaged making estimates and mapping out the most feasible routes."[44] The contract for a part of the first section of the canal was awarded on 20 January 1890.

By the time construction on La Grange Dam was started the District was again in need of more funds. The second bond election was held on 14 May 1892. The entire issue of bonds was sold to L. M. Hickman on the same terms on which he took the major portion of the District's first issue.

With money in view, the District had surveys and bids made for the construction of another section of the canal. The contract was awarded to Doe, Hunt and Company for constructing the remainder of the canal system as planned. For a few months this company tried to carry out the terms of their contract. In "less than six months after the contract had been awarded, it was declared forfeited by the District due to the Company's inability to carry out its part of the contract."[45] Work again stopped.

At this critical period a man appeared on the scene who well might be called the savior of the District, Judge James A. Waymire. From the time he became established in the legal profession until the time of his death he was constantly before the public; yet throughout that long career, he so acted and lived that he left in the memory of those who had even a slight acquaintance with him only a picture of a dignified, kindly, courtly and understanding friend.[46]

Judge James A. Waymire, savior of the TID.

The question has often been raised as to why a man of Judge Waymire's importance should have devoted his life and his fortune to a cause so far distant from the ordinary interests of his daily routine and profession. This question he himself answered:

I became interested by the purchase of the first bonds issued (part of the first issue of $600,000) having aided in the preparation of the bonds. By 1894 strong opposition to the Wright Law developed, and many law suits attacking the constitutionality of the law, the validity of the districts and their bonds, were brought. To make matters worse a great wave of financial depression swept over the world, so affecting values that even wheat could not be sold for a time in California. . . . Throughout the State all irrigation construction work ceased and the Wright Law seemed to be doomed. Firmly believing in the soundness of the policy and its ultimate triumph I determined to make an effort to vindicate the principles embodied in the law by making a success of at least one district. As I held some of the Turlock bonds and had induced others to buy, I naturally turned to that district.[47]

Accordingly, in July 1895 the Turlock District granted Judge Waymire permission to take over the old Doe, Hunt, and Company contract with the understanding that the system should be completed by 1 April 1896. By this contract Waymire agreed to complete the irrigation system at a total additional cost of not more than $382,000.[48] This contract was much more favorable to the District than the Doe, Hunt, and Company contract.

Nevertheless, Judge Waymire, confident of success, began work at once on the tunnel below the diverting dam. Work had just nicely gotten under way when an unforeseen difficulty appeared. After several years of court cases and decisions favorable to the Wright Act, a United States Circuit Court decision in *Tregea* v. *Modesto Irrigation District* held the Wright Act unconstitutional and the bonds issued under the law invalid.

Judge Waymire studied the Federal court's decision carefully and decided to carry the case to the United States Supreme Court, where he hoped to receive a favorable decision. The bondholders of the different districts raised the money to pay the expenses of the case and they left to Judge Waymire the choice of legal counsel. And well did he choose it.

To handle the case at Washington, he chose Hon. John M. Dillon of New York, ex-Judge of the United States Circuit Court, and Hon. A. H. Rhodes, ex-Chief Justice of California. Before the case came to trial Judge Waymire had, in the course of a friendly visit with Associate Justice Field at the Justice's own suggestion, discussed the case with him. He suggested that in addition, Judge Waymire secure the counsel of Joseph H. Choate, prominent New York lawyer. Justice Field, in recommending Choate, said that the latter "had such a pleasing way of presenting his cases and the Judges like to hear him."

Waymire wired Choate but found he had already been retained by George H. Maxwell, leader of the opposition, for the sum of $10,000.[49] The next step of the story is best related by Judge Waymire himself.

It seemed highly important to find a match for the eminent New Yorker. Finally I thought of Hon. Benjamin Harrison, ex-President of the United States. He was the equal of any man as a lawyer, his personality would certainly be as interesting and impressive as that of Mr. Choate, and the fact that he had appointed three of the Judges would do no harm. Fortunately I had a personal acquaintance with the General. A letter explaining the nature of the case, and offering a retainer met with a favorable response.[50]

When the case was finally tried on 16 November 1896, the decision was in favor of the Wright Act.[51] The dissenting voices of the Supreme Court were those of the Chief Justice and Justice Field. The issue settled by this decision was that the use of water for irrigation was a public use and as such the districts had the right to levy assessments.[52]

While Judge Waymire was preparing to test the legality of the Wright Act, he did not suspend the work which he had contracted to do. Before the decision was rendered he was already more than six months behind his contract schedule. When the decision was handed down, work on the canals was speeded up, and with the District assisting the contractor instead of canceling the contract, the canals were completed in 1902.

Horace Crane and George Bloss, both large landholders of Turlock, helped the District to take over the construction program. They completed all main canals west and some east of the main line of the Southern Pacific Railroad, a total length of eighteen miles. By 1902 water had reached as far as the railroad.[53]

Newcomers to the district report that at that time private individuals aided in construction. N. O. Hultberg, the promoter of the Swedish migration to Turlock, said that he, with the assistance of such men as Mr. Hubert Dunn, a TID director, undertook to aid the District. He stated in a letter,

> A great many canals had been constructed prior to my arrival but most of these canals had been neglected and had filled in with sand. They all had to be rebuilt. Still there were enough open canals so we managed to get water through to satisfy the first colonists. The district was broke and the land owners were broke. I had personally to spend thousands of dollars on the public canals in order to get water through. Mr. Hubert Dunn, now dead, was my stand-by in that work with his horses and men.[54]

This default on contract was not alone Waymire's fault. The contract he assumed carried with it the provision that the contractor should find purchasers for at least $60,000 of the District's bonds, the proceeds of which were to be used for construction. It was not until 2 March 1897 that L. M. Hickman succeeded in selling the bonds to R. A. Friedenrich, at the rate of 90 cents on the dollar. This man in turn tried to resell them, but found the market unfavorable to them.

One reason for the poor market value of the District's bonds was the opposition to irrigation by a group of "dry" farmers. They refused to pay their taxes and were strongly organized to oppose the progress of construction. T. C. Hocking in describing this organization, stated:

> The big wheat field owners in both districts joined forces to oppose the district. They formed a strong organization and after trying other methods they enjoined the collection of taxes. They caused dissatisfaction among many who were in doubt, and, for a while the districts were not able to collect taxes from more than a third of those whose property was assessed. These "anti's" carried their case to the Supreme Court three different times.[55]

Among the "dry farmers" were C. B. Byers, whose home was near the Crows Landing Bridge, and a number of farmers, such as Sam Foster and Ed Baxter, who lived west of Keyes. C. S. Bishop quoted Byers as saying, "I don't want water. I'll pay them to keep it off my land."[56]

Of Sam Foster, Mr. Mark Moyle told the following anecdote:

> While his suit against the District was pending, I met him one day looking rather gloomy. Upon inquiry I found he was afraid the District would win the suit. I told him, "Never mind worrying, Sam; you'll win anyway. Even if the District does win the suit, the appeals of the case will hold up payment for ten years and then by that time you'll be dead, so they can't collect." He didn't like my joke, but he did die before the case was finally decided. He was about seventy when we had this discussion. He was a man who was always dissatisfied with anything the rest of the world approved of.[57]

By their opposition the "dry farmers" were able to keep down the market valuation of the bonds and coupons. The latter they bought up at 75 cents on the dollar, and, after losing their long fight against payment of district taxes, they used these coupons to pay the taxes; in reality they were just paying a part of their real tax bill. These suits just referred to started in 1892 and were not ended until the decision in the case of *Baldwin et al* v. *Board of Directors of Turlock Irrigation District et al.* This case first started as an affair between taxpayers and the District, but with the continued use of injunctions to prevent the sale of lands for taxes, the bondholders joined the cause of the District. The decision of this case, rendered in 1901, was to the effect that the District had to pay the interest due bondholders and the bonds, also, as they matured.

In 1902 the District decided to issue a refunding series of bonds to the amount of $1,156,000 in exchange for the outstanding bonds. The exchange was made upon a par valuation set upon all bonds.[58] Work was started once more, this time with success.

The work of construction was done by section gangs, working at first for $1.00 a day and board. Later wages were raised to $30.00 a month. The gangs were fed at the nearest ranch houses; when these did not exist they resorted to the cook and feed wagon. They stayed in camps near the place under construction. The working hours were from daylight until dark.[59]

There were no labor difficulties reported by Horace Crane at the time he supervised the completion of a part of the canal system, but many times Judge Waymire had to find means of quelling strike threats. These were caused by the inability of the Judge to raise money with which to pay wages. The District treasury was devoid of funds, due to the opposition of the anti-irrigationists, and so Judge Waymire turned for help to outsiders who would trust him. Two very interesting cases relative to this subject are told.

At one time Judge Waymire went to Mr. C. N. Whitmore of Ceres, a man who owed the District $3,000.00 in taxes. Whitmore was willing to pay the taxes, but his property was already in the hands of a Modesto bank, due to heavy indebtedness. Whitmore, however, said that if the bank would lend him the money, he'd turn it over to the District. The bank consented and Waymire left the bank with the money in his possession, bought a pistol at a store across the street, and started for the labor camp. The arrival of Waymire with the gold quieted the men and the work on the canal continued.

At another time Judge Waymire reached Modesto Saturday evening, with $2000.00 in two checks. He had borrowed the money just before leaving San Francisco but did not have time to get the cash. In Modesto the banks were all closed, and, worse still, their vaults were closed with time locks which were set for Monday morning. In desperation he again appealed to a personal friend, this time to Judge Hewell. The two provided themselves with canvas bags, and making the rounds of the stores and saloons, cashed small checks drawn on Hewell's private bank account. The money secured, Waymire proceeded to the workers' camp.[60]

The District experienced little difficulty in securing rights-of-way because each farmer could see advantages in having a lateral on or near his land. Besides land was cheap.[61]

Chapter X

Turlock: a Center of Swedish Settlement

Carolyn Larson and Geraldine Johnson

During the spring in the early years of the Turlock district, green, grassy plains lay spread between the Merced and Tuolumne Rivers. The first pioneers began by farming the fertile river-bottom lands. As they prospered, thousands of acres of surrounding land were planted to wheat.

Then came the hot, dry summers. The fields were parched and dry. The winds came and whipped along huge clouds of dust. Sand, dust, tumbleweeds, jack rabbits, gophers, squirrels, horned toads, and lizards were a part of the scene in the little village of Turlock. Scattered wooden buildings could be seen between sandy streets covered with straw.

After the disastrous fires of the 1890s and the loss of the wheat business to towns on other railway lines, Turlock was desolate indeed. Nels O. Hultberg, who came to Turlock in January 1902, reminisced:

> The appearance of the town of Turlock was that of an abandoned mining camp with houses burned down years ago and never rebuilt, and other houses wrecked and leaning by the sand having blown away from their underpinioning and not fit to live in.[1]

But there was one ray of hope. Water had been promised to this dry and thirsty land.

With the coming of water, the entire area was opened up to colonization. John W. Mitchell, the original owner of 110,000 acres of land in this area, had passed away in 1893. His heirs, the Cranes, Geérs, and Blosses, decided to sell off the land. They formed the Fin de Siecle (end of the century) Investment Company in 1899. Horace Crane was the secretary-treasurer of this company. They soon found a man to promote sales for this company in the person of Nels O. Hultberg.[2]

Hultberg was born in 1865 in Skåne, Sweden. He came to America in 1887 and lived in Pullman, Illinois. He worked there for four years as a blacksmith.[3] In 1893 the Swedish Mission Covenant Church and the U. S. Government sent him to Alaska. He was supposed to organize a government industrial school for the Eskimos (Malamut tribe). The school never got started. Money had been appropriated by the United States Government, but the money never reached Hultberg.[4] He worked at a regular mission station located at Golovin Bay for five years. A herd of reindeer brought from Siberia by the government in the interest of the natives was also his responsibility.[5]

Hultberg met his wife in Galesburg, Illinois, before he went to Alaska. They were married in Alaska in 1894 and became the first white couple to be married on the Seward Peninsula.[6]

In 1898 Hultberg struck gold at Nome, on the Seward Peninsula. After two of his children died, he felt compelled to get out of Alaska to protect the health of the rest of the family. He made his mine over to an Eskimo, intending that profits should go to the church. Another Covenant minister bought the mine from the Eskimo for a nominal sum, and the ensuing controversy resulted in a suit between the Church and the minister which was settled only in 1920 in favor of the minister.[7]

Traveling around in California looking for a place to live that would meet his needs, Hultberg and his brother Olof reached Turlock on 1 January 1902. They hired a team of horses and rode around this area. The fires of the earlier years had burned and blackened the buildings, many of which the local citizens had not bothered to repair or rebuild. The Hultbergs investigated the Fresno area at the same time, but finally decided to settle in Turlock.[8]

Hultberg took samples of land in various sections. He sent these to the University of California at Berkeley for analysis. The laboratory sent a report back that the land was recommended for colonization if enough water was available. Hultberg then wrote to Washington to find out about the Supreme Court decision on the irrigation law.[9]

Mr. Bell, a real estate man from Modesto who had a branch office in Turlock, had been showing Hultberg around in this area. One day these two men met Horace Crane, the secretary-treasurer of the Fin de Siecle Investment Company, on Front Street where Central Park is now located. Horace had a hayrack and a pair of mules. Mr. Bell introduced Mr. Hultberg to Mr. Crane.[10] As a result of this meeting, Hultberg became the land sales promoter for this company.

In the *Missions-Vännen* Hultberg stated that his agreement with the Fin de Siecle Company permitted him to sell up to 1000 acres of land by the end of May 1902 at $25 an acre. After that, the Company could raise the price, and he expected it to go to $40 to $50 an acre. Land at Kingsburg was bought at $15 to $25 an acre by the promoters and was sold at $60 to $125 an acre. One could purchase Hultberg's land at one-fourth down, so no more than $250 cash would command forty acres, and there was a possibility of a crop the first year. There were no stumps to clear. ". . .for housing anything will do in California to start with. I myself," said Hultberg, "have contracted for a house and barn for 480 dollars. A barn need here cost no more than 125 dollars and a house less. It costs about 30 dollars to have a well sunk. . . . It costs no more than from 20 to 40 cents to get water for an acre of land."[11]

Hultberg formed a partnership with Walter Soderberg from San Francisco, whom he had known previously in Alaska. They called their firm the Hultberg-Soderberg Land Company. Soderberg seemed to be a silent partner and was seldom seen in Turlock. In a short time by various arrangements, purchase, long options, leases, and contracts, Hultberg secured about 35,000 acres of land.

Hultberg plotted out the largest piece of land (17,000 acres) he had purchased in 1902 and named the colony after his oldest son, Hilmar. He later wrote, ". . .it was not my purpose to make it a colony purely for people affiliated with the Swedish Mission Church as, of course, the different denominations established there would show. My dream was to establish the largest Swedish Colony in the State and possibly in the United States."[12]

Hultberg wanted stable, persevering Swedish settlers in this area, so he advertised in the Swedish paper, *Missions-Vännen (Mission Friends)*.[13] Other advertisements appeared in the *Minneapolis Weekly (Vekoblad)* of Minneapolis, Minnesota, and the *West Coast (Vestkuston)* of Seattle, Washington. These were religious papers. He also advertised in two non-religious papers, the *Fosterlandet* of Chicago, and the *Svenska Amerika Posten (Swedish American News)* of Chicago.[14] Rev. Andrew Hallner from Kingsburg, California, was asked to handle the advertising. He was a minister and he had had previous newspaper experience.[15]

After the first advertisements went out, on 4 February 1902, they received the first responses—nine letters in one day.[16] By the end of March, twenty-two families had arrived. In April 1902 whole carloads came and scattered over the area.[17]

With many families of settlers coming and mail pouring in, Mr. Hultberg needed a secretary who could speak and write in both the Swedish and English languages. Miss Esther Hall (later Mrs. Arthur Crowell) had graduated from business college in Minneapolis. She was visiting in San Francisco at this time. Hearing about this job opportunity, she applied for the position, was hired, and went to work immediately upon arrival in Turlock on 26 December 1902.[18]

Esther Hall Crowell.

August Johnson, Hultberg's first customer, and his family. From left, Mr. and Mrs. Johnson, Esther, Hilda, Edith, Aggie, May, and Aggie's twin, Bill. Courtesy Lorraine Johnson.

There were many responses to the advertisements in the church papers of the Midwest and East. The land office sent out pictures of San Jose and Kingsburg, telling how Turlock would look in the future. People came to investigate the area. Some bought land; others did not buy. Most of the people made down payments of one-fourth the cost on 20, 40, 60, or 80 acres. They would pay the one-fourth down on contract for three years at 8 percent interest. The preliminary contract was signed by Mr. Hultberg. Later, this contract was exchanged for a permanent contract with the Fin de Siecle Investment Company, signed by G. S. Bloss, President, and Horace Crane, Secretary. The money was generally paid in currency and drafts.[19] There was no increase in the price of $25 an acre for the first two years. The purchaser's name was placed on the map at the land office. This land was held until the buyer arrived to claim his land. Most of the settlers came with approximately $1,500.00. Quite a few came with only $300.00 to $600.00.[20]

August Johnson bought the first piece of land from this company, according to the records. He came first, purchased his land, returned to Illinois and brought his family to Turlock in December, 1902.[21] Many followed his example, the men arriving first to purchase the land and returning later with their families.

What motivated these settlers to come to the Turlock area? There were several reasons. The winters in the East and Midwest were severe. Cheap land prices and the promise of abundant water for irrigation were other factors. Then, too, these Swedish people were the hardy, adventuresome, pioneer type. Many had already left their homeland, Sweden, to come to this land. They were ready to seize what they thought was a better opportunity when it came along. One early pioneer said that with $800.00 and a cooperative wife, a man could go to California and make a fortune.[22]

The years of 1903-1904 brought the greatest influx of settlers. They came from Minnesota, Nebraska, Iowa, Illinois, Ohio, Pennsylvania, and other areas in the East and Midwest. About one-half of these settlers had farmed the land from which they came and the other half had worked in the mills and factories.[23]

How did the settlers come to Turlock? They came by railway. The women and children would often come by passenger train. The men and boys came in boxcars, filled with their furniture, belongings, farm implements, and livestock.[24]

When a train with settlers arrived in Turlock, Hallner was usually there to greet the newcomers. If he was not able to meet the train, August Erickson, the field man for the Hultberg-Soderberg Land Company, would meet them. If neither of these two men were able to meet the settlers, Esther Hall (Crowell), the secretary of the company, would meet them. Many people later told Mrs. Crowell that she was the first person they met in Turlock.[25]

Upon arrival, what accommodations were available to the newcomers? Hultberg had a boarding house located at the corner of East Main and Diablo (now Thor) Streets where the Masonic Building now stands. The boarding house was a story-and-a-half frame building. It stood back from the street in a grove of locust trees with a fence around the yard.[26] Settlers could stay here temporarily, free of charge, until they could move in with another family while their home was being built. There were some empty houses which the settlers were happy to rent. However, the influx of settlers exceeded the accommodations. Hultberg described the situation as follows:

> . . .the churches, none were in operation for church work at that time. . .were partitioned off with canvas walls and quarters were given temporarily the best way we could manage it until the newcomers got located on their respective lands and buildings put up. I had a carload of springs and mattresses sent down from San Francisco which were spread on floors all over. I had every vacant house and room in town rented with springs and mattresses put in every room. Everybody enjoyed the novelty of the whole situation and very few complained. There was no charge made for anything.[27]

As late as January and February, 1903, no new buildings had been built in Turlock. The city of Turlock consisted of two dozen old residences, three churches, a depot, a school, two general merchandise stores, a post office, and the Hultberg-Soderberg Land Office. There was also a hotel with a bar in it, a saloon, a livery stable, a blacksmith shop, a lumber yard, a few warehouses, and some empty buildings. The two main streets in town were Front Street and Main Street. They were bumpy, dirt roads. Main Street and a part of Front Street were covered with straw so the long mule teams (16 mules to two wagons) could haul the grain to the warehouses without bogging down in the deep sand. Because there were no sidewalks, everyone walked in the middle of the street. In rainy weather, the damp straw squished under foot. There were many trails leading from every direction through the tall weeds into town. They all led to Osborn's store and the post office next door.[28]

For transportation, horses, buggies, and wagons were used. If you wished to go some distance, it was possible to rent a livery rig. Wherever you drove, you were followed by a cloud of dust. Sometimes the wheels sank a foot into the sand because the roads were so sandy. Most people walked everywhere. In the summer, walking ankle deep in the hot sand was difficult, too. Women, following the fashion of the day, wore long skirts that had to be held suspended above the sand and dirt. In 1906, the first automobiles appeared. They frightened the horses in the beginning and caused accidents.[29]

Houses had to be built to accommodate the new settlers. Some of the newcomers were carpenters and they built their own homes. They had to go to Modesto to buy lumber, paying $12.00 to $14.00 per 1,000 board feet. Hultberg finally persuaded Charles Klein to start the Modesto Lumber Yard in the spring of 1902. In 1903, there was much hammering and sawing both day and night in order to accommodate the influx of settlers.[30] Usually, these first homes were two-room houses. Hultberg often advised the settlers not to put money into buildings but into the improvement of their land. He advised making the land more productive and paying for the buildings later. Many lived in their small homes for four to five years, but their land was clear of debt.[31] Some of the houses reflected their owners' Swedish origin, that of Mr. Bodén at Youngstown as much as any.

At first the only shade they had was the shadow of the house. Trees were soon planted. They gave shade and also provided protection from the strong winds.

Wells had to be drilled on the land for the new settlers. Most homes had an outside pump where they pumped their water into pails and then carried the pails indoors. Wood stoves were used for cooking and heating water for the washing. Wood for the stoves was not available in Turlock because of the lack of trees. Settlers had to go to the Merced River area to buy wood. The trees had to be sawed and the wood hauled home in lumber wagons. The boys in the family had the task of chopping the wood and carrying it to the woodbox by the stove.[32]

A water bucket on a stand with a washbasin nearby was standard equipment in these pioneer homes. For bathing, water had to be heated in pans on the stove and poured into a tin washtub in the kitchen. After being used for bathing, the water was often poured outdoors on the plants and trees. These settlers could not have indoor plumbing until they could afford a windmill and a tank. Then the households could have a kitchen sink with running water, and, later, a bathroom, if they could afford it.

There was no electricity in those days. There were no street lights. If a person went out on a dark night, he had to carry a kerosene lantern. Houses, stores, and homes were all lit by kerosene lamps. They had telephones (battery-operated) long before they had electricity.

One might wonder now about how this great, new system of irrigation was going to work out for the settlers. After all, the irrigation of the land was the main factor that was going to make this flat, wide expanse of desert blossom. The La Grange Dam had been built through the combined efforts of the Modesto Irrigation District and the Turlock Irrigation District in 1891-93. Litigation had hindered its use until 1901 when the dam actually went into operation. Wooden flumes now carried the water from the dam to the big canals on either side of the Tuolumne River, one serving the Modesto area and the other one serving the Turlock area. These main canals had been put in throughout the district, but the farmers had to put in their own ditches and headgates. Water did not reach Hilmar until 1903.

How was this system of dirt canals working out? Well, there were many problems, to be sure. Many times the canals washed out and flooded the land. Sometimes both animals and people had to be pulled out of the mud. Gophers in the area caused much trouble. They tunneled through the ditches causing many breaks. Often men and women sat in the breaks until the water was turned off and the ditch repaired. One jovial pioneer farmer said he was happy that he had a fat wife because she could fill a large hole when the ditch broke.[33] In the midst of their discouragement, the early settlers learned to sing a parody to the tune of "Oh, Susanna," while they sat on the sand banks watching and repairing the breaks in the ditches. It went something like this:

> Oh, Susanna, oh don't you cry for me,
> For we're sitting on the sand banks
> In the Hilmar Colony.[34]

Dairying was one of the early occupations of these pioneer farmers. Alfalfa, a very good food for the cows, was one of the first crops to be planted. The first field of alfalfa was twenty acres on Geer Road planted by Henry Geer. This was a show place. Everyone who arrived in the district was taken there to see the alfalfa. There was a ditch leading to the field.[35]

The dairymen separated the milk and the cream by means of a separator. The usual practice was to feed the calves the skim milk and churn the cream into butter. Butter could be taken to the store and traded for staple groceries. In 1903, the Western Creameries opened an outlet in Turlock.[36]

Many of the farmers' wives raised chickens. The eggs from the chickens were traded at the grocery store for other necessities.

It was discovered that fruit trees and vines would do well in this sandy soil. Soon the settlers began planting freestone peach trees, apricots, and grapes. The name of the first nursery that sold nursery stock to the Hilmar and Turlock farmers is not known. However, if a farmer purchased a certain amount of fruit stock, this nursery would give two ornamental trees as a bonus. This accounts for the fact that on so many of the older farms in this district, two tall, stately palm trees stand in front of the house, one on each side of the entrance.[37] From 1905 to 1911, Mr. Knut Knutsen, a pioneer settler in the area, had a nursery behind the Rochdale store (now the Mercantile). He bought nursery stock in the southern states and supplied the farmers with bare root fruit and grape stock.[38]

The peaches, apricots and grapes were all highly perishable crops. Clarence Ahlem and his father traveled from Hilmar to nearby Atwater to find out how the farmers were preserving their fruit by a drying process. They returned and demonstrated to their neighbors what they had learned in Atwater.

The process consisted of cutting the freestone peaches in half, placing them on trays, and putting them in a sulphur house. Smoke from the sulphur would first soften and then dry the peaches. Once they learned of this method, it became standard procedure. The farmer, his wife, and children would usually pick, cut, and dry the fruit from early dawn until dark during the season.[39] Dried fruit could be kept and held until prices were more advantageous. By about 1908, Mr. Knutsen was buying dried fruit from the farmers and selling it to the Rosenberg Packing Company of Fresno.[40]

Some farmers still continued to plant grain: wheat in the heavy soil and rye in the lighter soil, as John Mitchell had done for many years. Combines, pulled by 40-mule teams, harvested the grain. The straw from the harvest was used to cover the sandy roads to make more traction.[41]

Like all pioneers, these farmers faced many problems. When the alfalfa, trees, orchards, and vineyards were planted, the grasshoppers came. The Hilmar Colony area was the hardest hit in March, April, and May of 1903 and the north Turlock area experienced the plague in 1906. The grasshoppers ate everything in sight that was green.[42]

What did the farmers do to combat this plague? Large fields were burned in an attempt to wipe out the grasshoppers, but the plague continued. The State of California sent men to help in the fight. Poison was put out, but this was of no help. The cultivation of the ground, which destroyed and buried the eggs, offered the only solution to the problem.[43]

When the crops were planted again, the jack rabbits would come. They ate entire crops. They ate the bark of the trees. As a result, the trees would die. Some farmers built fences around their orchards. They dug the netting into the ground so the rabbits could not dig out beneath the fence. The farmers also rubbed hog's liver on the trunks of the trees. They discovered that the rabbits would not bite into the trees treated in this manner.[44]

The crops that were not eaten by the grasshoppers and rabbits were often covered or blown out by the terrific sandstorms.[45] Windstorms, lasting from five to seven days, were not uncommon. Sandstorms caused huge drifts, three to four feet high. The winds in these times were very strong. They would tear down trees and even some buildings.[46] These storms filled the ditches and covered the roads. People often got lost when they were caught in a severe sandstorm. Planting rows of trees as a hedge against the wind proved to be one partial solution to the problem.

The early pioneers were often discouraged. Most of them had put all their money into these farms so they had no choice. They had to stick it out and try again. Mr. Hultberg bought trees and vines by the thousands and had them replaced at his own cost. He had to do this to keep the settlers here. The Hultberg-Soderberg Land Company had to be careful not to allow the newcomers to talk to the old-timers. Many customers were lost through the discouraging remarks of the early settlers who were having problems.[47] Some settlers were dissatisfied enough to hold a mass indignation meeting in Hilmar. However, nothing definite resulted and the farmers settled down again to the routine of living.[48]

Many of the settlers, Swedish, Portuguese, and others, had very little cash money in these trying times. Ed Osborn, who had the Osborn General Store next to the early post office on West Main Street, had faith in these hardy people and also a feeling of compassion for their trying circumstances. He extended credit to them again and again. Osborn and other local merchants actually kept these people from starving at times. When payments were made on accounts, Osborn gave the children in the family some candy.[49]

Although they experienced many difficulties, the Swedish settlers were always friendly and hospitable. Their problems created a common bond between them. Their joys, too, they shared with one another. There was always time for a friendly visit over a cup of coffee. It took longer to brew a cup of coffee. A fire had to be made in the wood stove; the coffee beans had to be ground in a grinder. As there were no bakeries, each homemaker baked her own bread and pastries. The Swedish women became well known for their warm hospitality.[50]

In later years Swedish families' diet changed with the availability of a wider variety of fruits and vegetables. Hamburger drove out salt pork after 1920. However, holiday meals and festival occasions were celebrated very much in the traditional style. One early casualty was the Swedish Christmas ham, in part for lack of a cellar in which to store it; lutfisk, however, continued to be one of the Christmas delicacies.

American holidays were soon picked up: the Thanksgiving turkey dinner; the Fourth of July celebration; in Turlock, the annual melon festival. These were not religious in nature, and were celebrated outside the church.[51]

Life was simple and so they enjoyed the simpler things of life. Whole wagonloads of young people went fishing. The fish were plentiful; no one needed a license. The fish were caught in nets, and in a short while they had an abundant supply. The fish was often canned for later use, for fresh meat was very scarce.[52]

Social life revolved around the church. For the young people the choir and the Young People's Society were the main attractions. The Ladies' Aid Society was formed for the women, and they often raised money for missions.[53]

Church picnics were enjoyed by many and provided good entertainment for all. Many families had parties in their homes. Some of the games they enjoyed were: Drop the Hanky, Reuben and Rachel, "Skip Come a Lou," and Captain Jinks.[54]

In 1904 and 1905, Mr. Hultberg advertised again, but this time in American periodicals. He paid $160.00 a month for a year's advertisement in *Sunset* magazine. For a small ad in *Everybody's*, he paid $300.00. He also advertised in *The Earth*.[55] In 1905, Hultberg took in David F. Lane from Oakland, whom he had known in Alaska, as a partner in his company. They advertised heavily in 1907. There was a great influx of settlers again in 1908 and 1909. The invasions of the grasshoppers had stopped, the jack rabbit menace had subsided somewhat, and the winds and sandstorms were not what they were in the first years. People began to prosper, so land values rose. Many real estate men moved into Turlock at this time.[56]

While some of the Swedish settlers were farmers, others chose to follow business careers. Mr. Nels Shoreen from Galesburg, Illinois, had a general merchandise store where Hauck's Pharmacy West now stands (1971). Gust E. Johnson of Hilmar was a silent partner in this business for a short time. They handled "everything."[57] Mr. M. M. Berg came to Turlock in 1903 from San Francisco. Mr. Berg was born in Sweden and had come to the United States June 1, 1882. He had had business experience in Michigan and Ohio before coming to San Francisco. In 1903, he built a frame building on the north side of Main Street where J. C. Penney's store is now located. His store was a very complete general merchandise store, one of the very finest in the entire area at that time.[58] Mr. C. V. Lundahl from Ft. Dodge, Iowa, rented a corner of the Rochdale (Mercantile later) Store for a jewelry store. His business faced Broadway.[59] The Ramona Hotel on South Broadway, an early landmark, was owned and operated by Mr. and Mrs. Joe Samuelson. This hotel was a two-story wooden building, located on Broadway, in the block south of Main. In a corner of the hotel, Mr. Ed Rapp had a barber shop. Later,

M. M. Berg's store, built in 1903 by Gust Carlson. Note sidewalk in foreground. Courtesy Hazel Berg.

Sunset advertisement, showing La Grange Dam, 1904.

the Samuelsons sold the hotel. They started a restaurant across the street called "The Sweet Shop." This place later became "The Broadway White Lunch."[60]

There were several early Swedish building contractors. Swan Wakefield, an early builder, came to Turlock in 1903. He was born in Sweden and came to the United States at the age of twenty-one. He worked in New York for two years, returned to Sweden for a year, and came back to the United States to Halleck, Minnesota. Finally, after moving to Turlock, he began his contracting business. Among the buildings in Turlock built by him are the Osborn Building, the two Geer Buildings, the original Hawthorne and Lowell Schools, the first Bank of America (Commercial Bank), and the Mercantile Building.[61] Claus and Evar Tornell were contractors here in 1904. Gust Carlson was another builder and bricklayer who helped in the construction of the original Hawthorne and Lowell Schools.

These mentioned here are only some of the early Swedish pioneers. Others are mentioned in other parts of our story.

Two other Swedish colonies need to be mentioned at this time before we leave the colonization period. The first one was the Youngstown Colony. Rev. J. O. Bodén of Youngstown, Ohio, came to Turlock in the spring of 1903. He bought a tract of land south of town. It was divided into 10, 20, 30, and 40 acre plots.

Mrs. Hildur Erikson Olson recalled Bodén's coming to Anita, Pennsylvania, to advertise his colony. "With him he had a cloth bag. It was full of sandy soil from Turlock and he held it up in church and let the soil run through his fingers and said: 'Look, such fine loam. There is no need to clear stubs [stumps], just start planting directly.' "[62]

In October of 1903, Bodén, along with fifty-eight of his members, returned to settle in this colony.[63] These men had worked in the mines and steel mills. They were ready to try something different. In that same fall, a group came from Bessemer, Pennsylvania. They had worked in the limestone quarries and they, too, welcomed a change.[64]

Rev. J. O. Bodén and a confirmation class.

The Youngstown Colony settlers usually had families with five or six children. Money was not plentiful. They struggled to make down payments on the land, and they had to pay 8 percent interest on the remainder.[65] These settlers usually built two-room houses, 16' x 30'. Like Turlock and Hilmar, there was no electricity or running water. Many worked for other farmers to earn enough money to work their own land.[66]

In 1904, the first school in Youngstown Colony, Johnson Joint School, was built and named after Eric Gustav Johnson. Mr. Johnson was one of the first ditch-tenders in the area. He drove his two-wheeled cart down the dusty, sandy roads to contact the young parents and other settlers in the Youngstown district regarding a school for their young children. He went by horse and buggy to two county seats, Merced and Modesto, to make the necessary arrangements for a then unheard of "joint school district."[67] Farmers, working for $2.00 a day, helped in the construction. Edith Lindquist taught all eight grades in this two-room schoolhouse. Paper and pencils were furnished by the school; books and play equipment had to be purchased by the children.[68]

The settlers in this colony were from the Swedish Covenant Church. They asked and received permission to use the schoolhouse on Sunday mornings for Sunday School. Rev. C. J. Wideberg and Rev. P. M. Samuelson assisted in the services. They finally organized under the title of the Youngstown Colony Church. Services continued in the school building for a time. In lieu of an organ, a string band provided the necessary music.

Bethel Church, Youngstown Colony.
Ravnos photo, courtesy of Hazel Carpenter.

In about 1912, a church was built in this colony on the corner of Harding and Youngstown Roads. Its seating capacity was 175. Services were in the Swedish language. This church was later moved to Stockton to provide a sanctuary for the newly organized Stockton Covenant Church. They never replaced this church in the Colony. The membership dispersed to worship at the Beulah Covenant Church and the Evangelical Free Church in Turlock.[69]

Youngstown Colony shared hardships along with Turlock and Hilmar. The jack rabbits, the grass-hoppers, and the sandstorms were a part of their story, too. Through hard work, patience, fortitude, and stamina, these pioneer settlers finally brought progress and prosperity to this area as well.

The other settlement we must mention in our story is that of Irwin City. W. A. Irwin from Santa Monica bought up a piece of land in the Hilmar area in 1907. He promoted this settlement as Irwin City. As an enticement to buy land in his colony, he promised a railroad and other improvements. The town actually got started, but when the Western Pacific Railroad sought the right-of-way over the property of the settlers, they refused to cooperate. Because the railroad could not come to Irwin, Mr. Irwin's colonization plan failed.[70] Then the Tidewater-Southern Railroad (a feeder arm of the Western Pacific) laid out the town of Hilmar. The original Hilmar Colony was laid out at the intersection of Tegner Road and American Avenue, where the cemetery is located. In about the years 1916-1917, the Western Pacific established the town of Hilmar where it is presently located on Lander Avenue, two miles east of the original colony.[71]

The San Francisco earthquake of 18 April 1906 was felt in the Turlock area. One farmer in Hilmar reported that the water trough for his animals rocked back and forth.[72] Some San Francisco residents stayed in Turlock with friends or relatives until their homes had been repaired.[73]

Educational facilities were available in Turlock to the children of the first Swedish settlers. After the great immigration of 1903-1904, schools were organized in the Hilmar Colony. Five schools were constructed. They were North Elim, South Elim, Hilmar, Riverside, and Fairview. The persons in charge of organizing the school district made an arrangement with a man in Merced to furnish five teachers, one for each school. No trained teachers were available so this gentleman, whose name is not available, instructed these girls in teaching procedures during one summer. Some of these girls did not even have a high school education, but this was not known at the time. After some years, North Elim and South Elim were combined into Elim School. Later, Hilmar School was incorporated into Elim. Still later on, Fairview and Riverside were combined.

All of these schools were one or two-room schoolhouses with approximately twenty-five students to a room. They contained all eight grades and one teacher had the responsibility of instructing all grade levels. There was one exception to this basic pattern. A two-story schoolhouse was constructed in Hilmar where the present high school now stands. It had eight rooms, but the upper four rooms were not used until the high school opened.

In 1911, Hilmar High School was organized. Forty students attended the first class. This was a large attendance, but some eighth grade graduates from earlier years had been awaiting the construction of the school so they could attend high school. There were drop-outs in those days, too, and by the time graduation came in 1915, there were only ten remaining in the class. Four members of this class of 1915 continued their education at the University of California at Berkeley. The other six members attended San Jose State.[74] This would indicate the high caliber of students in this class and the value they placed on education even in the "rough and ready" pioneer days.

The Swedish settlers had no more than settled in the area when they, like the Puritans of colonial days, made arrangements to establish a church where they could worship God. A small group of worshipers had been meeting in the various homes. Then they began using the Methodist Church at the corner of Lander and West Main. This church had originally been built by the Methodists in 1888 on land donated by Mr. and Mrs. Stephen V. Porter.[75] The Brethren congregation had been using this church. A loan was secured in 1902 from Mr. John Brynteson, a wealthy Swedish benefactor, and the small Swedish Mission congregation bought the church from the mortgage holder for the sum of $2,000, a tremendous price in those days.[76]

Swedish Mission Church, formerly the Methodist Church, before remodeling and expansion.

The Brethren congregation concluded their last service in the church on 25 December 1902. They later renovated the vacant Congregational Church located on the corner of Olive and Center Streets, and continued to worship in that church for many years.[77]

This first Swedish Mission Church was an attractive, white, wood structure, with a tall steeple and a bell tower. Like most homes and churches in those days, it was surrounded by a white picket fence and locust trees.[78] The congregation and Sunday School had been officially organized on 18 December 1902. They held their first service, a Jul Fest (Christmas Program), in their newly purchased church.[79] Rev. Andrew Hallner led the congregation on New Year's Eve, 31 December 1902, when they held their first Wake Service. About twelve members were present. Since there were only twelve charter members registered at the close of 1902, it was decided to include those who joined in 1903 as charter members also. By the end of the year of 1903, the following charter members were listed:

Rev. and Mrs. C. O. Sundquist
Rev. and Mrs. P. A. Dimberg
Mr. and Mrs. A. G. Anderson
Mr. and Mrs. Peter Erickson
Mr. and Mrs. G. R. Larson
Mr. and Mrs. August Ivarsson
Mr. and Mrs. Henry Lundell
Rev. and Mrs. Andrew Hallner
Mr. and Mrs. John Rapp
Mr. and Mrs. Lars Norden
Mr. and Mrs. P. A. Elfblad
Mr. and Mrs. Gustaf Petterson
Mr. and Mrs. August Soderquist
Mr. and Mrs. P. E. Olson
Mr. and Mrs. Charles Hult
Rev. and Mrs. J. O. Bodén[80]

In the spring of 1903, this newly purchased building was dedicated. Esther Hall, Judith Hallner, and Amelia Johnson, resourceful young ladies in the church, picked blue lupin wildflowers from a nearby pasture to decorate the church for the special occasion. Kerosene lamps were used for lighting, and a wood stove provided the heating. A bucket of water and a common dipper in the entry hall provided water for the thirsty and an opportunity to build up a healthy resistance to germs.[81]

Until a regular pastor came, ministers who were living here such as Rev. P. A. Dimberg, Rev. C. O. Sundquist, Rev. J. O. Bodén, and Rev. Andrew Hallner, served the congregation. Finally, in 1908, the membership was able to call Rev. E. M. Carlson to serve as a full-time pastor. He received a generous salary of $60.00 a month.[82]

In August, 1908, due to an increasing membership, a new church was built on the same location as the old one. The original church structure was built into the new one, forming part of the Sunday School rooms of the new structure.[83] This new building was a gray, stucco building which was built for $12,000.00 and had a seating capacity of 600.[84]

Later, Beulah Covenant purchased the old high school property on Laurel and High Streets and built the present auditorium with a seating capacity of 1,500 at the cost of $55,000.00.[85] A social hall and youth building were added in 1955. Still another educational building was added in 1963-64. In 1968, the main auditorium was beautifully remodeled into a most attractive, modern church sanctuary.[86]

In these early years, the people rode to church by horse and buggy. Horses could be watered at the old watering trough, located near the church where Main and Lander meet. The horses were then tied up at hitching posts or stationed in stalls provided by the church.[87]

Many Turlock families can trace their origin to the romances that began at the Swedish Mission Church. Many of the young swains in town thought the Swedish girls most attractive. They came to the services, sat through long sermons in Swedish without understanding a word that was spoken. After church on Sunday evening, the young men would line up on either side of the path leading from the church to the gate. When the young lady he liked came along, he would ask to escort her home. The roads were very sandy. The ones who walked went directly home, but the ones that were fortunate enough to have a horse and buggy took the longer way home.[88]

Rev. August Delbon, Rev. E. N. Train of Hilmar, and Drs. Albert and Eric Julien were the men responsible for the establishment of the Emanuel Hospital in Turlock.[89] This Covenant-owned hospital is now a very modern, up-to-date institution located on Delbon Avenue. A mental health wing was added to its facilities and was dedicated on 1 August 1970.

In the early years, the majority of the Swedish people worshiped in the Swedish Mission Covenant Church. As other settlers arrived, other Swedish denominations organized their own churches.

Between 1904 and 1906, a few friends from a Swedish Free Church in Central City, Colorado, came to Turlock.[90] On the evening of 17 July 1906, these people and other friends formed a group of twelve who met for the purpose of establishing their own church organization. This first meeting was in the home of Rev. and Mrs. A. G. Bergstrom, 201 Lander Avenue. Rev. John Peterson of Kingsburg assisted in the organization. Mr. John P. Nylander was elected chairman; Mr. Henry Russell was elected the secretary. This group called themselves the Free Mission Church of Turlock.[91] Services were first held in a room rented from Mrs. Emma Hallstone at 213 South Broadway, across from where the Methodist Episcopal Church was located for many years. These services were held regularly every Sunday afternoon. Men within the group, traveling ministers, and missionaries conducted the services for the first two years.

Because of a growing membership, larger quarters were needed. Their first church building was erected in the spring of 1907 on Lander Avenue where the Nazarene Church is now located. A Sunday School consisting of seventeen members was organized.[92] Mr. Swan Johnson was chosen as the Sunday School superintendent. He continued in this position for the next twenty-five years.

Enjoying a steady increase in membership, five additions were made to this original building, the last one being in 1937. A new, modern structure was built in 1959 on Arbor and Johnson Road where the membership continues to worship at the present time.[93] The old church on Lander Avenue was sold to the Church of the Nazarene.

Another Swedish church in Turlock that had an interesting beginning was the Nazareth Evangelical Lutheran Church. In 1904, Rev. M. A. Nordstrom began his work in Turlock. The Ladies Aid had organized to bring the Lutheran people in the area together. Due to a lack of money and a lack of interest on the part of the Lutheran Conference, this work was discontinued. Rev. Nordstrom continued his interest in this work and when he was called to the Hilmar church, he continued the work in Turlock.[94]

On 10 March 1912, the church was organized in the home of M. J. Lundell at 300 Locust Street.[95] The Turlock congregation was included in the same parish along with Saron Church in Escalon and Berea Church in Hilmar.[96] A church was constructed in 1915 on the corner of South Broadway and D Streets by the men of the congregation. The first pastor called was Rev. W. X. Magnuson. A new structure was built on the corner of Orange and Columbia Streets in 1927. This building still stands and serves the present-day membership. In 1957, an educational-social building was added to the original church.[97]

The Calvary Baptist Church of Turlock is another church of Swedish origin. Rev. F. O. Nelson, the state missionary for the Swedish Baptist Conference of California, moved to Turlock late in the summer of 1907. Nelson visited many families in the Turlock area and finally assembled a group of Baptists for prayer and Bible study. On 22 March 1908, at Nelson's home at 329 South Broadway, the First Swedish Baptist Church was organized.

On Easter Sunday, 11 April 1909, their first church building on South Broadway was dedicated. This property was donated by the Joe Samuelsons. This building still stands in the 300 block of South Broadway, but it is now a private residence, the one with the four Ionic columns in front.

Because of the increase in their membership under the dynamic preaching of Rev. Axel Wall, the noise from the Tidewater-Southern Railroad, and the limited space for the parking of their horses and buggies, this church was sold to the Free Methodist Church for $1,600.00. They bought six lots at Locust and Columbia for $2,000.00. They then decided to put up an inexpensive, temporary tabernacle for $1,000.00 immediately. On the first Sunday in June 1915, the first service was held in this structure.

It is interesting to note that this building, originally planned for short-term use, served this new church for the next twenty-two years.[98] This structure, named the "Heavenly Barn" by Rev. Axel Wall, was replaced by a finer and more substantial building in 1937.[99] In March 1947, the name "Swedish Baptist Church" was changed to Calvary Baptist Church. Another modern sanctuary was built in 1971-72 on Monte Vista Avenue between Colorado and Geer Road.

Two other Swedish churches must be mentioned in any story of the early churches of this area. The first one is the Hilmar Covenant Church. Twenty acres of land were donated by the Fin de Siecle Investment Company for a church in Hilmar. A wealthy, prominent gentleman from Sweden, John Brynteson, contributed $4,000.00 toward the church. Mr. N. O. Hultberg built the first church two miles west of Lander Avenue on the corner of Tegner Road and American Avenue. They had the cart before the horse because they had a church before they had an organized congregation.

Rev. O. H. Myhren, the father of Mrs. Frank (Esther) Youngdale, was the first pastor. One offering a month was his salary. By 1903, the Sunday School and the youth groups had been organized.[100] In 1921, a new sanctuary was built on Lander Avenue, which was still in use in 1971.

Another church in the Hilmar area of Swedish background is the Berea Lutheran Church. It was organized in 1906. In 1910, the church was built in the old Hilmar Colony on Tegner between Crane and Turner. This location was two miles west of the present city of Hilmar. In 1948, the church was relocated in Hilmar on Lander Avenue. A modern kitchen, a large social hall, parish room, sacristy, and choir room were added at this time.[101]

All of these Swedish churches we have discussed held services in the Swedish language in the early years. Then came the period of transition with the gradual changeover from the Swedish to the English language. Naturally, this was a slow process over a period of many years. There were conflicts and adjustments in these times between the older and the younger members. However, the congregations survived the crisis intact and have continued to influence and mold our citizens, and have provided the spiritual leadership necessary to a young, healthy community.

Besides adjusting to a new language, the Swedes had to adapt to new climate, soils, crops, and other national and religious groups. How was this accomplished?

Phebe Fjellström, a University of Uppsala scholar who came to the Turlock area in 1966-67, interviewed many of the old-timers at Bethany Home and elsewhere. Appraising the Swedish community with the eye of an ethnologist, she concluded that there was little assimilation in the pioneering first

Swedish dancers at Centennial Dinner. Browning photo, courtesy TDJ.

decade. "The process of Americanization begins much later," she concluded, "when the struggle is over and the immigrant can let his gaze wander over and beyond his own social group and approach other groups."[102] One of the earlier shifts was in the matter of daily diet. "The constantly recurring ingredients of the Swedish diet—salted herring, salted pork, and rye-meal porridge—were gradually superseded by Californian items of food: hams, sliced pineapple, lettuce, peanut butter, turkey, clam chowder and other vegetables and fruits became important elements in the diet of the Californian Swedes." However, at Christmas the *lutfisk,* herring fixed in many ways, the tiny Swedish meatballs, the Santa Lucia ceremony recalled to their minds the land of their ancestors—even while the turkey was roasting in the oven.[103]

Early in the second decade of Swedish settlement, the Swedes gave up agriculture for town pursuits. By 1910, a number of hardworking Portuguese dairymen had bought out the Swedes, who then moved to town to pursue their crafts and trades.

C. G. Strom reported that in the early 1940s, when the early settlers began to die off, their farms were often sold to the Portuguese and Greeks instead of remaining in the family. As many as thirty-seven farms were sold thus during World War II.[104] The sons of the first Swedish generation were now attorneys, physicians, bankers, retailers, mechanics, truck drivers, and teachers.

Dr. Fjellström characterized the attitudes of the three generations of Swedes in Turlock thus: The original settlers adapted themselves to the economic situation, but refused to be absorbed either culturally or socially. Their sons and daughters were, for the most part, proud of their heritage, but were thoroughly assimilated. The third generation did not have the same personal emotional involvement with Sweden, but nevertheless found an intellectual interest in their families' past.[105]

In this chapter we have endeavored to tell you of the Swedish beginnings in this area. We have recounted some of the hardships, discouragements, hard labors, times of perseverance, and also some of their shared joys and accomplishments. Like all pioneers, these settlers brought with them their customs, religions, and culture. They established their schools and churches as soon as it was feasible to do so. Their stamina, endurance, and great faith in God helped them to endure, prosper, and establish the stable communities of this area of which we are most proud.

Fine sweet potato harvests made money for the Portuguese.
Courtesy Turlock Public Library.

Chapter XI

The Portuguese: an Important Element

Helen Hohenthal and Helen Manha Miguel

Portuguese have long been associated with California history. The commanders of the first two expeditions to explore the coast of Alta California were both Portuguese: Juan Rodriguez Cabrillo, the first European to sight its coast, in 1542; and Sebastian Rodriguez Cermenho, who was ordered to survey the coast on his return from Manila in 1595, and who lost his galleon in a November storm at Drake's Bay.

There were almost surely some persons of Portuguese descent among those who came to California during Spanish times, as the lists of settlers' names suggest. During the Mexican period Portuguese came to California in the whaling ships that stopped at the Azores to recruit seamen, for the Portuguese from those islands "were noted for their seamanship, hard work, and ability to spot whales." At San Simeon and Point Lobos there were whaling stations where Portuguese seamen brought in their prey as the huge schools of whales headed north in the spring and south in the fall. In 1855 there were seventeen Portuguese companies processing whale oil in the Monterey area.[1] With the discovery of petroleum in Pennsylvania and California, the demand for whale oil fell off, and the whaling stations declined.

Some Portuguese came to California during the Gold Rush, hoping to get rich. Many found the real wealth in the cheap, good land and the fisheries. The men returned to their Azorean villages and talked of California. In the Azores land was scarce, and the thought of owning broad acreages had great appeal.

In the 1870s "a number of Portuguese stevedores working in San Francisco learned that they could make good money driving teams and plowing in the San Joaquin Valley." So in the planting season several of them roamed the valley. Among these workers was Jose Mendonsa, father of Frank Mendonsa of Turlock. Jose Mendonsa spent four plowing seasons in the vicinity of Turlock but did not settle here, returning to his native island of Pico in the Azores.[2]

Before the turn of the century, Portuguese were found around Monterey, Mission San Jose, in the Hayward-San Leandro area, and in places south of Turlock in the San Joaquin Valley. They worked as tenant farmers, raising chickens, fruits and vegetables, until they had saved money to buy land and become independent farmers. A number of Turlock area Portuguese came from San Leandro; others moved in from farther south in the San Joaquin Valley. The Buhach and Atwater colonies attracted many of this nationality. For instance, John B. Avila bought twenty acres for $100 an acre, with water rights at $1 an acre annually. Starting with a few sweet potato plants, in a few years he built up a large production of high quality potatoes which sold at premium prices.

Portuguese settlement in the area around Turlock began in 1901 and was continuing in 1971, as economic conditions and the threat of volcanic activity in the Azores led them to seek other lands.

Space available in a general history does not permit the recording of all families and their achievements. The list below shows the essential information regarding many early families. A selection of stories of the pioneering families is given next. After that, examples are presented of the way in which the second and third generations have gone into many lines of work and have taken leadership roles in the community.

First Generation Portuguese Settlers
1901–1920[3]

Name	Birthplace	Came To Turlock From:	First Occupation in Turlock
1901			
John A. Santos	Flores	(Seaman)	Farmer
1902			
Celestino Goulart		Atwater	Farmer
Jose Goulart			
Joaquin Goulart (cousin of the brothers Celestino and Jose)		Atwater	Farmer
Manuel Pedras	Corvo	Atwater	Farmer: "Sweet Potato King"
Jose Silviera, father Samuel Silviera Joaquin Silviera Marie Silviera Pierce	Fayal		Farmers
Joe Novo	Flores	Flores?	Farmer
1904			
Frank Dias	Flores	Flores?	Dairyman
Alfred Machado	Pico	Pico?	Farmer: Field Crops
Manuel Machado, Sr.	Pico		Farmer: Field Crops; Dairyman
Jesse Santos	Madeira	Stockton	Saloonkeeper
Antone Rodriguez "Red" Vieira	Flores	Hughson	Dairyman
Antone Rodriguez Vieira (father of Joe)	Flores		Dairyman
Manuel M. Vincent	New England	Selma, California	Farmer, Subdivider, and Building Owner
1905			
Antone Coelho	Flores	Atwater	Farmer
Joaquin Coelho	Flores		
J. C. Fernandes	Flores	New England	Dry Goods Merchant
Joe R. (Coelho) Fernandes (brother of Antone and Joaquin Coelho)	Flores	Merced	Horse Breeder and Teamster
Manuel J. Frago	Flores	Montana ranches	Farmer

Name	Birthplace	Came To Turlock From:	First Occupation in Turlock
Frank Freitas	Fayal	Merced	Dry Goods Merchant
Manuel Garcia	Pico	Alameda County?	Farmer
Manuel S. Luis			Farmer; Poultry and Fruit Shipper
Manuel Vasconcellos	Flores	Oakland	Dairyman primarily
1906			
Frank M. Souza	Flores	Flores	Scraper and Equipment Operator; later Dairyman
1907			
Manuel Francis (John, Tony and Joe Francis later followed their brother to Turlock.)		Jamestown	Farmer: Sweets and Melons
1908			
Manuel Bettencourt	Graciosa	Graciosa	Dairyman
Ben Rogers		San Leandro area	Farmer
1909			
Frank Trigueiro	Flores	Suisun	Dairyman and Field Crop Farmer
John E. Souza	Terceira	Richmond, California	Farmer
1910			
Manuel Furtado	St. Jorge	Pinole	Large Dairy Owner (Cabinetmaker by Trade)
1911			
Antonio Silva Goulart	Pico	Oakland	Farmer
Matthew T. Manha	Flores	Oakdale	Blacksmith
1912			
Frank Caetano George, Sr.		Nevada	Farmer: Cows, Sweet Potatoes
Antone Gomez Frank Gomez, Jr. Joe Gomez Manuel Gomez (sons of Frank Gomez, Sr., who had settled on the lower Sacramento River)	Flores	Walnut Grove	Grocers
1913			
Joseph F. Fernandes	Flores	Alameda County	Large Dairyman
Tony Mendonsa, Sr.	Flores	Modesto, Patterson	Teamster
1914			
Joseph Jerome, Sr.	Corvo	Corvo	Farmer
1918			
Joseph H. Lewis and sons: Albert Lewis Norman Lewis Ray Lewis	Pico	Centerville	Farmers; later Nurserymen
1920			
Joseph Luis Freitas (son of Frank Freitas)	Fayal	Merced	Grocer

Stories Of The Newcomers

Most of the Portuguese who came to Turlock before 1920 had been born in one or another of the Azores. Quite a few of the men had been sailors or fishermen and had been attracted to California. In several cases they went back to the home island and claimed their brides before settling down in the United States. Some had worked as farm hands, sheep herders, and dairymen before moving to Turlock. Even those who were craftsmen usually turned to farming once they were settled in the Turlock region. Typically a family would buy twenty to forty acres, plant sweet potatoes the first season, and later start a dairy herd.

John A. Santos left home in Flores to become a whaler. He sailed aboard steamers operating off the Pacific Coast of the United States for fifteen years. When Joe M. Fagundes, his brother-in-law, told him about the Turlock Irrigation District, Santos moved his family to Turlock in 1901. From the Fin de Siecle Company, he purchased sixty-two acres at $35 an acre where Divine Gardens is today.[4]

The first real "success story" of a Portuguese in Turlock was that of Manuel Pedras. Pedras was born on the tiny island of Corvo. At sixteen years of age he earned his passage to the United States by working on a whaling ship. In 1890 he landed in Boston with the $40 he had earned as his share of the whale oil. He worked herding sheep from the Coast Range foothills to Merced and as far east as Yearington, Nevada. Then he farmed in Atwater and raised sugar beets for Adolph Spreckels on the coast. Drought struck, and he lost his sugar beet crop. On the way back to Atwater, he passed a sign advertising land for sale in Turlock and remarked that only a fool would buy in that sandy soil. But—in April 1902 he bought land on what is now Pedras Road. He planted a mere three and a half acres to sweet potatoes, but that one crop paid his mortgage and debts. By 1910 he was known as the "Sweet Potato King" of Turlock, and Turlock was the sweet potato center of California. Then Pedras switched to dairying and operated a dairy until 1915.[5]

The Vincent family had an especially interesting story. There were five children, Portuguese on their mother's side. The oldest brother, A. M. Vincent, was shanghaied off the streets of his native Boston about 1855. The vessel carried him around Cape Horn to San Francisco. Leaving the ship, he headed for the gold mines of Columbia and later homesteaded in the area. In 1863 he brought his wife; his mother; two younger brothers, Manuel M. and Marion; and two sisters to California.

In 1904 M. M. Vincent, then living in Selma, and a Mr. Willoughby purchased over 1600 acres of land east of Turlock and named it the Willoughby Tract. Vincent later bought out his partner. In 1919 the Vincent School was built in the tract.[6]

"Marion Vincent, the second brother, also purchased some of the tract land. When Vincent Properties acquired the St. Elmo Hotel and other holdings, Marion Vincent took over their management till his death in 1925. . .He met trains, got jitneys for women passengers, and played the 'father' for many lonesome arrivals."[7]

Still later, about 1915, three sons of A. M. Vincent moved to the vicinity: Joe, a blacksmith in Ceres; John; and Fred, a teacher. They and their uncle Marion constituted the Vincent clan in the vicinity for a number of years.[8]

Jesse Santos moved to Turlock from Stockton in 1904. He bought a saloon on the east side of Front Street (Highway 99), across from Central Park. Then he built a two-story brick building on Main Street, across Front from his original saloon. In it were a bar, a Greek restaurant, the town library for a time, and two offices which Santos rented out. No gambling or loitering was allowed in the bar. You downed your drink and walked out. Five years later the city discovered that J. W. Mitchell had deeded the property to the city for a park. The city then bought the Santos building and tore it down.[9]

In 1905 Joe R. Fernandes came to Turlock, having reached the United States as a stowaway when he was only sixteen. The family name was Coelho, but he adopted his mother's maiden name, Fernandes, after reaching California. First working on ranches around Merced, Madera, and Chowchilla, he came to Turlock and obtained a job on the Charles Geer ranch for $30 a month. The Geer ranch was a harbor for Portuguese immigrants. At times there were as many as twenty young fellows in the Geer bunkhouse.

*Santos' Saloon
stood at Main and Front Streets.
Courtesy Bella Santos Morchino.*

Fernandes first purchased twenty acres on Colorado Avenue while still working for Geer. During this time he spread straw on the streets of Turlock to keep the iron-rimmed wagon wheels from sinking in the sand. In 1907 he bought eighty acres on Crowell Road. He raised big draft horses for draying firms in San Francisco and Los Angeles, had a dairy, and for a while continued working part-time for Geer. Putting his fine teams to work, Fernandes contracted to level the 400-acre David Lane property. In 1907 he had a contract to oil Main Street from Canal Drive to the cemetery. When some of the first asphalt was laid in 1910, Fernandes put sixty head of horses to work leveling the streets and hauling the asphalt. At one time he had over a hundred head of work horses for his ranch and contracting business.[10]

One of the few businessmen in the first generation of Portuguese was J. C. Fernandes, who came to Turlock some months after J. R. J. C. Fernandes had come to California from New Bedford, Massachusetts, and lived in Merced for a while before moving to Turlock. He and a partner, Frank Freitas, established a dry goods and clothing store on Front Street. At the end of eighteen months, he bought out his partner. When Fernandes was ready to build a new store, he just moved the old building out into the street and continued business in the old store until the new one was ready.

Mr. Fernandes had had a good education and practical business experience. Soon many Portuguese, confronted with confusing legal terms in contracts and other business papers, asked for and received his help. He became active in church, lodge, and business affairs, serving at one time or another as a director of the First National Bank of Turlock, head of the Turlock Merchants and Growers Association, secretary of the Red Cross, and chairman of the Board of Directors of the County School of Corrections for Boys.[11]

Frank Gomez, Sr., the father of four Turlock settlers, came to California about 1870 on a whaling schooner. This Flores native was attracted to the area around the lower Sacramento River, so he bought a ranch. Part of his land was inundated annually by the river. Eventually the federal government built levees to keep the river in check.

About 1912 Frank's four sons, Antone, Frank Jr., Joe, and Manuel, established a grocery store on South Center Street near Crane. It was called the Farmer's Marketing Company and lasted until about 1919. After that, Frank Jr. worked for the TID and then for the County until he retired in 1956. Manuel farmed and was part owner of a produce shipping business. Antone returned to Walnut Grove. A sister, Mrs. Manuel Perry, and her family had a farm which is now part of the fairground at Turlock.

Joseph had a farm southwest of Turlock in the Tegner district, which his youngest son, Llewellyn, continues to operate. His elder daughter said, "We can now take credit for four generations of native

Californians on my father's side and five generations on my mother's side. So we feel pretty much like we belong."[12]

In 1920 Manuel Luis and Manuel Gomez formed a poultry and fruit packing and shipping company. Their first shed, which stood on Highway 99, was destroyed by fire. The other was on the south side of Crane Street just west of Center.[13]

Iria Mendonsa's story indicates what some of the women had to go through unless they were brought to California by sturdy husbands. Iria came from the Azores to New England when she was sixteen. For a time she lived in crowded quarters with girls who worked in a textile factory. Some of the girls shared their machines with her so she could earn a little money and learn the job. However, she had to hide when the foreman came by.

Iria's father decided that she should go to her brother in Atwater. She made the trip through Canada by train, crossed the Rockies, and came down the Pacific coast to Atwater. On arrival there was no one to meet her at the station. There were no trees, no flowers, no shade except for the shadow of the railway station. While waiting for her brother, all she could feel was the hot sun and the hot sand.[14]

Tony Mendonsa, Iria's husband, had come to the United States in 1903 as one of several young Portuguese stowaways from Flores. They landed on the east coast, and Tony made his way across the country to Modesto. There his first job was driving mule teams for plowing, scraping, and the like at 50 cents a day. Tony was an excellent "mule skinner" and could make a U-turn at the corner of Tenth and I Streets in Modesto with a six-mule team and two wagons. From Modesto he went to Patterson, and then to Nevada, herding sheep. In 1913 he obtained land west of Turlock and later moved to Denair.[15]

There were several independent Portuguese produce dealers operating in Turlock on a small scale. At first they shipped by train, later by truck, to markets in the San Francisco area. They sometimes dealt in a single product like eggs or melons. Shipping by express was fast and reasonable for the small buyer in those years.

An outstanding example of a successful produce merchant has been A. T. "Tony" Bettencourt. His ATB Packing Company ships melons all over the country from Turlock. He is also involved in the produce business elsewhere in the San Joaquin Valley.[16]

Upon his arrival from Pico in the Azores, Joseph H. Lewis first settled in Centerville, California, where he became a vegetable grower. In 1918 Lewis and his sons Albert, Ray, and Norman were established on a little farm on South Linwood Avenue south of Turlock. They raised sweet potatoes and Malaga grapes at first. In the 1930s they specialized in asparagus, onions, and chickens. As a hobby they had an aviary of unusual birds. They later turned to the nursery business, maintaining a selection of plants for landscaping under the name Lewis Nursery.[17]

While most of the individuals discussed so far have been farmers or merchants, Matthew T. Manha's career took a different course. Manha had heard of California from his father, who had been there twice, as well as from others in his village on the island of Flores. Borrowing the money, he paid $23 for his passage from the Azores to Brooklyn. Twenty other young men were in the party. At Golconda, Nevada, Manha got a job working in a mine's blacksmith shop. He worked on the night shift sharpening drills for $3 a night. He liked the job, the boss, the pay, and working with iron at the blacksmith's forge—it was creative work.

When the mine closed down, Manha came to Modesto and found work in the dairies. Later he worked on a grain ranch in Oakdale, plowing with a ten-mule team and seeding with a twelve-mule team for $1.35 a day.

In 1911 Manha went to work in a blacksmith shop in Turlock which was located on the corner of Highway 99 and Olive Street. Charlie Herbst, a German, and a Mr. Jessen, a Dane, owned the business. "In the shop they did wagon and buggy work and all the related woodwork, in addition to work on plows, scrapers, harrows and sweet potato planters. . . .

"After three years working for Herbst and Jessen, Manha and a partner, James Wilson, bought the Turlock Iron Works from them and became partners in a good business. Wilson kept the books and Manha worked at the forge. Two years later they joined the Board of Trade (predecessor of the Chamber of Commerce)."

The shop had many good customers who brought in big jobs and who paid their bills promptly. Charles Geer was the biggest customer, bringing in plowshares for his Stockton gang plow. Charles Dunn and Albert Chatom brought in four-foot scrapers used in digging ditches on contract with TID.

Matt Manha shod all the horses and mules. The latter came in literally by the dozens. The charge was $1.25 an animal, except for the large horses, for which it was $1.50. A horse was supposed to be shod within an hour. There was money in horseshoeing in those days, but no poetic memories.

Several novel jobs were remembered by Matt Manha. He told how there was no bridge over the canal at Canal and Geer Roads. To permit carriages and wagons to cross the canal when water was flowing during the summer, the canal was scraped and widened. To accommodate pedestrians, planks were put across the canal. Eventually a bridge was built, and TID turned to Manha for ironwork and bracing of the bridge.

Two of the jobs were for the fire department. Up to about 1916 it had a hand hose cart which could be drawn behind a wagon. The wheels were too close together, so it would turn over very easily when going around a corner. In 1912 Manha had the job of repairing it. Later the fire department purchased a Ford truck chassis. The Turlock Iron Works made a bed of white oak with the necessary metal framing. The bill for the job was $105.[18]

The only Portuguese woman to own a business during the early decades of Portuguese settlement was Mrs. Marie Santos Ripley, daughter of John Santos. She owned a hat store in the 1920s close to the corner of Center and East Main Streets.

The Second Generation

By 1925 a growing proportion of the Portuguese in Turlock had been born in the United States. Substantial numbers continued to come from the Azores, a few coming directly from Portugal. In a sense, even these were of the second generation, for those who had come during the preceding quarter-century had established themselves in the community, owned farms and stores, commanded credit at the banks, had organized several Portuguese associations, and were an active—perhaps the predominant—element in the Sacred Heart Parish.

Such a person was Frank Mendonsa, who came to Turlock from Newark, California, in 1925, attracted by the excellent conditions this area offered for successful farming. Like many others, he came without any capital, so he worked as a laborer at first to pay for the farm he purchased on Youngstown Road.

Mendonsa recalled that there was some discrimination against the Portuguese when he first came to Turlock, but that it had ceased. He himself played an active role in bridging the gap between the Portuguese and the rest of the community. He taught American Citizenship classes and also gave instruction in Portuguese in high school evening classes. Newcomers from the Azores and old-timers alike learned to turn to him for help and advice.

Mendonsa was perhaps best known to the community as the creator and director of the "Frankly Speaking" Portuguese radio program that ran for twenty-two years continuously on AM radio station KTUR and its successor, KCEY. On the state level, Mendonsa served as President and Director of the Union of Portuguese of the State of California (Union Portuguesa Estado California, abbreviated UPEC).[19]

William R. "Bill" Fernandes, son of Joe R., is a native of Turlock. A farmer and accountant, he has taken an active part in civic affairs, having been a director of the TID for twenty years from 1951 to his retirement in 1971. For twenty-six years he was auditor of the Chamber of Commerce, and for fourteen years (1958-1972) he was secretary-treasurer of the Rural Fire District. Fernandes served as master of the Turlock Grange; district director of the Farm Bureau; director of District 13, California, American Dairy Association; and director of the Poultry Producers Farm Cooperative.[20]

Like the two men just discussed, John J. Souza maintained a tie with farming after going into other occupations as well. Souza was brought to Turlock from Richmond, California, by his parents in 1909 when he was about a year old. His father, John E. Souza, had come to the United States from the island of Terceira in 1903. After several years working for the Santa Fe in Richmond, the elder Souza brought his little family to Turlock and bought a farm in the Tegner district.

Young John J. Souza bought his first farm on Bradbury Road in 1926. In 1934 he began driving a milk truck for the Carnation Company to eke out his income. Two years later he and his brother, Manuel J. Souza, bought their own trucks and began hauling milk to the Golden State Company.

Looking around for cheaper fuel for their trucks, the Souza brothers adopted propane. Customers on the route requested the Souzas to provide them with propane fuel also, so another line was added to their business. In 1938 they began selling appliances on Bradbury Road and were doing well enough that they moved to Turlock in 1941 and continued to expand their business, adding furniture in 1943. In 1946 Souza purchased land on Greenway Avenue and began a private airport, the Turlock Air Park. Souza's furniture and appliance business underwent major expansion in 1971 when he took over the former Safeway building at Highway 99 and Canal, diagonally across from his main location.[21]

Mr. and Mrs. Antone R. Vieira. Courtesy the Vieira family.

Mr. and Mrs. Manuel J. Frago. Courtesy the Frago family.

Like Souza, Anthony Ferreira was brought to Turlock when a small child, but a generation later than Souza. His father, like Souza's parents, was from Terceira; but they came to Turlock from Newman, California, in 1931. Ferreira's father was a farmer, while the son combined dairying, general farming, and the operation of milk trucks.[22]

Ralph Serpa is a member of the third generation of Turlock's Portuguese residents. During the 1960s he developed a wholesale milk route, and in 1967 he bought a small acreage.

Representative of the achievements of the generation coming to manhood and womanhood at the beginning of Turlock's second century was Richard Silva of Hilmar, who received the nation's top Future Farmers of America dairying award in 1971 and who at age nineteen was already a partner with his father, Frank Silva.

A few first generation and quite a number of second generation Portuguese left the farm and went into business. In turn, the second and third generation Portuguese began to select professional and sub-professional vocations. Clara Gonsalves and Alice Pimentel became registered nurses and nursing instructors at Modesto Junior College. Marie Ricardo Corvello taught physical education and became dean of girls at Central Catholic High School in Modesto. Vivian Manha taught mathematics and later was appointed assistant dean of students at Modesto Junior College. Joe Vieira was a manual arts teacher, and the late Ernie Jorge was a well known high school and college athletic coach.

Gilbert Goulart became an architect and has been responsible for several of Turlock's finest public buildings, which are pictured and discussed later in the book.

Ellis Ripley, an ichthyologist, spent a number of years in South America, one assignment being to aid the Brazilian government to establish fisheries. As of 1972, he was head of the World Fisheries Development Program under the United Nations. June Jane Ripley McVey, his sister, established her popular dance studio about the time she graduated from high school and was still operating it in 1972.

Richard Jerome became an announcer at station KCEY. Luverne Gomez served as pastor of the Mitchell Community Church west of Turlock before going to Oakdale. Eugene Lobo became chief pharmacist at Doctors Hospital in Modesto, while Flossie Lobo was appointed judge in a Merced court.

When a person of one's own nationality rises to community leadership, it seems that a goal has been reached for the entire group. It was thus significant for the Portuguese when Joe Miguel was elected president of the Chamber of Commerce of Turlock in 1959. Later he was appointed to the City Council. In 1962 A. T. "Tony" Bettencourt was elected to the Council and served two terms, until 1970. Representative of those who have taken administrative posts in local government is Dan Avila, who was appointed Planning Director of the City of Turlock on 1 January 1965.

Portuguese Associations

With the dedication of the Portuguese to their church, it is but natural that a number of their organizations are church related. The principal Portuguese festival in Turlock, as elsewhere, is the Pentecost Celebration. In Portugal the food was given only to the poor; here a barbecue is free for everyone. Here a grand ball is held on the evening before Pentecost Sunday to raise money; in Portugal this was not customary.

Belle Santos Morchino writes, "The first Holy Ghost [Pentecost Celebration] was out of my family home. I think we had the sopas near a canal. We had a parade. I carried the American flag and my aunt Rosalie Lima carried the Portuguese flag. The first Portuguese banner for the Holy Ghost was given by Manuel Serpa."[23]

Other religious holidays followed the same general pattern: a mass, a parade, climaxed by entertainment, dancing, and food.

The Pentecost Association was organized in 1912 with A. R. Vieira as the first president. Its first parade was held 18 May 1913. In 1915 Portuguese Hall was built by the Association as a social center.[24] The chapel was constructed in 1921. Still later the Turlock Ballroom was added to the complex, which sits on a portion of the triangle formed by Canal and Geer Roads and Highway 99.

The first chapter of the Ladies' Sociedade Portuguesa Rainha Santa Isabel was organized in Turlock by Mrs. Jesse Santos in 1901. Religiously oriented, its charitable fund has helped many in time of need; it has also become a focal point for cultural activities among the Portuguese.

The Conselho Mocidade No. 68 of the Irmandade do Divino Espirito (Brotherhood of the Holy Spirit) was formed on 1 September 1905. The first president was J. V. Gomes. After the organizing meeting a banquet was provided. "At a late hour everyone returned to their homes, wishing for such good times to come around often. . . ." This organization has confined its operations to California.[25]

Five years later, in 1910, the Union Portuguesa Estado California No. 75, a lodge of a Portuguese insurance society, was organized in Turlock. In 1921 the Turlock lodge first played host to the State Council, the Chamber of Commerce assisting in financing the convention with a grant of $1,000.[26]

The three groups mentioned above are among the earliest of no less than eight Portuguese lodges that exist in Turlock.

In Appreciation

Descendants of the first generation of Portuguese pioneers, as well as later comers, have become among the most successful farmers in the Turlock region. They are particularly noted for their dairies, which have helped Stanislaus County maintain its rank as second only to Los Angeles County in milk

Debi Miranda, Pentecost Senior Queen, 1971, and Louise Vieira, first Pentecost Queen, 1913. Browning photo.

Pentecost Association leaders, 1938. Left to right, front row, Theodore Cunha, Manuel S. Luis, Frank Gonsalves, Manuel Furtado; second row, Manuel C. Texeira, Frank Pereira, Frank Martin, Frank Linhares, Tony Silva. Courtesy Rose Lewis Frodelius.

Interior of the Pentecost Association chapel, 1921. Forsmark and Wedin photo, courtesy June Jane Ripley McVey.

Pentecost Association chapel, 1971. Caswell photo.

production. Individual Portuguese have continued to make outstanding records in sweet potatoes, although these are not raised as widely as in earlier years.

Socially as well as economically the Portuguese have made their contribution through their numerous organizations and festivities. The public at large has benefited through the Pentecost Association's operation of the Turlock Ballroom.

A worthy tribute to the early Portuguese settlers was penned by Helen Manha Miguel. "They were men of earnestness and determination who with dogged effort struggled with land, pests, weather, and sometimes ill health to get that precious piece of paper from the County Recorder's Office in Modesto." To this the writer would add another piece of paper they coveted: their American citizenship papers. Again and again in interviews and notes these Portuguese settlers have shown that they considered citizenship a privilege and a blessing.

Helen Miguel continued, "The inborn tenacity that came with them from the lava rock Azores where the inhabitants were always at the mercy of the elements, with no avenues of escape or protest, made strong men and women."

Samovar.

Chapter XII

The Assyrians: Settlers from the Near East

Sarah Sergis Jackson and Victoria Yonan Nevils

Background

The Assyrians were a minority long before coming to the United States. Without a country of their own, they have been a linguistic, political, religious, as well as an ethnic minority in the Moslem countries of Iran, Iraq, and Turkey. British diplomat Lord Curzon said that although they are a people small in number, "...with respect to race, history, religion, and sufferings [the Assyrians] excited greater interest in the world than any other community."[1]

Since Assyrians who migrate to the United States are considered to be of the nationality of their birthplace, seldom if ever are they listed among those making up the mass migrations to this country. Yet thousands have found haven in the United States after fleeing Moslem persecution and massacre. Perhaps no other people have found so welcome the proffer of the Statue of Liberty: "Send these, the homeless, the tempest-tost to me." Nor have any others looked more yearningly to the United States as the promised land. Like the Pilgrims, the Assyrians were seeking religious and political freedom.

Assyrians claim to be the direct descendants of the ancient Assyrians mentioned in Genesis 2:14, who are known in history as early as 2000 B.C. According to Fred Tamimi, Turlock Assyrian scholar, "No nation, ancient or modern, can trace its antiquity farther into the past than that of Assyria. Her recorded history can clearly be read upon her tablets milleniums before Christ, and her language [traced] to that of Adam and Eve."[2] The Assyrians have been called "the Romans of Asia." Like the Romans they were great conquerors. They won their victories by superb organization, weapons, and equipment.[3]

When Nineveh, capital of Assyria, was destroyed in 612 B.C., the remnant of the Empire was called Urhai and later Edessa. Many Assyrians fled to the secluded mountains of Kurdistan; some settled in Urmia in northwestern Persia, and others scattered throughout Asia Minor.[4]

Assyrians believe that the Magi who brought their gifts to the infant Jesus were Assyrians from Urhai. Eusebius tells of correspondence between Ogar, king of Urhai, and Jesus, who sent a disciple to visit Ogar. From this visit, according to tradition, the Church of the East arose. This church followed

St. Nestorius in rejecting the decrees of the Council of Ephesus in 431 A.D., hence it is commonly called Nestorian. It is represented by the St. Thomas Christians of South India. Nestorians were found in China in the seventh and eighth centuries. About 1550 A.D., a controversy resulted in a number of Assyrians becoming Roman Catholics, and these have been called Chaldeans.[5]

As the law of the Koran, the Moslem scriptures, is religious as well as civil, it could not be applied integrally to Christians, so non-Moslem communities were ruled through their religious hierarchies. Thus their church had a twofold importance to the Assyrians.[6]

With the coming of American, English, and Russian missionaries in the nineteenth century, the Assyrians became more aware of their national identity, thereby irritating the Moslems. As the missionaries hoped to revitalize the Church of the East and draw evangelists from it to carry Christianity to the rest of Asia, Moslem distrust grew.[7] There was perhaps no other mission field where so many rival Christian groups were found as in Urmia.[8] While the missionaries were allowed to establish schools and hospitals, mistreatment of the Christians was primarily staved off by the presence of Russian troops.

Increasingly, Assyrians sought to escape. Graduates of Urmia College and others went to America and England, hoping to earn money and eventually send for their families. Many men went to Russia to learn trades.

When Turkey attacked Russia during World War I, the Russians pulled out of Persia. Turks and Kurds swooped down and joined the Persians in plundering and massacring the Christians. Thousands fled to Russia. The American Presbyterian missionaries took as many as they could into their compound, but starvation and disease exacted a heavy toll. For several years the Christians withstood the atrocities, which were climaxed by the assassination of the Assyrian Patriarch, Mar Shimun. Assyrians and Armenians tried to stop the Turkish advance. The Turks surrounded Urmia on three sides and attacked it fourteen times. Finally on 31 July 1918 the Assyrians decided to evacuate Urmia and try to reach the British Army in the south. Over 50,000 men, women and children started out, accompanied by the American Presbyterian missionaries, Dr. and Mrs. William Shedd. After a month in which the refugees were looted, raped and murdered by Persians and Turks, the remnant reached safety at the British base in Hamadan, whence they were later moved to Iraq. Most of the Christians who did not leave Urmia were killed.[9]

Following World War I, many of the refugees stayed in Iraq. Some found their way back to Urmia; those who were able migrated to the United States and to other non-Moslem areas. Presently more Assyrians are coming to the United States from Iraq than from anywhere else. In Iran, however, Assyrians now have political representation, are not religiously persecuted, and are as successful as any other citizens.

The Assyrian Colony At Turlock

As long ago as 1867 an Assyrian came to California from Persia. For this feat, plus the fact he had visited Jerusalem, he was dubbed "maikdusee" (pilgrim) upon his return to the old country. But not until early in the twentieth century did Assyrians come to California to stay. A few came to San Francisco from eastern United States cities in answer to the call for workers following the 1906 earthquake and fire.

In 1911 Dr. Isaac Adams and a group of about forty-five arrived in Delhi, seeking a rural area which might be similar in climate and crops to their native Persia. They came by way of Canada and eastern and midwestern United States. Having reached these areas, they were still looking for something more like the old country. The sophisticated atmosphere of populous cities was in extreme contrast to their agricultural background, and the land and climate in Canada had not measured up to their expectations.

Paul Shimmon, author of *Massacres of Assyrian Christians,* thus describes Urmia in the province of Azerbaijan, from which these Assyrians came:[10]

> The plain of Urmia has a charm for all travellers. In the Spring and Summer it is
> a veritable paradise: its running waters, its gardens, its vineyards, orchards, melon
> fields, its tobacco plantations and rice fields give a variety of color and a beauty of
> scene seldom met with in the East.

The role of pioneer suited Dr. Isaac Adams extremely well: a Christian living in Moslem Persia, orphaned at the age of six by the Russian banishment of his father to Siberia, having lived in an orphanage supported by the Barclay bankers of England, educated in an American missionary college, imprisoned in an underground dungeon complete with Turkish cruelty, he was most anxious to seek a new life in **a new country.**

Dr. Isaac Adams, founder of the Assyrian colony at Turlock.

Dr. John Sergis.

As a boy in Deacon Knanishoo's orphanage in Urmia, Isaac Adams listened attentively to talk about America where people were free to have whatever religion they wished, to make of themselves whatever their potential made possible. Stirred by the example of missionaries, he resolved to become one. At the age of seventeen he was willing to face the hazards of a trip halfway around the world to study for the ministry. With practically no resources but faith that a better life was to be had, he migrated to the United States. In the latter part of the nineteenth and early twentieth centuries, other young Assyrian men also braved the uncertainties of life in a new world to come to America to get an education or work, or both, and eventually to send for their families. Adams' ambition was to return and help the people of his nationality to come to America.

As early as 1902 he wrote to Sacramento for homesteading information. The answer was that there were no longer lands sufficient in size and fertility for a settlement. Undismayed, he contacted Canadian immigration officials and was told such a settlement would be welcome in North Battleford, Saskatchewan. The same year Dr. Adams brought a group of Assyrians to Canada. The settlement succeeded, and in 1906 he went back to Persia to bring another contingent; but travel mixups delayed the small band in England where whatever little money they had was used up, and it was necessary to go into debt to complete the trip to Canada. Such unfortunate beginnings rather blighted the second settlement, so Dr. Adams again thought of taking some of his people to the United States where he had become a citizen while a student.

In 1910 Dr. Adams, accompanied by a few of the Canadian settlers, went to Chicago. There he saw the colonizing agent of the Santa Fe Railroad who recommended the San Joaquin Valley for a settlement. Recruiting more Assyrians from Chicago and points east, the prospective settlers at the agent's suggestion came to San Francisco to contact a Mr. Wilson who owned a large tract of land in Delhi. They were persuaded to settle there, the claim being made that the land was as good as that around Turlock. According to Mrs. Mary Benjamin, a niece of Dr. Adams, he was shown pictures of acreages in Fresno and Turlock which purported to be the Delhi land. What they were not told was that the land was very sandy, and since Delhi was then outside the irrigation district, they would have no water for their crops.[11]

All the section south of Delhi as far as the Merced River on the west side of present Highway 99 was bought by the Assyrians for $100 an acre. The unimproved land did not lessen the joy of these early settlers, for the climate and fresh air, which were free from the soot and dirt of cities, were just what they had been seeking.

Only one of these early settlers, Sargis Hoobyar, had brought his family. The rest had come to make ready land and homes before sending for their families.

Annually during this period in California history, sandstorms struck the valley in the spring and fall, lasting for at least three days. As these settlers were preparing their land for planting, one of the storms came on. For three days they were almost unable to see one another; each had to stay in his shack or tent. They couldn't move out of shelter for fear of choking in the sand swirling around their property. When the storm was over, the settlers decided their former homes were safer; all left with the exception of the Hoobyar family, which had no money to go anywhere else. Coincidentally there was also living in Delhi at this time George Andrews, a Syrian, with his family. Members of the Andrews family are still living on the east side of Delhi.

Dr. Adams purchased a ranch south of the Turlock overpass on the west side of Highway 99.[12] Mrs. Adams was still living on this property in 1971, and her son Albert, with his family, had a home adjacent. Quoting Dr. Adams, who was interviewed by Helen Hohenthal in 1930:

> Turlock was our shopping town. One day while driving into town, I stopped to talk to Mr. Bodén who was picking apricots. I had just sold my homestead in North Battleford to the Canadian government and I asked Mr. Bodén how much he wanted for his 23 acres. He said $8,000. I offered $7,000 and bought the place located 1-1/2 miles from Turlock on South Highway.
>
> Among others who had come out with me was Sargis Hoobyar. Hoobyar used to go to school with me in Persia. I met him again in Chicago. I sent letters to Assyrians in eastern U.S. cities and back to Persia to induce others to come here. I also enclosed literature from the Chamber of Commerce for those who read English. At our school English was one of the subjects.
>
> The products of the valley were the same as in Persia so my people knew the grape, melon, and orchard fruit crops. The climate is similar. Of those who came later many came by way of India, China, and Japan. Some were war refugees and didn't have much money. Many worked in cities until they made enough money to buy land. They were very good as plasterers, bricklayers, carpenters, etc. These later colonists bought land at peak prices, paying about a quarter down. Crops were bringing high prices, too, but two years later the prices dropped and the people had no money with which to pay for their land. Some lost it and some are very heavily mortgaged. I helped some of them to pick out their places, for example, the Koshaba Shimmon place from the Merritts. Shimmon, who had been a Persian rug dealer in Cleveland, Ohio, paid out on his place, then heavily mortgaged it to buy land for his son.
>
> Because the Assyrians had no homeland even in Persia, they will make good homes and good citizens here. Some have already left, but counting children there are about 500 in the district today. With the present low prices for crops, I do not encourage more to come. . . .A few years ago I received $2,300 for my apricot crop; last year the same size crop, only $125. I have a 40-acre place near Livingston for which I paid $28,000. There is a mortgage of $6,000 on it. I offered the woman who holds the mortgage the place for cancellation of mortgage and interest. She refused because she said the place wasn't making the taxes now.

When Lady Surma (sister of Patriarch Mar Shimun) was here in 1926, she was well pleased with my idea of getting Assyrians onto farms. Since then, wherever she goes, she advertises this colony.

I started the small Evangelical Assyrian Church. I thought it would be well for all the Assyrians (Methodist, Baptist, Presbyterian, etc.) to stay together. Then some decided to have a separate Presbyterian Church so the large new one was constructed (St. John's Assyrian Presbyterian Church, Palm and Minaret Streets). The old church is clear of all indebtedness. Rev. Eshoo conducts the services. He was a very prominent preacher in Canada.

The Assyrians have nice homes. They put in trees, flowers, etc., right away. That is because this is really the only homeland they have.

George Peters, now retired and living in Modesto, was the first Assyrian settler in the city of Turlock. Peters had attended Augustana College, a Swedish Lutheran school in Rock Island, Illinois. In Los Angeles he met Dr. Nelander, one of the organizers of the Berea Lutheran Church in Hilmar, who told him about Turlock. Coming to Turlock in 1911, Peters' first rooming quarters were at Mrs. William Fulkerth's home on Center and Mitchell Streets. His rent was $1.25 weekly. Mrs. Fulkerth, or "Aunt Abby" as she was known, informed him she had bought the property on both sides of Center Street from Olive Street to Geer Road for one mule!

In 1912 Joseph Adams and Odishoo Backus with their families arrived in Turlock from Canada, one the brother, the other the cousin of Dr. Adams. Land had already been purchased for Adams, but Backus shopped around for a while before purchasing acreage on F Street in partnership with Abel Tamraz, his brother-in-law, and George Peters. Each paid Andrew Johnson $450 for his share. The three opened up the present Eighth and Ninth Streets by digging up the peach trees on their land and making dirt roads. Peters also helped Johnson open up Fifth Street.

In 1917 Peters sold his share, and with Dr. Adams and George Inweeya as partners bought twenty acres from Fred Geer on the corner of Fifth and F Streets at a cost of $9,500. In 1918 the property was divided among the partners. Peters developed his section by putting in grapes and apricots. At that time F Street was a narrow dirt road. Joe Claes, a neighbor, and Peters improved the road, each donating forty feet for its widening before turning it over to the county. Peters had three wells dug on his property and built four homes.

In 1917 Peters, Inweeya, and Dr. Adams rented land from the vicinity of Arcade (Colorado) to Berkeley Road and from East Avenue to Canal Drive for $35 an acre from Horace Crane. Turlock High School and a residential area are now on the land. The partners planted Egyptian corn, spending over $3,000 and killing countless gophers, squirrels, birds, and jack rabbits to protect the crop. At the time Egyptian corn was bringing in a good price and grew even in isolated places without irrigation. But the partners took in only $450 income, for wild animals and a sandstorm took a heavy toll.

"Losing his shirt" made it necessary for Peters to go to work in San Francisco to replenish his purse. When finances ran low, other Assyrian men would do likewise, working for a while to make money, then returning to their land in Turlock; or they would work in San Francisco, commuting to Turlock on weekends until their farms were paid for and bringing in incomes.

Finally in desperation, because the Delhi soil was bad, snakes, squirrels, jack rabbits, and gophers ravaged the land, and water was difficult to obtain, Sargis Hoobyar left Delhi in 1915. He bought ten acres of land from David Brier's heirs, and later six acres from Homer Brier, with a small down payment. There were already peaches and grapes on the place, located between Linwood and East Avenues, a mile southeast of Turlock on Quincy Road.

Other Assyrians from the East who had moved to San Francisco and Los Angeles bought unimproved land from the Brier brothers near Hoobyar, paying $150 an acre, expecting the land to produce grapes, peaches, melons, alfalfa, and sweet potatoes. Bad soil and sand storms making their ventures unsuccessful, they abandoned their farms; but Hoobyar stayed into the 1960s.

*Mary Shimmon House,
Attorney-at-Law.
Courtesy Lillian
Shimmon Spielman.*

Mr. and Mrs. Sargis Hoobyar on their golden anniversary. Courtesy Arby Hoobyar, Sr.

In 1921 Odishoo Backus bought ten acres on Alpha Street east of Berkeley Road, adding more acres gradually. On his original unimproved land he planted melons, grapes, alfalfa, and kept a few cows. In 1971 Backus was still living in the same location; some of his children in their separate homes also resided in this section.

Likewise in 1921 the Elia Malick family came from Los Angeles to Madera, where they first purchased land. Mrs. Malick knew there were more Assyrians in Turlock, so she urged her husband to continue on to Turlock. They were about to buy a home in Turlock when Dr. Adams pointed out to them the wisdom of buying a farm and a home on Fifth Street which were available for the same price. Mr. Malick, an expert plasterer, worked at his trade in San Francisco and his wife managed the farm. The Elisha Khamis family bought the adjacent farm to the east, and the Abraham Jacobs family the farm across the road. Soon Mrs. Malick was thoroughly enjoying the neighborhood, to which were added the Lazar Benjamins, the Ablahat Kishtoos, the John Georges, the Avraham Nweas and others. When her brother, Walter Malick, moved to the farm on her west, Mrs. Malick felt almost as if she were in Urmia, but without the drawbacks of living in a Moslem country and with conveniences which she would never have thought of in Persia.

The first to venture out toward Denair were the Daniel Lazars, who arrived in Turlock via Canada in 1917. They established a charming home and grew apricots and grapes for drying. It would seem that their son Harvey, owner of Lazar Fruit Company, comes naturally by his interest in dried fruit.

The Lazars always had many visitors because Daniel was a great wit and because they had made their surroundings so reminiscent of the old country. Visiting among one another in the early days was the prime means of sociability for the Assyrians, who had not yet mingled very much with their American neighbors nor involved themselves in the affairs of the community. They loved to entertain each other. No matter when company dropped in, and it was usually unannounced because telephones were not in much use, the lady of the house somehow managed to lay out a spread of food: melons, grapes, and orchard fruits in season; nuts and raisins, and a flaky non-sweet pastry called *kada*. The *pièce de résistance* was always Samovar tea, served in small, delicate glasses with fine china saucers. The tea is sweetened by placing a small lump of sugar in the mouth. This is drinking tea *dishlama*. It is permissible to cool the tea in the saucer or even drink it from the saucer.

Not the least of the conversation had to do with expressions of gratitude for their good fortune at being in America, especially in a rural area so like the old country, yet enjoying freedom and protection and sharing in equal opportunities.

For the Khoshaba Shimmon family it was like the end of an odyssey in 1921, once more to have their own home and land. Before settling on Wolfe Road, they lived in Cleveland, Ohio, and before that for five years, 1913-18, persecutions and war kept the father and his family apart.

Little did the father know what was in store when he left Urmia in 1913 to come on business to the United States. Then World War I broke out and he was distraught by the reports that the Turks had attacked the Assyrians. He wanted to return immediately, but on second thought and on the advice of others, he realized he could accomplish more by eliciting help from this end. Besides he didn't know where to find his family.

Mr. Shimmon had left his banking and importing business in charge of his seventeen-year-old son, Yoaw. Now it became necessary for Yoaw to take charge of his mother, sister, and two brothers and flee for safety. Somehow they managed to get to Tiflis. There followed three and a half years of travail in which almost daily attempts were made to obtain passage for the United States. Wartime conditions, the Bolshevik Revolution, lack of transportation—all conspired against them. These were years of torturing suspense for the father: time after time money was sent, arrangements begun, careful plans laid, only to fail of fulfillment.

Because Yoaw could speak Russian, several other refugee families attached themselves to him. Finally in March 1918 they were able to leave Tiflis by way of Batum, for that was the only way to avoid the Moslems who were killing Christians. In Yoaw's own words:

> After many disappointments and long waiting we heard of a freight boat, the last that would leave. We could buy no tickets without passes; they would shoot one on the road if he had no pass. We would stand in line from dawn to 9:00 o'clock, then be sent to another part of the city, very far, and be told no more passes would be given that day. We must buy new passes in every city and pay what was demanded. The Bolsheviks were very lawless. We often found roads blocked and eight generals had just been shot in one place. But we all looked poor and forlorn in our old garments and they paid little attention to us.

Once on board the freight steamer, the refugees found only room to crowd on the deck, in spite of rain and cold. Then onto a cattle car, secured at great cost, foully dirty, with standing room only. Finally Vladivostock was reached, nearly three months after leaving Tiflis. The last papers, including border passports, were obtained and visas from the American Consul. On to Japan. Again no transportation. It took one week to obtain passage on a ship. Finally the boat moved—they were leaving Russia at last. At 9:00 the next morning the boat docked in Yokohama, but it was another couple of weeks before passage could be had on a Dutch liner for a nineteen-day trip to San Francisco.[13]

The daughter of the family, Mary Shimmon, became the valedictorian of the 1927 graduating class of Turlock High School. She worked her way through law school and in 1939 was a Stanislaus County Deputy District Attorney. She later became counsel for the California State Department of Employment.

Dr. John Sergis took up farming in Keyes, six miles northwest of Turlock, because failing eyesight made it necessary for him to give up the practice of dentistry. He purchased forty-three acres of good land from the Olivas brothers for $20,000 in 1923, built a comfortably large home, and moved his family there from San Francisco in 1925. The home was the first in the area to have a tiled bathroom, and for several years strangers would drop in and ask to see the bathroom. Twenty acres were already in grapes; peaches, apricots, and additional grapes were put in and some land left open for planting melons and beans. When the plants and vines were mature, the yields were exceptionally good: 25 tons of watermelons, 20 tons of apricots, and 16 tons of grapes to the acre.

His "American" neighbors looked rather askance at a "foreign" dentist trying to farm. But being a professional man, he applied professional techniques to his new vocation, and before long his neighbors began imitating him. Whereas they had tended to be rather sloppy in their surroundings, seeing in Dr. Sergis' example that one didn't have to be messy just because he was a farmer, they also started taking pride in the appearances of their farms, homes, and yards.

Prior to coming to San Francisco, Dr. Sergis was a dentist in the British Army stationed in Qasvin, Persia. When the Army started to leave Persia, Dr. Sergis consulted with the commander of the force, General Lord Ironside, as to which country would be best for him to take up residence in—England or the United States. He was an American citizen; but if he went to England, he could be retired by the Army. General Ironside's unequivocal answer was the United States, inasmuch as he predicted there would be another war in Europe within twenty years.

Two brothers-in-law of Dr. Sergis, with their families, moved from New York to equally good land nearby. One of them, Paul Shimmon, in the early '30s served as Rector of St. Paul's Episcopal Church in Modesto.

The family of Supervisor Joash Paul were also early settlers in Keyes, and his father, Philip, was an outstanding worker and farmer. Being of a more speculative turn than Dr. Sergis, Mr. Paul increased his landholdings in the area. The two men admired each other very much and helped each other in many ways.

Other Assyrians who could afford to pay a little more for the land also bought in Keyes. They came from various parts of the United States, having heard about the area from their relatives or friends and about the pleasant country living.

Another source of information which attracted these people was the *Assyrian Star,* a bimonthly magazine published in Chicago. Various persons from Turlock and Keyes were asked to supply information about life on the farm, the weather, the sociability, the crops, and other data that could be used by people contemplating a move to the area.

The first Assyrian to go into business in Turlock was Bob Abraham, who opened a hot dog and hamburger stand on Main Street and the Highway in the early twenties. He was immediately successful, and by the third year he had such a thriving business that the Chief of Police told him he had to move the stand elsewhere because other businesses were complaining of the traffic. So he purchased a lot from Henry Bowers and constructed a building for a restaurant which became even more popular than the stand.

The Assyrians with their penchant for nicknames began calling him Bob Hamburger, and some even Bob Lunch. To this day, even though Mr. Abraham is currently in the real estate business, he is still affectionately known as Bob Hamburger, with some people perhaps unaware that his surname is other than Hamburger.

These are only a few of the early settlers that space permits mentioning. Each decade sees more people of Assyrian descent moving to Stanislaus County, just as people of other ethnic origins are doing. Perhaps proportionately more Assyrians know about and move to the area than other minorities. A fairly large percentage of those in the United States have come to Turlock to live or visit, or have relatives and friends living here who urge them to come and see for themselves what a good place it is. Currently the people of Assyrian descent moving here are those who have achieved success in other parts of the United States and who can afford to retire in California. The area has been pleasing to the Assyrians: they have found some measure of similarity to their native country; they have been able to live in the rather unhurried and simple atmosphere they knew in the old country when the Kurds, Persians, and Turks weren't taking potshots at them or trying to relieve them of their possessions.

If there was criticism in the first years of the local settlement that the Assyrians were clannish, it may be said that it is only natural that people who had been persecuted, driven out of their native land, and who had a whole new language to master, would find pleasure and benefit in contacts with their own kind. But considering the very different background of these people in comparison with life and society in America, it can be said the Assyrians were quick to learn, quick to be respectful of the laws and customs of their adopted country, and were assimilated rather successfully in a fairly short time.

Perhaps one casualty in the eagerness of Assyrians to become Americanized has been the decline in use of their own language. Having common sense enough to realize that they could never succeed or be able to compete in their adopted country without mastering the language, Assyrians concentrated on learning English to the exclusion of use of their own language. While many can still understand Assyrian, the new generation coming up is not learning it, for in many cases only one parent is Assyrian;

or if both are, they don't know the language sufficiently to pass it on to their children. A few years ago, an attempt was made to revive learning of Assyrian by giving instruction, but insufficient response indicated there was not enough interest.

Assyrians are a convivial people—they like their native music, dances, and food. They are proud of all three of them and like very much to introduce them to other people and observe the enjoyment felt by non-Assyrians for things Assyrian. A very close-knit people because they have been minorities in non-Christian countries for so long, they have had to look to each other for security. They have learned to become self-sufficient because help has not been forthcoming to them from the governments, the educational systems, or the religious organizations where they have resided.

An example of the cohesiveness of the Assyrians is in the respect and affection given one by another: a younger person calls an older one uncle or aunt or teacher; a person of the same age or younger, brother or sister. Such practice cannot but promote unity, respect, affection, and loyalty. The tie of nationality is almost one of relationship; in fact, if they dig deep enough, two Assyrians will nearly always find they are related. For them relationship is not merely being first cousins: you are considered quite closely related if your great-great-great grandfathers were brothers.

Parents adore their children and will go to any sacrifice to help the child to find himself, to learn and to train for a life endeavor in which he can succeed. And his parents relish his success, readily exhibiting their admiration and satisfaction in him. An offspring rarely will let his parents down—they expect good behavior from him, and he tries very hard not to disappoint them.

The Assyrians have added four to Turlock's many churches. In the beginning, regardless of religious denominations, they attended the Assyrian Evangelical Church established in 1924. The building was located on Minaret and Crane Streets. Its first minister was Reverend David Joseph. In 1925 he was succeeded by Reverend Eshai Eshoo. Needing a larger building, a new church was built on the corner of Palm and Washington Streets in 1950. Reverend Abraham B. Badal has been serving the congregation since 1940.

Assyrian Presbyterian Ladies Aid.

As more Assyrians moved to Turlock, the predominant denomination, Presbyterian, decided to have its own church. Dr. Elisha David, a young minister called by the Presbyterians, spearheaded the drive to build the church. With the help of the Presbyterian Board of National Missions, fund-raising activities and labor contributed by the Assyrians, the church was completed and dedicated in 1927. Dr. David served the church until 1956, when it was reorganized under its present name, St. John's

Assyrian Presbyterian Church, located on the corner of South Palm and Minaret Streets. Incidentally, Dr. David's daughter and her husband are missionaries serving in Iran.

The number of members of the ancient Church of the East was also growing so they decided to start a church. At first services were held in temporary quarters belonging to the Episcopal Church located above the Montgomery Ward store on Thor and East Main Streets. The Mar Addai Church of the East was built on Canal and Olive Streets in 1948 and was consecrated by the Patriarch Mar Shimun XXIII in January 1950.[14] Reverend Mano Oshana is the minister in 1971.

In 1960 St. Thomas the Apostle Roman Catholic Church, Chaldean Rite, was started at 2901 Berkeley. Some Assyrian families, however, remained behind in the Sacred Heart Parish.

The Assyrians in Turlock have an Assyrian-American Civic Club which meets regularly at the Assyrian-American Hall. Nicholas Paul, uncle of Supervisor Joash Paul, has been a very popular master of ceremonies at the club's meetings. In addition to its monthly meetings, the club sponsors special dinners and arranges social affairs. There is an Assyrian-American organization in every city or town in the United States where a large group of Assyrians reside. Each year a national convention is held in which Assyrians from the various Assyrian-American Clubs all over the United States meet. The main purpose of these organizations is social; no political implications are involved. Emphasis is placed on what can be contributed not only to Assyrian culture but to American as well.[15]

Some of the important affairs held in the Assyrian-American Hall are weddings, which usually have upward of three or four hundred guests. Usually Assyrian weddings are hosted and put on by the groom's family. A sit-down dinner is given, with all the people waiting until the arrival of the wedding party. As soon as the bride enters, musicians are waiting at the door and the music starts. Relatives of the groom lead the wedding party through the hall with dancing until the wedding party reaches its tables. Music is played throughout the meal; and as the dinner draws to a close, *subkhta* is collected from the guests. This is money given as the wedding gift to help start the couple's new life together.

Music and dancing follow until the late hours. Both Assyrian and American music is played, usually by separate bands, and Assyrian and American dancing is alternated. However, it seems that many of the non-Assyrian guests enjoy the Assyrian dancing the most. The non-Assyrians, as well as the Assyrians, take great delight in the native foods served: dolma (stuffed grape leaves), baked rice, lamb Khurush, or lulu kabob (ground barbecued lamb). Other tasty Assyrian dishes are kifty (meatballs), booshala (yogurt with vegetables), and hareesa (chicken and wheat cooked slowly for approximately eight hours and then beaten).

> New American customs, new American names, and intermarriages—this is today's Assyrian-American in Turlock. And yet, through all these changes have come great rewards: freedom of religion, safety of home, and a wonderful new way of life. But one similarity remains. The ancient Assyrians lived close to the Garden of Eden; today's Assyrians who are American live in a new Garden of Eden—the United States of America.[16]

Indications are that the Assyrians have achieved what they were looking for in migrating to the United States: opportunity to develop their individual potential. Nothing really stands in the way of their doing so, unless it is whatever hampers anyone in this country, be he of longtime native stock or of recent ethnic origin. In other words, no special prejudices are exercised against the Assyrians. Assyrians are participating in almost every kind of endeavor; if they have the capability to accomplish, they are not denied the opportunity to do so because of their ethnic origin. Assyrians are engaged in almost every vocation: teacher, preacher, legislator, judge, lawyer, doctor, dentist, builder, salesman, journalist, plumber, carpenter, baker, merchant, candlestick maker, policeman, fireman, nurse, and many, many others. In honorably achieving their individual goals, they have contributed much to the community and the nation.

Fruits, Japanese Produce.

Chapter XIII

Japanese Colonies

Esther Noda

"Around the hearth where once we used to dwell
The smiles that bid us welcome bid fàrewell."
—*Issa*[1]

The Japanese immigrants arriving in California like other immigrants came for economic reasons, seeking their fortune, a better life and education. Some came to escape unhappy circumstances such as the draft or for political reasons. With the overcrowded condition in Japan most farms were only two to three acres in size, making it impossible to get ahead.[2]

The first group of immigrants to come to California was a group of war lords, farmers, tradesmen, and a teenager nursemaid named Ito Okei. Using the United States for political refuge, a European named John Henry Schnell, married to a Japanese woman, led the group across the Pacific into San Francisco Bay on 27 May 1869.

Stripped of influence at the end of the Tokugawa family rule, they came from around Aizu Wakamatsu in Japan. Settling near Gold Hill, the group called themselves the Wakamatsu Tea and Silk Farm Colony. Schnell brought thousands of mulberry trees to start a silk farm, but without irrigation, the trees died. After a couple of years most of the Japanese drifted away or returned to Japan with the exception of Miss Okei, who died in 1871 at the age of nineteen and is buried atop Gold Hill. A samurai carpenter, Sakurai Matsunosuke, lived some thirty years and is buried at Coloma; and Masamizu Kuninosuke, who died in 1915, is buried at Colusa.

The State of California recognized the arrival of the Wakamatsu Colony as a historic event; and a plaque dated 7 June 1969, commemorating one hundred years of Japanese immigration, was placed near Okei's grave on the grounds of Gold Trail School in El Dorado County.[3]

Starting from around 1870 a certain number of Japanese began immigrating to the United States. The first to come were professional men and those with more than average wealth—carpenters, clergymen, clerks, engineers, hotel keepers, tailors, merchants, publishers and students. However, very few of the early immigrants became permanent residents.[4]

Women began coming around 1884, but only about a fourth of the total passports issued were for women. After the men established themselves, they called for their wives or their "picture brides," and some returned to Japan and brought back brides.[5] For centuries in Japan it was the custom to arrange marriages and exchange pictures, especially if the parties lived far apart.[6]

After 1890 a great majority of Japanese coming to America were of the middle class farming group from the southern prefectures of Hiroshima, Kumamoto, Wakayama, Fukuoka and Yamaguchi. Male Japanese laborers also came from Hawaii.[7] Accordingly, the flow of immigrants continued until 1924 when a new immigration act was passed which excluded Japanese.

Nisaburo Aibara, one of the early Japanese settlers in Turlock, was born in Yamanashi Prefecture in Japan. He came to San Francisco in 1896 at the age of twenty-six, after completing his veterinary education and practicing for a short time. He moved to Modesto in 1906 and came to Turlock in 1913.[8] As Japanese families began to move in, he helped them and became their confidant.

More typically, those arriving in the United States during this period found employment in canneries, logging, mining, meat packing, salt industries, and the railroad.[9] Others were hired for domestic service as cooks, waiters, butlers in private homes, and as dishwashers, janitors and porters in restaurants and hotels.[10]

Students worked as "school boys" in families, doing general work around the house, including washing the car or yard work, in exchange for room and board while attending school.

Many of the young women who came from Japan as picture brides or to join their husbands spent a few years in domestic service to learn how to handle household chores and to learn the English language. At first some did not know a spoon from a fork.[11]

The only jobs available for Nisaburo Aibara, who was trained in veterinary medicine, were of the houseboy type, janitor, or fruit or railroad laborer. He was not even considered for any higher position. Aibara had come to America to further his education in veterinary medicine, but was unable to earn enough money to pay his way.[12]

Other types of employment using Japanese in great numbers were gardening and agricultural work. Since there were not many jobs available in the cities, the logical trend for the Japanese was toward agriculture. By 1909, there were 30,000 Japanese doing farm work. The Japanese were desirable workers because they were industrious and willing to work for low wages without complaint.[13]

Some of the business ventures entered into by the Japanese in the cities at the beginning of the twentieth century were hotels, boarding houses, restaurants, barber shops, poolrooms, laundries, tailor shops, art goods shops, jewelry stores, photography studios and supply houses.[14] In some cases the businesses were established especially to cater to the Japanese, who were not welcomed in many business houses.

Faced with overwhelming problems, the Japanese immigrant continued to pursue his ultimate goal. When Yonezo Yoshida of Cortez arrived in San Francisco as a young man in 1907 and looked out across the bay towards Oakland, his eyes were moist with mixed emotions, those of happiness and of loneliness. He was glad to be in America, yet wondered how he would be able to make a living in this new world with only three dollars in his pocket. Fortunately a friend of the family came to get him and he became a migrant farm laborer for a period of time thereafter. He did spend some time in 1917 as a school boy and attended a Christian school in San Jose.

Yoshida first worked in the potatoes in Stockton, but there was much rain that season and he contracted malaria. He was put in a hospital but was unable to pay the bill. He recalls looking forward to a free cup of coffee after ten o'clock at night at a Goodwill place because he had no money.

The migratory work took him to San Jose for the apricots, to Watsonville for apples and to Walnut Grove for asparagus and cherries. In Watsonville the professional Chinese gamblers would take all the money away from the young Japanese laborers. Becoming alarmed over the gambling problem, the Watsonville Japanese started a Recreation Club with activities such as "kendo" to keep the boys away from the gambling dens.[15]

The great number of laborers streaming into the country led to much criticism until a "Gentlemen's Agreement" between the governments of Japan and the United States went into effect in 1908. The agreement was to stop entry from Hawaii, Mexico and Canada; and only laborers who had been in the United States previously and their blood relatives could come. The primary responsibility for implementing the agreement was left to the Japanese. This put a stop to a large number of immigrants, but it was found to be not so effective in checking "picture brides" who came as relatives.[16]

The exclusionists criticized the coming of "picture brides" as immoral and termed it a breaking of the Gentlemen's Agreement by increasing the labor supply. Consequently, the Japanese government again obliged by proclaiming a "Ladies' Agreement" whereby the coming of "picture brides" was ended on 1 September 1921.[17]

The Japanese were quick to progress from ambitious laborers to economic competitors. Many purchased their own land or rented and planted crops. They applied intensive farming methods and succeeded well enough to be of great competition to the native farmers.[18] Japanese farmers succeeded in making barren acres productive and whole districts prosperous. They invested their money in farm machinery, automobiles and conveniences.[19] Because of their successes, the Japanese were severely criticized, and legislation was passed which affected them greatly.

After the first World War, in November 1920, a revision of the original land law of 1913 was passed by the legislature which prevented aliens from buying or leasing land. But when Japanese farmers still insisted on making a living, the legislature in 1923 passed a law to prohibit share-cropping contracts.[20] There were a number of legal cases over the right of an ineligible alien to be appointed guardian of minor children in whose name land was held. A decision in 1928 in the State Supreme Court upheld the right of an alien parent to act as guardian.[21]

E. Manchester Boddy, in his Introduction to his book *Japanese in America* (1921), wrote:

> It is inconceivable that fewer than 100,000 Japanese, willing to work exceedingly long hours at the hardest of tasks for economic success, could create an international problem. . .A certain section of the American Press has singled out the Japanese for vilification, abuse and slander, for the sole purpose of increasing its circulation by sensational methods.

On 26 May 1924, President Calvin Coolidge signed with regret the Immigration Act prohibiting admission of aliens ineligible to citizenship. He had preferred the continuation of the Gentlemen's Agreement.[22]

The underlying reason for prejudice towards Japanese in California was based on emotion, and emotion is a far stronger driving force than reason in human affairs.[23]

Japanese Arrive In Turlock

"There's Money in Melons" was the cry that brought many Japanese to Turlock around 1914-1924, a pattern similar to the Gold Rush Days. At first the Japanese settlers were raising sweet potatoes. Then watermelons took hold, and subsequently the cantaloupe became the main agricultural product.

When Aibara arrived in Turlock, he took a job as janitor for the Turlock Businessmen's Club located in the Geer Building above the present Hauck's East Drug Store. He got a room and $50 a month for his services.

Some of the early businesses operated by Japanese in Turlock were a laundry, an oriental food store and rooming house, a grocery store and service station, a chop suey restaurant and a pool hall. From around 1912 until 1917 Saburo Kitamura and Ichinosuke Kiyono were in partnership in a laundry business located at 326 South Center Street where Nisaburo Aibara is presently residing. The proprietors relinquished their business because they hoped to do better financially in the melons.[24]

Mr. and Mrs. Kumataro Ota opened an oriental food store and rooming house around 1916 on Highway 99, north of Marshall Street. Ota sold the store in 1918 to the S. Iwatas, parents of Buddy T. Iwata of Livingston, and went into melon raising. The store changed hands again in 1922 when Mr. Okamura took over the business, followed in turn by the R. Akunes.[25] Mr. and Mrs. Kaizo Tashiro and family were the last to operate the store before the mass evacuation.

The laundry operator, Ichinosuke Kiyono, who had gone into farming, tried another business venture. He started a pool hall on the southeast corner of Marshall and Highway 99. The establishment drew mostly single men and melon workers during their leisure hours. It changed hands later, and the Ren Kuges operated the hall for several years until around the mid-thirties.[26]

In 1927 Mr. and Mrs. Jyotaro Yokoi of Aichi Prefecture opened a grocery and service station on the southwest corner of East Avenue and Center Street. The business was named Y. M. T. after the names of their daughters Yae, Misa and Teru. A chop suey restaurant was started by them soon afterwards in a building just south of the store. Ballard White of Vignola and White Melon Shippers owned the property and helped them get started.

Several years later in 1934, when Highway 99 was rerouted from Center Street to its present location on Front Street, the grocery store was moved to the southeast corner of Highway 99 and East Avenue, where the family was in business until the evacuation.[27]

Some of the Japanese families engaged in farming in the Turlock area prior to 1920 were the Toyojiro Tomiyes, Tokujiro Nodas, H. Yoshinos, and George Furukawa. There were also several families who returned to Japan after farming in the area for many years.

It was in 1913 when the Toyojiro Tomiyes set out for Turlock and arrived at their abode near East Avenue and Daubenberger Road. Their eldest son, Nobuo, was born there in January 1915. They moved next to the northwest corner of East Avenue and Verduga Road, where daughter Aiko was born in 1917 and another son, Kiyoshi, in 1920. The children attended Roselawn, Keyes, Ceres, and Washington grammar schools and all graduated from Turlock High School. In 1930 a 20-acre farm was purchased on Faith Home Road where melons and row crops were planted. A dairy was also started there, along with the raising of some chickens.[28]

Following a disastrous year outside of Modesto when the barn was believed to have been burned by arsonists, killing more than a dozen horses and pigs and demolishing the family's Chevrolet, the Tokujiro Noda family came to the May D'Oley ranch on Sperry Road, Denair, in 1918. The very next year the family moved to an adjoining ranch belonging to Judge Robert S. Sayre. The family operated the 65-acre ranch which was planted in grapes until just prior to World War II when Jack, the eldest son, took over the place.[29]

The H. Yoshinos came to Denair in 1918 with their children James, Robert, Yuki and another daughter and son-in-law, the George Furukawas. Their farm was known as the La Paloma Ranch, which included 135 acres along Santa Fe Avenue and Barnhart Road.[30] Much of the ranch was planted in grapes. Later when James and Robert brought back their wives from Japan in 1931, James took over the farm and set up a dairy. Robert and the Furukawas went to Texas to farm, and Yuki moved to San Francisco upon her marriage.

Some families settling in the Keyes and Denair area later returned to Japan where family ties were stronger. Among those who went back to Japan around 1924 to 1930 were the Hinoda family, who resided on Sperry Road just north of Keyes Road; Mrs. Tsuda, widowed when her husband, a Japanese language news reporter and rancher, was killed in a car accident in San Francisco; Wakajiro Saimatsu, who was a ranch foreman for Gerard and Company, cantaloupe shippers; and the Yasuda family, residing on Keyes Road between Geer Road and the Santa Fe tracks.

The Watermelon

"The Watermelon alone sit serene,
Quite unaware of last night's storm."
                    —*Sodo, 1653-1716, Osaka*[31]

During the '20s when melons were the leading agricultural product in Turlock, a vast influx of Japanese melon pickers migrated annually from Imperial Valley from as far away as Yakima, Washington. They came by train with their bed rolls; and when they arrived at the station, employers would be waiting to take them to their ranches. The Japanese melon pickers were in great demand because they were hard workers, responsible and conscientious. Consequently, there was considerable agitation arising against them from the white workers since jobs were not available for all.[32]

Just before the peak season in 1921 an incident occurred in Turlock during the early morning hours of 20 July which hit the national news. Around midnight a group of 50 raiders gathered at a designated place and proceeded with two trucks to several bunkhouses, gathering some 58 laborers by force. The bunkhouses were located on Center Street, at a Front Street Japanese store (Iwata's Place), and at the ranches of Fred Vincent and Gerard and Company. The two truckloads of men were taken to Keyes and told never to return.[33] A passing freight train was also flagged down and many were herded aboard.[34]

Another mob action was prevented by the city police force patrolling the streets on the following days. Armed deputies kept watch over several ranches where laborers were staying.[35] Some laborers staying in other camps were known to have hidden in the alfalfa fields and vineyards for a night or two afterwards.

During the time prejudice towards the Japanese was prevalent in Turlock, the railroad was the dividing line. The businesses such as beer parlors, restaurants, barber shops and ice cream shops located west of the railroad would not serve the Japanese. The east side businesses did not discriminate. Matsunosuke Ishihara recalls that around 1924, after a long day's work, he and others returned to their bunkhouse on East Avenue to find a Ku Klux Klan sign painted on their Japanese bath house.[36]

Viscount Eiichi Shibusawa and his party from Japan stopped in Turlock in January of 1922 while traveling through visiting Japanese settlers in the Pacific States. The Turlock Businessmen's Club gave the group a luncheon. The Viscount chatted in English prior to the luncheon but gave his formal talk in Japanese, which was translated. He came representing the Japanese-American Relations Committee of Tokyo, "a society formed by leading financiers, businessmen and scholars of Japan. . .for the promotion of cordial understanding between Japan and America."

While visiting with the Japanese settlers, Shibusawa's party discussed "methods of removing obstacles in the way of smooth and cordial relations between them and their American neighbors" and "how their assimilation to American ways and ideals may be most effectively promoted."[37]

The center of all local Japanese activities until World War II and evacuation was the multi-purpose hall located at 326 South Center Street in Turlock. The property and buildings were acquired soon after the laundry operators Kiyono and Kitamara quit their business in order to go into melon farming. Nisaburo Aibara lived on the premises and served as caretaker from around 1918.

The building was the headquarters for the Central California Cantaloupe Company, the Stanislaus Nihonjinkai (Japanese Association), and the Turlock Social Club. Japanese language instruction and Buddhist Church services were held there, as well as Japanese movies, Christmas and special programs, New Year's Day celebrations, weddings and funerals.

Several organizations were established early to help the local Japanese with their livelihood, legal problems, and social activities. In 1914 Aibara was instrumental in organizing the Central California Cantaloupe Company for eastern shipment of melons since the Japanese were becoming more involved in farming of cantaloupes during that time. Aibara helped with the book work of the organization.

About the same time the Stanislaus Nihonjinkai was organized with T. Tomiye, George Furukawa and Aibara as its officers. The purpose of the organization was to assist in the legal matters of the San Francisco Japanese Consulate. The Japanese were quite mobile in going and coming from Japan and needed assistance in getting visas and passports. Since the San Francisco Consulate was too remote for immediate assistance, the organization was established.[38]

The Turlock Social Club was incorporated on 24 December 1925 with the help of Guy C. Calden, San Francisco attorney. The club was set up as a non-profit organization established purely for social reasons to benefit the local Japanese in their many activities.

The Japanese School was started around 1923 with Nisaburo Aibara as its instructor. Classes were held on Saturdays and Sundays from 9:00 to 12:00 noon. The ages of the pupils were from 6 to 18. Like schools in the Orient, students were encouraged to read their lessons aloud, but while the instructor was making his rounds most students were busily engaged in the day's conversation. The lessons were read to the instructor on an individual basis, and pupils were advanced according to their reading ability. Visitors would have been surprised at the constant din resounding in the large room.

Buddhist Church services were held on a Sunday afternoon once a month at the Japanese Hall. The priests of the Stockton Buddhist Church began conducting services in Turlock in the mid-'20s. Through the years Rev. Messrs. Terakawa, Sasaki, Unno and Hojo were some who came to Turlock and conducted church services as well as funerals and weddings.

Some of the happy events taking place before the war were the New Year's celebration and the annual picnic. New Year's festivities took several days. The women began the food preparation on the day before, and on New Year's Day tables were laden with appetizingly prepared rice cakes, boiled and flavored vegetables, chicken teriyaki, boiled whole lobsters, shrimp and fish, sweet bean candy slices, and cakes. All flavors of bottled beverages were available, including warmed saki and cold beer. After lunch, the young people looked forward to attending the local movie house where a film extravaganza would be billed for the pleasure of the holiday crowd. The day was not complete without the annual photo of all in attendance taken by N. Aibara, who was an expert photographer in those days. Following the feasting again in the evening, various persons were called upon to give musical renditions of Japanese songs accompanied by a samisen, a three-stringed Japanese instrument. In addition, some families made a practice of visiting one another in their homes for more feasting and New Year's greetings.

In the spring an annual event was the Japanese picnic which was held usually along the Merced or Tuolumne Rivers. Picnic lunches were prepared by each family, and ice cream and drinks were furnished. All types of races were planned, including prizes for all. A raffle held the attention of the picnickers during the lunch hour lull; and a costume parade, known as "kaso gyoretsu," followed soon after. Some of the costumes depicted characters out of a Japanese story book or history. The fun-filled day ended with "sumo," a Japanese wrestling contest, among boys and men. Winners often received great prizes, such as a 100-pound sack of rice or a keg of soy sauce, both coveted gifts during the depression years for the large families.

Turlock Japanese at annual picnic by the Merced River about the spring of 1925. N. Aibara photo.

Very often the Tokujiro Noda family benefited at the "sumo" tournaments as their sons Jack, Bill, George and Ben took home several sacks of rice as their sumo winnings. As a result of practicing for the picnic sumo matches, Jack Noda became one of the sumo champs in Central California in the early '30s. Both he and Bill Noda were invited to several invitational sumo tournaments in Fresno and Stockton around that time.[39]

Yamato Colonies

Through the assistance of Kyutaro Abiko, an agent of the Yamato Farm Company and a Japanese newspaper publisher of San Francisco, the Livingston and Cortez colonies came into existence.

Born in Japan in 1865, Abiko came to America in 1885 as one of the early pioneers following a number of successful years in the publishing business in Japan.[40] As a Christian, he had a dream of establishing various Christian colonies in California so that the Japanese would be accepted and integrated into the American way of life.[41]

Livingston's Yamato Colony consisted of three subdivisions, with Livingston on the southwest boundary and Cressey on the northeast. A total of 3,173 acres was divided into 40-acre parcels. The first subdivision was recorded in January 1907. At first the farms had difficulty in getting started because of the winds blowing sand over the crops and jack rabbits eating up what was left.

By 1910 there were 25 families tilling around 3,000 acres in a variety of crops, of which 1,100 acres were in grapes and the balance in apricots, almonds, figs, peaches, asparagus, sweet potatoes, tomatoes, eggplants, watermelons and alfalfa.

The colony was all of Christian faith, and the first service was held in the home of K. Naka on 6 October 1907. Later a church was built on ten acres of land which was set aside in the middle of the colony.

On 5 June 1914, S. Noda was hired as a shipping clerk in a small office located at Court and Simpson Streets in Livingston to take charge of the shipping of fruits and vegetables to the San Francisco and Oakland markets. This was the beginning of the Livingston Farmers Association. By 1971 the Nisei had spread out from the original colony and were farming approximately 7,000 acres in the Livingston and Cressey area.[42]

The Cortez Colony began with thirteen original couples who came between August and November 1919. They were Nenokichi Morofuji, Otokichi Kajioka, Chukichi Date, Tomezo Yotsuya, Tomekichi Toyama, Kasaku Kubo, Zenshiro Yuge, Yonekichi Kuwahara, Hachizo Kajioka, Suetara Narita, Tetsuzo Shiono, Yonezo Yoshida and Gentaro Nakayama. During the first years sandstorms literally covered up the young grapevines and fruit trees, which the families patiently uncovered by shaking the sand from the leaves. Chickens were buried alive in some of the worst storms.

Until 1925 when electricity was brought in, kerosene and candles provided heat and light. A whole day would be taken to go after supplies in Turlock with a team of horses and a wagon.

The children attended the one-room Madison School located at Cortez and Mitchell Avenues. Mrs. Nellie Armstrong came by horseback each day to teach the children.

In April 1924 eleven members of the community formed the Cortez Growers Association. The first president was Ninokichi Morofuji, and the first manager was Manroku Matsumoto.[43] The farmers' cooperative was the answer for a group such as theirs.

The first Christian Sunday School class was held in the front room of H. Kajioka's home. Around 1925 Kyutaro Abiko donated five acres of land for a church. The first building on this site was a bamboo shelter which was used for the Sunday School. Later, with the help of others in the community, a building was erected for use by the whole community. In 1963 a new chapel and Sunday School rooms were built, and the older building was refurbished during the succeeding years. Rev. Isamu Nakamura retired in 1969 after twenty-two years of service, and Rev. Mark Moon took the pulpit in February 1970.[44]

The Buddhist services were conducted by the Reverend of the Stockton Buddhist Church, who came to Cortez beginning in the middle '20s. Howa Kai and Sunday School were held at the Cortez Hall. Prior to the completion of the new Cortez Hall, the Buddhists acquired the older hall and completely renovated the interior around 1965.

In the middle of each July the Obon Festival is held by the Buddhists in memory of those who have passed on. It is held outdoors with colored lights and lanterns strung all around. The colorful kimono-clad girls, children and some boys do Japanese folk dances in a single or double circle. The music coming over the speaker system on a summer evening helps to set the mood for the dancers, who have been practicing for several weeks. The older girls are invited to the Stockton Church to

The new chapel of the Cortez Presbyterian Church, built in 1963. Debbie Noda photo.

Dancers prepare to participate in the annual Bon Odori (Obon dances). Shirley Baba photo.

learn new dances and then they return and teach the others. The public is invited to view the dancers at the festival, which is held in the open area between the Buddhist Church and the new Cortez Hall.

The War and Evacuation

The Japanese were just beginning to enjoy a taste of the fruit of their labors and were quite contented during the period before World War II. Prejudices had died down. Children were growing up and attending local schools and colleges. Some were marrying and establishing their homes.

When the news of the Pearl Harbor attack by Japan came over the radio, all Japanese families were stunned beyond belief. It was a nightmare that lasted for some time. The Japanese were faced with evacuation by Executive Order 9066, which gave authority to designate certain military areas and to exclude all persons from them.[45]

The Pearl Harbor attack was disastrous, and the military was subjected to extreme pressures favoring evacuation. The commanding general was impressed with the possibility that Japanese-Americans constituted a special danger, and he recommended evacuation in the firm conviction that it was demanded by military necessity.[46]

Buddy T. Iwata, who was president of the Turlock Social Club at the time of evacuation, wrote the following letter to area newspapers.

> Western Defense Command of the United States has considered it a military necessity that we evacuate very soon. To its decree we shall cheerfully cooperate in the conviction that in so doing we are making a practical demonstration of our loyalty and patriotism as well as our sincere belief in the principles of justice and democracy.
>
> Throughout our education we have been taught the American way—the democratic way of life. Most of us have never been out of California. In order that we may live, sleep and breathe in such an atmosphere in the future we shall do our part to help. Many of us farmers, especially in this valley, are still of the belief that we can do the nation more good by producing the crops than being evacuated, but that is not for us to decide.

We have received from many of our fellow Americans expressions of confidence in us, and the generous support and encouragement from these friends has given us strength, courage and hope to retain our self respect and to continue to have faith in the noble ideals upon which this country has been founded.

When the United States Government permits us to return to our homes in this community where we were raised, we earnestly hope that we can come back with a stronger conviction that this democratic way of life is best as we have been taught and experienced. We hope the community will accept us and our children then as one of you as you have done up to this time.[47]

Turlock Japanese gather for yearly New Year's photo, 1939. N. Aibara photo.

The Turlock Japanese were sent to Merced Assembly Center where they remained from 6 May 1942 to 15 September 1942.[48] Only a week's time was given them to set their farms or businesses in order and take with them merely necessities such as clothing, small utensils for household use and toiletries. Household furnishings were sold way below cost, and odds and ends were taken to the Auction Yard to be sold for whatever they were worth.

After 15 September 1942, those in the Merced Assembly Center were transported by train to the Amache Relocation Center in Granada, Colorado. The relocation camps were much larger than the local assembly centers. The long black tar paper barracks were separated into six separate units of about twenty feet by eighteen feet in size. A black cast iron coal burning stove was in the middle of each room. The walls were lined with sheetrock, which made the rooms more livable.

The typical relocation center was made up of thirty-six or more blocks. Each block was composed of twenty-four barracks served by one mess hall feeding 300 persons three meals a day, a shower and laundry room, and the latrines, in addition to the recreation hall.[49]

During the fall of 1942 after the move to the relocation centers, students by the hundreds were allowed to leave camp and enroll in schools in the Midwest. Jobs were opening up for the evacuees; by July 1943 the War Relocation Authority, WRA, had openings for 10,000 jobs from Chicago alone.[50]

Jack Noda relocated to Denver, where he was a supervisor of the Quartermaster's warehouse handling fruits, vegetables, cheese and meats until his return to Denair in 1947.

Buddy Iwata served as a Japanese language instructor at the University of Colorado Navy Language School between 1942 and 1945. He had a grocery and import business in Chicago from 1945 to 1953.

Bill Noda relocated to Deer Park, Washington, where he was a member of a cooperative farm venture known as the Bear Creek Farms, Inc., from 1943 to 1945. The farm produced garden crops such as celery, carrots, cabbage, lettuce and strawberries.

Around 43,000 persons had resettled in nine states, with Illinois topping the list with 15,000 followed in order by Colorado, Utah, Ohio, Idaho, Michigan, New York, New Jersey and Minnesota.[51]

Homeward Bound

On 2 January 1945, after nearly three years away from the West Coast, the exclusion orders were lifted.[52] Gradually the Japanese families began their trek homeward bound to the West Coast.

Those who returned permanently to the Turlock area were persons owning property. Members of the Cortez Growers Association returned to their ranches in September 1945.[53] Newcomers in the chick-sexing occupation arrived later to work for local poultrymen and settled here.

Of the forty families who lived in the Turlock area before the War, most were non-property-owners on account of the restrictions of the Alien Land Law and the land rotation by melon growers. A majority of this group was scattered in the Los Angeles and San Francisco Bay areas; others went to the Chicago area. Returning temporarily, some left for better employment elsewhere or to join other members of the family. Paul Yamamoto was employed in Modesto for a few years with an accounting firm and then went with his family to Oakland upon securing a position there. The T. Tomiyes sold their 20-acre ranch on Faith Home Road in 1948 and joined their daughter and son-in-law, Aiko and Mits Usui, in the San Fernando Valley.

The Japanese Hall on Center Street in Turlock was used for temporary quarters for returning evacuees, who remained there until their permanent homes became available or their employment destination was determined. The hall was also used as a home for older couples or single men who had no specific place to go.

The JACL

Through the Japanese American Citizens League and its leader, Mike Masaoka, who was a lobbyist, much effective legislation was passed to make amends to the Japanese families, especially their American-born children who had demonstrated a loyalty that could not be ignored.

In November 1946, the California Alien Land Law of 1920 prohibiting the purchase of agricultural land by Japanese aliens was repealed when Proposition 15, an amendment to strengthen the law, was defeated by the voters. The JACL's Anti-Discrimination Committee spearheaded the attack against Proposition 15.[54]

The Japanese American Evacuation Claims Act was signed on 2 July 1948, and 38 million dollars were paid out, which was only 10 cents on the dollar lost, based on 1942 prices. Many did not file claims because of insufficient documentation of losses. Masaoka observed, "This was not a generous program but it represents a major triumph for the evacuees. . .in that Congress recognized the error of the evacuation and the justice of the claims."[55] Most of the local Niseis who filed claims recovered the proportionate amount mentioned before.

There was another legislative goal left: to change the immigration and naturalization laws. In 1952 the Walter-McCarran Immigration Act repealed the Oriental Exclusion Act of 1924 and extended to Japan and other Asian nations a token immigration quota. It also eliminated race as a bar to naturalization, which had been in effect since Civil War days. This was the supreme triumph for Masaoka. Hundreds of Isseis enrolled in citizenship classes, and men and women in their 60s, 70s and 80s took the oath of allegiance.[56]

In Cortez citizenship classes for the Isseis were taught by former Rev. Isamu Nakamura, now retired, and in Turlock Vincent Keesey taught Americanization classes to these Japanese who, in their twilight years, were able to become naturalized for the first time.

In September 1971 Congress voted to erase a law passed in 1950, during the Korean conflict, allowing the detention of Americans suspected of being spies or saboteurs. Over the years, the abuses possible under the law continued to raise fears in the lawmakers.[57] The country can no longer detain its citizenry as it did during the mass evacuation of Japanese in 1942.

The Cortez and Livingston chapters of the JACL were organized. They actively supported the National JACL in its legislative efforts which brought justice at last to the Japanese.

Changes Evolving

The living standards of the local Nisei have risen since the war, a trend of all Americans in this affluent society. Within ten to twelve years after returning, many Niseis were able to build or buy new homes, to own several cars, and some, even a boat. Their leisure time activities include bowling, bridge, golf, fishing, travel and other hobbies or outlets.

Those who grew up in Turlock became involved in a variety of occupations with which their parents had not been associated. Among them are accountants, dietitians, insurance brokers, lab technicians, managers of fruit processing and farmers associations, officials in governmental agencies, realtors, architects and teachers. In addition, John Tashiro, whose parents operated the Japanese store in town, is a professor of pharmacology at the University of Rhode Island. Owning their businesses are Mr. June Taketa, formerly of the Hughson and Hilmar areas, who is a tool and die engineer and has the J. T. Tool Corporation in the suburbs of Chicago; and Ernie Yotsuya, a pharmacist, who has his chain of drug stores in Turlock, Hauck's East and West.

Sons of Japanese farmers who raised row crops for the market are now engaged primarily in orchard and vineyard farming. The back-breaking hand labor of their fathers' time has been eliminated. Although greater acreages are being farmed, the mechanization of farm labor has created more leisure time than during their parents' era. With the advanced farming techniques applied, the orchards and vineyards along both sides of the Santa Fe tracks in Cortez are the most highly productive in the Central Valley.

The Cortez Growers Association and the Livingston Farmers Association are organized for better purchasing power, for harvesting, packing and marketing purposes. They are considered to be the most successful cooperatives of this type in the state.

Local Niseis have made an effort to join civic, service and business organizations and churches, as well as the country club in Turlock, in order to better assimilate into the community. Some have attained presidencies of local clubs and chairmanships of school boards.

Buddy T. Iwata, who was president of the Governing Board of the Assembly Center located at the Merced fairgrounds during the 1942 evacuation, became the first chairman of the Merced College Board of Trustees twenty years later at the same site. Iwata also has been a member of the Stanislaus State College Advisory Board since 1962 to the present, serving as its chairman in 1969.

In spite of being uprooted from their homes and detained for almost three years, the Japanese Americans returned to their former homes and, starting from the bottom, were able to elevate themselves to responsible places in their communities.

The children of the Nisei, who are called Sanseis, are destined for the colleges of their choice. Their education is job-oriented; they enter "secure" professions.[58] Sanseis are becoming more Americanized and are shedding their parents' culture. With many intermarriages taking place, they will be bringing forth a homogeneous generation.

By 1971 some of the Sanseis were beginning to climb the ladder to new business ventures. Ernie and Don Yoshino, sons of the James Yoshinos of Denair, both passed their state architectural examinations after serving their apprenticeships. They jointly designed and built their elder brother's house on the home place on Barnhart Road in Denair. Eric Noda, son of the Jack Nodas, and nine other young men formed an advertising corporation.

In conclusion, the pioneering Isseis have largely passed on, leaving a legacy filled with struggle, hard work and heartaches. The Niseis have taken this foundation laid by the early Isseis and through education, organization and political influence have set up the future for the other generations to follow. And now they are beginning to drift into retirement age, while the Sanseis are pursuing their educational goals, seeking employment, businesses or professions of their own.

This could be termed a "Success Story" enveloping three generations.

"I raise my head, and gaze at the moon over the mountains;
I lower my head, and think of my native place."
—*Buson*[59]

Nisaburo Aibara receiving the
Medal of the Order of the Sacred Treasure
from the Japanese government
in July 1968. TDJ photo.

Gabriel and Elsie Arrollo, first Mexican family in Turlock,
on their golden anniversary. Courtesy the Arrollo family.

Chapter XIV

Original Mexican Settlers

Ernestine Rojas

The stereotyped picture of a Mexican peon, barefoot, drowsing under a huge sombrero, apparently waiting for *mañana,* is a mistaken image of those hardworking, gentle people of Mexico who began to settle in this area before 1910. In the economic development of Turlock, the place of the Mexican national group is unique, little known and often little appreciated. Certainly as early as 1912, probably even before, the Mexican worker formed the nucleus of the seasonal agricultural labor force of a wide local area, including Modesto, Hilmar, Ballico and Montpellier.

The first permanent Mexican settler, Gabriel Arrollo, established residence here in 1910. He came here from Daggett, California, in the Mojave Desert. He had worked for the Santa Fe railroad as a section hand there under the foreman, Charles Hohenthal, and when Mr. Hohenthal moved to Turlock, Mr. Arrollo came here to settle, too. Mr. Arrollo led an interesting life before coming to Turlock. He was born in the state of Michoacan in Mexico. He worked briefly in Argentina as a young man, putting up power lines and equipment. He later came back to Mexico and from there migrated to the United States where he worked for a time on the railroad in the area around Madera. He returned again to his home in Mexico; later he came again to this country and worked for the Santa Fe Railroad at Daggett, this time sending for his family. After leaving Daggett they stayed a short time in Livingston. While they were in Livingston there was a flu epidemic in which many children died. From Livingston the family soon moved to Turlock, making their home on Third Street for a time.

Gabriel and Elsie Ramirez Arrollo had five sons and five daughters. One of these children, Elsie Madrigal, tells about some of her remembrances of early Turlock. She says that there were frequent sand storms and the streets were very dusty. It was extremely hot in the summer. She used to like to watch the teams of horses pulling wagons loaded with beautiful watermelons and other fruits. For outside entertainment there were band concerts, carnivals and the July Fourth celebrations.

Mr. Arrollo worked at various occupations: in the grain fields, where he sewed the full sacks of grain by hand; in the warehouses and at Hume cannery where in 1911 he was appointed by Mr. Shannon to go to the bank to pick up the payroll—all gold and silver. It is said that he had to stop several times on his way back because of the weight of the coins on his back. Mr. Arrollo retired from the cannery and lived the remainder of his life in Turlock. The community is still enriched by his descendants who serve this community and the surrounding area in varying capacities: law enforcement officials, beauticians, secretaries, mechanics and businessmen.

These early workers such as the Arrollos usually came as loosely knit groups of families bound together by a common need, language and religion. They worked at any kind of work available. The women often packed grapes, cut peaches or worked in the laundry or shops. The rate of pay for this type of fruit work was five cents a box for packing the grapes, and six cents a box for freestone peaches. The laundry paid at that time a dollar a day—meaning from seven in the morning until six in the evening. The men worked long hours cutting and packing in the vineyards, or in the melon fields, hoeing, harvesting and packing. Many later worked for the Santa Fe and the Southern Pacific Railroads. Since the late thirties the young people have been employed in local stores, where their knowledge of the Spanish language has been needed. This was the type of work done by three members of the Meza family; Lupé, Ray and Jennie all worked as clerks in various Turlock stores.

Three more generations of Arrollos. Courtesy the Arrollo family.

Since housing was scarce, these families utilized any kind of building or used tents which some families brought with them. Lupé Meza Avila relates that one of her dearest childhood memories of coming to Turlock each year for the harvest is that of her father, immediately upon their arrival, arranging a shelter for his family, and of her mother making it into a home, with the delicious smell of fresh tortillas cooking and simple food bubbling on the stove, the comfort of clean bedding and fresh clothing for the children. No matter where they were or how humble their surroundings, Lupé remembers that her family were together and were not deprived of the security of home.

The "old-timers" like Henry Serna and Rose Valdez Serna (no relation) speak nostalgically about those times of a bygone era, when thirty-five cents an hour was a good wage for farm labor and bread sold for a nickel a loaf. The children of these families remember the sounds, smells and joys of a childhood lived in the warmth and closeness of family and friends.

To these early Mexican families, home and church were the two vital motivating forces in their lives. In a day devoid of electricity, radio or television, most entertainment was home-oriented around some specific religious or family event, such as the baptism of a new baby, a wedding, a birthday such as a "quincinerra." The latter is a girl's fifteenth birthday and is the traditional time for a young girl to pass from the status of a child to that of a young lady. Traditionally she was not to have danced prior to this time and on this festive occasion she was the recipient of many gifts and special honors.

These gay parties were times of fun, much good food, singing and dancing. For a few hours the cares and labors of the day were put aside. They were for young and old alike; there was no generation gap there. The old were honored and revered for their wisdom and experience, the young for the exuberance and promise of youth, and the babies for the evidence of the continuity of life. The lovely Mexican folk songs sung by Henry and Emma Serna at parties such as these are remembered by many of the people around Turlock. It was not then, and is not today, uncommon for the guests at family parties to provide spontaneous entertainment in the form of singing or playing a musical instrument at Mexican celebrations. This is just one of the many charming and delightful features of a Mexican party.

As a matter of record, Maria Jose Luna, daughter of Jose and Delphinia Seraphin Luna, was the first baby of Mexican parentage to have her baptism recorded in the newly formed Sacred Heart Parish. This was on 21 July 1912. How or why this family came here and where they went is unknown, but because of their faith, they are forever a part of the Mexican-American history of Turlock.

It can be assumed that up to the second decade of the twentieth century, most Mexican families came to Turlock only for the duration of the harvest season, regularly returning to their homes in the Brawley and El Centro area in the fall. One reason for this assumption can be gleaned from the Church baptismal records. This record shows that the baptismal dates (with the exception of the Arrollo family) range generally from June through October, the prime harvest months. Appearing there are such common Spanish names as Prado, Garcia, Rodriguez and Martinez. Many of those who came later, throughout the twenties and early thirties, found work with the Southern Pacific Railroad. However, during the hardest depression years from 1929 until 1933-34, some of those families, unable to find work, returned to Mexico; many later returned to this area in the forties.

Early day Turlockers will remember the long yellow section houses on the west side of the railroad tracks along First Street where these families were housed. Two such families were those of Salvador Mireles and Esteban Ramirez. Their children were born in Turlock, attended local schools, served in the armed forces during World War II, married and became an integral part of the diverse international flavor of this area.

It is often difficult to determine specifically whether any given national group influences an adopted environment or if that environment shapes that national group into a common mold. Probably it is some of both. The Mexican families who settled here learned to speak English, supported the schools and churches and contributed much of the field labor so necessary to the economic growth of the now flourishing agricultural and business community. At the same time, in their homes, by example and by precept, often around the dinner table, the children were taught the lovely customs and ancient traditions of Mexico; thus integrating the best of two great cultures to form a cohesive Mexican-American philosophy. Many young men like Sam Murillo and Mike Godinez, from homes such as these, gave their "last full measure of devotion" to this country during three wars and are now at rest in the Turlock Cemetery.

In the Mexican-American home, especially in earlier times, only Spanish was spoken. This made it difficult for the children when they started school, not only scholastically but socially as well. The language barrier set these children apart and caused them to draw more closely into their own groups. Many instances, some amusing, others pathetic, are remembered by early day residents. One little boy on his first day of school, when the bell rang for recess, went home, thinking that school was over for the day. Others, not understanding the language, spent the first few months of school in utter confusion. If this situation created a feeling of prejudice, it can be readily understood, considering the differences in language, customs and characteristics of the Mexican-American children from those of the Nordic and "native" American child. The children naturally adhered to that group with which they had most in common and where they found a sense of security and comfort.

In many cases the children's being exposed constantly to the English-speaking world would bring the language into the home and in this way teach it to their parents. Frequently these parents became naturalized citizens, many taking classes from Mrs. Daisy Brockway at the high school. The difficulty in passing a United States citizenship examination can only be fully appreciated by those who have had this experience. It is a rigorous discipline, made more so by an inadequate knowledge of the language. Those people who gained their citizenship in this manner are to be greatly admired. In many cases only the men of the family were able to get their papers. The women were so fully devoted and busy with the children and household chores that they too often lacked the time or the motivation for the long hours of tedious study required.

Descendents of early day Mexican families are proud of the many and interesting stories connected with their family backgrounds. They came from the several states in Mexico as varied in dialect and customs as are the regional differences found in the United States. Some states engaged chiefly in mining silver and gold, others in citrus fruits and row crops such as beans, corn, tomatoes and melons, etc. Still others came from the states on the coast which engaged chiefly in fishing. Given this diversity of background, it is impossible to lump all the early Mexican settlers together and say with accuracy that any one is typical of all. Each reflects his native environment to the degree that from state to state the geographical, social and economic situations shaped the personality and characteristics of the individual. Common to all groups, however, was the pride in a noble and advanced cultural and intellectual heritage dating back before the Conquest. The men who brought their families to this fertile area found dignity in work of any kind, which would make available to their children the opportunities and advantages of education which they felt was necessary for a better life.

If there is a typical blending of Mexico and America, perhaps it could be personified in a family like that of Esteban Meza. Born in a small mining town in the state of Sinaloa, he was a young man at the close of the Mexican Revolution. When the mines began to be mined out, Mr. Meza decided that there was no future in Mexico for him and his family and made the decision to migrate to the United States. He and his wife Guadaloupe and their baby daughter Juanita came by boat to California via Baja California. Their first home was in Los Angeles. Upon arriving there they had to take a bus from the coast to their home and through some misunderstanding they got on different buses. Mr. Meza was frantic, remembering the many instances in Mexico where during the Revolution whole families disappeared and were never heard from again. They finally found each other and set up housekeeping. Steve, as I shall call him, worked at many different kinds of jobs in Southern California. He worked in the cotton fields, on railroads, as a labor contractor, share-cropper (where he lost everything he owned) and as a clothing salesman. He worked for a time as a foreman of a silver mine in Arizona. The family finally made their way to the Brawley area where they were living at the time of the disastrous earthquake of 1939.

Steve and his family used to come to Turlock each summer for the growing season, then return to Brawley in the fall. They learned to like it here and eventually decided to move here permanently. During the war Steve worked at the bomb plant that was located at Faith Home and Harding roads where the Chemurgic plant is now. Following this he went to work for the Foremost Creamery in Gustine from which company he retired in 1961.

Steve Meza learned to speak English by reading books on philosophy, history and government, always with a dictionary by his side. His children remember him as a man who himself studied continuously and taught them a thirst for knowledge.

These parents, proud of their nationality and heritage, instilled this pride in their children. At the same time they taught them an ardent love and loyalty for the United States. This patriotism and love of their adopted country is one of the things that the children remember with warmth and affection, for it was during their growing-up years that the family discussed politics, constitutional principles and religious concepts around the dinner table.

Mrs. Meza was a remarkable woman, sensitive, affectionate and creative. As wife and mother, she devoted her life to her husband and children. She composed poetry and always had time for "cuentos" or stories for the children after dinner. In the afternoons she found the time to do needlework or to read. Almost all of her poetry was lost in a tragic fire which took her life in February 1963. In this fire Steve lost one eye and was severely injured. Being blind in one eye does not deter him from going to the library in Los Angeles each day to read and to study, both in Spanish and in English.

When the Meza family moved to Turlock permanently, several families moved from Brawley at the same time. Here all the children attended local schools—Lowell, Hawthorne and Turlock High School. One of the Meza sons, Ray, distinguished himself as being the first Turlock Mexican-American to be chosen a lifetime California Scholarship Federation member at Turlock High School. After high school Ray served as a captain in the Army during the Korean War, following which he attended the University of California at Berkeley and was graduated with honors. Needless to say, this was one of the proudest moments of his parents' life. Immediately after leaving the University he was accepted for training at the Thunderbird Foreign Trade School in Arizona. Ray went on from there to the American Foreign Insurance Association in New York. In 1971 he was in Sao Paulo, Brazil, where he was the branch manager of his company. In addition to this he was the president of the American colony there, in which he had the responsibility of organizing the celebrations appropriate to all the American holidays. He has exemplified the American tradition and brought honor to a proud name.

Other members of the Meza family have added their strength to the fabric of this area by their stalwart and upright character and industriousness. It may be said of this family that they have truly contributed to the community as Americans, simultaneously keeping intact their precious Mexican heritage.

The majority of the Mexican people who live in Turlock now came here during the 1940s and later. They came here basically for the same reasons as the earlier settlers did, the opportunities necessary for a better life. These later families, like the Rojas, Rodriguez, Avila, and Gallardo, just to mention a few of the families that are still here, are a vital part of the city of Turlock. They have become assimilated into community life and are making their individual and collective contribution to the growth of this area. The diversity of vocations held by Mexican-Americans attests to this fact.

Abe Rojas is serving very ably as Recreation Director for the City of Turlock and is well known for his work with the young people of this area. Mike Rojas has at various times served as captain of the Turlock Police Reserves, secretary-treasurer of the 12:10 Lions Club, and has been for many years active in Scouting and Little League.

Rojas youngsters about 1950.
Courtesy Abe Rojas.

Both Mike and Abe married girls who are not of Mexican descent. This has been the source of many jokes in Mike's family. One of the favorites has to do with genealogy in which they are both interested. Mike says that his wife's ancestors came over on the Mayflower, and his ancestors were here on the shore to greet them with bows and arrows. It is a source of great pride to their children (all ten) that their grandfather Rojas fought with the famous Mexican Revolutionary leader, Pancho Villa. They are equally proud of their mother's side of the family, since her great-great-great grandfather was with George Washington at Valley Forge.

There are many others of Mexican heritage who serve the community in various ways. Bob Hernandez is a member of the Turlock High School Board of Trustees. He is a local boy, a graduate of Turlock High School and a credit to his nationality, his school and his community. Another prominent Mexican-American is Raul Valle, who is in the appliance business here. He has long been active in the various community organizations. During 1970 he was lieutenant-governor of Kiwanis for his division.

The Avila trucking business is well known to Turlockers, especially the farmers and growers of melons and produce. Their fleet of trucks, family owned and operated, are a credit to their hard work and industry. Their contribution to the growth of this agricultural area has been substantial.

The Gallardo and Rodriguez families at one time had a trucking business, but are not now engaged in hauling produce. Both of these names are well known to local residents. Members of both families are still living in Turlock.

In addition to the families that have been in the Turlock neighborhood for twenty years or more are the recent comers from the Southwest and from Mexico. Those from the Southwest usually come as families, picking from early summer until late fall, then returning to El Centro, Arizona, New Mexico, or Texas. Those coming from Mexico are usually men, few bringing their families. Sometimes two or three brothers, a father and his sons, or cousins band together, following the ripening crops northward and living in labor camps.

Gradually migrant families from the Southwest find places to live in the Turlock region the year round. Pickers from Mexico find a likely spot and bring back their families the next year. Around 1970 there were probably a hundred families in Turlock that had followed this pattern and settled here within the decade. In the triangle from Hughson to Delhi to Hilmar there were probably four times that number.[1] These families are contributing to the continued growth of this rich agricultural area. It is to be hoped that they will retain some of the customs, traditions and the language pertinent to their nationality. In many instances when the Mexican-American marries outside of his nationality, the language is lost, since English is spoken at home. Many children from a mixed Anglo-Mexican family do not speak Spanish. This is unfortunate, since it is through the language of a people that those concepts which are unique to each culture are passed on from generation to generation.

It would seem that the major contribution of the Mexican people to the growth of the Turlock region can be summed up in one word—work. And this they did, on all levels and in a multitude of capacities. This then has been their great contribution to the economic and cultural growth of Turlock.

Armenians were grape growers and wine makers.

Chapter XV

Other Ethnic Groups

The Armenians: Agricultural Entrepreneurs

Helen Hohenthal

During and following World War I, a small but significant group of Armenians moved into the Turlock district.

They came as individual families, attracted to this section of the great and beautiful central valley of California because it had a long, warm growing season, productive land, a plentiful supply of irrigation water, an ideal climate for their crops, and a satisfactory transportation system to move the perishable crops to markets quickly. They could hope for maximum production and big profits.

A number of these Armenians already had growing and shipping experience in Fresno, Bakersfield, and the Imperial Valley before coming to Turlock. They had specialized in producing perishable fruits—strawberries, grapes, and a number of the varieties in the melon family—watermelons, cantaloupes, casabas, Persian melons, Christmas melons, and others.

Armenians are known the world over for skill in business management. This was a necessary ability in handling perishable commodities such as melons. But it was responsible also for our small group of Armenians investing money in local businesses such as apartments, stores, a theater, dehydrators, and others—which added to their profits and the community's progress.

So they came to live in Turlock, bringing their love of the land, their business skills, their special talents in preparing favorite foods such as the delicious shish kabob and rice pilaf, their love of music and drama, and a keen sense of humor.

The first three Armenian families arrived in 1915: the Dick Arakelians, the Vaughn Azhderians, and the Aspiar Vartanians. The Arakelians and Azhderians were relatives who had already gained expertise in the growing and shipping of melons.

Dick Arakelian built a home at 400 North Broadway. In 1917 he built the Broadway Apartments across the street from his home. The next year he constructed the Turlock Theater and brought in Wallace Reid, a popular actor-hero of the silent movies, for the grand opening. The theater was packed for the occasion. The four children, Violet, Lillian, Jack and Grace, attended local schools until the family moved to San Francisco.[1]

The Vaughn Azhderians began producing and shipping melons. Eventually the next generation, Shawn and Betty Azhderian Moozekian, took over and in 1971 were operating the original family enterprise, the only Armenian family to remain in melons.[2] For long the firm had seasonal shifts of operation between the Imperial Valley and Turlock.[3] For the families of both owners and workers, this meant children shifting from school to school.[4]

The Aspiar Vartanians were the third family to arrive. He was a minister and started a Presbyterian church for the small Armenian community. It held services in an upstairs hall on North Broadway.[5] The Vartanians eventually moved onto a small farm.[6] Araxie, the oldest daughter, was musically talented, and her talents were in constant demand for school activities during her years in high school.[7]

After a few years without many new families moving into the area, the Armenian church was dissolved. Most of the members joined the First Presbyterian Church on Crane Avenue.

The Vartanians remained in Turlock until around 1923, but eventually returned to Fresno where the father became minister of an Armenian Presbyterian church. Fresno by then had become a Mecca for Armenians.

The association of a particular nationality with some American church was due to the efforts of American mission boards to avoid duplication. Each mission field was designated for one Protestant denomination. As these immigrants came to the United States they joined the denomination with which they had had previous contact. For Protestant Armenians that meant either the Presbyterian Church or the Congregational Church.[8]

The year 1916 brought a larger number of Armenian families to Turlock. They were Harry Arakelian and son John, Harry's brother Joseph, Astor Akulian and son Leo, and the families of Y. B. Torosian, Oscar Dervishian, Mike Donabedian, and Aram Shahbazian.

John Arakelian first came to Turlock from Fresno to straighten out some problems that had developed in melon shipping.[9] Soon his father Harry and his uncle Joseph followed. Harry and Joseph, with their brothers Krikor and Ben, operated in the Imperial Valley and around Bakersfield and Fresno. They were considered to be the largest watermelon growers in California at the time.

The Harry Arakelians built a fine large home. The house with its seven bedrooms and three baths, a large dining room, and a very large living room cost only $2500 to build.

In 1917 Harry Arakelian and his son John started planting vineyards in Livingston. A couple of years later they built a raisin packing plant and a dehydrator in Livingston, operating their several projects as Arakelian Farms. John's sons, George and Albert, joined the operation in the 1940s. A few years later his son-in-law, Francis Gullo, an attorney, became an active partner. In 1969 Stephen Arakelian, George's son, became the fourth generation Arakelian to farm in the Turlock area.

Joseph Arakelian, Harry's brother, built the present Chevrolet garage on North Broadway. He also purchased several other business properties. Later he sold out, moved to Oakland, and retired at the age of forty-five. He then took up lawn bowling and twice won the world title![10]

Most of the newcomers of 1916 grew melons on a more modest scale. Aram Shahbazian started in with forty acres on the canal east of Johnson Road. Mike Donabedian had forty acres on a plot stretching north from the canal to the location of the present First Methodist Church. The Oscar Dervishians, too, grew melons. The Shahbazians and two of their six children were still in Turlock in 1971; the only remaining Donabedian was Tunney, who was operating a sporting goods store in Modesto.[11] The Akulians soon went elsewhere.

The last 1916 arrivals were the Y. B. Torosians. He established a small "racket store," now called a notions store, on West Main. The Torosian daughters, Esther, Betty, and Roxana, were popular in the art and music circles at the local high school. Only Mrs. Y. B. Torosian remained in Turlock in 1971.

In 1921 Y. B. Torosian's brother John came to Turlock and bought a small farm on Geer Road. John's sons, Rudy and Arthur, own and operate Rudy's Market on East Main Street.[12]

The Divanian brothers, Reuben, Pusant, Kalem and Jack, grandnephews of Dick Arakelian, arrived in 1920.[13] Their principal achievement was in starting a "garden" restaurant in 1934 which they called

John Arakelian.
Courtesy Mrs. John Arakelian.

"Divine." It had indoor and outdoor dining areas. The brothers worked in the garden by day and cooked their speciality, shish kabob, at night for the diners. It became a popular gathering place for many of the local citizens.

Divine Gardens was forced to close on 8 August 1949 when Highway 99 was widened to four lanes. It was reopened as an elegant restaurant, bar and bowling alley in 1961. By 1971 a fine 100-unit motel and additional banquet rooms had been added. A live band played for dancing every Saturday and Sunday night.

Three of the Divanian brothers were still active in the business in 1971. Pusant said, "Only a church town like Turlock could afford a name like Divine Gardens for a restaurant and bowling alley."[14]

Vaughn Azhderian's brother Mihran came from Cairo to join the small Armenian community in June 1921. He had been educated in the eastern United States and knew English. For his wife and children the trip to Turlock and establishing a home was a great adventure and not without many problems of adjustment.

His daughter Beatrice's interesting story, entitled "My Trip from Egypt," done for a history class at THS, gives some idea of the experiences of one of the more fortunate Armenian families on their way to America.

My Trip from Egypt

by

Beatrice Azhderian

For many years my uncle, in Turlock would write to us, telling of this beautiful country, America, more so the State of California. Telling us of the climate, good water, beautiful valleys etc.

My father, at the age of seventeen had left his native country, Armenia, and had come to America. He had his college education in the East. After that he traveled around Europe studying eight different languages. He learned eight languages. After traveling for awhile he went to Egypt, where he got married. We are seven in our family, and my father wanted us to have all the privileges that we could get, especially good education. So finally we decided to come to America. It took us months to get ready. We had to go through physical examination, it wouldn't be so bad if we went through it once, but about four times we had to go through it.

My mother had the hardest time, for she had five small children to take care of.

On April 1921, we took a train from Cairo to Alexandria, the seaport of Egypt. It was pretty hard for us to leave our native and accustomed land. From Alexandria we took a Greek ship to the port of Athens, Piraeus, it took us a day and one night.

Athens is a beautiful country, very quite. One thing I wont forget, is that we always had fish at the table never saw so many fishes in all my life. I am glad we stopped in Greece, because we saw the ruins of "Parthenon."

Took another ship from Greece. We traveled on the Mediterranean Sea for four days. Then we crossed the straits of Gibraltar; when we crossed it we could see land on both sides of us. The name of our ship was "Mehali Hellas". It took us seven days to cross the Atlantic Ocean. All we saw was water, only in the mid-ocean we passed the island of "Azoras." I was sea-sick almost all the way, so I can't say much.

Oh boy, when we saw the Statue of Liberty. But it was just our luck to arrive at Ellis Island on Decoration Day. We stayed in New York for three weeks and visited my father's old friends and relatives. For awhile we had in our mind to stay in New York for good. But with five children, New York isn't the place. So we crossed the continent to San Francisco on a five day trip on train. We rented a taxi from San Francisco to Turlock. Reached Turlock on June 1921.

It was an interesting trip, but I wish I could take it over again. I could enjoy it more now.

If one would ask me this question, "Would you like to go back to Egypt?" I'd say, "yes but not to live there. Just to visit."

Sometimes I can just see myself back in Egypt; I would not have any opportunity to take part in different activities, etc.

As my father had his education in America, so it made it easier for us to travel. But only my mother, everything was new to her, and she had a hard time to get use to things around here.

I can see how hard it must be to those Armenian immigrants, who knew nothing about this world and some of them with no education.[15]

In 1930 there were about sixty-five Armenians in Turlock, not a large settlement, but one that did leave its mark in the community.[16]

In 1971, "a few of the grandchildren and great-grandchildren of the early Armenian settlers are still in the community. Many moved to larger cities during the depression for the better opportunities of the city."[17]

In summary, an unusually high proportion of the Armenians have been entrepreneurs, typically starting in agriculture and branching out. The Harry Arakelians came to Turlock with an assured position in the agricultural economy of the State. Beginning with melons and a vineyard, they soon branched out into raisin production and the produce business. The Azhderians, starting in Turlock with much less, also made good in large-scale farming. The Divanians started out very modestly and did well in the restaurant and hotel business. Dick and Joseph Arakelian were in a position to invest in business properties by the time they came to Turlock, while Y. B. Torosian opened a shop. This is a remarkable record for so small a group.

How big the watermelons grew down in Turlock! Courtesy TDJ.

The Greeks

John E. Caswell

Two very small racial groups who have managed to retain a great deal of their individuality and culture are the Greeks and the Chinese. The principal factor in the Greeks' maintaining their cultural identity has been their loyalty to the Greek Orthodox Church. One man moved his family from Texas to Turlock so that his children could attend the Orthodox Church in Modesto. The Greeks of the Turlock region are in fact but the southern fringe of the Modesto Greek community.[18]

The earliest known Greek to settle in the vicinity of Turlock was Andrew Bollakis, who came to Turlock in 1910. A number of families seem to have come in the 1920s and 1930s who later moved on. Those remaining did not come at any one time or constitute a migration like that of the Assyrians. Several of the families were from Crete. About half of all families came directly to the area from their homeland; the others had originally located elsewhere and had later moved to Turlock. The climate, so similar to that of their homeland, was the characteristic of the region most frequently mentioned among factors enjoyed. Other items singled out for praise were the cleanliness, the schools and the opportunities.

Several Greeks mentioned the strain of adjusting to the new country. One can particularly sympathize with the plight of Mary Pantazopulos as she made her way to Turlock. Of her experience she wrote, "I came to Turlock in 1921 to get married. I traveled alone. It took us seventeen days to arrive in New York by boat. My papers were misplaced so I remained in New York for eight days. I did not know one word of English but they had a Greek interpreter to help. . . .They put me on a train with information written on a card. This was pinned to my dress. I did not like any of the foods. I could not communicate. I hardly ate on my trip to California."

The occupational range of the Greeks around Turlock has been limited. About half have had some experience as farmers. About half have worked in or operated restaurants at one time or another. According to Mrs. Mino Tavernas there were eight Greek restaurants in Turlock around 1930. Andrew Bollakis had come to California at age 16 and worked in the gravel pits at Richmond to earn the money he needed to buy a farm. Nick Megas had worked in the coal mines before coming to Turlock. John Flesoras had been a restauranteur in Oakland before coming to Turlock as a grocer. The Pallios family had been in Salt Lake City where their father had been a butcher and small farmer.

The Pallios family established a grocery store in Ceres. Then in 1965 John Pallios opened the Richland Market on East Canal Drive in Turlock. Its success established him as one of Turlock's leading Greek citizens.

Among the second generation of Greeks, Anastasios "Ernie" Vrenios received well-earned recognition in his home town on 15 March 1972. Vrenios got his start in music at Turlock High where he was graduated in 1958. Fourteen years later he returned to the familiar auditorium as an operatic tenor on the Community Concerts series, and won an ovation.

The state college brought Steve J. Grillos to Turlock as chairman of the Department of Biological Sciences. He had previously taught at Modesto Junior College before taking his doctorate at Oregon State University. He had married Georgia Pallios, so there were strong family attractions in the area.

The Chinese

John E. Caswell

From 1900 to around 1950 there were only scattering families of Chinese in Turlock. There was one Chinese restaurant around 1915 or 1920, but little is remembered of the families that came and went.

When the Ping Hoy Doo family came to Turlock in 1949, there were no other Chinese in town. The Doo family brought four sons, Jack, George, Ken and Quong, and two daughters, Mae and Nancy. Two other daughters had married prior to the family's removal to Turlock.

According to Ken Doo, "Ping Doo came from China and to the United States at the age of sixteen, worked in laundries in San Francisco, and turned to farming when tong wars broke out in San Francisco. He settled in Madera, and farmed there until 1949 when he decided to change occupations. The family looked up and down the valley for a grocery store, and finally found one located in Turlock. They noticed the friendly people, clean town and the more stable economy of Turlock over other cities. We also liked the small size of the town; we felt we could grow with it. We were well accepted.

"The Doo family is the largest group of Chinese in Turlock (24 out of 100 in 1971). Most have attended Turlock elementary schools and Turlock High School. Some have gone on to college.

"The Doos started their business venture with a small corner grocery store, expanding to two of Turlock's largest supermarkets, the Liberty Markets. Ping Doo passed away in 1966 and his four sons continue to operate the markets along with other enterprises."

In 1951 Guy M. Gong, born in Hong Kong, came with his parents to Turlock. They had operated a laundry in Merced. In Turlock they opened a grocery store; Guy went through Turlock High School, growing up in the grocery business at the same time.[19]

Still another successful grocery operation was that of Jing Ow, with his National Market on East Avenue.

Several other Chinese families in Turlock were operating restaurants in 1971. Andy and Sid Gin and Bob Chin opened the Golden Hour about 1968, while George Yee and his son Bill owned the Wah-Q-Food restaurant.[20]

The college attracted a number of Chinese to Turlock. The earliest arrival was Dr. George H. Yu, professor of French. Formerly a member of the diplomatic service of Nationalist China, he had doctorates from Lyons and Warsaw. Kitty Dean, wife of Dr. Britten Dean of the History Department, was the daughter of a ranking Nationalist ambassador. Several other Chinese taught mathematics, physics and philosophy, some of them living in Modesto.

Raymond R. Lee operated a grocery in Hughson and lived on the northern edge of the Turlock High School District. He had been born in Hong Kong and was living in the Pacific Northwest when he drove through the Turlock region on vacation. He stopped, liked it, and made arrangements to settle in the area.[21]

In both the Chinese and Greek communities were some conspicuously successful merchants. Both groups had contributed professional men to the town. Those in trade worked long, hard hours which limited their social life. What social barriers may once have existed seemed to have been pretty well overcome by 1971.

Raymond Le Cussan.
Courtesy Mrs. John Clipper.
Mrs. Donovan.
Courtesy Mrs. Clipper.

Martin Hedman.
Courtesy Mrs. Bert Towle.

Jack Osborn

E. B. Osborn.
Courtesy Mrs. Jack Osborn.

Horace S. Crane

Rex Ish (in uniform)
and Lewis Boies. Courtesy Mrs. Hazel Carpenter.

Alice (Mrs. Horace) Crane.
Courtesy Mr. F. H. Roselle.

Chapter XVI

Turlock, 1901-1940

Helen Hohenthal

The magical powers of irrigation water transformed the towns no less than the farm lands of the Turlock region. For more than a decade changes came fast. There was enough of the old in the town of Turlock that people, contrasting the new with the old, recognized the progress that had been made. To the writer, as a child, it was especially exciting—an adventure of sorts.

On the streets and in the stores a medley of foreign languages was spoken: at first Swedish and Portuguese; later, Assyrian, Japanese and others. The speed (to the uninitiated all foreign languages seem to be racing), the sudden exclamations, and the hand motions that accompanied the words were introductions to other worlds.

Sometimes classmates used foreign accents on English words. We who were foreign only to the area and not to the language were observers of the struggle of these newcomers to master English. Sometimes fellow students were not too sympathetic or helpful to the foreign-born who were trying to adjust to a strange town. While many of the Swedes had studied in eastern schools and knew some English, Swedish continued to be used in the homes and churches.

Teachers like Mrs. Lura Cottle Littler encouraged children to give an occasional song or recitation in their native tongue, especially at Christmas time when all knew the tune and words in some language. It was an important lesson for the entire class and reassuring to the child whose native language was not English. Sometimes language was a hard barrier to cross.

A few immigrants came along with the first assurance of irrigation water and the start of subdivisions in 1902, but the year 1903 was the real year of change for the Turlock area and certainly for the old town of Turlock.

Families often traveled in immigrant trains, the women and children in passenger compartments and the men or older boys in the freight cars with the stock (if they had any), household goods, tools, and farm equipment. Most families reported that family meals were packed for the entire trip—baskets of food of a non-perishable nature. On arrival at Turlock, the freight cars were put on the old grain warehouse sidetracks east of the depot until they were emptied.

One such young immigrant was Carl C. Carlson, who came in 1903. His father had bought eighty acres, paying $32.50 an acre plus $300.00 for buildings. They brought horses, three cows, and implements, along with household furniture. Carl took care of the stock on the trip. Until 1905 Carl worked on his father's ranch. Later he worked for the Turlock Lumber Company, beginning as a yard man. He finally became full owner of a large lumberyard and planing mill. His brother Paul stayed with ranching and served as a school trustee.[1]

For the most part, the newcomers chose the undeveloped part of town west of the railroad tracks. Here they built homes, hotels, stores, churches and theaters. Many financially successful newcomers chose locations on North Broadway and West Main streets for their homes.

A church of their own was an immediate concern of the first Swedish settlers. The Swedish Mission congregation bought the old Methodist church at Lander and West Main on 18 December 1902 and held their first service in it shortly after Christmas.[2] Ten months later, on 15 October 1903, a young people's society was organized. This small group included Judith Hallner, Amelia Johnson, Esther Hall, Victor Hallstone, Fred and Knut Knutsen, Oscar Anderson, and Otto Swanson. They "went immediately to work, holding meetings every Sunday afternoon. . .and assisting the church financially. . . .Then the ladies of the church formed a sewing society. . .sold articles at public auctions and by doing so helped the church financially."[3]

These early Swedish settlers set examples of church and community service for others and became leaders in all areas of community life, using their talents, energy and faith to help build a new Turlock. They joined hands with the grain farmers, townspeople and later arrivals, all of whom had a stake in the future of the town. We find names from all groups from an early date in the town's historical records.

New Stores

An example of such cooperation was the establishment of the Turlock Rochdale Store. The Rochdale Wholesale Company was a wholesale co-op in San Francisco which supplied a number of small member stores throughout northern California. Members of each local co-op purchased stock and shared in profits at the end of the business year. The Turlock Rochdale Company was incorporated on 21 November 1902, with Andrew Hallner, Nels C. Hultberg, Horace Crane, P. A. Dimberg, and August Eversen as original directors.[4] By the end of 1913 there was a list of over 100 members from whom to choose officers and directors. On the 1913 list were such pre-irrigation citizens as S. V. Porter,

The Turlock Rochdale Store, 1903. Courtesy TDJ.

A. L. McGill, and Henry Russell; Youngstown people such as Charles Hult, C. J. Ornberg, and Otto Swanson; new non-Swedish settlers, including C. H. Randall, Dr. Isaac Adams, J. J. Fleshman, and M. J. Frago; and a long list of Swedish people such as Claus and August Lindblom, Ole Ravnos the photographer, and Charles Emil Ellsburg.[5]

By this time the Rochdale store was in financial trouble, and was behind in its payments to the parent organization.[6] A deal was made with Charles A. and Claus Lindblom, Charles E. Ellsburg and E. A. Nicholson to buy the entire stock, the furniture and the fixtures, and to rent the building. The new owners contributed $3,000 apiece and incorporated as the Turlock Mercantile Company; in 1917 they purchased the building outright.[7]

The Lindbloms' Mercantile Store.

In the following year, two bachelor brothers, Nels M. and Jacob Lundquist bought four lots across the street from the Rochdale Store, paying $125 for the corner lot and $100 each for the other three. They erected a photo gallery and lived in the rear. In 1907 the People's State Bank bought the property for $3,000, moved the gallery around the corner onto North Broadway, and sold it to J. Emil Johnson, who opened a small stationery and bookstore.[8]

Many an elementary school student, the writer included, received an early lesson in business transactions at Johnson's store. We sold second-hand the books of the previous grade and bought second-hand books for the new grade. If no second-hand books were available, investment in new books was necessary. Occasionally an older brother, sister or friend helped the younger children, but the writer does not remember any parental supervision.

In 1903 M. M. Berg, a man of wide business experience, chose to make Turlock his home and business location. His first store, like most others in town, was a small general store. It was built for him by Gust Carlson and Ed Johnson at the northeast corner of Main and Broadway. It had big windows and a wooden sidewalk, a rarity in 1903. There was no street beside his store until later, when Berg constructed his new, big store. A few old locust trees were conveniently located along the side of the building to provide shade for customers' horses.

Across West Main from Berg's was a store built in 1903 by two Hilmar settlers, Nels Shoreen and Gust E. Johnson. To the east of their store was Detlof Sahlberg's shoe store, with living quarters upstairs. In 1910 George Keith bought the business and the building was moved off to make way for the two-story Union Block which Sahlberg and A. L. McGill intended to construct.

Hotels

Hotels and rooming houses were scarce in 1902. The old Turlock Hotel remained on Front Street, but the Fountain Hotel had been gone for a decade. In the next ten years two small and two large hotels were erected.

In 1904 John J. Vignolo, a newcomer from Raymond, California, acquired the old, dilapidated Turlock Hotel from Mrs. "Stony" Allen Swain. The Vignolos first built an annex to the hotel, then later tore out the old building entirely and replaced it with a fine two-story brick structure with a dining room, fifty spacious bedrooms, and office space for rent. This new Carolyn Hotel was opened to the public on 4 September 1909 with a big reception and dinner dance to celebrate the occasion. It was built by Swan Wakefield; the cost of the annex and hotel was $50,000. The Carolyn was a source of pride for Turlockers. The office space was filled quickly by the Turlock Land Company, the Rice barber shop, a drug store, candy store, cigar store, pool hall, and others.

In 1906 "Senator" Henry Hoskins began to promote a hotel for the west side. The St. Elmo Hotel was built on the site of the old Fountain Hotel at a cost of $40,000, and was nearly completed by the Fourth of July, 1908. It was a popular and attractive building with the lobby entrance facing on First Street. Meals had a good reputation as long as the dining room was operated.[9]

Meyer's Hotel was built in 1906 west of the site of the St. Elmo. There were ten rooms in the two-story building. It was said to be one of the first buildings in town to have plate glass windows. W. Litchfield, who came to Turlock in 1908, bought the building from John Vignolo for $7,000. It burned in the 1910 fire.

Another small hotel was built for J. Samuelson on Second Avenue (South Broadway), between Main Street and A Avenue. A restaurant and ice cream parlor were operated in connection with it.

Craftsmen and Contractors

The need for stores, hotels and homes kept all available men in the building trades busy. The town was lucky to have so many skilled carpenters, bricklayers and plasterers who had come in the Swedish and other migrations. Many a young Swede had had training in a trade school. Martin Hedman had had eight years' experience as a builder before coming to Turlock in 1902. He teamed up with Theodore Olson in 1903. Olson had been a big contractor in Central City, Colorado, sometimes having thirty to

Gust Carlson's crew working on school building, 1910. Carlson is in middle row, third from right.

forty men under him on a job. Hedman and Olson first joined business in the Turlock Lumber Company, then sold that to build the Turlock Hardware Company. The Turlock Lumber Company reported sales of 225 to 250 carloads of brick and lumber annually around 1910.[10]

Then there was Gust Carlson, who spent several years in Nebraska learning the trades of plasterer and brickmason. He located in Turlock and went into partnership with Ed Johnson for several years. He had a part in constructing the Berg Building, Hawthorne and Lowell Schools, the People's State Bank and other fine business buildings and homes in Turlock. Swan Wakefield's crew, and Claus Tornell and Peter Larson, carpenters, worked on many of the same buildings.

J. I. Bobst specialized in home construction. Among his early houses were the homes of Albert Chatom, A. J. Clipper, Ed Lyons, Emil Vignolo, and E. P. Mains.

Plumbers were a busy lot, especially after Turlock put in sewer and water lines. Dick Lander's shop was also referred to as a "pump and turning shop." Carl Hedman and Andy Thorsen came in the big post-irrigation migration to the area. Leonard McMullen's Plumbing Shop on Front Street was established around 1911 or 1912. The Olson Brothers' Plumbing and Well Drilling firm went into business about 1915. The older generation, Robert, Fred and Albert, has now been succeeded by Vernon, Weldon, and Emory, sons of Robert.

Charles Klein started the first lumber yard in Turlock, a branch of the Modesto Lumber Company. He told Howard Whipple that he came to Turlock in April 1902 because of a Hultberg ad, but kept his family in Modesto for the first year until he could get a house. He bought the Congregational Church manse on North Center for $1000, then improved it and planted trees and a grape arbor.

Society and Amusements in the New Turlock

In the very first issue of the *Turlock Weekly Journal* for 11 November 1904 there is a story of a Halloween party in a beautiful old home that dated back to the late 1870s. The party and the old house itself were evidences of gracious living. The hostesses were Mrs. Horace Crane and Mrs. A. G. Elmore. It was a costume affair, with the usual Halloween games, a great feast at 10:00 P.M., and finally the program in the parlor.

The program reflected a variety of talents and tastes in Turlock. It included "Tam O'Shanter," a piano solo by Mrs. A. G. Elmore; a selection from *Il Trovatore* by Max Strauss and Mrs. Elmore; a duet, "Come, My Loved One," by Mrs. Horace Crane and Mrs. Elmore; a lively violin, cornet and piano trio, "Every Nation Has a Flag but the Coon," Max Strauss, Horace Crane, and Mrs. Elmore; in more exalted sentiments, "The Holy City," solo by Mrs. Crane; violin solo, "Bohemian Girl," Max Strauss; an orchestra number, "In the House of Too Much Trouble," Strauss, Crane, and Mrs. Elmore; a piano solo, "Thine Own," by Mrs. Elmore; and in closing a romantic duet, "I've Got a Feeling for You," by Mrs. Crane and Mrs. Elmore.[11]

Not all parties were as elaborate as that one. Many represented a mingling of the new and old populations of Turlock, no matter who the hosts and hostesses might be. This was what the little town needed. Neither wealth, religion nor business established barriers. There were differences of opinion of course, as in all communities, but these people of the early 1900s recognized that mutual interests were paramount to individual differences.

Turlock's Literary Society was established somewhat before the beginning of January 1905. At one meeting there were piano solos by Misses Hicks and Chatom; Miss Klein gave a comic recitation; Miss Clara Powell (now Lundahl), a vocal solo; and a male quartet performed. Unfortunately, the article does not tell which Chatom sister or which Klein sister performed. Finally, four men debated the timely topic, "*Resolved:* that it would be more beneficial to the U. S. to have Japan win in the War with Russia." The affirmative was taken by Mr. Lamar, who had lived in both countries, and Dr. Hicks; negative, Mr. Hoskins and H. T. Randolph. The affirmative side won.[12]

In the same week that the Literary Society put on its program a meeting was held in Gaddis Hall to see whether sufficient funds had been pledged to build a town hall, and if so, "to decide on plans and location."[13] A month later, on 7 February 1905, it was announced that a "Hall Building" would be constructed for rental for public or private meetings or entertainments.[14] This was the building known as the Opera House, which was the scene of many entertainments and housed the high school **during its first year**.

Opera House in center, with Wonderland Theater just past it. Courtesy the Lindblom family.

"Minstrels and Dance a Success" was the headline in the *Turlock Weekly Journal* for 26 May 1905, over the article describing the first performance in the new hall.

"The Hall began to fill by 7:30 and later there was standing room only for the minstrel show. The songs were new and up-to-date, all being orchestrated, and the jokes new and catchy. As usual our popular citizens came in for a mention of themselves." Mr. Lane and Mr. Lundahl did a specialty act afterward, followed by E. H. Slissman of Merced, the director, who performed a cornet solo. It was a case of local talent making good—one of many such performances.

For a while the Opera House housed a stock company that came from San Francisco every week. The Dick Wilbur Company, with a stage curtain but no stage, gave such plays as "Girl of the Golden West" and "Uncle Tom's Cabin."

One of the town's most active musicians was a newcomer from Vermont, Jean Nelson. She helped to organize the dance orchestra that played for productions at the Opera House, and on many occasions elsewhere. The orchestra consisted of Jean Nelson at the piano, Bill Ady on the string bass. Dr. George Hodges on the clarinet, Ernest Siem and Clayton Cunningham on trumpets, and Hannibal Blewett on the trombone. Jean also played the violin. For a few years the Turlock Orchestra played throughout the area, from Roper's Barn halfway to Hilmar to La Grange in the eastern foothills, traveling by surrey very much as the Turlock Band had traveled twenty years before.

One of Turlock's annual events was a Fourth of July Parade. The *Journal* would have an old hand press on a wagon. Various stores and organizations would enter floats, some of them no bigger than a child's express wagon. After the volunteer fire department was established, its vehicles would be decorated and take their place in line. The Fourth of July parade soon took second place when a more ambitious undertaking was conceived.

From 1911 on for some years, the town's principal celebration was the Melon Carnival. The first one was held on Thursday and Friday, 24 and 25 August. The program began on Thursday morning at 9:00 with a band concert followed by an industrial parade. An address of welcome was given in the "Big Tent" at 11:30, and the crowd was invited to see the big stock exhibit and to eat melons to their heart's content.

Fourth of July Parade, 1908, looking east from West Main and Lander. Courtesy Hazel Berg.

Melon Queen Anna Lundell and attendants. From left, Jennie Wejmar, Queen Anna, Amy Clark, Esther Samuelson; Roger Quigley and Robert Eddy at their feet. 1911?

Entertainment at the second Turlock Melon Festival, 1912. Forsmark photo, courtesy TDJ.

After a lively fifteen minutes of band music at 1:15 the Melon Rolling Contest began, followed by boys' competitions grouped by age. Next came a free acrobatic contest, followed by a baseball game between Turlock and Oakdale. Meanwhile a Good Roads Congress met at the Wonderland Theater. The program lasted into the evening.

At 9:30 the next morning the band played again. Next was a parade featuring the fire department and decorated automobiles. A hose cart race in the afternoon brought neighboring fire companies into competition. This was followed by the start of a 50-mile motorcycle race and a Turlock vs. Modesto ball game.

The serious-minded could attend the State Irrigation Convention in the Big Tent. Meanwhile, the ferris wheel, merry-go-round, and sideshows entertained others. Sophisticates could dance during the afternoons and evenings "on the large Platform opposite the St. Elmo Hotel" to the music of Merrill's Orchestra. When one's throat became parched, he could repair to the Big Tent, where water-melons were served free, day and night.[15]

The Ladies' Improvement Club was formed in 1906. Soon afterward they staged a "clean up day." The men went out to the cemetery with shovels, hoes, and rakes, and cleaned up the place. Their reward was a lunch served in a tent on South Center Street. After that success the ladies had a ten-cent tag day. With the $300 raised, they hired three men for three weeks to complete the clean-up job at the cemetery and build a fence around it.

Next, the ladies decided the town needed a library. In 1908 a small room in the old Osborn Store building was made into a library. Mrs. S. R. Douglas, a lovely, gracious lady and wife of the first high school principal, was the librarian. The women put on a concert at the Opera House to raise money to support the library. Soloists came from Modesto, and fifty local singers made up the chorus. Patrons of the little library paid 25 cents a month to support it.

After the first few months, very little remained among the children's books which we had not read, but we young people were always hopeful that additional books would have arrived since our last visit. In 1909 the Women's Club donated $25 to be spent on children's books.

The city took over the library in 1910 and voted a tax to support it. About that time the library moved to the Santos Building, located on the Main Street side of the present Central Park.

Broadway Park was the next item on the Turlock Women's Club list, as the Ladies' Improvement Association seems to have been renamed. Mr. Claus Johnson gave the original lot and townspeople provided the trees.

Another project of these busy ladies was a drinking fountain for man and beast at the intersection of Lander Avenue and West Main Street. A small modern ornamental fountain commemorates the original, but cannot replace it in the memories of the old-timers.[16]

Turlock Becomes a Municipality

A Board of Trade, predecessor of the Chamber of Commerce, was organized in Turlock in 1905 and served as a means of stimulating town development. It was the Board of Trade that took the first steps toward establishing a high school in Turlock. Mr. A. G. Elmore, a member, reported that he had checked on the voters in the different elementary districts and found that those he talked to "were heartily in favor of the project."[17] The first high school classes were organized in the fall of 1906.

Fire was an ever present threat to any community where buildings were close together and not of fire resistant materials. An attractive new store, the Turlock Hardware Company, near Berg's store, was burned to the ground on 30 June 1907. Several citizens decided action was necessary to save the town. At Horace Crane's suggestion, merchants contributed to a fund for buying equipment. Then they secured county supervisors' permission to form a fire district. The supervisors appointed Horace Crane, John Gall, and Martin Hedman (whose building had been destroyed) as fire commissioners of the district.

The commissioners purchased a 60-gallon chemical engine and ordered a locally manufactured combination wagon to carry hose, hooks, and ladders. It could be pulled by six men or hitched behind a wagon. Eight wells were drilled at principal intersections to furnish water for the pumper. A Howe cylinder pump driven by a twenty-horsepower gasoline engine was mounted on a wagon body. The first of its kind in the state, the fire commissioners tried it out and found that it could pump a stream of water twice the height of the St. Elmo Hotel. In October 1909 it was first used on a fire that destroyed the Grange company warehouse. A still larger fire in 1910 burned everything west of the St. Elmo Hotel for 140 feet and wiped out a dozen businesses.

After organization of the fire department, municipal government was not long in coming. On 21 January 1908, the people of Turlock voted 61 to 42 for incorporation.

The first meeting of the Board of Trustees (original name of the Council) was held on 7 March 1908. H. C. Blewett was unanimously elected President of the Board. The other trustees were H. S. Crane, E. B. Osborn, Theodore Olson, and August P. Warren. A. G. Elmore was elected clerk.[18]

Fire on Main Street, 1910. Ravnos Photo, courtesy Turlock Public Library.

During March 1908 the Trustees of the City faced a group of citizens led by Rev. J. M. Hilbish, who called for a "local option" election to determine whether saloons should be outlawed in Turlock.

An election was called, and those wanting to retain saloons won the election; so the city of Turlock granted liquor licenses, but set the license for clubs and saloons at $100 a quarter when other businesses were paying around $15 a quarter. In the 1910 local option election the town voted against saloons, and when in 1911 the saloon forces raised the issue again, they were defeated for a second time.

There was no money in the city treasury for any of the expenses of government, so in April 1908 the Board set up a schedule of fees for all businesses.

On 3 October 1908 the Board granted its first franchise to the La Grange Water and Power Company. For its fifty-year franchise the company was to pay $110 in cash, and after five years 2 percent on its gross. The Board took the precaution of saying that "this grant of franchise is not exclusive and the governing body of said City of Turlock shall have the right to grant similar franchises to other persons or corporations."[19]

A month and a half later the City appointed George E. Steele as engineer to design a sewer system and estimate costs. As the cost of construction would be "too great to be paid out of the annual income and revenue of the city," a bond issue was suggested. On the same day a proposal for a city water system was passed and C. E. Moore was named the design engineer.[20]

A special election was set for 18 January 1909, to vote on a forty-year $27,000 sewer bond issue, and a $26,000 water bond issue, both bearing 5 percent interest. The assessed value of real and personal property which served as security for the loan was set at $485,647. Both sewer and water bonds passed by very large majorities.[21]

A series of ordinances passed in 1909 gave further protection to the city dwellers. One was a fire zone ordinance, requiring brick, iron or concrete construction of specified thickness for exterior and center walls in the central business district. This had the effect of transforming the downtown, for wooden buildings were gradually replaced with brick-faced structures. The downtown both appeared to be and was more substantial, and fires were thereafter contained more successfully. Related ordinances provided regulation of electrical wiring and plumbing.

Most of the basic services for the small city were established before 1910. A few ordinances of that era are amusing from the viewpoint of 1972. One forbade "any ball throwing games on streets and sidewalks" in a good share of the town; another made it a "misdemeanor for anyone to ride any roadster, tandem, safety or other bicycle or tricycle upon, on, or over any sidewalk." A third made it a "misdemeanor for children under 16 to get on or off wagons, trucks, or other vehicles while in motion." The first city speeding ordinance made it illegal for anyone to drive at more than eight miles an hour any horse, mule, or team "within three blocks of the Southern Pacific depot."[22]

A city volunteer fire department was created in July 1912, and the county fire district organization was dissolved. About 1919 a little Ford was purchased and equipped with pump and engine. In 1922 the city purchased a La France fire engine. Among the major fires was one that destroyed the Wonderland Theater on 21 July 1915. Knutsen's Wood Yard burned on 30 August 1915. On 4 May 1917 the Gall Denair building was destroyed in an early morning fire.[23]

In 1914 the Board of Trustees established the Board of Health as the first of a series of boards and commissions to serve as administrative or advisory bodies. The first Planning Commission was organized in 1916, and the Park Commission was created in 1918. Rules governing membership on these bodies were repeatedly revised.

In 1927 the titles of the President and the Board of Trustees were changed to Mayor and Council, respectively. For a long time the Council acted as a Commission, each member having supervision of some branch of city government.

Turlock Journal staff, about 1914. From left to right, Harry T. Randolph, owner; Al Thornton; Frank Harder; William Wright; and A. V. Hoffman, editor. Courtesy T. W. Randolph and SSC Library.

Newspapers

Although several newspapers had appeared in Turlock for short periods before the catastrophic fire of 1893, Turlock had been without a newspaper for years when the first issue of the *Turlock Weekly Journal* was published on 11 November 1904 by Jack and Harry Randolph. Turlock's population at the time was about a hundred. For their first shop the brothers rented an old one-story store on East Main near Center from Horace Crane. In 1905 they built the first unit and in 1907 the main part of their shop on North First Street. The machinery was operated by a small gasoline engine and by hand power. The paper was hand-folded.

The *Journal* was originally put out on an old-fashioned second-hand platen press for which they paid $1200.00. In August 1906 they purchased a Babcock cylinder press. Frank Harder came to Turlock in 1909 as their pressman and advertising salesman. In 1919 Harder left it and set up his own print shop on South Broadway.

Throughout the Randolphs' ownership, the *Journal* was a weekly paper except for the period 1 August 1911 to 2 November 1914 when both daily and weekly editions were issued. After World War I Harry Randolph sold out to Edwin Ullberg. From that time on the *Journal* has been a daily.[24]

Later, two other newspapers were started in Turlock: the *Turlock Tribune* and the *California,* now the *California Covenanter.* The *Tribune* was started in 1911 by C. W. Dockham and was issued three times a week. In 1916 Dockham sold it to Veda Calkins and Lou K. Neufield. Calkins became sole owner in 1920. The next owner was Thomas Crawford of Centerville, California. Eventually the rights were sold to the *Turlock Journal.*

Edwin Ullberg started the *California* in 1916, several years before he bought the *Journal.* It was for a long time published in Swedish and was especially enjoyed by older Swedish people. However, it has been printed in English for many years.[25] From 1916 to 1956 it was a weekly, and then a bi-weekly until May 1971 when it became a monthly. Milton Strom of Hilmar was its editor for about twenty years. Virgil Hanson succeeded Strom as editor. Its circulation in 1972 was about 6,000. The *California Covenanter,* to use its later name, was the official paper of the California Covenant churches.

Built in 1905 by Mr. and Mrs. George Simon, the J. H. Smith house was still a fine structure in 1972.

Effect of the 1906 Earthquake on Turlock

The San Francisco earthquake of 1906 was felt in Turlock. Hazel Ornberg Carpenter told how her father stood outside their home in the Youngstown Colony and watched the house sway back and forth. Mrs. Emma Abbott Simon told how the chandeliers in her big new house on Berkeley swayed back and forth and the rocking chairs on the porch started rocking. Dr. Harry D. Channing recalled how the hired man heard the coyotes getting their breakfast in the henhouse, grabbed a gun, and was rushing down the stairs when the quake hit, throwing him down in such a way that he broke a leg. Many people could see the red glow to the west, and later, the smoke all day long. Harriet Niman said her father rode about eight miles into town on horseback to find out what was wrong and was told news of the earthquake which had come over the telephone and telegraph. Stores quickly ran short of canned goods.

A later effect on Turlock was loss of a market for produce in San Francisco. Mrs. Simon had planted about 200 acres of cantaloupes and watermelons in 1906 in the hope of getting money to pay off on her land. As there was no market for them, she brought 3000 head of sheep in to get rid of the melons.

Communications and Transport

For many years merchants had been using the telegraph for emergencies. In 1898 a telephone toll station was opened in the back of the Osborn and Son store on West Main Street. This provided service north to Modesto and south to Merced. The firm operating the station was the Sunset Telephone Company. The customer placed his own call and paid Osborn for the toll charges. Sometimes people waited for hours to make their connections.

In 1902 an exchange was established in the Osborn building in a room facing North Front Street. The switchboard was of the type known as a magneto board, for it had hand generators which the operators cranked for ringing. Sunset Telephone Company appointed B. W. Childs as manager. His wife and two daughters, Lottie and Ruth, operated the switchboard.

The Sunset interests were bought out by five local men in 1908, who formed the Turlock Home Telephone and Telegraph Company. J. L. Randolph was appointed manager.[26]

The Home Telephone Company's service was increased by the Farmers' Union Telephone Lines with about sixty miles of lines radiating in all directions from Turlock. The farmers' lines in each area had a manager and linesmen to take care of the shareholders' needs. Each farmer paid for his share of stock and had to foot the bill for any service line necessary to reach his house.[27] Shares of stock were limited and people had to wait until an owner released his share. The farmers' phone lines were used for the usual neighborhood gossip and talking parties as well as business. On a given line most people knew the long and short ringing signals of all families on the line. A person receiving a call would often hear the click of other receivers being taken from the hook and would know that neighbors were listening to every word. The information thus received was rarely used to hurt others—it satisfied a listener's curiosity and kept her (or him) informed. The reader must remember that this was before television sets were in almost every home.

In 1958 there were still about 600 farmers' line phones in operation. The farmers paid regular phone costs of the city dweller and an added charge for necessary repair, replacement, and service for their private lines.

The switchboards were moved to 121 North Front Street. During one fire in a neighboring building the "hello girls" had the switchboards moved out on the sidewalk and continued their services to the public. In 1927 the Pacific Telephone and Telegraph Company bought out the Home Telephone Company.[28]

Street lights awaited the coming of electricity to Turlock for several years after local telephone service was available. Esther Hall Crowell and others told of taking a lantern with them when they went out on the streets in the evening. David Lane said that if a sandstorm wasn't blowing, the light in the barroom at Vignolo's Hotel was a welcome sight to anyone at night. There was no light in the depot except for the lantern the station agent lit when he was meeting a train. "Aunt Abby" Fulkerth volunteered to take care of the light by placing a lantern at the depot every evening. For some years after 1902 this seems to have been the only street lighting.

Turlock had excellent train service. In 1910, Turlockers had five passenger trains in each direction daily and fast freight service. Mr. J. A. Coveney, the local station agent in 1910, said that the SP was replacing wooden cars with all-steel ones that would not telescope or burn, that the cars were steam heated, and that there was a light for every seat.

Many farmers shipped small amounts of fruits and vegetables in the afternoon in order to reach the Bay area in time for the next morning's produce market. Perishables were shipped by Wells Fargo Express.[29] The writer's family shipped strawberries that way to a big Berkeley market. In 1908 Turlock shipped 12,000 turkeys to San Francisco markets by Wells Fargo Express, the market price ranging from 24 to 26 cents a pound.[30]

Original Southern Pacific Depot.

School Development

In Chapter IV the various moves of the grammar school were recounted. By 1884 or 1885 it was located in a two-story building with a bell tower on property which John W. Mitchell had deeded for school purposes on the north side of West Main at Lander Avenue.

Northwest of the schoolhouse were sheds for horses, and closer to the school building the hand pump and tin cups. Most young students carried individual collapsible cups. There were old locust trees in the yard, and a fence with a stile on the West Main side.

Pool's Van and Storage around 1925. A few horses were still used. Courtesy Don Pool.

In 1899 a school tax was levied to pay the expenses for a second teacher. Mr. A. G. Elmore taught the upper grades and Tillie Lewis taught the four lower grades, beginning a thirty-nine year career.

In 1902 four new school districts were created in the vicinity of Turlock to take care of the expanding population. At the same time a two-room addition was made to the old Turlock building. In 1903 a third teacher was added, and in 1905-06 two more joined the staff. By 1908 some temporary one-room, partially screened, open-air classrooms had been added. In September 1908, 337 pupils were enrolled, and 50 more were expected as soon as the harvesting was over. To accommodate the increased enrollment, a single-classroom building was added on the east side of town between Minaret and East Main Streets. There were now nine teachers, with Miss Della B. Heisser in charge of the single east-side classroom.

In 1906, the Turlock School District was six miles square. In 1908 it lost a quarter of its territory to the five new districts that were formed that year. By September 1910, two new "fireproof and modern" school buildings were occupied by classes. Both Lowell School and Hawthorne School started as eight-room buildings.[31] Before they were condemned under the Field Act in 1957 many additions were made to both buildings.

After World War II Hawthorne and Lowell Schools were first supplemented and then replaced by a number of one-story schools built in residential areas. These included the Julien, Crowell, Cunningham, Crane and Osborn elementary schools and the Walter Brown and Wakefield junior high schools. At most of these sites additional classrooms were built as the school attendance grew.[32] A good share of the pupils were taken to school by bus. Cross-town busing took place at times to equalize the load on schools, but the issue of busing for purposes of integration did not arise.

East-West Competition in the Business Community

Up to 1902, most of Turlock's commercial activity was east of the railway. Beginning in 1902, the new residents began to build stores west of the railway and homes along North Broadway and West Main. This led to a struggle for public buildings and whatever would enhance land values on one side of town or the other. Possession of the post office was a particular prize since many of the townspeople would come to it daily for their mail.

White-bearded Clois Doty in the first mail wagon.

When J. L. Brown was postmaster in 1901, he moved the post office to the old Osborn building on West Main Street. By 1910 Charles Geer had finished his building on the north side of East Main and needed a tenant. He made a deal with the Post Office Department to lease space for ten years. He had all the papers signed and sealed and had contracted for the fixtures when the west side heard the news. That was the real start of the east side–west side fight.

The west side merchants, headed by "Senator" Henry Hoskins, called a meeting, organized a holding company, raised funds, and took an option on the Litchfield Building. Hoskins got in touch with the congressman to see what could be done to keep the post office on the west side. Nothing could be accomplished until the inspector with whom Geer had done business quit his job. Then the decision was reversed, the holding company entered into a lease whereby it would furnish a large room in the new brick building, together with new fixtures, pay the upkeep and do the janitor work for the sum of $1 a year for a period of ten years. Needless to say, the Post Office Department accepted the west side's offer.

J. L. Brown and his son Walter had the post office until 1915 when Ralph Giddings took over. At the end of the ten-year lease the west side was fed up with the arrangement and offered to lease for a term at a fair rental. Then the east siders organized a company to provide post office quarters. Their choice was part of the Sierra Building at East Main and Thor. Meanwhile the postal authorities had added to previous requirements a very high ceiling so that a catwalk could be built the full length of the room to enable mail inspectors to observe the employees without being seen. The east side's quarters fulfilled this requirement and won. Giddings remained in office until April 1924, when Walter Brown succeeded him.

In 1935, Postmaster-General Jim Farley was handing out new post offices, and Turlock was notified that she was to have one. The Department invited the offer of sites. Both east and west sides agreed that they were not interested in donating a site. The location chosen by the Post Office Department's site inspector was at the corner of Lander and West Main Streets.

M. M. Brame was postmaster from 1936 to 1952. Then Ray Moen took over as acting postmaster until Warren F. Hollingsworth was appointed. He served for twenty years until his retirement in 1972, when his assistant, Don M. Swanson, was appointed postmaster.

With the growth of the town, the 1935 post office had become inadequate and in the 1960s the Post Office Department began looking for a new site. There was a move to put it in the Civic Center on Canal Drive. Both east side and west side merchants opposed that. The site chosen, on East Main opposite Hamilton, was a compromise.

Another east-west struggle was over the location of Turlock High School, the east side winning that struggle when several property-owners offered a larger site as a gift: that portion of the present campus lying between Berkeley and Arcade Streets.

A third conflict was over theaters. The old Wonderland Theater had burned in 1915, and there was no theater open in 1918 when Dick Arakelian built the Turlock Theater on North Broadway. This theater did a big business, as it was the only one open at the time.

In 1920 a group of east siders, headed by T. B. Whipple, built the Fox Theater on East Main. The fight was on. Both houses had vaudeville and legitimate shows, but neither made any profits. Then the east siders bought the lease of the Turlock Theater and closed it. The west side, without a theater, was bitter. When the east siders managed to break the Turlock Theater lease, the owner repaired the theater and reopened it. Finally the lease was sold to the Fox Theater. When the Fox was closed, the Turlock on Broadway was the only theater open in town.

In the days of silent movies, scores for the mood music were sent to the theater along with the film, said Jean Nelson, who provided the musical accompaniment. The piano player had to read the music at sight and synchronize with the picture for special sound effects. Playing for vaudeville was tricky, too, for the act often changed its timing between the afternoon and evening performances. Most vaudeville acts stayed a single night, but one Russian tenor stayed a whole week. Miss Nelson had a theater orchestra, too. Stanley Court of Livingston played the drums; Clifford Lee, the trumpet; Wheland Drew and Captain Roy Briggs played violins. One of the big films, *Birth of a Nation,* brought its own twenty-piece orchestra right along with the movie.[33]

Looking down East Main Street around 1912.

Steve Andrino, Labor Contractor

Irrigation had made possible the growing of melons, peaches, berries, and a variety of row crops. With these new crops harvest labor was needed in much larger supply than the grain harvest had ever required. Transient workers, labor bosses, cantaloupe packers, and warehousemen were needed in Turlock a part of each year. Following the ripening crops, many began the year in the Imperial Valley and worked their way north. Their children checked out of school regularly as soon as the perishable crops were in. Most returned to the Imperial Valley, but a few followed the fruit season northward. At times, the labor supply did not equal the demand. Laborers as well as farmers and shippers saw that the situation could create great hardships and losses. One such laborer was a Filipino named Steve Andrino.

Parade along West Main Street.

Steve Andrino's laborers relaxing. Courtesy Mrs. Steve Andrino.

Andrino first came to Turlock in 1917 to work in the cantaloupe harvest. Then he farmed for himself for several years. Recognizing the problem of getting a dependable labor supply, he decided to become a bonded and licensed labor contractor. He talked with some of his Filipino countrymen in Stockton and recruited about fifty men.

The farmers could depend on Steve, so in a few years he set up a large bunkhouse and mess hall that could accommodate a hundred men near the corner of Olive and Canal. Several bath houses were erected with large zinc tubs, the water being heated by a fire under the vats. Everything had to pass the health authorities' inspection. Children of the neighborhood used these baths for dressing rooms when they swam in the canal.

Mr. Andrino transported the workers to the ranches in trucks. His wife prepared the meals with the help of some of the other Filipino ladies. Lunches were packed for the men going into the field. After work, the men played volleyball, cards and musical instruments for recreation.

When the depression came in the summer of 1930, wages dropped to 20 cents an hour. Many of the men returned to the Philippines. Then Andrino recruited transients from the dust bowl area of Oklahoma and Arkansas. Many of these families settled in Turlock and the vicinity and became good permanent citizens.

By the late 1950s harvesting of nuts and the pruning of trees was becoming mechanized and the demand for labor slackened. The Andrinos had made a real contribution to this agricultural area by supplying trained farm workers.[34]

The Changing Business Scene

The general store—a category which covered all the early ones—was changing. Berg's, Osborn's, and the Rochdale were shedding some of their departments. For example, Berg dropped buggies in 1908 when cars were on their way in. He discontinued cream separators in 1919 when farmers started selling whole milk. About the same time farm implements and tools were dropped, so that by 1925 Berg's store was strictly "dry goods and men's and women's clothing."

In 1918 Rochdale discontinued its farm implement department. Edward Scanlon picked up the department, running it as a farm implement firm. The last owner of the business was Kenneth Monteith, who was burned out in 1966.

New Berg Building, 1911. An example of business buildings constructed to 1909 code requirements.
Courtesy Hazel Berg.

Osborn first dropped general hardware, then in 1948 eliminated groceries. Some time after 1940, Mercantile also dropped its grocery department.

Wood and coal yards like that of the Kiernans' (later owned by the McCues) hung on for a while, but fuel oil soon replaced coal although wood was still in demand for fireplaces. Livery stables and blacksmith shops were doomed, too.

By the 1920s there were specialty shops for a number of products on both the east and west sides. Seth Williams moved his clothing store from the west side to the east side, and with the Crescent Store on East Main helped to offset the drawing power of the Mercantile on the west side. The Palace Meat Market, operated by Shearer and Gotobed on South Center Street (east side) had a fine reputation for its meats. In addition to butcher shops, the west side had the very popular Martin's Fish Market. Both sides had good bakeries: on the west side Lundeen's became in turn Swanson's Bakery, then Marty's;

Osborn's Store, Henry Osborn in center. Courtesy Mrs. Jack Osborn.

Ruts in the sand along East Main Street. Ravnos Photo. W. W. Ferguson photo, courtesy Valesca Smith.

today it is the Honeycomb. On the east side were August Sisting's Bakery, Etcheto's and Ed Hutz's, whose son Ed operates the Polly Ann Bakery today.

Both sides of town had drug stores from an early date. Somewhat remarkable is the continuity of service of three stores which have survived under various owners for about sixty-five years. Their names in 1971 were Boies, Hauck's East (for long Turlock Drug), and Hauck's West. On the west side, James Shadle and son Herbert opened a pharmacy in 1906; they sold it to A. M. Jackson and his sons in 1908; this later was sold to Keller and Bennett, who sold it to Sweet. Sweet later took in Lewis Boies, who in turn became the sole owner; Kirk Sperry now operates the store under the Boies name.[35]

Across from Boies another pharmacy was started in 1916 by Fred Englesby, who sold it in 1922 to Ben Hauck. After forty-seven years, the Haucks sold it to Ernie Yotsuya and Richard Berger in 1968.

On East Main, Hudiberg and King opened a drug store at the corner of Center. After more than a decade, they sold in 1917 to Longstreth and Eddington. From 1947 to 1961 Eddington operated the store alone, then sold it to Franklin Schwoob and W. D. Plummer. In 1961 they sold to Raymond Heinrichs, who in 1970 sold out to Yotsuya and Berger.[36]

Another east side drug store was opened on 1 December 1927 by P. W. Johnson, who worked in the store thirty-four years to the day.[37]

In the 1930s Boies sought to forestall outside cut-rate drug firms by opening the Rite Price Drug Store. After several changes in ownership and location, Gordon Olson became the proprietor in 1949, moving it to the east side in 1958.[38]

Something of the atmosphere of the town would be lost if the smaller businesses were ignored. Only a few can be mentioned, such as Karl Barkdull's chicken and egg business, the Turlock Soda Works (predecessor of all the soft drink firms), which was bought out by E. C. Utendorffer in 1921. Utendorffer built a new soda water plant and acquired the Coca Cola agency. During the winter he sold wood and coal. There was Hazelle Mae's Beauty Shop, which opened in 1927 and was still operating in 1972. Mrs. Maud Britton had a "notions" store and Y. B. Torosian a racket (variety) store. S. V. Carkeet opened his candy factory in 1914 and operated it for years to the delight of the children. These are representative businesses; space limitations forbid a complete list. Whether in production or services, they all served the needs of the community.

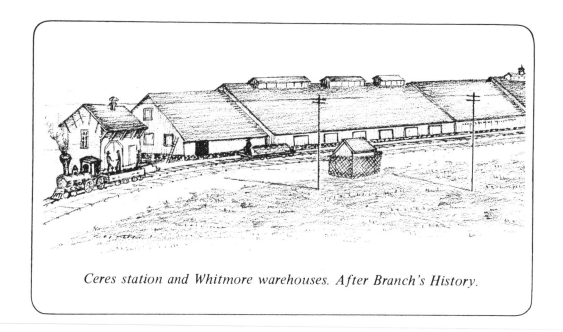

Ceres station and Whitmore warehouses. After Branch's History.

Chapter XVII

Ceres and Keyes: Neighbors on the Southern Pacific

Ceres, 1870–1940

Helen Hohenthal

Daniel Whitmore, the founder of Ceres, first came to California in 1854, crossing the plains in a wagon train. He located in the vicinity of Cherokee Lane, north of Stockton. Finding the soil too heavy for his liking, in 1867 he moved to Stanislaus County where he bought eight parcels of government land totaling 4,840.28 acres, recording the purchases on 20 and 23 March 1867.[1] Later he added to his holdings until at one time he had almost 10,000 acres south of the Tuolumne in the vicinity of Ceres.[2]

Whitmore seems to have built a cabin first, then in 1870 built the first house in the present town of Ceres and moved his family to it. The surveys had already been made for the Central Pacific railroad, and this undoubtedly influenced his choice of the site.[3]

Whitmore engaged in farming. When not busy with farm work, he contracted to build houses, barns, warehouses, and farm equipment such as cultivators.[4] He was described as a man of industry, honesty, and executive ability. He was always interested in the welfare of the community and up to the time of his death took an active part in shaping its history. He was one of the most prosperous and influential farmers in the county. Whitmore, like John Mitchell, rented much of his extensive landholdings out to tenants in large tracts; he operated large grain warehouses, founded a town, and outlived Mitchell by a year.

Mr. and Mrs. C. P. Warner were old friends of the Whitmores, and had been living at Auburn. At Whitmore's invitation the Warners and their daughter and young son-in-law, the John Services, joined the Whitmores at Ceres. The men went ahead and built houses, their families following later.

The Warners bought a section of land at $1.25 an acre and later acquired other farm land and town lots in Ceres. The Services first bought part of a section of land from Daniel Whitmore.[5]

Whitmore's landholdings eventually reached about 10,000 acres in Stanislaus County, 4,000 in Tulare County, and over 10,000 acres (27 sections) in Texas.

Ceres was a most unusual town for its time and area. Before Whitmore sold a lot, the buyer had to sign a strict temperance pledge, so Ceres was the only town in the early days where the majority of business houses were not saloons. Only once was a saloon opened, and that remained but a short while, for Mr. Whitmore put up $5,000 with which a Mrs. Woodbridge bought the building, later reselling it to Mrs. Conner, who opened it as a temperance hotel.[6]

When Whitmore applied for a post office, the question of a name came up. Ceres, goddess of the harvest, was the name suggested by Miss Elma Carter and accepted by Whitmore and the Post Office Department. For two years after the post office was granted to the town, Whitmore, as postmaster, had to carry the mail from Modesto. The post office was in his own residence.

The first public building was a boarding house built and run by two sisters, Mrs. Fellows and Mrs. Conner. Mr. J. J. Annear's blacksmith shop was built in 1872. In 1873 Whitmore put up a store building, but for four years it was used as a church. In 1877 it was opened as a store by Bradley and Rounds, being later sold to John Service.

The first railway station in the vicinity was built in 1871 about two miles south of Ceres on Eli Carter's property. It was only a flag stop and was named Esmar, a name made up of the initials of the first names of the five Carter children.[7]

According to one writer, the first Whitmore grain warehouse, a building 75 by 100 feet, was standing in 1872. When the station was built in 1874, Whitmore and Dr. Thomas E. Tynan, a rancher and ferry operator on the Tuolumne, each built a large warehouse to meet the demand.[8] The name Ceres was applied to the station as well as to the post office. Cyrus Lee, a nephew of Mrs. Daniel Whitmore, was appointed the first station agent. That same year the first townsite map of Ceres was filed.

Hoping to retain more of the grain profits within the community and increase its size through industrial enterprise, Whitmore built the Ceres Flour Mill in 1881 at a cost of $30,000. It had a Corliss engine and a straw-burning boiler. Its destruction by fire in late July 1883 was a blow. Said one writer, "It was probably worth more than all the personal property in the town besides."[10]

To the end of the grain era Ceres remained a shipping center. During the harvesting months hundreds of wagonloads of grain were hauled into the town, some of them from beyond Horr's ranch, seventeen miles east of Ceres.

Originally the small district school had been located two miles northwest of Ceres on the corner of the M. M. Williams farm. As the youthful population of Ceres increased, Ceres residents fought several election campaigns before they succeeded in getting the school and its teacher, Mrs. Aurelia Chapin, moved to Ceres. Mrs. Chapin taught in the Ceres school for nine years.[11]

The religious life of the community was at no time neglected. As elsewhere, church services were held as soon as a few families settled close enough to make meetings possible. The earliest services were Methodist, held in 1869.[12] Later, services were held in the Whitmore store building, then in the town hall, and after 1882 in the new Baptist church which had been organized in 1879. The Whitmores were active members of this church, serving in various offices over a long period of time. Clinton N. Whitmore served as superintendent of the Sunday School for twenty-one years until ill health forced him to resign. The Methodists held meetings in a variety of places, but did not have a building of their own until 1906.[13]

Although Ceres people worked as hard as the Turlockers for the establishment of the irrigation district, Turlock not only received the honor of the name of the district, but also, except for a short while, succeeded in having the business offices connected with it. Ceres residents evidently hoped for establishment of the TID office in their town as an incentive to new business, for in 1889 one newspaper correspondent wrote, "Ceres can't get the headquarters of the Turlock Irrigation District so I guess we'll have to start a bank, a newspaper, and get someone to start up in the real estate business so as to start a boom."[14]

The 1880s were good and happy years for the people of Ceres. The big warehouses were filled with wheat and barley. The settlers had all the essentials for happy living—good incomes and a town

Daniel Whitmore's home, built in 1870,
was still in use in 1972.
From Branch's History.

Ceres Flour Mill, 1881-1883.
From Branch's History.

made to their own specifications; the best of transportation, a fine climate, productive land, a church, a town hall for dances and other social gatherings,[15] a school, fraternal organizations, stores, and, before the end of that decade, a promise that an irrigation system, once established, would almost guarantee a crop income. By the late 1880s, however, wheat crops began to decline, and the end of the "Grain Era" brought lower incomes to the people of Ceres, as well as to those of Turlock. In 1903 Whitmore finally sold his grain warehouses.[16]

Although Ceres without saloons was a clean, quiet little town, a train holdup and attempted robbery in 1891 or 1892 provided very great excitement. After discharging a passenger at Ceres, the southbound evening train was picking up speed when it was halted by two armed bandits. Aboard the train were two railway detectives who took after the holdup men. In the darkness the robbers got away. Chris Evans and John Sonntag were partners in a Modesto livery stable, and the finger of suspicion pointed at them. Soon after the Ceres robbery their stable caught fire and a Negro stable boy was burned to death. Old-timers believed the fire was set because he might have known too much. After the fire Evans and Sonntag went to Visalia where Evans had a wife and family, and Sonntag had a brother.

Following a holdup at Collis (now Kerman), officers went to Evans' home to arrest the two. There was a shooting in which a deputy sheriff was "winged." Evans and Sonntag became fugitives, leaving a trail of wounded and dead across the southern San Joaquin Valley. Sonntag was killed, and Evans eventually was sent to Folsom prison minus an eye and an arm. By this time everyone in Ceres and Modesto "knew" they were guilty of the attempted train robbery at Ceres.[17]

Ceres joined the State's traveling library system in 1901 with a loan of fifty books. These books were changed every three months. The library was located in the old post office and store where Mrs. Allura E. Ulch served as librarian. The Farmers' Club paid the $3.00 per quarter for maintaining the traveling library. In 1905 a Ceres Library Association was formed. Its objective was eventually to have a free public library for Ceres. All over twelve years of age paid an annual fee of one dollar. Library books were added to the local collection by gifts and by purchase from funds raised at book socials. When the Stanislaus County Library was formed in 1910, Ceres was one of the first to join the county library system.[18]

With the coming of irrigation in 1901, towns as well as farms were changed for the better. Throughout the TID area real estate agents and promoters began to come in and subdivide the old wheat ranches into plots typically of twenty to forty acres. Clinton N. Whitmore was active in colonizing both at Ceres and around Denair.[19]

As dairying began to increase in the Turlock region, creameries sprang up. The Ceres Co-operative Creamery was established by Dr. C. W. Evans and Leslie Whitmore in the spring of 1904.[20] It was burned down shortly after that and rebuilt.

In January 1905 Ceres was reported to have a "first class hotel"; a combined blacksmith, wagon and machine shop; and an excellent butcher shop. There were three churches in the vicinity, including the Baptists' new building that seated 400 people, a Congregational chapel at Smyrna Park, and a newly organized Methodist congregation that was worshiping in Ceres Hall.

During late 1904 a new post office had been built and a forty-foot by seventy-foot general store with a full basement completed. Four houses were under construction, including Clinton N. Whitmore's $10,000 residence, long known as the "yellow castle."[21]

At about this time trucks and automobiles began to displace horses and mules on the farms. In the decade following 1910 gasoline tractors made their appearance, but old dobbin as a farm worker was not entirely displaced for several more decades.

The *Ceres Courier,* founded in 1910 by Clarence Humphrey Bronaugh, gave Ceres a medium for local news and for expression of public opinion on matters of public interest.[22] In 1971 it was still a living part of the town of Ceres as it recorded the town's day to day history.

The number of churches in Ceres grew slowly. In 1903 the Smyrna Park Congregational Church was organized; it moved into its own building in 1908. The Church of Christ was founded in 1908 and a building constructed in 1909, for members who had been attending church in Modesto found it too long a drive. The Glad Tidings Assembly of God held its first meetings in a home in 1919, but soon shifted to a pool hall until a church could be built.[23] On 8 January 1936 the Congregationalists voted to disband, giving their property and transferring their memberships to the Methodist Church.[24]

Ceres in the 1920s and 1930s was a typical small valley town. Driving south on the highway, one saw on the right a two-story yellow frame railway station, with three or four packing sheds strung along the railway siding. On the left was a cluster of stores in a couple of square blocks. Among these were a grocery, a hardware store, a drugstore, several service stations with perhaps repair shops attached, a newspaper, and a tiny local bank. The central business area was paved and had street lights. Beyond the central area most of the streets were neither paved nor oiled. On the edge of town were the Clinton Whitmore School and Ceres High School.

Beyond the business district were the Baptist and Methodist churches; nearby was Clinton Whitmore's big yellow house with its broad veranda and row of palm trees. By the 1930s orchards encroached closely upon the town, suggesting a clearing in a forest of peaches.

On the west of the tracks was Nail Park, an auto camp where travelers might pitch their tents or rent a cabin. In the 1930s many migrants fleeing the poverty of the Southeast and the dust storms of the Midwest set up their tents in the Nail family's grove. For many this was their first foothold in California.

From the park the migrants moved to tar paper shacks nearby. As they got a little money, many of the families built new homes, sometimes incorporating their first shacks in the newer structures. These newcomers constituted a colony in themselves. The older residents tended to ignore them. For some years their children attended Clinton Whitmore School, but when Don Pedro School was built, the children of "Nailville" went there and mingled less with the rest of the town. The very design of the freeway crossings, once the embankment was built, also isolated them from the main part of the town.

This group of settlers was important to Ceres, for they were familiar with farming, and even if they had to learn about new crops, their skill as farmhands was valuable. Their wives and older children found seasonal jobs in the three or four canneries of Modesto.[25]

Ceres, 1941–1971

John E. Caswell

With the coming of World War II, things looked up for farmers across America. Money rolled in and mortgages were paid off. This was true of Ceres as elsewhere. Now concerns were of a different kind.

Turning through the Ceres scrapbooks preserved by the City Clerk, one finds dozens of accounts of Ceres' sons in the service; of Ceres' daughters marrying and following their husbands from camp to camp across the nation, then coming back to mother or perhaps to their own apartments as their husbands sailed for foreign shores. Ceres' boys returned home to children they had known only through snapshots and their wives' letters. It was a story common to every town in America; Ceres has preserved the poignant record.

When the end of the war came, Ceres was not so very different in appearance from five years before. It was still an agricultural village, with shops providing services for the farm and home. Only in the late 1940s did things begin to change in response to the development of industry in Modesto. One of the first new plants was Stan Triplett's freezing plant. Then others began to fill in the Beard Industrial Tract. Ceres, little more than a mile across the river from the Industrial Tract, began to look attractive to people taking jobs in the new canneries and factories. Subdivisions were opened, the first within Ceres being the Caswell Tract in 1946. Later Morrow Village and other tracts opened up in the county and were only annexed to Ceres in later years.

With the new tracts came new schools: Don Pedro, Caswell (both in 1947-48), and Walter White (1956). The last to be built was Carroll Fowler School, constructed in two stages around 1960. On 1 July 1965 the Ceres Unified School District was formed of the Ceres Elementary Schools, the Ceres High School, and Westport School District, itself the result of combining the Jones, Laird, and Jennings districts in 1945.[26]

One of Ceres' revered leaders was Walter White, who had served as school principal and superintendent from 1923 to 1956. He was elected mayor three months before retiring and occupied that position until 1964. Under him, Ceres government began to forge ahead. In 1961 the first city administrator was employed, serving under the mayor and council.

Downtown Ceres had undergone minor surgery when Highway 99 was widened to four lanes around 1960. It underwent a radical operation when the highway was converted to freeway and a goodly slice of old Ceres was eliminated. By 1965 the operation was completed and the town began to return to normal. Among the businesses that had relocated in new quarters were the drug store, bank, and billiard hall. By the end of 1965 sales tax records indicated that business had again picked up. Some purchasers found it more convenient to bypass Modesto in order to do their shopping in a limited area where there were no meters and no ordinance against jaywalking. It was actually less noisy with the elevated freeway than it had been when the highway was at ground level. Until further improvements were made, however, pedestrians found crossing from the west side practically impossible.

In order to develop a long-range plan for the area that Ceres wished to stake out for herself, a San Mateo firm was employed. The area designated by the Ceres Council was bounded on the north by the Tuolumne River, on the south by Keyes Road, on the east by Faith Home Road, and on the west by Crows Landing Road. The plan was completed in 1964 and became a subject of heated discussion.

Hardly had the plan been received when one basic assumption was challenged: that the area north of Hatch Road would fall to Ceres rather than to Modesto. Sixty residents out of the 1700 in the area signed a petition favoring eventual annexation to Ceres. The inducement was the new general plan which showed parkways and low density housing in the area, whereas Modesto and the County would have admitted low-cost, high-density housing.[27]

The showdown on control of what had come to be designated "No Man's Land" came in 1967 when both Ceres and Modesto proposed to extend sewer service to a tract on Hatch Road at Highway 99, where a shopping center was projected. The "enticing tax revenues" were the spur to both cities. Eventually the County Local Agency Formation Commission awarded the 1,000-acre area to Ceres as a part of its municipal utilities service area.[28]

Mayors and councils, development plans, schools and shopping areas, however, do not make a community. A sense of belonging, of community pride, of cooperation is necessary to make the machinery work. In the period prior to World War II there was a strong sense of community, for many families had been in Ceres for a long time and there was much intermarrying. In the fifteen or twenty year period following 1945, when the community was growing fast, the newcomers tended to remain apart from the activities of the town. In part this was because their jobs and their friends were often in Modesto. In part, they considered themselves transient, expecting to move on and up. There were three groups in Ceres: the closely linked old-timers, the migrants of the thirties in Nailville, and the newer arrivals in the various tracts and subdivisions.

Only in the 1960s did the newer arrivals begin to join in community affairs other than school carnivals, possibly because they had felt themselves excluded from influence or responsibility. By 1970 it seemed that the town leaders were beginning to call upon the newer people. The different community groups began working together, and once more a sense of community, a larger community, was developing.[29]

If there was a single event that stimulated civic pride, it was the Ceres Paint-Up of 1961. The principal objective was to generate community spirit. A side benefit was the improvement in the town's appearance. Several men went to the Fuller Paint Company to see if they would supply the know-how to repaint the community in an aesthetic manner. Fuller Paints had sponsored such a project in Weaverville, and its movies made there were shown to every organization in Ceres. Members were asked to pledge their support in repainting downtown Ceres in a single weekend. Property owners agreed to allow their buildings to be painted in the colors proposed by the Fuller Company. On one Saturday morning in June the volunteer workers paraded down the middle of the street with their paintbrushes on their shoulders. The local bands were playing, and news reports were going out on TV and on local news broadcasts. In the one day approximately four blocks of store fronts and sides were painted, and new signs were put up through the downtown. Close to five hundred workers were served lunch and dinner. After a bit of argument, it was agreed that the workers should finish up on Sunday afternoon after church.

The paint-up was more than spreading fresh paint and relettering signs. Students in the Art Department at Stanislaus State College came up with a design for a mural on the side of one building. From the public school students other drawings depicting scenes of Ceres history were obtained and transferred to murals.

"When we got through, we had an awful lot of people who were proud of the town, which they hadn't been before." It was an excellent piece of promotion for the town because San Joaquin Valley newspapers, radio and TV stations carried it. San Francisco papers and others across the nation published accounts, and letters began pouring in. The final triumph was when the *Saturday Evening Post* did a centerfold spread.[30]

The Ceres community included many families who lived outside the boundaries of the city, but who identified with it. As new supermarkets went up, they tended to regret the passing of the older and simpler days. Conversely, some living within the city limits had not acquired any sense of community, but the proportion of those was diminishing. New plants, such as California Vegetable Concentrates built in 1957, drew workers from Ceres—perhaps twenty percent of its labor force. More important, they began to furnish a larger tax base for the schools. Ceres itself remained unindustrialized, although many of its dwellers were industrial workers. It seemed likely to remain a bedroom community for the immediate future.

Keyes

John E. Caswell

At about the same time that railway sidings were established on Dan Whitmore's and John Mitchell's ranches, a third siding, halfway between the two, was put on the land of Ephraim Hatch, who had also donated a right-of-way to the Central Pacific. The nearest settler was Thomas J. Keyes, an Ohioan who had come to California in 1850[31] and had a home a little east of the railroad.[32] The flag stop was called Keyes Switch, but in time the "Switch" was dropped. Almost a decade later, in 1880, all that was there was a warehouse and one dwelling.[33]

As early as 1892, residents of the Keyes area had petitioned for a school, saying that some of their seventeen school-age children had to go six miles to school.[34] When horses were needed for farm work, the parents were caught on the horns of a dilemma. Nevertheless, the Keyes Grammar School was not established until 1905-1906. At that time there were sixteen families with thirty-nine school-age children. The county superintendent reported that the average enrollment was thirty-three, and the average daily attendance was thirty-one. Rose McGarr, the one teacher, received $65 a month for nine months. The cost of the two-room school building was about $3600, which was financed by the sale of bonds.[35]

The next building of consequence seems to have been the little Methodist Church built across the road from the schoolhouse around 1908. For a time the Free Methodists also ran a Sunday School in the schoolhouse itself.

In the next half-dozen years shipping activity picked up at Keyes, and a village began to form. By 1915 Keyes was quite a melon center, shipping 1300 carloads of produce during each of several seasons and 1800 carloads in its peak year! Around that time Keyes had no less than five warehouse and produce companies: the Keyes Fruit Exchange run by local farmers, the Grange Company of Modesto, Peppers Fruit Company, and two collecting stations for large firms: the Hunt-Hatch Company and the Half Moon Fruit and Produce Company, which had a warehouse in the San Francisco produce district.

The first depot and station agent's home consisted of several boxcars set beside the tracks in 1914. In five months five agents quit because of the heat. In August 1914 Mr. and Mrs. Claude Warren took over the job, and in 1918 a two-story station was constructed. The Warrens stayed on until the depot was closed in 1931.[36]

Keyes, like many of its neighboring towns, had a creamery. Its life was short, for Keyes Creamery was incorporated on 29 January 1913 and it burned down in 1918. The next year the Milk Producers Association, which covered Stanislaus County, took over the property.[37]

The town's first grocery store was established by John Cross, one of the early teachers at Keyes. He also became the first postmaster. There were two blacksmith shops, and the Modesto Lumber Company had a yard there.

The pattern of crops around Keyes did not differ materially from what would have been found at Ceres or Turlock. Sweet potatoes were introduced by the Portuguese. When the Half Moon Fruit and Produce Company wanted to introduce sweet potatoes in its line, it paid George Nunes' father a half-cent a pound premium to put up a particularly attractive pack. Malaga grapes were planted before 1918, and

Keyes Grammar School.
Courtesy George H. Nunes.

Keyes' first railway station, built 1914. Courtesy George H. Nunes.

a little later some "gyp" corn and black-eyed beans were planted. By the early 1920s there were some peaches in bearing. While the Tupper family had the first almonds about 1926, most of the almond orchards were planted some time later. After World War II, walnuts were planted in limited quantities.

A number of Portuguese moved onto Hatch's land between 1915 and 1920, some coming directly from the Azores. They rented twenty to forty acre tracts, built redwood cabins, and planted sweet potatoes and melons. As opportunity arose, they purchased their own farms. These "energetic, friendly, vivacious and respected people" later became leaders in the Keyes community.[38]

Keyes' civic spirit has found expression in several different organizations. Old-timers recall the Keyes Improvement Club, which was one of the early social clubs. The Keyes Parent-Teachers Association was organized on 22 January 1925, and was still functioning in 1971.[39]

The Keyes Grange was organized in 1935. It was active in the district fair, helping to manage the Grange cafeteria. It sponsored 4-H Clubs, Boy Scouts, and other community activities. At first it met

Keyes' second station, built 1918. Courtesy George H. Nunes.

in the school, then for some years in members' homes. Finally a new Grange Hall was built, and in August 1955 the Grange held its first meeting in its new home.[40]

A month after Pearl Harbor, when no one knew what the war might bring, Keyes organized a volunteer fire department which has remained active ever since. It is connected to the county's fire dispatching service.

After the war the community picked up some momentum. The second school building, constructed in 1924, was relegated to service functions, and in the next decade several new units were built, the latest in 1956.

By 1972 Keyes Grammar School had an enrollment of 600, an increase of 40 percent in five years. Despite that rapid increase, over half the children were from families that had been in the area twenty to thirty years. Many of these families had either moved in from the southeastern states in the late 1930s or had come to Keyes after having worked in Bay area shipyards during World War II. Under Berne W. Feuerstein, the principal since 1967, new techniques of motivation and learning improvement known as Dr. William Glasser's "School without Failure" were being applied.[41]

To spur people on to becoming involved in the town's growth and progress, the Keyes Civic Group was organized on 7 April 1954; the group was incorporated on 29 November. The next year the Keyes Community Service District was created and served as the instrument for carrying out ideas that had usually been discussed earlier in the Keyes Civic Group. Among the Service District projects to arise from those discussions were street lights and a sewer system. The Civic Group itself raised funds, built and installed lights at the Keyes ball park at a cost of $3500. On 24 March 1955 it purchased land for future city offices. And on 25 June 1955 Raymond Hatch donated the land for Hatch Park, for which the Civic Group was most grateful.[42]

On 18 July 1955 Keyes took its first step toward organizing local government by approving a Community Service District. The first project the District undertook was to enter into a contract with TID to furnish street lighting at a cost of $70.95 a month. Next the District arranged to have sanitary engineer Homer W. Jorgensen of Ceres study the Keyes sewer problems. The solution recommended by the District to the voters was to run a sewer line from Keyes to the Turlock sewage treatment plant. This was put to a vote on 24 February 1959, and passed, 160 to 60. The sewer, however, was not completed until March 1965. The next undertaking was to install an improved water system. It was necessary first to purchase the Keyes Water Company, which was done on 10 August 1970. A year later, after the old and inefficient system was abandoned, an entirely new water system was completed on 26 July 1971.

Hardly more than a crossroads community up to 1971, Keyes was then facing the likelihood that the State Highway Department would take out a good share of its commercial structures for the third time. Unfortunately for local residents, the proposed overpass would be placed far enough away that they would derive slight economic benefit from it.

At that time the population of Keyes was gradually approaching 2000. By the year 1980 it was expected to reach 3500. Two projects had helped its growth. Between 1967 and 1971 some thirty Self Help Houses had been built (financed by the Farm Home Administration), in which the prospective owners, working under supervision, supplied the labor and at the same time acquired a skill. The other project was named Tempo Homes. Built by contractors for the Farm Home Administration, the payments were subsidized by the federal government.

Keyes' economic function in 1971 was quite different from that of 1914. There was little manufacturing, and rail shipping consisted of deliveries to two feed mills. Twenty-five businesses were listed in seventeen categories. Only the soap factory and the feed mills could be considered manufacturing. There was a wholesale petroleum plant. Among the other businesses were four grocery stores, three service stations, three trailer courts, two small bars, a drive-in movie, a beauty salon and a barber shop. Turlock was the nearest town with substantially better retail and service facilities. Linked to Turlock in the Turlock Union High School District, there was a strong tendency for Keyes citizens to go in that direction for items not available locally.

Why Ceres, Why Turlock, Why Not Keyes?

An interesting problem in geography is presented by these three crossroads villages, all of which were established as railway sidings at the same time, but only two of which developed. In the period 1871-1900, only Turlock had grown to any extent, but even it had lost its economic importance and its population had declined before there was a fresh surge of vigor in 1902. Ceres was exposed to the economic competition of Modesto; yet it, too, began to grow about 1905.

One factor against Keyes was the soil, which was not up to that of Turlock and Ceres. As a result, people in the Keyes area had less money to spend. A second factor is that Daniel Whitmore and John W. Mitchell were operating on a larger scale than Ephraim Hatch from the day that they came to Stanislaus County. They had larger crops of their own to ship, they were able to provide more facilities, and these in turn attracted more trade. The best years for Keyes were after 1914 when Portuguese began buying small tracts from the Hatch family and raising sweet potatoes and melons. Production was heavy enough to justify additional facilities, and Keyes was a more convenient shipping point than Turlock. However, when motor trucks and mechanized packing were introduced, followed by years of depression, Keyes lost out to the larger centers. Later, without adequate sewer and water facilities, Keyes failed to share in Ceres' postwar role as a bedroom community, However, with water and sewer facilities established by 1972, Keyes' population and its local retail and service shops may be expected to increase.

To recapitulate, for long little more than a railroad siding for loading wheat, Keyes at one time attracted branches of a number of wholesale produce firms. With the onset of the Depression of the 1930s, Keyes again lost ground. Highway construction twice threatened the tiny commercial core with extinction, but each time it was built back. In the 1950s Keyes again began to move forward and to develop community utilities through a district organization. Without anticipation of major growth, Keyes continued to provide a valuable service function to its rural neighbors and to improve the quality of life within the community.

Big John Davis' home, the first in the Denair area, 1870s.
Courtesy Les De La Mater.

Chapter XVIII

Santa Fe Towns: Denair and Hughson

Introduction

Helen Hohenthal

The neighboring communities of Denair and Hughson sprang up just after the turn of the century on land long under grain. A railroad had been built through the area a decade before, splitting the distance between the main route of the Southern Pacific, which passed through Ceres, Keyes, and Turlock, and the east side route, which passed through Hickman and Montpellier. With the coming of irrigation, landowners along the Santa Fe began to divide their great ranches into small holdings and sell them off. A railway station was considered essential for a town of any importance, and the promoters of both towns succeeded in getting the Santa Fe to build stations there.

The railroad was incorporated as the San Francisco and San Joaquin Valley Railway Company on 26 February 1895 with Claus Spreckels, a sugar baron and San Francisco capitalist, as the head. It was originally constructed from Stockton to Bakersfield. Records are lacking as to the exact time the line passed through the sites of Hughson and Denair, but it seems quite probable that it was during 1896 for construction into Bakersfield was completed in 1897. Although there seem to have been rumors that Spreckels was fronting for the Atchison, Topeka and Santa Fe Railway, that company did not acquire control of the line until 1901.

The station of Hughson was named after Hiram Hughson, who at the time the railroad was built through that point was a large property owner. A deed given to the railroad company by Hughson covering one hundred feet of right-of-way and station grounds was recorded on 28 January 1896. On 13 November 1898 a further agreement, covering certain townsite arrangements, was made between the railroad company and George W. McNear.[1]

The town of Denair, or Elmwood as it was first known, was laid out on the land of John T. Davis, who conveyed rights in the town to the railway company at about the same time that Hughson and

McNear did a little farther northwest. A plat of the town of Elmwood, drawn by the San Francisco and San Joaquin Railway, with a dedication to the railway of certain lands by Davis, was recorded on 8 March 1897.[2]

In neither town was there much development before 1906 or 1907. Then, with irrigation on the soil, promoters became interested and real promotional efforts took place. Each town developed a community spirit of its own, formed its own social organizations and maintained its identity. Depression days may have impoverished them. The coming of good roads and speedy cars offered escape to the inhabitants, but still they stayed on.

What did the newcomers of 1906 see in the land that induced them to settle, build their homes, and dedicate their lives?

History of Denair

Christine Chance

"It was a good land," Theodore Jessup said, when asked why he had chosen Denair as the spot to establish his dreamed-of Quaker colony. "Yes, the land was good, it was cheap, and there was plenty of irrigation water." Theodore Jessup had come from Iowa via Kansas and Whittier, California, one of those Americans seeking, still seeking the new, the fresh opportunity to better his condition.[3]

But Jessup was neither the first nor the last white man to look with favor upon this part of the San Joaquin Valley. Mr. Cutler, a teacher at Denair School in 1908, had often regaled his pupils with tales of his own boyhood. His playground, he said, had extended from Stockton to Fresno. He and his horse had roamed as they pleased, spotting herds of antelope and cattle as they fed amid acres of lupine and poppy. He had stopped nights at one cowboy camp or another.[4]

By the time Mr. Cutler was a man, Big John Davis and Charles Sperry, among others, had plowed under the poppies and sowed barley. Still later, after Mr. Cutler's hair had thinned and turned grey, and he earned his living explaining decimals to leggy children, La Grange Dam had blocked the waters of the Tuolumne River, sending them flowing between the sandy banks of miles-long canals to the relative flat of the valley below. This flow of water changed the great barley ranches into forty-acre diversified farms. The story of the Charles E. Sperry ranch could be, with modifications, the story of the entire area.

In 1880 Mr. Sperry purchased 966 acres of raw land and established his home on what is now Sperry Road, between Service and Keyes Roads two and three-fourths miles north of Denair. Here he and his sons, Charles, Louis and Willard after him, raised stock and grain until irrigation water changed the face of the land. The 966-acre ranch increased in size (whether by purchase or by lease, records are unclear) until the Sperry mule teams were turning the harvester at the section corner now marked by the intersection of Lander Avenue and West Main Street in Turlock, five miles from the Sperry home place.

As irrigation water had begun flowing soon after 1900, the Sperrys joined the movement to subdivide their holdings into twenty and forty acre farms. That was in 1906. Eventually the Sperry grain ranch became a community of small irrigated farms where grew alfalfa, beans, grains, fruit and nuts.[5]

Big John Davis had been the first to plat a subdivision. When the San Francisco and San Joaquin Railway approached him for a right-of-way across his land, a townsite was laid out in his barley fields and named Elmwood. A few homes and stores were built there around 1902 and 1903.

The first man to buy a small ranch around Denair was Harry Clark. He had worked as a hired hand on the Davis ranch and other barley ranches. With the coming of irrigation he felt rich enough to buy the forty that he had dreamed of. The plot chosen lay adjacent to the canal facing Gratton Road at the east end of the jog in the road a half-mile north of Denair. At the edge of the road Clark installed what could later have been a gateway to the dooryard. On a board hung from the posts he had lettered the sign, "Pioneer Ranch, 1902." A rose clung to one of the posts.

Sperry ranch, northwest of Denair, established in the 1880s. Courtesy George Sperry.

Harry Clark dug a well, set up a windmill, planted grapevines beside the mill, erected a barn and acquired a building for machinery and other farm needs. He and his wife Molly moved into this building "just for now." The intended house was never built. He and Molly lived out their days in the "temporary" home, the half-orphaned nieces and nephews of Molly sharing its shelter. Built onto, redecorated, repaired, that house rang with the shouts and laughter of many of the neighborhood's young ones. "Uncle Harry," "Aunt Molly," and the sign at the road are all gone now. One of the orphaned nephews and his wife, Leslie and Mary De La Mater, still lived on Pioneer Ranch seventy years after Harry moved that little house onto it and dug the well.

In 1905 Clinton N. Whitmore of Ceres, J. N. Lester, who had bought sections of the Davis ranch, and Charles A. Dickenson of Los Angeles laid out the Elmwood Colony in lots of roughly twenty and forty acres around the Elmwood townsite.[6]

A year later a small group of Quakers moved into the area, but their hopes of a Quaker colony and seminary came to naught. That same year John Denair, a former Santa Fe Railroad employee, came and bought up land. Incorporating the Denair Land and Development Company, he established its Colony No. 1 west of Elmwood. Denair and Whitmore continued their rival land developments for the next several years, Whitmore using the Elmwood title for his developments, and Denair his own name.

About this time Denair acquired the Elmwood townsite. After holding it until 1909, he decided the lots (apparently 25 feet by 150 feet) were too small. He had a new plat made, eliminating half the streets, and offered lots about an acre in size.[7]

The men who bought farms in the Denair vicinity came from Canada, Oregon, New England, the Southwest, the Mississippi Valley, and from other sections of California. Most of them were ignorant of how to irrigate, unaccustomed to small fields ("back home my pasture was as large as my entire farm here"), astonished by the sweep of the March winds that blew the seed out of the sandy ground and piled the top soil against a neighbor's barn. Their women, who had lived in tight houses "back home" now were continually sweeping sand out of the new barns where the families slept and ate, washing dishes not only after dinner but also before setting the table for supper. Sand seeped into everything. Children walked to school through seasonal fogs that vied with seasonal sandstorms, either of which muffled childish shouts of greetings and turned friends into faceless moving objects. In July, when these same children sought a spot of shade in which to build a playhouse or lay out a miniature farm, the only shade they found was that made by the eight-foot-tall weeds that grew along the ditch banks.

All this time ground squirrels built great underground villages which they shared with ground owls, commonly known as "Billy owls." Other wildlife commonly seen during their spring and fall migrations were great V's of Canadian honkers and wild ducks. They filled the sky. But there were no song birds— not a robin, not a thrush, not even a woodpecker or a jay. No trees to nest in? Likely.

Winter mornings the snow-capped Sierra Nevadas stood out in the east. (Still do, though trees and houses now block the view from many inhabitants.) Summer evenings the Coast Ranges rose silhouetted against the sunset, often streaked with fire. At sunrise only the tops of this range showed above the dust man stirred up and the smoke made by the forest fires.

Slowly, year by year, the newly arrived farmers learned how to raise crops by means of irrigation. They consulted old-timers, they observed, they tried and failed, they tried again and succeeded. They found that alfalfa roots kept down much of the blowing sand, that their soil and climate were adapted to peaches, apricots, figs, olives, grapes, sweet potatoes, nuts, feed grains, melons. They prospered enough to build houses and move their families out of the barns. They dug wells and erected windmills, the latter squeaking contentedly when the afternoon breeze finally sprang up. (Oh, blissful breeze!) They bought a few milk cows, a small flock of chickens, a plow, a harrow, a wagon, and a team of horses. Some of these horses had spent their best days on the streets of San Francisco as the city rebuilt herself after the earthquake of 1906; some others came bucking and snorting from the ranges of Nevada. Not first-class plow horses? Obviously not, but at any rate those gritty farmers managed to get their crops in with their help.

While the first farmers were sometimes confused about how to cope with the sand, the water, the wind, they could well have been confused about their address also, for the name of the post office kept changing. In the beginning, by stipulation between John T. Davis who owned the land and the railroad company which built the line, that name should be "Elmwood."[8] But the Post Office Department objected to this name, so it was changed to "Elmdale," although there was no dale in sight. Some time after December 1903 and before May 1904, the name became "Elms." On 14 July 1904 the name was changed again to "Elmwood." On 24 April 1907 the name was changed once more, this time to "Denair," and so it has since remained.[9] After repeated moves, the post office acquired its own building near the east end of Main Street in 1961.

The name Denair came from that of the promoter who formed the Denair Land and Development Company, buying up all available lots on the townsite as well as other land nearby. Denair was born in Germantown, Pennsylvania, and had served for a time during the Civil War as a member of Lincoln's bodyguard.[10] After the war he secured a job as messenger on an eastern railway. Later he went west and was a brakeman, then a conductor on the Southern Pacific. From that line he went to Albuquerque as superintendent of transportation on the Atlantic and Pacific. He then went to Needles, California, where he was division superintendent on the Santa Fe, successor to the Atlantic and Pacific. It is reasonable to suppose that he had inside knowledge that the Santa Fe was contemplating putting in a division headquarters in Stanislaus County and that he could win it for his colony. Denair's only son, Jack, was in the land company with his father.[11]

Although the Denair Land and Development Company failed, the settlement at Denair grew little by little. One by one, small businesses moved in to help supply the needs of the farm families. Of primary importance among them was the Tuolumne Lumber Company owned by Mr. Kewin of Modesto and operated by Clark Utterback. The yard was conveniently located beside the Santa Fe Railroad, adjacent to Main Street, at that time known as Alameda Avenue. Mr. Utterback, sometimes assisted by Glen Karnes, unloaded carload upon carload of pine boards, to reload the same onto waiting farm wagons. New, unpainted barns dotted the landscape.

The United Lumber Company later bought the lumber business and continued to serve the community. In 1953 the James Silvas of Turlock bought the business and changed the name to Denair Lumber Company.

Shelter is a basic need of man, and so is food. Consequently in 1903 the Crouch-Warner General Merchandise store was established. As the name implies, the merchants sold more than food. In 1904 Mr. Warner sold his interest in the store to Roy Crouch, and the sign over the door read, "Crouch Brothers'

General Merchandise." But the name was changed again when Norman Johnson, a cousin of the Crouches, came from Missouri and bought Earl Crouch's share of the business, Earl moved to Oakdale and the name of the store was changed to "Crouch-Johnson Mercantile Company," and so it remained until the business was discontinued in the early 1930s.[12]

The Bank Building, Denair.
Courtesy Mr. and Mrs. Merle Harmon.

Snider's Cyclery and the ice cream shop, Denair.
Courtesy Mr. and Mrs. Merle Harmon.

Various businesses came and went over the years. To encourage them to stay, a two-story, gray stucco building was constructed at the corner of San Joaquin and what is presently called Main Street in the summer of 1911. Over the main door one could read "Bank," in large letters. Thus that structure was dubbed "Bank Building," by which name it is known to this day. It did indeed house a bank, a branch of the Commercial Bank of Turlock. A. M. Morton was the sole employee.

A number of other businesses moved into the new building. There was the United States Post Office, Thake's Grocery Store, Martin's Meat Shop, Ludlow's Barber Shop with its single chair, also his Denair News Office and Print Shop, besides Atwood's Drug Store and a branch of the Stanislaus County Library. The second story, which was one large room, was used for community gatherings. Here the town wits entertained an appreciative audience with homemade doggerel and friendly insults. Here neighbors chatted and sang together.

In 1913 the Bank Building housed Denair's first high school. Turlock, the nearest high school, was four sandy miles away, an hour's drive by horse and buggy. Accordingly some partitions were built on the second floor to provide classrooms, and learning went forward with Lee C. Newby as principal.

More changes came to the Bank Building as time went on. The Commercial Bank moved its branch away, the post office and the various businesses moved out. The library and the high school moved to new quarters. But that did not mean that the Bank Building was unoccupied. Denair needed housing. More partitions were built upstairs, some remodeling was done downstairs, and the Bank Building became an apartment house, ugly, gray, shabby, with the title "Bank" gone from above the door. It has since provided temporary (or not so temporary) homes for newcomers, as hastily built barns had done for other newcomers sixty years earlier.

While the Bank Building was still new, in 1912, to be exact, young Stuart Snider set himself up in business across the street. He owned and operated Snider's Cyclery, for by that time every young blood longed for a motorcycle. Stuart himself demonstrated his prowess and startled the populace by driving his motorcycle "right down Alameda Avenue thirty miles an hour and looking backward." Needless to say, no other vehicle was traveling that sandy stretch at that moment.

About the same time Arthur Russell had a little shop on Alameda where he made ice cream in his ten-gallon freezer, selling his frozen sweet on hot afternoons. He repaired watches on the side.

J. J. Fairchild responded to the growing community's need by building and operating a hardware store in the weeds along Alameda Avenue. His family lived in an apartment upstairs. Eventually his store burned, and the Fairchilds moved away.

Among the firsts in Denair was Otto Abbott's garage on the corner of Alameda and San Joaquin. With the help of his family he sold gas and repaired automobile engines until his health failed.

During the years when businesses were moving out of the Bank Building new structures were built to accommodate them. Charles Pratt, who had bought Henry Thake's grocery store, built a new building on the next block and moved in. The Callahan family put up a small structure nearby, just big enough for the library and the post office. The library has never moved from that location.

From the beginning, the needs of the little town and of the surrounding farms influenced the founding of shops and of services and also their termination. By 1909 Henry Bowers was operating a creamery in Denair. After a few years he discontinued the service. About the same time a young man named Bill Caster did blacksmithing in a little shop. One smith or another hammered iron for his neighbors here until prefabricated parts and the welding torch made the forge and anvil obsolete. Roger's Truck Repair and Wood's Machinist Repair have taken the place of the blacksmith.

But care of the hair is never obsolete. In 1941 Oley Haile moved his barber shop into the new building on the corner of Main and San Joaquin. In a room adjacent to the barber shop Helen Moss (later Mrs. Thornton Snider) set up her shampoos and towels. In the thirty ensuing years other beauty parlors sprang up on converted front porches, but only two were in operation in 1971.

In the 1960s Denair had another spurt of growth. Contractor Bob Runyon started building a group of homes and a shopping center, Denair Village, immediately west of the Santa Fe tracks. This shopping center could house seven shops. In the older part of town, east of the Santa Fe tracks, one could find the post office, the county library branch, and ten other shops and services.

Man does not live by bread alone, and the farmers needed more than groceries, hardware and haircuts. They needed churches too. Eight churches were established in Denair since 1905. The first in point of time was the Christian Church, pastored by James N. Lester. The entire community joined in Sunday services in the schoolhouse. After the new school building was finished and the children moved into it, the Christian Church bought the little old schoolhouse, refurbished it and continued worship there. Much later, the property came to belong to the Church of Christ, which razed the old building in 1953 and erected one better suited to their growing needs.

Two other churches were organized in 1906 at about the same time. A number of families of the Society of Friends, commonly called Quakers, had moved to Elmwood in the hope of establishing a colony and a seminary. Fifteen families were charter members of the local society and erected their church building on the corner of Gratton and Zeering Roads, with William Mills as pastor.[13]

The other church was the Missionary Alliance, young Noah Witmer, pastor. Members of this church built their sanctuary at the corner of Sperry and Zeering in 1910. It still stands beside a more impressive new sanctuary, the old one serving now as an educational building.

Other churches moved in during later years. The Church of the Nazarene was first, with William Allen as the original pastor. Since 1933 the church has been located at the corner of Gratton and Walton. The Southern Baptists built a church at the corner of Main and Madera Streets. After they moved away, the Landmark Baptist Church took over the property in 1958. The Assembly of God under Fred Kirkwood perfected its organization in 1948 and built a handsome little church on the east side of Lester Road.

As the farmers around Denair prepared for the business of living, they did not forget that mankind must also die. Consequently they organized the Denair Cemetery Association in 1907 and bought approximately four acres of land at the corner of Zeering and Quincy Roads.[14] Since then some 650

Original Missionary Alliance Church, built 1910.
Courtesy Mr. and Mrs. Merle Harmon.

Hotel Denair, about 1910.
Courtesy Mr. and Mrs. Merle Harmon.

citizens have been buried there. As Helen Robertson Hornbeck was heard to remark on one Memorial Day as she looked about, "All the people I ever knew!"[15]

The more elemental matters of living and dying provided for, the growing community began organizing for other more sophisticated interests. In 1914 the farmers organized the Denair Branch of the Stanislaus County Farm Bureau. For years from 20 to 125 of them assembled monthly to hear talks by experts on growing crops, marketing them, protecting them from insects, blight, excessive water, and weeds. They listened to reports on the progress of construction of Don Pedro Dam and the accompanying power house (1922, 1923). They heard politicians electioneer and discussed farm-related politics. They ate uncounted dozens of doughnuts and drank gallons of steaming coffee. But at last, by 1971, with farmers fewer and distractions greater, the Denair Branch meets but seldom.[16]

The County Farm Bureau, centered in Modesto, is still active and mails to members a weekly news sheet carrying information of interest to farmers.

The sister organization of the Farm Bureau, the Home Department, was begun in Denair on 7 January 1922.[17] Like the men's branch of the Farm Bureau, the Home Department was well attended at first. But first the radio, then the television as well, poured out instruction on cooking, entertainment, home decoration, sewing, gardening. Thus it was that women learned at home as they worked, presumably. At any rate, attendance at Home Department meetings dwindled until the last remaining members disbanded in June 1963.

Another community organization is Gratton Grange #528, organized on 2 August 1933 with fifty charter members.[18] Throughout the years Gratton Grange has worked for the betterment of the community. Famous cooks among the members have served public dinners, the proceeds from which helped finance worthy projects, not the least of which was to provide scholarships for ambitious students. Mutual participation in work and in play has developed a high degree of loyalty among the members. In 1971 there were 118 active members. The Home Economics Department of the Grange, as the name implies, offers instruction in matters of homemaking. This branch of the Grange is still active, though it is now known as the California Women's Activities.

While all this activity was going on out in the country, the businessmen were not idle. A Board of Trade was formed on 22 November 1911. This became the Chamber of Commerce on 26 March 1923, with forty-five members. Glen Karnes was president at that time, and Roy Crouch was secretary. The Chamber has been active continuously since, sometimes more vigorously than others. An achievement of which the 125 members were proud was the remodeling and redecorating in 1971 of the Community Clubhouse.

Before the end of the first decade of this century the country folk enjoyed rural free delivery services. William H. Fowle was the first rural mail carrier. He traveled many miles daily by horse and buggy. In 1971 Denair had two rural routes: Route 1, more than 55 miles long and serving an estimated 153 persons; and Route 2, 45 miles long and serving an estimated 770 persons. With some 680 persons served in post office boxes, there were approximately 1603 inhabitants in the Denair postal area in 1970.[19]

Another community organization was born of dramatic need: fire, fire, breaking out in June along the road in dry weeds, spreading to standing barley, racing to ranch buildings. It was one of the ranchers' worst enemies, even before the turn of the century. After irrigation brought settlers with their makeshift dwellings, their cow sheds, their stacks of hay, the losses were compounded. To be sure, neighbors rushed to a fire and gave such help as they could, with such tools as came to hand.

Because these means were too often futile, the Denair men organized a volunteer fire department with one truck furnished by the Stanislaus County Mutual Insurance Company. They erected a fire house in May 1942. By 1959 Denair had become a legal fire district, operated on tax money. Since 1969 the fire trucks, now increased to five in number with another on order, have been housed in a new and larger fire house at the corner of Gratton and Zeering Roads, on land that was once a school playground. The firemen put out fires not only in their own district, but respond to calls from other fire departments upon occasion. Besides, they rush their resuscitator to the aid of a drowning victim or to a heart patient.[20]

There was one fire in Denair that must have astonished the whole town. It was the fire that consumed the warehouse. To know about the warehouse one must start back when Barley was King. The warehouse stood at the intersection of the Santa Fe Railroad track and the road now known as Main Street. To its door strings of mules hauled creaking wagons loaded with sacks of grain, where sweating men unloaded the barley and turned their teams, heading out again for another load. The Santa Fe trains, in turn, shipped the grain to distant markets. Though irrigation added other commodities to the piles of barley sacks so that additions had to be built, the warehouse still served as a community storage place until these crops could be sold.

The succession of owners coped with infestations of rats and weevils, and with business losses on account of trucks and paved roads. Then one foggy night in November of 1961 the old warehouse burned to the ground. Stealthy, it seemed, for the fog was so dense that few heard the fire whistle or saw the flames. It was never rebuilt. The Santa Fe Railroad, which owned the site, tore out the great cement foundation where the building had stood and leveled the ground. Like the "beautiful Village of Grande Pré" in Longfellow's poem, "naught but tradition remains" of the bustling, bulging warehouse that once stood along the Santa Fe tracks.

The people felt another need, less dramatic than fire fighting, but nonetheless real. It was the need to read. To satisfy this desire, a branch of the Stanislaus County Library was established in the office of Lee Newby, the high school principal, on 23 January 1913. Soon thereafter the library was moved to a room of its own on the first floor of the Bank Building, with Maude Hubbard as librarian. Since the 1950s the library has been located at 4609 Main Street. Seven women have served as librarian. Thousands of books have been issued to readers in the neighborhood during those 57 years.

As time went on and more people moved to Denair, other community organizations were formed. In April 1949 the Denair Lions Club was chartered, with twenty-eight original members. True to tradition, the Denair Lions have always responded to community needs, such as the loan of a hospital bed for the sick, supplying the temporary need of crutches, donating furniture or clothing in case of fire.[21]

There is change and adjustment, wherever people live, in Denair as elsewhere. When the inhabitants became unhappy enough about the dim street lights (which seemed so bright when they were first installed in 1923), the uncertain water system and the septic tanks that took care of the village sewage, they formed the Denair Community Service District in 1961. This district included not only the original Denair townsite, but also such surrounding territory as was served by street lights, thus approximately doubling the territory.

In the ten years that the Service District has been in existence, it has installed better lights, bought and improved the water system, dug a sewer system and connected it to Turlock's.[22]

The Service District finally purchased much of the School District property on Gratton and Zeering Roads. Here they erected the fire house mentioned above, installed a community well and water tank, and encouraged an amateur theater company to refurbish the school auditorium, all that was left of the abandoned elementary school building. That theater has been named the Golden Gaslight Theater. An amateur cast puts on performances throughout the year, a portion of their earnings going to the Service District.

The Denair Golden Gaslight Theater was used by several regional theatrical groups in the early 1970s. Browning photo.

More change. Once loading sheds along the Santa Fe Railroad at Zeering Road served peach and melon growers at shipping time. After paved roads, trucks, and melon blight changed farming practices, the sheds ceased to be used and were torn down.

Still more change. Better water, light and sewer systems encouraged home builders, happily so, as people continue to move to California to live. New housing developments appeared, both in Denair itself and on the fringes.[23]

So it was from the beginning of the little settlement of Elmwood to the present small town of Denair, when people needed homes, goods or services, they got them. If buildings or businesses lost their usefulness, they were eliminated; and better ones took their places. One need, however, Denair has not yet felt—the need of a saloon, either by the early settlers or by the present citizens. They get for themselves hardware stores, farm stores, food stores, clothing stores, garages and gas stations, furniture stores, laundromats, machine and welding shops, yes; but saloons, no. Not interested.

East of the Denair area lies all that remains of two wheat shipping communities, Hickman and Montpellier. Hickman still has a service station, several stores, a bar or two, and a quaint church where services are still held. The huge wheat warehouse stands by the old railroad right-of-way where the last passenger train ran in the 1920s, and the last freight train before World War II. About five miles south of Hickman is Montpellier. At one time it had three warehouses and two grain elevators, a dozen houses, a general store, depot, post office, and schoolhouse. The warehouses stand empty, only half of the houses survive, the store is no more, the post office was closed in 1937 and the territory annexed to the Denair School District in 1942. The schoolhouse is kept in repair, and a ladies' social organization, the Barmont Club, meets there several times a month.

The empire of wheat has gone, but with the development of sprinkler irrigation, the hillsides once covered with wheat, barley, or rye are now being planted to almonds and grapes. New ranch houses crown the hilltops, and families who measure their ancestral landholdings by the sections rather than by acres are entering a new era of prosperity.[24]

Jake Wassum, Sr., harvesting with huge steam tractor in the Hickman-Montpellier area about 1904. Courtesy Mrs. Fern Wassum.

One further matter should be noted—the story of Denair's War Memorial. In 1918 slim, blond, fleet George Rodman, who lived on the family dairy farm north of Denair, said goodbye to his parents and his sisters, joined the army and was shipped to France. Communications between commanding officers on a battlefield were carried by runners. When his commander had to send a message, he called for volunteers. George was one that stepped forward. So it was that George and two other lads sped across No Man's Land. George fell.

Eventually Mr. Rodman drew an envelope from his mail box. It had a wide black border and was addressed to "The Parents of Private George Rodman, 151 M.G. Bat., A.E.F." There was a long silence in the post office lobby where the elder Rodman stood alone, before his heavy footfalls announced that he had started home.[25]

The American Legion remembered. They planted a little pine tree near the intersection of Gratton Road and Main Street and placed a cement slab at its base. It reads:

Dedicated
to
Geo. A. Rodman
151 M. G. Bat. A. E. F.
by
Am. Legion
Post 88 and Auxiliary
May 30, 1937

His tree, now grown tall, still stands. Children have helped to beautify and keep the bit of ground around it.

At Denair nothing ends. It just changes.

History Of Hughson

Margaret Sturtevant

There was still a pioneer spirit in Central California in 1900 and new towns were not unusual. The men who founded the town of Hughson in 1907 probably dreamed that it might some day become an important and large city, for it did meet the first requirement of success: the presence of a railroad. In this instance it was the Atchison, Topeka and Santa Fe.

A second important factor was a hotel. Charles Flack and C. W. Minniear, the founders of Hughson, purchased the Gillette Hotel of Ceres and had it moved to Hughson in 1908. Not only did they believe that it would increase the prestige of Hughson but also that it would handicap Ceres to be without the hotel.

Moving hotel from Ceres to Hughson. Note the two steam tractors and a dozen span of mules. Courtesy Margaret Sturtevant.

A third factor was abundant irrigation water from the Turlock Irrigation District. After fourteen long years of paying district taxes, bringing teams and scrapers to work on the ditches, of argument and frustration, water had reached the Hughson area in 1901. This was the essential economic foundation for truck gardens and dairies, orchards and vineyards.

The writer of the 1912 Hughson Board of Trade folder proclaimed that this area

> was in the midst of good surroundings, where the people are law abiding, where there is fine soil, a good market, excellent transportation facilities, a mild summer and winter climate, fine schools, churches, up-to-date stores, and other advantages of a splendid community. . .an empire in the making. . . .Hughson has the best location for a splendid little city of any in the country. Drainage is excellent, the water is soft and of the purest, and the mountains in the distance add to the beauty of the scene. The climate is well nigh perfect. The summers are long, dry, bracing and it is never too hot to work in the fields during the middle of the summer. . . .Our rains come in the winter, and few people use more than one ton of coal during the wet weather. . . .Our peaches are as perfect as can be produced, with a delicate flavor and large size which makes them sought for in

Once relocated, the hotel in its time played many parts. Photo 1968 by David Griffith, courtesy of Margaret Sturtevant.

all markets wherever shown. The Turlock Irrigation District contains the finest soil the sun shines upon. When the land is irrigated its production is little short of marvelous.

The first settlers in the Hughson area were James M. Hudelson, a brother Will (William F.), and a sister Sarah Browder, wife of William Browder. They moved to this area in 1851 and over some years purchased about 2500 acres of land on the south bank of the Tuolumne River. Most of it was south and east of the present Tuolumne River bridge on Geer Road.

In 1876 John Fox bought 560 acres of James Hudelson; in 1900 Thomas Alonzo Owen bought 160 acres of Will Hudelson. Sarah Browder's daughter married Albert Crow and the Browder property became known as the Crow ranch. Parts of it were sold at various times. The last 160 acres were bought in 1935 by Warren Hudelson, grandson of James Hudelson.[26] In 1892 Forrest Hudelson, James' son, purchased 240 acres north of Whitmore and west of Tully Road from James W. Stetson. There were descendants of the Hudelson, Fox and Owen families still living in Hughson in 1971.

Starting in 1887 Nathaniel L. Tomlinson purchased and leased a total of 6000 acres, including some property owned by Hiram Hughson. Mr. Tomlinson harvested the last crop on the land which became the townsite of Hughson in 1907. His sons, Everett and Arthur, continued to farm the family ranch on the corner of Service and Berkeley Roads.

About 1880 Charles E. Sperry bought land on the extreme southeastern part of the Hughson area. A son and daughter, William E. Sperry and Florence Sperry Sorenson, still lived near the site of the original family home on Sperry Road in 1971.

In October 1887, Daniel Baldwin bought 160 acres west of Hughson between Hatch and Whitmore Roads from A. E. and Mary Stetson Cowles for $6400 "in gold coin." In 1971 his grandson Edgar was living on this Baldwin Road ranch.

Schools were the first community institutions established. They have always played an important role in the life of Hughson. In the last half of the nineteenth century the Hudelson family and the few others living in this area attended school on the river bluff, probably east of Waring Road on the property that was later Frank Zambruno's.

There was also a little school in the middle of Hiram Hughson's grain field, about where Hughson Avenue and Charles Street now intersect. This burned down. Since Hughson did not want the school on his property, the next one was built at Tully and Whitmore Roads. This one also burned in 1892 when a defective stovepipe broke and ignited the ceiling. The new one-room school with its little belfry was built on land that Forrest Hudelson bought that year from James W. Stetson. While it was being constructed the students attended classes in the Hudelson home. All these early schools were in the Empire School District, named after the original Empire City which was located on the south bank of the Tuolumne.

Gradually the one-room school was enlarged; in 1903 a second room was added. In 1909 a four-room wooden structure was built on the northeast corner of Charles and Whitmore, and the old building on Tully became the high school, except for one year when high school classes were held in part of the new grammar school. During World War I the fifth through eighth grades were housed in "chicken coops" which were canvas-sided buildings with big pot-bellied stoves in the middle.

The town continued to grow. In 1925 a lovely new brick elementary school was built on Whitmore for $60,000. This was torn down in 1955, as was the wooden building. A new high school was built in 1920-21 on the corner of Seventh and Whitmore. This in turn was replaced in 1966 with a new building. In 1958 an office and classrooms were constructed on the campus.

A high school auditorium had been constructed in 1925. At that time the trustees were convinced that dancing was very sinful and they were not going to allow the students to be corrupted. They, therefore, had the cement floor slanted and also had the seats bolted to it, so there was no possibility of ever having any dancing. The building was planned to include a balcony, but there were insufficient funds to put it in. As a result the acoustics were so poor that the sound died before it reached the back wall. The building was limited in its use and was torn down in the·1950s.

In the years following World War II, two new elementary schools were built on Fox Road to handle the increased student population. They were named after two long-time teachers. The (Mattie) Lebright School was built in 1948 and the Emilie J. Ross School in 1962.

Before the town of Hughson was established there was at least one church in the vicinity. Services were held in the schoolhouse on Tully Road until 1906. In that year the Methodists, with the help of the Seventh Day Adventists, built their sanctuary on the southwest corner of Tully and Whitmore. This building was later moved to the corner of Second and Locust. In 1966 the Methodists built again, this time on Fox between Fifth and Sixth, and sold their former church to the Missionary Baptists.

The Seventh Day Adventists worshiped in the Methodist Church until 1908 when their own edifice on the southeast corner of Fifth and Locust was completed. For a number of years the Adventists shared their building with the First Baptists. In 1914 the Baptists constructed their own sanctuary on the northeast corner of Sixth and Pine. In 1962 the Adventist congregation moved to Ceres and the building was sold to the Primitive Baptists.

Up to 1921 Catholic services were held above Northway's store on Hughson Avenue, next to the Bank of Hughson. St. Anthony's Catholic Church was built on the south side of Whitmore in 1921 and was used until 1967 when the members moved to their new building on Euclid and Fox. Their former church was taken over by the United Pentecostal congregation.

In the early years there was apparently a friendly rivalry among the Baptists, Methodists and Seventh Day Adventists. They also respected each other's observances. For instance, school plays were not given on Friday evenings because that was the beginning of the Adventists' sabbath.

Other churches in Hughson in 1971 were an Assembly of God on the southwest corner of Fifth and Fox; a Free Will Baptist Church on Charles south of Whitmore; a Pentecostal Church of God on the southwest corner of Hughson and Second; and the Church of the Nazarene on the northeast corner of Seventh and Fox.

Community income has come almost entirely from agriculture and related businesses. This was originally cattle country which was later planted to wheat. The land was rolling and quite uneven. Stories are told that the harvesters and other equipment could go out in the field for a very short distance and completely disappear from sight when they reached a low spot. Irrigation changed this: the land was leveled and it was possible to have alfalfa and dairies, then vegetables and fruit. The dairies remained fairly stable but the story of the peach orchards is quite different.

Shipping melons from Hughson in 1915 or 1916. Courtesy Margaret Sturtevant.

There were a number of small acreages planted to peaches prior to and during the first World War. Much of the fruit was shipped fresh to nearby markets or hauled to the Pratt-Low cannery in Modesto and also to the Hume cannery in Turlock. Most of the peach trees, both clings and freestones, were planted during the 1920s. As plantings increased, the number of canneries increased accordingly.

Some of the peaches, particularly the Lovells and Muirs, made fine dried fruit. The dry yards with their cutting sheds provided ample summer work for students and women in the area. One of the best known cutting sheds in Hughson was the one owned by William Carson, Sr. The original site was north of Hatch Road on Santa Fe; it was later moved farther east. The days of dry yards ended about 1940 when fruit began to be dehydrated mechanically.

Because of the war there was a great need for dried fruits of all kinds. In 1943 Evan Hughes built a dehydrator on his property on Santa Fe Road. In 1944 about 65 tons of peaches were processed each day. In addition, approximately 400 tons of raisins were delivered each year to the government. The dehydrator ceased operating in 1949 or 1950.

Mr. Hughes' fruit terminal, which had started the same year and on the same property as the dehydrator, was expanded until there were docks for thirty canners and freezers at one time. In the 1945 season the terminal handled 30,000 tons of fruit, which was the greatest volume of any shipping point in California for that year. The *Hughson Chronicle* for 4 March 1946 quoted Evan Hughes as saying, "We not only shipped the most peaches, but we shipped the world's best." Local farmers proudly claimed that Hughson was the peach bowl of the world. Such a record was far exceeded in later years when as many as 95,000 tons of fruit were delivered to Hughes' docks.

In the early days most of the labor for the ranches came from local residents. There were a number of single men who lived in the hotel or in rooms above the stores; others lived on the ranches and worked year around in the fields and orchards. As the peach acreage increased during the 1930s there was a need for greater numbers of workers. Farm families in the Midwest were suffering from the drought, so many of them came West to help harvest the crops. Gradually some found more permanent jobs and settled locally. Others returned to the Midwest to stay, so that by the 1950s the harvest labor problem was again crucial. Busloads of people were brought down from the San Francisco Bay area, but since many of them were picked up from skid row, they were generally not satisfactory.

The farmers thought they had the answer with the bracero program that was developed during World War II. Workers were brought from Mexico for the harvest, housed and fed, and then returned to Mexico when the harvest was over. Permanent residents in the area objected and said they were losing their jobs to the braceros, so this program was ended in 1964.

Some Mexicans continued to enter legally on work permits, but others, attracted by the high wages, entered illegally. These were called "wetbacks" because they were supposed to have swum the Rio Grande. Instead of coming just for the harvest, they frequently stayed all year—or at least until they were caught and returned to Mexico by the Border Patrol. Unlike the braceros whose contracts were supervised by the federal government, these later comers often did not have adequate housing and food; there were increasing numbers of complaints that they took work away from those who lived legally in the area. Up to 1972 a satisfactory solution to the labor problem had not been found.

One answer to the farm labor shortage was the increased mechanization of orchard and harvesting equipment so that fewer workers were needed. However, peach production had become so expensive by the end of the 1960s, there were so many problems in connection with labor, crop surpluses, weather and insect damage, that few peach growers were left who were not planting at least part of their land to other crops, particularly nuts and grapes. Some were working at other jobs so they could afford to live on a ranch.

The number of businesses in Hughson remained about the same from the early days to 1971. Only a few remained in the same buildings, however, since some of the early wooden structures burned and others were torn down. The livery stables went, and with them the watering trough that stood in the middle of the intersection of Hughson Avenue and Charles. The merchandise in the stores changed to keep up with the times but continued to meet the same common needs. For a brief period there were automobile and tractor dealers in Hughson, but when it became easier to travel longer distances, people went to the larger cities to shop for major purchases.

The merchants worked very hard to keep the shopper in Hughson. Starting in 1915 and continuing until sound movies came in, the stores remained open on summer Saturday evenings, and free outdoor silent movies were shown. The film was projected on the wall of the Kennedy (Pedreira) building. This provided entertainment for the community for a number of years. Previously Mr. Date had shown movies for a small charge upstairs in the annex of Hotel Hughson.

Hotel Hughson was for years the center of Hughson's social and business life. It had been cut in half in 1908 and moved from Ceres to Hughson, where it was jacked up and an additional floor placed beneath the others; an annex was added in 1912. Among the guests were drummers (traveling salesmen), teachers, and farm workers. J. V. Date managed the hotel for a few years; he then branched out to other businesses. He was very active in civic enterprises and was sometimes called the "unofficial" mayor of Hughson.

The number of occupants declined so there was no longer need for a hotel in Hughson. It was purchased by the Odd Fellows in 1934 and was used thereafter for lodge activities. The first floor was rented to various businesses, and housed the town library. For a long time the doctors' offices were there.

The first major industry was the Hughson Condensed Milk Company, later called Dairymaid Creameries. It was built in 1911, but got on its feet only after H. W. Low bought it in 1912. In 1942 he sold out to Marin Dell Company. Ten years later it became part of the Foremost Company. In 1971 it was processing powdered skim milk, anhydrous fat, bulk butter and some ice cream mixes. Over the years it has done an unusually large volume of business.

A sorghum mill was started in 1919 by E. F. Sawdey and others. It was located across from Hudelson's on the northeast corner of Tully and Whitmore. The cane grown in this area was of high quality and the syrup was very good, but the prices paid were not sufficient to make it worthwhile. After a couple of years it had to shut down.

The railroad was extremely important to the community until automobiles became common. Besides being used for shipping products, it brought the mail several times a day and transported passengers. People would get on the Santa Fe in Hughson, go to Empire and board the Modesto and Empire Traction Company's motor car to go to Modesto. They would do their shopping, go to the dentist or perhaps the circus, and return to Hughson the same way. There were seven possible stops in the five miles between Empire and Modesto and in 1915 it took about twenty minutes to go that distance. Hughson residents also went to Oakdale by way of Riverbank, where they changed to the Southern Pacific. Sometimes they would drive their buggies to Hickman and take the train on the eastside SP line to Oakdale from that point.

Originally the railway depot in Hughson was a little shack, then a boxcar was used, and in 1909 a depot was built. This was torn down in the early 1960s, and thus ended the relationship of Hughson and its railroad.

There was a great deal of community cooperation in Hughson and its different organizations worked well together. There were just a few hundred people in town for many years and almost everyone participated in the parades, Fourth of July picnics down at Fox's Grove by the Tuolumne and other community events. The farmers regularly helped each other during the harvest and in emergencies and they were used to working together. When anyone was going to Modesto, he would send his children around the neighborhood to see if he could buy supplies for others who might need them.

During the Depression of the 1930s there was an effective welfare committee which was praised by the county chairman, C. H. Ramont. He "commended the committee for the efficient manner in which they had carried on. Hughson was the only community in the county that was wholly self-sustaining and did not call on the county for assistance."[27] This welfare committee was the forerunner of the Hughson Community Emergency Fund established in the late 1960s.

Each May of the years 1939, 1940 and 1941 a "Peaches and Cream Festival" was held. These followed the pattern of early times when "Hughson Days" were also held in May. In 1939 the Festival program included a 4-H Club clothing exhibit and fashion parade, a 4-H livestock show, a drum and bugle corps drill, a picnic dinner, a coronation ceremony,[28] a dance program, music and speeches. There was a softball game between the peach growers and the dairymen, and a playday for youngsters. At 9 p.m. there was a festival ball with a grand march led by the queen, her attendants and escorts.

Each year the Stanislaus County Farm Bureau held its annual picnic, 4-H Club fair, and fashion show in conjunction with the Hughson Peaches and Cream Festival. Claude Nation, Festival chairman, reported that 4000 people attended. United States involvement in World War II ended the festivals.

Hughson's "golden age" was probably in the 1940s, just after World War II. The servicemen returned home, many times bringing with them young wives from other parts of the country. The Lions Club had just been organized and was a very active group. There was a great deal of enthusiasm in all the local clubs.

One of the most ambitious projects undertaken was the building of the community swimming pool in 1947 and the consequent formation of the Hughson Youth Center. Thousands of young people

Elevator and abandoned wheat warehouse at Montpellier. Caswell photo.

and some adults, too, learned to swim there. Nearby communities brought their children for swimming lessons. The money for the pool was all raised locally. A three-day carnival was organized by the towns-people which netted almost $7000. Part of this money came from "bonds" which were sold for $25 each. There was also a big scrap iron drive as well as other money-raising projects.

In addition to building the swimming pool, the Hughson Sanitary District was formed and bonds were sold to construct the sewer system. Plans for a 30-bed hospital in Hughson were completed and incorporation papers drawn up when the Memorial Hospital project in Ceres took precedence.

It seemed there was no project that was too big to tackle. People were not yet in the habit of having the government do everything for them. They knew that if anything was to be done, they themselves had to furnish the manpower, the time and the money. Great things were accomplished.

During this same period there was an adult softball league in which almost all the organizations in town entered a team. The community supported this summer recreation program most wholeheartedly. Money was raised for lights for the baseball field. After Dr. Glen Sweeley had a heart attack and died while playing in one of the games, the community named the field in his honor.

In 1950 the California Young Farmers started their annual Hughson Tractor Rodeo and Implement Show, the first of its kind in the Central Valley. Since then other towns have had similar shows.

In response to a county-wide need a Community Family Planning Clinic, the first in the county, was established in 1969. It was held two nights a month at first; and after one year, on a weekly basis.

From very early days there was occasional talk of incorporation. Homer Newberry mentioned this in his "History of Hughson."[29] In the past there was not sufficient interest to carry it through. There is currently (1971) a revival of enthusiasm which may be strong enough for it to pass.

Almost all of the people in Hughson have been of European stock. The Portuguese, most of whom were from the Azores, were very early residents and have been dairymen for the most part. There are also many Italians and Swiss in the fruit business. There have been a few Oriental families from time to time, and occasionally a Negro family.

In recent years many Mexican people settled in Hughson. They started as farm laborers. As they became more fluent in English they gradually found other kinds of work and some were able to buy their own homes. The first Mexican-owned business in Hughson was Fortuna's Tortilla Factory on Hughson Avenue. One result of the Mexican influx has been that ranchers and businessmen have learned to speak Spanish so that they might communicate better with the growing number of Mexican people in the community.

Nels O. Hultberg, founder of
the Swedish colony of Hilmar.
Courtesy Albia Hultberg Erickson.

Chapter XIX

Hilmar and Delhi: a Church Colony and a State Colony

Hilmar and Delhi, neighboring agricultural communities, were established in 1902 and 1906, respectively. The nucleus of the Hilmar colony was a group of settlers belonging to the Swedish Missionary Alliance. The Delhi colony took on its distinctive character after 1920, when a State Land Settlement was opened.

Both colonies went through trying times before they became solidly established. The reader may find it of interest to compare them as to agricultural experience of the settlers, harmony within the colony, methods of finance, and eventual success. We have sought to avoid belaboring the comparisons in the hope that the reader will make his own.

Development of Hilmar and Irwin

John E. Caswell

How Nels Hultberg established the Hilmar Colony has been recounted in an earlier chapter. The colony remained solidly Swedish for only a few years. Soon Portuguese farmers began to come into the colony. At the same time some of the Swedes moved into town to ply their trades. Hard-working Portuguese dairymen bought their ranches.[1] On Johnson Avenue alone, twelve houses were soon built by the Portuguese.

Harry Johnson recalled that when the boys in Hilmar High wanted to play baseball, it was easy to choose up sides—it was the Portuguese against the Swedes. Despite racial and religious differences, each respected the scrupulous honesty of the other. Clarence Ahlem agreed that the two nationalities got along fine.[2]

In 1907 a more diverse element entered the community when W. A. Irwin began promoting a townsite on Lander Road just south of a TID lateral canal, a little over a mile southeast of the center of the original Hilmar Colony at Tegner Road and American Avenue. He named the site Irwin City and launched an electric interurban project to connect Turlock and his new town. The project never developed.[3]

Several years afterwards the Tidewater Southern Railroad proposed to run its line through Irwin to Fresno. However, the people of Irwin refused to grant a right-of-way, so Tidewater Southern encouraged the development of a site to the north.[4] B. T. Cowgill and Tom Petigo surveyed and gained Merced County's approval for the "Townsite of Hilmar" north of Irwin on Lander Avenue.[5] In 1918 the Tidewater Southern reached Hilmar. Electrified as far as Modesto, steam locomotives were used on the twenty-mile stretch to Hilmar. At the height of operations there was only one train a day, consisting of two or three freight cars. The rise of trucking in the 1920s cut into the railway business.[6] On 20 August 1953 the freight service was eliminated, and on 15 July 1954 the tracks were removed south of West Harding Road.[7]

About 1914 several small businesses were built along Lander in Irwin. Hochleitner's blacksmith shop arose where the Elim Unified School stands; a lumber yard and a hardware store were also established. Later Hilmar and Irwin had a garage, a drugstore and several other stores, a bank and warehouses. A cannery operated for a short time.[8]

A flurry of excitement over oil occurred in 1916 or 1917. The first well was drilled on the Stattler Ranch; there were the usual rumors of striking a gusher and plugging it. Three other wells were drilled but produced nothing.[9]

Public utilities came to Hilmar in rather haphazard fashion over a period of fifty years. The San Joaquin Light and Power Company was the first to enter the area. In 1921 the Hilmar Lighting District was established to furnish street lighting. The Turlock Irrigation District entered the colony from the north and offered domestic electricity at about half the price of SJL&P's power. To avoid costly competition, an election was held and the colony voted in the ratio of 25 to 1 for TID power. The Merced River was made the dividing line between the two systems.[10]

Water was first distributed from a wooden tank built by B. T. Cowgill. After he left town, seven families took over the system and eventually made an operating agreement with TID. About 1967 a water and sewage disposal district was organized to take over the water supply. In 1971 it was decided to develop a sewage disposal system as well.[11]

Although much of Hilmar's social life centered in its churches, the Hilmar Concert Band was an exception. Organized in 1905 with about twenty-five members, the group was directed by Earl Mauer of Turlock. A practice session was held weekly in the Irwin town hall. Each member purchased his own green and gold uniform. Outdoor concerts were given weekly in the summer for a number of years.[13]

The formation of six school districts in the Hilmar area and the consolidation of the North and South Elim Schools in 1908 were discussed in the story of the coming of the Swedes. The union school was located in Irwin. It was a two-story building with a single flight of stairs. The elementary grades had the first floor and Hilmar High had the second floor down to 1918, when the high school was given its own building. By the 1930s the fire danger inherent in the elementary school's design was recognized and it was condemned; a new elementary school was built in 1936, and four rooms were added later.

In 1947, when the "Little Hilmar" district found it difficult to retain teachers, a consolidation agreement was made with the Elim district. Two years later, a school unification election led to the elimination of the Hilmar, Prairie Flower Joint, and Fairview elementary districts with their little two-room schools. Residents of the Riverside district objected so strongly that their building was retained for the first and second grades until it burned and the insurance money was used to build two more rooms at Elim.

Shortly after unification, Mrs. Ruth Larson became teaching principal at Elim and served over twenty years until her retirement in 1970. Said Mrs. Larson of the community, "The people are really and truly interested in their children and want to cooperate in every way possible. If there was a problem, all one needed was to "talk to the parents and it was settled." As a unified district, by 1970 Elim had been able to obtain and administer several special programs. These included a class for the mentally retarded, one for the emotionally or neurologically handicapped, and a special reading program. A speech correction teacher came in one and a half days a week, and a psychologist was available through the county schools office.[14]

Elim Union Elementary School with original school buses. Courtesy Mrs. Grace V. Watrous.

In the early 1940s the first generation of Swedish settlers of Hilmar began to die off and their farms were sold to Portuguese and Greeks.[15] After the war most of the people who lived in Hilmar town either worked on a nearby ranch or in a neighboring community like Turlock, or were retired.

During the seventh decade of Hilmar's history the community grew about 20 percent in population, from 4,097 to 4,888.[16] It had several fine dairies. Although the trip to Turlock's stores had become a matter of ten minutes rather than a day's pilgrimage by buggy, several new stores were opened, and older ones received a face-lifting. Among the new businesses were a lumber yard where the Tidewater-Southern track terminated, a beauty parlor, a small "department" store, and similar retail and service industries. For a time both Hilmar and Irwin had post offices only a few hundred yards apart, but the Irwin post office was closed, leaving the name Hilmar on the books.[17]

Hilmar, unlike many crossroads communities, was far from extinction. Community loyalties could center on the elementary and high schools. The churches continued to command the support of the community. The annual smörgasbord prepared by the Hilmar Covenant Church was an event that attracted many from neighboring towns. Even the cemetery and water district proclaimed Hilmar's individuality. Many families had lived there for over a half-century. So long as members of these families, Swedish or Portuguese, continued to operate their own farms, it appeared that both the town and the larger community would continue to survive.

Early Delhi

Henry T. Schendel

There is something about our "early Delhi" that invites our imaginations to run wild. Did any white man see the Merced River before Lt. Gabriel Moraga, who named it *El Rio de Nuestra Señora de la Merced* in 1806?

There were many flowers in spring and early summer. California poppies, hundreds of acres of them, bloomed as they did all over California. Light colored buttercups; a deep colored, almost orange flower that looked much like a buttercup; and wild pure white primroses were scattered all over the area. A light blue flower about six inches high, with five or six petals, and perhaps an inch in diameter. In some secluded spots baby blue eyes and a few bluebells grew. The whole area was one vast carpet of color, a picture never to be forgotten by this writer.

Along the Merced River during the days of the early settlers there was much evidence of Indian camps, fire-scorched trees, and small fireplaces ringed with stones. There was a sandblow west of Delhi where the grass over the ages had encroached on the sand and then had been covered by sand until there were some mounds six or seven feet high and fifty feet in diameter. Among these the grass grew quite rank, making a rather nice campground for the natives. Many fire pits could still be seen. Small mounds of sand held the carcasses of rabbits, squirrels, and magpies with the yellow bills still in evidence. Sea shells of several kinds and sizes, many arrowheads and some large pieces of flinty material that might have been used for chopping. Sticks with pointed ends that could have been used for digging.

When the Central Pacific ran its line through John W. Mitchell's property in 1871, he built a siding and warehouse a little north of the center of his holdings and called it Delhi. As elsewhere, Mr. Mitchell built houses and barns for his tenants. These houses were made of rough redwood, nearly all on the same pattern. The ordinary home had four rooms on the lower floor: two bedrooms, dining-living room, and kitchen with pantry. Upstairs was a loft for the help to sleep in. Back of the house were a well with a hand pump and a long barn, used for feeding and stabling the work stock. Off to the side about 300 feet was a second barn for hay and grain storage.

Mitchell tenant house, the Delhi "white house," about 1910. Courtesy Henry T. Schendel.

A typical house was built at the Delhi Station. Another ranch house was on the Merced River south of Delhi. This, we were told, had been at times a hideout for the Dalton brothers and later for the holdup men, Evans and Sonntag. The Weaver home was located on Letteau Avenue about a quarter of a mile west of Merced Avenue and several hundred yards north. In 1907 this house was surrounded by a swamp, the only standing water in the Delhi area.

The "Waite" ranch on the corner of Lombardy and Sycamore had a large shop building and blacksmith shop in addition to the other buildings. The Hinksons' home, also on this model, stood east of Cortez Avenue. This was the only family still farming when a new wave of settlement began around 1907.

Methods of grain farming described in Chapter III were essentially unchanged in 1907. After 1910 gasoline engines were placed on the harvesters and a few years later tractors were used to pull them.

After the death of John W. Mitchell, the Fin de Siecle Investment Company managed his estate and pastured sheep and cattle in the area. A large sheep shearing barn was built about a quarter of a mile east of Delhi and a bit north of El Capitan Way. This was a large structure, perhaps sixteen feet high.

The sheep were driven into small pens, sheared by hand, the wool gathered into a ball and packed into a jute bag about eight feet long and perhaps four feet in diameter. The balls of wool were tossed into the bag. After a bit of wool had been thrown in, a man would jump into the bag and begin to tramp the wool down while others would throw in the wool balls. When the bag was tramped and full, it was sewn up and rolled into a heap to be hauled to market.

This whole area was covered by a wild "needle" grass, so-called because the seed pod had a needle-sharp point and serrated sides. This pod would work its way into the wool of the sheep or long hair of the stock and into the mouths of the animals eating the ripened grass. It would get into the clothing and was almost impossible to pull out. One pushed it through and took it out the back side. The grass was very good feed until it got ripe.

In places where there was more moisture "alfillaree" grew. It looked somewhat like alfalfa and many times was cut, put up, and fed like hay. On the west side of the railroad there was a weed that might grow from three to seven feet tall. Because of its bushy tail it was called "cow tail." A woolly weed about a foot high we called "sheep weed" for the same reason. These soon disappeared for they could not stand irrigation or cultivation. Tumbleweeds grew in large balls. In the fall the wind would uproot them and blow them across the fields. Russian thistle was brought in later. There were other small weeds, most of which are still present. The blue lupin was considered more of a flower than a pest.

In 1904 or 1905 J. K. Mills and Edgar M. Wilson of San Francisco bought 8,000 acres in the area surrounding Delhi from the Fin de Siecle Company. Later that year a syndicate was formed that included Mills and Wilson, a Mr. Seagraves, and a Mr. Black. Somehow Mr. Ed Shanks and Mr. G. H. Letteau were interested in the project. This syndicate purchased additional land from Fin de Siecle until they had a total of 23,000 acres. The land lay in roughly a triangle, following the bluffs north of Merced River to a point a quarter of a mile east of Golf Road, then northward to Letteau Avenue, where the boundary went eastward with several northward jogs to a point about in line with Sycamore Avenue and a mile east of Ballico, where it turned southward to the Merced River. The land was surveyed, and an area of several thousand acres where the railroad crossed the northern boundary was assigned to Ed Shanks as "Shanks Delhi Tract."

In the summer of 1906 George Schendel came from southern California, moved to Turlock and became the agent for "Shanks Delhi Tract." He purchased 160 acres himself. In January 1907 the Schendels built on their acreage a storage building to be used for living quarters until a house could be built, together with a lean-to barn. The George Schendels' building was the first new structure built in "New Delhi." The Andrew Schendel family arrived from Kansas in the fall, took up 80 acres, and built a house. Others who moved in during 1907 were John McCarty, Chilton Wilson, the Duffields, the Nortons, and the brothers Frank and Ted Cooney.

The main problem was the lack of water. TID had finished its No. 6 Lateral, and in the winter of 1907-1908 the Schendel community ditch was begun with the help of the Cooneys and McCarty. The ditch was nearly completed when a March wind almost blew it down. The ditch was rebuilt, a short section at a time, and covered with weeds to protect it from the winds.

The settlers planted orchards and small vineyards, but after watching the rabbits feeding on the bark, they found it necessary to protect the trunks with a cover of sorts. Alfalfa was covered to protect it from the windstorms, mostly with weeds. When irrigation was begun, the water seemed to find all the squirrel dens and disappear. This probably drowned the squirrels, but the water had to be rerouted and the holes filled before irrigation could be resumed.

The first crops were a bit of alfalfa, barley and some Egyptian corn which resembled milo. Potatoes were planted on sub-irrigated land on the long abandoned Weaver ranch. This proved to be an excellent crop, but the market was poor.

During the spring and summer of 1908 about eight additional households moved into the area, including the Leedoms and the Ratzlaffs. Nearly all these families came too late to put in crops for 1908, but they put up their buildings and were ready for the fall plowing.

More families came in 1909, including the Francis Fiorini family. This family lived in tents until a small house was built on their 320-acre ranch. The next year the house was enlarged and they began

Sitting on the break.

dry farming as ditches had as yet not been dug. Samuel Rixey and his family moved into the "old Delhi house" built by John Mitchell. This family was from San Francisco. When they had been there only a few months, they applied for a post office, which was granted on 18 June 1909. Theretofore everyone had gone to Turlock for his mail.

The settlers of 1907 came too late in the fall for arrangements to be made for schools, so that year's schooling, such as it was, had to be at the kitchen table. The west side of the Delhi community belonged to the Elim District, which provided a school bus in 1908-1909. The bus, said to be the first school bus in the United States, was a farm wagon with a row of seats on each side and a bow top covered with canvas to keep the wind, sand and rain off. Leaving Delhi at 7:30, the driver would take the children to Elim Elementary School in Irwin City, farm during the day, then deliver the children home in the afternoon. He would camp in the McCarty barn at night and repeat the process the next day. There were nine children from Delhi and seven or eight others to be picked up farther along.

In 1909-1910 the Elim District provided the material, equipment, and a teacher for a school in the Delhi area. The parents removed the partitions between the two bedrooms in the "old Delhi house" which the Rixeys occupied. Somewhere a heating stove was found, and the Delhi school was on its way. The teacher's name was Mrs. Grace Watrous of Hughson. She taught all eight grades. About seventeen children were in attendance. During the year the Delhi School District was formed from portions of the Elim District, the Johnson District to the northwest, and the Madison District to the northeast of Delhi.

The next year the arrangement was the same, but the teacher, Mrs. Margaret Schattenberg, each day drove a little black pony hitched to a two-wheeled cart from Turlock. The first two graduates from the Delhi school were Henry Schendel and Tinley Leedom. During the year a bond election was set for a new school. Edgar Wilson insisted on no less than a four-room school. As he would pay 90 percent of the taxes, he contended that he should specify the size.

The new school was completed in time for the year 1913-1914. Much grading and landscaping was yet to be done; while a tank house provided running water, outdoor sanitary facilities were still the rule. The next year enrollment had gone up, so it was necessary to have two teachers. This was pretty much the arrangement until the State Land Settlement was established at Delhi in 1920.

Meanwhile, there were many obstacles to overcome, as in every new community. There were only trails wandering from here to there. The only bridge across No. 6 Canal was on the road paralleling the railroad. At other places the canal had to be forded.

Perhaps the first pests to be encountered were the ground squirrels. Hundreds of colonies with up to forty or fifty holes apiece were scattered all over the area from the sandblow to Ballico. These pests would denude their neighborhood of everything edible. The abandoned holes harbored rattlesnakes by the dozen. Farmers tried to poison the squirrels with grain, but this did not help much. The most successful method seemed to be bisulfide of carbon gas, but it took years. A bit of the liquid was applied to a small lint ball which was rolled into the center holes of the dens.

The rattlesnakes probably lived on squirrels and field mice. The brothers Henry and Dave Schendel saved the rattles from 350 that they killed in one year. The Schendels' turkeys would locate the rattlers, making it easy to destroy them. Sheep were pastured all over the territory east of the railroad. The rattlers would strike at the sheep, get their fangs caught in the wool, and be dragged to death or killed by the sheep's sharp hooves. The snakes did not harm the sheep as they could not strike through the wool.

Grasshoppers! These pests would swarm into a green field by the thousands. They ranged from big, green ones three inches long to rather yellowish ones an inch long. They could eat a swath around an alfalfa or corn field in a few days. The best method of controlling them seemed to be to burn an area around each farm where the grass might harbor them. This not only destroyed many of the pests but also their potential for another year.

Jack rabbits! There were thousands of these pests that could ruin a field in a little while. Three professional hunters used a buckboard drawn by a horse or mule. The men would stand in the buggy and could kill from forty-five to sixty rabbits a day. The rabbits were semi-dressed, packed about a dozen to the sack, and shipped by train to San Francisco markets. In 1915 the community organized a rabbit drive. A large pen was installed and a circle of men from nearby communities started to march toward this pen driving the rabbits ahead of them. The first year over 600 rabbits were taken. The next year shotguns were used, and 2,300 rabbits were netted and sent to market. The next few drives reduced them to a reasonable number.

Coyotes were really no problem, as they helped to reduce the squirrel and rabbit population. The loss of a few chickens was a small price to pay for the pests they destroyed.

Windstorms were much of a problem unless a crop could be planted in the fall, which was not always possible. Alfalfa borders and ditch banks would disappear during a windstorm. Farmers soon learned to cover these with weeds, which were never hard to find. Many of the early farmers planted trees and bamboo for windbreaks. About 1911 or 1912 J. K. Mills criss-crossed the old sandblow with

John Hinkson plowing, about 1910.
Courtesy Henry T. Schendel.

with furrows and planted bamboo roots, about thirty-five miles of them, trying to hold down the drifting sand. It looked hopeless for a while, but after a few years the bamboo held the sand long enough for the grass to take root and prosper, thanks to a man who had the imagination to try something. Now there are good farms where there was nothing.

Despite hard work and hard times, there were occasions for social activities. The first Thanksgiving dinner in the new settlement made it possible for the neighbors to meet each other at the same table. It was held at the Leedoms' home on the shady side of the house in the sand. This became an annual event and was held down to the 1920s. A Fourth of July picnic was held each year on the Merced River at the Livingston bridge. The last day of school was also celebrated with a picnic.

In the early days "before trees" the summer temperature would go to 115 degrees most days. Many of the early settlers would escape the heat of the week by seeking the bank of the Merced River to spend a Sunday in the shade. A potluck dinner, a bit of swimming and perhaps a bit of fishing, made it possible to stand another week of heat and sand.

During the summer of 1915 a Sunday School was organized with an average attendance of twenty or more. Ministers from Irwin City and Livingston began to come and hold services.

Although chapters have been devoted to the Assyrians and Japanese, it should be noted here that the first farms the Assyrians owned were in the Delhi area. The Adams and Hoobyar families moved into Delhi in 1911. For some time they lived in tents near the Delhi house, then built a small home on property about a half-mile south of Delhi. There was no irrigation in this area at the time, so these folks raised what they could and worked for other farmers in the area. The Adams family soon moved to a farm near Turlock.

Japanese had been working in the Turlock area since about 1907. The Livingston colony was established in 1910. The Cortez colony was established in 1919 with thirteen families; twenty-nine families moved in during the next year. They demonstrated great ability in developing their ranches and became respected and appreciated members of the Delhi area.

The Delhi State Land Settlement, 1920–1931

Tony Kocolas

In the decade preceding World War I, there was a great deal of agitation favoring a State land settlement in California. Most proponents were humanitarian socialists or agricultural expansionists who felt that such a project would be advantageous for both the State and the settlers involved. In 1907 Dr. Elwood Mead, an agricultural economist at the University of California, took a sabbatical leave to go to Australia and set up a land settlement project. After Mead's return he used his experience as proof of the workability of a land settlement.

Partly as a result of Dr. Mead's urgings, the California State Legislature in 1915 created a Commission to investigate the possibilities of such a project; the report was very favorable. In 1917 the California Legislature passed the Land Settlement Act authorizing the appropriation of $260,000 for a land settlement project. In 1918 land was purchased for the Durham colony near Chico. In 1919 the Delhi colony of 8,600 acres was purchased from Edgar Wilson of San Francisco for about $92.50 per acre. The site was on two railroads and a good state highway. It had a water supply from the Turlock Irrigation District. Sale of land to colonists began in 1920.

One of the principal reasons for the Land Settlement Act was the desire for closer settlement.[18] In 1920 California had vast areas of good land that were not in productive use. It was argued that California should employ a settlement technique that had helped populate other nations.[19] Further, the first official report stated, "It helps people who aspire to be farmers, but who, under ordinary conditions could not make the attempt."[20] With assistance in getting new farmers started, the American system of free enterprise and independent farms could be maintained.[21] Under a properly sponsored state settlement, the colony could provide an adequate social life and local government for people living on the farms, at the same time that their chances for success were increased.[22]

Assistance to Army veterans and farm laborers was also a purpose of the Act, and preference was offered to veterans.[23] Rural life should be made pleasant to farm laborers, as many were being lured to the city.

Not all the reasons for creating the colony were humanitarian. One of the main stimuli was the anti-Japanese sentiment in California. The first report was most explicit: "The question that needs to be always in the forefront is—Is this land to be peopled by Americans or aliens?" It was said of the farm worker, "He will not stay on the land if he has to compete with Asiatics and will not bring up his family where his wife and children have no status." A six-point evaluation of the threat of Japanese domination of California's agriculture concluded, "In a very short time the Japanese control over certain essential food products will be an absolute one." Said the report, "The more Durhams and Delhis there are, the more certain it is that rural California will in the next half century remain the frontier of the white man's world."[24]

The initial requirements for becoming a Delhi settler were that a person have $1,500 in cash, a good character, be able to make a 5 percent down payment, and have enough money to buy needed tools and livestock.

The State had paid $92.50 an acre during the 1918-19 land boom for land which had gone begging at $25 a few years earlier. It now put up the land at $250 an acre and gave preference to ex-servicemen.[25] The land did not sell well. By 1922 the postwar boom was over, agricultural prices were depressed, and land values sank to a new low.[26]

The managers of the project advertised it across the United States. The bulk of the new settlers had had no experience in farming.[27] The colony, at its peak, had over 200 families; over 20 of the settlers were disabled veterans.[28]

The project had an elaborate staff, with engineers, architects, surveyors, agricultural specialists, and a Veterans Welfare Board. To develop a pleasant community environment, the Land Settlement Board planned two townsites, one of 300 acres at Delhi, the other of 200 acres at Ballico, with provision for stores, schools, and even a movie house.[29] At first there was only one store in Delhi, but it was soon joined by other enterprises.[30]

The State originally required a 40 percent down payment before house construction could begin, but this requirement was soon eased.[31] Under the guidance of chief architect Max Cook, one building was constructed every 1.5 working days.[32] By September 1922 there were 454 structures of all kinds in the settlement.

Initially no irrigation was available, and the land was in need of leveling. Eventually all land was irrigated. To reduce costs of installation and furnish employment, a pipe factory was built at Delhi. At full capacity the plant employed thirty men.[33] A 1923 report stated that in three years Delhi had saved "about four times the cost of the factory."[34]

One of the first community activities was the Delhi Cooperative Association, which promoted cooperative agriculture.[35] Its meetings were originally major social functions. Wilson Hall, donated by the former landowner, was the place where most games, dances, watermelon feeds, political rallies and church meetings took place.[36] A Community Sunday School was soon established, and in 1923 the Delhi Community Presbyterian Church was organized with 108 members. Masonic and Catholic Clubs were formed a little later. A fair put on by the Delhi community in 1922 attracted 1200 people for the barbecue.

Delhi's colonists had to endure physical discomforts, wind and sandstorms such as earlier settlers had experienced. Some of the settlers could not afford decent housing, though most of the homes were comfortable. Two or three years passed before electricity was installed.[37]

An interesting aspect of Delhi's struggle to obtain public utilities was its telephone problem. The Hilmar Phone Company and the Livingston Phone Company divided the area at El Capitan Way. A phone call across the street was a long distance call. The service was poor, the phones obsolete, and the wires non-galvanized. A number of settlers wanted neither company, preferring service from Pacific Telephone and Telegraph, which had a line through Delhi. Several applications to PT&T for phone service were submitted, without reply. Even Mrs. Walter Fox was unable to get satisfaction, although she had connections with the phone company in Los Angeles.

Since Dallas Bache was the settler most urgently in need of a good phone, he led the Delhi committee in demanding phone service. Discovering that the real reason for denial of service was the company's feeling that the settlers lacked ability to pay, Bache took a petition to the Railroad Commission (later the Public Utilities Commission) requesting that phone service be ordered. Within a week, work of installation began. Settlers east of the townsite also had to file protests; it was not until 1926 that all settlers wanting phones had them.[38]

The colony at Delhi, which was expected to become the model for future agricultural colonies, ended in financial failure. The State lost over $2,000,000, while numerous settlers suffered severe financial losses. There was no single reason for the failure, nor were there any villains to be blamed.

The soil at Delhi was sand and sandy loam, and very poor in the mineral and clay content needed for good crops. Most of the land had to be leveled for irrigation. Windstorms in 1920 damaged much cultivated land.[39] The final report admitted, "The selection in the case of Delhi was extremely unfortunate."[40]

Initially most colonists grew seasonal crops to obtain cash income. A few settlers attempted to plant orchards and vineyards, but most of these died for lack of sufficient minerals. After numerous crop failures and severe financial losses, considerable organic substance was added to Delhi's soil and the land became good for trees and vines.[41] With new vegetation, jack rabbits multiplied and became a major agricultural menace, destroying bark, young shoots and crops. Again jack rabbit drives were instituted.[42]

Perhaps the real tragedy was that after stable crops developed, such as grapes, peaches or apricots, there was no decent market price. After a 65 percent drop in prices between April 1917 and January 1922, agricultural prices remained depressed during much of the 1920s.[43] At a time when the California Canning Peach Growers estimated that they needed $28 a ton to break even, the canneries offered $22, and the farmers had no option but to accept.

Settlers who had livestock fared little better than the others. Thousands of chickens were being raised, and neither eggs nor chickens brought an adequate price. Dairy cow owners temporarily fared better, but in 1924 a severe case of hoof and mouth disease swept the West and wiped out most of the cows in the Delhi colony.[44]

A final factor contributing to Delhi's economic chaos was lack of agricultural experience. Among the 740 people who ultimately occupied the Delhi settlement, numerous professions were represented. Most of them had had some experience in farming, but some had never farmed before and lacked the basic knowledge.

In the light of these conditions it is understandable why the Delhi experiment was doomed. Too high a price was paid for the land, great difficulty was experienced in growing orchards, many of the settlers were inexperienced, crop prices were low, and herds were decimated by disease. By 1922 the State and the settlers had incurred a deficit of $352,837.61.[45] As the situation grew worse in 1922, the Delhi colonists organized political rallies and registered protests at what they felt was injustice on the part of the State. Numerous letters were sent to Sacramento, and committees were organized to stimulate action.[46] Walter Packard, superintendent of the Delhi colony, became more and more unpopular as it seemed he was doing nothing to improve the desperate financial situation.

Governor William Stephens promised to authorize emergency State loans to the colonists, but he was succeeded in office by Frank C. Richardson before taking action. Richardson felt that too much money had already been wasted on Delhi.

In 1923-24 a Ku Klux Klan was organized and at one of their night meetings hanged Dr. Mead, head of the settlement projects, in effigy. Superintendent Packard, feeling helpless to improve the situation and fearing for his safety, resigned. Before Packard left, a time bomb was planted to kill him, but it stopped five minutes before it was to detonate.[47]

Max Cook, the colony's architect, was made acting superintendent. Packard's job was offered to many prominent people, but all refused. In desperation the State sought out J. Winter Smith in Montana. He was a former Army officer who had distinguished himself in similar projects. Smith accepted with the proviso that he be given full authority, that he would tolerate no political overtones, and that he would be fired if no results were obtained. Smith took over in April 1924.

Smith first attempted to get a $40,000 loan from the State's emergency fund to tide the settlers over. Governor Richardson initially refused, but after Smith and a settlers' committee had frantic meetings with the Governor and his Council, the loan was approved. To obtain more funds the energetic new superintendent sold all the official cars and the entire pipe factory. He cut his staff from twelve to six after finding jobs for those dismissed. In 1925, after further meetings with the Governor, Richardson agreed to defer the settlers' payments.[48]

To improve morale, Smith encouraged the creation of various organizations, including the Boy Scouts, Campfire Girls, and a Community Council. An elaborate community Christmas celebration was held, as well as a Pioneer Day celebration that attracted statewide attention. Virtually the entire colony joined in a Jamboree and picnic on the banks of the Merced. Through these activities Delhi made front page news across the state just as the Legislature was contemplating Delhi's plight.[49]

When Governor Clement C. Young assumed office in 1927, he declared his interest in cleaning up the Delhi problem. Smith and the more reasonable settlers wanted a fair settlement for those colonists who could not succeed financially, and reduced payments for others. Young appointed a committee to investigate the problems of the Land Settlement project, while the settlers created a committee of three to negotiate on behalf of Delhi. J. Winter Smith and Charles Cleary, the Governor's representative, also participated in the discussion. Two basic concepts were agreed on: (1) all settlers should be treated equally; (2) after a final settlement was decided on, the Federal Land Bank should pay off the State, and the Land Bank would hold the settlers' mortgages.

The Governor's committee proved to be conciliatory, and a proposal called Plan "A" was drawn up. This plan was unacceptable to many settlers, some of whom had threatened to embarrass the State by walking out *en masse;* and only mediators such as Oscar Shattuck (one of the colony's great leaders) kept the hotheads from taking drastic action.

The two committees finally came up with Plan "W", which was ultimately accepted. According to this plan the settlers owed the State $375,000, which would be advanced by the Federal Land Bank. The balance of more than twice that sum was written off by the State. A satisfactory method of distributing the debt was worked out which left no one owing more than the appraised value of his land and gave small refunds to those who had best kept up with their payments.

To insure that Plan "W" would be acceptable to the State, the settlers employed two respected appraisers, Wells Lee Brown of Berkeley and Ed Varner of Turlock. They appraised every piece of property in the colony. When Plan "W" came up for approval, about 60 percent of the settlers were in favor of it; the rest, including most of the politically powerful disabled veterans, were undecided or opposed. The State demanded 100 percent approval before it would agree to the settlement.

Assemblyman E. G. Adams agreed to take up the veterans' cause. Faced with this new dilemma, the settlers' committee met with Adams to find out what terms the veterans would accept. Adams demanded $30,000 more for the dissident colonists he represented. As Governor Young's term was drawing to a close and the next administration might not be so interested in a settlement, the other settlers in desperation agreed to Adams' terms. Virtually the entire colony then acquiesced to Plan "W." The legislature approved the arrangement and the State's proprietorship of Delhi was terminated. The bill was approved by Young's successor, James Rolph, Jr., and took effect 14 August 1931.

The State had lost $2,097,520.80 in the final settlement. Despite the generous settlement, bitter feelings remained from the long struggle. Many Delhi area farmers outside the colony were embittered because they had had to overcome equal obstacles without State aid. Nonetheless, when the final agreement was made, most parties involved were happy that the experiment was terminated and an acceptable solution had been reached.[50]

Delhi Since 1931

John E. Caswell

Although a compromise had been reached between the settlers and the State, and it had been embodied in legislation, several years elapsed before the State received the last of the money owed it.

Some settlers sold their property and left the colony, but many stayed. Those who had recently planted trees or vines rented their properties out so that sweet potatoes or field corn could be planted between the rows. As the Delhi soil lends itself to growing very good sweet potatoes, a lot were planted. Settlers who were in dairying raised enough feed between the vines and trees to carry their costs.

Peach trees were growing in popularity in the region, and Delhi ranchers began planting them. There was some sort of deficiency in the soil that caused a lack of chlorophyll in the leaf. The leaves would turn yellow, the branch would die, and finally the tree would die. Dr. William Henry Chandler of the University of California was working on the problem in several locations through the State, but the deficiency showed up more plainly at Delhi because of the very light sandy soils. Dr. Chandler tried a hundred and forty-two different compounds, looking for the missing factor.

Dallas Bache was interested in Chandler's study and worked with him. As Chandler had obtained good results with iron, Bache put on thirty pounds of iron sulphate per tree and his trees improved. Chandler was getting good results with iron sulphate made from local scrap. The next year he brought in some Swedish iron, and no improvement was noted—it was pure while the American iron had zinc as an impurity.

The experimenters actually found out that small traces of zinc were needed when they started shipping trees and soil to the University. After a while, they began to use zinc-coated garbage cans. When plants were set in the cans, they started growing, just from the zinc sluffing off from the cans. Chandler guessed that the zinc on the galvanized cans was the answer and brought down a five-pound package of zinc to try on the trees of Delhi. "Strange as it might seem," said Dallas Bache in relating the story of Chandler's work, "you could watch that green creep down the tree. It started with the top leaves, and after a few days it got greener and greener until it got clear to the bottom branches of the tree."

Among those who came to Delhi in 1921 were William and Ruth Zierenberg, who bought about ten acres. Mrs. Zierenberg told how they lost their alfalfa, and how the chickens they bought had chicken pox. Finally Mr. Zierenberg took a job in Merced and they moved there, renting out their acreage. They had planted a number of fruit and nut trees, including three varieties of almonds. While other trees perished, the almonds survived.

During the Depression Zierenberg was out of work. He was talking one day with his friend Bert Stribling, the Merced nurseryman, when the latter suggested that he would furnish the almond trees to plant his acreage if Zierenberg would paint the Stribling house. This worked out. The Zierenbergs came out on weekends to care for the orchard, which was the first almond orchard in the vicinity. The almonds grew so well that others began to plant orchards.

Bache had an interesting theory regarding the heavy production of almond trees in the Delhi area. "It takes a certain amount of suffering," said he. Delhi's soils were poor, so ranchers there had learned to add as little or as much fertilizer, minerals, and water as were needed for best production. Because of that "suffering," the trees naturally set more. "A person who has to work hard learns to give up and do without, and a tree planted here has to do without and learn to do without. So, since he's afraid he isn't going to be remembered in heaven, he produces more children." In the Le Grand area were "the most beautiful walnut trees and almond trees that you can imagine. . . .They grow fine almonds down there, but they don't get the tonnage. . . .I tell them we have areas here where we get a ton of meats to the acre. They look at you in disbelief."

The transformation of Delhi from one of the poorest areas of the region to quite a prosperous area was due largely to two factors, the application of scientific knowledge and the enduring tenacity of the farmers. The man who had made available the fertilizer, sprays and chelated minerals that the farmers needed was Dallas Bache.[51] He was also the man who bought their peaches for California Canners and Growers and their almonds for California Almond Orchards, Inc.

Although there was a movement from peaches to almonds in the period following 1940, the biggest success story of the Delhi area involved peaches. Albert Ferrari, according to Dallas Bache, was in 1971 the biggest peach grower in the world. In 1971 he had delivered 16,000 tons of peaches to Del Monte Corporation. He also raised some 200 tons of almond meats, as well as some grapes.

Albert Ferrari's father was a day laborer. The family came to Delhi in the very early days and built a little cabin on El Capitan Avenue. He had one brother and three half-brothers. Albert could attend grammar school only part-time, but eventually graduated from the Ballico School. He and two other young men started out threshing beans with a rented thresher, and eventually ended up owning it.

His first purchase of land came about when a bank foreclosed on a farm which had been allowed to run down during World War II. The bank begged Ferrari to take it over on a "you pay us what you can when you can" basis. Ferrari agreed, got married, built a little home, and established a family. He went on to take over other properties. Typically, he leveled the land and put pipeline on it—tax deductible expenses. As his income went up, his investment in land spiraled. A partner on one piece of property was Ugo Caviani; a partner on another was Herk Shamgochian. Ferrari had come a long way from the '30s when he received ten or fifteen cents an hour for irrigating, or ten cents a tree for burning brush pruned in the neighbors' orchards, to ownership or control of thousands of acres.

By the 1960s another element was becoming conspicuous in the Delhi population: families that wanted to get their children out of the cities into the country. In Delhi, partly as a legacy of the Land Settlement, there were many small acreages available. The youngsters would go to one of several small schools in the area, then to Livingston High School. Dad might work in Turlock or Merced or Modesto, perhaps as far away as Stockton. The orchard and garden, rabbits, chickens or sheep would give the children worthwhile tasks to perform, and an environment where it was not hard to keep up with the Joneses.

Relations between Delhi leaders and the Japanese of Cortez and Livingston seem to have been friendly since World War II, except for a few unpleasant incidents immediately after the return of the Japanese. In the early 1920s there was a sign perhaps four feet by eight feet in dimensions as one entered Livingston, "No Japs Wanted." Now the children of those Japanese are thoroughly respected.

At the same time that Delhi's population has been growing in numbers and the older residents have become comfortably well off, there has been a loss of civic unity. The difficulties of the 1920s, despite deep differences between factions in the community, seem to have brought the town together. Further, they had a single Community Church with one Sunday School and a single women's association, although it was made up of people from many denominational backgrounds. By 1955 there were seven churches, and the community was no longer drawn together to a single focus.

In 1971 there seemed to be slight chance of Delhi's becoming incorporated in the near future. Sewage and water districts provided those essential services. The Delhi Investment and Development Company had been formed to channel federal assistance in rebuilding the business section after freeway clearance had taken place. Otherwise, Delhi residents depended on Merced County services.

The original Don Pedro Dam under construction, 1922–23.

Chapter XX

An Engineering History of the Turlock Irrigation District

Roy V. Meikle

The San Joaquin River, the main stream of the San Joaquin Valley, rises in the high Sierras southeast of Yosemite National Park. The Tuolumne River, the largest tributary of the San Joaquin, drains a basin of 1,880 square miles and flows westerly for about 150 miles until it joins the San Joaquin. From its headwaters on the northern slope of Mount Lyell it flows through upland meadows, then through a canyon eighty miles long in granite. The upper end of this canyon has a depth of between 3,000 and 4,000 feet for 25 miles. At its lower end is Hetch Hetchy Valley, now flooded by the Hetch Hetchy Reservoir of the City and County of San Francisco.

Next the Tuolumne River reaches the Don Pedro Reservoir above La Grange. Finally, at La Grange Dam water is diverted to canals of the Turlock and Modesto Irrigation Districts on the south and north banks of the river. At La Grange Dam the Tuolumne River leaves the lower canyon and enters the San Joaquin Valley, crossing the valley to its confluence with the San Joaquin River, a distance of about 55 miles.

The average run-off of the Tuolumne River over a long period of years is about 1,800,000 acre-feet, a quantity that makes irrigation a profitable enterprise. However, there is a great variation in the run-off from year to year, from 600,000 acre-feet up to 5,000,000 acre-feet, which makes control of the flow essential.

The Turlock Irrigation District's System of Dams and Canals

The principal structure of the original irrigation system was the La Grange diversion dam. This dam is a notable structure, even now after years of service. In planning to distribute the waters of the Tuolumne River over the plains, it was necessary, on account of the elevation of the area to be irrigated and because of the difficulty of obtaining a practicable canal location, to build a very high diverting dam at the La Grange site, in fact, the highest overflow dam built up to that time. The dam as constructed was 129 feet above stream bed, and later was raised 3.5 feet to increase the capacity of the main canal. The length of the dam's crest is 336 feet. It is 90 feet thick at the base, and 24 feet thick at the top. The rock for the dam was quarried out of a bluff on the right bank of the river. Cost of the original dam was $550,000.

The distribution system consisted of rock-cuts, flumes, wasteways, tunnels, fills, deep earth-cuts, large canal structures, and miles of canals built in earth. Millions of cubic feet of earth and rock had to be moved, and millions of board feet of timber built into the flumes and trestles to bring the water 23 miles from the La Grange Dam to the division gates at the northeastern corner of the District. From this point the main lateral system spread out and irrigated the 180,000 acres lying between the Tuolumne and Merced Rivers. The irrigation works had cost $1,200,000. They were thought to be comparable with any other system in the United States.

Development forged ahead as predicted. By 1913 irrigation had reached 85,002 acres, and the main canal carried 1,140 second-feet.

A new problem now faced the District. Early in July of each year, the natural flow of the river began to fall off, and by August the flow was totally insufficient to meet the demands of the ever-increasing irrigated area. Additional water storage was imperative.

The Davis Reservoir, later renamed Owen Reservoir and now called Turlock Lake, was built in 1913. It covers 3,000 acres, has a capacity of 50,000 acre-feet, and cost $488,000. It is located in the foothills about halfway between the eastern boundary of the District and the La Grange Dam. Seventeen dams and levees and one outlet gate structure were required. This reservoir made it possible to deliver the required water to all irrigated lands up to and sometimes during the month of August. Later, with additional storage capacity and power at Don Pedro Dam, it became indispensable for regulating purposes.

While the Turlock Reservoir was being built, extensive improvements were made on the main canal. The 600-foot hard rock tunnel at the head of the main canal at La Grange was enlarged. The Morgan Flume and the Delaney Flume were replaced by hydraulic fills carrying a reinforced concrete conduit 30 feet wide on the bottom and 13 feet deep. The Delaney Fill was 746 feet long and 81 feet high. Other improvements included replacing the Snake Ravine Flume with a 900-foot concrete wall 11 feet high.

To deliver water to the southern part of the District which lay adjacent to the Merced River, the Highline Canal was built along the western edge of the District. It was completed in 1912, as were two cross ditches and Lateral No. 5-1/2. When Lateral No. 4-1/2 and the Ceres Main Extension were completed in 1914, the main canal and lateral system totaled 240 miles. The area irrigated was 94,000 acres, or about half the eventual irrigated area. The system now had the capacity to deliver an ample supply to meet irrigation needs, but the storage capacity was not sufficient to carry through the entire season, and in dry years the supply was far short of meeting requirements.

A new phase of canal improvement began after completion of the original Don Pedro Dam in 1923. All the old wooden flumes, drops and gates in the main canal and lateral system were replaced by reinforced concrete structures, and hundreds of watertight cast iron gates replaced the old wooden slide gates at the heads of the community and private ditches. The lining with concrete of the main canal and laterals progressed year by year, until in 1971 193 miles, or about three-fourths of the 250-mile main system, was concrete-lined.

Drainage Problem

In the first years of the District's operation farmers tended to over-irrigate during the months of May and June when Tuolumne's stream flow was ample, hoping that water stored in the ground would mature the crops when the supply from the river and Turlock Reservoir fell off in the late summer. This practice, together with the great mileage of earth ditches in sandy soil and the large amounts of water used to flood rough checks of too great an area for careful or even reasonable irrigation use, caused a steady rise in the ground water level. By July 1917 the average depth to ground water was only 4.1 feet over a large area of the District. This level dropped during the winter months. Numerous lakes appeared over the western area of the District with a combined area of about 1,800 acres. Banks refused to make further loans to the farmers on such land.

To meet this most serious situation the District undertook a four-pronged attack. About 52 miles of gravity drainage ditches and drain pipes were installed. More careful use and distribution of water was practiced. Farmers were urged to recheck their land. Between 1915 and 1924, 55 miles of canal were concrete-lined. Some experiments in pumping from wells to control ground water were made as early as 1907, but the cost of operating gasoline-driven pumps was high. As electric pumps became available, the gravity drains became obsolete. Between 1917 and 1924 the average ground water level was reduced from 4 to 5 feet below the surface. By 1970, the underground water level was held at about 7 to 9 feet during the irrigating season. The District operated 181 deep well drainage pumps and pumped 191,571 acre-feet of water back into the canal system, most of it during the irrigating season when it formed a valuable supplement to the reservoir system.

Don Pedro Storage and Power Project

To provide adequate water throughout the growing season, many landowners favored a larger reservoir in the Tuolumne River canyon, but the cost was long considered prohibitive by the majority. Preliminary surveys and plans were made for a high masonry dam to be located about six miles above La Grange near Don Pedro Bar.

In 1913 an application for a permit to build a reservoir on federal land was filed with the Department of the Interior. The permit was granted in 1916. During 1918 a comprehensive preliminary engineering report was submitted to the District's Directors.

An agreement was entered into by the Turlock and Modesto Irrigation Districts on 19 July 1919, making a joint undertaking of the Don Pedro Project. The two Districts agreed to share the expense and benefits in proportion to the number of acres in each District. Turlock transferred 31.54 percent of all Don Pedro water rights, dam site, lands and privileges to the Modesto District, retaining 68.46 percent.

Plans and specifications were completed for the Don Pedro Dam and bids were received in February 1921. As the bids exceeded the Engineer's estimate and the amount of bonds available for the work, they were rejected by the Districts. Considerable time was lost in the consideration of various cost-plus proposals submitted by contractors. At a joint meeting of the two Boards on 4 April 1921, the District's engineers were authorized to build by force account a standard gauge construction railroad from the gravel bars in the Stanislaus River east of Oakdale to the Sierra Railway, whose track the gravel trains would use to Hetch Hetchy Junction, where a new line would carry the trains 8.5 miles to the Don Pedro Dam site, an overall haul of 33 miles. To avoid further delay, the Engineers were instructed on 28 April 1921 to proceed at once to construct the dam and appurtenant works under the Districts' superintendence.

"Old" Don Pedro Dam was completed early in 1923, just ahead of the very dry year of 1924. It was 284 feet high and was rated the highest in the United States, if not in the world, at the time. It was concrete, and arched in plan. Its capacity was 289,000 acre-feet, and it covered 3,276 acres at high water. The concrete placed in the dam and spillway amounted to 296,552 cubic yards.

Power Generation and Distribution

The Old Don Pedro Power Plant was located immediately below and adjacent to the dam. Three 5,000 KVA generators of the vertical type were directly connected to water wheels which were supplied through three conduits 6 feet in diameter and 210 feet long. In 1928 two additional 9,370 KVA generators were installed and the power house enlarged. The rated capacity of the plant was 30,000 KW, while the peak carried was 37,000 KW. The project as completed in 1923 cost the Turlock and Modesto

Turlock Irrigation District's Board of Directors, 1923. From left, clockwise: Fred Moffett, John Chance, S. A. Hultman; attorney P. H. Griffin; chief engineer R. V. Meikle, standing; Anna Sorensen, secretary; directors John Sisk and Claus Johnson. Courtesy TID.

Irrigation Districts $4,744,113. This was $95,562 below the Engineer's estimate. The 1928 addition to the power plant cost $625,856.

The La Grange Power Plant is located at the lower end of the TID's 600-foot diversion tunnel. It cost $230,000 and was operated for the first time in December 1924. Its capacity is 4,300 KW. It is operated only during those months when there is surplus water over irrigation requirements which can be wasted into the river from the canal. The plant can furnish some standby service to the District in an emergency and is used for peaking when the water supply is short.

A complete electrical transmission and distribution system has been constructed. It served 28,889 customers as of 28 December 1970. This has also made possible the installation of electrically driven turbine pumps to control the ground water level. These wells have an average depth of about 200 feet. They consist of a 28-inch diameter hole, a gravel envelope, and a 16-inch perforated casing. These deep well turbine drainage pumps deliver on the average about 1,800 gallons per minute with an average draw-down of 43 feet. In addition to the Turlock Irrigation District drainage pumps, 75 private pumping plants have pumped up to 70,000 acre-feet into the canal system at $5.00 and $4.00 per acre-foot.

The Turlock Irrigation District's electrical distribution system has been a successful enterprise. Many difficulties were surmounted by the Directors of the District. The large amount of power available during the irrigation season when water is released for irrigation and the small amount of water available for power after the irrigation season presented a problem. This was overcome by a sale of surplus power to the Pacific Gas and Electric Company during the summer months and by a contract for the purchase of power when required by the District. The power distribution has been confined to the Turlock Irrigation District area. Since 1924 and until 1954, the Turlock Irrigation District generated practically all the power required for distribution and to meet the wholesale contract delivery to the Pacific Gas and Electric Company, but as the distribution load has increased the District has been required to purchase more power. However, the contract with the power corporation, which has netted the District seven and one-half million dollars, ended in 1954; and this power has been applied to the District's growing distribution load.

Rural distribution with but few customers available per mile of line is expensive and could not be undertaken successfully in competition with lines already built by the power corporation. The District met this difficulty by purchasing the competing lines in the area from the San Joaquin Light and Power

Turlock Irrigation District Offices. Caswell photo.

Corporation and from the Pacific Gas and Electric Company. At the present time the District purchases power from the City and County of San Francisco and the Pacific Gas and Electric Company. The District operates 135 miles of 66 KV transmission line and 1,117 miles of distribution line. The electrical system represents an expenditure of approximately $17,000,000 plus $40,000,000 at New Don Pedro Powerhouse and its related facilities.

Improvement Districts

Under the Improvement District Act of 1927, there are about 990 Improvement Districts within the Turlock Irrigation District. The formation of Improvement Districts within the District has resulted

The First National Bank of Turlock, 1905. It later housed the TID offices. A second story was added and the building was still in service in 1971. Courtesy Turlock Public Library.

in a greatly improved community ditch system. These districts represent 135,000 acres and have concrete-lined or piped 464 of a total of 1660 miles of community ditches at a cost of about $6,300,000. The 79 Improvement District pumping plants cost an additional $477,000.

It is the policy of the Turlock Irrigation District to operate only the main canal and main lateral system, delivering water to the heads of these various community ditches. Under the Improvement District Act, two-thirds of the landowners on any community ditch or in any given area may form an improvement district for the pipe construction or concrete lining or auxiliary pumping plant and for maintenance costs. The cost of construction work is paid for over a period of ten years, one-tenth each year, with warrants bearing 4 percent interest. Maintenance costs may be levied each year as necessary. All principal and interest payments and maintenance costs are collected by the Turlock Irrigation District with the regular District tax. The Turlock Irrigation District invests reserve funds in the Improvement District warrants. All warrants are now purchased and held by the Turlock Irrigation District.

New Don Pedro Dam

The Irrigation Districts made filings on the waters of the Tuolumne River as far back as 1887. Under the Raker Act of 1913, the City and County of San Francisco has a right to develop 400 million gallons daily for domestic supply from the flood run-off of the river. The wide variation of flow in the Tuolumne River from year to year makes large reservoir storage capacity desirable to regulate the river and carry over storage from wet to dry years.

The requirements of the Districts and the City and County of San Francisco amount to approximately 1,500,000 acre-feet annually. Prior to the building of New Don Pedro Dam, six reservoirs had been completed by the Districts and the City: Hetch Hetchy, Lake Eleanor, Lake Lloyd, Don Pedro, Turlock Lake and Dallas Warner—a total storage capacity of one million acre-feet.

The final storage project which completed a comprehensive plan for the development of the Tuolumne River was the New Don Pedro Reservoir. Preliminary surveys and investigations had been carried on by the Districts since 1960. One of the five sites between Old Don Pedro and La Grange Dam was selected by geologists and was explored by several hundred feet of tunneling and found to be very satisfactory for either a concrete or an earth-rock dam.

Bechtel Corporation engineers were appointed in 1958 by the Districts to make a preliminary report and recommendation as to the most favorable type and height of the proposed New Don Pedro Dam, suitable generating facilities, spillway and appurtenant works. The Bechtel Report was received in July 1959, and the cost of the project was estimated at $78,620,000, exclusive of lands, relocation of highway, roads and services, and general expenses.

The New Don Pedro Dam is an earth-rock fill structure, 580 feet high. The reservoir covers 12,960 acres and has a capacity of 2,030,000 acre-feet. When full, it backs the water 22 miles up the river and has a shoreline of 159 miles.

The City and County of San Francisco paid about half the cost of the project for the use of 570,000 acre-feet of exchange storage space plus one-half of 340,000 acre-feet flood control space when available. This storage space insures the City's water right of 400 million gallons daily and transfers flood control operations from the City's reservoirs to the New Don Pedro Reservoir.

A hydroelectric power plant belonging to the Districts immediately below the dam contains three 70,000 H.P. turbines operating under a maximum gross head of 530 feet, connected to three generators with a combined capacity of approximately 150,000 kilowatts. The plant generates annually about 600 million kilowatt hours of electrical energy.

Request was made to the California Districts Securities Commission by the Turlock Irrigation District on 23 May 1961 for approval of the engineering report entitled "New Don Pedro Dam" dated July 1959 and of a bond issue. Approval was received by the District in September 1961 for a bond issue of $34,000,000. This was voted by Turlock Irrigation District (5,754 yes – 126 no) on 7 November

1961. The voters were advised that neither taxes nor power rates would be increased as a result of the new project.

In May 1961 the Districts made application to the Federal Power Commission for a license to build the project. By July the State Department of Fish and Game and the U.S. Department of the Interior had voiced a demand that 219,000 acre-feet, the equivalent of an acre-foot for all irrigable land in MID and TID, be released annually to protect the dwindling salmon run. Numerous other demands were made in respect to wildlife and recreation facilities. The Districts would not agree to release water for fish when it was needed for agricultural purposes.

Meetings were held through the spring and early summer of 1962, and an agreement was threshed out, only to be repudiated by the Fish and Game Commission. On 16 October 1962 a ten-day hearing began before the Federal Power Commission, without the parties having reached agreement. Very complete evidence was presented by the Districts' experts covering all phases of the project and its operations. Meanwhile the engineering firm of Stone and Youngberg had reported in August that the potential capital value of New Don Pedro to TID was about $28,000,000. The Bechtel Corporation's estimate of the total cost to the three participants was $92,415,850.

The Federal Power Commission issued its opinion on the license on 10 March 1964. It made no adjudication that water for fish should be assured ahead of municipal and agricultural rights. The Department of Fish and Game and the Department of the Interior filed suit in the Ninth U.S. Circuit Court of Appeals to require that the FPC's order be revised in line with their contentions.

The Court handed down a far-reaching decision on 18 May 1965, approving the Federal Power Commission's order. But the court held that the Commission had the authority to take irrigation and municipal water held pursuant to State-granted rights and reallocate that water for salmon. This not only affected District rights held under State law, but threatened San Francisco's rights under the Raker Act.

When a petition for rehearing was denied by the Court, a petition for review was submitted to the U.S. Supreme Court, but this, too, was denied. No further legal remedy was sought.

By February 1966 the Districts and the City of San Francisco were close to agreement. In March Bechtel engineers came in with an up-to-date cost distribution:

City of San Francisco	$48,423,538
Turlock Irrigation District	28,216,904
Modesto Irrigation District	15,881,658

On 23 May 1966, the "Fourth Agreement" was signed by San Francisco and the two Irrigation Districts. When bids were opened on 22 June 1967, Guy F. Atkinson Company was the lower bidder at $49,693,960, well under the engineers' estimates. Later, bids were received and orders placed for reservoir clearing and electrical equipment. A ground breaking ceremony was held at the site on 6 October 1967.

The New Don Pedro Dam was located a mile and a half downstream from Old Don Pedro at a site recommended by the Districts' consulting geologist in 1957. An earth and rock fill dam had been decided on. The central core of impervious clayey material was covered with a heavy shell of gravel obtained from gold dredge tailings downstream of the La Grange Dam. These tailings were brought to the dam site over a specially constructed road in vehicles capable of carrying 75 cubic yards of material at a maximum speed of 35 miles an hour. The exposed lakeside surface of the dam between minimum operating level and the top of the dam was covered with heavy rock riprap. The thickness of the dam at the base was about 2,800 feet—an enormous prism which no anticipated natural catastrophe could overwhelm.

	Old Don Pedro	New Don Pedro
Height	280 feet	580 feet
Length of crest	1040 feet	1900 feet
Acre-feet, total	290,000	2,030,000
Acre-feet above minimum operating pool	258,000	1,721,000

Turlock Irrigation District's Board of Directors, 1968. Left to right; Tilden Genzoli, William R. Fernandes, Samuel Kronberg, J. Homer Clark, and Everett L. Tomlinson; Reynold S. Tillner, Secretary and General Manager; Roy V. Meikle, Chief Engineer. Gordon Ham photo.

On 2 November 1970 valves in the face of Old Don Pedro were opened, and water began filling in the storage space between the two dams. New Don Pedro was dedicated on 22 May 1971, with Mayor Joseph Alioto of San Francisco making the keynote address to more than three thousand people attending the ceremonies and barbecue.

A secondary benefit to the public was the creation of three recreational areas at Don Pedro Reservoir at a cost of about $6,200,000.

Eighty years after construction had begun in the Turlock Irrigation District, and seventy years after the first major water delivery, the last anticipated major dam project was finished. The first directors of the District could hardly have imagined the series of engineering works that had been developed on the Tuolumne River to serve Stanislaus County and the City and County of San Francisco. Neither could they have anticipated the legal complexities involved.

The Turlock Irrigation District had been blessed by nature with a generous stream flow on the Tuolumne, combined with several excellent dam sites. It had been fortunate in finding partners to share the cost of the projects. It had been lucky in having several generations of leaders who doggedly overcame opposition and difficulties of all sorts. The District's wealth has been in its agriculture, abundant water supply and electric power.

Boat dock at Old Don Pedro. Walters photo.

Chapter XXI

The Human Side of the Turlock Irrigation District

Helen Hohenthal

In the history of the Turlock Irrigation District 1901 was a memorable year, a turning point away from discouraging and costly litigation toward the fulfillment of the leaders' great dream of adequate irrigation water for farmers. Directors and farmers alike were sure that the thirsty sand plains would become beautiful fields of grapevines, melons, beans, alfalfa, vineyards and orchards.

The attitude of their opponents was reflected in Judge J. D. Works' *History of the Bench and Bar*, published in 1901. He wrote, "...the law of irrigation districts has ceased to be of general interest. It has become important only to the unfortunate bond holders of the districts, now in existence, and the more unfortunate property owners therein, whose property is subject to taxation to pay for the redemption of the bonds. The law has proved such a dismal failure in its practical workings, that it is not likely that the formation of any new districts under it would ever be attempted."[1]

But in 1901 the United States Supreme Court handed down a decision favorable to the Turlock Irrigation District which defeated the "dry" farmers in their last big effort to kill the District. As the District had to pay interest on its bonds and redeem them when they matured, the Court ruled that the District had the right to tax property to secure money for this purpose. In this case Turlock and Modesto Irrigation Districts' bondholders had joined forces with the Districts to fight the "dry" farmers.[2]

By 1901 water from Canal 1 had reached the plains around Hughson and Ceres. Over 3700 acres were irrigated that year. Some of the original members of the Board of Directors lived to see this successful ending to their fourteen-year struggle, as did Judge Waymire, Judge C. C. Wright, and the District's able attorney, P. J. Hazen. John W. Mitchell did not.

The District now faced such problems as draining, storage space for water needed later in the summer and fall, and building of farmers' ditches to get the water on the land. Both the District's officers and the farmers had to learn how to use and control the water supply properly.

In April 1904, the Modesto and Turlock Irrigation Districts held a "Jubilee of Completion" in Modesto, at that time a small town of about 2500 people. It was hard put to it to provide accommodations for the crowd of 5000 visitors who attended the two-day celebration.

As part of the celebration, a special thirty-car train carried visitors north to the new villages of Salida and Ripon, and south to Turlock to take a look at the changes brought to the area. They were amazed at the rapid progress of the little town. More than 200 Swedish families, migrants to Turlock since irrigation had become available, proudly showed the visitors their farms. Land prices had doubled since the arrival of the new settlers.

Farmers ready with scrapers to clean out the sandy ditches, 1909. Courtesy I. Andrew Bert Riise.

Among the visitors were California's Governor, George C. Pardee, and his wife. Dr. Elwood Mead represented the U. S. Department of Agriculture.

In a speech at one of the programs, President Benjamin Ide Wheeler of the University of California predicted a population of ten million for the San Joaquin Valley.[3]

In 1913-14 a foothill reservoir was built to store water so that the irrigation season could be extended. At first called Davis Lake, it is now known as Turlock Lake. Soon after the reservoir was filled, a defect developed near the outlet gate. "Early in the morning of 27 June 1914, the 48,740 acre-feet of water in Davis Reservoir burst through the south wing of the outlet gate and roared down the main canal, partially inundating three ranches and finally breaking through the canal banks and over a 100-foot bluff toward the Tuolumne River, tearing a mile long 400-foot-wide gorge in sand and hardpan. The ravine still remains, a geographical memorandum of the district's foremost dam break. . . .No one ever satisfactorily explained the crack-up of the outlet wing, puddle filled and faced with from six to twenty-four inches of reinforced concrete. . . .A terrified night watchman telephoned to La Grange Dam ordering dam tenders to close the gates and turn back into the Tuolumne River the head of 1600 second-feet of water which was feeding a roaring flood that swirled down the main canal below the buckled outlet wing. Dan E. Kilroy, then a TID foreman, received orders from Water Superintendent Milo J. Caton to rush all available men and stock to the Davis Reservoir.

"The water continued to flow out of the reservoir until 8 July. It was not until 17 August that water flowed normally in the ditches again; after huge crews of men, stock, and equipment under Milo Caton, A. G. Chatom, and Engineer Roy V. Meikle had labored day and night to construct a detour canal."[4] The cost of this break was estimated at $50,000 in 1914 dollars.

There was another tragic loss associated with the reservoir break. Three of the members of the TID Board, T. A. Owen, N. J. Witmer, and Ed Kiernan had a car accident on an inspection trip to the reservoir. Kiernan died as the result of injuries received when the car overturned.

The Directors and Chief Engineer continued with the extension of the canal system, replacing outdated and unsatisfactory flumes with earth fills and lining the canals with cement. As the land under irrigation increased, there was an approaching need for more water storage, a larger dam, and electric power.

Don Pedro Bar comes into the District's story at this point. A Frenchman, Pierre Sainsevain, known to his California friends as Don Pedro, set out from the Santa Clara Valley in 1848 for the gold fields. He struck it rich at a bar on the Tuolumne which was henceforth known as Don Pedro's Bar. A boom town sprang up on both sides of the river. Reputedly thirteen million dollars worth of gold dust and nuggets was shipped out of the camp by the Wells Fargo Express Company. By 1864 the bar had been worked out, and when the town burned it was not rebuilt.[5] At the bar was a spot where Indians camped and held dances.[6] It was this romantic spot that was selected for the monumental Don Pedro I.

Some years before the irrigation districts became interested in the site, a local cattleman, Albert Chatom, who knew the country from river to river, often gazed upon the valley behind Don Pedro Bar and dreamed of a great storage reservoir and power plant. When he heard that a power company was planning to survey the site, he took an option on the land to hold it for TID.[7] Details of the erection of Don Pedro Dam have been given in the preceding chapter.

TID performed a variety of services for its customers. With the completion of Don Pedro I and its accompanying power plant in 1923, the Modesto and Turlock Irrigation Districts could supply not only irrigation water, but additional electricity for the homes, the milking machines and other power needs of the farmers, as well as for city homes and industries. The Turlock District also established a retail appliance store until a sufficient number of reliable businessmen were established to furnish high quality appliances and repair service.

An important service to farmers was supplied under the Improvement District Act of 1927. This permitted the District to purchase ten-year warrants of each new Improvement District, thus providing convenient financing and professional supervision at the local level. Farmers now found it both profitable and convenient to put in cement pipelines or cement-lined ditches. No longer did the farmers need to be much concerned with water losses from leakage, with washed-out ditch banks and consequent damage to soil and crops, and the undesirable weeds in the ditches or along their banks.

The introduction of tractors, trucks, and power tools, together with diminishing maintenance problems, caused a rapid decline in the number of horses and mules owned in the district. Beside the barns that had formerly housed the horses and mules were erected a new style of barn, designed to conform to state milk production regulations.

Old Don Pedro Dam
was a joy to the eye.
Harry M. Channing photo.

At the time that Don Pedro I was built, engineers identified another site a little downstream as a desirable one, and deliberately saved it against the time when a larger dam would be needed. The City and County of San Francisco had water rights at Hetch Hetchy on the upper Tuolumne, and it was both legally necessary and economically desirable for the two irrigation districts to gain San Francisco's cooperation in building a greater Don Pedro. The big city leaders and the farm-oriented groups joined hands, to the mutual advantage of both the farmers and the city dwellers.

The site was ideal for construction of the new Don Pedro Dam. Geologists and engineers said it was excellent from a builder's viewpoint—fine rock conditions, materials located conveniently nearby, a wide working space, and a climate where work was possible most of the days in the year.[8]

As with any accomplishment of the magnitude of the Turlock and Modesto Irrigation Districts' systems, success depended on many factors. Two important ones have been leadership and cooperation. From the first elected Board of Directors in 1887 down to the present time, the Turlock Irrigation District has had outstanding leaders. Among the early ones, education was mostly a matter of experience, self-education beyond public schools, reading and observing—not college degrees. They were storekeepers, farmers, blacksmiths, teachers, and shrewd businessmen. They gave all their talents to developing a legal and workable irrigation system for their district.

The directors consulted with others in the community to get the best available legal, managerial, and engineering advice. These directors needed courage to withstand the many years of legal maneuvering of the minority opposing irrigation. By their conduct the District's directors won the faith and support of those who furnished the financial resources that carried the District through lean and discouraging years. Later elected boards completed the canal system, solved the problems of drainage, and transformed the agriculture and daily living patterns of the people.

The District originally planned to sell power to help reduce taxes and redeem bonds, but there was no authority in the law for districts to do so. Large quantities of power could be generated at Don Pedro. "In the early 1920s," said R. V. Meikle, "the idea of an irrigation district's selling power to provide for additional revenue was unheard of. The TID directors put the problem in the hands of [the law firm of] Griffin and Boone; went ahead with the construction of Don Pedro and finally Griffin was able to get a measure passed by the state legislature which legalized sale of power by an irrigation district for the purpose of retiring its bonded indebtedness." Patrick H. Griffin was a great attorney. Meikle had only praise for him. "If it had not been for old P. H., we would never have been able to build that dam."[9]

When the District first began distribution of electric power, it had a surplus, for few houses were equipped to use it and time was required for wiring to be put in.

One of the familiar sights of the town around 1920 was the old TID corporation yard at the corner of Pioneer Avenue and East Main. It had barns for the District's mules and horses and sheds for the equipment. These were torn down and a new corporation yard put in on North Broadway. There TID has a modern repair and electric shop, warehouse, electrical dispatch office, a cement warehouse, and various sheds.[10] A portion of the original store is used for selling electrical wiring materials and lamps, and for repairing appliances.

Anna Sorenson's Reminiscences

For TID's Golden Jubilee in 1937, its long-time Secretary, Mrs. Anna Sorenson, gave one woman's view of the organization at work in the early days. She first worked in the office of the District's attorney, P. J. Hazen. The Directors met only once a month. After the meeting the books were sent to her. Her husband, Martin Sorenson, was accountant and bookkeeper for TID from 1899 to 1902, and upon his death she was offered and accepted his job. In 1906 she was appointed Secretary, and served in that post until retirement, except for a short period of temporary retirement.

During part of her service Mrs. Sorenson added assessment rolls and estimated taxes. Among her duties were a number not in the Secretary's job of today. "I did all the blueprinting for Engineer Burton

Smith in a heavy wooden frame, carried it from the office into the back yard in the sun. . .then washed the prints and hung them on a clothesline to dry.

"It was also my duty to make out the ditch tenders' reports and act as timekeeper. At the end of every month, I drove with my horse and buggy to the camps to get their time. . .this took two days. The first day I visited the camps between Ceres and La Grange. In the evening, I checked supplies with the foremen and storekeepers. In the morning I made out the payroll and wrote out demands on the Turlock Irrigation District. These had to be approved by the Directors in their meeting. I then made out the checks from the demands, registered them in the warrant book and mailed them. When the Don Pedro project was started I did the secretarial work for the joint meetings. When the Improvement District Law was passed, I was appointed to see that each petition was checked to see that all signers were on the assessment roll."[11]

Mrs. Sorenson had a keen memory for details. When on a witness stand one time, her statements were challenged. The books were ordered as evidence. She had quoted accurately long details of facts and figures from memory.

Staff and Structure

The Turlock area owes much to its citizens who have served on the Board of Directors. They have picked engineering experts, legal advisers and other professional, technical and clerical staff carefully and wisely. Then the Board has trusted them to carry out their share of the work.

The dedication and efforts of the Board of Directors have been praised by Roy Meikle, long-time Chief Engineer. He said that he has "always been impressed with the Board's open discussions on all questions during its Monday meetings. . . .During the years there was no side-politics going on. We've never had that. In fact," he added, "the boards have been so united after discussions that most important votes have been unanimous since 1922."[12]

Relations with the taxpayers of the District have been equally good. Once a year the Board sits as a board of equalization to review protested assessments. A former board member said, ". . .the board of equalization meetings have been set each year (a legal requirement for the last 25 years), but in the 21 years I have served we never had even *one taxpayer* appear at these meetings to protest tax rates set by the board.

"We have had many other hearings on irrigation problems and improvement district formation, in which the board has carefully examined arguments and made fair decisions to the best of their ability."[13]

The key figure in the TID organization for years was Roy V. Meikle, Chief Engineer of the District, who retired in December 1971, after fifty-nine years' service—a most unusual record. He served the District well.

After completing his civil engineering course at Stanford, Meikle gathered experience in engineering jobs with the City of Tacoma, the Rogue River Canal Company, and the United States Department of Agriculture at Berkeley. In 1912 he was employed by Burton Smith, Chief Engineer of TID, to work on the Hetch Hetchy Report prepared by the District in connection with the Raker Act, in which Congress granted water from the Tuolumne to the City of San Francisco.

Meikle said that when he joined the District's staff, "it owned one automobile and sixty mules."

Don Pedro I was Mr. Meikle's first great and beautiful project and one of which he was justly proud. Later, the Modesto and Turlock Districts again chose him as chief engineer in enlarging the Don Pedro power plant. The last great service of Mr. Meikle was planning for the construction of Don Pedro II and its facilities.

As chief engineer, Meikle planned the Turlock Irrigation District's construction program: dams, reservoirs, improvement districts, drainage, extension of the canal system, power plants, and power distribution. Harmony and cooperation have prevailed in his coordination of the work, a tribute to the quality of his leadership and the staff's deep respect for him.[14]

At first the functions of assessor, collector and treasurer were assigned to different individuals who served only part-time. J. V. Davies was the first Assessor, A. N. Crow the first Collector, and C. N. Whitmore the first Treasurer. Whitmore served from 1887 to 1905; the others served for only a short time. In 1905 J. H. Edwards was appointed Collector; in 1909 the duties of Assessor were added, and in 1911 he succeeded E. B. Osborn as Treasurer. On his resignation in 1923, J. A. Clipper was appointed to the post, being succeeded by Elwood Nelson in 1946, and in turn LaMonte Thornburg took over the office in 1968.

The office of Secretary was held by Anna Sorenson from 1906 to 1936 with a two-year intermission. Her successor, James F. McCoy served eleven years until Reynold S. Tillner was advanced from Assistant Auditor to Secretary-Auditor in 1947. Tillner was given general oversight of the operation in 1968 with the additional title of General Manager.

From the days of P. J. Hazen, the TID's first attorney, down to the present the directors have had good legal help, some of it volunteered, as with L. S. Dennett who assisted Hazen in connection with the refinancing of the District's bonded indebtedness in 1902. P. H. Griffin and then his nephew and partner, Thomas C. Boone, were the District's attorneys from 1908 to 1943. Coburn Cook was then appointed in 1944; his sons Jeremy and Hilary succeeded in turn, and with their appointments to the Superior bench, another member of the firm, Lin H. Griffith, was appointed in September 1971.[15]

TID has seen a remarkable continuity in its top management. This has given the organization great stability. At the same time there has been every evidence that TID has kept up with the times and has encouraged the best practices.

A friendly and cooperative spirit has prevailed among the people serving the Turlock Irrigation District. The employees, numbering close to 300 in 1971, have their own organization which provides a retirement system and other business services for the needs of the group. The staff includes employees at Don Pedro and La Grange Dams as well as the staff in the headquarters. They cover a wide range of occupations. Customers have become accustomed to a courteous and quick response, whether the emergency is major, like the 1914 break in the Davis Reservoir, or a power outage that interrupts preparations for a family meal or the machine milking of a string of four hundred cows.

The trouble shooting crews must know the huge territory between La Grange and the San Joaquin, and from the Tuolumne to the Merced River. Following them come the linemen to repair the damage and restore power.[16] How important their service can be is illustrated by the case of the local chicken rancher whose chicken house depended on air conditioning for regulating the temperature during the

The "old swimming hole," Turlock region's version. Courtesy Turlock Public Library.

hot summer months. When the power was off for several hours on a very hot day, he had heavy losses in his flock.

An efficient and trained army of ditch tenders regulates the time and amounts of water allowed each farmer. Without these trained men, there would be utter confusion and great losses. These men are seasonal workers of the District, their employment time dependent on the length of the irrigating season. Canals are dry from about late October to early March. This is the time the District checks and cleans the canal and lateral system and has necessary cement and construction work done.

But back to the ditch tenders. Each man is given a territory and a canal-lateral section to watch over for the season. The length of his "beat" is determined by the number of outlets to farm lands and the type of crops irrigated in the area. His reports to headquarters are sent to the Water Superintendent—Ted Holden in 1971.

Farmers do not use water without permission. The ditch tender is completely in charge, making his assignments as requests come in. Sometimes a farmer will exchange his reserved time with a neighbor, but all changes go through the ditch tender's records. At the peak of demand for irrigation water, farmers take the water as soon as it is released by the preceding user, day or night. Farmers today, with few exceptions, have had their lands checked and leveled, graduating heights from the watergate to the far edge of the check being irrigated, so as to complete the irrigation in a normal amount of time and avoid too much or too little water on any part of the field.

Irrigation permits double-cropping on lands; for example an early-harvested crop of oats in the early growing season and a crop of beans planted in the summer·and harvested in the fall. Irrigation and warm summers make it possible to have up to six cuttings of alfalfa on most of the land for the season's production. Almond growers have a last irrigation before knocking the nuts, then level the land to facilitate the harvesting.

All property owners in the District pay TID taxes, even though many areas of business and homes have no access to the water. The tax is small. There are still a few town property owners of lot size pieces of land who use the irrigation water for family gardens and orchards because they have easy access to the ditches. Some business holdings and school properties on former farmlands also use the irrigation privileges.

The Turlock Irrigation District is big business. Its own payroll is large. By its services to the people, the land produces better and more profitable crops, and indirectly it has attracted many new businesses to the area. It has brought pleasure as the canals have become "the old swimming holes" to thousands. The beauty of the orchards, the grateful shade of the parks, the amelioration of the climate, is all due to the waters of TID. It has proven to be a most valuable investment for all generations.

The people of the State of California have seen the spectacular Greater Don Pedro project completed in 1971; they have seen a network of canals and ditches which has transformed the dry sandy plains into a garden spot. They will see the continued development of recreational facilities in the New Don Pedro area. We, locally, see fellow-citizens working to make these things realities. For us, the story of the Turlock Irrigation District is a proof of democracy at work in the good old American traditional way.

Fruit drying in Claus Lindblom's orchard.

Chapter XXII
New Crops, New Industries, 1901-1940

John E. Caswell

The actual flow of water down the ditches of the Turlock Irrigation District in 1901 was the beginning of a revolution in the region's agriculture. It formed the basis for new industries and caused drastic reduction in the size of landholdings as the great ranches were broken up for dairies, orchards and row crops. New towns sprang up, and the Turlock region, once famous for wheat, now excelled in melons, grapes, and peaches. Year by year the amount of irrigated land increased. In 1901 only 3757 acres were irrigated in the northern part of the District. By 1903 the acreage had trebled; in 1906 it reached 32,587 acres; and in 1908, about 58,000 acres were under irrigation in the Turlock district alone.[1] Eventually, the amount irrigated would increase to over three times that figure.

Despite the declining production of wheat in the county, there was still much land devoted to cereals in the Turlock region and in the foothills beyond. In 1906-07, Stanislaus County still had 180,000 acres in wheat, 88,000 acres in barley, and 24,000 acres in oats.[2] The decline in cereal crops thereafter was sharp. Countywide grain acreages went up again in the war years, down immediately thereafter, then leveled out for the next fifteen years at about 100,000 acres.[3]

As extensive farming gave way to intensive farming, the "scattered population of grain growers" became a "dense population of dairymen, vineyardists, orchardists, truck and melon growers, and others who farm intensively." In 1900 the average farm in Stanislaus County had 873.5 acres. The typical new irrigated farm was one of twenty to forty-nine acres. This size had been found quite adequate for a family dairy, an orchard, a truck farm, or a berry patch.[4]

At Turlock John Mitchell's heirs put his holdings on the market, and Nels Hultberg brought in Swedes who purchased some thousands of acres. At Ceres Clinton N. Whitmore split up his family's ranches and developed the Elmwood Colony northeast of Turlock.

One of the first things the new settlers needed was a source of ready cash. About the quickest source of cash was to plant alfalfa, buy a few dairy cows, and sell the cream to the nearest creamery. Poultry were another source of ready money. Others turned rather soon to planting fruit trees or grapes, then put in melons, beans, or the like between the rows for several years until the ground was too shaded to continue.

The pleasure of those years, so often missed, has been caught by Erik Hawkinson who wrote, "There was exhiliration in following a plow and turning a furrow on a fine spring day, with birds following in the furrow to see what the plow had turned up. Nor can one exaggerate the sheer joy of sowing grain by hand and harrowing it into the soil.

"The crops themselves were rewarding. To go out into the vineyard on an early morning with the hoarfrost on the vine and pick Thompson Seedless, Tokays, Malagas or wine grapes was a delightful experience in taste perceptions. To pick apricots—Orange Clings or Muirs—ripe on the tree gives a taste that we in the cities cannot know. The smell of a new-mown alfalfa or clover field was something more than bottled fragrance and far more encompassing."[5]

Experimentation went on with a variety of crops. Even within the Turlock region there were differing soils, hardpan encountered at varying depths, smooth land and uneven land, and, most undependable of all, a varying ground water level. Peach orchards were planted at Turlock but were soon pulled out, while they continued to thrive at Hughson. Between Ceres and Keyes Clinton Whitmore put in a 30-acre experimental orchard where he tried out different varieties of apricots, peaches, grapes, prunes, and practically every tree crop that has since become established in the region.[6]

The first University of California Farmers Institute in this region seems to have been the one held at Turlock in Gaddis Hall on the 14th and 15th of December 1904. Professor D. T. Fowler, Conductor of Farmers Institutes for Central California, delivered eight talks in the two days, one of which was on "Alfalfa Culture," and another on "The Dairy Herd and the Creamery." John S. Dore of Fresno spoke on "Some Uses and Abuses of Irrigation," and later on "Planting of a Vineyard." Mrs. L. F. Fowler gave several talks to the ladies on domestic science. The *Turlock Weekly Journal* commented, ". . .at no meeting of the Institute was there over a half dozen Americans present and the showing of the ladies was very slim. The audiences were almost entirely composed of Swedish farmers."[7]

Grape-laden gondola cars.

After operating for about a decade, the Farmers Institutes were replaced by county farm advisers working under the Agricultural Extension Service of the University of California, and by short courses in agriculture offered ordinarily at the Davis campus of the University of California. C. M. Conner was the first Stanislaus County farm adviser.

The Stanislaus County Farm Bureau was organized in 1914, some three years after the Farm Bureau movement got under way across the United States. Under the County Farm Bureau, local Centers were organized in the Turlock region at Turlock, Keyes, Denair, Hughson, Mountain View, Mitchell, Jennings,

Hickman, and Fairview. The advisers made the rounds, speaking at each Center once a month. In November 1917 A. A. Jungerman succeeded Conner as Farm Adviser, and served for over thirty years. In the fall of 1921 the first Home Demonstration Agent was appointed for the county.

Before the Farm Bureau entered the field, the Farmers Union had begun cow testing, one of the principal dairyman backers being Guy Miller. When the Dairy Department of the Farm Bureau was organized in 1917, the older cow testing program was taken over. That year, 2800 cows were tested. This activity later was organized as the Stanislaus County Dairy Herd Improvement Association.

By 1926 there were no less than fourteen cooperative marketing services operating in the county under the Farm Bureau and Extension Service. In the next few years the number of Stanislaus County members of the Bureau increased from 600 to 850. A U.S. Weather Bureau frost warning service was established, and peach cost studies were started which spread throughout the state.[8]

Haying and Dairying

First of the new crops in importance for some years after 1901 was alfalfa, which was used for both pasturage and hay. After the first season a field could be cut four to six times, often yielding five to ten tons per acre for the season. Although alfalfa did best on the deeper soils, it could be grown on land that would not support an orchard.

Irrigated land sold for $60 to $100 an acre; when put into alfalfa another $15 to $30 had to be spent on leveling the land, raising small levees to check the water, and on seeding. W. P. Stephenson, who lived near Ceres, reported that in 1907 he had 30 dairy cows on 30 acres of land and grossed just less than $3000 on the operation—close to $100 an acre.[9]

The impact of irrigation on pasturage and secondarily on the dairy industry in Stanislaus County can be seen in the following table.

Growth of Dairying and Cattle Industry, 1900–1939[10]

Year	Alfalfa	Acreage Alfalfa + Sudan grass + Ladino	Cows and Heifers 2 years old and over kept for milk	All Cattle
1900			4,427	21,446
1910	40,917	Same	20,678	49,132
1920	58,214	Same	36,297	78,855
1925	61,225	Same	37,206	69,217
1930	61,706	61,906	47,467	95,960
1935	67,416	88,313	47,957	109,743
1939	69,938	110,450	43,000, est.	105,000, est.

Some of the earliest dairies were run by Swedes in the Hilmar area.[11] Somewhat later the Portuguese began to go heavily into dairying and became outstanding in the field. The children early learned to milk and when they had completed elementary school started working in the dairy until they eventually obtained their own. For a while the nearest creamery was in Ceres, a half day's haul.[12]

The Turlock Creamery was started in 1908 and had a building on South First Street.[13] It put out about 1700 pounds of butter a day. After the day's churning was over the buttermilk wagon could be seen on its way out to dump the buttermilk and waste into some nearby ditch for want of economic use or sewers to carry it away.

The smaller creameries soon vanished, for introduction of trucks made it possible to consolidate in this industry, as in others.[14] By 1935 milk for manufacturing was hauled directly to the condensed milk factories at Modesto or Hughson or to the larger creameries.

After almost five years of depression following 1929, cut-throat competition broke out in the California dairy industry. Although there was more efficient utilization of manufactured milk products, per capita demand for fresh milk fell off. Milk at times sold for only a few cents a quart, well below true production costs. Prior to this time there had been sanitary regulation of the dairy industry. At the request of dairymen, pricing and marketing controls were now created through the Desmond Milk Control Act of 1934. The Bureau of Milk Stabilization was established to assist the Director of Agriculture in setting and enforcing wholesale and retail market prices.[15]

The Desmond Act and later acts provided for contracts between the creameries and the individual dairymen. Those whose dairies reached Grade A standards received contracts for given percentages of Grade A milk. If they delivered more and the creamery did not have the market for Grade A, it could pay the dairyman at a lower rate and use the surplus for manufacturing milk. The whole thing became very complex; creameries were from time to time charged with buying at Grade B prices and using the milk as Grade A. Those who got poor contracts complained about their more favored brethren with "sweetheart" contracts. Nevertheless, the dairy industry did survive the depression years. One Turlock banker said he could not recall that a single dairyman of his acquaintance had lost his dairy.[16]

The Turlock Area, a Melon Center[17]

Doran Kopp

Who the first person was to plant a field of melons in the vicinity of Turlock, old-timers are reluctant to guess. They agree that some time between 1900 and 1908 melon fields began to appear in the Turlock area.

In the early days melon raising was usually a family affair on a five to ten acre farm.[18] The melon season started for the grower in February when he began to plow, disk and harrow his land in preparation for seeding. Seeding generally took place during the first week in April. About ten days later, the farmer could expect to see the first of his infant melons breaking top soil. It took the melons anywhere from 90 to 100 days to reach maturity. Consequently, by July Fourth most Turlock growers were preparing to bring in their first harvest. Then, as in the 1960s, the field was picked five times, generally about a week apart, with the third picking being the big one. The end of July was generally the peak of the melon season in the Turlock area.[19]

In late 1907 the Southern Pacific reported that Turlock, which it had considered abandoning as a station in 1900, was now seventh in car loadings in the entire Western Division, with 410 carloads shipped during the year.[20] Presumably most of these cars were laden with melons.

When melons were first grown around Turlock they needed none of the irrigation or expensive fertilizers that they required in later decades. The virgin soil was rich with the necessary nutrients, and the water table was so high that the melons received all the water they needed directly from the soil. It was not uncommon for early Turlockers to see swamps around the area resulting from the unusually high water table caused by over-irrigation.[21]

These early years were good, as tonnage ran from 18 to 22 tons per acre in the watermelons, and prices ranged from early season highs of $10 to $15 a ton. As the season neared its end the prices generally dropped as low as $4 a ton.[22] Cantaloupes sold in 1915 for about fifty cents a crate. Occasionally, if the market was exceptionally good, the price would soar to a dollar. The cost of the wooden crate and the packing was about twenty cents, and the hired hand who picked the melons was paid two dollars a day for his efforts.[23]

By 1911, with the rapidly increasing melon production, Turlock entered upon a golden age. From 1911 until about 1925 Turlock was known as the "Watermelon Capital of the World." Melons of all varieties were being grown in Turlock and south to Delhi, east to Denair, and north to Keyes.[24]

Perhaps the first of the produce companies that specialized in melons was the Central California Produce Company, which was formed early in 1908.[25] On 25 March, an enthusiastic meeting of over 100 growers was told that the company has bought a warehouse and grounds, and that roads would be graded immediately. A down payment of $5 was required on each $20 share of stock, and the company would be operated as a cooperative.[26]

A banner year in the development of Turlock's melon industry was 1911. The Arakelian Brothers of Fresno, a prominent produce firm, had been buying grapes and cantaloupes in the vicinity of Turlock for the preceding six years. On 7 June work began on building a 40-foot by 60-foot packing shed where two cars at a time could be loaded.[27] Likewise in 1911 O. G. Olson organized his first company, the Turlock Shipping and Supply Company, which he managed until 1917 when the company was dissolved and he became an independent shipper.[28]

The *Journal* predicted that 500 refrigerator cars of watermelons and 150 cars of cantaloupes would be shipped from Turlock, while Atwater would have 60 to 70 cars of cantaloupes and Livingston 25 to 35 cars. In addition, Turlock would ship about 400 cars of sweet potatoes, while the Merced district would ship about 800 cars.[29]

In 1915 the Turlock Merchants and Growers Association was formed in order to develop new outlets for the melon crop. Approximately 350 subscribers took one $25 share each to begin the corporation. It had a number of management problems and was dissolved in 1935 after twenty-two years of life.[30]

In 1920 J. H. "Cantaloupe" Smith, a former employee of O. G. Olson, began the Cantaloupe Smith Packing Company in Denair. In 1926 the operation was moved to Turlock and the name was changed to the Turlock Fruit Company.[31] It was still family-operated in 1971.

In the early years of the melon industry there was a great deal of speculation involved in shipping to eastern markets. When a buyer purchased melons he was gambling that eastern prices would be good when his shipment arrived. If he guessed wrong, he stood to lose a great deal of money.[32]

Packing cantaloupes for shipment was originally done on the farm. The grower would haul a wagonload of melons from the field to a bamboo shed, so that his family and helpers could crate the melons under shade. After crating that day's harvest the farmer would load the melons on his wagon and drive to market. The market place was located on North Front Street (Highway 99). Here wagon after wagon lined up as each grower waited patiently for a chance to sell his load to the buyers who had come from all over the country. Eventually each grower received a bid on a piece of paper from every shipping representative who was interested in his fruit. After the grower decided to whom he would sell his fruit, he would unload it at the designated place and be paid in cash. He would then wend his way home and

Melon market, 1 August 1919. Courtesy Turlock Public Library.

prepare for the following day. Watermelons varied only slightly from the pattern of cantaloupes. They were, and still are, sold by the ton.

Immediately after paying for the melons the shippers began making preparations for shipment. During the early years nearly all melons were shipped by rail. One of the major problems of early shippers was to keep the melons from spoiling while en route to market. To retard spoiling, buyers demanded that the farmers pick their melons three-quarters ripe. Initially, ice was placed at the front of the freight car and a fan blew cold air over the melons. This technique worked rather well, and Turlock's melons arrived in prime condition to be enjoyed by hungry easterners.

About 1918 a new man appeared on the scene: the county melon inspector, who was responsible for making sure that all local melons met minimum county standards.[33] The most common reasons for rejecting a load were too high percentage of green fruit, too low sugar content, or rind rot entering the flesh of the melon.[34] Fortunately, a load of melons was seldom rejected and the Turlock melon industry grew at a fantastic pace in the years from 1911 to 1925, in part because of the establishment of certified quality.

In the early 1920s state inspection was established under the Agricultural Commissioners Act in order to set standard grades.[35] Marketing melons had been a risky business. A carload of melons might have its destination changed two or three times while en route in order to avoid saturated markets.[36] On arrival at its final destination, the purchaser might say, "Although I agreed to purchase this load at $2.00 a crate, they have deteriorated in shipping, so I'll pay you only $1.00 a crate." This "market blight" became so serious that the melon growers and brokers asked for state inspection. If inspection showed a grower's load to be of high quality, he generally received good bids.[37] In turn, the purchaser bought to specification. He received a certificate which was attached to the bank draft and had to be honored. If there were genuine deterioration, a claim could be filed against the railway.[38]

All good things must come to an end, and Turlock's melon industry was no exception. After 1925 melon raising in the immediate vicinity began to decline slowly; then in the 1930s rapid deterioration set in. The biggest single cause of Turlock's reduced melon output was the lowering of the water table by pumping to help the orchards and to protect the soil from alkali intrusion. With a lower water table, melons had to be irrigated and this seemed to cause their quality to decline. Another factor instrumental in diminishing the quality and quantity of local melons was the appearance of aphids. By 1930 Turlock's famous melon boom was only a memory. The melon growers moved their main operations west of the San Joaquin but still shipped them by truck to the now mechanized packing sheds in Turlock.

Packing melons in the Turlock Fruit Company's shed, 1945. Courtesy Turlock Public Library.

Fruits and Fruit Processing

Spring is a lovely time in the lower San Joaquin Valley. The brown hills of winter are tinted with green. Then come the blossoms, the pale white of the almond and the pink blush of the peach. At close range some of the fragrances can be almost overwhelming. Grain fields send up their tiny spikes in serried rows. The grape leaves seem to increase in size from hour to hour. The large trumpet-shaped flowers of the melons lie half-concealed in beds of green.

Summer is a good time, too, as the red-gold apricots and peaches cause the boughs to droop under their weight. Melons and squashes are stacked high at the roadside stands, dark green, light green, yellow, and striped. In the years of which we are speaking pickers climbed tall ladders to gather the peaches and apricots, filled their buckets, and descended to empty them in the boxes that would carry the fruit to market. Wagons, and later trucks, carried the fruit to the cannery where skilled women pitted them and prepared them for the cooking. What a farmer could not sell to the cannery was often "cut" in his own cutting shed, processed in sulphur, and set out in the sun on large wooden trays for the sun to dry. Raisins, grapes and prunes likewise were sun-dried. The picking, cutting and packing of the fruit constituted an important source of income for families throughout the area, particularly for youths out of school for vacations. Harvest hands followed the crops from south to north and gave the extra assistance needed for the harvest.

Cutting and drying peaches on the Gust E. Johnson ranch on Lander Avenue about 1911.

Vineyard acreages in the Turlock region increased gradually during the war years. With the coming of nationwide prohibition, there was a shift in demand from bulk wine grapes to fresh grapes and raisins which could be shipped nationwide for home wine production under the National Prohibition Act. The price of fresh grapes, which had been ten dollars a ton in 1916, soared to eighty dollars a ton in 1921. These high prices caused heavy plantings between 1920 and 1923. Where the Turlock region had averaged 2800 acres in grapes between 1915 and 1919, the average was 14,600 acres for a comparable period between 1924 and 1928.[39] Grape acreages then declined to a low of 11,000 acres in 1937 before resuming their upward trend.

For a time grapes were the major fruit crop of the Turlock region, following the decline of melons in the early 1920s. Grape prices reached a peak of over $65 a ton during World War I and immediately thereafter. Helen Hohenthal's father received $75 a ton for Zinfandel grapes on one occasion. But even when an exceptionally heavy grape crop ran seven tons to the acre, the per-acre profit never reached the peak received for cantaloupes.[40]

Orchard land in the Turlock region amounted to just over 5,000 acres in 1920, went up to almost 11,500 acres in 1927, then declined to 7,500 acres in 1933 before beginning a rise which continued year by year to 1970 with the single exception of a 200-acre dip in 1948![41]

Peaches have been pre-eminent among tree crops in the Turlock region. Peach roots need rapid intake of water and good drainage, a damp soil and plenty of oxygen. The light soils of the Turlock region provide these so long as there is sufficient depth of soil and good drainage. Hughson is near the center of the best peach land of the region.

Another factor which has contributed to Hughson's leadership was John Halford's discovery of a peach that will produce 12 to 15 tons to the acre and ripen in mid-season, filling in a gap in the canneries' production schedule. Later, Pierce Miller discovered the mildew-free "Halford No. 2" strain. These have remained the most popular variety in the region.

Pierce Miller is also remembered as being the first in the Hughson vicinity to get a big yield by adopting the long hanger method of pruning.[42] Warren Tufts at the University of California, Davis, had noted that pruning practices were removing much of the young, fruit-bearing wood. By pruning so as to leave long hanging branches, more of the new wood was saved. Many "practical" orchardists scorned the "prof's" idea until Miller demonstrated that his yields had doubled.[43]

By the early 1940s Stanislaus County was producing more peaches than any other place in the world. One of the principal rivals had been the Sutter Basin; peach yields per acre were higher in the north, but in Stanislaus County there was a greater area that was good for peaches, so that the total yield was larger.[44]

Establishment of Canneries and Dehydrators

Important alike to the fruit and vegetable growers were canneries where they could conveniently sell their fruit and produce. Prior to the opening of canneries in Stanislaus County, fruit growers in the county had to haul their figs, apricots and peaches to San Jose and Santa Clara for processing.

The first cannery to operate in Stanislaus County was established at Oakdale in 1907 by the Kaufman family. The next year the Modesto Canning Company opened its doors. It had a capacity of 1,000 cases daily and a peak seasonal employment of between 125 and 175 workers.[45]

In 1910 the George W. Hume Company built a cannery at Turlock that was approximately twice the size of the Modesto operation. The Hume family had operated a salmon cannery, the first in the world, on the Sacramento River in 1864. Later the Humes opened others on the Northwest Coast and in Alaska. They also operated several fruit and vegetable canneries in California. The last Hume cannery built was that at Turlock. G. W. Shannon was brought to Turlock to operate the cannery.[46]

During the cannery's first season of operation, 50,000 cases of fruit were packed.[47] In 1911 sales grossed $79,102.76 and the end-of-year inventory of peaches, pears, and apricots was valued at $29,670.22.[48] Spinach was another item canned in early years.

By 1917 the Turlock cannery was employing 400 men and women during the season and the output had risen to 80,000 cans (about 3,300 cases) daily. As such a labor force was not to be found in Turlock alone, that year the Humes built about twenty-five small houses, each intended for three persons, across Front Street from the cannery.[49] Said one reporter, "It has one of the best systems of houses for its employees in the state. The houses are well built and nicely arranged and the grounds are neat."[50] To young women who had spent the winter isolated from companions on some outlying farm, the opportunity to work in the cannery and live in Hume employee housing was a social as well as an economic boon.

Over the years the Hume cannery was an important asset to Turlock, furnishing a substantial amount of summer employment and taking a good share of the area's fruits and vegetables.

Closely linked to the Turlock area was the Turlock Cooperative Growers, founded by David Lane, Ed Osborn, Roy Meikle and Earl Neill (a partnership), all of Turlock; Fred Moffatt of Ceres, Haswell Leask of Waterford, and Dr. Carmichael of Empire. These men were large orchardists, producing 500 to

Hume Cannery, winter of 1910–11, Courtesy TDJ.

A display of Hume Cannery products.

Hume workers' housing.
Courtesy Harriet Hume Krusi.

Interior of Hume Cannery, 1930s. Courtesy Harriet Hume Krusi.

1000 tons of cling peaches each season. Their production in 1928 exceeded Hume's capacity, so they established TCG. In 1929 the company leased a cannery in Emeryville. Frost had damaged half the state's peach crop and prices soared to between $90 and $110 a ton.

After the stock market crashed in October, the pack netted less than $30 a ton. The Growers, however, did not give up. They leased a cannery near Salida and later purchased it. This was operated until TCG combined with other canneries to form the Tri-Valley Growers. The combined firm operated a total of seven canneries in San Jose, Stockton and Modesto. Its newest plant, completed in 1971 in southeast Modesto, was the largest cannery of any sort in the world.[51]

The California Cooperative Cannery was organized in San Jose in 1918. A Modesto plant was opened in 1920 with Armour Packing Company as the distributor. At that point the federal government entered an anti-trust suit against Armour which ended in a consent decree. With full warehouses, CCC had lost its distribution system. George Parr, a Hughson schoolteacher, bought out the other members at ten cents on the dollar, eventually sold off the peaches in storage, and owned the cannery. This in turn became part of Tri-Valley.

The California Packing Company (Calpack) came into the area about 1920, shipping by rail from Turlock to San Jose, San Leandro and Emeryville plants of the firm. The next year Jack Harmon became the Calpack representative and began shipments from Denair.[52]

The drying of fruits had been an orchard operation, familiar from Hilmar to Hughson, prior to 1936. Freestones were normally used, but clings could be diverted when canneries refused to take them. Grapes were also sun-dried into raisins.

R. L. Puccinelli's mother had an orchard near Los Gatos, and he himself was studying engineering and food technology at the University of California when unseasonable rainstorms caught their crop on the drying trays and ruined it. This experience turned Puccinelli's thoughts to more dependable means of dehydrating fruit. Acquiring several patents, he built dehydrators for various operators.

In 1929 Puccinelli built a raisin dehydrating plant in Livingston, which he afterwards bought. Seven years later, in 1936, he decided to move to Turlock and to build a dehydrator and packing plant here. "Until World War II," wrote Mrs. Puccinelli, "our products were all dried fruit of which a large part was exported—the majority to Europe. We dried raisins and peaches and packed prunes, peaches and apricots. During World War II we dehydrated vegetables, principally cabbage which was important for the prevention of scurvy for the armed services, and onions. After the war we continued the dehydration of vegetables including onions, garlic, carrots, potatoes, asparagus, tomatoes and peppers." At the peak of operations under the Puccinellis there were probably about 750 employees at the Turlock plant and an equal number at Livingston.[53]

The two Turlock plants, Hume and Puccinelli, managed to survive the Depression years and to expand during succeeding decades. They are representative of the entire group of fruit and vegetable processors that have played an important role in the economy of Turlock.

Poultry and Poultry Processing

One of the customary features of many family farms across the nation until well after 1900 was the chicken house. Sometimes there was a fenced chicken yard, but often the chickens had the run of the barnyard and lawn, picking up seeds, worms and grubs where they could. Feeding the chickens was under Mother's jurisdiction, although the children might be drafted to get a panful of feed for the hens from the sack in the shed.

The "egg money" was Mother's, too, and provided her some ready cash or the wherewithal for barter at the general store. Once or twice a week the surplus eggs were taken in to the grocer to trade for such items as a pound of sugar or a box of tea. Some families made a bigger thing of egg production and took eggs regularly to the broker who would ship them to San Francisco.

In 1900 there were approximately 66,000 chickens over three months old in the county, or perhaps 75,000 all told. By 1920 there were over 330,000 chickens, or more than four times as many. In 1939 the number had reached about 575,000.

There were about 40,000 turkeys raised in the county in 1930; this dropped to 20,000 in 1935. In the next three years turkey growing spurted up to 150,000.[54] Two years later, in 1940, 300,000 turkeys were raised. Their estimated value was $651,000.[55]

Turkeys were rather a rarity in the Turlock region until well after 1920. The first turkey raiser around Turlock was A. C. "Pat" Rapp. In 1916, Rapp acquired land a couple of miles southeast of Turlock and built a turkey hatchery. He used patent incubators at first. Then about 1927 Rapp acquired some insulated refrigerator cars, fixed them up with heaters, ventilators, and thermostats which he fabricated himself, thereby substantially increasing the capacity of his hatchery. From March through July he hatched three or four thousand poults a day.

Around 1920 Turlock began going crazy about turkeys, Rapp recalled. He himself helped many young fellows get started in the turkey business, giving them 250 to 300 poults each for a start. He never billed them, and frequently went unpaid.

Rapp stayed in the turkey business until 1945, when his hatchery no longer met the rising requirements of the State's veterinary inspectors. As turkey prices were falling, he retired rather than rebuild his plant.[56]

Enoch S. Christoffersen was Turlock's prime example of the successful poultry processor. Christoffersen started in the poultry business in 1923. At his little shop the eggs were packed, chickens plucked, and at Thanksgiving and Christmas turkeys as well. At that time the birds were shipped "New York style," without eviscerating or freezing. The containers full of fowl would then be taken to the express office and shipped by rail to San Francisco.

As business expanded, Christoffersen Bros., as it was known at that time, moved its plant to north Broadway. Express shipments were replaced by trucking to San Francisco. The truck would leave around midnight, snake its way over Altamont Pass, cross the Bay on a ferry and deliver the poultry and eggs to the produce market a few blocks west of the Ferry Building by seven o'clock in the morning.

Around 1934 the turkey season was about ninety days, and Christoffersen packed somewhat over 100,000 turkeys a year. This was a substantial figure, but a trifle compared to the 1,700,000 birds processed annually by Christoffersen alone at the peak of the turkey business three decades later.[57]

Trends

From the standpoint of agriculture, the years from 1905 to 1920 in the Turlock region were ones of growth and development. They were pioneering times. Many a family lived in one end of a barn with the cattle in the other until they could afford both a barn and a house. Then with the coming of World War I, prices of agricultural products increased sharply. The gross farm income in the county had been $14,300,000 in 1910; by 1919 it had soared to $34,204,000. This total reflected the inflationary prices of the years immediately after the war. Then came a crash and a slow revival of farm prices. Stanislaus farmers' gross for 1930 was below that of 1920. Not until the years of World War II was the gross farm income of 1919 exceeded.

With the coming of irrigation, alfalfa could be planted on much of the land. This was a boon to the dairymen, who were an important factor in all stages of the region's development. The area immediately around Turlock saw a great boom in melons from 1911 to the early 1920s when physical conditions became less favorable and the major growers shifted to the west side or points farther south in the valley. Grapes next took the ascendancy for a short time. During the 1930s production of peaches increased materially. Poultry became more important, and the foundation was laid for the turkey bonanza of later years. There was a continuing trend to smaller farm units during the forty years under consideration. The average size of farm in Stanislaus County fell from 874 acres in 1900 to 93 acres in 1938. In 1900 there were 258 farms of 1,000 acres or more and 458 of 500 acres or more—48 percent of the total number. By 1938 the largest single category of farms was that of 20 to 49 acres, representing 41 percent of the whole. Even more spectacular is the shift in farm size if one considers all farms of from 10 to 49 acres, for they represented 59 percent of all Stanislaus County farms in 1938. As many of the large "spreads" were in the foothills, the proportion of small farms in the Turlock region was even larger.[58]

Wally Lindskoog's prize Holstein, Arlinda ABC Daffy.
Strohmeyer photo, courtesy of Arlinda Dairy.

Chapter XXIII

Agriculture Turns to Science and Technology

John E. Caswell

A visitor taken on a drive through the Turlock region in 1940 might well have been struck by the diversity in crops. On the rolling foothills were great fields of barley. South of the Tuolumne from Gratton Road to Ceres, 40 percent of the land was devoted to peaches with an admixture of apricots and almonds. Throughout the region were vineyards and field crops, including melons, sweet potatoes, peanuts, blackeye and lima beans. As one moved southward, hayfields, forage crops of milo, and pastures increased in number. Forty years of experimentation had enabled the farmers to utilize almost all the land, although there was comparatively little first-class soil. Except for the towns and stretches near the rivers, more than 95 percent of the entire region was under cultivation.[1]

The war years, 1942-1945, were difficult ones for the farmers. Labor was in short supply, even after contract laborers or *braceros* were brought in from Mexico. Farmhands were drafted, and young farmers anxiously awaited the renewal of their deferments. Internment of the Japanese left the Turlock region particularly short-handed. Farm implements were repaired when they should have been replaced.

There was a brighter aspect. As prices for farm products were uncontrolled, they rose to a very comfortable level and many a mortgage was paid off during those four years.

In the ten years or so following 1945, Turlock area farmers did reasonably well. Specialty crops such as almonds were not greatly affected by the ups and down of the general commodity market. It was only around 1955 that the cost-price squeeze began to be felt. By 1970, however, it had become acute.

Characteristic of the quarter-century following World War II was the farmer's growing dependence on science laboratories. Chemists were now able to detect and measure trace elements with an accuracy not theretofore possible. Highly specialized new insecticides, synthetic hormones for animals, chelated metals—all were available in wider variety. Geneticists were making new discoveries, and nutritionists were producing more efficient diets. Engineers produced ever more powerful tractors, while mechanical harvesting was applied to a wide range of crops.

The high cost of the new equipment often made it uneconomic for the small farms that had characterized the Turlock region for a half-century. The trend toward smaller units was reversed as the little grower had to get big or get out. A forty-acre orchard had long been considered adequate for a one-family enterprise. In 1965 perhaps 120 acres in orchard was needed for comfort.[2] By 1970 syndicates were planting almond orchards and vineyards, several thousand acres at a time. As many of these investors were taking advantage of the tax shelter provided by farm development, it was the United States Government that was subsidizing the syndicates' competition with the family farm.

Let us now consider in some detail what was happening in the principal departments of agriculture in the Turlock region between 1940 and 1971.

Dairying

As in previous decades, dairying continued to be an important factor in the area, particularly from the standpoint of dollar earnings. Stanislaus County quite consistently ranked second only to Los Angeles County in milk production within California; it also placed high among the counties of the nation. By 1971, however, Stanislaus County had dropped to third place, behind Tulare County, which had become the home of some large dairy operations that had moved from Los Angeles County.

A conspicuous change in the dairy industry was the growth in the size of herd. Around 1930, as Joe Domecq recalled, the typical herd was no more than ten or twelve cows. "One would take the cream," said he, "and feed the hogs skim milk."[3] Such a dairy had a minimum investment in barns and equipment, and would have had to sell its milk as Grade B for manufacturing purposes.

Several factors tended to force out the small operator. Sanitary standards were raised, requiring more investment. Milk marketing orders controlled the industry, cut down competition, and strengthened the hands of the large milk processors who handed out contracts. As Don Hall explained it, in order to get a contract you had to be under health regulations and you had to have a certain minimum production. In order to guarantee that, you had to become larger. The good "sweetheart" contracts went to the Grade A dairymen, and the Grade B men were gradually edged out. After 1960 the selling of any kind of milk in ten gallon cans was forbidden, and the dairyman had to have a cooler, an insulated tank, and meet much more stringent health regulations. "Now the family dairy is 200 cows, and the corporation dairy is 700 to 1000 or so cows," Hall concluded.[4]

Despite the growth in size of farms and herds, very few corporation farms had sprung up in the county. During the first decades of irrigation the large wheat ranches had been broken up into smaller plots, many of them from twenty to forty acres. In the 1960s it was difficult and expensive to get enough adjoining farmers to sell their plots to make tracts of hundreds of acres that most corporate operations required.[5]

An idea of the tremendous change in herd size can be obtained by contrasting Joe Domecq's statement about herds of a dozen cows with the table below giving the number of herds in each size category and their production in terms of milk and fat.

Standard Herds on Test — 1969–1970
Stanislaus County[6]

No. cows	No. herds	Production of top herd Av. milk per cow	Av. fat per cow
1–50	5	15,812 lbs.	594.0 lbs.
51–100	45	16,678	629.6
101–150	60	19,414	757.0
151–200	21	17,152	620.5
201–300	34	18,642	659.0
Over 300	35[7]	19,511	697.0
Cows in standard test: 51,838		Over-all average: 13,579	531.9

Changes in the nation's milk-consuming habits, evident since the early 1930s, continued. Margarine could now be sold with the coloring worked in, and vegetable oils in "imitation ice cream" replaced butterfat. Dried milk was used to enrich an increasing variety of manufactured foods. Yogurt was packaged with fruits added.

The dairymen's response to the shifting market was to turn from their long-time favorite Jerseys to the Holsteins that produced a far larger volume of milk.

A great deal of effort was put into developing high-producing genetic strains. One method concentrated on tabulating productivity in terms of butterfat, and later on milk solids as well. Wally Lindskoog, who had been a prizewinner since his days in the Turlock High School Future Farmers of America, preferred to place more reliance on the body proportions of the animal. Failure to take the animal's physique into consideration, he believed, would result in an inferior strain. That his attention to these additional considerations paid off was shown by his Arlinda Holsteins placing tops in the county in 1970 with a phenomenal herd average of 19,414 pounds of milk per animal and an average butterfat production of 757 pounds. One of his prize cows, Daffy, produced over 30,000 pounds of milk and over 1,200 pounds of butterfat a year for six years in succession![8]

"It used to be," Carl Muller said, "that the cows in the better dairies that were being tested ran 240 pounds of butterfat, and if a cow ran 300 she got her name in the paper. And this is primarily the Jerseys that were making it. The Holsteins were lower. Now if you have a Holstein cow that doesn't make 500 pounds on her first calf, she's pretty likely to go to the butcher's. . . .We had Jerseys from 1942 until 1969, and they are beautiful things to have. . .but you have the choice of going out of the dairy business or making the switch to Holsteins. However, several Jersey dairies like Bill Ahlem's in Hilmar—mostly with special market outlets—are continuing in successful operation.

"The odd part of it is now that the Holstein cow in terms of butterfat is the equal of the Jersey. We've improved our dairy herds in thirty years more than has been done in two hundred years prior to that."[9]

Increase in Butterfat Production, 1930–1970

Stanislaus County Dairy Herd Improvement Association[10]

Year	Average butterfat/cow All tested herds	Decade's gain
1930	317.3 lbs.	
1940	346.0 lbs.	28.7 lbs.
1950	381.0 lbs.	35.0 lbs.
1960	445.6 lbs.	64.6 lbs.
1970	531.9 lbs.	86.3 lbs.

Another factor in Stanislaus County's high milk production rate has been careful dieting. Wally Lindskoog came to the conclusion that one can overfeed as well as underfeed a cow. He developed a device for giving each cow a quarter-pound of feed for every pound of milk in the pail, experimentation having shown this to be an optimum diet.[11]

With cows producing milk equivalent to their own body weight in as short a time as two weeks, not only caloric intake but minerals and vitamins became important. The relation of dietary deficiencies to a number of diseases of cattle was established by Lyle A. Baker, D. V. M., Turlock veterinarian. Baker first became interested in control of dairy cow diseases through improved nutrition at a professional meeting held in Corvallis, Oregon, during October 1961. His initial skepticism turned to active study. He had some outstanding successes in saving prize herds. To answer university critics, Baker bought his own herd in 1963 so that he could establish a control group for his experiments.

Baker noticed that some of the finest herds were among those worst hit by milk fever, retained placenta, and mastitis. It became apparent that the cow that was "giving her all" was suffering from lack of energy and calcium, a problem of diet. A further refinement, based on the work of Dr. John J. Miller, was establishment of the need in metabolism for chelated trace metals.[12]

By 1971 Baker had set up a system of quick analysis and reporting on blood samples and on the chemical constituents of a herd's diet. Airmailed samples were analyzed by atomic spectrograph at Pennsylvania State University. A wire hookup gave the data to a computer in Chicago, which transmitted its results to Atlanta, Georgia, for appraisal and drafting of dietary recommendations.[13]

Like the Chinese who traditionally paid their physicians to keep them well, a number of dairymen accepted Baker's proposal for continuous monitoring of herd health and diet, with the fee related to the increased profits.[14] While others had made the basic scientific discoveries, Dr. Baker had applied them in a clinical situation, had devised a highly precise and speedy reporting system, and had worked out the economic implications for both dairymen and veterinarians.[15]

Concentration on dairy cow breeding has lifted Stanislaus County repeatedly to first place in volume of milk production in the United States. Higher prices in Los Angeles County have placed that county ahead of Stanislaus County in value of product.[16]

Poultry

In several respects the dairy industry's history has been paralleled by that of the poultry industry. For years flocks were small. Many a farm family had a few dozen laying hens that kept the table supplied with eggs and put some cash into the farm wife's pocket when she sold her surplus to the village grocer.

With the coming of World War II, flocks increased in size, many ranging from 500 to 3,000 birds. Runways were provided, so that the hens got plenty of sunlight and exercise.

During the quarter-century following the war, the size of the flocks soared and the runways disappeared. A single henhouse might house 50,000 hens, crowded four to a cage. Food and water were rationed out continuously through the day, artificial light was provided to extend the day, and evaporative air conditioning provided temperature control.

Many poultry producers banded together in cooperatives. One of the biggest was the Nulaid Farmers Association, formed in 1916. It was vertically integrated from feed mills through processing plants and offered financing to its members. Following the industry trend, Nulaid sought to grow during the late 1950s. "Producers were encouraged to expand operation. Breeder flocks were developed, hatcheries were built, processing plants were constructed, and feed mill facilities were enlarged to take care of anticipated increases in volume."[17]

At the same time that Nulaid was expanding, its membership began to fall off under the pressure to "get big or get out." Between 1959 and 1970 membership fell from 1,269 to 61! Yet production remained just under 2.2 million cases of eggs a year.

Geared to a large membership, Nulaid put in a general purpose feed mill at Turlock. Its tall silos with their blue neon "NULAID" sign were a landmark on the horizon. Unfortunately it was unable to compete with smaller special-purpose mills. Elsewhere a large Nulaid egg packing plant to serve small ranchers was forced to close when the big ranches put in their own facilities.[18]

The growth of Rainbow Farms between 1955 and 1971 illustrates the trend toward scientific, highly mechanized and cost-conscious operation in poultry. Oscar Holt, who had grown up in Turlock, graduated from the University of California with a major in Accounting, as did his friend, Roland Ramsey. After handling poultrymen's accounts for a time, they decided the real money was in egg production.

Up to that time, Petaluma had been the center of the poultry industry. It had been the egg basket of the world in the 1920s, and the methods had not changed materially since then. Meanwhile the small cage system had been introduced in southern California. Holt and Ramsey chose Turlock for their location. Land prices were right, labor was available, the climate was good, excellent connections existed with the San Francisco market, and the State Poultry Pathology Laboratory on the edge of town provided an important scientific service. Rainbow Farms' first flock in 1955 consisted of only 3,000 baby chicks.

Inspecting turkeys at the Armour plant. Browning photo.

Valchris poultry feed mill.
Caswell photo.

Ramsey and Holt proposed to integrate vertically, from hatchery to retailer. As opportunity arose, Rainbow Farms became the nucleus of an expanding operation. They branched out first with Oregon Skylane Farms, near Woodburn. Later they obtained elevators to receive feed from grain ranches in the Sacramento Valley. A holding company, Valley Fresh Foods, Inc., was formed. By midsummer 1971 Valley Fresh had eleven different plants. About half the production was in the Turlock area, with eggs at Rainbow Farms and poultry processing at Valley Fresh. An idea of the size of the entire operation can be gained from the fact that in the fiscal year 1971, 1.5 million laying hens were in the cages (average), 29 million dozen eggs were produced, and 36 million pounds of fryers were processed.[19]

Since 1955 significant developments had taken place in poultry genetics, feeding, and facilities. Continuous inbreeding of high production strains of poultry had resulted in thin-shelled eggs and other deficiencies. The newer genetic technique called for developing separate strains of males and females and crossing the strains to produce a sturdy, cross-bred laying hen.[20]

In poultry feeds, energy, essential elements, drugs, and costs played the key roles. In 1955 barley was the staple poultry grain. Then barley went up in price, and by 1960 raisers had switched to milo. By 1971 new high producing varieties of wheat were being used, and the proportion of corn was increased because it had the highest metabolizable energy per pound. For flocks that became ill, sulfas, terramycin or aureomycin were added to the feed.

Chicken houses where the hens were permitted the run of the floor were replaced by houses where the hens were kept in cages, the eggs rolled down onto conveyors, and feed was carried to the hens continuously. By the late 1960s these were being replaced by "deep pit" houses. Fully automated, they were also air conditioned, sealed against flies, and the cleaning problem was solved by deep pits in which chicken droppings might accumulate for as much as five years before it was necessary to send in a tractor and scoop to clear out the manure. Automation was approaching the point where an egg would not be touched by human hands from the time it left the hen until it was broken into the frying pan.[21]

One of the more important hatchery operations was run by Wally Lindskoog, who was mentioned as a top Holstein breeder. Lindskoog bought his first turkey poults at 35 cents apiece in 1938. The first years were a struggle against disease, but by the late '40s he was clearing $3.50 on birds raised from the egg. In 1944 he set up his first hatchery on Berkeley Avenue. Later he expanded with a second hatchery near Ceres and a third in Fresno. In 1967 he hit a peak, with ten million eggs. That year the industry overproduced, so Lindskoog cut back to five million eggs in 1968. In 1971 he hatched turkeys at Fresno only.[22]

Lindskoog's primary technical contribution to hatchery operation was in developing methods of getting antibiotics inside the shell to control "air sac" in turkey eggs. This cut culls by 80 percent during the growing period.[23]

The largest independent poultry processor in the nation during the 1960s was Enoch S. Christoffersen. From the standpoint of employment furnished the community, he was also the most important industry in Turlock, although Armour's Turlock plant was a not inconsiderable rival.

Christoffersen had been processing both chickens and turkeys up to World War II, but dropped chickens because of the petty graft and black marketeering. Around that time he was raising many of his own turkeys and financing farmers whom he had under contract.

Introduction of automatic plucking machines in 1943 was a major technical development. When the temperature of the hot dip used was raised in 1951, it required that the turkeys be eviscerated, but they came out oven-ready and were much more acceptable to the housewife. Next boned turkey rolls were introduced. After contracting out the boning for a time, Christoffersen began doing his own boning on 1 July 1953. The federal government has bought great amounts of boned turkey, largely for the armed services. Up to 1971 about half of it had come from Valchris, the Christoffersen organization. At one time 60 percent of the Valchris boned turkeys went to the government.

Turlock's reputation as a leader in turkey processing did not rest on Christoffersen's leadership alone. The Acme Poultry Company had been operative for some years when Armour and Company acquired the plant in 1957. At that time the pack was about 15 million pounds a year; by 1971 it was 60 million pounds, including "whole turkeys, stuffed turkeys, the popular self-basting turkeys, turkey rolls, turkey roasts, frying chickens and cut-up chickens."[25]

With the growth in production of eviscerated turkeys in Turlock, increased freezing capacity was needed. As mentioned elsewhere, the Turlock Refrigerating Company was organized to serve the various poultry plants as well as fruit processors.[26]

As turkey production grew, eastern markets became of increasing importance, and freight rates a serious competitive hindrance. By the 1950s Valchris and others were large enough to ship in freight car lots. Although truck rates were cheaper than rail, the latter was more dependable and cars could be more easily diverted to other markets en route. With a guarantee from the packers of the area that they would ship 70 to 90 percent of their interstate freight by rail if a better rate were obtained, Christoffersen first got the Trans-Continental Freight Bureau, representative of the western railways, to agree to accept a lower rate. He then tackled the Interstate Commerce Commission. Its three-man panel seemed determined to stall action although the Thanksgiving shipping season was upon the processors. Using telephone and telegraph, Christoffersen obtained the needed information and agreements and gained the desired 0.7 cents a pound reduction in rate—during the course of one morning. This saving, Christoffersen promised, would be passed on to the growers.[27]

In 1967 overproduction caused a shakeout of turkey raisers which eliminated those who had been surviving with flocks of 6,000 to 12,000 a year. With the smaller operators eliminated, a typical turkey ranch in 1971 raised three flocks a year of 25,000 birds each. Costs aside from labor amounted to two dollars a bird.

Use of turkeys was increasing by about 2.5 percent a year nationwide around 1970. Minnesota was raising more birds than California. As these were primarily of frying size, California remained ahead in pounds produced. Despite California's position, Mr. Christoffersen believed that turkey processing in the Turlock area and in the West generally had passed its peak. Eastern growers had picked up west coast innovations, and transportation costs effectively shut Pacific Coast birds out of eastern markets.

Turkey processing still remained a big business in Stanislaus County in 1971. The sales of feed, the amounts paid farmers for the birds, and the gross realized by the processors added up to a 50-million-dollar annual volume. With the increasing population and industrialization of the Turlock area, it was possible that the center of turkey operations would move to other parts of the San Joaquin Valley.[28]

One must not neglect the Far West Turkey Show. In September 1940 a "Turkey Day" was planned for Turlock.[29] The next year E. Glenn Drake proposed a turkey show to advertise Turlock and its turkey industry. Drake and Harry Nystrom studied turkey shows from Hemet to Oregon. That fall the first show was held, but the war put an end to the shows until 1946.[30]

In 1946 the Chamber of Commerce reactivated the Far West Turkey Show and advanced $500 for promotional purposes.[31] From 1946 to 1965 the show was held each fall in Turlock. Turkey growers

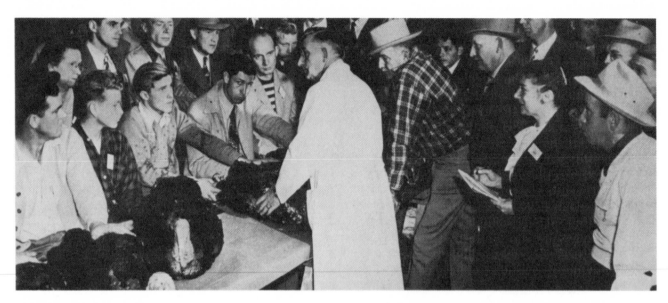

Turkey judging, Far West Turkey Show. Courtesy Chamber of Commerce.

at times came several thousand miles to participate. There were prizes for live birds and dressed birds, more prizes for the junior division, prizes for intercollegiate turkey judging—which Stanislaus State won in 1961, to the chagrin of colleges with agricultural schools. To growers young and old the Show furnished an opportunity to share ideas and problems, to see the latest equipment, and to hear pharmaceutical houses' detail men describe new drugs.

By the early 1960s, the number of independent growers had declined sharply. One by one the other turkey shows closed, and in 1966 the directors decided to drop the Turlock show. Said Arthur St. George, "The turkey business has been changing. When we first started the show 20 years ago we had an attendance of more than 1,000 growers. The last few shows have been largely dominated by major growers."[33] The funds remaining were put into an endowment for agriculture students at Modesto Junior College.

Changes in the Melon Industry after 1940[34]

Doran Kopp

With reduction in the subsurface water table during the 1920s, it became necessary to provide surface irrigation for melons. Deterioration in melon quality was blamed on the necessity for irrigation. Fertilizers were also found necessary. Long before 1940 there was a shift in the center of melon production. After 1940 many changes took place in the industry: in the varieties, organization, shipping, and marketing.

The bulk of the melons were now grown on the West Side, in the Patterson and Westley areas, or south of Turlock around Los Banos and Firebaugh. The soils of those areas were found to be much better suited to growing the high quality melons that once grew in Turlock.[35] The degeneration of the Turlock soils had made it necessary for watermelon growers to turn to Blue Ribbon wilt-resistant melons such as the Striped Klondike No. 11.[36]

Another major change in the local melon industry took place in the early 1940s. A business that had been essentially a family affair now developed into a strictly grower-shipper relationship. When a grower took his crop to market, he already had a contract to sell to a particular buyer, although he was still at the mercy of the market's fluctuations and didn't know how much he would be paid. The buyer could dictate to the grower exactly what type of melon he wanted grown that year. Actually, from the time of seeding the melons belonged to the buyers and not to the growers. In economic terms, the buyers were now vertically consolidated.[37] After this consolidation, the growers were no longer responsible for crating the melons. Thereafter all melons were hauled into town loose, just as watermelons always had been, and the shippers crated them themselves.

Between 1915 and 1969 the cost of growing and packing melons increased enormously. A crate of melons that could have been picked and packed for twenty cents in 1915 cost three dollars to pick and pack in 1969. In 1915 the wooden crate cost a mere thirteen cents, while in 1969 the crate cost a dollar and ten cents. In 1920 fifteen dollars a ton for watermelons was an enormous price to pay. By 1970 it was not unusual for watermelons to sell for as much as forty dollars a ton, with the pickers getting three dollars a ton just to pick the watermelons in the fields and roll them on end so that the pitching crew could see them. A five-man pitching crew following the pickers received three dollars a ton for pitching the melons onto a wagon. When the final tally was in, it had cost the grower somewhere between ten and twelve dollars a ton to get his watermelons from the field to the market. This is a far cry from the days when he used to sell his melons for that much per ton.

In the early 1940s shippers began using a different method of cooling the melons on the way to market. They started putting "top-ice" on the melons in the refrigerator cars, instead of leaving all the ice at one end of the car. With ice on the melons and fans blowing across the cars, the melting water would drip down among the melons. So effective was this method of cooling that the melons began to be picked "full slip," or ripe, instead of three-quarters ripe, as they had been previously.[38]

A further change in shipping methods was the introduction of long distance truck shipping. Straw was generally placed on the sides and bed of the truck to protect the melons. Trucks from all over the country would pour into Turlock packing sheds at the height of the season. However, approximately sixty percent of the cantaloupes were still shipped by rail in 1969.[39] Turlock's principal buyers and shippers were the A. T. B. Packing Company owned by Tony Bettencourt, and the Turlock Fruit Company, still owned and operated by the Smith family.

Turlock inspection continued to be important in the industry, as it had been in the two decades before World War II, although there were other inspection points in the state. It was difficult for a younger generation to imagine the sensation of pride that older residents of Turlock experienced during Turlock's melon boom. Nonetheless, the highway fruit stands in Turlock were heaped high with melons in the late summer, and visitors were taken to see the trucks rolling in from the fields to the packing sheds. The Turlock melon industry still survived.

Peaches Reach a Plateau

Late summer is one of the pleasantest times to drive through the orchards of the Turlock region. The limbs of the peach trees droop under loads of the golden fruit that are almost too heavy to bear. The sweet, warm scent of the nectar is as much of a treat to the nostrils as the sight of the fruit is to the eyes. The whole scene speaks of Nature's abundance spread out to reward man for his labors.

Repeatedly Stanislaus County has ranked first in the nation for peach production. Approximately half the acreage during the thirty years since 1940 has been in the Turlock region. There have also been heavy plantings of peaches in that portion of the Turlock region between the county line and the Merced River, including those of the largest single producer, Albert Ferrari.

For that portion of the Turlock region in Stanislaus County, a fair estimate of plantings for 1940 was 3,500 acres of cling peaches and 1,500 acres of freestones. By 1944 the acreage had increased to about 5,000 acres of clings and 2,000 acres of freestones.[40] By 1953 there were 8,019 acres in clings, of which 6,363 acres were in bearing. The years of most rapid expansion were between 1956 and 1958, when plantings of clings increased by almost 1800 acres, although only 250 acres came into bearing. In the next dozen years down to 1970 the acreage increased by only 1,500 acres, an average of 125 acres per year. Although productivity varied somewhat from year to year, the general trend was upward. In 1953 productivity was 11.8 tons per acre; in 1956 it reached 13.27 tons per acre.[41]

The increase in plantings between 1956 and 1958 can be explained by the phenomenal 1955 price of $73 per ton, plus a $7.50 per ton bonus. Prices dropped to $70 without bonus in 1956, and kept falling during the rest of the decade. In 1959 the price hit $50 a ton, then went up to $57 per ton, including premiums, in 1960. Of the 1960 season, the California Canning Peach Association stated, "More than half the growers failed to cover their production costs. Grower losses are estimated to exceed $7½ million for the season."[42] Statewide, growers' costs exceeded returns every year from 1958 to 1970, despite production controls.[43]

If one asks why so many ranches were in an unprofitable crop, one must look at the record of peaches from 1935 down to 1958. After several bad years from 1930 to 1934, peach growers again began to make money, and the return per acre climbed steadily until 1945. With the peace, peach prices followed the inflationary trend, reaching a peak in 1948. This was probably the growers' best year, statewide. The next year profits took a sharp drop, and in anticipation of the drop the first postwar Cling Peach Marketing Order was issued for the 1949 season. Until 1958 cling peach growers were able to show a profit.

Under peach marketing orders, the principal method of control is to order a "green-drop," by which each cooperating grower knocks the fruit from a specified percentage of his bearing trees. An alternative allowed the grower is to pull up trees representing the same proportion of his crop. At first trees pulled were credited for one year only; later credit was allowed for two years on each tree uprooted. As a result of the marketing orders, the net increase in plantings during the decade 1960-69 in the northern part of the Turlock region was held down to less than one percent a year.

In the thirty-year period since 1940 much experimentation has gone into methods of peach production and harvesting. One of the simplest improvements was in changing the method of pruning so that a higher proportion of new wood is left on the trees in "hanger" branches.

Many new varieties of cling peaches were introduced. By 1970 there were 98 recognized varieties, of which no less than 57 had been introduced into the Modesto District since 1940.[44] Almost half the cling peach acreage was in the newer varieties. Although many of the new ones offered one advantage or another, many varieties had come and gone and the old standbys, particularly the Halford No. 2, remained.

The chemical industry provided a number of aids to the peach grower. Around 1948 DDT was added to the grower's weapons, as the peach tree borer had become resistant to lead arsenate. By about 1956 DDT was becoming ineffective as genetically resistant strains of the borer appeared. Parathion was brought in next. Although not noticeably harmful on occasional contact, thinners and pickers had to be kept out of orchards within two or three weeks of spraying because of the dangers of continuous contact.[45]

Fertilizers have been used in increasing amounts, while their cost has gone down. Chilean sodium nitrate presented problems in Stanislaus soils, so other fertilizers were introduced: ammonium sulphate, ammonium nitrate and urea.[46]

There were important changes in irrigation practices, based on better understanding of trees' physiology. Around 1940 the standard practice was to withdraw water for three weeks before harvesting. Canneries spelled this out as a requirement in contracts as late as 1937, their idea being that too much water made the fruit soft and more subject to damage. Later it was found that adequate, regular and continued water supplies were needed for a healthy tree which in turn would bear a healthy peach. Withdrawal of water produced undesirable physiological changes. There were experiments with sprinkling peach orchards in the late 1940s. While sprinkling helped on some soils, most ranchers stayed with flooding, which was cheaper, faster and easier.[47]

Harvesting practices changed dramatically around 1960 with the introduction of bulk bins and mechanical peach harvesters.[48] Two or three bulk bins put on a flatbed trailer by means of a forklift truck replaced the repeated handling of the old field lug boxes. They were not nearly so likely to spill on the highway as the old lugs had been.

Harvesting machines consisted of a shaker mounted on a tractor and some sort of a catcher which would decelerate the falling peach in such a way as to minimize bruises. In 1971, 80 machines were being used in the state, of which 35 were in the Modesto district which stretched from Escalon to Merced.

Each machine replaced twenty to thirty workers, but the investment was sufficient to deter purchase by smaller ranchers. The main advantage in using a mechanical harvester was reliability rather than cost saving. With a small skilled crew, it could be operated during the cool hours of night, with less damaged fruit. Rain was no serious deterrent, and if showers should strike a limited area machines could move in and recover the fruit in the three-day period before brown rot set in. The amount of fruit left on the trees was found by some to compare favorably with that left by pickers.[49]

California cling peach growers had done well during the first decade following World War II. They had done so well that some sought to expand and others entered the industry. In 1956 warning signs were seen when nearly 7,000 acres were planted across the state. The following year, 1957, 10,000 acres were planted. Just at that time canners were integrating their production and mass distribution was forcing out the small retailer. To the growers, control of a cannery operation of their own seemed to promise greater influence in the industry. The California Cling Peach Association sponsored California Canners and Growers, a canning cooperative. In cooperation with growers of other fruits and vegetable producers, "two of the largest independent canning companies, Richmond Chase Co. and Filice & Perelli Canning Co."[50] were purchased. A number of Hughson ranchers became members of Cal Can, shipping their peaches to the former F & P plant in Stockton.[51]

Regulating production and orderly marketing became an increasing problem. Growers complained that canners were bonusing a few large producers at the same time that efforts were being made to keep production down. The small producer was suffering because it suited the convenience of the canners to deal with only a few suppliers.[52] With over-planting, the Cling Peach Advisory Board regularly called for a green-drop or, alternatively, the removal of half the trees represented by the green-drop order. In 1970, 10,000 acres were uprooted across the state. In 1971 the situation became so acute that as a substitute for green-drop, about 13 percent of the cling acreage in the Stanislaus district was pulled early in the season, and a little later 13 percent of the remaining trees were pulled. Still later a seven percent green-drop was ordered, resulting in the stripping of every fourteenth tree. This was still insufficient, and 53,000 tons of clings were destroyed after picking in a cannery diversion program. The net result was that cling growers sold but 60 percent of their potential output. The price received, $79 a ton, was a substantial increase dollarwise over prices received in the 1950s, but was definitely behind the general price increases of the intervening decade and more.[53]

Some ranchers had long since seen the handwriting on the wall, and had moved to other crops. The most attractive tree crop from about 1940 on in the Turlock region was almonds.

Almond Growing in the Turlock Region

In 1939 there were 4,320 acres of almonds in Stanislaus County; thirty years later, in 1969, there were 14,303 acres, more than a threefold increase.[54] Cling peach acreages had increased almost as much, while grape acreage had increased at half the rate of the almonds and the clings. Freestone peaches had suffered a slight decline. In the area from the Tuolumne to the Merced county line, cling peach acreage had increased quite slowly for more than a decade from the late '50s down to 1969. Almond acreages were increasing more rapidly both in percentage and in absolute number of acres, although exact figures are lacking. The great increase was in the late 1960s. About half the county's almonds were then south of the Tuolumne, some 7,000 acres. Some 41 percent of the county's acreage in 1971 was still young and non-bearing.[55]

One of the first ranchers to experiment with almonds was J. B. Tupper of Ceres, who carried on experiments from around 1920 to the 1940s. His own holdings were not large—around forty acres. The biggest almond orchard in the district was Bertel Rutherford's in South Modesto, which had been planted some years before.

Several reasons have been advanced for the growing popularity of almonds. For one thing, a very considerable amount has been learned about their culture. "We have learned to give almonds plenty of TLC," said Norman Ross, Specialist for Tree Crops in Stanislaus County. "TLC? Tender, loving care." A rancher formerly expected to get a good almond crop once every two or three years. With improved methods, he could expect a good crop almost every year. An almond crop is seldom a total loss; on the other hand, it responds as well as any crop to highest quality treatment.

Five factors in improved production have been irrigation, fertilization, frost control, pruning and pollination. As with peaches, irrigation practices have been improved so that the tree can put forth its best effort. Two or three times as much fertilizer was used in the late 1960s as had been the rule some years earlier. Frost control included prompt warning, the use of heaters and of wind machines. As for pruning the rule had become, "Keep the top forever young." Finally, the most dependable variety has been the cross-pollinating Nonpareil, originated around 1900 by A. T. Hatch of Suisun. For best cross-pollination, the quality of bees and the arrangement of the hives in the orchard are important. All these factors had contributed to a dramatic increase in the yield per acre. In 1958 2,000 pounds of nut meats per acre was exceptional; in 1971 there were twenty men in Stanislaus County alone who were producing 2,500 pounds to the acre.[56]

While peach ranchers were facing a series of problems in the late 1950s, the production rate in almonds was beginning to soar, the market was good, and almond growers had some very good years. Both groups of growers faced labor problems, but almond growers had an advantage in having a crop easily adapted to mechanical harvesting.

An important element of strength was a superb marketing organization, the California Almond Growers Exchange, under its General Manager, Glenn Stocker.

The secret of the Exchange has been vertical organization, a structure that has spelled success in other fields, such as poultry. Here the growers operate their own receiving stations and process a good share of their product, although a part of the pack goes to almond salters and candy manufacturers. Such flavors as hickory-smoke and barbecue have made almonds welcome among the hors d' oeuvres on many a sideboard.

Another factor has been the advertising carried out by the Exchange. Still a third factor has been the effort to push sales overseas. Between 1950 and 1970 the United States has ceased to be an importer and has become an exporter of almonds, with one-half the crop going overseas.[57]

A spectacular increase in exports occurred between 1968 and 1969. Sales to the "Top Ten" importers jumped from just under 11 million pounds to over 31 million pounds. Japan had been the best overseas customer, taking bulk almonds literally by the shipload. Then the Almond Growers helped finance a processing plant in West Germany, and imports shot up from three-quarters of a million pounds to 10.5 million pounds in one year.[58]

Continued marketing efforts would be required if almond growers were to continue enjoying good times. Around 1970 heavy plantings of almonds took place on the foothills where irrigation by sprinkler was necessary. A substantial share of this acreage was owned by "tax loss farmers" who could thus convert highly taxed current income to a long term capital gain situation. This was checked in 1971 by legislation which placed almonds in the same tax category as citrus fruits. However, with 41 percent of the county's acreage coming into bearing in the early 1970s, and approximately the same increase holding true across the state, an increase of 50 percent over 1971 production was anticipated.[59]

As the Turlock region moved into its second hundred years of agriculture and almonds began to lose their glamour, the newest bonanza crop was varietal grapes.

Vineyards

For more than a decade, from 1933 to 1944, the acreage in vines within the Turlock region was remarkably constant, falling below 11,000 acres in but one year, and never exceeding 12,000 acres. Between 1945 and 1947 acreages rose to over 14,500, but fell back to an average of under 12,000 acres. In 1958 acreages began to climb to around 16,000 acres, where they were stabilized until 1966, when they fell off to under 14,000 acres. In the late 1960s raisin acreages decreased, while wine grape acreages increased.

The region did not experience the general increase in vine plantings which had been going on in the state for the preceding fifteen years. Only in the summer of 1971 were there heavy plantings on the foothills in the Hickman area, but these were balanced by acreages taken out of production elsewhere.

The shift in demand from Thompson Seedless to varietals was likely to have an adverse effect on the Turlock area unless further foothill plantings replaced raisin types within the region.

Like other phases of California agriculture, machine cultivation has replaced much of the hand labor in viniculture. Pruning has remained an off-season task for which there is no machine substitute although machines lighten the labor. Experiments have been conducted with grape pickers, but as of 1971, much more work was needed before they became practicable.

Grapes now moved to the winery in bins on flatbed trailers. There were no commercial wineries within the Turlock region, but just north of the Tuolumne River in Modesto was the Gallo winery, the largest in the world. One of the latest developments harked back to the oldest methods, where the crushing was done in the vineyard. Gallo set up a crusher at Livingston, and trucked the juice to Modesto. Grapes had previously moved long distances from vineyard to winery; now even more efficient methods of transportation were in store.

Despite rapid growth in the demand for California wines, overproduction threatened the industry, as it did the almond growers. Across California 30,257 acres had been newly planted to wine grapes in 1971, an increase in acreage of one fifth in a single year. Vineyardists had not achieved the legal protection against tax loss farmers enjoyed by the citrus and almond industries, and with additional water available from the California Water Project to increase irrigated acreage, there was reason for concern in the years just ahead.[60]

A Specialty Crop: Boysenberries

Carl W. Muller[61]

Boysenberry production in the Turlock region began in the 1920s, when they were grown for sale fresh in the San Francisco market and elsewhere. Shortly they were moving out of the area, a refrigerator carload at a time. This was a large volume for the short four-weeks season, and was more than the market could economically absorb. By the end of the decade production was serving only the very small local demand.

In 1945 Pacific Grape Products, headed by Stanley Triplett of Modesto, developed a process of quick-freezing Boysenberries by placing them in square cans designed for home refrigerator storage, then immersing the tins in alcohol at -20°F. Pacific Grape Products contracted for about 300 acres for 1946. Following Pacific Grape Products, many freezer-processors encouraged new plantings, and some offered financial assistance. The California Boysenberry acreage practically doubled within two years. The high competitive 1946 field prices for almost all produce for freezing was followed by a postwar market adjustment when inventories became excessive. This caused economic disaster for processor and grower, when Boysenberry prices dropped from $440 a ton in 1946 to $120 a ton in 1947. Thereafter Boysenberry prices fluctuated widely from year to year.

Growers initiated the California Bush Berry Marketing Order in 1954, assessing themselves $6.00 per ton to provide market stability and expansion through research, advertising and trade promotion. Despite these efforts, in the following years wide fluctuation in Boysenberry prices continued. Factors included expansion of competing colored pie fruits: blackberries, blueberries and red sour pitted cherries; weather-induced irregularities in supply, and changing socio-economic pressures.

The Bushberry Advisory Board reported that the crop for commercial processing had fallen from 19,480,000 pounds in 1958 to 11,985,016 pounds in 1961. Production recovered by about a million pounds in 1962, but no significant expansion occurred in acreage. Grower costs were increasing, and declining prices had brought some competing fruits down to one-half their previous prices. "Each acre of Boysenberries requires 700 to 1200 man hours of labor per year," the *Report* stated. "This high labor requirement subjects growers to welfare legislative pressure restricting the employment of women and minors, organization harassment and increased cost. Only the higher producing, more efficient or tenacious growers remain in the business."[62]

The decade of the 1960s witnessed the development of successful mechanical harvesters for black-berries, blueberries and cherries. Boysenberries were the most difficult to mechanize because of their large, tender fruit suspended from a small, flexible stem on thorny vines. When mechanically agitated, the berries were pierced by the thorns, causing bleeding and loss of quality. In order to concentrate on research, the Advisory Board terminated advertising in 1969 and devoted its efforts to mechanical harvesting, improved processing, development of new strains, and refining horticultural techniques. Preliminary research produced a prototype Boysenberry harvester which included in-field freezing. Some limited success was experienced in 1971, encouraging further development.

The technique for in-field freezing consisted in direct immersion of the raw product in -20°F freon. This cryogenic freezing process appeared adaptable to most fruits and vegetables, constituting a breakthrough in frozen food processing by improving quality and reducing cost on all commodities, including Boysenberries.[63]

Boysenberry acreages in the early 1970s were relatively small, with high payroll costs for both the growing period and the harvest. If through management skill and mechanization unit costs are reduced, Boysenberries may be able to compete more effectively with domestic and foreign fruits.

Trends in Review

The Turlock region continued to be an important agricultural area of a leading agricultural county from 1940 through 1971. Its dairies and orchards produced ever more efficiently. It was the home of the leading independent turkey processor. The Hughson area in terms of tonnage was the leading peach center of the world. The region's almond production was significant and increasing.

The region, however, did face difficulties in competition. The reduction in size of farm unit that accompanied the introduction of irrigation made difficult the application of mass production methods. The decreasing profit margin from about 1937 on tended to squeeze out the smaller operator. Although the area escaped the worst of the labor troubles that afflicted the San Joaquin Valley, the threat was sufficient to turn ranchers to mechanical harvesting equipment despite the high investment required.

The very success of farmers in increasing their yields posed a threat of overproduction. To meet this, marketing orders were issued, after elections, for peaches, almonds, and other crops. These orders were issued by the crop advisory boards and provided for limitations on production. Growers likewise formed associations. The various peach associations played an important role in negotiating prices with the cannery owners. The Canning Peach Association established its own cooperative canneries which handled a portion of the crop. Similarly, the Almond Growers processed a large share of their own crops and did their own advertising.

One major consolidation within industry originated in Turlock as Valley Fresh spread its control over more and more egg producing and chicken processing plants. Foster Farms was also rising rapidly to become an important factor in dairying and fryer production.

The trend toward intensive farming was likely to continue in the Turlock region. The number of family farms remained large, despite a trend toward corporate farms.

The Draper Building at right with Osborn's store and the Blewetts' real estate office in 1907. The TID offices were in the second building down.

Chapter XXIV

A Businessman's History of Turlock, 1940-1971

John E. Caswell

The coming of the Swedes to Turlock, as has been noted, produced a period of activity in which new firms were established and new frame buildings constructed. After a series of fires, a building code was adopted requiring brick fire walls between structures in the business district. Gradually the frame buildings disappeared, and by the middle 1920s much of the downtown had brick walls and fronts.

A person returning around 1940 would have seen many of the buildings that had been constructed around 1910. Even in 1971 many of them were still standing, although covered over with glossy modern fronts. For some years before 1940 the eastern edge of the business district had been stationary at Thor Street, with a few scattered businesses in the next block. By 1960 Main Street was pretty well filled up to Palm, while by 1971 business blocks filled the north side and a portion of the south side of the street as far as Hamilton.

Little expansion of the business district took place on North or South Broadway during the three decades. Business development on Lander Avenue was spotty and growth could not be gauged as accurately as on East Main.

Between 1960 and 1970 the business district underwent considerable renovation. The Saint Elmo Hotel was torn down, and almost every one of the older shops had its brick front covered with enameled metal or glass panels. Public parking lots replaced some of the sadder structures. At the intersection of West Main and Lander old buildings were pulled down to open Olive Street through to the Lander and Main intersection. On West Main the old Hawthorne School was replaced with a modern shopping center, of which Safeway, the Bank of California, and SavMor Drugs were the principal occupants. Widening of Lander Avenue began at the south end of town and moved north until in 1971 the bulldozers and wrecking balls had cleared the western side of the street. On East Olive several new buildings went up, principal of which were the redwood trimmed Wells Fargo Bank and another housing the Sears order office and the Don Pedro Savings and Loan.

Creation of neighborhood shopping centers did not add materially to the retail facilities. The principal center, at Canal and Johnson Road, had a large grocery, a service station, pharmacy, variety store, sports shop and four smaller shops and offices in 1971—not a serious threat to the downtown.

Adjacent to the college a single building housed the Liberty Market, a restaurant, and two or three small shops. In 1972 a larger shopping center was under construction across Geer Road. As its principal clientele would come from the hundreds of student apartments in the neighborhood, it seemed unlikely to cut into the volume of downtown trade.

Various claims have been made for Turlock retail business. One was that for cities of its population it consistently stood near the top in per capita retail sales. Another was that Snow's Bottle Shop had more dollar sales per square foot than any other liquor store in the state. More solid evidence of retail prosperity was in a comparison of sales subject to state tax in 1960, 1965, and 1970:

Growth in Retailing, 1960–1970

Fiscal Year	Sales Tax Collected	Rate	Volume of Taxable Sales
1960	$191,595	5%	$3,839,180
1965	$285,650	5%	$5,713,000
1970	$378,252	5%	$7,565,040[1]

The evidence is very simple: approximately the same number of firms took in twice as much money in 1970 as in 1960; and when due allowance is made for inflation, the increase was still significant.

One factor frequently cited for the perennially high retail sales volume in Turlock is that it has been a convenient and popular place for farmers to shop. Related to this is the fact that promoters sold off land in rather small parcels around Turlock, Hilmar and Denair, thus creating a relatively dense rural population. While true of Ceres and Hughson as well, the volume of shopping of that area has been drained off to Modesto.

Nothing succeeds like success, and Turlock was able to develop a variety of specialty shops catering to the vicinity. The number of shops increased slowly in some lines, if at all. Darrell Woods pointed out that, while furniture stores came and went, there were usually about eight at any one time, catering to different tastes and purses. Turlock alone would hardly have been able to support eight furniture stores.

Another characteristic of Turlock that had an impact on the retail trade was the "quiet wealth" in the community. Many couples worked hard, lived comfortably and modestly, acquired some wealth and bought what they wanted without thought of or desire for ostentation. C. K. Sanders told the story of a farmer in clean, faded overalls coming into his display room one day and looking over the Cadillacs on the floor. Sanders advised his salesman that the farmer in the faded blue overalls would probably end up by buying a Cadillac and paying cash. Such stories well express one phase of the region's character.

Saving the Downtown

The merchants of downtown Turlock realized that it was entirely possible for community shopping centers to be organized on the periphery that would leave the downtown decaying. Starting in 1948 the Turlock Chamber of Commerce suggested that whenever possible merchants should improve both their store fronts and the interiors of their stores, thereby enhancing the appearance and character of the downtown.[2] Much improvement took place in the early 1960s.

Creation of offstreet parking through formation of a parking district did much to make the downtown more attractive to shoppers. At the same time, the parking district eliminated some of the older and more disreputable buildings.

Other changes in the appearance of the downtown resulted from a campaign to break up the continuity of concrete surfaces by establishing islands of trees and shrubs at every corner along Main Street from Thor to Lander. New shopping areas were required to landscape their off-street parking and to bring in plans with some artistic merit. Mansard roofs found favor with the City Council. The Wells Fargo Bank plan featured a warm-textured natural redwood exterior, while Safeway chose a grey stone-like stucco with a fine greenish aggregate pressed into it. Snow's Bottle Shop was resurfaced in red brick, while stained glass in a gable suggested a chapel rather than a temple to Bacchus.

Efforts to Attract Industry

The need to attract industry in order to build a town has long been an article of faith with American businessmen. Merchants reasoned: attract industry—create new jobs—attract new population—increase your retail market without proportional increase in competition.

The city fathers and landowners reasoned: attract industry—tax industry's expensive plant—raise your per capita assessed valuation—spread the tax burden without proportional increase in cost of services.

Only in the late 1960s did other lines of reasoning become popular. Economists pointed out: attract industry—increase the demand for city services—overtax sewer and other public utility capacities—generate a new cycle of expenditures for which the whole city is taxed. Ecologists protested: attract industry—ruin the landscape with unsightly factories—poison the air and water with obnoxious byproducts—ruin the land—drive people away.

Turlock's leaders recognized the validity in both lines of reasoning. While continuing to seek new industry, they became more selective. Their *Turlock General Plan, 1969-1990,* reflected a growing concern to improve the physical environment and to develop the amenities of small town life.

The first move toward attracting new industries originated in the Chamber of Commerce. Enoch Christoffersen, vice president of the Chamber of Commerce, proposed a dinner meeting to discuss ways and means of attracting industry. About 225 of Turlock's leaders turned out.[3]

It was soon determined that more information was needed regarding Turlock and its opportunities if business were to be attracted. On 27 June 1949 President E. Howard Hale of the Chamber of Commerce presented to the Chamber's Board and its Industrial Committee a proposal for an industrial survey. Earl Davis of Industrial Survey Associates stated that "the survey would show what the area has, what it does not have and how to develop what it has."[4]

Early the next year the survey was completed, compiled largely from U. S. Census, California Chamber of Commerce, and State Department of Employment statistics.[5]

Chairman Christoffersen reported that the Committee was working with a fertilizer firm, a furniture manufacturer, a cold storage plant, and a frozen foods firm.[6] In April 1951 he reported that a refrigerating plant had purchased property, and a large paper manufacturer was interested in Turlock.[7]

In 1953 the need for one new industry was forcefully brought to Christoffersen's attention. He learned that Armour and Company was considering removing its poultry processing plant from Turlock due to lack of cold storage facilities. Getting on the phone, he found that the decision was not final and irrevocable if someone would come up with the necessary cold storage space. Within 90 days, on 15 April 1953, Christoffersen and others had completed incorporation of the Turlock Refrigerating Company, and that fall brought in W. O. "Ted" Thompson, Jr., as manager. The firm was capitalized at $300,000.[8]

The Industrial Committee of the Chamber seems to have made little headway in bringing in outside firms down to 1954. Lack of funds to operate with was one of its major problems. To remedy this lack the Committee was transformed into the Industrial Division late that summer. A twenty-five-man Board was formed and set out to collect funds specifically for attracting industry.[9] Enoch Christoffersen remained as head of the expanded Industrial Division.

The semi-independent status of the Industrial Division was maintained for three years until 20 September 1957, when it was reorganized as a special committee of the Chamber.[10]

Among the firms that were brought to Turlock by the activities of the Chamber were the carton-making plant of International Paper Company, Bright Foods—now Banquet Foods, Miller Manufacturing, the Schuckl Company cannery, and the west coast distributing operation of the American Thread Company.[11] It was the Industrial Committee of the Chamber that stood behind the efforts of Stanley Wilson to bring Stanislaus State College to Turlock and paid for the incidental expenses.[12]

Attention was drawn to Turlock as an agricultural center through the Far West Turkey Show. This was organized just before World War II, then put in cold storage until after the War. Annually thereafter from 1946 to 1965 the show was staged on the Fairgrounds in the fall and attracted turkey growers from all over the United States and Canada. At that time turkey-raising was still largely in the hands of independent farmers. The show was a tremendous boost to Turlock.[13]

One other vehicle for bringing industry to Turlock was Turlock Industrial Opportunities, Inc., which was set up under the Chamber of Commerce. It was established to comply with the requirements of the federal Small Business Administration in coordinating aid to small businesses. Under this scheme, the small business itself was required to put up a very limited amount of capital, local business was also required to contribute, and the federal government would then guarantee a bank loan for the remainder. Its one success was bringing Cuckler Steel to Turlock in 1963. After that it faded out of the picture.[14]

The most effective phase of the effort to bring new industry to Turlock was the Chamber of Commerce's development of two industrial parks. An industrial park brings together at a convenient site those services and public utilities ordinarily needed by factories. The advantage to Turlock in having an industrial park was in being able to show potential customers a site zoned for industry with utilities in, and reasonably priced. The first park was of five acres on South Avenue across the street from the Cuckler Steel plant and was financed out of the Chamber's current budget during 1965-66. By 1968 this had been sold off in one-acre plots.

A questionnaire was then sent out to Chamber members by the Industrial Development Committee to see if they would be willing to contribute to a revolving fund to finance development of future industrial sites.[15] The response was favorable, and a "kitty" of $30,000 was raised. The Chamber was in the process of acquiring twenty acres on Tegner Road when the Varco-Pruden Corporation learned from the Chamber of its availability and bought the whole piece.[16] The Chamber then began developing twenty acres immediately to the south and offering it in five-acre tracts. By the close of 1971 there were five industrial plants on the Chamber's industrial park or adjacent to it.[17]

Jack Phillips, Secretary-Manager of the Chamber, commented, "We are unique in that we are the only Chamber of Commerce in the state of California that owns its own industrial park. When an industry looks us over, we have property ready and available at a reasonable price. They also learn that the business community believes in the town enough to put up their own money for development. It makes them believe we really want industry."[18]

With the success of the Chamber of Commerce's industrial parks, Turlock appeared to have found an effective means of drawing in light industry to help balance its seasonal agricultural and cannery jobs. Those in a position of influence were aware of Turlock's limitations and had come to realize that many types of industry would not be an asset to the town. The *Turlock General Plan, 1969-1990,* for instance, recommended that industrial regulations should include standards for "sound transmission, odor, smoke, sewage generation and potency, landscaping features, debris and building maintenance," while future industries should have "low sewage and water demand. . ."[19]

Banking, 1905-71

The *Turlock Weekly Journal* for 20 January 1905 ran a front page editorial which said in part, "Turlock is very much in need of a Bank. At present the banking business of this town is done in Modesto, which, by the way, is no small amount. It seems strange to us that some one has not started a bank here before this, for there is ample business here to support one, and it would be a good investment."

There must have been scurrying behind the scenes, for three weeks later the *Journal* could report that the First National Bank of Modesto had purchased two lots between Osborn & Son and M. M. Berg's store. Oramil McHenry would be the largest stockholder. "This with the new Hall building, will make the 7th new building that has been added to Turlock in the last couple of months," said the editor with satisfaction.[20]

Not until July was the First National Bank of Turlock actually ready for business. Deposits had risen to $55,000 [21] but had fallen off by the end of the year to $48,000.

Two months later, on 21 February 1906, Oramil McHenry died, and liquidation of his estate probably accounts for the sale of the First National to Horace S. Crane on 2 November 1906. Crane promptly took it under state charter as the Commercial Bank of Turlock on 27 February 1907. It is

J. E. Weaver, President, People's Bank. Courtesy Roy Weaver.

rather remarkable that in two and a half years the deposits in the First National–Commercial–Bank climbed to almost half a million dollars. The deposit record shows:

31 December 1905	$ 48,005.12
30 June 1906	78,391.02
31 December 1906	240,003.25
21 June 1907	353,819.87
31 December 1907	477,152.50[22]

Establishment of the Peoples State Bank took place on 6 May 1907. Claus Johnson was the president, M. M. Berg the vice president, and C. O. Anderson the first cashier. It was capitalized at $50,000, twice that of the older bank.[23] Despite the larger capitalization it grew much more slowly, for when it changed hands at the end of five years, its resources (not deposits) totaled only $266,279.60.[24] The Cranes' bank was linked with the heirs of John Mitchell, who had seen their land sales soar since the coming of the Swedes and Portuguese. Peoples State Bank was the "Swedes' Bank" in popular parlance, and when one considers the destitute condition of many of the Swedes when they arrived over the preceding six years, the accumulation of even a quarter of a million dollars is a matter for congratulation. In a measure, the one bank's clients had made the other bank's clients wealthy.

Peoples State Bank tried several methods of strengthening its position. In 1909 it applied for charter as a national bank, but was refused.[25] The officers' first application to establish a savings bank in conjunction with it was granted by the State Banking Commissioner, then for reasons unexplained the Turlock Savings Bank was suspended in November.[26]

On 5 April 1912 sale of the Peoples State Bank to J. E. Weaver and his son Roy was announced in the *Turlock Journal.* The Weavers had come directly from Palo Alto, but had been established before that in Colorado Springs.[27]

In 1917 or 1918, Howard Whipple and his brother T. B. Whipple bought the controlling interest in the Commercial Bank from the Cranes and their relatives and took out a national charter as the First National Bank *at* Turlock.[28]

The last bank to be established in Turlock for over forty years was the Security State Bank, incorporated on 19 April 1922 with a capital of $75,000. This was a "Swede bank," too, for J. N. Johnson was the first president and J. F. Swensen the cashier.[29] In the 1940s when the brothers Carl and P. L. Peterson took over, Security State retained its Swedish flavor.

The process of losing local control of banking to chain banks began when the Whipples sold out to the Giannini interests, and First National became the Bank of America. Howard Whipple went to the central office. Shortly, Roy Brown became the manager.

With the name now available, the Peoples State Bank became the First National Bank *in* Turlock and remained so until 25 June 1946, when Weaver finally agreed, after numerous approaches, to sell a controlling interest to Transamerica Corporation, receiving the title of vice president and remaining in control until his retirement in 1957. On 1 December 1954 the bank was transferred to the First Western chain, and in March 1961 to the United California Bank.[30]

Last to succumb to the blandishments of the big banks was Security State. In 1963 the Petersons and other stockholders sold out to the Bank of California. In exchanging Security State stock for Bank of California stock, the stockholders received stock with a market value ten times the nominal par value of the stock surrendered.[31] This was, however, a forty-one-year capital gain due in some measure to retention of earnings in surplus and also to long-term inflation.

The fourth local banking institution began in 1929 as the Turlock Guarantee Building-Loan Association. Incorporated on 13 May, the charter subscribers took a quarter of the authorized capital of $100,000. The principal shareholder was E. E. Pratt of Los Angeles, who subscribed $18,100. Ernest A. Hale and Arthur G. Crowell put in a thousand dollars each; most of the rest of the participants put up but $500. Five years later there were only 400 shares of $100 each outstanding, representing an effective capitalization of $40,000.

In late 1935 Turlock Guarantee took over a portion of the assets of El Capitan Building-Loan of Merced for $16,250 in investment certificates.[32] This represented the establishment of a boundary between the operations of the two firms.[33]

In 1948 Turlock Guarantee changed its name to Stanislaus-Merced Savings and Loan Association. It eventually sold out to State Savings and Loan of Modesto.[34] It was reported by one who should know that the sale price of the $100 par shares was $5500 each.

What was it like to do banking in Turlock? For long there was a very close relation between banker and client, for the banker could know each one personally. He knew how good a farmer or merchant the client was, how deeply he was in debt, and whether he was "good pay."

Up to the 1930s many families had credit established with the grocer and the department store rather than with a bank. Farmers would run up a twelve months' bill for groceries and dry goods and pay off when they received checks for the wheat or peaches or grapes. If crops failed or the cannery was slow to pay, Osborn or Berg or Lindblom had to wait for his money—sometimes for two or three years.

Fortunately for Turlock businessmen, many of their customers were small dairymen who received fortnightly checks from the creamery. These customers contributed materially to the liquidity of the community's assets.

For the most part there was a close business and social relation within the banking community. The banks got together on interest rates. And if one bank turned a man down for a loan, the other banks would usually get wind of it and turn him down, too. For a long time the *Journal* published the "called reports" of the financial condition of the banks. When that was stopped, the editor visited the banks and published town totals. For a long time the heads of the banks shared their figures, but when one stopped cooperating, the others just waited for the town totals, and with two quick penciled calculations learned the third bank's condition.[35]

After 1930 many stores followed Safeway and J. C. Penney onto a cash basis, and more people were forced to establish credit at a bank. Between 1942 and 1947 many ranchers around Turlock started raising turkeys. In addition to household expenses, this meant expenditure for poults and feed, which had to be financed in one of two ways: either through the bank or through a contract with the feed mill. The banks probably picked off the most dependable customers. One banker considered it a favorable sign if the women of the farm fed the turkeys. The turks had to be fed regularly and as women were more dependable, the turks got off to a better start.[36]

Those who could not get a line of credit at the bank had to depend on the feed mill. This gave the feed supplier the opportunity to lay down certain standards. He had knowledgeable field men who regularly called on the various accounts, thus reducing the chances of failure.[37]

A related factor that forced ranchers to look more and more to banks for financing was the trend toward greater investment in stock and machinery. Dairy herds went from 30 or 40 head to 100, and then to 200 and 300 cows. Dairymen were forced by the State to maintain ever higher standards of sanitation. The hand milker was replaced by the milking machine, and near the barn a milking parlor was built with its cooler and stainless steel tank.

In the 1960s other branches of agriculture faced labor problems. Braceros, Mexican field hands brought in on government-supervised contracts, disappeared. Good laborers became scarce. Unionization drives at Delano and elsewhere showed what was in the wind. As our century drew to a close, farm owners were responding by replacing the gangs of pickers in orchard and field with harvesting machinery. And the machinery required financing, usually over a period of several years.

Admittedly the bankers, too, played a role in forcing out the smaller farmer. The larger farmers were often able to offer better security and tended to command somewhat better interest rates, and the banks realized larger returns for the same effort on the big loans. "To him that hath shall be given. . ."

In 1966 Wells Fargo Bank entered Turlock. Established at first in small quarters on the northwest corner of East Main and Highway 99, its new building on East Olive was completed in early 1967. In 1971 Security Pacific, a Los Angeles based bank, moved into the former Bank of America building. Turlockers took the entry of these firms as a sign that well-informed outsiders had confidence in the community's future.

Summary

Downtown Turlock grew rather little between 1940 and 1970, but there was a conscious effort to improve the appearance of the downtown and to make it convenient and pleasant to shop there. Taxable sales doubled in dollar volume during the 1960s, while the number of firms did not change materially. Such neighborhood shopping centers as had arisen so far posed no threat to the downtown. Turlock traditionally had a large trade from farms and neighboring small towns, and it seemed to have held much of that trade because of the variety and quality of its shops.

Around 1948 the Chamber of Commerce became concerned to attract industry to Turlock. Several firms came in during the late 1950s, but the biggest catch in Turlock's history was Stanislaus State College when in 1959 Stanley Wilson managed to unite the town behind a single site. Cuckler Steel was induced to locate in Turlock in 1963 with the aid of a loan underwritten by the Small Business Administration. Later the Industrial Committee of the Chamber of Commerce undertook to develop several industrial parks with the aid of a revolving fund donated by businessmen. This acted as an effective inducement for a number of firms, and has provided orderly and controlled development at the same time.

Turlock's first bank was opened in 1905, its second in 1907, and its third in 1922. Not until 1966 did another come to town, and a fifth came in 1971. During most periods in the town's history per capita deposits have been high. Turlock did not experience the bank failures that plagued many agricultural communities during the 1930s. Gradually the private banks were absorbed in chains, with the advantages of strength and the disadvantages of remote control inherent in such a situation.

For a town that did not reach the 10,000 mark until after 1960, Turlock retailing and banking has been a solid success.

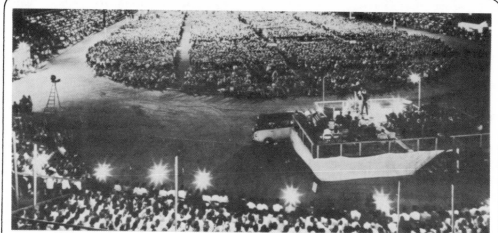

Billy Graham addresses 15,000 in an evangelistic meeting opening the semi-centennial celebration of Turlock's incorporation, 1958. Lindblom photo, courtesy Chamber of Commerce.

Chapter XXV

Turlock's Religious Enthusiasm

John E. Caswell

One of the first things a newcomer is ordinarily told about Turlock is that it "has more churches for its population than any other city in the nation." Robert Ripley made such a statement around 1930 in his nationally syndicated "Believe it or Not" cartoons. If true in 1930, the chances are against its having been true in 1970, for the city's population had trebled while the number of churches had increased by less than half.

The founding of the original Methodist Church in 1881 and its demise in 1896, the establishment of a Catholic mission in 1888, and the efforts of the Congregationalists have been treated in an earlier chapter. The religious life of Turlock, like the morale of the whole community, had sunk to a low ebb in the late 1890s.

Revival of religion, like that of community life in general, came with the Swedes. Hultberg's colony had been extensively advertised in the journals of the Swedish Mission Church. Many of the settlers were members of that denomination, and naturally enough the first church in Hilmar, now Hilmar Covenant, was founded in 1902, shortly after the first Swedes arrived. The first Hilmar pastor was the Rev. O. H. Myren. The church building was on Tegner Road near American Avenue, which was the original center of the Hilmar colony.

In Turlock the old Methodist church building was available and was taken over by the Swedish Mission congregation.[1]

A Seventh Day Adventist Sabbath School was begun in 1903, but the congregation was not in a building of its own until 1908.

In 1906 alone six churches were founded in the vicinity of Turlock. As more and more Swedes moved in, three additional Swedish congregations were established: Berea Lutheran in Hilmar, Nazareth Lutheran and the present Evangelical Free Church in Turlock. Likewise Methodist work was reestablished in Turlock after the interval of a decade. A number of Quakers moved into John Denair's colony on the Santa Fe line and organized the Friends Church; other residents founded the Denair Missionary Church. Both congregations shared the school building for the first year, then shared a sanctuary until 1910.

In 1907 only one denomination, the Free Methodists, entered Turlock.

The three years 1908-1910 saw no fewer than seven churches begin work. Both the Swedish Baptist Church (Calvary) and the First Christian Church were founded in 1908. In 1909 the First Baptist Church and two Presbyterian churches were organized: First Presbyterian, which built next year on Crane Street, and the Turlock Park Presbyterian several miles out West Main. These two were consolidated in 1916.[2] In 1910 the Church of Christ and a Christian Science Society were established. Thus in nine years, five distinctively Swedish churches had been built, and four major Protestant denominations and six smaller ones had entered the field.

The major forward movement in 1911 was the establishment of the first resident Roman Catholic priest, Father Denis Bailey, to minister to the rapidly growing number of parishioners, particularly the Portuguese of the outlying areas. The following year the beautiful Sacred Heart Church was completed. Certain features were clearly Romanesque, but its white-trimmed red brick strongly resembled American colonial architecture.

Pentecostal enthusiasm entered Turlock in 1915 when the nucleus of Bethel Temple, Assembly of God, was formed by a group from the Evangelical Free Church that desired more fervor in worship and encouragement to pentecostal "speaking in tongues."[3] It was followed two years later by the Full Gospel Tabernacle, established in the wake of a tent revival by a group of recent arrivals from the east.[4]

Although other Pentecostal churches may have flourished briefly, the next which survived until 1971 was the Good Tidings Assembly of God in Delhi, established in 1939 by a mission from Bethel Temple headed by Enoch Christoffersen. With that exception, there seems to have been a gap of three decades before the Pentecostal movement began to expand in the Turlock region. The seeds of the later enduring churches were sowed first in 1957 with the establishment of the Northside Assembly of God, the Denair Assembly of God, and in Delhi the Free Pentecostal Holiness Church. These were followed in 1959 by the Faith Temple in Turlock, in 1962 by the Irwin-Hilmar Assembly of God, and in 1963 by the Delhi Pentecostal Church.

Returning to the years following World War I, a person is struck by the fact that there were only two significant developments. One was the hiving off of Assyrians from other churches. The Assyrian Evangelical Church was established in 1923-24, and Saint John's Assyrian Presbyterian congregation left First Presbyterian in 1926. The other development was the establishment of Sunday Schools by the American Sunday School Union. A Sunday School founded in 1924 eventually became the Mitchell Community Church; one founded in 1927 became the Mountain View Community Church.

The decade of the 1930s saw a large migration into the San Joaquin Valley from the southeastern United States. Churches which were strong in the southeast were eventually established in Turlock and the vicinity, but only following 1940. Whether this delay was primarily due to lack of roots in the community or to poverty, we do not know. Only three churches existing in 1971 were established during the decade: Denair Nazarene in 1932, the Delhi Good Tidings Assembly of God in 1939, and the Free Will Baptist Church in Turlock in 1940—the first congregation of this two-hundred-year-old creed in California since the San Francisco Fire of 1906 dispersed a congregation there.

In 1941 the East Side Church of Christ was formed by a conservative secession from the First Christian Church. Despite the pressure of war, four churches were established in 1942 and 1943: the Delhi Church of Christ, the Church of the Good Shepherd (Lutheran, Missouri Synod), St. Francis Episcopal Church, and the Church of the East.

A number of German Lutherans from Turlock had been attending Missouri Synod churches in Livingston and Modesto. With the cooperation of those churches a congregation was established in Turlock in 1942.

Episcopal missions had been organized in Turlock on four different occasions between 1919 and 1943. Attorney Coburn Cook was one of the first lay leaders. Finally in 1943 an ordained priest was assigned full time and a sanctuary was built.

The delay in establishing a Nestorian congregation in Turlock has been ascribed to the fact that the heir to the patriarchate was a minor until 1940 and could not carry out the functions of his high office. The congregation was organized in 1942, and the sanctuary built in 1947.[5]

With the end of World War II, two groups, the Southern Baptist and the Pentecostal, spread rapidly. Both were characterized by fervor, literal interpretation of the scriptures, and mass appeal. The Southern Baptist Church had not been established in California as a denomination before 1940, but after that it grew rapidly. In Turlock the West Avenue [Southern] Baptist Church was established in 1945, followed in 1946 by the Delhi First Southern Baptist Church. In 1954 a portion of the West Avenue congregation wanted a more central location and founded the Broadway Baptist Church, using the old Methodist sanctuary. In 1970 it moved into a bright new building on Berkeley Avenue and changed its name to correspond.

The first Mormon family in Turlock, that of Daniel S. Anderson, came in 1911. For thirty-five years Turlock Mormons had to go to Modesto to attend services. Finally in 1946 the 115 Mormons received permission to hold services locally. By 1955, when their own building was completed, there were 273 members. Resembling the Congregational, Christian Science, and Unitarian churches in springing from American soil, the Church of Jesus Christ of Latter Day Saints was the only one of the four churches to have gained a strong position in Turlock.

Only two churches seem to have been formed in Turlock during the 1960s. Both of these were created by a group hiving off from an established congregation, although in quite different circumstances. A portion of the Assyrians within Sacred Heart parish formed Saint Thomas the Apostle Church, using the Chaldean Rite and the Aramaic tongue in the Mass.

Monte Vista Chapel was established as a local congregation without denominational ties in 1966. For a long time there had been divisions of opinion within Beulah Covenant Church. These were crystallized when the Rev. Gordon F. Rasmussen, a gentleman of commanding personality, a former FBI agent, and a conservative theologically and politically, became the minister at Beulah. When issues had reached an impasse, Rasmussen and a portion of the congregation withdrew from Beulah. After five years, it appeared that both congregations were strong enough to carry on an active ministry both locally and through their mission activities.

As one looks back over almost seventy years, certain patterns become plain. Several Swedish churches were first established. Somewhat later, the old-line Protestant churches came in. A few Pentecostal churches were formed; then the Assyrians arrived in sufficient numbers to establish several churches. The Southern Baptist drive began immediately after World War II. The Pentecostals established several new churches in the late 1950s and early 1960s. By this time, however, despite Turlock's growth by half during the 1960s, the period of rapid church formation seems to have drawn to a close. The significant developments of that decade were a strengthening of Catholic and Pentecostal congregations, a plateau in membership for some Protestant congregations, a surge of church buildings, and a growth in interchurch fellowship for the churches in general.

On the basis of evidence presented so far, it becomes clear that the diversity of nationalities in Turlock and vicinity explains in considerable measure the diversity of churches. Two nationalities brought not one but four churches each in their train. The Swedes brought not only their national church, the Swedish Lutheran, but Mission Covenant, the Swedish Baptist, and the Evangelical Free Church. The Assyrians likewise established four churches. The Portuguese practically made a national church out of Sacred Heart parish for several decades but did not create a separate parish as the Chaldeans did later. We may apply the same principle and point out that migrants from the South carried with them their own sectional churches.

This by no means explains all the variety in Turlock. Monte Vista Chapel was created by the ultra-conservative wing of a congregation which had never been considered particularly modernist. The Eastside Church of Christ likewise split off from a relatively conservative congregation. Some of the Eastside congregation objected to instrumental music and hymns in church; others objected to affiliation with national groups.[6] Some of the division then was along conservative-less conservative lines. One hesitates to use either "modernist" or "radical" in the Turlock context.

The large number of tiny Pentecostal churches is probably due to two factors. First, anyone who feels that the Spirit has called him to preach is free to do so with little restraint—no minimum of seven years of higher education is demanded of him. Further, the local congregation is practically autonomous.

The pastor in numerous instances does not expect to be entirely supported by the gifts of the congregation. Unlike the staid old-line churches, the newer churches emphasize enthusiasm rather than discipline. Whether the Turlock region has turned out to be especially fertile soil for the Pentecostals would be hard to answer. The writer feels that many other areas have been equally fertile. It is only that the eyes of those who write books are blind to the little stucco chapels in the poorer suburbs of our cities.

If the period of rapid church formation may have drawn to its close, it does not mean that the churches of Turlock have failed to make progress. Indeed a stranger coming to Turlock in the early 1950s might have been more perplexed than a later arrival to hear that Turlock was a strong church town. If the business section was shabby, some of the church buildings were disgraceful—battered, weathered and dingy. Between 1954 and 1971 a real transformation took place.

One of the most spectacular changes came when the Methodists moved from a worn brown frame bungalow to a large concrete block structure set amidst spacious lawns and parking lots. Its beautiful sanctuary with royal purple and deep red stained glass harked back to the Anglican tradition. Comfortable church school rooms, a large social hall, and an elegant reception room made up for years of austerity. Later the church school plant was expanded.

The First United Methodist Church, 1972, typical of the solid and attractive church buildings constructed during the 1950s and 1960s. Caswell photo.

The Evangelical Free Church moved from the tiny triangle formed by Lander and "A" Streets to a site on Johnson Road that was even more spacious than the Methodist site, and there they erected a church that was equally lovely. Beulah Covenant's congregation tore down their old Sunday School building (the original Turlock High School) and erected modern classrooms. Later the main sanctuary was refurbished and a very fine pipe organ installed. Bethel Temple built one of the largest sanctuaries in town next to an older building. Behind the choir was a silhouette of Calvary and three stark crosses. The Seventh Day Adventists built a new sanctuary on East Olive, next to their school, where the light filtering through the stained glass produced a particularly fine glow at the end of a summer's day.

Berkeley Avenue became a new "church row" during the period. The Methodists and the Latter Day Saints built on it. The Presbyterians began what they expected to be a multistructure complex by building an Olympic-size swimming pool as the core of a fellowship center. Saint Thomas Chaldean Church built a little farther out; and Broadway Baptist, as was mentioned, relocated there and took the name of Berkeley Baptist. Monte Vista Chapel built at the intersection of Berkeley and Monte Vista, and after once expanding its main structure, built a commanding office tower on the corner.[7]

In 1971 the Free Methodist Church built several hundred yards east of Berkeley Avenue on Tuolumne Road, and Calvary Baptist Church began construction on Monte Vista Road at Olive, the nearest church at that time to the college campus.

The most significant architectural triumph among the churches was the new sanctuary of Sacred Heart Church, designed by Gilbert W. Goulart, a local architect who was a son of the parish. The structure brought many elements of modern architecture to the service of a great traditional church in the midst of a decade of modernization. High above the main entry, for all who approached to see, stood Christ as Teacher, inviting worshipers. Inside, the abundant decoration of many Roman Catholic churches was missing. Pulpit, lectern, and communion table were in the midst of the congregation, while beyond the altar was poised another figure of Christ.

The churches of Turlock, for the most part, finished the century in good physical condition, with attractive sanctuaries, church schools, and social halls. It had required sacrifice and faith, but one could no longer say that Turlock's homes were bright while her churches were dingy.

Three churches operated day schools in Turlock at the end of the first century. The Sacred Heart Parochial School enrolled about three hundred students in grades 1 through 8. Tuition was $20.00 a month per family, regardless of the number of children enrolled. Because of a shortage of nuns, the upper four grades were taught by lay personnel. Students could continue through high school in the Saint Stanislaus parish in Modesto.[8] The Seventh Day Adventist School normally enrolled about sixty students in grades 1 through 8, with tuition at $32.00 per student. Its graduates could attend the Adventist Academy on Hatch Road in Ceres.[9] Newest of the schools was the Turlock Christian School begun in 1968 and sponsored and housed by the Evangelical Free Church. It had between forty and fifty students in kindergarten through the third grade, and tuition ranged from $25.00 to $35.00 per child. About two-thirds of the children were from churches other than the Evangelical Free Church.[10] This pattern of parochial schools was not conspicuously different from that of many other cities across California.

The Seventh-Day Adventist Church, 1972, like others in Turlock, suggested the Gothic in the sanctuary's design. Caswell photo.

Figures on changes in Turlock's church membership were sought from only a few churches for it was rightly anticipated that some would be reluctant to release them. However, the pastors of several of the larger parishes were most cooperative, and the information obtained suggests some interesting trends.

Father Manuel V. Alvernaz came to Sacred Heart Church in 1959. By 1970 attendance at all Sunday masses had increased from an average of about 1200 to about 2300. There were seven Sunday masses, including one in Portuguese and one in Spanish. In 1970 there were 122 confirmations, and 55,000 individual communions were administered. Within the city itself, Catholics had increased from 8 percent of the 1960 population to 20 percent of the 1970 population, which was still below the statewide figure of 26 percent. Father Alvernaz attributed the increase to the growth of the town and the influx of people with a wider range of national and religious backgrounds following establishment of the college. There had been, however, no particular increase in number of Catholics among the rural population. Sacred Heart's congregation was mixed, with Anglos, Portuguese, Mexicans, and Assyrians. Rather surprisingly, Father Alvernaz felt that the proportion of Mexicans had increased only slightly during the decade. Most, but by no means all, of the Assyrians had hived off when Saint Thomas Church was established.[11]

Among the Protestants, two old-line Anglo-American churches admitted some loss in membership over the decade, although there seems in one case to have been an actual increase in attendance. In neither case did there appear to be any decrease in activities. A third old-line church reached a peak early in the decade, had suffered its downs and ups since then, and was probably weaker than it had been in 1963, although it should have profited as much as any by the coming of the college.

The churches originally founded by the Swedes now had a strong admixture of other national elements. The total number in Beulah Covenant and its offshoot, Monte Vista Chapel, was greater than for the single church a decade previously. Overall, there was probably some small growth in membership for the entire group, but not in proportion to the town's growth.

Bethel Temple, oldest and largest of the Pentecostals, had increased its average attendance for all Sunday services from about 1050 to 1550 between 1960 and 1970. The number of communicant members increased from 150 to 375, and the Sunday School enrollment rose from 750 to 1250.[12] This increase materially exceeded the rate of population growth at the same time that the number of Pentecostal congregations was increasing.

In the decade we have been considering, the basic fact is that Turlock's population increased by one-half. Sacred Heart Church and Bethel Temple very nearly doubled in size, gaining slightly on the general population. The Swedish group of churches gained but still did not get their proportional share of the general population increase. This is to be expected in view of their lingering ethnic identification. The old-line Protestant churches were the ones that probably would have shown the least growth if a full census had been made, and this despite an increasing number in the community with white, Anglo-Saxon, Protestant backgrounds.

The dramatic Sacred Heart Church, 1972, placed the altar in the center of the worshiping congregation. Mark Vasche photo, courtesy Modesto Bee.

Explanations for the standstill reached by the Protestant churches in Turlock differ little from those offered across the nation. The new families that might have made them grow were often a little younger, a little better off, a little more likely to have been to college, a little more involved in other community activities, and a little more often transplanted from community to community than the typical Turlock family. Uprooted, busy, skeptical, with a sailboat in the garage, they had no time for the churches of their fathers.

There were gaps among the churches, as well as within the churches. Conspicuous by their absence were several of the liberal wing of American Protestantism: the Congregational church, the Quakers, and the Unitarian-Universalists. Despite a growing Jewish element, there was no Jewish synagogue, although Modesto had one.

Christian activities were by no means confined to the churches, whether evangelistic, social, or welfare. The evangelistic and missionary impulse has been strong in Turlock. The *Turlock Journal* reported a series of evangelistic meetings in 1905, and these probably were not the first. One of the earliest evangelists was Dan Shannon. Between 1910 and 1920, John Brown conducted several evangelistic campaigns. In 1919, and probably at other times, evangelistic services took place in a wooden tabernacle on West Main opposite the Hawthorne School (later the site of the Norton Mortuary).[13]

After its establishment about 1937, the Turlock Christian Businessmen's Committee sponsored an evangelistic series almost every year for a quarter-century. Held at first in tents, they were later transferred to the fairgrounds. Beulah Covenant, Bethel Temple, Calvary Baptist, the Evangelical Free Church, and for a while the Methodists and the Presbyterians, as well as others, sponsored evangelistic meetings.

The high point in evangelistic services was reached on 25 May 1958, when the Rev. Billy Graham opened the Semi-Centennial of Turlock's incorporation with a mass meeting. At this service on the Turlock High School football field 15,000 people crowded in to hear him—twice the population of the town—and 1300 sang in the massed choir.

Evangelistic services continued to attract crowds in Turlock. David Wilkerson's Youth Crusade at the Fairgrounds in 1970 brought a total attendance of about 10,000 in three nights. In 1971 Marvin Schmidt conducted a Spiritual Renewal Crusade at Bethel Temple with a total attendance of over 40,000 in seven weeks. Closed circuit television had to be used to accommodate the crowd.[14]

Turlock's missionary impetus extended around the world. Monte Vista Chapel had one end of its high foyer covered with pictures of missionaries it supported, some of whom had gone out from the Chapel itself. Bethel Temple contributed to the support of seven missionaries in the United States and thirty-three abroad. Beulah Covenant fully or partially supported fifteen missionaries.[15] Other churches could identify amounts allocated to missions.

Summary

Turlock in 1971 hardly lived up to its reputation for having more churches relative to its population than any other town in the country. However, it did have a high proportion of church membership and attendance, particularly for a western town. The number of new sanctuaries erected since 1954 indicated both enthusiasm and financial support. The large number of churches is explained in part by the diverse national and sectional origins of the population, and in part by the appeal of the Pentecostal churches. Some Anglo-American churches had reached a membership plateau, due in some measure to the worldly success of their upper middle class clientele. The smaller denominations that concentrated on a fundamentalist gospel message, however, were continuing to grow. In this part of grass-roots America the Christian church was still vigorous and a strong motivating force in the lives of individuals and of the community.

Turlock's 1907 baseball team. Courtesy Rex Ish Post No. 88, American Legion.

Chapter XXVI

Recreation in Turlock

John E. Caswell

Since the days of Turlock's resurrection around 1905, it has provided a variety of amusements for its citizens. Newcomers have not always known where to look, but those who are reasonably outgoing personalities have usually found plenty to do. From the time that an association was incorporated to build the "Opera House" and home talent shows were put on, down to 1971 when Turlockers were writing and preparing to produce their centennial pageant without outside direction or talent, much initiative has been displayed in providing entertainment and recreation.

By 1907 Turlock had fielded a team in a valley league. Among the players were Pat Rapp and Walter Brown, both well known to three generations of Turlockers. One of the first fields was at the corner of East Main and Colorado; another was between Front Street and the railroad tracks, south of Canal. In the 1920s and 1930s baseball was played on the American Legion field at the present fairgrounds.

In the 1930s the first softball league was organized. The teams are reported to have been the *Swedes,* the *20-30 Club,* the *American Legion,* the *National Guard,* the *Gratton Grange,* and the *TID.*

In 1924 the Turlock Golf Club was founded and a nine-hole course built. Later this was extended to eighteen holes, and a new clubhouse and pool were added.

The 38th District Fair

For many the high point of the year was the Fair. One can trace the idea from the Fourth of July parades of the 1900s to the Melon Carnivals of 1911 and the next few years. World War I put a stop to these celebrations. Then in 1924 Rex Ish Post 88 of the American Legion and the Women's Auxiliary put on a very successful Fourth of July celebration. The next year the Legion revived the carnival. A second carnival was held in 1926 in the baseball park which lay between the railroad and Front Street north of Olive.

A better site was needed, so the Legion and Auxiliary bought a twelve-acre plot of land at North Broadway and Canal. It was named "Legion Field," and an entry arch was built of river boulders. In succeeding years attendance grew. There were 21,893 paid admissions in 1932. In 1933 three days were dedicated to the Future Farmers of America and to the 4-H Clubs. This was signaled by changing the name to the "Turlock Melon Carnival and Junior Stock Show."[2]

By this time the carnival had become more than the Legion and Auxiliary could handle alone. Other areas had fairs to which the State contributed through District Agricultural Associations. How could Turlock transform the carnival into a district fair?

Two men turned the trick. In 1934 Dr. Harry D. Channing was an active supporter of Frank Finley Merriam in his primary campaign for governor. If Merriam won the governorship, Channing was to receive an appointment to the Board of Dental Examiners. Meanwhile attorney W. Coburn Cook was active in the campaign of the incumbent, Governor Clement C. Young. He had been promised that Turlock would receive a charter for a District Agricultural Association if Young won. Cook proposed that Channing ask for the charter in place of the Dental Examiners appointment, and the one that was successful in bringing the district fair to Turlock could be considered the "daddy" of the fair.

Channing's candidate won, and a bill was put through the Legislature creating the 38th District Agricultural Association to manage the fair on behalf of the State.[3]

The fair was sponsored jointly by Rex Ish Post and the Agricultural Association down to 1941, when the title was changed to the Stanislaus District Fair. The Legion sold its tents and equipment and interest in the site to the District. Meanwhile, the site had been expanded to 32 acres and an armory-exhibit building had been constructed by the federal Work Projects Administration.

Fairs were discontinued during World War II. For a short time during 1942 Japanese were interned in the camp while awaiting transfer to inland areas. In 1946 the fair was revived and the site increased to fifty-two acres.[4] The armory became the industrial building. A new building was constructed for agricultural displays. Other buildings included a cafeteria operated by the Pomona Grange and one especially constructed for flower and garden exhibits. Stock sheds and metal buildings were erected, expanded and improved.

In 1960 the fairground was chosen as the temporary campus of Stanislaus State College. Rental of the facilities provided additional funds for the fair, and a number of improvements were made, including surfacing of most of the roads.

There was seldom a year in which attendance at the fair did not exceed previous years. Increasing urbanization did not dull its delights.

The fair took place during the first week in August. On a hot summer's night people would pour in from miles around, the men in shirtsleeves, the women in summer dresses or slacks or shorts, many walking hand in hand.

First would come the home economics exhibits: prize cakes and pies, canned fruits, dresses, embroidery, knitted garments, weaving. Next, the flower exhibits: orchids beside a mossy waterfall, roses, early chrysanthemums, and dozens of others. Outside the building were booths in which contestants had designed gardens: Japanese, English, Mexican, Southern—each an invitation to repose. Now on toward the stage, where under bright lights contestants for the title of Miss Stanislaus paraded in bathing suits and formal dresses, doing little numbers as demonstrations of their musical, dancing or other talents. Nearby were the bandstand and concrete dancing floor where the music blared loudly and many found pleasure in motion.

The next natural stop was the agricultural hall. Here fairgoers could wander contentedly, noting the quality of the peaches, melons, squashes, grapes, strawberries, beans, bell peppers, and a score of other products of field and orchard. Then a quick circuit of the Industrial Building, where *Britannica* competed with *Americana,* Hoover with Electrolux, Republican voter registrars with their Democratic opponents, and all sorts of vendors plied their wares as the litter of discarded leaflets accumulated on the floor.

The 4-H Clubs' and Future Farmers' exhibits came next. The first building housed the girls' sewing projects; then followed shed after shed filled with Holsteins, Jerseys, porkers, sheep, rabbits and assorted fowl. Adjacent was the judging ring where Future Farmers persuaded their cattle to show off their finer points.

Last came the mixed joys of the Midway. Here were all sorts of catch-penny games: toss a dime into a bottle and win a gaudy prize! Shoot the ducks that move along the gallery—once in a while a crack shot comes along and makes a killing! Talk your girl into going on a scary ride in the hope that she will cling tightly to you. Walk through the House of Horrors. Ride a boat on a river of steel links through the Tunnel of Love. Stop for a foot-long hot dog and a coke, or perhaps an enchilada.

By now the night was cool, so tired and happy, the fairgoers sought their cars on the many seemingly identical side streets and headed homeward.

Older fairgoers could recall features that attracted special interest. Some liked the Hi Tail Horse Shows, with the handsome horses being put through their paces by adept riders. The women recalled the cute Kiddi Kapers Parades. Rodeos attracted young and old alike, while some got their thrills from watching drivers mash up their junk cars in the Destruction Derby.

At other times in the year the District Fairgrounds were made available for other activities. Among the annual events at one time or another were a poultry show, the Far West Turkey Show, demonstrations by the Turlock Cavalier Colts, evangelistic meetings, and cattle sales.

The Youth Center

For thirty years an extremely useful facility was the Youth Center, built in 1941 on East Avenue near Minaret. Such a center had been dreamed of for some time when Dr. Marion C. Collins sparked the drive that made it a reality. The Exchange Club furnished much of the muscle power, under Rex Abraham, chairman of the construction committee. The original Turlock Women's Club contributed $1500 that it had been holding for some time for a public purpose. From Exchange Club and other sources another $1800 was raised. When completed, the structure was appraised at $8,500.[5] It was dedicated on 25 February 1942, with Mayor Roy M. Day presiding. The ceremony "marked formal acknowledgment of the completion of years of effort on the part of Turlock Exchange Club, with the cooperation of the Turlock Women's Club and other civic groups."[6]

Prior to the formation of a Recreation Commission, the building was administered by five trustees appointed by the City Council, on which the Exchange Club was represented. It was reported in 1946 that "One or more youth groups meets there almost every afternoon and evening."[7] Later, the Senior Citizens met there until they had quarters of their own. In 1971 the Youth Center was still in active use and was a convenient size for groups up to 140.

The City Parks and Recreation Department

The City of Turlock made what was probably its first significant contribution toward providing recreation when it built the Turlock Plunge, a swimming pool, beside Highway 99 about 1925. Sheltered from the winds by a high white wall, with a tall diving tower, dressing rooms and a sun deck, it was a cool oasis in what was still a hot and dusty land. It was leased out to various operators over a period of close to thirty-five years, until it was finally torn down about 1959. For long, this was the only pool in town. The common alternative, which was by no means safe from disease or drowning, was to swim in an irrigation canal. Indeed, one of the favorite swimming places in town until the high school pools were built in the early 1960s was directly across from the high school, where the depth of the canal seems to have been about right.

Organized recreation was first developed by the high school and was conducted by it for several years down to 1945. On 15 May of that year, the principal of Turlock High School, Charles Perrott, went before the City Council to ask aid for the City Recreation Program. Three weeks later the Council was requested by the Turlock Softball Association to develop Columbia Park for softball. The same night, 5 June 1945, a Recreation Board was created, consisting of Councilman E. R. Gaster, Superintendent Robert Lee of the Turlock Elementary Schools, and Principal Charles Perrott of the High School. An amount not exceeding $350 a month was authorized for recreational activities by the Council, and shortly thereafter Cliff McKay was hired as summer recreation director at $250 a month. Earlier in the year tree planting had begun at Columbia Park.

The year 1947 saw a major step forward in the development of a city recreation program. A Recreation Commission was appointed on 15 April, with attorney Oliver K. K. Nelson as chairman.[8] McKay was again appointed summer recreation director, serving from May through September. The next month Ed Frank, who had prepared a report on recreation in the spring, was appointed the first full-time recreation director at a salary of $300 a month. Somewhat after the fact, a formal agreement was signed that the Turlock High School and the County Superintendent of Schools Office would contribute $500 each for recreation expenses in 1947-48.[9]

Late in 1949 the project of a War Memorial Auditorium got well started when Mrs. Jennie V. Starr gave a piece of land on the northeast corner of Canal and North Palm for the project.[10] After searching unsuccessfully for government funds, the townspeople furnished money, materials, and labor, completing the building and turning it over to the City Council almost exactly two years after Mrs. Starr's gift, on 20 November 1951.

The availability of a large multipurpose auditorium opened many opportunities to the Recreation Department. Now dances could become a regular part of the program. Active games could be played in wet weather. Craft classes could meet the year around.

Rentals became an important source of revenue to offset the cost of operating the auditorium. Local groups rented the building to put on breakfasts and dinners as a means of financing their own projects, many of which were youth programs. Close to 10 percent of the whole population of the town would turn out for the more popular dinners. The Methodists and Episcopalians had beef dinners; the Presbyterians, their chicken barbecues. In some years there must have been a full dozen pancake breakfasts staged by one group or another. People enjoyed coming to these affairs, not only because the cooking was good and the meals more reasonable than restaurant prices, but also because they were sure to find old friends there, and their money was going to some charitable organization.

Although planned so that it could be used as a basketball floor, few athletic events were ever staged in the War Memorial. In 1967 the building was remodeled, the kitchen modernized, and a small meeting room substituted for the stage. A false ceiling and new lights were installed, and the Auditorium became even more acceptable as a social hall.

Before the War Memorial was finished, the Girl Scouts donated the Girl Scout House and the land on which it stood to the City as an extension of the Columbia Park facilities. The house was then available for other affairs when the Girl Scouts were not using it.[11]

Meanwhile Turlock's favorite game, baseball, was thriving. A Junior Softball League was organized early in the summer of 1950. That winter Turlock High School was approached for use of its baseball field for night baseball. The G. W. Hume Co. guaranteed the necessary money to light the field, and it was agreed early in 1951 that the Recreation Department would have use of the field during the summer.[12]

After financing the War Memorial Auditorium the good citizens of Turlock took a deep breath before embarking on the project of obtaining a new pool site. Fifteen months after the War Memorial was completed, Mrs. Arthur Sanders and Mrs. Mabel Endorf began their drive to obtain a public pool, but it was not until the summer of 1956 that things began to move. On 18 September Harold Larson proposed pools for both the East and West sides. In March 1957 the Council authorized a pool at Columbia Park if funds became available. A committee was formed with Harold Larson as chairman. Councilman Gilbert Moody suggested that $25 Life Admission tickets be sold to finance the Columbia pool, and this was done. Turlock Community Pool, Inc., was organized to handle the funds drive and to contract for construction. In December 1957 Larson reported to the Council that a bid of $25,000 had been received for building the pool, except for the deck and wiring, which would be completed with volunteer labor. On 21 May 1958 the pool was turned over to the City. There were, however, no dressing rooms, so the Council voted $10,000 for their construction.[13]

For several years there had been both mechanical and personnel problems in operating the City Plunge, which was now more than thirty years old. With Columbia Pool available, it was closed down and shortly thereafter was demolished. This left the youngsters of the East side with a long trek and a

Columbia Pool. Courtesy Turlock Parks and Recreation Department.

dangerous highway crossing to reach Columbia Pool. A joint Turlock High School-City Recreation Department Pool had been proposed at the time that a drive was begun for the Columbia Pool. On 7 December 1960 the City Council agreed to contribute $25,000, estimated to be a quarter of the cost, toward a new pool complex consisting of a regular pool for recreation and racing and a deep pool for diving. Matters moved along slowly. Two years later the City agreed to increase its share to $30,000 provided bath houses were built. Finally in the spring of 1963 the pools were completed.[14]

About this time the Parks and Recreation Department undertook a new long-range project—the creation of a large community park in the area of future housing development south of the college. The *Turlock General Plan* issued by the County Planning Department in January 1962 had shown need for both a park and a storm water holding basin in that vicinity. It was proposed to combine the two by developing a lake that could be supplied by TID in the summer and used as a holding area and settling basin during winter storms.

On 14 September 1962 the Park and Recreation Commission recommended that a north area park site be acquired and that it be named in honor of retiring State Senator Hugh P. Donnelly, a long-time resident of Turlock. Twenty-three acres of land were acquired on the south side of Pedras Road, with the aid of a 30 percent grant from the federal government. Development proceeded slowly. In 1966 the Lions Club presented 200 trees for the park, and a basin was scooped out. Some time later additional land was acquired, bringing the total up to 38.7 acres.[15] In 1971 arrangements were made with the contractor building the freeway bypass by which he would complete excavation and grading in partial payment for dirt removed for overpasses. It appeared that a full dozen years would elapse between the time the site was acquired and the opening of Donnelly Park to the public. Fortunately, land had been acquired at a favorable price and planning begun in ample time prior to actual construction of sub-divisions in the area.

A Town Hall Forum on drugs held on the SSC campus in November 1968, followed by a forum for high school students at the War Memorial, helped focus attention on the fact that Turlock, like many other towns, did not have a real social center for young people. Several church leaders formed a Christian coffee house, the Rapping Post. For high school age students, Sally Gillispie and Abe Rojas undertook to establish a center which was soon given the name Kaleidoscope. As the old City Library building on North Broadway had recently been vacated, the Council granted the use of the building, along with $700 for materials to renovate and adapt it for the new use. In the spring of 1969 teams of young people and parents set to work to renovate it. Furnishings and appliances came from service organizations and individuals, including a fine radio-stereo donated by the former Superintendent of the Turlock High School District, John Pitman. Thornton Snider donated pool tables. In the fall of 1971 attendance remained good, running from twenty-five to fifty a day. The emphasis was on recreational activities.[16]

In 1971 the principal facilities available through the City for recreation were Columbia Park with its swimming pool, Broadway Park with a tots' wading pool, Crane Park with its tennis courts, the high school pools during the summer, the War Memorial Auditorium for dances and large meetings, the Youth Center for meetings up to 140, and the Girl Scout House for smaller groups. The Senior Citizens Center had just become available under certain restrictions. And there were ball parks on Soderquist Road and at the Julien and Wakefield Schools.

Diane Domingues and Beverly Finley give tennis lessons, 1971.
Courtesy Turlock Parks and Recreation Department.

To provide maintenance for the parks, Rojas had thirteen year-round employees. Guidance and supervision of the recreation program was furnished by fifty part-time employees in the winter and by some 125 summer employees.

Activities

The philosophy that animated the city officials and the Parks and Recreation Director, Abe Rojas, was summarized by Rojas in the phrase, "total involvement." Ideally he would have liked to see every member of the community involved in some sort of recreational activity under his department.[17] This was no new idea, for Mayor Enoch Christoffersen had voiced the same idea more than a dozen years before. Mary Ellen Leary of the *San Francisco News* had come to Turlock to write an article headlined "Why Turlock is Leading Fight Against 'Bad Comics' in California." She found that the program of the mayor and community was much more positive than negative. Believing that a busy child would be both happy and out of trouble, the town had provided ample opportunities for children to participate in constructive and wholesome recreation. "Literally there is something going on for them every day and every evening: Bands, hikes, butterfly-collecting, stamp clubs, coin clubs, supervised hot rods, Bible classes, baseball, football, horseback riding. And parents here cheerfully pay the bill for such activities.

"Said J. S. Bainbridge, phone company manager and Boy Scout organization leader: 'My life in other communities in California didn't prepare me for Turlock. I've never heard of such a place. It's terrific.' "[18]

Summer activities in Broadway Park, about 1955. Courtesy Turlock Parks and Recreation Department.

The principal phases of the recreation program in 1971 were swimming, baseball, dancing and crafts. Swimming instruction was given at both pools in the mornings (in 1971 as part of the high school's summer session program at the east side pools), and the pools were opened to recreational swimming in the afternoons and evenings.

A full series of softball leagues flourished from early May of each year until early August. Typically, the City furnished and maintained the facilities and paid the umpires. Management and direction was left in the hands of private groups. The Little League was for boys aged 9 to 12 and had 27 teams participating in 1971. The Babe Ruth League took boys of 13 to 15 and had eight teams, including two "minor league" teams. The American Legion and the City co-sponsored a city softball team of 15 to 20 players that finished third in the state in 1969. For those over 18 there was a softball league which used the Wakefield diamond. Over eight years it had grown to a 30-team league. A girls' softball league was started in 1971 with four teams of 20 high school girls and young adults each. That same summer baton classes for girls from 6 to 16 were begun in the War Memorial.

The oldest of the dance groups was the Rhythm Beaters, whose membership was confined to THS students. It met once a month the year round. As a result, the high school had reduced its dances to approximately five a year. The students, it appeared, liked the dances better away from the atmosphere of school and the supervision of teachers. At the War Memorial, furnished free by the City, parents and members of the Recreation staff were the chaperones. The membership fees went to finance live bands.

Junior high age youngsters had monthly dances, the City likewise supplying the facility and the students financing the program itself.

The Turlock Dance Club originated in October 1971. This was a club for married couples of 21 and older offering both ballroom and folk dancing. There were 300 members by the fall of 1971. Dancing lessons were offered weekly, and dances were held once a month.

Craft activities were a part of the summer program at Columbia, Crane, and Broadway Parks. They involved youngsters between the ages of six and fifteen. Boys and girls took part in about equal numbers. Among the handcrafts available were candlemaking, woodcraft, papier mache, and plaster of Paris.[19]

Private Groups

Outside the official recreation program were a number of private groups and individuals that provided recreational activities. These ranged from the Turlock Horsemen's Club to the June Jane Ripley Dance Studio and Beverly Payne's Turlock School of Ballet.

Turlock seems to have had a band of some sort during most of its existence. In 1945 Weldon Leonardson, conductor of a big Oakland band, started making regular trips to Turlock to direct the Weldonian Band. He continued to do so until 1949. After that the group became known as the Musicadets and has continued in existence down to 1971 as a semi-professional group, playing for Portuguese festivals and similar occasions when called on.

The Turlock Junior Band was organized in October 1947, with a parents' organization financing it through catering dinners and a food booth at the Fair. Taking youngsters ranging in age from eight to eighteen, it provided musical training and some disciplined group activity. John Wing was the conductor from its founding until 1969 when Keith Peterson took over. It played on many civic occasions.[20]

The Turlock Aquatic Club likewise was backed by a parents' group which for long had no formal organization. Begun in the late 1950s, Stan Sondeno was the coach for a decade. Columbia Pool was used free of charge. The program was competitive swimming and diving. Almost every weekend through the summer there was a meet somewhere between Merced and Sacramento. Swimmers were loaded into station wagons, sometimes for an all-day meet, sometimes for an evening competition. Costs of medals and ribbons were covered by the fifty-cent admission fees. Late in the summer would come the Turlock Invitational Swim Meet. Held at the THS in later years, the meets were refereed by parents and members of the Kiwanis Club. The Club also guaranteed any losses. By 1969 the program had become too big, and the parents, with a bit of nostalgia for the days when they had been deeply involved, turned the Aquatic Club over to the Parks and Recreation Department.[21]

As a service to the youth of the community another pool was opened to the public in 1962 by the First United Presbyterian Church. Mornings were devoted to swimming lessons. During the afternoons the pool was opened without charge to the community. For some time migrants' children were bused in from Patterson for swimming lessons.

A Turlock Horsemen's Club was officially organized on 2 November 1944, with forty members. W. L. Linn was the first president and Earl Bradley the second president. A uniformed group, they have taken part in parades and rodeos, three-day rides, bus trips to horse ranches, and have staged field day events at the fairgrounds and a gymkhana. Their social activities have included club dances and box socials. To raise money for their activities, they have operated a breakfast booth at the Fair.

The Junior Horsemen were organized in March 1945 for children under fourteen. At first they were called the Cavaliers. Under Earl Bradley, they became a junior drill team. They took part in shows at the San Francisco Cow Palace and many other competitions, winning a number of awards. In 1949 they won the state title for drill teams. "I have never come in contact with a grander group of young

Turlock Cavaliers, 1951. Courtesy Mrs. Joe Mills.

people, perfectly organized and beautifully disciplined," Carl L. Bosworth of the Santa Cruz County Fair wrote to Earl Bradley on 9 October 1951.

As the first group passed the age limit, fifty-four youngsters competed for thirty spots on a new drill team, the Turlock Cavalier Colts (1953). It was believed to be the largest drill team in the country.

Bowling leagues were developed at the Turlock Bowl, and later at the College Lanes and the Divine Gardens. A good share of these were financed by downtown stores and local industries. Some service clubs fielded teams.

Many other recreational organizations came into being: the Camera Club, the Pistol Club, and the Steppin' Pards (folk dancing), to name a few.

If one were to qualify Abe Rojas' commitment to "total involvement" as Turlock's policy toward recreation, it would be the City Council's often-expressed position that it would support a project with city funds only if the individuals concerned would make a substantial effort to obtain what was needed. This was true of Columbia Pool, of the War Memorial, and other projects. The main example was in the building of a Senior Citizens Center. What follows may be considered a classic case study of the difficulties that can be surmounted by dedicated individuals in achieving a significant goal in the community.

The Senior Citizens

It has become increasingly apparent that, thanks to modern medicine, there is a growing proportion of elderly retired people in American society. Friends from shop and factory have dispersed. Their children, in many cases, have moved to distant cities. Few churches are likely to have enough elderly people to justify and sustain such a variety of programs as to serve their differing tastes and interests. A community-wide organization is often the logical answer.

In 1957 Mrs. Alice Phillips, Turlock's cordial City Hostess, and several others recognized that Turlock, small as it was, needed to take positive steps to develop activities for the growing number of elderly people who had retired in Turlock.[22] Through their efforts a senior citizens group was organized on 7 September. Shortly thereafter A. V. Jensen was elected its president, and the Youth Center was offered as a meeting place.

Dr. John C. Walker suggested to the Exchange Club that the Senior Citizens needed a meeting place of their own. The Exchange Club contributed $1,000 and the Soroptimists $400 to establish the Senior Citizens Building Fund.[24] In January 1962 the club was incorporated as a non-profit organization, so that tax-deductible pledges might be given to the building fund.[25]

The club's programs while at the Youth Center consisted of one evening meeting and three recreational afternoons a month. Attendance averaged around 90. One long summer bus trip and several shorter bus trips a year were scheduled; for several years a journey was made annually to the Rose Parade in Pasadena. One of the longer summer trips was to Montreal to visit Expo '67.[26]

By 1966 about $16,000 had been raised by the Senior Citizens and the Exchange Club, with the intention of expanding Youth Center facilities. At a crucial meeting of the Directors on 22 July 1966, it was decided that remodeling the Youth Center would be unsatisfactory; a new Senior Center was needed. Later a Building Committee was appointed, with Walter F. Commons as chairman.[27] The possibility of obtaining federal money was explored, but the matter was dropped after Walter Commons had put forth much time and money.[28]

Extending the War Memorial Auditorium to furnish quarters for the Senior Citizens was discussed and, on review, abandoned.[29] Then the Senior Citizens, with the encouragement of the Mayor and Council, came up with a proposal that the Senior Center be financed by public subscription and deeded to the City, with the City donating a site next to the newly completed City Library and doing all landscaping, grading and surfacing; it later donated the kitchen equipment as well. The Senior Citizens would then lease the Center back from the City, which could rent it to other adult groups when the Senior Citizens were not using it.

Turlock's Senior Center, an excellent example of her public buildings. Browning photo.

The Council approved the proposal on 4 February 1969. Architect James W. B. Shade prepared plans and specifications, and on 8 May the financial drive began. At the end of a year, $110,000 had been pledged. Ground was broken on 6 March 1970, and the building was dedicated on 17 April 1971.[30]

The main room of the Senior Center could seat 300 for a performance or about half as many at dinner; at either side were smaller public rooms, separated by folding doors from the main room. A fireside room,[31] crafts room and kitchen completed the building. With carpets and full air conditioning, it was a very pleasant structure. Walter Commons reflected the general opinion when he wrote, "This lovely room, along with all the many other special features, makes us feel our Senior Center is one of the most beautiful buildings, inside and out, in California."[32] With their own building available, the Senior Citizens expanded their programs, doubling the hours of utilization.

Once again, as with the Youth Center, the War Memorial, and Columbia Pool, private citizens had gained their objective "the Turlock way." They had not depended on the federal or local government to give them what they wanted; but having demonstrated their desire and dedication by personal contributions and fund-raising activities, they were assisted by the City in completing the project.

Ladies' Improvement Association parade, 1911.
Joyce and Eugene Farr were the horses, Gertrude Smith (Markley)
the driver, with her sister, Dorothy Smith (Fiorini), to the right.

Chapter XXVII

Organizing for Community Service

John E. Caswell

The key to the tremendous variety and dynamism in American community life is found in its myriad of voluntary organizations. With *Roberts Rules of Order* as their guide to democratic action, groups with common aims organize, conduct their business, and work toward their goals.

In Turlock alone, the Chamber of Commerce in 1971 listed sixty secular clubs and organizations, very nearly twice the number of churches found within the city limits of Turlock.

Were one to seek to write a history of these sixty clubs, an entire volume would be needed. The modest aim of this chapter is to present a history of several organizations which have had considerable influence on the community, in order that the reader may discern something of how they have operated.

The term "service club" in American society has come to mean a club meeting weekly for fellowship, fun, inspiration and community service. The nature of the schedule and the costs tend to restrict the clubs to middle or upper management, professional people, and self-employed. In many clubs election is a mere formality; the screening process customarily takes place in the preliminary visits the prospective member makes to the club. During these visits he decides whether its goals are his goals, and whether he will feel comfortable in that particular club. In one Turlock club, probably half the members are non-smokers, non-drinkers, and active churchmen. Another Turlock club is noted for the speed with which its members dispose of the program and stack up the poker chips. Both provide useful service to the community.

For a long time most of the service clubs met in a large, bare inside room at the Carolyn Hotel. With the completion of the Divine Gardens in the early 1960s, there was a mass movement to the new location where all was fresh and new and the chef was different. Eventually most clubs agreed to buffet meals in an effort to maintain quality at a reasonable price.

A person sitting in on a mid-morning coffee session at one of the town's cafes or bakeries might well have heard the principal service clubs characterized somewhat as follows. The Exchange Club was the "old men's club"—said jocularly or even affectionately, for a number of older community leaders had been members, a few as far back as its founding in 1925. Rotary was the "big one." It had many of the town's corporate managers and commanded many excellent speakers, thanks in part to a close tie between some of its farmer members and the University of California at Davis. Soroptimists were the "little sisters" of the Rotary Club, but as they met at the same time and next door to Kiwanis the two clubs began to hold occasional joint meetings, and it looked as if Rotary's "little sisters" were being wooed away. Kiwanis had been founded as recently as 1958, hence was one of the smaller service clubs during most of the 1960s. It managed to acquire a number of rising junior managers, shop owners, and college faculty members.

Several clubs became known for their fund-raising projects. The Lions Club book sale was looked forward to by many as a means of replenishing their fiction supply or picking up some gem not recognized by its former owner. The weekend before Halloween the Kiwanis appeared at downtown corners in carpenters' aprons, selling apples by the bag or box to replenish their Boys' and Girls' Fund. Other organizations had booths at the Fair in August or at the Home Show in the spring.

Each club had its individual way of contributing service to the community. The Exchange Club had made notable contributions through the years in initiating drives for the Youth Center and the Senior Citizens' building. The Rotarians rather prided themselves in carrying on service projects without advertising, although their participation in Rotary International's overseas scholarship program was well known. The Lions had furnished playground equipment. Kiwanis, with a youth emphasis, had sponsored athletic competitions for the grade schools and junior high schools, a Little League team, trips for Turlock High athletes to the Fellowship of Christian Athletes, as well as various scholarship programs. The list of contributions from all the clubs would be long.

Women's Clubs

The first Turlock Women's Club was established in 1906 as the Ladies' Improvement Association and disbanded only in 1942. The best remembered of its civic projects were the establishment of the city library and creation of Broadway Park, an area still enjoyed by mothers and their children.

In 1928 the Tuesday Reading Club was established, with about twenty-four charter members. The first president, Mrs. G. C. Saunders, was "a jolly, vivacious person, eager to be creating. . . .She was very cultured and interested in bettering the lives of Turlock residents."[1]

The stimulus to organize the club arose from dissatisfaction with the Literary Guild's book selections. The members decided it was better to buy and review their own books. Each member was originally expected to read all the books and take part in discussion. Later a member reviewed a book, and it was passed around and formed the basis of a "book chat." Still later, outside speakers were brought in once a month, and at the second meeting of the month, a member led a "book chat" and a business meeting was held. For a time books which the club bought went into a library, but these were eventually sold off to the members.

The club grew rather steadily. The problem of finding an adequate room for meetings at times restricted the growth and a waiting list was quite common. At first there were eighteen or twenty active members who met monthly in a basement room of the City Library. This was increased to thirty members and thirty associates, later to fifty and fifty, still later to seventy-five and fifty. One won associate membership by giving a book review or taking part in a "book chat." If elected a club officer, she moved to active status with voting privileges thereafter. This distinction was abolished in 1961, when the membership was increased to 145 a little while after the Florence Porter Room at the new Methodist Church was made available to the club.

Honorary membership was originally awarded only to librarians who had "rendered continuous professional service to the club." Among them were Mrs. Susan B. Love, Miss Minette Stoddard, and Miss Bertha Simms. Then in 1970 the bylaws were changed to make those who had been members for forty years or more honorary members.

The first May Tea was held in 1929 and continued thereafter—an occasion when guests were invited. In 1930-31 the club decided to have an invited speaker on the second Tuesday of the month, and a book review or "book chat" led by one of the members on the fourth Tuesday, when club business would be conducted as well. A tea at a regular meeting was first held on 8 September 1931, but does not seem to have become a regular part of the afternoon's socializing until later.

In the autumn of 1932 "Dr. Willard Smith of the English Department of Mills College was engaged to speak at the first regular meeting of each month. Then the members discussed the lecture at the second regular meeting." Among his topics were "The World as Women See It," "The Newer Psychology in Fiction," and "Novels of Epic Sweep."

The selection of books for review was varied. One was Tolstoy's epic *War and Peace;* another, the *Autobiography of Clarence Darrow;* a third, *Lost Horizons.* Nobel Prize novels were regularly reviewed— Mrs. Albert Julien said she enjoyed those best. In a lighter vein, many reviews were of "whodunits." Agatha Christie's books were favorites. Miss Alice Cooper of Modesto Junior College was a favorite poetry reviewer.

Over the years the format of the meetings changed, partly in response to the increasing number of cultural groups in town. After more than forty years of activity the Tuesday Reading Club has continued to be a valued organization, as its waiting list demonstrates.

The Soroptimists, founded in 1939, were a business and professional women's service club. By 1971 their most senior member was Mrs. Esther Cooper, who for long had been secretary of the G. W. Hume Company. The Soroptimists had played an active part in establishing the Senior Citizens, along with the Exchange Club.

The Newcomers Club was a direct outgrowth of the activities of Mrs. Alice Phillips, who had undertaken the job of City Hostess under the sponsorship of the Chamber of Commerce. With lists of new families furnished her, Mrs. Phillips called on them, answered their questions, left a brochure and coupons for small gifts from her individual sponsors among the downtown merchants. She also found many lonely women who needed an instant social circle.

Accordingly, the Newcomers Club was organized on Friday night, 9 December 1955, at a dinner held at the Youth Center.[2] A few months later a "Mr. and Mrs. Group" was formed.[3] During the first few years quite a variety of programs was staged. They included dinners, illustrated talks, demonstrations of making floral arrangements, card games, a picnic in Hagaman Park, and many more. While Mrs. Phillips had expected the club to be a first step out into the community, some women have remained active over a number of years, a factor that has given continuity to the club.[4] In 1971 the club was going strong, with good attendance at their monthly meetings.

The year after she organized the Newcomers Club, Mrs. Phillips formed the Turlock Woman's Club. The Tuesday Reading Club's waiting list was long, its interests were literary, and there was a real need for another women's cultural club. An article in the *Turlock Daily Journal* invited participants, saying, "A tea or a luncheon will be held once a month for members. . . .As each group becomes interested, different sections will be formed in arts and crafts, literature and travel, music and choral and an evening section. . . .

"Women of all ages in Turlock and surrounding areas are eligible to join and become charter members."[5]

By its second year, the membership had reached 46 active members and 6 associates. In 1970-71 there were 54 active members and 13 associate members, with Mrs. Phillips the sole honorary life member.[6] The variety of interest groups Mrs. Phillips had anticipated did not develop. However, programs covered a wider variety of topics and had a more flexible format than those of the Tuesday Reading Club.

The handiwork of no women's organization was more conspicuous than that of the Turlock Garden Club, organized 29 July 1948 by Mrs. Fran James. "She gave generously of her time and talent, interesting women in the art of handling and using cut flowers properly and in the joys of gardening and thinking flowers." Its civic activities have included oleander plantings on the north and south approaches to the city, the landscaping of Central Park, the spectacular pyracantha plantings and trees along Canal Drive, and the landscaping of the Senior Center. The club's annual clean alley contest has been particularly needed in sections where unpaved alleys have been hard to keep tidy.

These women's clubs are but the more conspicuous examples of those that have been vehicles for civic activity and cultural stimulus. Space fails to tell of the Antique Club, the Republican and Democratic women's clubs, the church groups, lodges, sisterhoods, and Greek letter organizations in which women have found friendship, further education, and a means of personal and community improvement. To understand their function in women's lives, one must recognize that the pattern of modern living does not encourage the formation of mutually supportive neighborhood groups. Women tend to look elsewhere for likeminded souls with whom they can discuss problems of husbands, children, schools, finances. It is over the coffee as much as during the program that a woman is likely to find what she perhaps unconsciously came to seek.

Red Cross ladies welcomed the doughboys with food, 1918. At other times they made bandages and knitted and knitted!

The Turlock Grange

Jacqueline Harris

The National Grange, the Patrons of Husbandry, was organized on 4 December 1867 to unite farmers and promote their interests through a cooperative effort. The Grange was organized as a secret, ritualistic organization, but each meeting had a period devoted to discussion, educational work, and recreation and entertainment.

One of the earliest, if not actually the first organization in Turlock, was the Turlock Grange, established in 1873. One evening Aunt Abby Fulkerth, as she was affectionately called, invited friends, neighbors, and farmers of the district to a barn dance at the Fulkerth ranch. Unbeknown to her guests, Aunt Abby arranged to have Dr. J. A. W. Wright, first State Grange Master of California, present. A delicate form of bribery was employed when Aunt Abby made her guests organize a Christian Endeavor for the young people and a Grange local for the adults before she would let the dance begin.[7]

The Turlock Grange operated for only two years before relinquishing its charter, probably due to the economic hardships of the seventies. One remaining offshoot of the early Grange is the Grange Company, organized in 1874 by Grangers in the area.[8]

On 11 September 1934 the Turlock Grange was reorganized and rechartered with seventy-five local residents becoming charter members. A Booster Celebration Parade marked the installation of the officers. It featured a prairie schooner reputedly driven by Asa Wilder, a member of the Donner Party, and with "Aunt Abby," the oldest Grange member in California, riding in the schooner. It was later revealed that a younger woman took the role of 97-year-old Aunt Abby.[9]

Nine committees were set up, among which were "Legislative and Taxation," "Dairy," "Community Projects and Utility," and "Literary."[10]

At the end of the first year the total membership had risen to 161. Soon the problem arose of determining the eligibility of candidates that had an interest in farming, but possibly a greater interest in business.

It was immediately apparent that the newly reorganized Grange would become a very active community organization. During the first year, the Grange was instrumental in establishing a countywide bovine tuberculosis eradication program and a rural fire district. Social activities were numerous. Card parties, potluck dinners, and dances not only provided entertainment but made money as well.[11] The Ladies Home Economics Committee had monthly meetings at members' homes for business and pleasure. This active group also accepted invitations from other groups to cater dinners.[12]

Around the end of 1949 the Grangers began discussing the possibility of building their own meeting hall.[13] Delwin Thornburg and his wife Petra donated an acre of land on Walnut Avenue and the barn standing on it to the Grange. Grange members voted to labor *gratis* on construction of the hall, and set out to raise money for building materials.[14]

During the two and one-half years of construction and afterward the Grangers made a concentrated effort to raise money. As charter member Mrs. Effie Freeman recalls, "We did anything to make a dime."[15] Card parties, box socials, bazaars, cake walks, auctions, and dinners were held for the benefit of the building fund. At one Grange meeting the men had their waists measured and were made to pay one penny per inch.[16] Galloping parties were another favorite way of making money. Grangers would arrive unexpectedly at a member's home bringing refreshments and paying twenty-five cents admission fee. The rest of the evening was spent playing cards and games.[17]

On 16 March 1950 ground was broken for the new Grange Hall. Several months earlier members learned that war surplus buildings on the fairgrounds were to be auctioned off, and decided to bid on them. Their $750 bid for two 40' x 80' buildings was accepted.[18] The first stage of the hall was the kitchen and dining room. A contractor was hired to lay the foundation; the rest of the construction labor was done almost exclusively by Grange members. On 12 March 1951 Grange members used the hall for the first time, inviting the public to a whist party.[19] Nearly two and one-half years after groundbreaking ceremonies the main hall was completed. Dedication ceremonies were held 27 September 1952. Among the 200 guests were the twelve remaining charter members. During the ceremonies, State Master George Sehlmeyer and State Senator Hugh P. Donnelly praised the resourcefulness of the Turlock members.[20] Grange members were very proud of their new building, hailed as one of the best in the state.[21]

No longer in debt, the Grange decided to help fund other worthwhile projects. In 1956 the Grange put on dinners with proceeds going to the Faith Home Teen Ranch. Another service project was sponsorship of a local Future Farmer of America. The Grange provided a heifer for a youngster to care for for three years. He was then expected to give a heifer to the next project recipient.[22]

In later years Grange activities diminished. Effie Freeman stated, "Back then people came out for card parties and socials. That's all we had. But now, people stay home and watch television."[23] The once weekly card parties by 1971 were held twice a year. Catered dinners and breakfasts featuring ebelskivers, a Swedish specialty, became a thing of the past. Annual ham dinners and turkey dinners celebrated Grange birthdays and anniversaries. The ability to produce prize-winning fair exhibits had definitely not diminished over the years. Hard work and cooperation among members continued to be very much a part of all Grange activities.

Musical, Theatrical, and Artistic Groups

In various other contexts we have had occasion to discuss some of the performing groups that were established in Turlock: the various bands and Jean Nelson's ladies' orchestra. Most of the churches had choirs which absorbed much of the musical energy of the town. When Frank Mancini organized the Modesto Symphony Orchestra, instrumentalists went from Ceres and Turlock and probably from other parts of the region to participate. After Stanislaus State College was established, a College-Community Orchestra was formed under Dr. Joseph E. Bruggman, and performers from communities as far away as Sonora came regularly to rehearse. The Modesto Symphony gained several good players from among the State College faculty and their families, and the two orchestras were probably mutually supportive rather than rivals. Nevertheless the College-Community Orchestra was dropped after Alexander Capurso became president of the College, presumably in an effort to improve community relations.

Although the town's musicians complained about the lack of support given music in the schools, a rather spectacular part of the high school year beginning in 1957 was the production of an operetta or Broadway musical every year or two. The first production was an operetta, "Mississippi Melody," directed by Sylvia Sateren. One of the singers was a tenor, Ernie Vrenios, who went on to make a career of music and returned to Turlock on the Community Concert Series during the spring of 1972.

Stepping up to the "big time," Turlock High put on "The Boy Friend" in 1959. Among later productions were "The King and I," "Oklahoma," "Finian's Rainbow," and "The Music Man." These required the cooperation of drama department, band, orchestra, chorus, and other parts of the school to insure proper staging and performance. These were sufficiently ambitious that they were not staged on an annual basis.[24]

The principal agency for bringing professional musical talent before the Turlock audience was the Community Concerts Association. This was founded in 1940 as the Cooperative Concerts Association when a young man came to town to promote a concert series. He got into touch with Mrs. Rose Hosley Ireland, who in turn called on Mrs. Bernice Weaver for assistance. These two women brought together other interested women and organized the Association.[25] The first fund drive was put on in 1941.

Despite predictions of failure, the project was a success from the beginning. The first drive netted 363 adult and 200 student memberships, when the minimum required was 300 adult memberships. The Association kept growing until in 1949 it reached a peak of 820 adult and 154 student memberships. A part of the initial success was due to the fact that Modesto had no concert association until about 1950, for Frank Mancini had begun to build the Modesto Symphony and his backers wanted no competition. The Turlock Association, however, was free to sell tickets in Modesto and did so. The slump following 1949 was largely due to the establishment of the Modesto Association.

Essential to continued success was the skill of the Community Concerts Board in picking superior artists who would appeal to the Turlock audience. The Board developed considerable ability in identifying artists who were on their way up—before their prices went up. Turlock thus heard Bidu Sayao, the Brazilian soprano, during her first year in the United States. Others whose fortunes were rising when they came to Turlock were Dorothy Warenskjold, Leontyne Price, and Licia Albanese. A balance was also needed between artists: soloists and groups, vocalists and instrumentalists, classical and more popular.

The first artist brought in was a baritone, Lansing Hatfield. He had been a contestant in the Atwater Kent Metropolitan Opera contest for young singers. He had a wonderful, warm voice and personality, and captivated his audience. A few weeks later, Turlockers were glad to hear that he had received the Metropolitan Opera award.

Among groups that came to Turlock were the General Platoff Don Cossacks, the De Paur Infantry Chorus which appeared twice, the Vienna Boys Choir, the Robert Shaw Chorale, and the Trapp Family Singers.[26]

Carrying on the traditional Green Room reception for performers, the Association Board has regularly entertained the artists at some home after the concert. Over punch and coffee, cookies or cake, Turlock's musicians, professional and amateur, have been able to extend their acquaintance with musicians from many cities and distant lands. At the same time, they have been able to reenforce the feeling that a number of artists have mentioned: that Turlock's audiences are warmly responsive.

In 1905 funds were raised for an "Opera House." Although a very modest hall, it furnished the stage and facilities for putting on shows, for which the Grange Hall and Gaddis Hall, built thirty years or so earlier, were either not available or were no longer acceptable.

About 1906, Jean Nelson, Turlock's durable orchestra conductor and pianist, was a leader in establishing what was apparently Turlock's first group of players.

Shortly, traveling stock companies began coming to Turlock on a circuit through the valley. At times they came as frequently as once a week. One of these groups was the Dick Wilbur Players. Jean Nelson played the piano for them, and local people took bit parts.

Lura Critser Flint, drama teacher at Turlock High, became the principal organizer of town dramatics from the early 1920s to the middle 1930s. The Fox Theater on East Main and the THS auditorium were used for the productions.

In 1935 Lamar Jackson became president of the drama group, which took the name of the Turlock Community Players. It used both the Little Theater and the auditorium at Turlock High. Among its productions was the dramatic and eerie "Outward Bound" by Sutton Vane, in which the characters were unaware that they were dead and heading for Paradise. In the late 1940s "My Sister Eileen" and the favorite chiller "Arsenic and Old Lace" were among the shows staged.

In 1952 the Turlock Community Players was incorporated. Raymond and Margaret Hume made available the cafeteria of the Hume Cannery. Here was staged "Bad Seed" by Maxwell Anderson, along with many other productions. Then a small building that belonged to the high school, the Tigers' Den, became available. It was purchased by the Community Players and moved to a site just off North Broadway.

When Stanislaus State College opened on the Fairgrounds it lacked both the staff and facilities for drama. Lamar Jackson was employed at the beginning of the second semester to teach speech and drama. A joint program was worked out between the Community Players and the College, and a number of performances were put on in the former Tigers' Den. Among these were Tennessee Williams' "Glass Menagerie," and "Everybody Loves Opal," by John Patrick, better known as the author of "Teahouse of the August Moon." This arrangement lasted until 1964.[27]

In the autumn of 1965, the Little Theater opened on the new SSC campus. In a day when "theater in the round" was popular, the architect had taken advantage of the trend and designed a "theater in the half-round." Both stage and seating were semicircular. This imposed very considerable limitations on the stage sets, but brought the audience close to the actors and thus minimized the difficulties of hearing the actors from the side seats.

During the first year Dr. Daniel Witt was director of the Little Theater. The next year Bruce Hood took over. During the first three years of his directorship three plays a year were produced, and Hood assisted Giovanni Camajani of the Music Department in producing an evening of opera.

The first touring production of the Little Theater was George Orwell's "Animal Farm," produced in the fall of 1966. Molière's "The Imaginary Invalid" was the first period piece, and was rated a major success. In 1969 Jere Wade became the second full-time member of the Drama faculty. During the year he directed Claude Van-Itallie's "America, Hurrah!"[28]

With the opening of the Performing Arts group of buildings in 1970, the Drama Department, as it had now become, acquired its first major facilities. Small productions were staged in the Studio Theater, while major productions went onto the full-sized stage of the Mainstage Theater. Unfortunately, State formula had limited the size of the house to 300 seats, which meant that popular productions had to be staged over several weeks.

In 1970 Dennis H. Ehrp and Bill Stothart, two SSC students, took the lead in making the abandoned auditorium of Denair High School into the Golden Gaslight Theater, which they rented from the Denair Service District. The students put in literally hundreds of hours in repairing the leaky roof and refurbishing the building, materials being paid for by the District. During that summer and the following, student groups put on old-time melodramas, to their own edification and the audience's delight. Perhaps more important, they demonstrated to the Denair community that long-haired, freaky-looking kids could be good workmen, steady characters, and creative individuals.[29]

About the same time that the students were "doing their thing" a movement got under way to revive the Turlock Community Players. Rick Smith became president of the group, which inherited the corporation papers and treasury of the earlier organization. As the group now was playing outside Turlock and attracting actors from the surrounding area, it began doing business as the Central Valley Players. It was active during the eight winter months, so the Golden Gaslight Theater had one active group or the other throughout the year.

Theatrical activity in Turlock had reached a new high as the first century closed. Probably a larger proportion of the town had been involved in the productions of 1906. Nevertheless, there was a wide variety of offerings during the year, something for every taste, in the Studio Theater, the Mainstage Theater, and the Golden Gaslight Theater.

Painting and sculpture as outlets for amateur talent have not flourished in Turlock in the same way that music and the theater have. One reason is the more individualistic nature of the discipline. Another may be that the Protestant churches have not encouraged an interest in the plastic arts in the way that they have developed music. The fact remains that the number of practicing amateurs has been small, and the audience has been restricted. Professional and amateur artists of the region have found common ground in the Central California Art League, located in Modesto.

Turlock, or rather Denair, has had one outstanding home-town talent in the person of Robert R. Coffin, Sr. After growing up in Denair, Coffin went away to study, spending some time in Italy, and later spending much time in the Southwest, where some of his best studies have been of the Navajos.

With the coming of the college, the community gained a number of practicing artists. Aside from members of the Fine Arts faculty, the outstanding talent was Edith Dinkin (Mrs. Lawrence D. Berkoben), whose works were chosen for the first show in the SSC Art Gallery when it was opened in the autumn of 1965. In 1970 the Gallery moved to larger quarters in the Performing Arts complex. Since its opening the Gallery has presented the works of the Art faculty and students and has also brought in exhibits of many artists in various media. These have been open to the public, and have drawn members of the community as well as students, faculty and staff.

Conclusions

Voluntary organizations have played an important part in Turlock life, providing fellowship, opportunities for service, and cultural enrichment. In the cultural field, the college has furnished valuable additional resources, but only in the fine arts has it provided a nucleus where one was previously lacking in the town. For some time it was the town that was helping the college get its programs in music and the theater under way. For a town of its size, Turlock was abundantly supplied with voluntary organizations and cultural outlets at the close of its first century.

THS girls' basketball team, 1910, San Joaquin Valley champions.
Miss Maud Clark was coach and principal. Courtesy Ada Thornburg Crow.

Chapter XXVIII
Schools of the Region

Helen Hohenthal and Others

Introduction

Schools are a vital part of a community's life. Here are centered the parents' fond hopes for their children's bettering themselves in life. Here is the common meeting ground where Swede and Portuguese, Japanese and Assyrian, Briton and Mexican come to know each other and absorb the elements of a common American culture. Here are the meeting halls, gymnasiums, and playing fields that serve the entire community.

The stories of most of the elementary schools have been covered briefly in the histories of the towns. Here we shall discuss the high schools, the unified school districts that had both elementary and high schools, and some of the rural elementary school districts. Fully to cover the region's schools is impossible in the space available. We shall at least record some of the basic information and several of the most outstanding developments. Hopefully these brief sketches will serve as an incentive to further investigation. The reader who does so will be richly rewarded.

I am grateful to the several writers for their help and to others for memoranda which are cited in the footnotes. As teachers and citizens, they are deeply interested in their schools.

The Ceres Schools

Fleming E. Haas

The first small district school to serve the Ceres area was built in 1870 two miles northwest of Ceres. As the number of youngsters in the town increased, their parents fought several election campaigns before they succeeded in getting the school and its teacher, Mrs. Aurelia Chapin, moved to Ceres in 1874. The school was ungraded until 1887.

For years the eight grades of the Ceres School met in that two-story building with one long room on each floor. Later another room was built on at the side. On 4 January 1908 it was noted that the five rooms (perhaps two of the rooms had been divided) were full to overflowing, and a new school was needed.[1]

In 1910 a fine new grammar school was erected, with a small primary building nearby. There were now eight teachers and 294 pupils.

The high school, founded in 1908, had 62 pupils in 1910.[2] It had met for the first couple of years in the Grange Hall, then moved into the vacated elementary school building.[3]

As the Ceres Elementary School District grew, the Whitmore School, and later the Caswell, Don Pedro and Carroll Fowler Schools were added. A junior high, Walter White, was opened in the 1960s, and the Mae Hensley Junior High School was slated to open in 1972. The old Whitmore building had become unsafe, so the children attending there were scheduled to move into Walter White.

The high school was able to move out of the forty-five-year-old frame grammar school into a new building at the Central Avenue and Whitmore site in 1915. It was considered a model school for its day. After fifty years' service, it was demolished in 1965 to make way for another building.

A major change in organization of the Ceres schools took place in 1965, when the Ceres Elementary and High School Districts and the Westport Elementary District were combined. Westport itself was the result of a consolidation about 1948 of the Jones School on Grayson Road at Carpenter and the Laird School on Grayson and Laird, both constructed some time before 1900, and the Jennings School at Zeering and Jennings Roads, built in 1916.

Under the unified district several programs have been introduced to provide greater flexibility in responding to children's needs. In the "language experience" approach to reading, a youngster's own words, drawn from his own familiar world and personal experience, are written down for him to form the basis of his reading instruction. Ceres High has been a pioneer in individualized learning through modular-flexible scheduling that provides widely varying periods for different subjects and also permits more direct student involvement and more personalized instruction through small group instruction.

Chatom Union School District[4]

Helen Hohenthal

Chatom is a unified elementary school district located west of Turlock on Clayton Road. It was formed in 1958 by the union of four smaller school districts: Washington, Mitchell, Central and Tegner. A new schoolhouse was built shortly after consolidation.

In 1968 the Mountain View District petitioned to come in with Chatom. After a successful bond election, a new school was built on the Mountain View site. As of 1971-72, a kindergarten and grades 1–6 were housed there.

At Chatom, all nine grades are taught. The seventh and eighth grades include students of both Chatom and Mountain View. There are 29 teachers and 740 students in the unified school system. Covering a broad rural area, the schools recently acquired their own buses.

For students of the two upper grades, with high school not far away, special introductions are given to a variety of subjects and activities by "short course" periods of instruction. Most appropriate to young people in an agricultural community without a town center is an introduction to ornamental planting and horticulture. A local junior college student teaches wrestling. There are short courses in sewing, Spanish, square dancing, knitting and photography. A chess club and other groups are active. The 4-H Clubs also serve the community and its youth.

Both the PTA and the Parents Club are strong and active in the district.

Mitchell School.

The Denair Schools

Margaret Harmon

The original 160-acre townsite of Denair was owned by John T. Davis, who had had the townsite surveyed and recorded under the name of Elmdale in 1897. In 1902 Davis deeded fifteen lots on Gratton Road to the Elmdale School District. On this property a one-room schoolhouse was built. Miss Arletta Scott was the first teacher. Three of the five pupils were Harry, Hazel and Leslie De La Mater. The other two were Jack and Mary Pickford, stepchildren of the first postmaster. On Sundays the schoolhouse was used by the Christian Church, families of that denomination coming from Turlock for several years until they could have a sanctuary of their own.

Five years after the little one-room schoolhouse was built, a two-story frame building was erected across the street, with Jacob Witmer as contractor. On 18 February 1907 the new building was occupied, with the two teachers, Miss Elsie Cottle and Miss Leta Haworth, carrying the desks over to the building, one by one. The site of the first school reverted to J. N. Lester, who had bought Davis' interest in the land.

A horse-drawn vehicle, called the "Kid Hack," was a familiar sight, and was greatly welcomed by the school children who lived at a great distance from school. With the friendly drivers, the children's trips to and from school were made much more pleasant, especially in stormy weather. Reports show that at the end of the 1911-1912 school year, the property was valued at $475. The library of twenty-six volumes was appraised at $62. Operating expense for the year was $3,395.38.

The year 1912 saw a significant expansion in Denair's schools. Denair High School was established as the result of an election held on 20 June 1912, with 26 out of 28 voting in favor of a high school district. A year earlier, a brick and stucco building, often called the "bank building," had been built on the corner of what was later Main and San Joaquin Streets. The upper story of this building was used for a time for Denair High School. There were 26 students and two teachers. On the first floor were a bank, library, drug store, grocery store, meat market, post office, barber shop, and the *Denair News* office. A basketball court adjoined the bank building, and tennis courts were a half-block away.

The same year, 1912, the "Little Brown Schoolhouse," a one-room school on the Denair Community Park site, was built for use of the first grade. Miss Pearl Brown was the first teacher.

The two-story frame building constructed in 1907 was destroyed by fire in 1916. For the next two years classes were distributed among the old one-room school, the Friends Church, and temporary buildings

First Denair school,
Robert Coffin at right.

moved onto the site. The new brick building, constructed of bricks made on the grounds, was finished in 1918. A year later a domestic science room was constructed. It was used not only for instruction, but also for a cafeteria, for 4-H meetings, and for various civic groups, such as Farm Bureau Home Department meetings and the organizing meeting of the Denair Lions Club.

The last class to go through high school in the bank building was graduated in 1921. That fall the school moved into a new brick building on Hawthorne and Fresno Streets. Physical needs made the occasion for an instructional project. The student body of somewhat under 70 members was divided into classes, and a definite area was given to each class to hoe, rake and plant. The upper floor of the new building was used for home economics classes. In 1923 the high school students built the first shop building under the supervision of the instructor, Mr. Benton. Still later they built a manual training building on the grammar school grounds.

In 1925 the PTA and the Home Department of the Farm Bureau started a cafeteria in the domestic science room of the grammar school. Mrs. Bella Neill did the cooking, assisted by Mrs. Marion Nye, through the spring of 1929. In 1927 the high school students began walking over to the grammar school for hot lunches. Mrs. Neill was in charge from 1929 to late 1931, when the cafeteria was closed because the patronage was too small. Various other women kept it open for short periods until 1933, when it was closed for several years.

In 1927, twenty-five years after the first school was built in Denair, the first gymnasium was constructed. It stood on the high school grounds. The grammar school auditorium was remodeled in 1933 and the dressing rooms enlarged, thus making it more useful for assemblies, plays and graduation exercises, as well as for community programs and meetings.

In 1939 the first school bus was purchased and a service reestablished that had been missing since the days of the "Kid Hack." Two teachers alternated in driving during the mornings and afternoons. Later other buses were added.

The Denair Community Clubhouse grew out of a 4-H activity on the grounds of the "Little Brown Schoolhouse." C. W. Moore set his club to building an outdoor barbecue pit there in the late 1930s. Oliver W. Chance and other men assisted. Rocks were hauled from the river to build the fireplace and a three-foot-high wall. Later a roof was added, then walls, and finally a floor, and the clubhouse was complete. It was enlarged and improved several times thereafter, the latest being in 1971. In 1942 the first firehouse in Denair was built on the same grounds.

In 1942 the elementary and high school districts were unified. Students from Montpellier had been coming to the high school, so it was an opportune time for the Montpellier District to join the unified district. The high school board ceased to exist, as the elementary board had precedence.

In 1947 the board purchased the first part of a new elementary school site at Hawthorne and Madera Streets. The next year more adjoining land was purchased. In 1949-50 both the old schoolhouse and the "Little Brown Schoolhouse" were used for school purposes for the last time. A four-classroom wing was begun on the first parcel, and in January 1950 Mrs. Frances Hale and her fifth-graders moved desks and supplies in her car to the first room completed. Through the spring the other three upper grades were moved in. In 1952 the second wing and the administrative office were built. The old gymnasium was replaced by a new and larger one in 1954. A few years later a new shop and agriculture building was constructed. Various other structures were added, including a multipurpose building named "Larson Hall" in honor of W. O. Larson, who had served as a board member for twenty-two years, and as chairman for eighteen.

With the growth in Denair's population, more room was needed. In 1959 forty acres was purchased across Lester Road from the school campus. The Thomas Simms Science Building was built in 1963 and named in honor of the school superintendent whose retirement was approaching. Under his administration the elementary school and other structures mentioned above were built.

During John Allard's four-year superintendency, 1966-1970, a teachers' room and Wing IV were built, and the multipurpose building was enlarged. The first unit of the new high school was built across Lester Road, consisting of six classrooms and a central auditorium seating 350. It was occupied during 1969-70.

In early 1972 two additional projects were begun on the new high school campus. One was a 4,000-square-foot shop with facilities for drafting, welding, and automobile washing and lubrication. The other was an athletic field which was undertaken as a community project, local organizations furnishing money, labor and equipment.

After being closed for almost a decade during the depression years of the 1930s, the school cafeteria was reopened in the fall of 1943 under a government subsidy program, with Mrs. Mildred Ayres in charge. In 1947 Mrs. Lorene Haworth became manager and was still serving in 1971. An average of 450 lunches a day was being served.

The Denair schools have had a variety of activities, including the Future Homemakers of America and the Future Farmers of America. Annually several girls and their advisor attend the FHA Conference in Asilomar. One year two girls and their advisor went to the Youth White House Conference in Long Beach, the money for the trip being raised by a smorgasbord.

The Future Farmers group has been a Master Chapter since the early 1960s and has produced twenty State Farmers, an award of excellence! David Reiswig won the coveted American Farmer award and went to Kansas City to receive it.

Athletics has always been part of Denair High School activities, basketball having been played continuously through the years. Baseball was started several times before the school entered the Joaquin League and fielded a team regularly. Track was begun in 1920-21. In 1922-25, Denair won the statewide trophy for all-round athletes in schools under 100, and it became a permanent possession. In 1924-26, Denair won the state decathlon for schools in the same class. Denair started football in 1946-47. Since then it has won two League championships and was undefeated in 1956.

Girls' athletics has been a part of the high school since its establishment. Trophies have been won by the girls and are on display in the trophy case.

Our primitive little country school of 1902 with its five pupils has grown to 488 elementary students and 224 high school students housed in a complex and modern plant.

The community has felt, "This is ours—our home; these kids are our kids; everybody belongs to us; let's do all we can for them." Young and old have attended the sports activities, plays, benefit dinners usually put on by the Women's Service Club, the graduations, and the summer baseball games. Never a basketball game in the old gym but that there were many elderly people "rooting" for the home team. Mrs. Blanche Johnson, when she could no longer drive, would walk over to the schoolgrounds to watch the baseball games. Whole families, young and old, followed the team to the out-of-town games.

Hilmar High School Chorus directed by Jean Nelson, about 1925. Courtesy Jean Nelson.

Hilmar High School

Douglas Boehme

In writing the history of Hilmar High School, it is necessary first to go back to 1864 when the Fairview Elementary School was formed. From that time on for the next forty-seven years, the countryside was dotted with small elementary schools. The need for a high school became ever more apparent. Out of this need and under the leadership of O. C. Anderson, Ed Rose, Harry Ahlem, Charles Dahlquist, K. A. Peterson, and P. A. Johnson, the Hilmar Colony Union High School was established.

In September 1911 classes met for the first time on the second floor of the Elim Union Elementary School. With a few dozen reference books, meager equipment and supplies, and thirty-six students, Mr. Pettitt, the principal-teacher, and Miss Emma Loomis officially started the first high school classes in Hilmar.

From this beginning, Hilmar High School has grown until in 1971 it has a library of over 8,000 volumes, modern teaching aids, 450 students, and 32 professional staff members. Coupled with this growth have come expanded curricular and extra-curricular programs.

In keeping with the rural nature of the district, Hilmar has developed an outstanding agricultural program. Under the leadership of the agriculture teachers, the agriculture classes and the Future Farmers of America have earned honors on both state and national levels. As an example, in 1970 the Hilmar Future Farmers of America had State Farmer degrees awarded to eighteen of its members, a record which has never been equaled by any other school in California, regardless of size.

In the extra-curricular areas, Hilmar has been able to provide its students with opportunities to express and develop talents which lie outside the academic classrooms. A typical example can be found in the sports program, which has had more than its share of championship teams.

With the moral and financial support the community has given throughout the years, the efforts of dedicated board members, and the leadership of some fine administrators, Hilmar High School has been able to grow and offer its graduates to the community and society as citizens of whom it can be justifiably proud. Undoubtedly the founding board of the Hilmar Colony Union High School would feel that its efforts in 1911 have resulted in a most worthwhile educational system.

Hughson High School

William Hurd and Marjorie Brooks

Hughson High School was organized in 1910, and classes were started in the fall. To accommodate the high school, a vacant room was made available in the new elementary school at the corner of Charles and Whitmore Avenues. Professor Mower was the principal, and about nineteen students were enrolled. The first class of ten students was graduated in 1914.

In 1912 the high school was moved to the school building on the property at the corner of Whitmore Avenue and Tully Road. The building originally had one room; as the school system grew, it was enlarged several times.

In 1920 a new high school building was constructed on the northeast corner of Whitmore Avenue and Seventh Street. The buildings erected at that time have been replaced by modern buildings.

In some minds, the most outstanding development at Hughson High School was its introduction of Learning Activity Packages, popularly known as LAP. In a community with a high proportion of agricultural workers, it was not surprising that there was a great deal of absenteeism. Many failed to finish high school, and comparatively few went on to further education.

School and community people determined to provide the "best that's humanly possible in mass education," according to Hughson Union High School Board Chairman Cordie Qualle. "Ours is a small school in an agricultural area, and our students were going off to find employment in the cities. We wanted to give them an education that would allow them to compete easily in the job market.

"We also wanted no 'end of the line' for anybody while they were in school. If algebra is hard for somebody when he's a freshman, he can stop and take it some other time, when *he* sees the need for it. We wanted each student to find out for himself that he is educable. That's the time he learns best."

Qualle and HUHS District Superintendent Robert R. Reeder decided to seek government funds for educational improvement. They secured an Elementary and Secondary Education Act Title III (innovative) grant of three yearly $150,000 installments. Their application was based on the philosophy that each student can learn best at his own speed and in his own manner. Thus each student should be given the chance to work fast and well by offering him an individualized curriculum with a wide variety of academic and vocational options, and an emphasis on developing salable vocational skills.

Reeder and Qualle were able to convince federal officials that a small school could pioneer such a drastic change from tradition and that Hughson High School was the place where dreams of a better education for students of all backgrounds, abilities and aspirations could be realized.

Much of the federal money was used to train the thirty faculty members in the principles of individualized instruction and the art of converting whole segments of a secondary curriculum into sets of written goals and instructions for reaching them. Associate Professor Dr. Richard V. Jones, Jr., of the Stanislaus State College Department of Education, provided the technical expertise needed to adapt the Learning Activity Packages originated by the Nova Schools of Fort Lauderdale, Florida, for use in the Hughson Union High School's "Continuous Progress Program." Jones served as advisor throughout the life of the grant.

Community support for the new program was strong from the beginning. Mrs. Judson Sturtevant first developed a parent volunteer group and coordinated the work of over fifty interested parents and community members. They produced and typed Learning Activity Packages, manned evening vocational and academic laboratory centers, and explained the program to over 4500 visitors who came from many parts of the world. Parents and friends have also proctored the testing center from 8:00 A.M. to 3:00 P.M. each school day since the inception of the new curriculum.

By 1971-72 the program was in its fifth year. Over 80 percent of the curriculum was available directly to the students because of its conversion to the written Packages. Students have taken advantage of the choices thus afforded them. They have found they can carry heavy academic majors and yet plan their time so as to develop personal projects in sewing or art or electronics. Others budget their time and energy so that they can participate in a variety of extra-curricular school activities that would not be possible in a traditional setting. It is not unheard of for a student to be actively involved in band, forensics, and a major sport all at the same time.

The HUHS graduation requirement is higher than that of most high schools, yet many HUHS students have been able to finish their required subjects earlier than is possible in the usual high school schedule, and have then devoted much of their senior year to service projects in the school. Others have elected to develop a particular talent or personal interest, such as journalism, auto mechanics, or a foreign language.

They have done satisfactorily in the annual state-mandated tests and in college. Many have gone from high school vocational training to full-time jobs in the same firm or industry. Others have won jobs on the basis of the personal responsibility and initiative developed under the Hughson program.

Qualle believes the innovative program is succeeding and bases his proof on the reactions of students. "These kids go and visit other places and they realize just what they have here. They find out they're proud of their school." School personnel report they find the attitude of Hughson students toward education to be the most stimulating and rewarding of any groups with whom they have worked.

Turlock Union High School

Helen Hohenthal

In the spring of 1906, six grammar school districts, Washington, Central, Mitchell, Tegner, Keyes, and Turlock, joined to form the Turlock High School District. This was followed on 23 July 1906 by approval of a bond issue for building a high school.

"School started on 10 September 1906 in the town hall on the corner of Broadway and Olive in Turlock," Crystal Klein Brown recalled. There were twenty pupils and two teachers. The principal was S. R. Douglas, a graduate of West Point; his assistant was Miss Maud Clark. The subjects were Latin, history, mathematics and English. Handicaps existed—no desks, no classrooms, no library, no laboratory. Miss Clark's classes used the stage and Mr. Douglas' classes the main floor of the auditorium. Debate was the only possible inter-school activity."[5]

Turlock High School, 1907-1922. Forsmark photo, courtesy TDJ.

The new building at Locust and High Streets was ready for classes in September 1907. Now there were four teachers and fifty students. There was a library of one hundred books, among them a donated encyclopedia. Seventy more books were added in 1908. Inter-school competition was begun and included track, baseball, and basketball for both boys and girls.

By 1910 the school was overcrowded. The trustees, upon advice from Miss Boggs, county superintendent of schools, secured a loan to build the science and art annex. In 1912 temporary structures were built for a gymnasium and a study hall.

Bond issues for further expansion were defeated. Overflow classes were being held in churches. Both the trustees and the voters realized that more land was needed. Two sites were available, one of about six acres on Lander where the Bethany Home was built later, and a tract of over twenty acres offered by Horace Crane and Ed Lyons a few hundred yards east of Main Street and just south of the TID lateral. The east side location was chosen. Since then additional land has been purchased and several acres donated for streets, leaving a net of about forty acres.

Turlock High School as it was from about 1940 to 1972.

In 1922 the Junior College (see last section in this chapter) was moved to Modesto, and the entire high school was moved to the Canal Drive site: students, faculty, and such movable buildings as the old Annex, the study hall and gym. Continued building of permanent structures on both sides of Berkeley by direct taxation still goes on to meet the needs of increased enrollment and an enlarged curriculum. Fire in the summer of 1963 gutted the band hall, the pilot light in the water heater igniting fumes from fresh varnish. Several years later it was rebuilt. Replacement of much of the main classroom building and auditorium is scheduled to occur, under earthquake safety requirements of the Field Act.

Some courses that started out as extra-curricular activities have become popular in fulfilling the graduation requirements. The orchestra that was started by Dr. George Hodges as an after-school activity was the forerunner of a large department with regular classes in vocal and instrumental instruction. Public speaking, debate and journalism have become regular classes.

The school has also experimented with on-the-job work experience for graduation credit. An early example of this was when students in advanced electricity were getting credit for on-the-job work in TID shops under experienced personnel.

Agriculture was rightly made a regular department in the fall of 1914, when B. E. Porter taught the first courses. The department has kept pace with changing practices in all phases of farming. Turlock students have won many awards on state and national levels in agricultural shop work, livestock competitions, and other branches of agriculture. The community has been grateful for the fine leadership of its agriculture teachers, such as Lawrence ("Buck") Clausen and Don Hall.

During the school's history, the faculty has grown from 2 to 104, and the student body from 20 to 1936, exclusive of the Continuation School at the old Roselawn building and the Adult Education classes.

High School Principal John H. Pitman and his immediate predecessors, Leroy Nichols and Charles F. Perrott, served a total of forty-two years from 1924 to 1966. Their policies were essentially the same. There was to be no bonded debt, and the taxpayer was to get the maximum benefit for each dollar spent. There was to be "compassion and concern for each individual," championship of all departments, improvement of services to pupils, and "ample opportunities for student participation in athletics, art, drama, music, public speaking, clubs, etc."[6]

In 1966 the Elementary and High School Boards agreed to employ a single superintendent, and brought Thomas N. Hedden in from Patterson. The following year the boards agreed to have common personnel and pay policies. In this way they have sought to gain the benefits of larger-scale operation when it has not been possible to consolidate the two districts because of differences in boundaries.[7]

As in most California communities, Turlock High is the center for adult evening classes, and many activities such as concerts, plays, games, and community meetings.

Adult Education in Turlock

Joe Debely

Adult education in Turlock High School started in 1920 with classes in citizenship, typing, sewing, and occasionally some special subject. Over a period of twenty years from the late 1920s, Mrs. Daisy Brockway taught citizenship classes to individuals seeking to take the citizenship examinations. Physical education for adults was promoted from the 1930s on by Joe Debely.

In 1945 the Adult School started a series of very popular adult forums with film-lectures and speakers. One of the most popular speakers was Dr. Alonzo Baker, who returned annually to keep the people of Turlock informed on world affairs and entertained by the accounts of his travels.

At the beginning of the 1967-68 school year, the Turlock Adult School was set up as a separate administration with Joseph S. Debely as half-time principal. The programs which were continued or initiated included: citizenship, elementary diploma, high school diploma; elective education: arts, crafts, homemaking, health, first aid, physical fitness, industrial arts, English for foreign born, family life, securities and investments; and an enlarged forum series.

Between 1967-68 and 1970-71, enrollment in the Adult School program increased from 2,343 to 3,306, while individual attendance increased to such an extent that the average daily attendance went up from 58.98 to 115.76. In those four years, 15 elementary diplomas and 214 high school diplomas were earned. Attendance at the Adult Forum increased from 4,253 to 7,594, while the number of programs offered went up from 11 to 15. Average attendance went up 14 percent.

Other phases of adult education include the Modesto Junior College courses brought to Turlock in the evenings and the Continuation High School for students who are working during the day.

Education is now from the cradle to the grave, and there is a definite place for adult education. It may take certain new forms, but it will be an essential part of the overall educational picture.

Turlock Junior College

Helen Hohenthal

Junior colleges in California developed from post-graduate courses offered by some of the larger high schools around 1910. In recommending students with post-graduate credit for admission to universities and colleges, the high schools sought to have the post-graduate work counted toward graduation.

The University of California began collecting information and in July 1915 published a circular, "The Junior College in California." In 1916 it sent a group of men to visit these colleges to work out problems of transferring their students to the University.[8]

On 20 August 1917, the Board of Trustees of TUHS, by unanimous vote, established Turlock Junior College, the first junior college in Stanislaus County. The college opened that fall with seventeen students representing four different high schools.[9]

By attending a junior college, students postponed by two years their departure for Berkeley and other campuses, and saved much money otherwise spent for fees and board and room. Regulations for completion of the lower division requirements were the same as at the University of California.

The Dean of the Turlock Junior College was Murray K. Martin, who also taught French and Latin. Offerings were the basic lower division courses, with the same description and number as used in the

University of California. They included courses in history, economics, English, logic, chemistry, physics, botany, zoology, Spanish, mathematics, drawing, business, music, home economics, including dietetics, and special night classes given for nurses in training at the new Emanuel Hospital.

Students who attended Turlock Junior College reported happy memories and top quality instruction when they assembled at luncheon a half-century later to share reminiscences, notes and pictures. They mentioned Kate Marks' English classes; Gertrude Hunt Julien in chemistry; C. J. Carpenter in physical education, which in World War I days included some military training. J. P. Ratzell introduced the interesting subject of logic to them, and M. K. "Polly" Martin was remembered with affection. There were others, too.

The alumni mentioned ditch days, picnics, class plays put on for the school and the community, parties, banquets, and above all, close friendships with classmates and faculty in their junior college days. They talked about the popular trio from Hawaii: Afoop Ung Soy and Ernest and Lionel de Silva, who shared their musical talents with their classmates. One bright memory of the men was the time they were able to muster up a thirteen-man team to defeat the high school in baseball and track.

A list of close to eighty names of Turlock Junior College students was drawn up. It was known that many went on to finish college at the University of California, Redlands, and other universities. There were several Phi Beta Kappans among them. Others had transferred to four-year institutions at the end of one year, and their names were not on the list.

Turlock Junior College shared the faculty and facilities of an already overcrowded Turlock High School on its High Street campus. The high school was going through a trying period, short of funds and space. The Junior College was becoming an extra burden. Modesto had already acquired a large grant of land and starting capital for her junior college. It is understandable that worried trustees and feuding east side-west side citizens expressed little regret at the passing of Turlock Junior College.

Summary

Between 1906 and 1917 five high schools and a junior college were established in the Turlock region. Temporary quarters were usually established, at times in the elementary school, before high school buildings were constructed. The various special programs have given character to the schools. Several have had outstanding agriculture curricula. Hughson's experiment with individualized learning has been the most unique development within the area. The trend toward unification of districts is clearly evidenced. The growth of high schools has paralleled the growth of towns, and they have largely taken over the functions as community centers that the district elementary schools had prior to 1900.

Emanuel Hospital student nurses in 1930s.

Chapter XXIX

A Valley Medical Center

Mernell Thompson, Chrissie Collins, and John E. Caswell

Turlock has been blessed by having had a number of able physicians who have served the region long and faithfully. The practice of medicine before 1920 was thus described by the widow of one of the physicians, Mrs. Albert Julien. ". . . ninety percent of the people were Swedish, and only a very small part lived in the village of Turlock. The surrounding area was the social, religious and economic part. At that time 'the Juliens' brothers Albert and Eric were both spending 75 percent of each day, including Sundays, driving miles to deliver babies, set broken bones, operate by lamplight for appendicitis or whatever was wrong. There was no hospital. That came later. This service included Newman, Patterson, Livingston, Atwater and even Fresno at times."[1]

Like so much of Turlock's history, the growth of medical institutions began with the coming of the Swedes. There is a recollection of one physician before 1900, but his stay must have been fleeting. Of hospitals there were none. The best one could do with the sick or injured was to bundle them on the train and take them to Modesto where there was a county hospital as well as small private facilities.

In 1903, Dr. H. Virgil Monett opened an office in his home, a large two-story house on Front Street between Main and Market (now Crane) Streets. He practiced until 1923. Around 1906 three or four other physicians came to Turlock. The physicians took offices either over People's Bank or on the second floor of the First National Bank building on the northeast corner of Main and Center.[2]

One of the physicians who arrived in 1906 was Dr. P. N. Jacobsen, who owned what seems to have been the first hospital facility in Turlock. This was a hospital cottage on Vermont Avenue at Lander. Mrs. Valesca Ferguson Smith, who was one of Dr. Jacobsen's first patients, recalled how "Miss Jean Nelson who lived next door with her mother cooked the meals and carried the trays over to the hospital assisted by Miss Post one of the nurses."[3]

Long-time residents debate as to the number and locations of the small hospitals that were established in the decade following 1906. As best we can determine, the second hospital was located on West Olive; a third was located on the northeast corner of Marshall and Hamilton streets by the fire station; the fourth, established by Dr. Florence Cheney in 1916, was located on the east side of Lander a little north of Fourth.

The Doctors Julien had a few rooms for the temporary accommodation of patients in their office suite, and probably other physicians did likewise.[4]

The two Julien brothers played a prominent role in Turlock for a half-century. The earlier arrival was Dr. Eric Julien, who reached Turlock in 1911 and opened an office above M. M. Berg's new store. Becoming ill, he called on his brother Albert to take over his practice while he went for treatment to the Mayo Clinic in Rochester, Minnesota.

Dr. Albert Julien arrived in 1915. "The two Doctors met in 'the Weaver' Bank. Dr. Eric said hello, Dr. Albert grunted. Dr. Eric said, 'The office is over there,' and pointed across the street to the Berg Building.

"Word of mouth took it from there and by afternoon everyone in town had a complete description of the 'New Doc,' his history, his qualifications and the fact that he was a 'black Swede.'

"Weeks later it was known that Dr. Eric was graduated from Northwestern Medical School and Dr. Albert from the University of Minnesota. Both had had graduate work and both had had tremendous surgical experience, Dr. Eric in Seattle, and Dr. Albert as police surgeon in Superior, Minnesota. To the people of this area this meant that 'they were pretty good.' " By the time that Dr. Eric had returned from Rochester, the practice had grown to the point that it could support both brothers.[5]

Dr. Albert Julien. Courtesy Mrs. Eric Julien.

Dr. Eric Julien. Courtesy Mrs. Eric Julien.

Development of Hospitals

Mernell Thompson, Chrissie Collins, and John E. Caswell

With more than a half-dozen physicians in town, even the two-story sanitarium built by Dr. Florence Cheney in 1916 was inadequate.[6] Two Swedish Mission pastors, Rev. August G. Delbon and Rev. E. N. Train of Hilmar, joined their forces with the Doctors Julien and gained the interest of the Swedish Evangelical Missionary Association. The sponsoring association took up the financial campaign with such vigor that construction could begin in 1916, and the hospital opened its doors to patients in 1917.

Named Emanuel after the Great Physician, the new ivory-brick two-story hospital on East Canal could accommodate approximately thirty patients. The setting was attractive and peaceful with gardens and lawn adding to its serenity. Most of the rooms were private, in order to provide as complete quiet as possible for the promotion of speedier recovery.[7] There were two operating rooms on the top floor; these were provided with skylights, many windows on the sides, and strong lighting for use in emergency night operations. Two years later the hospital's bed capacity was increased to fifty patients.

Hospital rates in those simpler days were inexpensive, even after allowance for the generally lower cost of living. Room rates ranged from $4.00 per day for a two-bed room to a top of $7.00 a day for a private room. Major surgery cost from $12.00 to $20.00. Convalescence, however, was usually much slower, which may have more than made up for the lower daily rates.[8] Incurable and contagious cases were treated in the County Hospital in Modesto.

Despite donations from the community, the hospital was in financial trouble by 1923. Dr. Albert Julien loaned the hospital $10,000 for eight years, and provided that the interest on the loan was to be put into a fund for charity patients.[9] Such acts of kindness were typical of Dr. Albert, Miss Eva Nelson, former superintendent of nurses, recalled. He would charge some patients and treat others totally free of charge, depending on his knowledge of their economic situation. Families often could not pay cash, so paid in every kind of farm produce imaginable.[10]

Two years after Emanuel began operation, Dr. James L. Collins moved to Turlock and took over Dr. Jacobsen's practice. Collins had practiced in Iowa before World War I. He had dreamed of coming some day to California and opening a hospital of his own. After his service in the Army Medical Corps, he came to the San Joaquin Valley in search of a suitable location. Four years later, in January 1923, he opened a fifteen-bed hospital on the second floor of the new Sierra Building on the corner of East Main and Thor Streets. He called it the Lillian Collins Hospital in honor of his sister and his daughter. The superintendent of nurses was Miss Goldyn Carter, a sister of Mrs. Collins.

With limitless faith in Turlock Dr. Collins began to plan for the erection of a new hospital building on the southwest corner of Crane and Thor Streets. At the opening ceremony in March 1925, Dr. Collins said, "I believe that Turlock will continue to grow and this community deserves a first class hospital where all of the latest aids to medical science can be found."[11]

Lillian Collins Hospital before additions. Courtesy Dr. and Mrs. Marion C. Collins.

For almost two decades there was no significant expansion in Turlock's medical institutions. Emanuel established a school for nurses, but it was forced to close its doors in 1934.[12] The depression years of the 1930s were no time for expanding private hospitals. The war years of the 1940s were no better, with private construction virtually cut off due to shortage of building materials. Nevertheless, Dr. Marion C. Collins, who had practiced with his father until the latter's death in 1941, was able to add two four-bed wards to the Lillian Collins Hospital in 1944 to accommodate the growing population of Turlock.

After World War II, Dr. James W. Collins came to Turlock and became associated with his elder brother, Marion. Finding the hospital too small for their growing practice, they built a new $120,000 wing which was dedicated late in December 1947. It incorporated the latest equipment and building techniques, and recent changes in fire protection and public health requirements—one of the first hospitals in the state to meet these standards. Eighteen beds were added to the hospital capacity, plus a new kitchen, obstetrical labor and delivery rooms, and the latest in nursery facilities.[13]

Although expansion of medical facilities was limited for a number of years in Turlock itself, a project in the northern part of the region resulted in the establishment of a new hospital that materially extended medical services. This was Memorial Hospital, opened in Ceres in September 1951.

As early as 1943 a group of interested citizens began preliminary studies of the need for such an institution. Three years later a formal feasibility study was made and the Memorial Hospital Association of Stanislaus County was formed. Lawrence R. Robinson, Sr., internationally known seedsman, was elected first president of the Association and a financial campaign was launched. The million dollar goal was exceeded when 4,840 individuals pledged $1,020,570. The achievement was celebrated by a victory dinner held on 7 November 1947.

Six years after opening the first unit, a half-million dollar second unit was completed. In the first ten years, 10,000 babies were born in Memorial, a testimony to its popularity with the young matrons of the region!

Looking ahead, the Board of Directors in 1965 purchased thirty-five acres of farmland on Coffee Road northeast of Modesto, and in 1970 completed the first 99-bed unit of a new facility planned for an eventual capacity of 400 beds. By that time, the older facility, then known as Memorial South, had 104 acute care beds and 48 beds in its extended care facility.[14]

Emanuel Hospital completed a major expansion program on Canal Drive in the 1950s. Even this appeared to be inadequate for the future, and the Emanuel Board immediately began planning expansion of "patient capacity, diagnostic and emergency facilities," of which more later.[15]

Medic Alert

Chrissie Collins

Meanwhile, a unique world-wide service, Medic Alert, was initiated in Turlock by Dr. Marion C. Collins. Medic Alert may not have brought the name of Turlock before as many people as the lithographs on melon crates, but its bracelets have been more widely distributed across the face of the earth.

Linda, daughter of Dr. and Mrs. Collins, cut her finger in a minor accident and was taken to the hospital to have it treated. After suturing the wound, her uncle, Dr. James W. Collins, instructed the nurse to test Linda for sensitivity to tetanus antitoxin. Linda's reaction was immediate and violent. She went into anaphylactic shock and it was several days before physicians were confident that she would recover. They also knew that another test could be fatal.

In the spring of 1956 Dr. Collins began seeking some form of permanent identification for his daughter. The family devised a bracelet with the medical caduceus and the words "Medic Alert" on the face, and the engraving of her allergy on the reverse side. Seeing Linda's bracelet, other patients began asking for similar identification for allergies and other medical conditions.

This brought home to Dr. Collins the great need of many people with hidden medical problems for permanent identification. He corresponded with Dr. W. W. Bauer of the American Medical Association, seeking his advice regarding establishment of an organization to distribute such emblems. Dr. Bauer agreed that such a device was necessary. Knowing of no medical identification emblems or any organization providing such identification, he encouraged Dr. Collins to develop his idea.

In October 1956, Medic Alert bracelets were introduced to the medical profession at the Congress of the American College of Surgeons in San Francisco. Again, Dr. Collins received strong encouragement to pursue his idea. During 1957 posters emblazoned with the words "Don't Ignore This Emblem" were sent

Linda Collins Maurer with her
Medic Alert bracelet,
her parents and husband.
Courtesy Dr. and Mrs. Marion C. Collins.

to every hospital in the United States and Canada, to every county sheriff in the United States, to all division headquarters of the Royal Canadian Mounted Police, and to all police chiefs in cities of over 10,000 population. Free articles about Medic Alert were solicited in all papers in California, Oregon and Washington.

In January 1958 the California Peace Officers Association accepted the Medic Alert emblem as a standard means of identification of persons with medical problems. Miss Lillian Collins began calling on hospitals in California, asking them to place literature in their reception rooms. Drug stores were asked for space to advertise the emblem, and publicity continued to go out to the medical profession. By the end of the year about 8,000 people in the United States and Canada had chosen to wear the Medic Alert emblem, the greatest percentage being diabetics and persons allergic to drugs or antibiotics.

During all this time the correspondence of the Foundation was conducted by Dr. and Mrs. Collins. The teenage members of the family assisted with the mailings. All funds for producing the emblems and the educational literature came from Dr. Collins' personal income. All members of the family served without salary, and all work was directed from Dr. Collins' residence. In the early months of 1960 the program began to pick up in volume. The activities were moved to two rooms in the Lillian Collins Hospital and a part-time secretary was employed. By March Dr. Collins realized that the task was too large for one family, and the non-profit Medic Alert Foundation was incorporated on 29 March 1960.

Meanwhile, peace officers urged Dr. Collins to put serial numbers on the emblems and to maintain a file where the name, address, nearest of kin, and name of the wearer's physician might be recorded and be available in case of emergency on a 24-hour basis.

On 6 June 1960, the syndicated Sunday magazine supplement, THIS WEEK, carried the story of Medic Alert in the newspapers of forty major American cities. The following Friday a large canvas mail sack containing 10,000 letters was delivered to Dr. Collins' residence. In the next six months more than 100,000 letters were received as a result of this story. To handle the deluge, a downtown office was rented and thirty people were employed to answer the mail and send out identification emblems. Fred Hamann, vice-president of the Foundation, was made managing director of Medic Alert. Later Stafford Garrett became business manager, and Hamann devoted full time to public relations.

In 1961 the American Medical Association formed an *ad hoc* committee to study the problem of medical identification, and Dr. Collins was asked to serve on it. All of the standards set forth by this committee are met in the Medic Alert emblem. Service clubs and life underwriters' associations across the nation began to assist in distributing educational literature, and a Canadian Medic Alert Foundation was established with offices in Toronto. Tax-exempt status was granted the Foundation in 1962 by a U.S. Treasury ruling. Between 1962 and 1964 foreign affiliates were established in New Zealand, Spain, the Netherlands, the Philippine Republic, the United Kingdom and the Republic of Ireland. A 1965 world trip by Dr. Collins resulted in new foundations in Australia, Rhodesia, South Africa, France and Belgium.

Back in Turlock, Medic Alert moved into a new building adjacent to the Civic Center on 14 July 1967. With the tremendous growth of the files and the increase in long-distance telephone requests for information, a high degree of mechanization became necessary. Under the able direction of executive director Alfred A. Hodder, computerizing and microfilming of members' records were begun in the spring of 1970.

As of 30 June 1971, over 450,000 people in many parts of the world were protected by Medic Alert. The emblem originally designed to protect one girl had become the universally recognized symbol for medical identification.[16]

Worldwide Medic Alert headquarters. Courtesy Dr. and Mrs. Marion C. Collins.

Lillian Collins Becomes Community Hospital

John E. Caswell

With the challenge of developing the Medic Alert idea before him, Dr. Collins found it desirable to dispose of the hospital which he and his father had operated for thirty-five years. In October 1960 he sold it to the Turlock Community Hospital Corporation. The stockholders in this corporation were a group from Redding who already owned a hospital there. Jay Akin became the administrator.[17] The new owners continued to operate Community, as it was now familiarly called, as a general hospital. There was a continuous upgrading and updating of the facilities, with a major remodeling of the lobby, offices, doctors' lounge and nursery in 1966. That same year saw the organization of the Turlock Community Hospital Foundation with Forest Fiorini as its president. The function of the Foundation was to identify community health needs and to provide the funding for specific projects of general significance.[18]

A new phase of expansion and upgrading was begun in 1970. By 1973 it was expected that the oldest section of the hospital would be replaced, the number of beds increased from 39 to 63, a third surgery recovery room and physical therapy department added, and the emergency rooms, laboratory, and X-ray department completely rebuilt.[19]

The New Emanuel Hospital

Mernell Thompson and John E. Caswell

In 1960 there were ninety beds in the two Turlock hospitals, and estimates showed that by 1975 twice that number would be needed. The Emanuel Board decided it was time to consider expanding their facilities. Three different consulting firms were brought in to see whether the old hospital on Canal Drive could be upgraded; they agreed unanimously that it could not.

It thus became necessary to buy a new site. One was chosen which lay between Olive and Colorado Streets. A street was put through, and named "Delbon" in honor of the Board's first president, Rev. August Delbon. The estimated cost of construction was $1.7 millions, of which $500,000 was needed in gifts. Mayor Enoch S. Christoffersen undertook to chair the fund drive, which raised pledges and cash of about $517,000. This was the more remarkable in view of the fact that the largest community fund drive up to that time had raised no more than $60,000.[20]

Preparation of the site was begun when only a few thousand dollars in pledges were in the bank. Almost three years later, on 15 November 1966, the main building was occupied. It had a total of 90 beds, including 12 bassinets.[21]

Hardly was the general facility completed, when plans were begun for a mental health wing that would "offer emergency services, inpatient and outpatient services, partial day care and consultation."[22] It was expected that grants from the federal and state governments would cover most of the financing required. A grant was also obtained from the Ben and Gladys Arkelian Foundation of Fresno. At this point the federal government indicated that no funds would be available for the mental health wing. Again a campaign was conducted in the town and $339,218 was subscribed. Then federal funds were once more made available and local subscribers were invited to permit their pledges to be used to pay off the loans that had been necessary.

When the mental health unit was ready for occupancy in August 1970, it had twenty-five beds which could be used either for night, day, or continuous care, with additional facilities for the treatment of 100 outpatients daily.[23]

Chosen as head of the new unit was Dr. John I. Maurer, husband of Linda Collins, the inspiration for Medic Alert. Working in close cooperation with Stanislaus State College and other regional facilities, Dr. Maurer and his staff quickly began to receive commendation through the community for their constructive approach to mental health problems.

Shortly after the general hospital unit on Delbon Avenue had been completed, permission was obtained from the City to use the old hospital building on Canal as a convalescent home for a maximum of five years. It was actually phased out in October 1970, when a bright new convalescent home, Brandel Manor, was opened west of the main hospital.

As the centennial year 1971-72 drew to a close, Emanuel was engaged in still another expansion program which would provide eight beds in a "modern intensive care and coronary care unit, five pediatric beds and 19 general acute beds." Additional physical therapy and other ancillary facilities were also being provided, the whole costing some $800,000.[24]

One effect of Emanuel's move to the north edge of the city was to attract a number of physicians who built offices across from the new hospital on land made available by the Emanuel Board. The third unit of Boies Drug Store was also placed in "Doctors' Row."

By no means all physicians followed Emanuel. The group of physicians headed by Dr. V. S. Todd remained close to Community Hospital, with a pharmacy just a block away. The Seventh Day Adventist physicians' group, Turlock Medical Clinic, remained at the corner of East Main and Colorado, with Boies' second unit adjacent to it.

Turlockers increasingly found their need for specialists met in their home town. One of the attractions to physicians, George Perrine of Community Hospital has suggested, was that Turlock had an "amiable medical community—physicians get along well with each other."

While the Turlock facilities served a considerable area, residents of the northern half of the region found Memorial Hospital and Modesto physicians more conveniently located. Turlock as of the autumn of 1971 had no orthopedist, dermatologist, no oral surgeon, nor full-time ophthalmologist. For such specialties one still had to go to Modesto. Two hours away were the facilities of the Bay Area, including the hospitals and clinics attached to the medical schools of the University of California, Stanford University and the University of the Pacific.

For a town of about 15,000 population, Turlock could congratulate her physicians and herself for the excellent health facilities provided.

Emanuel Hospital about 1958.
Courtesy Chamber of Commerce.

New Emanuel Hospital in center, with Mental Health Wing to right, and Brandel Manor, the convalescent home, in upper left. "Doctors' row" is in foreground. Shutters photo, courtesy Emanuel Hospital.

Victory dinner, 29 December 1959. From left, Senator Hugh Donnelly; J. Burton Vasche, Associate Superintendent of Public Instruction (not yet appointed President of SSC); Ralph Brown, Speaker of the Assembly; and Stanley T. Wilson. Courtesy Stanley T. Wilson.

Chapter XXX

Turlock Wins a College

Stanley T. Wilson

One might say the Stanislaus State College story should start on January 8, 1957, when Assembly Bill 4 was introduced in the legislature to provide $500,000 for the acquisition of a site for a new college to be located in Stanislaus County, and that the ending should be December 9, 1959, when the State Public Works Board decided by unanimous vote that the new college would be located in Turlock.

But the site selection was not the end. Passage of the college bill had stimulated a contest between sponsors of locations at Modesto, Ceres, Oakdale, Riverbank, Salida and Turlock. Eventually all sites were eliminated but two west of Modesto and one just north of Turlock. Modesto's leaders assumed that its population and facilities made the choice obvious. When the Turlock site was chosen, the Modestans continued the struggle for several months seeking to upset the decision.

Efforts to get legislative approval of a state college in Stanislaus date back to 1949, but the county's two representatives—Senator Hugh P. Donnelly and Assemblyman Ralph M. Brown—were not successful until 1957. Brown's bill, co-authored by 19 of his colleagues, was the one that made it through the legislature and to the desk of Governor Goodwin J. Knight, who signed it into law on July 5, 1957. A similar measure had been introduced by Donnelly as a protective move, in case the first bill got tied up in committee.

William N. Bucknam of Ceres, a member of the State Board of Education, played no small role in providing ammunition for Brown and Donnelly to round up the needed votes for passage. In fact, the turning point came on March 11 when the State Board of Education made a recommendation to the Assembly Ways and Means Committee, giving Stanislaus a high priority following issuance of a *Study of the Need for Additional Centers of Public Higher Education in California.*[1]

Based on projected enrollment alone, the study committee previously had told the legislature (on January 18) that Stanislaus ranked no better than a three-way tie for fourth, but that "other factors are worthy of note." It said these included "presence or absence of junior colleges, percentage of area students eligible to enter a state college, the existence of private colleges and universities, and the presence of existing or proposed campuses of the University of California." Taking all these things into consideration, the Board of Education later made an "immediate priority" list for new state colleges, and Stanislaus County was third.

Thirteen days after Governor Knight signed Assembly Bill 4, the Turlock Chamber of Commerce scheduled a dinner in Merced and invited school and civic leaders of that county to attend. Thirty persons were present, including Merced's two legislators—Senator James A. Cobey and Assemblyman Gordon D. Winton—and nearly all expressed the opinion that a college located in the southern end of Stanislaus would better serve Merced County.

The Turlock group left the meeting encouraged, even though Stanislaus County School Superintendent Fred Beyer predicted there would be "quite a hassle" over location of the college, and that there already was a strong west side (of Modesto) committee working. Beyer's prediction proved correct and 29 months later he found himself in the middle of the hassle.

A problem of money with which to finance an effective campaign faced the Turlock Chamber. But it had one committee with a healthy bank account. The Industrial Division, under the chairmanship of Mayor Enoch Christoffersen, had gone store-to-store in the business district to raise funds to help bring in new industry. At this group's next meeting, someone asked, "What better industry could we get than a college?" All agreed, and Orville L. Gross proposed that a special college committee be set up. I was voted its chairman, and others named were Richard Ward, Gross and Christoffersen. Ward later moved away and was replaced by Jack Rickenbacher.

When the committee was announced, rumors began making the rounds in Modesto that I had an inside track with Governor Knight, who had appointed the three men who would make the site selection—part of this based on a published report two years earlier that Governor Knight had offered me a six-year appointment to the Public Utilities Commission, and that I had turned it down. These rumors led to an inquiry by Modesto, and in a speech to the McHenry Lions Club, Lorne A. Campbell said: "The chairman of our committee, Ian Hardie, was informed by state officials that their every move in arriving at a decision will be open and above board and that rumors to the contrary are without base."

In September, the Department of Education issued a lengthy report titled *Factors in the Selection of a State College Site in Stanislaus County*[2] and Turlock was rocked back on its heels by a subsequent headline in the *Modesto Bee* that read:

COLLEGE SITE IN MODESTO AREA IS FAVORED

The story beneath it read: "The State Department of Education today recommended that the site for a planned new state college in Stanislaus County be located in the vicinity of Modesto. The recommendation. . .pinpoints the probable site location within a seven and a half by 15 miles rectangle. The alignment of the rectangle roughly parallels US 99 from five miles north to 10 miles south of Modesto. . ."

I began re-reading the report—not once but many times—in search of a loophole. The first thing I found was this. The report did not say the college should be located within the 7½ x 15-mile rectangle which had been drawn on a map of the primary service area. In two places it said a site should be found within or VERY NEAR the rectangle. One of the four Turlock sites we were going to propose—at Geer and Monte Vista—was near the rectangle and near US 99.

Another point made by the Department of Education reflected its feeling that "extension of publicly supported institutions to the degree that the continued operation of private ones long in existence and seemingly serving the community well is jeopardized, is not in the public interest."

The College of the Pacific (now University of the Pacific) was such a private institution, so I made a trip to Stockton to enlist the support of Dr. Robert Burns, president. Dr. Burns not only agreed to help Turlock, but got the support of Senator Alan Short of San Joaquin County. This made three legislators so far in the Turlock corner, Cobey, Winton and Short. Stanislaus' two—Donnelly and Brown—made it clear that they would remain absolutely neutral in the matter of a site selection, for they both represented the entire county.

It was not known whether it would be important to have friends pulling for you. I took the position that no poor location would be chosen, population center or not, but tried to be realistic enough to believe that if Turlock and Modesto came down to the wire with two sites of equal quality, both acceptable to the state, then it wouldn't hurt to have some pretty important people in your corner rooting for you. In an effort to build this "rooting section" I wrote or telephoned every friend I had with any connections in Sacramento. Resolutions of support also were obtained from the County of Merced and various cities.

In November of 1957 the first of two brochures went to the Public Works Board, detailing what we thought were the advantages of six proposed sites, and making a strong pitch for locating the new college halfway between two existing state colleges in Fresno and Sacramento.[3]

The brochure was updated many times, as new information became available, and particularly since Governor Knight decided in 1958 not to seek re-election, thus resulting in many changes in the complexion of the Public Works Board. Modesto did likewise. Six sites were proposed there in 1957, and on January 13, 1958, studies of 20 possible sites were presented in a booklet taken to Sacramento by Modesto chairman Ian Hardie, City Planning Director George Smeath, and Harold Pederson, Chamber industrial director.

That same month, Chairman Hardie revealed that the Modesto college committee had been in existence for more than a year, and that when Governor Knight signed the bill making the college possible, the committee was increased to include representatives of Modesto city government.[4]

The Modesto committee told the state: "The geographic center of population of the six county area is near Modesto and has been moving northward over the years. The Modesto-Ceres urban area has over half the population of Stanislaus county. More than 70 percent of the high school enrollment of the county is in the Modesto, Ceres and Oakdale High School Districts. The geographic center of high school enrollment for the six counties is 4.72 miles north and .56 of a mile east of Modesto. Modesto business firms are sources of more part-time jobs for college students than will be found in other cities in the county. In addition, the area provides more housing, jobs, recreational and cultural opportunities, library facilities and professional services than other locations."

All these features, the committee said, indicated the state should pick a Modesto area location for the campus. Close proximity to the Modesto Junior College "which would supplement a four year college" also was cited as in favor of a Modesto location.

One thing that disturbed me was that three of Modesto's sites, on the Ed Mape Ranch west of town, had been offered to the state at no cost.

By mid-year, with Knight out of the race for governor, resignations began to pour in. T. H. Mugford became director of finance and C. M. Gilliss was appointed director of the Department of Public Works. Both happened to be friends of Forest Fiorini, who was on the State Aeronautics Commission, and I asked him to write them regarding the college site selection.

Their replies were non-committal, but Mugford, who had been Deputy Finance Director and thus familiar with the college matter, offered this opinion: "I believe that problems of site selection and purchase will be less severe in Stanislaus County than we anticipate in the North Bay area. Even though there is understandable rivalry between Turlock and Modesto, I feel very sure that the two communities can find common ground for support of a location when we have secured all facts and data concerning the sites that are suitable for State purchase."

Gilliss later resigned as Public Works Director and was replaced by T. Fred Bagshaw of Mill Valley, who had been a friend of mine since 1945 when I purchased the *Mill Valley Record.* But a wholesale change in the Public Works Board came after Edmund G. Brown was elected governor. He named Bert Levit as his Finance Director, Robert B. Bradford as Public Works Director, and W. A. Savage as Real Estate Commissioner. This team stayed in the saddle until after the college site was chosen, with the exception of Levit. He resigned and was replaced by John Carr.

With the election of Governor Brown, the Democrats also gained control of the Assembly and elected Stanislaus' Ralph Brown as Speaker. This would put him on the Public Works Board, where he wouldn't have a vote but could perhaps get the various site selection matters moving along faster.

On February 25 I attended the new board's first meeting, primarily to get acquainted with Levit, Bradford and Savage, and to chat again with H. C. Vincent, Jr., the state's Property Acquisition Chief and Board Secretary.

On May 4 the Stanislaus County Board of Supervisors approved a road department proposal for widening Geer Road from the Turlock city limits to Taylor Road, and I immediately wrote Vincent to tell him that this would enhance the desirability of our proposed site at Geer and Monte Vista. I also got data from Merced Supervisor Neill Galloway showing the projected development of Lander Avenue, which would place Los Banos within 33 miles of Turlock.

On May 11, the Modesto Board of Education offered "full cooperation" to the proposed new college, and implied it would consider sharing the use of facilities wherever feasible and mutually beneficial, including classrooms, stadium and auditoriums, until the college was self-sufficient. "This might help the state set up here a year or two earlier," said School Superintendent James H. Corson.

At a meeting on June 29, the Public Works Board set July 20, 1959, as the date for an inspection tour and public hearing in Stanislaus county. Plans were made for the meeting to be held in Modesto and the state officials to have lunch in Turlock.

Meanwhile, the Public Works Board had directed its staff to inspect all of the sites proposed—there were some 40 of them—and weed out all that could not qualify. When this was done, there were seven sites "in the running," including one in Turlock. Originally the staff had narrowed the selection down to six, but the West Modesto Committee—which was working independently of the Chamber of Commerce of Modesto—put up such a fuss when the site at California and Pauline Streets was eliminated, that the board decided to take a look at it. Oddly enough, it was still in contention when the choice had been narrowed down to three.

Late in June, I wondered if Turlock might receive some help through Neil Haggerty, an official of the AFL-CIO who had connections in Sacramento, so I made inquiry of former Governor Knight. For reasons which he explained, Knight advised against asking him. But Knight did say he, himself, was "greatly impressed with the sturdy fight you are waging" and added that "I am going to Sacramento next week and will put my ear to the ground and see if I can be of any help."

On July 16 Knight wrote again, "I did what I could when I was in Sacramento in my conference with Bert Levit. Can you tell me anything further I can do or any other person I can contact between now and the time when the decision will be made?"

Turlock made big plans in preparation for the July 20 site inspection and hearing. While Vincent had insisted, when we were discussing where the group would have lunch, that "we'll pay our own way," I was equally insistent that the bus load of officials be our guests at noontime. While the Chamber Industrial Division had given me a free hand and a blank check—with instructions to spend whatever was necessary to get the college—I nevertheless took up the matter of playing host to the state when the Division next met. It was decided to go all out, with an elaborate steak barbecue; hopefully at a private home. Thornton Snider had just the right home.

Without hesitation, Snider agreed to our plan.[5] The guests included people from the Departments of Finance, Architecture, and Education—as well as the Public Works Board including Assembly Speaker Brown and other legislative members. Mayor Don Hammond of Modesto and Mayor Ray Carter of Turlock likewise were included.

No formal pitch was made (we saved that for the afternoon meeting) but displayed prominently was a large map, drawn by Ron Hawkins, which showed how the major roads feed into Turlock.

As we had boarded the bus in Modesto that morning for the tour of all sites, City Manager Ross Miller of Modesto handed everyone a folder containing the presentations to be made that afternoon by four members of the committee—Ian Hardie, Dr. Corson, Dr. Hansberry, and Mayor Hammond. Each presented good arguments. John H. Pitman, Jeremy C. Cook and I did the talking for Turlock at the packed-room hearing, and others to speak were from Salida. Riverbank, Newman, Ceres and Keyes.

The seven sites inspected that day were located as follows: Rumble Road and Prescott Road, Coffee Road on both sides of Floyd Avenue, Yosemite Blvd. between Lincoln Avenue and Riverside Avenue,

Whitmore and Crows Landing Road west of Ceres, Geer and Monte Vista in Turlock, Pauline and California, and Maze Road at the corner of Dakota.

My next trip to Sacramento was on August 24, and by this time John Carr had replaced Levit as Finance Director and chairman of the Public Works Board, which had placed the Stanislaus site matter on the agenda for that day. The board had before it a cost analysis of the seven sites under consideration. The total cost of 300 usable acres ran all the way from Turlock's $713,000 to $1,350,000. There would be a reduction of from $103,000 to $250,000 in each of the six Modesto sites if Modesto assumed the storm drainage, as Turlock had agreed to do. At the time the figures were prepared, the Modesto Irrigation District apparently had not yet agreed to the use of its ditches for drainage purposes.

The Turlock Irrigation District always had maintained a policy of permitting the city to empty storm waters into its ditches, so drainage was no problem at Geer and Monte Vista, which the city had promised to annex. But the Modesto Irrigation District would never allow such a practice. All of us thought that in the area of drainage, Turlock had a built-in advantage. Modesto must have thought so too, for the city went to the Irrigation District board and got the directors to make an exception—for the college.

After some discussion, the Public Works Board on August 24 eliminated four sites from further consideration, and Turlock had survived the axe. Both of Modesto's remaining sites—California and Pauline, and Maze Road at Dakota—were on the west side of town, and this brought forth a brand new ball game for it became possible to develop a new set of figures giving even better reasons why the college should come to Turlock.

For one thing, it put Oakdale and even some of eastern Modesto closer to the Turlock site; it gave us a whole new set of figures to present, and I began at once to prepare a new brochure. I also wrote a number of letters to Turlock supporters, including Senators Cobey and Short and Assemblyman Winton, asking them to write the Public Works Board again and "pour on the steam." Also I wrote to former Governor Knight, who replied:

> Just received your letter written Aug. 25 and will answer immediately. By good chance I am meeting John Carr for the first time tomorrow morning here in Los Angeles. The purpose is to discuss with him the selection of a portrait painter.
>
> As you no doubt know he worked for years for Buffums in Long Beach. Mrs. Norman Chandler is a member of that family.
>
> I will get all the info I can about him and report further to you.

By September the Department of Education had begun making plans for opening the new college number 15 in the chain of state colleges—which meant that a president would have to be appointed as soon after January 1 as possible so that he could begin gathering a staff.

In reporting this, the *Modesto Bee* said that the college would operate at first in rented quarters and "in other areas the state has preferred to tie the state college in with a junior college if possible" as this "permits more easy transition of students into upper division work."

The story didn't make good reading in Turlock.

Meanwhile, the City of Ceres threw its support to Turlock, making a total of 15 communities that were backing us. My appeal to Paul R. Leake, chairman and veteran member of the State Board of Equalization (as well as a Woodland newspaper publisher) brought immediate support in the form of letters to Governor Brown and Chairman Carr of the Public Works Board. Subsequently Leake wrote me, "Have just talked to John Carr. He is very favorably impressed with the site at Turlock."

Later, after the site selection was made, Leake wrote me: "It is my feeling that your site would not have been chosen if it were not the best one. While Mr. Carr is partial to your community, he would not have by-passed another site if it had more advantages than yours."

In the weeks preceding the site selection, it just seemed that more and more roadblocks were being set up. Although he insisted that it was intended to be objective, and not detrimental to any proposed location, County Planner Martin L. Schueller gave the County Supervisors a site analysis that seemed to me would work against Turlock. I replied to it in considerable detail. Later the staff in Road Commissioner

Ellis Delbon's office came up with figures on access road costs which caused quite a hassle. Delbon didn't see the figures until they went to the Board of Supervisors, but he later called them inaccurate and gave different ones to the state. He was accused by pro-Modestans of using "varying sets of cost estimates." An attempt was made to ask the state to disregard his figures. This motion lost 3 to 2, only the two Modesto supervisors supporting it.

Before the access road storm was kicked up, I had finished our new brochure, which Ernie Zuick of the *Journal* advertising staff illustrated with clever cartoons to fit the text. I took three copies to Sacramento on October 26 and handed them personally to Carr, Bradford and Savage of the Public Works Board. Each brochure was personalized. For instance, the one that went to the chairman had this message—in large letters—on the cover:

MR. CARR
THE FIGURES
FAVOR TURLOCK

Those figures claimed that 53.6 percent of the high school graduates in Stanislaus county were closer to the Turlock site. In addition, it was pointed out that "Many students living on the east side of Modesto will find it an easier drive to the Turlock site than to either of the west side Modesto sites."

The brochure pointed out that since 1950 Merced County's population had increased 32.4 percent, while in Stanislaus County the increase had been but 18.1 percent, and in San Joaquin County 2i percent. This would support our claim that the college should be located convenient to Merced County.

Completion of Geer-Albers Road, the brochure said, would put Oakdale just 16.8 miles from the Turlock site, as compared to 19.5 and 18.2 miles from the two Modesto sites.

In repeating the suggestion that the college go midway between Fresno and Sacramento, the brochure pointed out that 67 percent of the high school graduates in Stanislaus and Merced Counties lived closer to the Turlock site. It said that if every 1959 high school graduate in the two counties attended the new college, the potential student miles per day would be 48,642 if the college were placed west of Modesto, but only 43,508 miles if the college went to Turlock.

Site cost figures were dealt with (the Maze Road site was carried on the county assessment rolls at a figure 19 percent higher than the Turlock site, and the other Modesto site was 11 percent higher) and finally the brochure gave 23 reasons why the Turlock site was felt to be superior.

Turlock's efforts to get the college, it was stated, had been endorsed in resolutions passed by the Merced County Board of Supervisors as well as city councils and/or chambers of commerce in Atwater, Ceres, Delhi, Dos Palos, Gustine, Keyes, Livingston, Los Banos, Merced, and Oakdale. Later there were endorsements from Hughson, Denair, Patterson, Newman and Hilmar.

The illustrated brochure was eye-catching, and I am sure it was read thoroughly. I remember that while I was talking with Public Works Director Bradford he kept thumbing through it, approvingly. He later wrote:

> Thanks for presenting me with the illustrated booklet on the proposed College site.
> I have read it through with interest; also, with admiration for the imaginative way it
> is put together.

As we waited for the college site selection to be made, new trouble developed—this time of equal concern to Modesto and Turlock. Arthur G. Coons, president of Occidental College and chairman of the Master Plan Survey of Higher Education (a liaison committee) wrote a letter to Superintendent of Public Instruction Roy E. Simpson urging that the college be delayed.

The letter claimed that not less than five areas had greater needs for state colleges than those of Stanislaus and North Bay, and then it said:

> If delay is not possible, then the Public Works Board might like to have our judg-
> ment that sites should be selected in locations that could serve adjacent areas that

have rising needs for state college services. For example, a site in the extreme north of Stanislaus County might serve a clientele from the Stockton (San Joaquin County) area that will be, in 1975, about as large as that from Stanislaus.

Assembly Speaker Brown issued a public statement deploring any delay, and I challenged Dr. Coons's assumption, using some of the figures from our brochure.

Perturbed by Dr. Coons's contention that more students could be served if the college were placed in the northern part of Stanislaus County, and equally disturbed by Hayward's ability to get Governor Brown to ask that the Alameda college matter be re-opened, after a site at Pleasanton had been chosen, I made an appointment to see the Governor on November 27.

I didn't mention Dr. Coons's letter, but told the Governor that the purpose of my visit was to talk about population centers, and to explain that while it might appear so on the surface, there was no comparison between the situation in Stanislaus and that in Alameda County. I recited figures to show that the west side sites in Modesto were not the center of student population.

While in Sacramento, I dropped in at the Division of Architecture and quite by accident learned of something that was highly detrimental to Turlock's site. I was chatting with one of the staff men when he let a remark slip to the effect that state engineers were concerned that they would find the same situation in Turlock that they had in Tracy when the state built the Deuel Correctional Institution.

As soon as I could, I called Allen Cook, superintendent at Deuel, to inquire what kind of problems they'd had in construction. I learned that at Deuel, the water table varied from three to five feet; also that the institution is located outside the Banta Irrigation District so there was no way of controlling the water table as is done in Turlock. Furthermore, initial construction at Deuel was during an extremely wet year when everything around was flooded. In addition, the soil has a high gumbo content and spread footings were not used, as was planned with SSC. They used pilings and it was hard to find solid ground to support the buildings.

Sure enough, the Tracy situation was thrown at us at the December 9 site selection hearing, but I had answers which seemed to satisfy the Board.

On my November 27 visit to Sacramento, I also learned that the Division of Architecture had completed its work and filed a comprehensive report, based on test borings and other factors. I was anxious to get my hands on this report, but Acquisition Chief Vincent couldn't release it without Carr's approval. Carr gave it, and I received the report—which was very detrimental to Turlock—on December 3. The next day I had to be in San Francisco so I asked Orville Gross if he would go to Modesto and talk with someone in the farm advisor's office about nematodes, high water tables, and other things that the Division of Architecture had brought up.

Gross learned that Architecture had received a report from the farm advisor and then had drawn its own conclusions. Just as one example, the report said the nematode condition was "medium to heavy." The Division of Architecture chose to leave out the word "medium" and call it "heavy."

J. L. Meyer, with whom Gross talked, said there is no means of measuring nematode infestation other than to judge from damage to root stocks of existent plants or trees. The conclusion that the area had "medium to heavy" infestation was based on findings in a peach orchard at the corner of Geer and Monte Vista that was planted 25 or 30 years before, prior to the time a root stock (S 37) was developed that is nematode resistant. Meyer said both of the Modesto sites had nematodes but that they were of little consequence as the property had not been used for crops that were susceptible to nematodes.

My letter to the Public Works Board was lengthy and claimed that Architecture had over-estimated the site preparation cost in Turlock by $125,000. This claim was backed up by letters from Howard F. Luther, president of Chemurgic Corporation, and Ray Lewis of Lewis Nursery, as well as a University of California map showing soil types in the college site area, and a Stanislaus County Soil Survey showing that the Turlock site has good soil and the type which produces a heavy yield.

As for the water table, I referred them to a previous letter—from Roy V. Meikle, chief engineer of the Turlock Irrigation District—saying what steps the district would take to control the water table, if necessary. Point by point I attempted to answer the architectural report.

During a sleepless night on the 7th, I suddenly wondered what effect this latest report would have on the Department of Education. Dr. Simpson previously had told me he had visited all three sites, and liked Turlock's.

The next morning—the day before the all-important site selection hearing—I called Dr. Simpson's office in Sacramento. He was out of town—attending a conference at the Claremont Hotel in Berkeley. I placed a call to him there and asked, "Have you made your college site recommendation to the Public Works Board?"

He prepared me for what was to follow by saying that the Division of Architecture had dealt Turlock a pretty severe blow. Then he added, "I have in my possession a letter to be signed, which Dr. Vasche has prepared, recommending a site in Modesto."

My heart seemed to stand still momentarily. Then I managed to ask, "Will you do one thing for me?"

"What is it?" he inquired.

"Will you not sign that letter until I can get some information into your hands—facts that will prove the architectural report is slanted and inaccurate?"

Dr. Simpson promised me he would hold off signing it. I inquired how long he would be in Berkeley, and when told, I stated that the material would be delivered to him there.

I didn't see how I possibly could drive to Berkeley myself, for I had to work on the speech that I intended to make at the Sacramento hearing the next day. So I called Mayor Carter:

"Ray, we're in trouble and I need some help," I said.

"All right, what can I do?" he responded quickly.

I explained our predicament and asked if there was anyone the city could send to Berkeley. He volunteered City Administrator Larry O'Rourke.

As soon as I could get the material together, O'Rourke hopped in his car and drove to Berkeley, where he personally handed the envelope to Dr. Simpson.

On behalf of Dr. Simpson, Dr. J. Burton Vasche the next day recommended the Turlock site to the Public Works Board.

Carr and Bradford both voted for the Turlock site, and Savage—who was testifying at a federal trial in Southern California—made it unanimous when his ballot, given to Carr in advance, was brought forth.

The news was greeted with excitement in Turlock, where Mayor Carter proclaimed the next day as "College Day," but with disappointment in Modesto. Townspeople in Turlock said the decision would take its place in history along with the coming of the railroad in the 1870s and the formation of the Turlock Irrigation District. The Chamber of Commerce, then planning for its annual installation of officers, changed the meeting date to December 29 and called it a "victory dinner" to honor the college committee. At this dinner, my wife and I were presented a sterling silver candelabra set.

An indication of what was to be forthcoming from the county seat was given in a *Modesto Bee* story on December 10:

> The announcement that Turlock has been selected as the site for Stanislaus County's new four year state college threatens to turn what had been termed 'a friendly rivalry' between that city and Modesto for the campus into a bitter feud.
>
> In some Modesto quarters the news brought cries of 'investigation' and 'restudy.'
>
> The Modesto City Council last night sought an explanation of the state public works board's decision.
>
> Stanislaus County Schools Superintendent Fred C. Beyer said the issue should be taken to Gov. Edmund G. Brown for reexamination.
>
> Despite a reported Turlock claim that he was misquoted in yesterday's *Bee*, Beyer today reiterated his stand that there 'should be a complete investigation' of the state decision.

Beyer, who the next day called Dr. Vasche for an explanation of the Department of Education's action, said later that a site selection "based solely on a few dollars seems a peculiar way to settle the cultural destinies of a community." Beyer insisted that the board's decision "is by no means final."

The *Bee* also on December 9 reported that "The Modesto City Council, shocked at yesterday's selection of the north Turlock site for the. . .college. . .devoted a portion of its meeting last night to calling names and asking for an explanation."

Mayor Don Hammond said it was "in the realm of a political decision." Councilman Tom Spaulding said, "Months ago there were persistent rumors that we were wasting our time in providing facts on the college sites, that this had all been signed, sealed and delivered to Senator Donnelly." City Manager Ross Miller said, "We must have proceeded on a wrong basis. We did not go out and seek endorsements of other groups. We assumed the selection would be made upon facts and we felt we could help best by providing facts."

Councilman Spaulding's comment about the political gift was labeled as "ridiculous" by both Senator Donnelly and Assembly Speaker Brown, who reiterated that they had remained neutral throughout the struggle between Turlock and Modesto. And most people must have believed them, for they were re-elected.

The year 1959 ended, hardly quietly, and on January 20 the Modesto City Council scheduled a meeting which lasted two and one-half hours and attracted an overflow crowd to the basement of McHenry Library. The City Council had asked Dr. Simpson to be present to "explain" the Department of Education's recommendation favoring Turlock. He did not attend and did not send a representative.

There were many speakers, and tempers flared. Donnelly, Brown, and Bucknam all warned that the college could be lost by undue wrangling. Mayor Hammond said that political pressure favoring Turlock came from Merced and San Joaquin legislators "while Modesto was left in the middle without representation in this matter." Several brought out that the Public Works Board's decision had been reversed in the matter of Alameda County, and it could happen again.

With this thought in mind, it was decided that Mayor Hammond should name a committee of citizens to attend a Public Works Board meeting to ask questions about the site selection. Such an opportunity came on March 2.

Prior to the hearing in Sacramento, Mayor Hammond mailed a five-page, single-spaced presentation to the Governor, the Department of Education, the Public Works Board, and to Stanislaus' two legislators. At the hearing itself, spokesmen were Leslie Knoles, a Modesto Junior College faculty member and city councilman: Herbert Baum, Dr. Robert Walton and Hugh Barton, representing a citizens' committee; Mrs. Ada Hubbard, a housewife; Ross Miller, City Manager; Dr. Ray Shearn, a Planning Commissioner; and John Feltes, chairman of the West Modesto College Committee.

The pleas of this delegation—some impassioned, others calm but firm—did not change the Board's decision. The three members refused to budge from their previous position, telling the audience they believed the best site had been chosen; that the processes of government had functioned properly and that all factors had been weighed carefully.

A week later the Modesto City Council voted 5 to 2 to send a letter to Governor Brown protesting the procedures used in the site selection, and Councilman Thomas Spaulding read a 1200-word statement which was rather strongly worded.

By March 14 the city council had its letter to the governor drafted, but there was considerable discussion as to whether it should be sent. The motion to mail it passed by one vote, but the council seemed unanimous on one point—it wouldn't do any good. Mayor Hammond urged that the matter be dropped, pointing out that the city had been unable to "generate any local support from organized groups such as the schools, chamber of commerce, merchants or service clubs."

The letter to Governor Brown protested "the manner in which the Public Works Board reached its decision" and asked that "in the interest of sound government" he investigate the matter.

He did so, and his reply to Mayor Hammond was made public on April 6. It closed the door on the site selection squabble, and cleared the way for Stanislaus State College to open its doors—in temporary quarters at the fairgrounds—the following September.

There was some uneasiness, though, right up to the day the first concrete was poured on the new campus. And let me say parenthetically that after my problems with the state Division of Architecture, I was pleased that Stanislaus State College became the first state college to be completely master planned by private architects.

Library lobby at night. Courtesy SSC

Chapter XXXI

Stanislaus State College's Crucial Formative Years, 1960-1971

John E. Caswell

The nineteenth of September 1960 was fair and warm in Turlock. At 11:00 A.M. a group of about 1100 notables, faculty, staff, students and townspeople gathered on the Fairgrounds to see the symbolic ribbon cut, listen to speeches, and share a luncheon provided by the Turlock service clubs. State Senator Hugh P. Donnelly and Assembly Speaker Ralph M. Brown, legislative sponsors of the college, were the ranking guests. There were mutual congratulations and best wishes all around. Stanislaus State College had been launched.

Official registration figures showed 756 students, of whom 579 were taking six units or less. Many of these were provisionally credentialed teachers, for whose upgrading Bill Bucknam of Ceres had secured endorsement of the college from the State Board of Education, of which he was a member. Others were qualified teachers continuing their education. Still others were matrons who sought teaching credentials in order to help finance their children's education. Among the men were flyers from Castle Air Force Base, well-trained and ambitious. The excellent motivation of the first students set a high standard of expectation of future classes.

There were at first only eight full-time teaching faculty members. To cope with the unexpectedly large enrollment, which stood at 299 full-time-equivalent students (total credit hours attempted divided by 15) when 175 had been expected, President J. Burton Vasche turned to Modesto Junior College, neighboring county and city schools offices, and to talent in Turlock. Soon the faculty was supplemented by close to a dozen part-time instructors, some of whom later became full-time faculty.

Planning for the college had been going on only since May, four months before the college opened. Ordinarily one or two years' lead time was granted a president to assemble a staff and library and get temporary buildings constructed. Vasche felt that this was a waste. He would show what could be done, and soon Gerard J. Crowley, Tom Emmons, and Ernie Rives, who were picked by Vasche from the State Department of Education staff, were spending their weeks in Turlock planning facilities, enrolling students, and handling business matters.

Temporary buildings could have been placed on the permanent site, but Vasche would not hear of it. Once a temporary building was put up, he observed, the college would be stuck with it indefinitely. Hence the choice of the Fairgrounds. The agricultural exhibit hall was transformed by grey gypsum panels into classrooms, a laboratory, faculty offices, and the registrar's office. Administrative offices and the snack bar went into the industrial exhibit building, whose main hall was still the site of weekly National Guard drills, the Far West Turkey Show, and a week of revival meetings annually.

The character of the college was determined in large measure by the personality of its first president. Vasche had grown up in Oakdale, only twenty miles north of the college; later he taught there for ten years, then put in additional time in the county schools office in Modesto. After obtaining a doctorate from Stanford in 1947, he spent several years in the Washington State Department of Education and a year as Colorado Commissioner of Education before returning to California in 1952 as Chief of the Division of State Colleges and Teacher Education in Sacramento. Thus he was well versed in the state colleges' operation and was aware of national trends as well as California's demands for the improvement of public education generally.

In President Vasche's first address to his fledgling faculty, he said that the very reason for the college's existence was "that the young men and women may gain the finest education possible. . ." The college should stress the liberal arts, those subjects whose principles and subject matter form the basis for Western man's thinking, communication, and professional studies. To prevent too early specialization, he favored a requirement that a substantial part of each student's course be taken in the liberal arts outside his major.[1]

Stanislaus State College's first faculty and administration, September 1960. Seated, Lola Johnson, Tom Emmons, J. Burton Vasche, Paula Loeffler, Mary Byrne. Standing, Charles Farrar, Ernie Rives, Joseph E. Bruggman, Lloyd Bevans, Enoch Haga, R. Dean Galloway, James Hanson, John E. Caswell, Richard Reinholtz, Gerard J. Crowley. Courtesy SSC.

Faculty and committee meetings during those first few months were frequent and stimulating. With his own knowledge of the state colleges and of the area, Vasche did an excellent job in directing the thinking of his faculty along practical lines. The multiple tasks of finding housing, moving families, preparing lectures, advising students, planning programs, and making speeches placed a heavy physical burden on the faculty and staff. Yet there was an exhilaration about developing a college a little nearer to one's ideals that compensated for the weary days and sleepless nights.

The permanent Stanislaus campus was the first one to be planned under the direction of the State College Trustees, who took over control of the state colleges from the State Board of Education on 1 July

1961. In a number of respects, Stanislaus became a proving ground. One fortunate "first" was the appointment of John Lyon Reid of San Francisco as master plan architect, the first private architect so engaged. His initial task was to design a campus for the college's projected enrollment of 10,000 students in 2015 A.D. He also laid down a few basic specifications for the architects of individual buildings, permitting them to exercise initiative in design and materials, while creating harmony of height and structural module.

The excess of initial enrollment over estimates generated great enthusiasm, and an effort was made to include money for both planning and construction of buildings in the State's 1961-62 budget. Although funds were voted for plans and site development, money for building construction became available only in 1963-64. The first buildings were ready for occupancy in June 1965.

Summer sessions were held in Turlock High School's new east wings from 1961 through 1964. Financially a speculative operation, the success of the first summer session was assured by a very popular pre-session in reading under Maude H. Edmonson. Few classes had to be cancelled in the first three years, and students could be confident of getting the courses announced. Consultants on loan from neighboring school districts played an important role during the summer sessions.

A faculty organization began to function during 1961-62, recommending policy to the president. Later a Faculty Senate became the legislative body. From the first, faculty committees participated in the sensitive retention, promotion and tenure process, with the final decision always firmly in the hands of the president.

Student activities and student government were likewise encouraged. On a commuter campus, with most of the student body married and having social ties in their own communities, the number involved was never large. Nevertheless, the Christmas dances were festive affairs with the selection and crowning of Mary Christmas and King Cole. Springtime brought an afternoon of frivolity on Warrior Day, when Chief Stanislaus made his appearance, riding à horse. Later, on the permanent campus, a boat race in the reflecting basin became the chief feature of Warrior Day.

Commencement was a semi-annual event during the first two years, as a number of the first registrants lacked but a few units of graduation. Speakers usually consisted of a graduating senior and a faculty member. Refreshments were served afterwards by community organizations amidst a cheerful crowd of families and friends.

During the college's first year, President Vasche had a recurrence of an old illness; soon its terminal nature was clear. Aware that he could no longer delay appointing deans, Vasche appointed Gerard J. Crowley as executive dean and John E. Caswell as dean of instruction in July 1961. In September Joseph E. Bruggman was named dean of students. Dr. Vasche continued to direct the institution until he took disability retirement on 12 May 1962, a fortnight before his death.

The resignation of Vasche brought a period of uncertainty to the campus. The faculty was dedicated to Vasche's goal of a liberal arts college while some other state colleges were still steeped in a normal school tradition. Various faculty members, aware of Crowley's close association with Vasche, influenced the Faculty to petition the Chancellor to appoint Crowley acting president, and this was done.

The first step in a college's acquiring academic respectability is its achieving accreditation. Temporary accreditation of the credential programs by the State Department of Education was automatic. Teams from the Department and from the Western Association of Schools and Colleges visited Stanislaus on 18-19 March 1963. Members of both teams talked to students, faculty and administrators, looked over course outlines and examinations, inspected the primitive classrooms and the nucleus of a library. Early in the second afternoon came the verdict: a two-year accreditation would be recommended. The inside word was that initial skepticism had been changed to enthusiasm for what was being done.

Recruiting faculty for an unknown institution housed on fairgrounds, a hundred miles away from major research resources and metropolitan delights, was not an easy task. There were, however, factors that appealed to some very desirable candidates. Turlock was a good family town. The prospects for rapid advancement were good, and there was no pressure to "publish or perish." Success in recruiting depended in large measure on the professional acquaintance and personal standing of the division or departmental chairman.

The Trustees had by now authorized faculty-elected screening committees to nominate presidential candidates to the Chancellor and Board. A committee was elected, which soon found that the same difficulty in recruiting faculty applied to obtaining presidential candidates. Some months earlier, however, a man had visited the campus and had impressed several who met him with his grasp of academic matters, his vigorous manner, and his service as head of faculty organizations. Dr. Alexander Capurso was known to be on close terms with the Chancellor, so when his name was submitted among others, it was no surprise when he received the appointment as president of Stanislaus State College, effective 1 July 1963.

The college's commitment to the liberal arts continued undiminished, and the fine arts expanded. In the crucial area of instructional administration Capurso brought in his own lieutenants from San Francisco State College. The acting dean of academic affairs returned to San Francisco after a year. In six years there were four men in that position. This lack of continuity, together with the annual influx of new faculty members, resulted in constant conflict over the curriculum. Unit requirements for some departmental majors reached levels more appropriate to a professional school than to a liberal arts college.

The New Campus

On the new campus site, the land was leveled, drains were laid and utilities installed. Finally the library and classroom buildings began to rise, with a small boiler plant to the rear. To the impatient faculty it sometimes seemed as if the buildings would never be finished. The move to the new campus was made in the summer of 1965. Invitations were sent far and wide to attend an Open House on Sunday, 18 October 1965. It was a warm autumn afternoon; an estimated 14,000 people toured the campus, saw the exhibits, and were served punch and cookies—until supplies ran out.

Student enrollments had hung around the 300 full-time-equivalent mark from 1960 to 1964, usually rising in the spring with an influx of teachers taking a single course. With the move to the new campus, the doors were opened to freshmen, but only 47 enrolled.[2] In retrospect, several reasons appear. Local high school graduates often wanted to make the break with home or desired a livelier social life than SSC afforded. On the other hand, students elsewhere learned only gradually of the intimate campus and relatively high academic standards. Further, housing continued to be a problem for the resident student. Upper division students, however, crowded in. The full-time-equivalents increased from 318 to 486. This 53 percent gain was the basis for a substantially expanded budget.

Glimpse of new campus. Speakers' platform in foreground. Classroom Building at left, tennis and basketball courts and baseball backstop at right. Courtesy SSC.

Lounge in Student Union, opened March 1971. Courtesy SSC.

The new campus was attractive to faculty as well as to students. With bright new buildings, private offices, carpeted floors, clocks replacing clanging bells, high quality library and laboratory facilities, and grassy lawns, the image of Stanislaus State began to change. Increasingly, students in top-ranking graduate schools who preferred teaching to research began to look over Stanislaus.

On the fairgrounds faculty members had coached baseball, tennis and some other sports. With the enrolling of freshmen in 1965 a Physical Education Department was required. Soon Stanislaus teams were competing up and down the coast in basketball, baseball, tennis, track, cross-country, women's volleyball, and golf. As of 1971, Stanislaus had not yet joined a conference. Football was still in the future. A field house was authorized and planned, but the State Department of Finance cut it back to a single basketball floor without even standing room for spectators; neither was there a single classroom for professional courses.

The next instructional building to rise on the campus was the Performing Arts Complex, actually three buildings in one, linked by sheltered walkways and dominated by the unique prism of the theater's fly gallery. Again, the original plans were cut back, both in space and quality of construction. The major space loss was in reducing the theater from 700 to 300 seats, thus creating a problem in financing stage productions. Nevertheless, the new building group permitted Music, Art and Drama to increase their offerings and their staffs. With greater variety and balance, the number of students rose steadily.

A student housing problem arose as more and more young people came to Stanislaus seeking escape from city environments and campus turmoil. At the beginning of the second year on the new campus, a privately owned dormitory, Yosemite Hall, was opened on Geer Road. More and more Turlockers offered rooms to students. Tenant houses on ranches, trailer courts in the country, apartments in Modesto were put to use for faculty and student housing. In 1967 Verne Crowell opened up his first sixty-apartment complex just west of the campus in time for fall quarter. By September 1971 Crowell had built a total of 240 apartments, and other interests had built apartments, town houses, and modest homes within a half-mile of the edge of the campus.

Change at the Helm

In September 1968 the faculty assembled in the cafeteria for luncheon. They shared vacation experiences, met their new colleagues, and awaited President Capurso's message. Shortly before the end of the meeting a stir was created when it was announced that Dr. Maurice Townsend, the Academic Dean, was resigning as of 31 December to take a position in Indiana. That sensation was as nothing to the bombshell which followed: President Capurso announced that he himself was resigning at the end of the academic year to return to teaching. How the halls echoed with speculation!

Again a presidential screening committee was elected to interview candidates and make recommendations to the Chancellor. Candidates called; teams traveled throughout the state, to the Pacific Northwest; and finally one team crossed the nation interviewing the principal candidates. Meanwhile the Chancellor announced that the faculty's finalists would be interviewed by a "rainbow committee" chaired by himself and consisting of representatives of his office, of the faculty committee, of SSC's Local Advisory Board, and of the Trustees. The interviews were held, a candidate was accepted by the Trustees, and then withdrew for compelling personal reasons. The hunt was renewed. One candidate, Dr. Carl Gatlin, had just become available. He passed the searching review and was appointed effective 1 September 1969.

During President Gatlin's first year several changes and reassignments were made in the administrative staff. Dr. William J. Mason of the Chancellor's academic planning staff was brought in as academic dean and subsequently raised to the rank of academic vice president. The host of faculty committees was pruned back severely. The sovereign remedy for ills was the president's open-door policy. To all his door was open, his reception cordial, his explanations clear, his confidence monumental.

In 1970-71 four Schools were created: Natural Sciences, Behavioral and Social Sciences, Arts and Humanities, and Professional Studies. In structure this was a return to the original divisional organization, but in the interim departments had attained a large measure of self-government. The new deans provided a level of interdepartmental coordination and administrative expertise that was needed in the growing institution.

Changes on the statewide level also affected Stanislaus. With the cutback in college construction programs, SSC profited by the diversion of students to the less crowded colleges. This enabled the president to fill almost all authorized positions in 1970 and 1971, materially strengthening a number of departments. In number and scope of courses, the larger departments compared favorably with those of major institutions.

The Student Body

The composition of the student body began to change in 1965 with the admission of freshmen and a decrease in the number of part-time students. The proportion in their late teens and early twenties increased sharply. In 1968 a nationwide effort to bring college education to youthful leaders of the black and brown minorities led to the establishment of an Educational Opportunities Program. From the very first, SSC had had a sprinkling of Orientals, Blacks, and Mexican-Americans. Now the numbers in the two latter groups multiplied. Most of those admitted were fully qualified academically, although a few were admitted in exempt status. EOP orientations were held before school opened. There friendships were formed and a group identity established. This was reenforced by the tendency of the EOP students to concentrate in certain majors and to seek out sympathetic professors.

A program which was often confused with the Educational Opportunities Program was the Ethnic Studies Program, which sought to encourage understanding of racial minorities' problems by courses set up in appropriate departments. It naturally appealed to many EOP students.

A trickle of foreign students began early in the 1960s. Ordinarily the students had had some college experience, either at home or in Modesto or Merced Junior Colleges, before coming to Stanislaus. From an educational standpoint it would have been desirable to have had an even wider variety of foreign students for the benefit of the Americans.

Despite radical elements in both the student body and the faculty, Stanislaus largely escaped the campus chaos that characterized the late 1960s. Several simple rules were established: due notice must be given the administration of outside speakers being brought to the campus; and there must always be opportunity for questions and debate. After the college was moved to the new campus, Freedom Rock was set up in front of a small platform on the plaza northeast of the library. Here any member of the college was free to speak, so long as he was willing to expose himself to debate. More than one speaker had his arguments torn to shreds by sharp student questions or comments.

Townspeople, not surprisingly, were disturbed by some of the speakers who appeared on the campus. Bettina Aptheker, daughter of the leading Communist theoretician in the United States, was one. At the opposite pole was George Rockwell, neo-Fascist leader. *Turlock Journal* editor Lowell Jessen came to the defense of First Amendment liberties on the college campus, pointing out that both Aptheker and Rockwell had been shown up in their true light by student questions.[3]

The indifference of much of the student body to campus politics furnished an opportunity to radical insiders; on the other hand, it prevented massive confrontations unless outsiders were called in. A number of the standard ploys of the left were tried. Student moratoriums (strikes) were held on "Vietnam Day." The president was confronted in his office over the non-reappointment of a radical instructor. Proposals were made to siphon off student body funds by paying inordinate fees to leftist speakers. The student newspaper, the *Signal,* for several years was in the hands of radicals, and sank to a low level of scurrility while the news content vanished. This called forth an "underground" newspaper, the *Free Warrior,* which furnished both campus news and moderate opinion columns.

Stanislaus was undoubtedly fortunate in having cool-headed leadership and a student body which was willing to express its concern with social and political issues, by and large, in the framework of democratic government. There was, however, a certain element of good fortune, for dissident elements in the Bay Area were but two hours' drive away. On at least one occasion SSC student body officers turned down an offer of "help" from that source.

The Community and the College

To the average tourist traveling along Highway 99, Turlock used to be one of those hot little valley towns where one stopped for gasoline or a coke, and whether Turlock was north of Tulare or the other way around was hard to remember. Little did the tourist know of the green lawns, the giant sycamores, and the shady gardens that made delightful the best parts of the valley towns. Why put a college in Turlock, many a person asked. Yet a wise and sensitive old-time resident of Ceres opined, just after the site selection had been made, that Turlock would make a very good college town.

When the new faculty and staff moved into town they received a cordial welcome. The Kiwanians invited them to luncheon. The Chamber of Commerce gave them breakfast and took them for a tour of the town's industries. Scores of individuals performed acts of kindness for one faculty family or another. The faculty reciprocated by quickly lending their support to many of the town activities.

Soon students and townspeople were sharing in drama productions under the leadership of ex-Mayor Lamar Jackson, who had been appointed to teach speech and drama. Dr. Joseph E. Bruggman, head of Music, organized a College-Community Orchestra. A year later Clifford Cunha of the college Music Department organized a College-Community Chorus. College teams competed in local leagues. Faculty members addressed many groups throughout the six-county service area of the college.

A College Area Planning Committee was created jointly by Stanislaus County, the City of Turlock, and the President of the College to formulate zoning recommendations for the college area and transmit them to the City and County Planning Commissions. The recommendations were embodied in the *Turlock General Plan, 1962.* Although some recommendations were later modified, the community had pledged itself to produce a high-quality environment for the campus.

Many members of the college community, having known the hurly-burly of urban centers, were pleased to find a town where they could raise their children in a reasonably quiet environment.

In 1962-63 a Local Advisory Board was established with representatives from the colleges' service area in order to get community opinion and, in turn, to present college viewpoints on matters of mutual concern. Nevertheless, the close college-community relations of the Vasche regime deteriorated.

Recognizing what had taken place, President Gatlin made a determined effort to strengthen community ties. College-community joint undertakings were once more encouraged. The college Drama and Music Departments collaborated in staging several productions appropriate to the centennial year, and a

Mainstage Theater in Performing Arts Complex. Courtesy SSC.

new warmth began to pervade town and gown relations.

The economic impact of the college on Turlock was substantial. The college was in effect a basic industry drawing dollars to Turlock, which were spent on a variety of retail and service industries. One possibly optimistic estimate was that every fifteen full-time students created two jobs on the campus and two more in the area, a majority of which were in Turlock.

One phase of the college's story that should be recorded is the fact that efforts were made on several occasions to kill it. Three different reports had been made on the need for state colleges between 1948 and 1957. The first and third favored placing some state colleges outside metropolitan areas. The second favored enlargement of existing institutions. The third found Stanislaus County ranking fifth among nine areas deserving state colleges.[4] These reports had given ammunition to both sides.

Periodically the press carried stories of proposals to eliminate the college, and after it had its own campus, to make it a junior college. In 1966-67 a study committee of the State College Trustees considered disposing of the college as a possible means of reducing the budget, but decided to retain it. At a later time a cost analysis was made by the Chancellor's office with the same object in view.[5] By 1971 SSC had reached a size that brought per-student costs fairly well into line with those of larger institutions. There was also a certain public disenchantment with the violence-prone larger campuses. It now seemed unlikely that there would be a time in the foreseeable future when serious thought would be given to closing Stanislaus.

The spring of 1972 saw a change in the name of the college to California State College, Stanislaus, as part of the Trustees' program of standardizing designations of the colleges. When it would receive the designation "university" would depend on the rate of growth of its graduate and professional programs.

Summary

Stanislaus State College was established primarily to raise the qualifications of teachers in central California. After five years in rather primitive accommodations, the college moved to a pleasing, comfortable and efficient campus. It was designed as a liberal arts college which would avoid duplicating high-cost vocational facilities available at some of its older and larger sister colleges. In the spring of 1972 it had a student body of almost 3000, a full-time teaching faculty of more than 150, and had attained a reputation for high academic standards.

Turlock City Hall, completed 1961.   Caswell photo.

Chapter XXXII

Politics and Planning

John E. Caswell

The political issues that arose during the first three decades of corporate life have been discussed by Helen Hohenthal in "Turlock, 1901-1940." In those years, control of the town was largely in the hands of people who had come before 1910. The principal division seems to have been between the older propertyholders, whose lands lay east of the railway and the highway, and the newcomers, many of them Swedes, who had bought up land west of the railway. This was seen in the fight over relocation of the high school and in the struggle as to whether Highway 99 would go down Center Street or Broadway. An old-timer has pointed out to the writer how well lighted Center Street is—a reminder of the efforts to make it a major thoroughfare.

In the years since 1940 the east-west conflict diminished but did not entirely disappear. The Swedish west side, which was once the new side, had become the old side as residential districts developed to the east. Many old Swedish families left the west side and built modern homes on the east side, and the geographical polarization was muted.

If one were to characterize the attitude of some of Turlock's older leaders, it might be summed up in the phrase, "What was good enough for me is good enough for your children." This came out most clearly in the fight over bringing the elementary school buildings into compliance with the earthquake safety code. It came out also in the almost yearly conflict over salaries and working conditions, where the majorities on the school board were content to leave classroom salaries at almost the bottom level for districts of its category. The attitude is perhaps understandable in those who went through the struggles of the early 1900s.

By contrast, from the middle of the 1950s on a movement for town improvement was evidenced in the development of several general plans, in efforts to bring light industry to Turlock, in progressively raising requirements for subdivisions, in planting trees and erecting benches along Main Street, in the development of parks and a recreation program, and in the extension of water and sewer facilities to care for years of future growth.

Progress thus took place in the more visible features of community life. Even in the schools many good things happened. There were excellent teachers who stayed in Turlock, quite frequently because their husbands' jobs were there. But for the student who needed special help or advanced opportunities, facilities remained inadequate.

"Who Runs The Town?"

Over luncheon one day the writer was asked by a sophisticated newcomer, "Who runs Turlock?" Who does run Turlock? Certainly there is no one political boss who can deliver votes and make or break a council. There are a number of individuals in town who, by their opposition, can go far to defeat any candidate for public office or any local measure on the ballot. This "veto power" is perhaps the most significant feature of Turlock politics.

Power comes through identification with one or more groups in the community. It is important to have a Scandinavian name. It is important to be a churchman, particularly if you are affiliated with one of the larger and more conservative churches. It is important to have held office in the Chamber of Commerce. It is important to have headed a successful drive for the United Crusade or the Heart Fund.

It is important to be a businessman. An attorney may make the Council, but few other professional men have done so. A physician may serve on a school board. A college administrator has served on the Planning Commission, and a college professor has been appointed to the County Planning Commission. For a school teacher to be elected to the Council has been unthinkable. And no college faculty member down to 1972 has had the temerity to run either for a school board or for the Council.

The most influential organized group in Turlock government is probably the Chamber of Commerce. It has proposed several development programs through the years. These have been considered by the Council, but the Council has not always accepted Chamber suggestions.

Issues and Accomplishments of the 1940s

On 6 April 1940 Turlock was momentarily in the news when its 1,247-foot-long overpass, the longest in the state and costing $330,000, was dedicated. The Turlock High Band played, and the drum majorettes cut the ribbon. Assemblyman Hugh P. Donnelly, fortyish and wavy-haired, was in the picture, as was plump Mayor Roy M. Day. That the overpass had been built was in part due to Day's perseverance with the State Highway Commission. The president of the Chamber of Commerce, E. Glenn Drake, presided at the luncheon that followed the dedication.[1]

The completion of the overpass symbolized a major stage in a series of tasks undertaken by the Chamber of Commerce and by the Council: obtaining good road connections with other parts of the county and state. In such minutes of the Chamber of Commerce as survive this was the principal theme of the 1930s. It continued to be the theme as better connections were sought to Los Banos and to Oakdale. Roughly twenty years after the overpass was dedicated these connections were opened.

In an era when "ecology" has been a favorite topic, it is interesting to look back over thirty years and to find that in April 1940 the Chamber of Commerce sponsored a drive to clean up and paint up the town. With the backing of the Exchange and Rotary Clubs, the Ministerial Union and other groups, 150 tons of rubbish were removed between April 18 and 28.[2] "Concern" was not invented in the 1960s.

Following Pearl Harbor there was a spate of ordinances establishing air raid precautions and dealing with enemy aliens, interference with radio broadcasting, and the creation of a Department of Civil Defense.[3]

Of greater long-range importance was the creation of the Turlock Planning Commission, which held its first meeting on 22 January 1941. Roy Day, the mayor, was elected chairman of the Commission.[4] As a consultant, the Commission employed H. H. Jaqueth at $40 a day for two days a month. Jaqueth was also serving the City of Modesto and the County as consultant. Don C. Davis was made the resident engineer. Roy E. Weaver was recommended to the Supervisors as a member of the County Planning Commission.

Planning Commissioners must be among the unsung heroes of city government. Their regular diet consists of the approval of subdivision maps, which must be in accordance with all local ordinances and the general plan, if one exists. They must hear requests for variances and listen to the complaints of neighbors who object to the variances. They must approve requests for authorization to erect signs. They must make recommendations to the Council on plumbing, electrical, and other construction codes. And when a promoter does not like their interpretation of the rules, he takes his case to the City Council, which is likely to overturn the Commission's ruling. This is painstaking and often dull work, but when well done, it can make the difference between a well planned and soundly built town, where property values are maintained, and a shoddy, depressed village.

Only in 1944 did the Commission appoint a committee consisting of Roy Meikle, Coburn Cook, Ed Leduc and Lowell Jessen to work with Don Davis, the resident engineer, on a master plan map for Turlock and the vicinity. A year later the Commission recommended to the City Council that it consider inaugurating the proposed master plan. Nothing seems to have come of their effort.[5]

The spring of 1946 brought new faces to the Council, including Lamar Jackson, Oliver K. K. Nelson, and Harold Markley, who was elected Mayor because of having the largest plurality of the popular vote.[6] Roy Day now retired, after having served as mayor for over eleven years.

On 18 June 1946, the structure of the Planning Commission was revised. Councilman Nelson moved that the Commission consist of six members not officials, appointed by the Mayor and approved by the Council. There should also be three *ex officio* members, one of whom would be the City Engineer. The measure was duly passed.[7] Among the members appointed by Mayor Markley were Day, Weaver and Leduc from the original Commission, with Fred Fredine of the Bank of America, Lowell Jessen of the *Journal*, Engineer Don Davis, Attorney W. Coburn Cook, and Lloyd Cunningham, Fire Chief.[8]

In 1946 a special census showed Turlock's population to be 6,105. At about the same time, the Council chose to install parking meters. Reasons stated by the mayor included helping with the parking problem, reduction of the property tax, and financing off-street parking.[9] As no parking lots were bought prior to the creation of a parking district in 1957, the money seems to have gone into the City's general fund.

A major forward step during Harold Markley's term of office as mayor was the creation of the first Recreation Commission. The development of the City's recreation program has been recounted at some length in the chapter entitled "Recreation in Turlock."

In 1948 Lamar Jackson was elected mayor by his colleagues on the Council. Theretofore there had been no separate Planning Department to support the work of the Commission. One was now created, and Bryant Hall, Assistant Planner for the City of San Francisco, was employed as Consultant Planner. Mayor Jackson had been serving on both the City and County Planning Commissions, and as a result of his experience, proposed a land use permit system whereby Turlock and other cities might have an important voice in controlling the areas within about three miles of their limits. The County Supervisors adopted the proposal, and soon Modesto, Patterson and other cities in the county were taking advantage of it.

Within the city, Jackson and Walter Brown took the lead in putting a series of bond issues on the ballot. These covered new industrial waste and domestic sewer systems, street improvements, parks, and firehouses. With the firehouses and other improvements, Turlock was assured of 10 percent reduction in fire rates, and possibly could obtain a 20 percent reduction.[10]

At the election the bond issues carried by ratios ranging from 4:1 to 6:1. The domestic sewers were put in; the first section of Canal Drive was constructed as a major artery; the new firehouses were built and fire rates were reduced. The industrial waste system, though funded, was delayed for several years because of changes in design.

The city administration was put on a more businesslike basis in 1949. For some years the Council had actually operated as a commission, with each councilman responsible for supervising some branch of city government. Now a chief administrator's post was authorized and Recreation Director Ed Frank, who had a master's degree from Columbia University in Administration, was advanced to that position.[11]

The Elementary Schools and the Field Act

In March 1933 an earthquake struck Long Beach which produced more damage to structures than any other in California history, except for the San Francisco earthquake of 1906. If the earthquake had occurred during school hours, the loss of life would have been frightful. Many solidly built schools were flattened. The Field Act of 1934, in consequence, set rigorous standards for school construction and instructed all school districts in the state to bring their schools into conformity with the new standards. The Turlock districts, like many others in the state, did nothing.

Anson Boyd, the State Architect, inspected the old Hawthorne and Lowell Schools in the spring of 1949 and advised the Elementary School Board that both schools were unsafe and that state loans were available for rebuilding. A private architect confirmed the finding and the Board instructed Superintendent Robert Lee to prepare an application for State aid. The application was turned back for revision because the Board proposed to buy a twenty-acre tract for one school.[12]

By January 1950 opposition had arisen to the rebuilding proposal, and the Chamber of Commerce sponsored an open meeting. Enoch Christoffersen, the chairman, said the Chamber was "interested in the progress and welfare of the community...[but it was] also interested in holding taxes as low as advisable."[13]

John Beatty, school trustee and civil engineer, presented the information furnished by the State Division of Architecture. The availability of State aid and the personal liability of every trustee under the Field Act was pointed out.

William Graybiel, long-time school trustee and chairman of the Chamber's Tax Committee, attacked the proposal and denied that the Field Act created a personal liability for the trustees.

Mayor Lamar Jackson suggested that people coming into the state would not settle in Turlock if the schools were poor. The buildings were about forty years old, and it might be cheaper to construct new buildings than to maintain the old ones.[14]

Two weeks later Beatty told the Turlock Parent-Teacher Association how new school plans were functional, safe, simple and economical. School design had improved vastly in twenty years. In the older schools lighting was bad, seating inadequate, and at least 52 percent of elementary school children in such classrooms had 1.8 preventable defects each. Further, exits were inadequate and furnace rooms directly under the main exit. Wakefield School conformed to the new standards.[15]

Arguments against rebuilding were based on several assumptions: (1) that a severe quake in the Turlock area was highly unlikely; (2) that the schools were well built; (3) that fire danger was minimal; and (4) that the effects of poor lighting and badly designed desks and seats could be safely ignored.

The showdown came in May when Beatty was opposed for reelection. Beatty's opponent took a half-page advertisement in the *Turlock Journal* to express his views. Ignoring the danger from earthquake and the possible loss of life from fire, the advertisement concentrated on the undesirability of a loan. "Industry will not come to a community with heavy indebtedness or taxation. Turlock wants industry."[16] It was that simple. Beatty's opposition harped on the possibility of a sharp increase in the tax rate. The many elderly people on fixed incomes felt this as a threat, and the rebuttal failed to reach them.

The election of Beatty's opponent was the signal to drop the proposal for new schools, despite one last effort by the State Division of Schoolhouse Planning.[17]

The matter was reopened only in 1957 when a simple request to the Elementary School Board on 10 September developed into a full-blown crisis. Said next day's *Modesto Bee,* "Parents...turned the opening day of school into a nightmare for trustees by dragging two skeletons from the board's closet and rattling them vigorously in its face." The principal issue was school safety.

In 1956 John Beatty III had been in the first grade at the modern Julien School; he had now been transferred to Lowell. His father refused to send young John to Lowell in view of the State Fire Marshal's reports of 1950 and 1957 that the school was unsafe. Further, his attorney had advised him that he could not be compelled to do so. The public learned that the Board had been told the previous spring by the Chief of the Division of Schoolhouse Planning, "I have never seen such frightening structures for school children." Finally Trustee James Day asked Beatty to head a new citizens' committee to sponsor a bond election. Reluctantly, Beatty once more took up the cudgels.[18]

At the first meeting of the citizens' committee on 16 September the four elementary school trustees in attendance were asked (1) to seek financial aid for school construction *immediately,* and (2) to take interim action to get the children out of the unsafe buildings.[19] This meeting generated a wide popular response backing the committee's position.[20] A teacher asked how Turlock could expect good teachers to teach in such buildings when new ones were available in Modesto.[21]

One woman wrote the State Fire Marshal in wrath at nothing having been done in the eight years since the fire and panic inspection of 1949. "It is my opinion that the town of Turlock has had some seven years of grace without a catastrophe. . .While these two buildings stand, looking substantial and quite impressive. . .those people who have no children in the buildings will certainly laugh away any suggestion that drastic action is needed."[22]

A letter from C. F. Richter, seismologist who designed the Richter Earthquake Scale, convinced many doubters. He wrote, "I continue to be astonished at the willingness of many California communities to gamble with the lives of their school children." He recalled that in the great earthquake a century earlier, on 9 January 1857, water was thrown over the banks of the Mokelumne River, while heavy shaking was reported from both Los Angeles and San Francisco.[23] Such a quake was the one most likely to spell disaster for Turlock.

About this time an award of $300,000 damages against the Dunsmuir School District demonstrated that multiple claims could bankrupt a school district.[24]

People asked why the old school buildings could not be brought up to code by remodeling. It was replied that they no longer met "basic conditions as defined in the laws of the State and Uniform Building Code." Their very design was not acceptable, so it was unnecessary to point out that they would have to be completely relathed with metal and replastered, that all metal heating ducts would have to be replaced, and the buildings rewired.[25]

Several members of the Board were quickly convinced that new buildings were inevitable. The matter had indeed been discussed during the spring, but failure of a tax override had caused the matter to be dropped. The Board and Superintendent wanted the citizens' committee, now called the Safe Schools Association, to educate the public.[26]

The Trustees appointed a consulting engineer, Milton G. Leong, to give an independent opinion on physical condition of the buildings.[27] Leong made his report personally on 27 December. He reported, as Board members well knew, that bricks were ready to topple from the walls and had been picked off the parapet by hand. After three hours of wrangling, the Board voted 3-2 to close the schools and put the classes into neighboring schools on double sessions. Closure of the schools had been won.[28]

The issue was now squarely before the people of Turlock. The Board appointed a New Schools Committee under Attorney Jeremy Cook to obtain support for the bond issue and State loan. Mrs. Paula Frayer, who had served as publicity chairman for the Safe Schools Association, agreed to continue as publicity chairman for the new committee.[29]

The need to pass the $230,000 bond measure and to authorize the $1,950,104 State loan was made clear. The immediate increase in the tax rate would be only three cents, and payments on the principal would not begin until 1971. If after thirty years there were still sums unpaid under the formula, the balance of the loan would be forgiven. The drive was successful, and the election was won.

Ten years later people were still talking about how hard it was to batter down the old schools. The difficulty encountered was in knocking down a fairly new steel and concrete cafeteria at one school. The beautiful old structures with their wooden cores and eroded mortar crumpled before the wrecker's ball.

Had it not been for the dogged persistence of a few individuals in educating public opinion, the town might have gone on indefinitely under the illusion that all their children were in safe schools.

The Struggle Over the Freeway Location

If the Field Act fight may be likened to a civil war, the freeway struggle began as a minor power holding a great power, the State Division of Highways, at bay; but eventually factions formed. Politicians failed to read the public's mind. At last the majority had its way, thanks to the determination of a few stubborn leaders; but Turlock was made to pay for its intransigence; instead of being the first town in the Valley to obtain a freeway, it was the last.

In October 1954 it first became known that the Division of Highways was planning a freeway that would take out buildings over a strip a block wide and almost a mile long. Somewhat over half would be earth-fill, with the central portion a viaduct.

Arthur G. Crowell, representing the Chamber of Commerce, and Dr. Harry D. Channing asked the City Council to appoint a committee to investigate the rumors. The Council named a committee with Councilman Ray M. Carter as chairman.[30]

In reply to the committee's inquiry, John G. Meyer, the District Engineer, said the Division of Highways favored no particular route, but would examine all possibilities and determine how each route fitted into the well-being of the community. "When and if we do arrive at a plan," he said, "it will certainly be brought before the people and be thoroughly discussed."[31] Favoring a route west of town, the Turlock Planning Commission instructed its consultant, Harold Wise, to plan such a route.

On 25 October Richard Ward, the City Engineer, explained the Division of Highways' Route A to the Freeway Committee. An earth-fill embankment would take up the block between Thor and Palm Streets from Canal to Olive. The freeway would be carried over the business district on a viaduct, then descend to earth and tie in with the railroad overpass. Carter was opposed to the embankment. Crowell favored the western route, and so moved at the conclusion of the discussion. The resolution carried unanimously.[32]

Three weeks later Sam Helwer, representing the State, presented arguments for Route A to the Committee. While it would cost $5,900,000 and the western bypass would cost only $4,400,000, Route A would produce greater savings to motorists, and the joint cost would be smaller. Other advantages included visibility of the central business district. Finally, it was stated that the embankment and viaduct would not create a barrier to development.

The arguments in favor of the western bypass as listed by Harold S. Wise included its location near present and future industrial sites, the removal of heavy truck traffic from town and the shunting of west side traffic around town, reduction of the downtown noise level, avoidance of condemnation and destruction of real property and the attendant displacement of many families and businesses.[33]

Helwer said the Citizens Committee would be called in before a decision was made. He added, "Do not get people excited—wait for definite plans to be presented."[34]

Despite Helwer's advice, the *Journal* editorialized, "We appreciate the consideration given to the convenience of the motorist [but]. . . .In plain language, it would not be 'convenient' to have valuable property destroyed by an overpass just east of the present Highway 99."[35]

For over a year there seems to have been an impasse, despite a Committee discussion of alternatives.[36] On 17 January 1956, the Committee met with Stanislaus County's legislators, Senator Hugh P. Donnelly and Assembly Speaker Ralph Brown. Brown pointed out the City's strategic advantage, for no freeway could be built through town without an agreement signed by the City. If necessary, he suggested appealing to the Director of Public Works or the Governor himself. Consequently the Council asked the Director of Public Works to halt land purchases until a route agreement was reached.[37]

Despite the Council's request, in May Dr. Channing spotted a Division of Highways survey crew at work on Route A. Channing quickly organized a Citizens Freeway Committee. On 21 June a delegation went to Division headquarters and were shown completed drawings of Route A and sketches of a second route closely following the railway.[38] Arthur G. Crowell commented bitterly, "They propose to put the freeway just exactly where the business section of Turlock is now expanding. . .In years to come it will develop into a district of saloons and second class stores."[39] The next week the City's official Freeway Committee voted in favor of a western bypass.[40]

Just when it seemed that unanimity had been reached in opposing a through-town route, Joash Paul organized a group of seventeen to oppose any bypass. He estimated that seventy cars a night stopped in Turlock for lodging, gasoline and meals, and spent $1,000 nightly. This revenue, he claimed, would be lost to the town.[41]

Shortly before the Division of Highways held a public hearing, the *Journal* polled the public on its preference. Three-quarters of the 740 ballots favored the western bypass; the balance were divided between various through-town routes.

At the hearing on 18 July Routes A through E were discussed, the economics of freeways and the calculation of benefits explained.[42] Following the hearing, the City Engineer was instructed to draw up a bypass plan. When this was proposed at the official Freeway Committee's meeting on 2 August, it was strongly opposed by residents of the area because it chopped up farmlands and came too close to Wakefield School.[43] This led to still another plan which swung farther from the town and minimized the increase in mileage by taking off from the current route farther north and south of town. This was the plan finally adopted as Route G. In due course the Committee approved the plan and the Council adopted it, notifying the Division of Highways of its decision.[44]

In reply, Meyer stated that the revised plan was entirely unacceptable. As he was adamant, the Freeway Committee began studying a new proposal, Route K, which would bring the freeway down the highway to Olive, with an overpass over Main and the railroad. This eliminated fewer new buildings than either of the two routes proposed by Highways. After several meetings the Committee recommended Route K to the Council, which endorsed it "in principle, but not in detail."[45]

Convinced that Route A had been sidetracked, Channing's Citizens Committee had become inactive. Paul's downtown group was still busy, but was now opposed by a group spearheaded by Carl and P. L. Peterson. The encounter came at a Freeway Committee meeting on 18 March 1957, when a petition with 150 signatures was presented opposing Route K. Said Ernie Gaster, "If you want to hang a piece of crepe on the west side, get Plan K."[46] The Committee now seems to have caved in, for it reported to the Council that it "strongly favored" the bypass, but because of opposition among neighboring farmers and Highway's refusal to give it further consideration, the Committee was recommending Route K.[47]

After considering holding an election on the issue, the Council approved Route K.[48] The combined Peterson and Channing committees now forced the Council to put the issue on the ballot in April 1958. The vote was 1050 to 211 in favor of the western bypass.[49]

The Highway Commission now realized that the Council could not approve any through-town route and began designing Route G. Further public hearings were held in 1959, with Highways now arguing that the benefit ratio was in favor of the bypass, while construction difficulties and disruption of Turlock would be avoided. Of no mean significance, the bypass would cost $3,000,000 less. Supporters of the through-town route were furious, but the majority had won.[50]

The five-year struggle had forced the Division of Highways to consider cultural as well as economic values. "The choice of the bypass by the state commission," said the *Journal*, "brings victory to the local group which, from the start, refused to compromise its belief that a through-town elevated freeway would be disastrous to Turlock growth and community beauty."[51]

Although the freeway location had been decided, ten years passed before an agreement was signed by the Division of Highways and the City of Turlock. Many details had to be agreed on, and the desired railway overpass near the college was not obtained. Ground was finally broken for the freeway in late 1971. Instead of being the first town in the San Joaquin Valley to obtain a freeway, Turlock was the last—but the freeway was where the majority of Turlockers wanted it.

Planning, 1951–1971

While school rebuilding and freeway location absorbed the attention of Turlock during much of the decade 1950–1960, there were a number of other significant developments in the realm of city government. After the State extended the privilege of levying a sales and use tax to counties and cities, Turlock adopted a 1/2 percent sales tax in June 1952, raising it to 1 percent in April 1955 when additional revenue was needed to pay for sewer construction.[52]

A Civic Center fund was started rolling on 15 May 1956 with a substantial donation by Mayor and Mrs. Enoch Christoffersen. In July a five-acre site was purchased on Canal Drive, next to the War Memorial

Auditorium, with TID buying a smaller site adjacent. First built was the TID Building. The City Hall was dedicated in 1961, and the Police and Justice Building in 1964. The whole formed an attractive and useful civic group.[53]

In the 1950s a General Plan was developed with the cooperation of the Stanislaus County Planning Commission. It apparently was never adopted, but was referred to as a point of departure in developing later plans.[54]

In 1961 the Chamber of Commerce became concerned with the physical condition of the downtown business area. Although some old buildings had been eliminated by the City's purchase of sites for off-street parking, it was now clear that the freeway would not be cutting through town and knocking out other eyesores.

There were vacant and deteriorating store buildings and shops with fronts that had not been refurbished since they were built forty years before. Burt Gartin reported the comment of a returning friend who declared that downtown Turlock "looks worse than it did twenty years ago." Some blamed absentee landlords, others over-regulation.[55] "Why spend money when business is good and we've kept out the chain stores?" was perhaps nearer the attitude.

On the basis of the Chamber of Commerce's preliminary study, several downtown businessmen organized FORWARD TURLOCK, with P. L. Peterson of Security State Bank as president. Its goal was "to revitalize older areas with specific attention to Turlock's downtown area." Such a renovation, said a brochure, was "long overdue, and must be carried to a successful completion if our community is to maintain a minimum tax rate and at the same time provide municipal protections, services and solvency." In view of later demands, it is worth noting the organization's statement that "FORWARD TURLOCK is not looking to the City, the State, or the Federal Government for its financing or its direction."

To lay a foundation for future action, FORWARD TURLOCK proposed a "comprehensive economic analysis" of the community, including the need for new stores in the downtown area, improvement of traffic routes, and renovation or rebuilding of downtown properties, as well as the impact of Stanislaus State College on retail business and commercial land values.[56]

Local merchants were invited to subscribe to a $10,000 fund for the study and for support of FORWARD TURLOCK. Leon Rimov of Berkeley was employed to make the survey and analysis.[57]

On 8 November 1962 Rimov presented the results of almost a year's labor to the organization in the form of a 37-page brochure entitled "PROJECT 70." He proposed in the next eight years to built a mall along Main Street from Center to Lander, with a broad pedestrian tunnel under the railway. Cross streets would continue to go through, but about half the downtown buildings would be destroyed to make way for parking. A dozen possible means of financing were suggested by Rimov, without analysis of their feasibility. There was no suggestion as to means of obtaining compensation for the owners of buildings destroyed. The 33 people at the meeting, by a show of hands, unanimously accepted the Board of Directors' proposal to adopt the fundamentals of Rimov's plan and to send it to the City Council for study.[58]

In presenting Rimov's plan to the Council on 4 December, Peterson opposed either bonds or an improvement district as "too expensive to finance." Assessment of downtown property for either purpose, Peterson said, would put an additional burden on the overloaded commercial property. Federal redevelopment was likewise opposed—"we feel we can do the job without this help." Instead, FORWARD TURLOCK proposed that the City freeze its budget for all other purposes and make available tax moneys realized from the increasing assessment rolls as loans to downtown businessmen for improvements.[59] The effect would have been to decrease the levels of service of the police, the fire department, parks and recreation, and all other City general fund-supported agencies as population grew and prices rose.

Several months after FORWARD TURLOCK was organized, but almost a year before the Rimov report was submitted to the Council, the City and County issued the *Turlock General Plan: a College Community*. Some items were in both plans: for instance, connecting West Olive and Lander Avenue and developing additional off-street parking, in part by leasing a strip of the Southern Pacific's right-of-way along First Street.[60]

Two weeks after the Rimov report was laid before the City Council, the Council appointed a 32-member committee under pharmacist Kirk Sperry to study the Rimov plan.[61] After a year's work, Sperry's committee was cut to ten members and continued as the Redevelopment Committee. At the earlier committee's recommendation, the Council had established itself as the Turlock Redevelopment Agency in order to qualify for federal funds. When it became apparent that redevelopment under federal law was impractical in Turlock, the Agency was dissolved.

Among the developments that came out of the proposals and discussions was the cutting through of Olive Street to the West Main-Lander intersection. Additional off-street parking was developed. Later trees and benches were put in, making Main Street much more parklike and pleasant. Store owners were stimulated to spruce up their own buildings, and the downtown took on a brighter, livelier and more attractive appearance. Much was done at City expense, but the trees in concrete planter boxes were contributions of the merchants through a campaign of the Chamber of Commerce, captained by Ernie Yotsuya.[62]

In 1969 the City Council and Planning Commission jointly issued a revised plan, entitled the *Turlock General Plan, 1969-1990.* A number of committees had been involved, one of the principal ones being charged with developing a scheme for sewer trunk lines.

The plan anticipated that Turlock would be a compact community of 51,000 inhabitants by 1990, so designed as to eliminate urban sprawl and unnecessary destruction of farm lands. It would be bounded

After World War II, ranch-style homes predominated. This was built along Lester Road about 1966. Browning photo.

"Town houses," an innovation allowing medium density housing, were introduced around 1970. Caswell photo.

For three decades the Albert Julien home, this colonial house was purchased by the Donald L. Smiths in 1970. Caswell photo.

on the north by Taylor Road, on the south by Linwood Avenue, on the east by Waring Road, and on the west by Tegner Road. It would be planned as a series of neighborhoods of about 4,000 each, with comparatively few points of access to main arterials. There would be a variety of types of housing available, and within any one area the population density would be about the same as in any other. Apartments would thus be compensated for by parks or low-density housing. Each neighborhood would have its own elementary school and small park, often adjoining the school's playground. At intervals of two or three miles larger community parks would be placed. Donnelly Park, expanded to 37 acres, was expected to serve as the single regional park down to 1990.

Turlock was envisaged as a city of homes with services appropriate to a college town and diversified light industry. Tree planting and landscaping of shopping centers would be encouraged. Emphasis should be on the quality of life. When the freeway bypass was completed, garish signs should come down, and a low-pressure, pleasant community would be developed.

Such a town was not merely a planner's dream. It was gaining acceptance by business and political leaders. Whether the reality would approach the dream lay in the hands of young leaders who were just beginning to be identified as Turlock's second century opened.

NOTES

Chapter I – From Discovery to Settlement

The portion of this chapter dealing with the Indians was revised and updated by Dr. Thomas E. Durbin, Department of Anthropology, Stanislaus State College.

1. *Tule* [too'li] – any of the several bulrushes growing in the marshes of California and the Southwest.
2. For the 1806 expedition, see Hubert Howe Bancroft, *History of California* (7 vols., 1886-1890), II, 52n, summarizing Fray Pedro Munoz, Diario de la Expedicion hecha por Don Gabriel Moraga...1806. MS.
3. George H. Tinkham, *History of Stanislaus County* (1921), pp. 37-38.
4. There are three works that one may consult profitably on the Yokuts Indians. Dr. Alfred L. Kroeber, *Handbook of the Indians of California* (1923), is the briefest and the most authoritative regarding tribal boundaries. See p. 485 and elsewhere. Frank F. Latta, *Handbook of the Yokuts Indians* (1949), gives many insights into their culture. The first extensive scientific study was Stephen Powers, *Tribes of California* (Contributions to North American Ethnology, III, Washington, 1877), which was used by L. C. Branch in his *History of Stanislaus County* (1881), p. 88 and elsewhere.
5. Branch, *Stanislaus County*, p. 16.
6. Kroeber, *Indians of California*, p. 523.
7. Branch, *Stanislaus County*, p. 90.
8. Kroeber, *Indians of California*, p. 523.
9. Tinkham, *Stanislaus County*, p. 33.
10. Branch, *Stanislaus County*, p. 94.
11. Elk horns, Indian mortars, pottery and flint arrowheads were found by the Crane family when they moved to what was long known as the Kehoe Ranch on East Avenue. The Edward L. Conyers family was living there in 1907. Later families were those of Arthur J. Eddy, and Ray Stough. Mrs. Wilbur Trent, daughter of Tony Lawrence, was living on the property in 1971.
12. John G. Marvin, Scrapbook, 1851-52.
13. Marvin, Scrapbook, 1851-52.
14. Carvel Collins, ed., *Sam Ward in the Gold Rush* (1949), pp. 45n, 51n, 54n-55n, 59n, 104, 177-78.
15. Marvin, Scrapbook, 1851-52.
16. Branch and Tinkham set the date as 1820, but Branch is probably referring to Smith's expedition. Branch, *Stanislaus County*, p. 29. Tinkham, *Stanislaus County*, p. 40.
17. Harrison Clifford Dale, *The Ashley-Smith Exploration and the Discovery of a Central Route to the Pacific*, (Rev. ed., 1941), p. 181, draft letter of 1825 which reflects Smith's ideas before setting out.
18. Dale, *Ashley-Smith Exploration*, p. 187. This account depends on a comparison of that volume and Dale L. Morgan, *Jedediah Smith and the Opening of the West* (1953).
19. Morgan, *Jedediah Smith*, p. 207.
20. Robert Glass Cleland, *Pathfinders*, (1929), p. 268.
21. Cleland, *Pathfinders*, pp. 276-283.
22. Charles Wilkes, *Narrative of the United States Exploring Expedition*, p. 302.
23. Cleland, *Pathfinders*, p. 329.
24. Branch, *Stanislaus County*, p. 29. Neither Dale nor Morgan lists these two men, while Bancroft (*History of California*, III, 767 and 779) ties Hawkins alone to Ashley's outfit.

Chapter II – Pioneers and Pioneer Days

1. John C. Fremont reported seeing wild oats four feet high in this valley.
2. L. C. Branch, *History of Stanislaus County*, p. 226.
3. In the early 1850s wild cattle belonging to Louis Belcher and John Lewis were seen in large herds in the territory between the Stanislaus and Tuolumne rivers. With so much land to graze over and only the two groups of owners competing, it is not likely that they used the same ground. In the early days the area south of the Tuolumne was always referred to as the "Laird Range."
4. Branch, *Stanislaus County*, p. 224. John Kendall Wallis, in his *Journal, 1851-1868*, (1970), p. 11, for 31 Jan. 1851, uses the phrase, "three ounces and four dollars or fifty-five dollars." This would mean gold was worth $17.00 an ounce at that time.
5. According to Mark Moyle, himself a representative of these river settlers, this area was settled by men from England or descendants of Englishmen.
6. John Vincent Davies was the uncle of Mark Moyle. The name, according to Moyle, was originally Davis, but the Davises became so plentiful that he changed it to Davies.
7. John Carpenter was the great-grandfather of Mr. Vernon Thornburg of Turlock.
8. Branch, *Stanislaus County*, p. 179.
9. Mr. Moyle located on the south bank of the Tuolumne on land next to that of his uncle, John Vincent Davies. The land was bought from Joe Lord and Stephen Thomas of Sonora. T. K. Wallis was a brother of William K. Wallis, and Joe Vincent was a relative of J. V. Davies. By 1880, most of these English families were related through intermarriage.

   Another prominent family in the neighborhood, the Quisenberrys, came a generation later, in 1879. James F. Quisenberry and his wife, Katy Prince, came with their year-old son, Jackson A. Jackson later married Minnie A. Muncy, whose father James came to California in 1850. He and his wife, Juliette Squires, settled on the banks of the Tuolumne. Fay Quisenberry, daughter of Jackson and Minnie, noted, "Moyle, Muncy, Quisenberry, McCabe, Chapman, Brush, Sanders, Vivian, Magladry – these are some of the old neighbors." —Letter to Helen Hohenthal, 27 Sept. 1971.
10. Wallis' autobiography in Branch's *Stanislaus County*, p. 169.
11. *Ibid.*
12. Settlers in the area around the town of Empire reported deer, elk, antelope and even bears in plentiful numbers in 1852. —Marvin Scrapbook, 1852.
13. Mark Moyle, interviewed by Helen Hohenthal, June 1930. Mr. Moyle recalled the time when, as a young boy, he assisted in corraling a number of these mustangs. The place where they did this was on the Laird lands next to the Tuolumne City Bridge.
14. *Ibid.*
15. Mrs. M. H. Kittrelle, "Floods During 1861-1862," *Modesto News-Herald*, 21-22 Sept. 1927.
16. Mrs. Abby Fulkerth, interviewed by Helen Hohenthal 1930.
17. Branch, *Stanislaus County*, p. 243.
18. *The Stockton Daily Independent*, 16 Jan. 1867, and John Ross Browne, *The Policy of Extending Local Aid to Railroads*, p. 41.

INITIALS FREQUENTLY USED

JEC	– John E. Caswell	TDJ	– Turlock Daily Journal
TID	– Turlock Irrigation District	TWJ	– Turlock Weekly Journal

19. Branch, *Stanislaus County*, p. 211.
20. Moyle interview.
21. *Stanislaus County News*, 14 July 1871.
22. *San Joaquin Valley Argus*, 25 Sept. 1869.
23. Dr. Adams, Mrs. M. H. Kittrelle stated, was the first doctor to practice his profession in the county. *Modesto News-Herald,* 21-22 Sept. 1927.
24. Moyle interview. Also M. H. Kittrelle, "Floods During 1861-1862," *Modesto News-Herald,* 21-22 Sept. 1927.
25. There was no cemetery there; Mr. Moyle said the reason was "that people never knew when to die." Moyle interview.
26. 9 Statutes-at-Large 519. Swamp and overflowed land grant act of 1850. 2 California Statutes 189 (1852), An Act... for the sale of swamp and overflow lands.
27. Stanislaus County, Recorder, Overflow Lands Book, p. 1. *See also* Abstract Book (spine title: Map Book), in which the first ten numbered double pages are devoted to purchasers under this act.
28. Paul W. Gates, *History of Public Land Law Development* (1968), pp. 335-36.
29. Stanislaus County Recorder, Abstract Book (Map Book), pp. 69-91.

Chapter III – Settlement Spreads to the Sand Plains

1. *Stockton Daily Independent*, 16 January 1867.
2. Branch, *History of Stanislaus County*, pp. 243, 246. Dr. Ashe was one of the oldest settlers in the county. He located first in the Keyes section (Township 4, Range 10, east) but later the Ashe ranches southeast of Turlock, around present Ballico, were better known. Before moving into Paradise, he had resided in Stockton. After his death his son, William Ashe, took charge of the extensive estate.
3. H. S. Crane, interviewed by Helen Hohenthal, 1930.
4. Mrs. Roscoe Service, interviewed by Helen Hohenthal, 1930.
5. Annette Service Van Norman, "The Beginning of Agricultural Development in Stanislaus County," (Senior Thesis, Dept. of History, SSC, 1971), pp. 4, 11-13, citing Fred Field Goodsell, *John Service, Pioneer* (1945), *passim.*
6. Mrs. Abby Fulkerth, Diary and Notes. The diary describes the trip of the Fulkerth brothers, Tom, Will, and Asa, and their sister and families across the plains from Iowa to Stockton, California. All of these brothers were pioneers in this district and helped to mold its history and direct its destiny. Many other pioneers of this district came either across the plains or around by Panama or "the Horn" at a much earlier date but none, to the writer's knowledge, has left us such a complete story. "Aunt Abby" was active in the community and church life of Turlock until near her death on 16 February 1935. Born 29 July 1837, she was over 97 at the time of her death.
7. Sources for this table include Branch, *History of Stanislaus County*, the Thornburg Notes, and others. All known settlers from 1846 to 1880 are given in the Supplementary Material to Hohenthal thesis, available in SSC Library.
8. Henry Osborn was a step-brother of John W. Mitchell, according to his widow, Mrs. Belle Osborn. Mrs. Mary Geer and Mrs. S. H. Crane were nieces of Mitchell.
9. *Tuolumne City News*, 29 May 1868.
10. H. S. Crane interview, 1930.
11. David F. Lane, letter to Hohenthal, 18 June 1930.
12. *Modesto Herald*, 17 October 1878.
13. H. S. Crane interview, 1930.
14. Extracts from the *Tuolumne City News* of the above dates.
15. Col. E. Wood, interviewed by Helen Hohenthal June 1930. The straw was first used in 1877.
16. This description is taken from pictures and statements in Branch's *History of Stanislaus County*, and has been verified by several pioneers.
17. *Tuolumne City News*, 12 June 1868.
18. *Modesto Herald*, 22 August 1878.
19. *Ibid.*, 12 September 1878.
20. *Stanislaus County News*, 28 June 1878.
21. E. V. Cogswell said that he used a combined harvester as early as 1878, but they were not in general use. He cut 1475 acres in forty-two days. Branch, *History of Stanislaus County*, p. 208.
22. Branch, *History of Stanislaus County*, p. 74.
23. *Stanislaus County Weekly News*, 30 July 1886.
24. Crane, Moyle, Wood, and others who themselves worked on the harvesters disagreed as to the exact amount paid, but all agreed that the common laborer did not receive over $2.00 a day.
25. H. S. Crane interview, 1930.
26. *Modesto Herald*, August 1878.
27. One-arm Hughson, after whom the town of Hughson was named, lost his arm in a mowing machine accident.
28. *Modesto Herald*, 18 July 1878.
29. Chinese cooks were usually employed at a rate of $25 to $30 a month and board. The generosity with food was shown in other situations as well. John Mitchell is said to have left standing orders at his warehouses that no hobo was ever to be turned away hungry.
30. Col. E. Wood interview, 1930.
31. The *Stanislaus County Weekly News* for 30 July 1886 contains this comment: "Plenty of drunks in town every Sunday now. If Turlock were only a prohibitionist town, we could blame it on the prohibitionists, but as it is we must attribute it to bad whiskey and beer."
32. Col. E. Wood interview, June 1930.
33. *Stanislaus County Weekly News*, 30 July 1886.
34. Mrs. Tom Menzies, letter, June 1930. Mrs. Menzies was born near the town of Turlock in 1870—before there was a town. Her uncle gave the town its name.
35. *Stanislaus County Weekly News*, August 1886. These stories are all verified by old timers' statements.
36. *Modesto Herald*, 14 August and 22 August 1878.
37. Sam Strauss and his brother Max came to Turlock in 1880 and for many years thereafter ran a general merchandise store here.
38. *Stanislaus County Weekly News*, 30 July 1886.
39. *Modesto Herald*, 17 October 1878.
40. *Modesto Herald*, 8 August 1878. The Ceres Flour Mill, built by Daniel Whitmore in 1881 at a cost of $30,000, was burned to the ground a few months later. *Ceres Courier*, 19 April 1923.
41. Col. E. Wood interview, June 1930.
42. J. M. Moyle, interviewed by Helen Hohenthal, June 1930.

Chapter IV – School Life "In the Olden Days"

1. Branch, *History of Stanislaus County*, p. 226. This school was established only six years after the first San Francisco school (Bancroft, *History of California*, V, 656.) Stanislaus County claims as her own the first two State Superintendents of Public Instruction, J. G. Marvin, elected in 1850, and Paul K. Hubbs, chosen in 1853. Hubbs had made his home near Oakdale. He was the first to recommend that "school funds be apportioned according to average daily attendance instead of the number of census children."

2. Mr. J. R. Broughton in a letter to the writer of 5 June 1930 wrote that he attended the Laird School of the Adamsville District from October 1870 to June 1871, while Joseph Vincent was the teacher.

3. In 1854 the teachers' salaries were made up in the following way. The State appropriated $95, county taxes provided $159, and the rest was raised through rate bills or subscriptions.

4. Mrs. F. L. Walsh, who taught in the school when it was in its original location said, "People living within a radius of four or five miles who sent children to school were the two Russell families, the Kellys, the McCabes, Allens, Osborns, Thompsons, Hendersons, Warners, McClouds, Fulkerths, and Blatchleys. . . . Most of the children rode on horseback . . . I rode an old ranch horse named 'Old Blue.'" –Mrs. F. L. Walsh, Letter to Howard Whipple, 21 August 1921.

5. Ralph Giddings, who had attended the school, said that later the Ladies Aid Society built on a 40′ x 50′ addition when it bought the building and renamed it Washington Hall.–Ralph Giddings, Interview by Howard Whipple. The old Union or Grange Hall on Front Street, which was used as a school from 1881 to 1885, was a little larger, about 40′ x 75′.

6. All the facts, with a few exceptions, concerning the Fairview School were given to the writer by Mr. Horace S. Crane, who attended the school, and Mrs. A. G. Chatom, who taught there in 1885. One exception is Mrs. Walsh's letter to Mr. Whipple.

7. Even as late as 1910 this practice was still in vogue. The writer recalls in her own school days at the old Hawthorne School the rush made for the school pump the minute the recess bell rang, and the way the cups were passed around.

8. Mrs. Walsh wrote, "The school library at that time (1870) consisted of Webster's Dictionary and a very dilapidated copy of State Superintendent John Swett's report on the schools of California for the year 1865. I was told the dictionary had been donated to the school by a traveler who had taken refuge in the school house one night from a severe storm. . . . At that school I read a chapter every morning from the Bible and most of our singing was of Sunday School songs. I thought that the proper thing to do . . . ."

9. In 1863 the State series of school books adopted were: Eaton's *Arithmetic*; Greene's and Quackenbos' *Grammars*; Wilson's *Readers*; Allen's, Cornell's, Warren's, and Shaw and Allen's *Geographies*; Hooker's *Physiology*; Quackenbos' *History of the United States*. Two other books were also recommended, Robinson's *Algebra* and Cowdery's *Moral Lessons*. In 1880, the Stanislaus Board of Education dis-

carded all of the above except Cowdery's *Moral Lessons*, and adopted the following: Robinson's *Shorter Course in Arithmetic*; Duff's *Bookkeeping*; Payson, Dunton and Scribner's *Penmanship*; Bartholomew's *Drawing*; Harper's *Geography*; Anderson's *History of the United States*; McGuffey's *Readers*, revised; Cutter's *Physiology*; and Hatze's *Natural Philosophy*.

10. One day Henry Ward yelled his number at the teacher and immediately the latter got into action with a barrel stave. Henry dodged behind the crowd which formed, and the barrel stave, missing its mark, hit a big queer fellow by the name of Grimes. He yelled that his arm was broken by the blow and actually stayed out of school several days nursing it. Each school had its favorite "victim" as well as a bully; Grimes was Washington School's victim.

11. Because Captain Ward was one of the few men who willingly served as a school trustee, he was on the board all the time.

12. These were brothers of Judge Fulkerth. They were Charles, 7; Sydney, 4; and Asa, Jr., 2 years. These facts and the poetry were taken from "Aunt Abby" Fulkerth's scrapbook.

13. *Stanislaus County Weekly News*, 10 April 1874. For April, 1874, the honor roll for the Fairview (Washington) School included Ed Osborn and Horace Crane in the third grade, and Loren Fulkerth and Lucinda Bonnett in the second grade. Four years later, when W. S. Chase, later secretary of the TID, was the teacher, the following names appeared on the lists for October and November: Freddie Hill, Henry Ward, Albert Russell, Ed Osborn, Stonewall Allen, John McCabe, Alex McCabe, Armanda Mills, Florence Barney, Mattie Allen, Julia Geer, May Fulkerth, Maggie Casey, Lizzie McCabe, Annie McCabe, Mary Kehoe, Eugene McCabe, and Ralph Giddings.–*Modesto Herald*, 17 Oct. 1878, 21 Nov. 1878.

14. Mrs. Belle Osborn, interview Notes, 1929. For this reason, the site was used for the Hawthorne school, although it was then really too close to the business center.

15. In the summer of 1886, the school census marshal, P. R. McCabe, said there were 125 children in the Turlock School District, 91 of whom were of school age. *Stanislaus County Weekly News*, 30 June 1886.

Chapter V – Community Life and Society During the Grain Era

1. Mrs. Tom Menzies, letter to Hohenthal 10 June 1930.
2. *Modesto Herald*, 19 December 1878.
3. Thomas Gaddis was a prominent business man and farmer in the community. He was at one time associated with the Osborns in their store.
4. *Daily Evening News*, 5 December 1888.
5. *Stanislaus County Weekly News*, 3 December 1886.
6. *Ibid.*, 1 March 1889.
7. *Ibid.*, 30 June 1886. This was a moral play sponsored by the Prohibitionists.
8. *Ibid.*, 1 March 1889.
9. Will H. Osborn, interviewed by Howard Whipple, 5 August 1921.
10. *Modesto Herald*, 24 October 1878.
11. H. S. Crane, interviewed by Helen Hohenthal, 1930, and *Stanislaus County Weekly News*, 23 July 1886.
12. *Stanislaus County Weekly News*, 23 April 1886.

13. In the *Stanislaus County Weekly News*, 1 March 1889, the following item is found to bear out the statements made by Mr. Moyle, Mr. Crane, and others: "Tom and Charlie Baldwin and H. M. Liston started Friday for the Coast Range with guns in their hands...we speak for the first bear."

14. E. M. Moyle, interviewed by Helen Hohenthal, 1930; H. S. Crane, interviewed by Helen Hohenthal, 1930.

15. Since pelicans are no longer seen in the valley, the writer somewhat doubted this story from Mr. Moyle until Branch's *History of Stanislaus County* verified the existence of the blue pelican along the San Joaquin River.

16. Horace Crane interview.

17. On the fifth birthday of the band, 21 July 1886, the Turlock ladies presented the band boys with a beautiful silk banner. *Stanislaus County Weekly News*, 23 July 1886.

18. Will H. Osborn interview.

19. H. S. Crane interview. At one time a Dr. Jackson of Modesto was the only physician serving the region.

20. Rev. Mr. E. B. Winning, letter to Hohenthal, 10 April 1930. Mr. Winning's father, Rev. Mr. E. A. Winning, was a Methodist preacher for the greater part of the present Modesto and Turlock districts from 1876 to 1879. The son was a small boy at the time. In the 1930s he was pastor of a Methodist Church on Shattuck Avenue, Oakland, while another son was pastor of the Santa Cruz Methodist Church.

21. H. S. Crane interview.

22. The Westport Primitive Methodist Church was organized 13 March 1861. It was then known as the Adamsville Methodist Church. The services were first held in the John Davies home, then in the schoolhouse. The church was built in 1880.

23. The first church service ever held at Turlock was held in the Porter home. A Baptist missionary, a Rev. Mr. Reese, preached the sermon in 1869.—Florence Porter papers.

24. This statement was made by "Aunt Abby" Fulkerth. Horace Crane was of the opinion that its affiliation was determined by the fact that there were more members of the Congregational Church in Turlock than of the Methodist Church.

25. *Stanislaus County Weekly News*, 1 March 1889.

26. H. S. Crane interview.

27. N. O. Hultberg, letter to Helen Hohenthal, 5 June 1930.

28. The facts concerning the Catholic Church were obtained by Helen Hohenthal from Mrs. A. G. Chatom and Miss Margaret Casey, both of whom were members of the church and pioneers of the area.

29. *Modesto Herald*, 10 October 1878.

30. Sam Strauss, interviewed by Helen Hohenthal.

31. *Stanislaus County Weekly News*, 7 May 1886.

32. *Ibid.*, 1 March 1889.

33. W. D. Adams, interviewed by Howard Whipple, 8 August 1921.

Chapter VI – Road and River Transportation

1. Stanislaus was a part of Tuolumne County until 1854.

2. These boundaries were defined on page 1.

3. John G. Marvin, Scrapbook, 1850-1852. Mr. Marvin was the first to establish a newspaper printing office in Sonora. The prices charged were $20.00 for a year's subscription, and 50 cents for a single copy. "Ads" were inserted at the rate of ten lines or less, $4.00 for the first insertion or $8.00 a month.

4. H. S. Crane, interviewed by Helen Hohenthal, 1930.

5. J. S. Bishop, interviewed by Helen Hohenthal, 1930.

6. These boxes were first used by Wells Fargo to carry gold out of the mines.

7. In their appearance these drivers had none of the adventurous character of the pony express riders. They were just ordinary laborers, often too old to do other work, or men who were glad to get such a job during the winter months for $45.00 or less a month. H. S. Crane interview.

8. The heavily wooded territory along the San Joaquin was for long a place of refuge for criminals. One was Charles Wiley, who in a drunken rage killed three men in 1930.

9. *Stanislaus County Weekly News*, 10 Sept. 1886. The Turlock end of this road is now East Avenue.

10. J. S. Bishop interview.

11. Col. E. Wood, interviewed by Helen Hohenthal, 1930. The writer also used notes from her interview with J. S. Bishop, a bridge tender at Crows Landing; from her interview with Mark Moyle, who lived on the south bank of the Tuolumne; and parts of a Journal written by J. K. Wallis, who lived along the San Joaquin next to the ranch of his brother-in-law, John Carpenter. Horace Crane's interview notes and E. B. Winning's letter were also helpful.

    Ferries on the Tuolumne River, in order from the mouth upstream, were (1) Tuolumne City ferry, earlier called Dr. Ryer's ferry; (2) J. V. Davies' ferry; (3) Paradise City ferry; (4) Whitmore's ferry at Modesto; (5) Empire ferry or Eli Marvin's ferry; (6) Roberts' ferry (called Dickenson's ferry before 1862); and (7) Ward's ferry above Jacksonville.

    Ferries on the Merced river started with (1) Turner's ferry or (2) Hawkins' ferry not far from the Merced river's mouth; (3) McSwain's ferry (perhaps near present Cressey); and (4) Snelling ferry. Wallis also mentions a Russell ferry which may be east of Turner's ferry.

    Ferries in this region on the San Joaquin river started with (1) Grayson ferry, also called Durham's ferry; (2) Carpenter's ferry, four miles north of Crow's Landing; (3) Liggett's ferry, mentioned in T. K. Wallis's Journal, may be the one that Bishop refers to as the Mahoney Landing ferry, one mile north of Crow's Landing; there was also a Ward's ferry in that area; (4) Crow's Landing ferry; and (5) Hill's ferry, three miles north of the present town of Newman.

    This list may not be complete; it includes all the writer has found in references or in her interviews with old-timers. The only maps found by the writer proved to be inaccurate, not only in locating ferries but towns as well. One of these was a map of Central California in 1867 filed at the Bancroft Library, and another was that in Branch's *History of Stanislaus County, 1881*.

12. Dr. Ryer later became identified with other phases of development in the district. The station of Ryer, on the Southern Pacific Line east of Turlock was named after him. His son was a well-known and well-liked citizen of Turlock in early days.

13. Rev. Mr. E. B. Winning, letter to Hohenthal, 10 April 1930.

14. *Modesto Herald*, 12 December 1878.

15. *Modesto Herald*, 19 December 1878.

16. J. S. Bishop interview.

17. *Stanislaus County Weekly News*, 3 Sept. 1886. The contract bid of the Pacific Bridge Company for $35,280 was the bid accepted. Since the San Joaquin was a navigable stream

the State Engineer had to approve of the plans before the drawbridge could be constructed.

18. Branch, *History of Stanislaus County, 1881*, p. 245.

19. J. G. Marvin, Scrapbook, Year 1852.

20. Mark Moyle pointed out the place where the river boats came right up to the bank of the river along his uncle's land. Here he, as a young man, often helped load the grain sacks on the barges and steamers.

21. J. S. Bishop interview.

22. *Modesto Herald*, 17 Oct. 1878.

23. *Modesto Herald*, 18 July 1878.

24. *Modesto Herald*, 1 August 1878.

25. J. S. Bishop interview.

26. The point at which the Tuolumne River first broke through her bank was the exact spot used by the Davies and Moyles as a landing place during the shipping season. The enormous fissure formed by the force of the water was pointed out to the writer by Mr. Moyle in 1930.

27. M. H. Kittrelle, "Floods of 1861-1862" in the *Modesto News-Herald*, 21-22 Sept. 1927, and J. M. Moyle, Interview Notes, June 1930. Mrs. Kittrelle was the daughter of Capt. Humphrey Jones and the niece of Capt. J. P. Ward. Mr. Moyle pointed out the route taken by the boat across the grain fields; it landed in the field opposite the Laird School because it could not reach a pier in the swollen river. Later the *Alta* was stranded near old Elk Horn Stage Station, when rapidly falling waters blocked her return from Tulare Lake to Fresno Slough. There were still remains of her there in 1930.

28. Branch, *History of Stanislaus County*, p. 222. Not at the present city of Fresno, but somewhat farther west.

29. *Modesto Herald*, 18 July 1878.

30. Mr. J. S. Bishop, who told this story, said, "Yep! the captain had an eye for the ladies all right."

31. At the place where the Tuolumne River in 1862 overran its banks and flooded the whole plains for miles, the water in June of 1930 was perhaps thirty feet below the top of the banks.

Chapter VII – The Railroad Transforms Transportation

1. Stuart Daggett, *Chapters on the History of the Southern Pacific* (1922), *passim*.

2. *Tuolumne City News*, 6 August 1869.

3. John Ross Browne, *The Policy of Extending Local Aid to Railroads* (1870), pp. 6, 40. This proposed law was to allow the people to determine by vote whether the counties would donate bonds to the amount of $6000.00 per mile (bearing seven percent interest and payable in twenty years) toward the construction of a railroad which would connect Stockton (or some point on the Central Pacific Railroad) and some point on the Colorado River line. These bonds were not to be issued until the railroad was completed.

4. The Southern Pacific was incorporated under the laws of California 2 December 1865. By 1868, Governor Leland Stanford, Charles Crocker, C. P. Huntington, and their associates in the Central Pacific had bought controlling interest in the Southern Pacific. *Southern Pacific Bulletin*, June 1928.

5. *Southern Pacific Bulletin*, June 1928.

6. This section was constructed under the name of the San Joaquin Valley Railroad, a company of men interested in bringing trade to Stockton.–Bancroft, *History of California*, VII, 587.

7. From Goshen on, the rest of the construction was under the name of the Southern Pacific Company instead of the Central Pacific in order to take advantage of the federal land grant and right-of-way.–*Southern Pacific Bulletin*, June 1928.

8. The Central Pacific offered Mitchell free passage over the road at all times; although he rejected the offer, the railroad officials would stop the train anywhere along the way to pick him up.

9. H. S. Crane, interviewed by Hohenthal, 1930.

10. R. E. Kelly, letter to Hohenthal, May 1930.

11. *Stanislaus County News*, 16 June 1871; 6 October 1871. It was estimated that it would take the crew about four weeks to complete this bridge.

12. H. S. Crane interview. Mr. Crane gave the story of the construction crews at work in this area. Trains were running to within three miles of Turlock before the summer of 1871 was over. For the hundreds of Chinese laborers there was a city of white tents moving south as construction progressed toward the Merced River.

13. The trains did not operate on regular schedule to Merced until 25 January 1872.–*Southern Pacific Bulletin*, June 1928.

14. By 1878 the Southern Pacific timetables showed two northbound trains and two southbound trains daily.–*Modesto Herald*, 12 December 1878.

15. The second line to go down through the valley was the west side line. According to the *Southern Pacific Bulletin* for June 1928, this line was started during 1888, and was opened for operation from Tracy to Newman on 1 July 1891.

16. *Southern Pacific Bulletin*, June 1928.

17. Being a rival to the pioneer line already established, the Government granted this railroad no aid, aid going only to the first line constructed.

18. The line was completed to Bakersfield in 1897, therefore passing through the Turlock District about 1896.–C. G. Fluhr, letter to Hohenthal, June 1930.

19. *Modesto Herald*, 8 August 1878.

20. Stuart Daggett, *History of the Southern Pacific*, pp. 262-334.

21. This is not high when it is remembered that ferry transportation across the river was not less than 50¢. About 1928 Mr. Crane found an old unused Central Pacific ticket among his papers. He presented it to the conductor on the train and the conductor said it was still good, because, when it was issued, there was no time limit placed on a ticket.

Chapter VIII – Early Turlock, 1871-1900

1. Loren Fulkerth, Sam Strauss, and Horace Crane interviewed by Hohenthal, 1930. *See also* Whipple File, Turlock Public Library.

2. Whipple File, Turlock Public Library. The "old Jim Allen Hotel," long known as the Turlock Hotel and later as Vignolo's Hotel, was moved from Westport to Turlock in the winter of 1871-72. It is probable that additions were made to the original structure.

3. Horace Crane said that the first Giddings and Ward store was located on the southwest corner of Center and East Main, but Pete Le Cussan bought a Giddings and Ward store on Front [Highway 99] and East Main Streets in the late 1870s.

4. Bernard Le Cussan, Interviewed by Whipple 19 August 1921. Joe Blanc worked in both the Tom Fulkerth blacksmith shop and wagon-making shop and in the Donovan (later McGill) blacksmith shop in the early 1880s. He later quit the blacksmith shop and rented 700 acres of Mitchell land in the present Chatom-Mountain View area. The Fulkerth blacksmith shop burned down after 1885. Joe Blanc's son Emil and grandson Joe live in this area now, 1971, and gave an interview for the later family history.

   Blanc's friend, Pete Le Cussan, in the late 1870s borrowed $1400.00 and bought the one-story Giddings and Ward empty store on the corner of Front Street and East Main. Two years later he bought the rest of the block facing East Main and rented the Fulkerth blacksmith shop to Joe Blanc.

   The older Le Cussan brothers moved in and out of the story of Turlock until they returned to France to stay.

5. Horace Crane, interviewed by Whipple, 26 July 1921: "Part of the old Turlock Hotel was moved from west of Keyes in 1872." Mrs. Stephen Crane, interviewed by Whipple, 4 August 1921: "The hotel was first. It was moved in a fog in the fall of 1871. Horace Crane thought that the movers were lost in the fog."

6. *San Joaquin Valley Argus*, 20 January 1872. *Stanislaus County News*, 5 April 1872.

7. A general store "carried everything from threshing machines to needles," an old-timer said. Ward's store also served the community as a substitute bank to accommodate those who did not bank in larger communities.

8. *San Joaquin Valley Argus*, 20 January 1872. *Stanislaus County News*, 5 April 1872.

9. Florence Porter, interviewed by Whipple, 1921.

10. Abby Fulkerth, interviewed by Whipple, 29 July 1921. "Aunt Abby" said that Capt. J. F. Ward had not informed Mrs. Ward that the building was to be moved then. She kept on with preparation of the dinner while the building was in transit. Later Ward added a two-story section to the original building. When Stephen Crane bought the building, he tore down the old part and moved the two-story part across the street.

11. Sam Strauss, interviewed by Hohenthal, 1930.

12. Walter Brown, letter to Hohenthal, 14 June 1930.

13. U. S. Bureau of the Census, Census of 1880. Enumerators' Sheets, Stanislaus County. Microfilm in Stanislaus State College Library.

14. Two pioneers of Turlock, Mr. and Mrs. Charles M. Wilson, worked in the Farmers' Hotel before their marriage. Mr. Wilson was a classmate of Ed Osborn in Turlock's first schools. His father, Sam Wilson, lived in the Denair area. A home of the Charles Wilsons was at Marshall Street and Johnson Road.—Opal Wilson Morrison, Interviewed by Hohenthal, 1971.

15. Horace Crane, Abby Fulkerth, interviewed by Helen Hohenthal, 1930.

16. Sam Strauss and Horace Crane, interviewed by Whipple, 1921(?).

17. *Stanislaus County Weekly News*, 30 July 1886.

18. E. B. Osborn, interviewed by Whipple, 4 August 1921.

19. Ralph Giddings, interviewed by Whipple.

20. Pete Johnson, interviewed by Whipple, 6 August 1921.

21. H. S. Crane, interviewed by Whipple, 26 July 1921.

22. Sam Strauss, interviewed by Helen Hohenthal, 1930.

23. *Modesto Daily News*, December 1888.

24. See Chapter V for early Turlock church history.

25. *Stanislaus County Weekly News*, 27 December 1889.

26. Sam Strauss, interviewed by Helen Hohenthal, 1930. Also E. B. Osborn, interviewed by Whipple, 1921. The front page of the *Turlock Item* for 6 Feb. 1890 was reproduced in the TDJ for 14 Oct. 1971, p. 3. The *Turlock Times* for 25 Dec. 1891 was reproduced in TDJ for 15 Oct. 1971, p. 2.

27. One of the general stores was established by H. A. Osborn in the Fountain Hotel building in 1892.

28. *Turlock Journal*, 11 February 1910.

29. William Ward, interviewed by Whipple, 1920.

30. Tom Gaddis, interviewed by Whipple, 26 July 1921.

31. A. L. McGill, interviewed by Whipple, 17 August 1921.

Chapter IX — Creation of the Turlock Irrigation District

1. John Mitchell, the founder of Turlock, frequently said irrigation would again make the valley prosperous.

2. *Stanislaus County Weekly News*, 1 June 1886.

3. *Stanislaus County Weekly News*, 22 October 1886.

4. Mr. Wright is described by those who knew him as a tall, slender, red headed young man; a man of self-assurance and determination. Upon his death on 11 January 1906, a Los Angeles paper paid him the following tribute: "No citizen of Los Angeles was held in higher esteem than was Judge Wright . . . it was a priceless privilege to seek and secure his wise and able counsel when some great question required solution, or some movement was contemplated."

5. *Laws and Resolutions Passed by the Legislature of 1885-6, Extra session*, XXXIV, 29-45. Mr. H. S. Crane said that he was present in Modesto when Wright returned from Sacramento, after his law was passed. The people of Turlock and Modesto, about 300 in number, met him at the station, and to the accompaniment of band music and cheers escorted him to the Rogers Hall where he told them the story of his fight at Sacramento. Before this meeting was over, a row started between the "dry" farmers and the "wets."

6. J. R. Broughton, letter to Hohenthal, 5 June 1930.

7. Mrs. C. C. Wright, letter to Hohenthal, 28 May 1930.

8. The bill was passed without a vote of opposition in either the Assembly or the Senate. Mrs. C. C. Wright makes this most interesting comment: "In 1887 when Mr. Wright wrote the Bill, there was not a typewriting machine in town—at least I never remember hearing of one, and as he always considered my writing more legible than his, I made a copy of the Bill, and I have always been proud of the fact that it is now on file in Sacramento, in my handwriting."

9. C. E. Grunsky, letter to Hohenthal, 9 June 1930.

10. *Daily Evening News* (Modesto), 11 December 1888.

11. *Daily Evening News*, 11 December 1888.

12. The votes recorded were 291 for organization and 73 against organization.—Stanislaus County Board of Supervisors, Minutes, 6 June 1887.

13. California, Irrigation District Bond Commission, *Report on Turlock Irrigation District*, p. 32.

14. Turlock Irrigation District, Minutes, 15-16 June 1887. Ceres was keenly disappointed in not securing the location of the Turlock Irrigation Offices. After shifting around in the different Turlock buildings for a while, J. W. Mitchell donated, for the use of board meetings, rooms below the Public Hall in his Fountain Hotel. Later the offices were moved to Ceres, then returned again to Turlock.

15. TID, Minutes, 7 July 1887. Mr. Manuel is described by one person as short, stout, dark, and not overly inclined to vigorous actions.

16. One such company was the Merced and San Joaquin Irrigation Canal Company, 1873.

17. C. E. Grunsky, letter to Hohenthal, 9 June 1930.

18. TID, Minutes, 16 September 1887.

19. Mrs. Anna Sorenson, statement to Hohenthal, 1929.

20. The people had approved of a total of $600,000.

21. TID, Minutes, 7 November 1887.

22. U. S. Dept. of Agriculture, Office of Experiment Stations, *Bulletin 158*, p. 99.

23. Turlock Irrigation District v. Williams, 76 Cal 360.

24. *Daily Evening News*, 8 and 13 December 1888. John Mitchell, the founder of Turlock, had great faith in irrigation. He often stated that if irrigation came, wealth and bumper crops would be the result.

25. The Southern Pacific Railroad's irrigation taxes amounted to $812.35 for that year. It was taxed on rolling stock and roadway, 18.87 miles, valued at $188,700, on 18.87 miles of telegraph lines, $943, and on its Turlock reservation and improvements $1500.–*Daily Evening News*, 26 December 1888.

26. TID, Minutes, 4 September 1888.

27. Hickman was considered one of the few "wet" farmers in and around Denair. Hickman's bid was again the only one received.

28. On 18 September 1888, the Board set the fees of the District's attorney at $1000.00 per year. P. J. Hazen was described as a man rather small in stature. He was decidedly the "studious type." While somewhat eccentric and sometimes inclined to magnify the importance of legal technicalities, nevertheless, he was a fine man and an efficient counsel of the District. Of him Judge L. W. Fulkerth of the Superior Court of Stanislaus County wrote:

"His good judgment and advice had much to do in piloting the new enterprise to success . . . . He was skilled in the law, a close student, diligent in the discharge of his official business, and faithful to his clients. His work for the Turlock Irrigation District was of inestimable value . . . . Mr. Hazen was my neighbor for some thirty years and I had the highest regard for him as a friend and as a neighbor."

He served as the Turlock District's attorney up until the time of his death.–L. W. Fulkerth, letter to Hohenthal, 1 June 1930.

29. *San Francisco Daily Alta California*, 8 December 1888.

30. "A written contract was made by L. M. Hickman and a syndicate of S. F. capitalists . . . by which the syndicate agrees to purchase 1000 bonds of $500 each. The bonds are to be delivered and paid for as needed in the construction of the canals and works; no more bonds to be delivered than necessary to complete the works. Interest on the bonds will not start until the bonds are delivered." *Daily Evening News*, 13 December 1888.

31. *Ibid.*, 13 December 1888.

32. California, Irrigation District Bond Commission, *Report on TID, 1914*, p. 30.

According to John R. Freeman, the custom of filing water claims was distinctly a western custom, originating in the days of placer mining. The claims are filed like the *ad damnum* in damage suits. Later, when agriculture was developing in the valley, certain men saw the possibility of making claims and then later selling their water rights. In making a claim the party concerned usually demanded far more than he thought he might ever need.–John R. Freeman, *Reports on the Uses of Water from the Tuolumne River*, 01-08.

33. That Col. M. A. Wheaton was not wholly popular is indicated by the rather amusing incident recorded in the 11 June 1886 issue of the *Stanislaus County Weekly News*.

"M. A. Wheaton, a San Francisco attorney, dammed up a creek and ignored the neighbors' wishes and the orders of the Deputy Fish Commissioner to take it down. He is now on trial before Justice Eastin."

34. C. E. Grunsky was manager of the C. E. Grunsky Company, Engineers, in San Francisco, and the first engineer for the Modesto Irrigation District.–C. E. Grunsky, letter to Hohenthal, 9 June 1930.

35. California, Department of Public Works, Bulletin 21, p. 187.

36. U. S. Dept. of Agriculture, Office of Experiment Stations, *Annual Report of Irrigation and Drainage Investigations, 1904* (Bulletin 158), p. 104. Henceforth cited as USDA Bulletin 158.

37. *Report of the State Engineer, 1880*, p. 79.

38. California, Irrigation District Bond Commission, *Report on Turlock Irrigation District, 1914*, p. 20. Also J. H. Dockweiler, *Water Needs of the Turlock and Modesto Irrigation Districts*, pp. 13-15.

39. Because of the fact that Turlock had full ownership of the Wheaton Dam site before negotiations with Modesto were entered into, she held Modesto to this 50-50 proposition, instead of proportional costs according to the acreage of water needs of the two districts.

40. USDA Bulletin 158, p. 106.

41. C. E. Grunsky, letter to Hohenthal, 9 June 1930.

42. California, Irrigation District Bond Commission, *Report on Turlock Irrigation District, 1914*.

43. The Turlock Irrigation District as of 1970 had 250 miles of canals and laterals, of which 193 miles were concrete-lined. Nine hundred and ninety-one improvement districts had been formed and completed, with 464 miles of lined ditches and underground pipelines. Turlock Irrigation District, *Report, 29 October 1970*.

44. *Stanislaus County Weekly News*, 1 March 1889.

45. Frank Adams, *Histories of Irrigation Districts in California, 1887-1893*, pp. 30-32.

46. As an influential person in the state of California, Waymire succeeded in carrying the state in the presidential election for his close friend, William McKinley. For his service it was thought that McKinley would appoint him to a cabinet position, but at the last moment he selected McKenna instead. McKenna later served on the Supreme Court. Judge Waymire was in the midst of his Turlock District troubles when the newspapers got wind of the cabinet talk.

47. *Modesto Morning Herald, Irrigation Jubilee Supplement*, 22 April 1904. Signed statement by Judge Waymire.

48. Frank Adams, *Histories of Irrigation Districts in California*, p. 32.

49. George H. Maxwell, Letter to Hohenthal, 3 April 1930.

50. *Modesto Morning Herald, Irrigation Jubilee Supplement*, 22 April 1904.

51. Tregea v. Modesto Irrigation District, 164 U. S. 179. On the same date Fallbrook Irrigation v. Bradley, 164 U. S. 112, was decided, upholding the Wright Act.—Frank Adams, *Histories of Irrigation Districts*, pp. 26-27.

52. Aside from the legal victory, this case was of much personal interest to the people of the District. Two men who meant much in the history of the District, Judge Waymire, who saved the District, and Judge C. C. Wright, "Father of Irrigation Districts," were in the thick of the fight. Mrs. C. C. Wright stated: "Mr. Wright had the satisfaction of taking part in the argument before the United States Supreme Court in Washington and after thirteen years of litigation the 'Wright Irrigation Bill' became a 'Law!'"—Mrs. C. C. Wright, Letter to Hohenthal, 28 May 1930.

53. Horace Crane, interviewed by Hohenthal, 1930.

54. N. O. Hultberg, letter to Hohenthal, 21 May 1930.

55. T. C. Hocking, interviewed by Hohenthal.

56. C. S. Bishop, interviewed by Hohenthal, 1930.

57. Mark Moyle, interviewed by Hohenthal, 1930.

58. Anna Sorenson, interviewed by Hohenthal, 1929. The 6% bonds of 1888-1892 were replaced bond for bond with 5% bonds.

59. Horace Crane interview.

60. *Modesto Morning Herald, Irrigation Jubilee Supplement*, 22 April 1904.

61. Horace Crane interview.

Chapter X — Turlock a Center of Swedish Settlement

1. N. O. Hultberg, Letter to Harry B. Ansted, 29 March 1925. Henceforth cited as Hultberg to Ansted. In Helen Hohenthal's possession.

2. Mrs. Esther Hall (Arthur G.) Crowell, Interview by Carolyn Larson, 28 Oct. 1965. Henceforth referred to as Crowell Interview by Larson. Mrs. Larson also made notes from three manuscripts prepared by Mrs. Crowell; these will be referred to as Crowell-Larson Notes.

3. Nels O. Hultberg, Interview by Howard Whipple, 12 August 1921. Henceforth referred to as Whipple Interview. Original in Turlock Public Library.

4. Nels O. Hultberg, Letter to Helen Hohenthal, 5 June 1930. Henceforth referred to as Hultberg to Hohenthal.

5. *Ibid.*

6. *Ibid.*

7. Phebe Fjellström, *Swedish-American Colonization in the San Joaquin Valley in California: a Study of the Acculturation and Assimilation of an Immigrant Group* (Studia Ethnographica Upsaliensia, XXXIII, 1970), pp. 60-62. Henceforth cited as *Fjellström*.

8. Hultberg to Ansted.

9. *Ibid.*

10. Hultberg interview.

11. *Missions-Vännen (Mission Friends*, published by the Swedish Mission church), 29 April 1902, cited in *Fjellström*, p. 63.

12. Nels O. Hultberg, letter to Wallace Smith, Los Gatos, Cal., 9 Nov. 1931. Quoted in Wallace Smith, *Garden of the Sun* (Fresno, 4th ed. 1960), p. 432.

13. Hultberg to Ansted.

14. Hultberg interview.

15. Mrs. Esther Hallner (Magnus) Lindgren, interviewed by Geraldine Johnson, 24 Oct. 1968. Cited in Geraldine Johnson, "Early Swedish Settlement in the Turlock Area," (Senior Seminar Paper, Department of History, SSC), p. 3. Henceforth cited as *Johnson*.

16. Hultberg Interview.

17. Hultberg to Ansted.

18. Mrs. Esther Hall (Arthur G.) Crowell, interviewed by Geraldine Johnson, 26 Oct. 1968. Henceforth cited as Crowell interviewed by Johnson. In *Johnson*, p. 3.

19. Hultberg interview.

20. *Ibid.*

21. Crowell interviewed by Larson and Crowell-Larson Notes. August "Gus" Johnson was the father of Mrs. Esther Cooper, Mrs. Agnes (Gail) Cooper, Mrs. Edith (Claude) Wood, Mrs. Hilda Hamm, and the late William M. Johnson. The latter was the father of Turlock physician Everett Johnson and of Lorraine Johnson, secretary to two SSC presidents and an acting president.

22. Mrs. Esther (Frank, Sr.) Youngdale, interviewed by Geraldine Johnson, 8 Nov. 1968. In *Johnson*, p. 4.

23. Hultberg to Ansted.

24. Crowell interviewed by Johnson. In *Johnson*, p. 5.

25. Crowell interviewed by Larson, 2 Nov. 1965.

26. Crowell interviewed by Larson, 9 Nov. 1965.

27. Hultberg to Hohenthal.

28. Crowell-Larson notes.

29. *Ibid.*

30. Hultberg interview.

31. Rev. J. O. Bodén, interviewed by Howard Whipple, n.d. Interview probably took place between July and October 1921. Henceforth cited as Bodén interview.

32. Clarence Ahlem, interviewed by Geraldine Johnson, 17 Nov. 1968, in *Johnson*, p. 7. Henceforth cited as Ahlem interviewed by Johnson.

33. Crowell-Larson notes are the source for the four preceding paragraphs.

34. Carolyn Larson, Notes from conversations with my father, Mr. Knut Knutsen. Henceforth cited Knutsen-Larson notes.

35. Hultberg interview.

36. Ahlem interviewed by Johnson. Cited in *Johnson*, p. 8.

37. Clarence Ahlem, telephone interview by Carolyn Larson, Nov. 1971.

38. Knutsen-Larson notes.

39. Clarence Ahlem, interviewed by Ramon J. Desagun, 29 Aug. 1970, in Desagun, Hilmar, (Individual Study Paper, Department of History, SSC, 1970). Henceforth cited as *Desagun*.

40. *Johnson*, p. 9.

41. Harry Johnson, interviewed by Ramon J. Desagun, 31 July 1970, in *Desagun*, p. 11.

42. Crowell interviewed by Johnson, in *Johnson*, p. 9.

43. David Lane, letter to Helen Hohenthal, 18 June 1930, in *Johnson*, p. 10.

44. Ahlem interviewed by Desagun, in *Desagun*, p. 9.

45. Crowell-Larson notes.

46. Ahlem interviewed by Desagun, in *Desagun*, p. 8.

47. Bodén interview.

48. Crowell-Larson notes.

49. Mrs. Valesca Smith, interviewed by Geraldine Johnson, 14 Nov. 1968, in *Johnson*, p. 11.
50. Mrs. Crowell also gave Miss Johnson the use of her three MSS. Cited as Crowell-Johnson notes, in *Johnson*, p. 11.
51. *Fjellström*, pp. 117-122. Among those interviewed on the transfer of Swedish customs were Mrs. Ellen Olson, Mrs. Ellen Nordkvist, Mrs. Maria Hall, Mrs. Liliane Johnson, Mrs. Eleonora Warn, Mrs. Hildur Olson, Mrs. Jennie Nordfeldt, Mrs. Esther Crowell, and Mr. Erik Hawkinson.
52. Crowell-Johnson notes, in *Johnson*, p. 11.
53. *Fjellström, loc. cit.*
54. Crowell-Johnson notes, in *Johnson*, p. 11.
55. Hultberg interview.
56. Bodén interview.
57. Dr. Harry D. Channing, telephone interview by Carolyn Larson, 22 Oct. 1971. The son of Gust Johnson, Channing changed his name because there were so many Johnsons in Turlock. The Ahlem family also changed their names from Johnson.
58. Crowell-Johnson notes, in *Johnson*, p. 12.
59. Crowell-Larson notes.
60. Valesca Smith interviewed by Johnson, in *Johnson*, p. 12.
61. Weva Wakefield Devitt, interviewed by Helen Hohenthal, Sept. 1971.
62. *Fjellström*, p. 68. The name Bodén was anglicized to Bodin, but was still pronounced Bo-deen'. Mrs. Esther Crowell recalls Bodén to have taken a jar of sand and postcards of lovely palm trees to show how beautiful Turlock would be some day.—Crowell-Johnson notes.
63. Bodén interview.
64. Warner Swanson, interviewed by Geraldine Johnson, 7 Nov. 1968, in *Johnson*, p. 22.
65. Swanson interview, *Ibid.*, p. 23.
66. Warner Swanson also loaned Miss Geraldine Johnson his MS notes, henceforth cited as Swanson notes. *Johnson*, p. 23.
67. Violet Johnson Martinson, letter to Carol Ann Evenson Lundell, 9 April 1970. Eric Gustav Johnson was the husband of Jessie Johnson and the father of Royal Johnson, Leslie Johnson, and Violet Johnson Martinson.
68. Swanson notes, in *Johnson*, p. 23.
69. *Ibid.*, p. 24.
70. George W. Clark, *History of Merced County* (Merced, 1955), p. 42, cited in *Desagun*, p. 3.
71. Ahlem interviewed by Desagun, in *Desagun*, p. 3.
72. Knutsen-Larson notes.
73. Crowell-Larson notes.
74. Ahlem interviewed by Desagun, in *Desagun*, pp. 11-12.
75. Tinkham, *History of Stanislaus County*, p. 172.
76. Beulah Covenant Church, *Sixtieth Anniversary Publication, 1902-1962*, cited in *Johnson*, pp. 13-14.
77. Crowell-Larson notes.
78. *Ibid.*
79. Crowell-Johnson notes, in *Johnson*, p. 14.
80. *Sixtieth Anniversary Publication*, cited in *Johnson*, p. 14.
81. Helen Moline, Notes of translated Covenant Church Minutes; Helen Moline, interviewed by Geraldine Johnson, 6 Nov. 1968; both cited in *Johnson*, p. 15.
82. *Sixtieth Anniversary Publication*, cited in *Johnson*, p. 17. O. G. Olson, a former minister, was one of the early choir directors. He was the father of Mrs. Lamar (Carmen) Jackson.
83. Levi Ahlberg, Interviewed by Carolyn Larson, 1958.
84. Ernest Skarstedt, *California och desa Svenska Befolkning*, (Seattle, 1910), p. 197.
85. Swedish Covenant Church [Beulah Covenant], Minutes, 1929.
86. Helen Moline, telephone interview by Carolyn Larson, 22 Oct. 1971.
87. Moline-Johnson notes, in *Johnson*, p. 17.
88. Crowell-Larson notes.
89. *Sixtieth Anniversary Publication*, cited in *Johnson*, p. 19.
90. Swan Johnson, interviewed by Carolyn Larson, 12 April 1931, at Berkeley, California.
91. Evangelical Free Church, Turlock, *Fifty Years, 1906-1956* (Turlock, 1956), p. 9. This name (Free Mission Church) was later changed to the Evangelical Free Church. Mr. and Mrs. A. G. Bergstrom, Mr. and Mrs. S. J. Booge, Mr. and Mrs. John P. Nylander, Mr. and Mrs. Henry Russell, Mr. and Mrs. Carl E. Anderson, and Mr. and Mrs. Peter Tuveson were the charter members. Several days later, Mrs. Emma Hallstone and Mrs. Lovisa Wickstrom were added to the list of charter members. Pastors are listed as: Rev. C. G. Nelson, Rev. C. E. Cedar, Rev. Carl Liljekvist, Rev. Gottfried Stone, Rev. A. J. Thorwall, Rev. Arthur P. Peterson, Rev. Hugo G. Rodine, Rev. Willard Eckman, Rev. Joy Cummings. The Rev. L. E. Hagstrom succeeded Cummings, and was pastor in 1971.
92. Swan Johnson interview.
93. Rev. L. E. Hagstrom, telephone interview by Carolyn Larson, 22 Oct. 1971.
94. [Nazareth Lutheran Church], *Illustrerat Album Utgivet Av Svenska Evangeliska Lutherska Nazareth Forsamlingen, Minneskrift, Turlock California, 1912-1922*, p. 7. The charter members were: Mr. and Mrs. John A. Erickson, Mrs. Hannah Lundahl, Adolf Swanson, Mrs. Jenny Swanson, John A. Anderson, Mrs. Jenny Anderson, L. Moberg, John Lundin, Mrs. Alida Lundin, M. J. Lundell, Mrs. Christine Lundell, Axel Hoff, S. A. Norquist, Mrs. Hannah Norquist, John Lewis, and Mrs. Amanda Lewis.
95. M. J. Lundell, interviewed by Carolyn Larson, 5 April 1931.
96. Rev. Neal Pearson, "Nazareth Lutheran Church," in *History of California Conference of Augustana Evangelical Lutheran Church in North America, 1893-1953* (Kingsburg, Cal., 1953), p. 22.
97. Nazareth Lutheran Church, Turlock, Church records. MSS. The pastors who followed Rev. W. X. Magnuson were: Rev. John Billdt, Rev. C. W. Samuelson, Rev. F. J. Ellman, Rev. Paul Engstrand, Rev. Neal Pearson, Rev. William Conrad, Rev. Adolph Dickhart, and Rev. Lloyd Hanson, who was serving in 1971.
98. Calvary Baptist Church, Turlock, *Fiftieth Anniversary, Turlock, March 22, 1958*, pp. 4-6. The charter members were Rev. and Mrs. F. O. Nelson, Miss Nellie Nelson, Mrs. S. C. Nelson, Mr. and Mrs. C. A. Nystrom, Mr. and Mrs. Joe Samuelson, Mr. and Mrs. William Ternstrom, Mrs. Anna Ahlquist, Mrs. Mathilda Anderson, Mr. and Mrs. John A. Carlson, Mrs. J. E. Eklund, Mr. and Mrs. Axel Hagstrom, Mr. G. Andrew Johnson and Mr. Andrew Nelson.
99. *Ibid.*, p. 10.
100. Hilmar Covenant Church, Hilmar, *Fiftieth Anniversary Publication, 1902-1952*, cited in *Johnson*, p. 21.

101. Pastor M. A. Odell, "Berea Lutheran Church," in *History of the California Conference of Augustana Evangelical Lutheran Church,* p. 20.
102. *Fjellström,* p. 72.
103. *Ibid.,* pp. 147-148.
104. C. G. Strom, Hilmar, MS (Covenant Archives, North Park College, Chicago), cited in *Fjellström,* p. 129.
105. *Fjellström,* pp. 148-149.

Chapter XI — The Portuguese an Important Element

1. August Mark Vaz, *The Portuguese in California,* pp. 40-45.
2. TDJ, 10 November 1964, p. 24.
3. Most of the information given in this table has been obtained from questionnaires filled in by family members. See appropriate notes below.
4. John A. Santos, interviewed by Hohenthal, June 1930. Also June Jane Ripley McVey (Santos' granddaughter), Notes, November 1971.
5. Frank Pedras, Notes, deeds, to Hohenthal, March 1972.
6. Ida Vincent Fernandes, Notes to Hohenthal, December 1971. Mrs. Fernandes is a granddaughter of A. M. Vincent.
7. Ida Vincent Fernandes, letter to JEC, 7 May 1972.
8. The approximate date of 1915 was supplied by Bruce Vincent, son of Fred.
9. Belle Santos Morchino, Notes on the Jesse Santos family sent to J. J. R. McVey, November 1971. Mrs. Morchino is a daughter of Jesse Santos. (The John and Jesse Santos families were close friends, but not related.)
10. William R. Fernandes, Notes; interview by Hohenthal. Henry Arline, "Horseman Joe Fernandes Helped Pave City Streets," TDJ, 10 November 1964.
11. J. C. Fernandes, interviewed by Hohenthal, 1930. Mrs. Clara Rogers Fernandes, interviewed by Hohenthal, October 1971. Pamphlet on the UPEC.
12. Henrietta Gomez McMahon, Notes to Hohenthal on the Gomez family, December 1971.
13. Rose Luis Frodelius, Notes to Hohenthal about the Luis family and business, April 1972.
14. Iria Mendonsa, Tony Mendonsa, Jr., and Jim Mendonsa, Notes obtained by Christine Chance, January 1972.
15. *Ibid.*
16. See Chapter XXII, "New Crops, New Industries," for a discussion of the melon business based in part on interviews with A. T. Bettencourt.
17. Helen Manha Miguel, Notes on the Lewis Brothers, 1972.
18. Helen Manha Miguel, Biography of Matthew Manha, November 1971.
19. Frank S. Mendonsa, Questionnaire Notes, December 1971.
20. William R. Fernandes, Questionnaire Notes, November 1971. Also "Dairyman of the Month," *The Refresher* (California Branch, American Dairy Association), August 1968.
21. John J. Souza, Sr., Questionnaire and Notes, April 1972.
22. Anthony Ferreira, Questionnaire Notes, April 1972.
23. Belle Santos Morchino, Notes, November 1971.
24. William R. Fernandes, Questionnaire and Notes, November 1971. Underwriters of the cost of Portuguese Hall were Joe Fernandes, Manuel Furtado, Manuel Lorango, Manuel Garcia, Manuel Cardoza Goulart, and A. R. Vieira. Dates supplied from Pentecost Association, Minutes, courtesy Mrs. Anthony Ferreira.
25. J. C. Fernandes, "Portuguese Insurance Order Organized 1 September 1905." Other officers were Thomas Dutra, vice-president; J. C. Fernandes, secretary; J. I. Rocha, treasurer; A. A. Silva, master of ceremonies; J. A. Silveira, guardian; M. D. Martin, marshal; J. F. Silveira, J. S. Goulart, and M. R. Pereira, trustees.
26. TDJ, 15 October 1921.

Chapter XII — The Assyrians: Settlers from the Near East

1. John Joseph, *The Nestorians and their Muslim Neighbors* (1961), p. 168. Henceforth cited as Joseph, *Nestorians.*
2. Fred Tamimi in the *Turlock Daily Journal,* 28 August 1968.
3. *World Book Encyclopedia,* s.v. "Assyria."
4. Kurdistan is the mountainous area west and south of Lake Urmia. It is inhabited by the warlike Kurdish tribesmen and since World War I has been divided between Iran, Iraq, and Turkey.
5. Victoria Yonan, "A History of the Assyrian People in the Turlock Community" (Graduate paper, Division of Social Sciences, SSC, 1962; 71 pp.), pp. 14-22, citing transcript of a 1952 radio broadcast by His Holiness, Patriarch Mar Eshai Shimun XXIII.
6. W. A. Wigram, *The Assyrians and their Neighbours* (London, 1929), p. 6.
7. Mary Lewis Shedd, *The Measure of a Man* (1922), p. 31.
8. Joseph, *Nestorians,* p. 123.
9. Shedd, *Measure of a Man,* pp. 170, 271ff.
10. Renamed "Rezaiyeh" for Reza Shah, ruler of Iran, 1925-41.
11. Dr. Isaac Adams, Interviewed by Helen Hohenthal, 1930.
12. Yonan, "Assyrian People," pp. 39-40.
13. Jessie C. Glasier, "Down a Trail of Torture from Persia to Cleveland," *Cleveland Plain Dealer,* Sunday Magazine Section, 3 November 1918. Also Mrs. Lillian Shimmon Spielman, interviewed by Sarah S. Jackson, October 1971.
14. Yonan, "Assyrian People," pp. 55-56.
15. *Ibid.,* pp. 34-35.
16. *Ibid.,* p. 69.

Chapter XIII — Japanese Colonies

Acknowledgment is given to Helen Hohenthal for materials collected by her on the first generation Japanese and made available for this chapter.

1. Harold Stewart, trans., *A Chime of Windbells* (1969), p. 125.
2. Matsunosuke Ishihara, interviewed by Esther Noda, 27 May 1971.
3. Bill Hosokawa, *Nisei, The Quiet American* (1969), pp. 31-33.
4. E. Manchester Boddy, *Japanese in America* (1921), pp. 25-28.
5. Yamato Ichihashi, *Japanese in the United States* (1932), p. 10.
6. *Ibid.,* p. 293.
7. Harry H. L. Kitano, *Japanese Americans* (1969), pp. 7-10.
8. Nisaburo Aibara, interviewed by Prof. and Mrs. Emery Fleming, Jr., J. Carlyle Parker and Esther Noda, 22 May 1971.
9. Kitano, *Japanese Americans,* p. 15.
10. Ichihashi, *Japanese in the United States,* p. 111.
11. Mura Sekine, interviewed by Esther Noda, 20 May 1971.

12. Aibara interview, 22 May 1971.
13. Kitano, *Japanese Americans*, p. 15.
14. Ichihashi, *Japanese in the United States*, p. 119.
15. Yonezo Yoshida tape, Japanese American Citizens League dinner honoring Issei, November 1969.
16. Hosokawa, *Nisei*, pp. 92-93.
17. Ichihashi, *Japanese in the United States*, p. 296.
18. Kitano, *Japanese Americans*, pp. 16-17.
19. Helen E. Hennofrund and Orpha Cummings, *Bibliography on the Japanese American Agriculture* as cited in *San Francisco Bulletin*, 1 September 1919.
20. Hosokawa, *Nisei*, pp. 102-104.
21. Bradford Smith, *Americans from Japan* (1948), p. 212.
22. Ichihashi, *Japanese in the United States*, pp. 309-310.
23. Smith, *Americans from Japan*, p. 216.
24. Aibara interview, 22 May 1971.
25. Buddy T. Iwata, Note, 7 June 1971.
26. Matsunosuke interview, 27 May 1971.
27. Yae Yokoi Questionnaire, 18 June 1971.
28. Nobuo Tomiye Questionnaire and Interview, by Esther Noda.
29. Jack Noda, interviewed by Esther Noda, 23 May 1971.
30. T. Noda, interviewed by Helen Hohenthal through Mary Noda, 1930.
31. Asataro Miyamori, trans., *Anthology of Haiku, Ancient and Modern* (1932), p. 228.
32. Aibara interview, 22 May 1971.
33. *Modesto Herald*, 21 July 1921.
34. *San Francisco Examiner*, 21 July 1921.
35. *Modesto Herald*, 22 July 1921.
36. Ishihara interview, 27 May 1971.
37. "Japanese Peace Party Headed by Viscount, Sees Progress, Peace, Prosperity in Turlock," *Turlock Daily Journal*, 4 January 1922.
38. Aibara interview, 22 May 1971.
39. William Noda, Notes, 15 June 1971.
40. Boddy, *Japanese in America*, p. 186.
41. Helen Yuge, "Cortez Growers: An Oasis Created," *Turlock Daily Journal*, 5 May 1964.
42. Kazuo Masuda, Notes on Yamato Colony at Livingston, California, 18 June 1971.
43. *Turlock Daily Journal*, 5 May 1964.
44. Helen Yuge, "Cortez Presbyterian Church History," *Turlock Daily Journal*, 6 November 1970.
45. Hosokawa, *Nisei*, p. 285.
46. Morton Grodzins, *Americans Betrayed* (1949), pp. 365-366.
47. Buddy Iwata, Commencement Address, Stanislaus State College, 13 June 1970.
48. Hosokawa, *Nisei*, p. 283.
49. *Ibid.*, pp. 341-342.
50. *Ibid.*, pp. 355-356.
51. *Ibid.*, p. 436.
52. *Ibid.*, p. 435.
53. *Turlock Daily Journal*, 5 May 1964.
54. Hosokawa, *Nisei*, p. 450.
55. *Ibid.*, pp. 445-447.
56. *Ibid.*, pp. 90, 452-453.
57. Mark Vasche, "Japanese-Americans Recall 'Bitter Years,'" *Modesto Bee*, 19 September 1971.
58. Kitano, *Japanese Americans*, p. 142.
59. R. H. Blyth, trans., *Haiku*, IV (Autumn-Winter 1952), xxvii.

Chapter XIV — Original Mexican Settlers

This chapter has grown out of the personal experience and contacts within the Mexican community of Ernestine (Mrs. Mike) Rojas.

1. Raul Valle, telephone interview by John E. Caswell, 1 Nov. 1971.

Chapter XV — Other Ethnic Groups

1. George Arakelian, Notes, 15 April 1971.
2. Betty Azhderian Moosekian, interviewed by Hohenthal, Nov. 1971. Mrs. Moosekian is a niece of Dick Arakelian. Shawn Moosekian was serving as a member of the Stanislaus State College Advisory Board in 1971.
3. Betty Moosekian, interviewed by George Arakelian, 15 April 1971.
4. Helen Hohenthal recalls the general seasonal exodus of students whose families followed the fruit as shippers, buyers, packers or laborers, some following the fall fruit season northward, others returning to the Imperial Valley to prepare for the next crop there.
5. George Arakelian, Notes, 25 April 1971.
6. Rudy Torosian, interviewed by Hohenthal, Nov. 1971.
7. Araxie Vartanian was a high school classmate of Helen Hohenthal. She was the first Armenian to attend Turlock High School, graduating in 1917.
8. George Arakelian, Notes, 25 April 1971.
9. Statement by John Arakelian to Helen Hohenthal in 1963.
10. George Arakelian, interviewed by Hohenthal, July 1971.
11. George Arakelian, Notes on Shahbazian and Donabedian, 25 April 1971.
12. George Arakelian Notes, April 1971, and Rudy Torosian's additions to the Arakelian Notes, Nov. 1971.
13. Betty Moosekian, interviewed by Hohenthal, November 1971.
14. Kalem Divanian, interviewed by George Arakelian, 18 April 1971.
15. This paper, "My Trip from Egypt," and a questionnaire interview of her father by Beatrice were part of a high school paper assignment in 1930 in a U. S. History Class. Helen Hohenthal was the teacher.
16. Mihran Azhderian, Questionnaire for Helen Hohenthal, 1930, by his daughter Beatrice.
17. George Arakelian Notes, 25 April 1971.
18. The following section is based on questionnaires returned by the following individuals or families: Andrew Bollakis, John Flesoras, Nick Megas, Mrs. Athena Pallios, Mary Pantazopulos, and the children of George Steve Tavernas (deceased). The assistance of Steve and Georgia Grillos in circulating the questionnaires is gratefully acknowledged.
19. Statements of George and Ken Doo to JEC, 18 Nov. 1971.
20. Response to questionnaire.
21. Statements of Raymond R. Lee to JEC, 1971.

Chapter XVI — Turlock, 1901-1940

1. C. C. Carlson, interviewed by Howard Whipple, 27 July 1921. Also, Marjorie Carlson Bussinger, interviewed by Helen Hohenthal, 25 February 1972.
2. The charter members are listed in Chapter X.
3. Beulah Covenant Church, *History Horizons, 1902-1962* (pamphlet).

4. California, Secretary of State, Corporation files. Caswell notes.

5. List printed by the *Turlock Journal* for stockholders.

6. Letter of 9 February 1905, Turlock Mercantile archives.

7. Various documents in Turlock Mercantile archives, courtesy of Harold Lindblom.

8. Carl C. Carlson interview.

9. Hazel Berg Memory Book, assembled by her for her father, M. M. Berg.

10. Ernest Skarstedt, *California och dess Svenska Befolkning.*

11. TDJ clipping and invitation in Hazel Berg's Memory Book.

12. TWJ, 6 January 1905.

13. TWJ, 13 January 1905.

14. Directors of the association were E. B. Osborn, H. S. Crane, C. V. Lundahl, D. F. Lane, and G. F. Donkin.—California, Secretary of State, Corporation Files.

15. "First Annual Melon Carnival, Official Program," TDJ picture files.

16. Mrs. Alice Crane, "Pioneer Ladies Join Men in Pushing Progress," TDJ, Semi-Centennial Edition, 1958. For the city's establishment of a library, see Ordinance No. 45, 5 October 1909.

17. "The Turlock Board of Trade," TWJ, 22 September 1905.

18. Turlock, Board of Trustees, Minutes, I, 1.

19. Turlock, Trustees, Ordinances, No. 24.

20. For sewer system, see Ordinance No. 25; for water system, see Ordinance No. 26, both of 17 November 1908.

21. Turlock, Trustees, Ordinances, No. 28.

22. For the last, see Ordinance No. 42, 7 September 1909.

23. TDJ, 7 August 1954, and 10 November 1964.

24. TDJ, 10 November 1964, p. 38.

25. Beulah Covenant Church, *History Horizons, 1902-1962. California Covenanter*, February 1972. Virgil Hanson, Interviewed by Helen Hohenthal, March 1972. The permanent file of the *Covenanter* is in the Chicago archives of the Mission Covenant Church.

26. The owners were Will Thornburg, Arthur J. Eddy, Thomas Adams, Jack Williams and J. L. Randolph. The office was in the Decker Building at about 226 East Main Street.

27. Mr. Leon Unger was line manager for the East Turlock Farmers' line for many years. The writer thinks she paid $50.00 for her share of stock.

28. "Turlock's First Phone Installed 56 Years Ago," TDJ, (special issue), 1958.

29. J. A. Coveney, "Railroad Transportation," Industrial Edition, TWJ, 11 February 1910.

30. An important factor in handling business transactions on perishable commodities such as fruit and poultry was the establishment of banks in Turlock in 1905 and 1906.

31. Lowell School stood on Minaret Street, on the site later occupied by the City Library and Senior Citizens' Center.

32. For information on the high schools of the area, see Chapter XXVIII.

33. Jean Nelson, interviewed by Helen Hohenthal, 1971. Clipping from TDJ in Berg Memory Book, n.d. E. J. Cadwallader, manuscript stories of Turlock, 1945. Betty Moosekian, Interviewed by Helen Hohenthal about her uncle, Dick Arakelian, 1971.

34. Steve Andrino died in 1960. The information was supplied by Mrs. Elizabeth (Steve) Andrino, who is well known in Garden Club and other activities in Turlock. She and part of the family still reside (1972) at the home place on Canal Drive.

35. Valesca Ferguson Smith, Turlock History Memoirs. Hazel Ornberg Carpenter, interviewed by Helen Hohenthal, November 1971.

36. Recent dates courtesy of Ernie Yotsuya, D. Pharm.; Mrs. O. E. Longstreth; Franklin Schwoob, and L. Englesby.

37. Mrs. Irene (P. W.) Johnson, telephone conversation with JEC, 24 March 1972.

38. Details courtesy of Gordon Olson.

Chapter XVII – Ceres and Keyes: Neighbors on the Southern Pacific

Grateful acknowledgment is given to Mr. and Mrs. Homer Jorgensen for arranging and hosting a group interview on Ceres since 1940. Others present on 21 February 1972 were Robert Jorgensen, Mr. and Mrs. Grant T. Lucas; Mrs. Caryl Fowler; Mr. Roger Strange, and JEC, the interviewer. George H. Nunes supplied most of the data on Keyes. Valuable information was also furnished by Helen Hohenthal and Fridolph E. Nelson.

1. Stanislaus County, Recorder, Abstract Book (Spine title: Map Book), pp. 80ff.

2. Information on Daniel Whitmore's reason for leaving the Stockton area, and on his eventual landholdings, was kindly supplied by his grandson, Charles N. Whitmore.

3. L. C. Branch, *History of Stanislaus County* (1881) shows three houses built by Daniel Whitmore in the illustration following page 12. The cabin was probably built in the summer of 1867 and may have been at Hatch and Mitchell. According to Charles Whitmore, the house with a narrow front was the one built in 1870 by Daniel Whitmore for himself. This was still standing on the east side of Fifth Street north of North in 1971. The third house was built for Daniel's son Clinton and his family and stood on the southwest corner of Whitmore and Moffett. Clinton built a spacious house in 1905 somewhat north of his parents' home. It was occupied by his wife until her death in the late 1930s. Wallace and Jennie Whitmore Caswell occupied it until their deaths. After July 1966 it was occupied by Charles Whitmore's son, Robert E. Whitmore.

4. George H. Tinkham, *History of Stanislaus County, California*, p. 235.

5. Statement by Mrs. Roscoe Service. They had an old deed signed by President Andrew Johnson and dated 1 June 1867. It does not seem likely that the deed was to land purchased from Whitmore.

6. Mrs. Lucy Jane Whitmore, "A History of Ceres from 1871 to 1895," *Ceres Courier*, April 1923. (Reprinted in Centennial Edition, November 1971.)

7. Estella Updike Service, Interviewed by Helen Hohenthal, June 1930.

8. The informant was Cyrus Lee. His report, however, gives the date of building the station as 1876, rather than the usual date of 1874. *Ceres Clipping Books*, article dated 19 Feb. 1887. Charles Whitmore indicated that Lee was not necessarily accurate.

9. The plat was filed by R. K. Whitmore, but the section of land was owned by Daniel.

10. *Ceres Clipping Books.*

11. See also Chapter IV, "School Life in the Olden Days."

12. Gladys Moore, "United Methodist Church," Centennial ed., *Ceres Courier*, 30 Sept. 1971. A report of the Ceres Sunday School for 1878 showed forty scholars on the rolls. *Ceres Clipping Books*.

13. Moore, "United Methodist Church."

14. *Stanislaus County Weekly News*, 1 March 1889.

15. Built in 1880 by the Ceres Hall Association capitalized at $2500 with $5 shares. *Ceres Clipping Books*.

16. Charles N. Whitmore Interview, 1971.

17. For events at Ceres and Modesto we follow the order of events and interpretations of Sam Strauss, interviewed by Helen Hohenthal April and May 1930, and Estella Updike Service (Mrs. W. Roscoe), interviewed by Helen Hohenthal May 1930. For later events, see Wallace Smith, *Garden of the Sun*, 4th ed. (Fresno, 1960), pp. 313-327. To secure funds for her father's legal assistance, Evans' daughter Eva was instrumental in getting the story on the stage, reputedly having had a hand in writing the play itself. She and her mother Molly took their own real-life roles. The play was put on in a San Francisco theater and was seen by Mrs. Roscoe Service.

18. Linda Rowland, "History of Ceres Library," Centennial Ed., *Ceres Courier*, 30 Sept. 1971.

19. Charles Whitmore Interview, 1971.

20. *Ceres Clipping Book*, 10 April 1904.

21. "Items from Ceres," TDJ, 27 Jan. 1905, pp. 1-2.

22. "Newspaper's Founder," Centennial Ed., *Ceres Courier*, 30 Sept. 1971.

23. "Church of Christ," *Ibid.* "Glad Tidings Assembly of God," *Ibid.*

24. *Ceres Clipping Books* and Charles Whitmore conversation, 4 Jan. 1972.

25. Grant Lucas in Group Interview, Jorgensen home.

26. See Chapter XXVIII, "Schools of the Region."

27. Caryl Fowler, "Ceres Adapts to Living in Shadow of 99 Freeway," *Modesto Bee*, 4 Jan. 1966.

28. Caryl Fowler, "Ceres Looks Forward to Expansion During 1968," *Modesto Bee*, 28 December 1967, p. B-3.

29. Several members of the group interview entered into this discussion. Mrs. Caryl Fowler made some very perceptive remarks. For opinions expressed above, the author assumes final responsibility.

30. Abridged and paraphrased from Roger Strange's account in group interview.

31. Mrs. Anne Warren to George H. Nunes, 1971.

32. Mrs. W. R. Service, interviewed by Helen Hohenthal, 1930.

33. Sam Strauss, interviewed by Helen Hohenthal, 1930.

34. "A New School District," *Turlock Times*, 5 February 1892.

35. Annual Report of the Condition of the Public Schools in the County of Stanislaus for the year commencing July 1, 1905, and ending June 3, 1906. *California State Archives*.

36. Mrs. Anne Warren to George H. Nunes, 1971.

37. Directors of the creamery were J. F. Snowen, J. W. Mann, W. J. Middleton, J. W. Scott, and R. F. Wells, Jr.

38. Fridolph E. Nelson, letter to Helen Hohenthal, 4 February 1972.

39. First officers of the PTA were: Mrs. Cochrane, president; Mrs. Alma Austin, vice president; Mrs. Mabel Updike, secretary; Mrs. Jessie Oberkamper, treasurer; Mrs. Via Stetson, auditor; and Miss Pearl Olson, a teacher, historian. Keyes PTA, Minutes.

40. Information on the Keyes Grange was supplied by Mrs. Alfred H. Bolter, based on Grange records. The first officers of the Grange were: Charles Austin, master; A. G. Jones, overseer; Mrs. C. A. Talbott, lecturer; Jack Orr, steward; C. W. Austin, assistant steward; Mary Ford, lady assistant steward; Mrs. M. C. Jessup, chaplain; John Orr, treasurer; Chester Talbott, secretary; Ross Munch, gate keeper; Mrs. Evelyn Pudas, Ceres; Mrs. A. H. Bolter, Pomona; Mrs. Clyde Stafford, Flora; Peter Olson, Egbert Jones, and T. F. Elam, executive committee.

41. Berne W. Feuerstein, principal, Keyes Grammar School, Telephone conversation with John E. Caswell, 11 March 1972.

42. Keyes Civic Group, Minutes (in the possession of George H. Nunes).

Chapter XVIII — Santa Fe Towns, Denair and Hughson

1. The deed and contract were recorded on 24 June 1898 in Stanislaus County.

2. Stanislaus County, Recorder, Map Book Vol. 1, p. 51.

3. Mr. Jessup, an old-time neighbor, gave Christine Chance this information when she interviewed him in his home in Denair, 1941.

4. Mr. Cutler was Christine Chance's seventh-grade teacher in Denair in 1908.

5. Tinkham, *History of Stanislaus County*, 1921, pp. 1136, 359.

6. Plat of Elmwood Colony, 14 April 1905. Recorder's Map Book, II, 13. Lester continued to live in the Davis ranch buildings down to about 1913. Christine Chance's parents, the Hollingsworths, lived next door.

7. Plat of J. D. Subdivision, 9 Nov. 1909, Recorder's Map Book IV, 37. Others who were active in Denair real estate were the aforementioned Theodore Jessup and his associate D. J. Wood, who operated Wood's Hotel for a time (this structure still stood in 1971, in use as a private dwelling). L. A. Walker was another; E. J. Cadwallader later moved his real estate office to Turlock where he lived out his ninety-odd years.

8. In honor of the young elms he had planted about his home? Christine Chance said, "These elms continued to shade the crumbling ranch house for some half a century, when elm beetle slowly destroyed them. As a neighbor, I watched them die."

9. C. G. Fluhr, Letters to Helen Hohenthal, 16 and 21 June 1930.

10. Birth date, 10 November 1846.

11. A number of Denair's fellow workers on the Santa Fe followed him up to the Turlock area. Among these were H. W. Rickenbacher, E. C. Hoover, A. J. Eddy, W. T. Vary, and C. T. Hohenthal. Denair is remembered by Hohenthal as a kindly white-haired man who always brought the children boxes of candy when he visited the family. Other instances of his generosity were remembered by the community. For the last ten years of his life he was active in Denair and Turlock real estate and in supervising railway construction near Blythe, California. He died in Los Angeles, 4 October 1915. [Personal information on John Denair and this note are by Hohenthal, based on her personal recollections and on letters from C. G. Fluhr, then Coast Division Superintendent

of the Santa Fe, to Hohenthal of 16 June and 21 June 1930. Fluhr had worked with Denair from 1897 to 1906; part of his information was based on an article in the *Santa Fe Magazine* for November 1915—Ed.]

12. Information supplied by Mrs. Roy Crouch.

13. In 1971 there were 91 families on the rolls.

14. The Board of Trustees at the time of incorporation consisted of D. J. Wood, chairman; E. J. Cadwallader, secretary-treasurer; J. B. Kinser; C. S. Shafer; Joseph Oyer; G. Hier; and Jacob Witmer.

15. Helen Robertson spent much of her childhood and youth on her father's farm on Sperry Road a quarter-mile north of After her marriage to Louis Hornbeck she returned to live for some years in the converted Hotel Denair.

16. The earliest records that could be found by this writer named Jim Roberts as president of the Denair Farm Bureau in 1916. Subsequent officers include dairymen, field-crop farmers, orchardists, vineyardists, berry growers.

17. Stella Perry, long an officer of Denair Home Department, is the source of this information.

18. The first master was Jim King; the first secretary, Helen Kisling, who was also chairman of the Home Economics Department.

19. Information from postal records supplied by Kennard C. Bratten, Postmaster.

20. Records in Jack McCauley's possession show that the first president of the board of directors was Walter Commons.

21. The first slate of officers for the Lions Club was: President, Ray Drake; 1st Vice President, Stanley Martin; 2nd Vice President; Thomas Simms; 3rd Vice President, Wilford Moore; Sec.-Treas., Larry Griffin; Tail Twister, Art Watkins; Lion Tamer, Melvin Horine.

22. The establishment of fire hydrants has resulted in the lowering of fire insurance costs by as much as 45 percent. The improved sewer system not only eliminated the use of septic tanks, but also made it possible to have more homes and businesses, including a laundromat. Information supplied by Robert Heans, chairman of the Service District.

23. In 1971, recent additions included Martin's Mobile Homes in Denair and another mobile homes park on Waring Road (Country Squire Estates). Albert De Palma was subdividing his land at the corner of Lester and Tuolumne Roads; Bob Runyan was developing a handsome housing project on Lester Road; Charles Schultz had erected some low-cost houses at Story and Zeering and was beginning others on Sperry just north of Zeering; Mr. Sutherland had built small apartments on Zeering near Lester, and across the road from him, Glen Brown did the same.

24. Notes on Montpellier by Mrs. M. L. Harmon, March 1972.

25. The writer was a mail clerk in the Denair Post Office at the time of this incident and observed it.

26. The story of the Crow ranch ended rather sadly. The Crow family refused to have anything to do with irrigation. As land in Hughson became more valuable, taxes increased, expenses were greater, and the non-irrigated crops did not bring in much money. Finally the bank had to take over what was left of the property. It was then sold for almost nothing—just enough to cover the amount that was owed. It became the H. W. Low ranch and was later purchased by Harold Schmidt, D.V.M.

27. *Hughson News*, 24 November 1933.

28. Jean Sinclair was elected queen that year.

29. Edited by R. Dean Galloway (SSC Library, 1966), p. 19.

Chapter XIX – Hilmar and Delhi: A Church Colony and a State Colony

The portion on the State Land Settlement is extracted from Tony Kocolas, "California's Experiment at Delhi: Evaluation of the Delhi Land Settlement Project of 1920 to 1931" (Graduate Paper, SSC, 1971). That on later Delhi is based on a group interview of 27 July 1971. Present were: Dallas C. Bache, Sr., host; Mr. and Mrs. Walter Fox, Mrs. Sybil Hill, Mrs. Ruth Zierenberg, and Mr. and Mrs. John E. Caswell. Unless otherwise indicated, the information is from Mr. Bache. The assistance of the participants is gratefully acknowledged.

1. Phebe Fjellström, *Swedish-American Colonization in the San Joaquin Valley in California* (Uppsala, 1970), p. 129.

2. Harry Johnson, interviewed by Ramon J. Desagun, 31 July 1970; Clarence Ahlem, interviewed by Ramon J. Desagun, 30 July 1970. In Desagun, "Hilmar" (Individual Study paper, Department of History, SSC, 1970), p. 13.

3. Johnson interview, in *Desagun*, p. 14.

4. Ahlem interview, in *Desagun*, p. 3.

5. *Ibid.*, and Carl Larson, interviewed by John E. Caswell, 11 Dec. 1971.

6. Terrance Shireman, "Tidewater Interurban: a Short History of Electric Interurban Service between Modesto and Stockton" (Senior thesis, Department of History, SSC, 1970), p. 32, *passim*. The Western Pacific Railroad bought up the Tidewater Southern in 1917, at the time the extension to Hilmar was being planned (*Shireman*, p. 30). Mr. Shireman's paper also discusses a second railroad that lost out to Tidewater Southern—hence the title.

7. Information from Tidewater Southern records, courtesy of Lincoln A. Hupp.

8. Johnson Interview, in *Desagun*, pp. 13-14.

9. *Ibid.*

10. William Ahlem, telephone interview by JEC, 8 Dec. 1971.

11. Clarence Ahlem's statement to JEC 30 Dec. 1971.

12. William Ahlem telephone interview.

13. "1905 Hilmar Concert Band," TDJ, 10 Nov. 1964, p. 32. In *Desagun*, p. 15.

14. This account of the schools is based on an interview with Mrs. Ruth Larson, long-time principal of Elim Elementary School, by JEC on 11 Dec. 1971. Dates have been checked in the official records through the kindness of the district superintendent, Eugene R. McSweeny.

15. C. G. Strom, "Hilmar," MS (Covenant Archives, North Park College, Chicago, Ill.). Cited in *Fjellström*, p. 129.

16. U. S. Bureau of the Census, *Population, California, 1970*, "Counties and Minor Civil Divisions."

17. Carl Larson interview.

18. J. Winter Smith, Interviewed by J. Carlyle Parker, 25 Feb. 1971; Dallas C. Bache, Sr., Interviewed by Tony Kocolas, 18 May, 1971.

19. California Legislature, 44th Session, *Appendix to the Journals* (1921), I, p. 45.

20. *Ibid.*, p. 46.

21. *Ibid.*, p. 48.

22. California Legislature, 45th Session, *Appendix to the Journals* (1923), IV, pp. 13-14.

23. *Appendix to the Journals* (1921), I, pp. 59-60.

24. *Ibid.*, pp. 45-51.
25. *Ibid.*, p. 57, and Bache Interview.
26. *Appendix to the Journals* (1923), IV, pp. 23-25, and Bache Interview.
27. Bache Interview.
28. Smith Interview.
29. *Appendix to the Journals* (1921), I, p. 55.
30. Bache Interview.
31. *Appendix to the Journals* (1921), I, p. 55.
32. *Appendix to the Journals* (1923), IV, p. 50.
33. Bache Interview.
34. Roy J. Smith, "The California State Land Settlements at Durham and Delhi," *Hilgardia*, 15 (October 1943), p. 414.
35. *Appendix to the Journals* (1921), I, pp. 39-42.
36. Bache Interview.
37. Bache Interview and Letter of Naomi Bache to other former settlers, 30 January 1970.
38. Bache, Interviewed by Kocolas, 3 June 1971.
39. *Appendix to the Journals* (1921), I, p. 34.
40. California Legislature, 50th Session, *Appendix to the Journals of the Senate and Assembly* (1933), IV, p. 18.
41. Bache Interview; Smith Interview.
42. *Appendix to the Journals* (1921), I, pp. 34-35. *Livingston Chronicle*, 4 March 1927.
43. *Appendix to the Journals* (1923), IV, p. 24.
44. Smith Interview and Letter of Naomi Bache.
45. *Appendix to the Journals* (1923), IV, p. 24.
46. Bache Interview. Smith Interview.
47. Smith Interview.
48. *Livingston Chronicle*, 25 May 1925.
49. Smith Interview.
50. Information on final settlement is from Bache Interview of 18 May 1971, Smith Interview, and the report on the final settlement, *Appendix to the Journals* (1933), IV. Mr. Bache was a member of the Settlers' Committee.
51. Bache is a descendant of two notable American scientists: Alexander Dallas Bache, Superintendent of the Coast Survey, and Benjamin Franklin.

Chapter XX – An Engineering History of the Turlock Irrigation District

Roy V. Meikle served the Turlock Irrigation District from 1914 to 1971, most of that time as Chief Engineer. This chapter is an abridgement of a longer paper, written from his own vast experience, with the records of the District at his command.

Chapter XXI – The Human Side of the Turlock Irrigation District

1. J. D. Works had served as a Justice in the California State Supreme Court and as a United States Senator.
2. Baldwin *et al.* v. Board of Directors of the Turlock Irrigation District *et al.*
3. John Patton, "Turlock, Modesto Held Jubilee to Fete Completion," TDJ, Golden Jubilee Edition, 9 June 1937.
4. Andy Curtin, "Story of 1914 Dam Break Writes Drama into Turlock Irrigation History," TDJ, Golden Jubilee Edition, 9 June 1937.
5. Harry L. Villinger, "TID's 67 Years of Progress Demonstrate Both Foresight and Ability," TDJ, 7 August 1954.
6. Ernest Forsmark, Interviewed by Helen Hohenthal, 1930. The story of seeing the Indians dancing was told Forsmark by the Flemings, father and son, who were old residents of the district.
7. Villinger, "Turlock Irrigation District's 67 Years..."
8. William R. Fernandes, interviewed by Helen Hohenthal, November 1971.
9. TDJ, Golden Jubilee Edition, 9 June 1937, Sec. III, p. 8. Boone was a nephew of Griffin.
10. Reynold Tillner, interviewed by Helen Hohenthal, 1971.
11. Elnore Hatfield (Mrs. Joseph Debely), "Veteran Secretary of TID Watched Growth," TDJ, Golden Jubilee Edition, 9 June 1937, Sec. IV, p. 6.
12. Diane Chittock, "Roy Meikle Steps down as TID Chief Engineer," TDJ, 14 December 1971.
13. William R. Fernandes, written statements to Helen Hohenthal, 7 February 1972.
14. Chittock, "Roy Meikle."
15. A list of the officers of TID has been compiled by Reynold S. Tillner, and is available in the SSC and Turlock City Libraries.
16. Carl Fallquist, "Trouble Shooters," TDJ, Golden Jubilee Edition, 9 June 1937.

Chapter XXII – New Crops, New Industries, 1901-1940

1. A. T. Sweet, J. F. Warner, L. C. Holmes, *Soil Survey of the Modesto-Turlock Area, California.* (U. S. Department of Agriculture, 1909), p. 60. Henceforth referred to as *Sweet.*
2. *Sweet*, pp. 13-14.
3. A. A. Jungerman, "Statistical Information on Stanislaus County Agriculture" (Stanislaus County Agricultural Extension Service, Jan. 1939, processed), Table 10. Henceforth cited as Jungerman, "Statistical Information."
4. *Sweet*, pp. 7-8. See also A. A. Jungerman, "Statistical Information," Table 1.
5. Erik Hawkinson, "Memories," MS, quoted in Fjellström, *Swedish-American Colonization,* p. 149.
6. Charles N. Whitmore, interviewed by JEC, 13 Sept. 1971. This was sometime prior to 1912.
7. TWJ, 9 Dec. 1904, p. 1; 16 Dec. 1904, p. 1.
8. A. A. Jungerman, *History of Stanislaus County Farm Bureau to...November 1948* (Mimeographed), pp. 1-5.
9. *Sweet*, p. 49. This was twice the average value of land in the county, $54.40 per acre, three years later in 1910. See Jungerman, "Statistical Information," Table 1.
10. Adapted from U. S. Census figures reproduced in Jungerman, "Statistical Information," Tables 10-11. Years given are correct for cattle; for acreages they are based on the preceding 31 December.
11. Clarence C. Ahlem, conversation with JEC, January 1972.
12. T. C. Hocking, interviewed by Hohenthal, June 1930. Mr. Hocking described the establishment of the first creameries east of the San Joaquin River in Stanislaus County.
13. Organizers of the Turlock Creamery Co. were J. B. Kinser of Denair, W. D. Wood of Stevinson, G. W. Jenkins, A. T. Kinser, and Philip Rutherford of Turlock—the latter living near Keyes. Authorized stock was $25,000. The charter was forfeited on 28 February 1920, probably a couple of

years after its actual closing.—California, Secretary of State, Archives, Corporation File, Inactive.

14. Helen Hohenthal, "History of the Turlock District" (M.A. thesis, University of California, MS), pp. 275-276.
15. Dean W. Larson, "Bureau of Dairy Service and Bureau of Milk Stabilization" (Term paper, SSC, Fall 1961), *passim.*
16. Roy Weaver, conversation with JEC, January 1972.
17. This section is from Doran Kopp, "A Brief History of the Turlock Melon Industry" (Senior Seminar paper, SSC, June 1969), with minor extension and revision.—*Ed.*
18. Tony Bettencourt, interviewed by Doran Kopp, 30 April 1969.
19. Joe Espinola, interviewed by Doran Kopp, 6 May 1969.
20. "Turlock Important Shipping Point," TWJ, 15 Nov. 1907, p. 6.
21. Mrs. J. H. Smith, interviewed by Doran Kopp, 22 May 1969.
22. TDJ, 10 Nov. 1964, p. 26.
23. Smith interview.
24. Tony Bettencourt and Carl Bianchini, interviewed at A.T.B. office by Doran Kopp, 30 April 1969.
25. "Meeting was of Great Interest," TWJ, 27 Feb. 1908, p. 1.
26. "A Big Crowd Attends Meeting of Produce Company," TWJ, 27 March 1908, p. 3.
27. "New Packing House Going up Here," TDJ, 9 June 1911, p. 1. Later several members of the Arakelian family moved to Turlock. See index.
28. On his death in 1929, his son Milton took over and expanded the company. When Milton passed away in 1951 his wife Winifred (later, Mrs. E. M. Raney) took charge and operated the company until 1968 when its doors were closed.
29. "Watermelon shipments," TDJ, 28 July 1911, p. 1. See also "Fruit Prospects in the Turlock District," TDJ, 14 July 1911, p. 11.
30. First directors were David F. Lane, M. Furtado, C. C. Carlson, George Scherer, W. H. Lockwood, D. E. Johnson, and Frank McVey. During its later years Realtor H. W. Rickenbacker was president and Attorney William N. Graybiel was secretary-treasurer.—California, Secretary of State, Archives, Corporation File, Inactive. *See also* Helen Hohenthal, "History of the Turlock District," pp. 282-83.
31. Mrs. J. H. Smith, interviewed by Doran Kopp, 22 May 1969.
32. A. T. "Tony" Bettencourt, interviewed by Doran Kopp, 2 June 1969.
33. Bettencourt interview, 2 June 1969.
34. Joe Espinola, interviewed by Doran Kopp, 6 May 1969.
35. Carl Muller in Group Interview, "Agriculture in Stanislaus County," recorded by John E. Caswell, 2 July 1971.
36. Tony Bettencourt interview, 30 April 1969.
37. Mrs. J. H. Smith interview.
38. Carl Muller in "Agriculture in Stanislaus County."
39. Countywide data is from A. A. Jungerman, "Statistical Information on Stanislaus County Agriculture" (1939), Table 9. For the Turlock region, see Turlock Irrigation District, "Comparison of Crops" (annual).
40. Hohenthal, "Turlock District," pp. 286-286n.
41. TID, "Comparison of Crops" (annual).
42. M. L. "Jack" Harmon and Carl Muller, interviewed by JEC, 23 January 1972.
43. Norman Ross, interviewed by JEC, 25 January 1972.
44. Norman Ross interview.
45. Lu Gandolfo, "Stanislaus Canning Industry Started with Pea Packing in 1907," *Modesto Bee,* 12 April 1965, p. B-3.
46. George W. Hume Company, Board of Directors, Minutes, *passim.* Hume file, SSC Archives. Gift of Mrs. Harriet Hume Krusi.
47. Diane Foster, "Hume Family—Scottish Castle to Turlock Cannery," TDJ, 18 March 1964, p. 14.
48. G. W. Hume Co., Turlock Cannery, Trial Balance Sheet; All-cannery Inventory, both for 31 December 1911. Hume files, SSC Archives. Gift of Harriet Hume Krusi.
49. Clipping, Hume files, SSC Archives.
50. Robert H. Nicol, article in Turlock Chamber of Commerce Scrapbook, 1921. Reference in clipping to 1917 as the year past.
51. Carl Muller, statement to JEC, 16 January 1972. Muller worked for David Lane at the time, and had direct knowledge of the circumstances surrounding establishment of the firm.
52. Harmon and Muller interview.
53. Mrs. R. L. (Jane) Puccinelli, letter to Hohenthal, 14 August 1971.
54. Jungerman, "Statistical Information," Table 11, "Numbers of Livestock on Farms—1900-1939."
55. Stanislaus County, Agricultural Extension Service, "Acreage and Estimated Value of Crops, Livestock and Livestock Products for the Year 1940" (November 8, 1940; processed), p. 5.
56. A. C. Rapp, interviewed by JEC, 6 October 1971.
57. Enoch S. Christoffersen, interviewed by JEC, 25 June and 26 September 1971.
58. Jungerman, "Statistical Information," Table 1, pp. 1-2.

Chapter XXIII — Agriculture Turns to Science and Technology

1. This description is derived from: University of California, Agricultural Extension Service, *Brief of Land Use Survey of Stanislaus County...Recommendations by County and Community Committees of Farmers.* George H. Sawyer, Chairman, A. A. Jungerman, Secretary, Stanislaus County Land Use Committee, Modesto, 1940 (?), 100 pp.
2. Earl Caswell, Conversation with JEC, 1965.
3. Group Interview, "Agriculture in Stanislaus County, 1930-1971," by JEC, 2 July 1971.
4. Group Interview, "Agriculture in Stanislaus County, 1930-1971," p. 1. In 1971 Hall was a member of the Turlock High School agriculture faculty.
5. Gene Stevenson, *Ibid.,* p. 2.
6. Stanislaus County Dairy Herd Improvement Association, *Forty-eighth Annual Report.*
7. Max Foster's Herds I-IV are counted individually.
8. Stanislaus County Dairy Herd Improvement Association, *Forty-eighth Annual Report.* In 1969 and 1970 Daffy produced over 35,000 pounds of milk and 1400 pounds of butterfat.
9. Group Interview, "Agriculture in Stanislaus County, 1930-1971," pp. 4-5.
10. From Stanislaus County Dairy Herd Improvement Association records, courtesy of the Stanislaus County Farm Adviser's Office.

11. Wally Lindskoog, Interviewed by JEC, 25 Sept. 1971.
12. Lyle A. Baker, D.V.M., *Bovine Health Programming* (Cleveland, Ohio, United Publishing Company, c1968), pp. 16, 18, 27.
13. Lyle A. Baker, speech of May 1971.
14. Baker, *Bovine Health*, pp. 141-150.
15. Based on several conversations between Dr. Baker and the writer.
16. E. E. Stevenson in Group Interview, p. 7.
17. Milton R. Dunk, "The Nulaid Story—an Epic of Change," *Poultry Tribune* 77 (June 1971), pp. 12-19.
18. Dunk, "Nulaid Story," p. 18 (membership) and elsewhere.
19. Valley Fresh Foods, Inc., *Business Summary and Financial Statements, July 1, 1971*, p. 12.
20. Rainbow Farms was west coast distributor for Babcock Poultry Farms of Ithaca, N.Y., and Homer Vilas was the area representative for Dryden Farms males and Kimber Farms females.
21. For the description of the Valley Fresh organization and the developments in egg production I am indebted to Oscar Holt in interviews of 20 July and 26 July 1971. He also showed me through the Rainbow Farms operation.—*Ed.*
22. As of 1971 Lindskoog was hatching chicks in Turlock, using Heisdorf and Nelson bloodlines from the state of Washington. At the Ceres hatchery he was using Hyline stock.
23. Wally Lindskoog, Interviewed by JEC, 25 Sept. 1971.
24. Enoch S. Christoffersen, Interviewed by JEC, 8 Oct. 1971.
25. *Armour News*, Memorandum prepared by editorial office, courtesy of Harold Lovell, October 1971.
26. Christoffersen Interview, 8 Oct. 1971.
27. Christoffersen Interview, 25 June 1971. See also "ICC Approves Cut in Freight Rates...," TDJ, 11 Oct. 1955, p. 1.
28. Christoffersen Interview, 8 Oct. 1971.
29. Turlock Chamber of Commerce, Scrapbook, 1940.
30. "Co-founder of Turkey Show recalls how it all happened," TDJ, 1 Dec. 1964.
31. Turlock Chamber of Commerce, Minutes, 4 January and 1 February 1946.
32. "FWTS Show is Lone Survivor," TDJ, 7 March 1964.
33. "Turkey show dropped as local group cancels annual event," TDJ, 23 June 1966, p. 1.
34. From Doran Kopp, "A Brief History of the Turlock Melon Industry" (Senior Thesis, SSC, 1969), with minor editorial changes.—*Ed.*
35. A. T. "Tony" Bettencourt and Carl Bianchini, Interviewed by Doran Kopp, 30 April 1969.
36. Joe Espinola, Interviewed by Doran Kopp, 6 May 1969.
37. Donald J. Smith, Interviewed by Doran Kopp, 22 May 1969.
38. Bettencourt and Bianchini Interview.
39. Espinola Interview.
40. Assuming approximately half the Stanislaus County acreage was south of the Tuolumne River. See Stanislaus County Agricultural Service Reports for years given.
41. Cling Peach Advisory Board, "Orchard and Production Surveys, Zone 8," years cited. Cling peaches are the canning peaches *par excellence*, although some freestones are canned.
42. California Canning Peach Association, *Annual Report, 25th*, 1961 Season, 1960 summary. Henceforth referred to as CCPA:
43. "Gross Returns vs. Total Costs for Cling Peaches 1925 to 1970," *Cling Peach Almanac, 1972*, opposite September calendar.
44. Cling Peach Advisory Board, "Varieties by Varietal Group by Code Numbers," Rev. 7/20/70. Annotated by M. L. Harmon.
45. Norman Ross, Interviewed by JEC 15 February 1972. Mr. Ross is Specialist, Tree Crops, in the Stanislaus County Agricultural Extension Service.
46. Norman Ross, Interviewed by JEC 25 January 1972.
47. Carl Muller in Harmon and Muller Interview.
48. California Cling Peach Association, *Annual Report, 1961.* 1960 Summary.
49. "Machines Stand Ready to Take Over if Needed," *Modesto Bee*, 12 September 1971, p. F-6.
50. CCPA, *Annual Report*, 1961. 1957 and 1958 summaries.
51. Information courtesy of Susan (Mrs. Leo) O'Brien.
52. CCPA, *Annual Report*, 1961. 1960 summary.
53. "Economic Problems Plagued Growers in '71," *Modesto Bee*, 26 December 1971, pp. F3-4.
54. Stanislaus County Agricultural Extension Service, Total Acreage of Principal Fruit and Nut Crops, 1939-1969 (compiled for use in this volume).
55. Earl W. Caswell, interviewed by JEC, 23 Jan. 1972.
56. Norman Ross, interviewed by JEC, 25 January 1972. On frost control and Nonpareil, see Earl W. Caswell interview.
57. Caswell interview.
58. "Spectacular Growth Pattern," *Almond Facts*, November-December 1971, p. 15.
59. Caswell interview, and *Almond Facts*, p. 15.
60. "Wine Sales Boom, but Growers Could Run into Trouble," *Modesto Bee*, 28 January 1972, p. D-6.
61. Formerly Chairman, Bushberry Advisory Board.
62. Bushberry Advisory Board, *Annual Report, 1962-63 Marketing Season*, p. 1.
63. Work on the cryogenic process was undertaken jointly by the Departments of Agricultural Engineering and Food Science at the University of California—Davis, and the United States Department of Agriculture's Agricultural Research Laboratory at Albany, California.

Chapter XXIV — A Businessman's History of Turlock, 1940-1971

1. California. Controller. *Annual Report of Financial Transactions Concerning Cities of California, 1959/60; 1964/65; 1969/70*; various pages.
2. Enoch S. Christoffersen, conversation with JEC, 4 Jan. 1972.
3. Christoffersen, conversation with JEC, 6 Jan. 1972.
4. Chamber of Commerce of Turlock, Minutes, 27 June 1949. Members of the Industrial Committee at that time were Enoch Christoffersen, chairman; Lamar Jackson; Thornton Snider; John Souza; Jess Blaker; P. Leroy Peterson; and Hale.
5. Industrial Survey Associates, "Industrial Payrolls for Turlock..." (January 1950), 40 leaves.
6. Chamber of Commerce, Minutes, 16 Feb. 1951.
7. Chamber of Commerce, Minutes, 30 April 1951.
8. Enoch Christoffersen, interviewed by JEC, 8 Oct. 1971. Also, California, Secretary of State, Corporation files, active.
9. Chamber of Commerce, Minutes, 19 July 1954 and following. "Industrial Division is formed by Chamber," TDJ, 4 June 1954, p. 1.
10. Chamber of Commerce, Minutes, 20 Sept. 1957. Orville Gross was vice chairman; M. S. Johnson, secretary; and W. F.

Fredine, treasurer.—"C of C Industrial Division Elects," TDJ, 8 June 1954.

11. TDJ clipping, about Dec. 1962, on Enoch Christoffersen's resignation after fourteen years as chairman of the Industrial Committee and Division. Also W. F. "Fred" Fredine, interviewed by JEC, 11 Oct. 1971.

12. See Chapter XXX, "Turlock Wins a College."

13. Fredine interview. Fredine was at first president and later treasurer of the Show. The Show's Board worked closely with the Chamber of Commerce down to the last year or two of its existence, sharing office space and clerical help.

14. Walter O. "Ted" Thompson, Jr., was chairman of the Board, and Donald L. "Chevrolet" Smith was secretary.—W. O. Thompson, Jr., interviewed by JEC, 31 Dec. 1971. *See also* Chamber of Commerce, Executive Committee, Minutes, 11 Dec. 1962.

15. Turlock Chamber of Commerce, "Industrial Park Questionnaire." Filed with Board Minutes for 9 Sept. 1968.

16. Varco-Pruden by this time had risen to be the third largest metal building manufacturer in the world. Its 142,000 square-foot plant employed 150 people.

17. Jack Phillips, interviewed by JEC, 31 Dec. 1971.

18. Phillips interview.

19. Page 4.

20. "Turlock's Building Boom," TWJ, 10 Feb. 1905, p. 1. Final capitalization was $25,000.

21. "Has Done Excellent Business," TWJ, 12 Jan. 1906, p. 1.

22. Advertisement, TWJ, 3 Jan. 1908, p. 1. The original building was later taken over by TID and a second story added. In early 1971 it was occupied by the Turlock office of the Title Insurance and Trust Company (117 West Main).

23. Ira B. Cross, *Financing an Empire: History of Banking in California* (San Francisco, 1927; 4 vols.), II, 696.

24. "Peoples State Bank Strongly Officered," TWJ, 17 Jan. 1908, p. 1.

25. Files of the application for a national bank charter were loaned to the authors by Mrs. Sam Hackett.

26. California, Secretary of State, Corporation files, inactive.

27. J. E. Weaver took the presidency; M. M. Berg remained as vice president, Roy Weaver and Ellen White were bookkeepers, and O. H. Olson was cashier.

28. Cross, *Financing an Empire*, II, 766. Roy Weaver, interviewed by JEC, 21 July 1971.

29. Cross, *Financing an Empire*, II, 777. Ernie Hale, the Ford dealer, D. J. Walton and M. M. Berg were interested, too. A. E. Malberg was the cashier and held the power.—Roy Weaver interview.

30. Roy Weaver, on basis of his personal records. Exception: date of transfer to UCB from Harold Larson, Manager, UCB, from bank records. On 30 January 1930 the First National Bank *in* Turlock was organized as the commercial bank. Peoples State Bank was continued as the savings bank. On 31 August 1939 it was merged into the First National Bank.

31. "Security State Bank's Holders Okeh Merger," *Modesto Bee*, 28 Oct. (?) 1963.

32. California, Secretary of State, Corporation File, active. "Stanislaus-Merced."

33. George G. Voight, a former director of El Capitan, in conversation with JEC.

34. California, Secretary of State, Corporation File, active.

35. Weaver interview.

36. Fredine interview.

37. Enoch Christoffersen, interviewed by JEC, 8 Oct. 1971.

Chapter XXV — Turlock's Religious Enthusiasm

1. Except as otherwise noted, dates of founding of churches and information on their early pastors have been obtained from brief histories published in the *Turlock Journal.*

2. Mrs. Crystal Klein Brown, "Historical Sketch [of the First United Presbyterian Church]," *Church Directory*, 1961 (and later years).

3. Rev. Robert Carrington, Interviewed by Ron Harrelson, 9 May 1969, in Ron Harrelson, "Why Turlock's Many Churches" (Graduate Seminar Paper, Department of History, SSC, 1969), p. 11.

4. Mrs. Molly Frost, interviewed by Ron Harrelson, 20 May, 1969, *ibid.*, pp. 18-19.

5. Fred Tamimi, telephone conversation with John E. Caswell, autumn 1971.

6. Harrelson, "Why Turlock's Many Churches," p. 11.

7. Monte Vista Chapel, the Sunday School building at Beulah Covenant, and the sanctuary at Bethel Temple were all designed by Turlock architect James W. B. Shade.

8. Father Manuel V. Alvernaz, interviewed by John E. Caswell, 25 August 1971.

9. Pastor Marvin Seibel, telephone conversation with John E. Caswell, 29 Dec. 1971.

10. Rev. Lloyd E. Hagstrom, interviewed by John E. Caswell, 26 Aug. 1971.

11. Father Manuel V. Alvernaz, interviewed by John E. Caswell, 25 Aug. 1971.

12. Turlock Centennial History Church Questionnaire: Bethel Temple.

13. Gilbert Moody, interviewed by John E. Caswell, 14 Sept. 1971.

14. Turlock Centennial History Church Questionnaire: Bethel Temple.

15. Turlock Centennial History Church Questionnaire: Bethel Temple and Beulah Covenant. Rev. Gordon Rasmussen kindly showed the author through Monte Vista Chapel's unique and efficient church buildings.

Chapter XXVI — Recreation in Turlock

Research notes from City records were kindly furnished the writer by Abe Rojas, City Recreation Director.

1. Information from Les De La Mater, through Abe Rojas.

2. Jack Bliler, "It Started with a Melon Carnival," TDJ, n.d. Hazel Berg Scrapbook.

3. H. D. Channing, "Stanislaus County Fair," MS (1971). Members of the first Board of Directors were Dr. A. J. Ronsse (first fair manager), Eric Oken, Lester Shock, Earl Bradley, E. B. Leduc and H. D. Channing from Turlock; Joe Fritz of Hughson; and R. B. Flower and Sam Cornell from Modesto.

4. Bliler, "Melon Carnival."

5. "Turlock Youth Center," *California Exchange*, February-March 1946, p. 2. Exchange Club Scrapbook.

6. "Youth Center Dedication in Formal Rites," TDJ, 25 Feb. 1942, p. 2. For photographs, see TDJ, 24 Feb. 1942, p. 1. Exchange Club Scrapbook.

7. *California Exchange*, Feb.-March 1946, p. 2.

8. Other members of the Commission were Ed Frank, John Pitman, Robert Lee, G. D. Godfrey, Edwin Washburn, and Ray Hume.—City of Turlock, Council, Minutes, 15 April 1947. See also the Minutes for 4 and 18 March 1947.

9. Turlock Council, Minutes, 6 May and 14 Oct. 1947; 6 Jan. 1948.

10. Turlock Council, Minutes, 1 Nov. 1949. Members of the Executive Committee were Roy M. Day, Arthur Crowell, Ed Leduc, John Arakelian, and Lowell Jessen.

11. Turlock Council, Minutes, 16 Jan. 1951.

12. Turlock Council, Minutes, 19 Dec. 1950 and elsewhere.

13. Turlock Council, Minutes, 16 Feb. 1954; 6 June, 18 Sept. 1956; 19 March, 2 April, 3 Sept., 3 Dec. 1957; 21 May, 5 Aug. 1958.

14. Turlock Council, Minutes, 7 Dec. 1960; 17 Jan., 21 Feb., 5 Dec. 1961; 2 April, 1962. See also 2 April 1963, 4 April 1964.

15. Turlock Council, Minutes, 14 Sept. 1962; 5 Feb., 20 Aug. 1963; 4 Jan. 1966.

16. Abe Rojas, telephone interview by John E. Caswell, 11 Oct. 1971.

17. Abe Rojas, interviewed by John E. Caswell, 27 Dec. 1971.

18. "S. F. Writer Points to Turlock as Model City Under Crusading Mayor," TDJ, clipping from about 1956-57.

19. Rojas interview.

20. John G. Wing, telephone interview by John E. Caswell, 28 Dec. 1971.

21. Mrs. Arnold Richard, telephone interview by John E. Caswell, 28 Dec. 1971, as well as the editor's own recollections.

22. Glenn M. Haldeman, interviewed by John E. Caswell, 22 Dec. 1971.

23. Glenn M. Haldeman Memoranda (5 unnumbered leaves). Mr. Haldeman was for several years treasurer of the Turlock Senior Citizens, Inc.

24. Otto E. Zimmerman, "History of Turlock Exchange Club," MS, p. 2.

25. Walter F. Commons, "History of Turlock Senior Center: Turlock, the City that Cares (3 pp., mimeographed, n.p., n.d.), p. 2.

26. Haldeman interview.

27. Haldeman Memoranda; Commons, "Turlock Senior Center," p. 1. Other members of the committee were: Axel Hallberg, assistant chairman; Glenn Haldeman, secretary-treasurer; Julius Huntsman; Alice Graf; Emma Carlson; and Vada Stewart.

28. Haldeman Memoranda. Compare Commons, "Turlock Senior Center, p. 1.

29. Haldeman Memoranda. Date of notification to City that the Senior Citizens were no longer interested was 26 Oct. 1968.

30. Commons, "Turlock Senior Center," p. 2; Haldeman Memoranda.

31. Donated by Mrs. Selma Berg and Miss Hazel Berg, the widow and daughter of early-day merchant M. M. Berg.

32. Commons, "Turlock Senior Center," p. 3.

Chapter XXVII – Organizing for Community Service

The section on the Turlock Grange is excerpted from Jacqueline Harris, "The History of the Turlock Grange" (Senior Thesis, Department of History, SSC, 1971).

1. Material on the Tuesday Reading Club down to 1963 is based on Helen (Mrs. Vernon) Thornburg, "Notes for Talk on History of Tuesday Reading Club, September 24, 1963." Her paper in turn was based on the club's archives.

2. TDJ, 10 Dec. 1955.

3. TDJ, 17 March 1956.

4. Mrs. Alice Phillips, interviewed by JEC, 27 Dec. 1971.

5. "Organization of Woman's Club Slated Friday," TDJ, 18 March 1958.

6. Turlock Woman's Club Yearbooks, 1959-60, 1970-71.

7. TDJ, 28 November 1949.

8. Alvin Turner, Jr., Secretary, Grange Company, Inc., interviewed by Jacqueline Harris, 19 May 1971.

9. *Modesto Bee*, 24 September 1934, and TDJ, 1 October 1934. In 1933 and 1934 there was a general revival of the Granges of the area, and the establishment of new ones. The first to be reorganized was the Ceres Grange on 27 April 1933. Dates of foundation of other granges were: Keyes, 7 June 1933; Gratton, 2 August 1933; Hilmar, 13 October 1933, all by M. B. Stearns. Mountain View, 30 April 1934, by E. R. Parrish. Delhi was founded over a decade later, on 17 September 1948, by Edwin Koster. Source: Helen Kisling, Secretary, Gratton Grange, telephone conversation with JEC, 24 February 1972.

10. TDJ, 10 October 1934.

11. Turlock Grange, Minutes, 7 December 1935.

12. Turlock Grange, Minutes, 10 December 1935.

13. TDJ, 24 February 1949.

14. Turlock Grange, Minutes, 23 September 1952.

15. Effie (Mrs. Ernest) Freeman, interviewed by Jacqueline Harris, 1 June 1971.

16. Turlock Grange, Minutes, 9 September 1952.

17. TDJ, 17 April 1950.

18. TDJ, 14 November 1950.

19. TDJ, 15 March 1951.

20. TDJ, 26 September 1952.

21. George and Ann Bill, interviewed by Jacqueline Harris, 6 June 1971.

22. TDJ, 18 January 1958.

23. The Gratton Grange's experience was much like that of Turlock, although it was a larger and more active group. It had 50 charter members, and first met in the Gratton School. At its peak it had about 360 members. It then declined until by 1971 it was down to about 125 members. Source: Helen Kisling, telephone conversation with JEC, 24 February 1972.

24. Sylvia Sateren, telephone conversation with JEC, 18 Feb. 1962.

25. Bernice (Mrs. Roy) Weaver, interviewed by JEC, 21 July 1971, based on her review of the Community Concerts Association Minutes and files.

26. *Ibid.*

27. Lamar Jackson, telephone conversation with JEC, 19 February 1972. Information on authors of the plays was kindly furnished by Dr. Douglas McDermott.

28. Bruce Hood, Chairman, Drama Department, SSC, telephone conversation with John E. Caswell, 19 February 1972.

29. Lamar Jackson interview, 19 February 1972.

Chapter XXVIII – Schools of the Region

Credit is due the following individuals for research on and initial drafts of portions of this chapter: Introduction by Helen Hohenthal; Ceres by Fleming E. Haas; Chatom by Helen Hohenthal; Denair by Margaret Harmon; Hilmar by Douglas Boehme; Hughson's early history by William Hurd; the Learning Activity Package program by Marjorie Brooks; Turlock High School in general by Helen Hohenthal; Adult Education and Continuation classes by Joe Debely; the Junior College by Helen Hohenthal. The final draft is the responsibility of the editor.

1. Ceres Clipping Books. Probably from *Modesto Morning Herald*. Clipping Books are in the custody of the Ceres City Clerk.
2. Mrs. A. E. Ulch, "Ceres, Example of County's Progress," *Modesto Morning Herald*, 22 March 1911, in Ceres Clipping Books.
3. Charles N. Whitmore, conversation with JEC, 4 January 1972.
4. Materials for this section were given Miss Hohenthal by Mrs. Pearl Ream, teacher, and Mr. Richard Pritchard, principal of Chatom School.
5. Crystal Klein Brown, letter to Helen Hohenthal, 1930.
6. John H. Pitman, "Over the Years," memorandum for Helen Hohenthal, 1971. Pitman was raised to Superintendent of the District in 1956, retaining the principalship except for one year.
7. Thomas N. Hedden, Memorandum to Helen Hohenthal, 25 February 1972.
8. "The Junior College Bulletin," University of California, *Bulletin*, XI (May 1928).
9. Turlock Junior College, *Circular of Information*, 1920-21.

Chapter XXIX – A Valley Medical Center

Emanuel Hospital is by Mrs. Mernell Thompson. Collins family practice, Lillian Collins Hospital and Medic Alert are by Chrissie (Mrs. Marion C.) Collins. Other topics are by John E. Caswell.

1. Mrs. Albert (Gertrude) Julien, letter to John E. Caswell, 17 July 1971.
2. A partial list of physicians who established themselves in Turlock between 1903 and 1930 was kindly supplied by Mrs. Eric Julien. It has been checked so far as possible against records of the California State Board of Medical Examiners.
3. Valesca Ferguson Smith, "Turlock History Memoir, 1971," p. 6.
4. Helen Hohenthal, memorandum and conversations with John E. Caswell, October 1971.
5. Mrs. Albert Julien, letter to John E. Caswell, 17 July 1971.
6. Mrs. Eric Julien, "Some Doctors Having Practiced in Turlock Since 1900."
7. Mernell Thompson, "History of the Emanuel Hospital," (Senior Thesis, Department of History, SSC, June, 1971), pp. 1-2, *citing* Eva Nelson, R. N., "A Short History of Emanuel Hospital (1947?), pp. 1-2. Except as noted, the history of Emanuel Hospital has been extracted from Mrs. Thompson's thesis.–*Ed.*
8. *Thompson*, p. 3, citing *Nelson*, p. 3.
9. *Thompson*, p. 4, citing Emanuel Hospital, Board of Directors, Minutes, March 1923.
10. Eva Nelson, interviewed by Mernell Thompson, 16 April 1971.

11. Mrs. Marion C. Collins, "History of the Lillian Collins Hospital."
12. Nelson interview.
13. Collins, "History."
14. Leonard Bartlett, [Memorandum on Memorial Hospital], Nov. 1971. Also Memorial Hospitals, "At Your Service," leaflet.
15. *Thompson*, p. 6, citing Board of Directors Minutes, 15 July 1957.
16. Mrs. Marion C. Collins, "History of the Medic Alert Foundation" (1971), 4 pp. The material is an abstract of Mrs. Collins' paper, substantially in her words.
17. George L. Perrine, Community Hospital administrator, telephone interview by J. E. Caswell, 20 Nov. 1971.
18. Photo and caption, *Turlock Daily Journal*, 6 May 1966, p. 4. Also article on "Long-range study set on Community Hospital needs," TDJ clipping, n.d.
19. Perrine interview.
20. Enoch S. Christoffersen, [Notes on Emanuel Hospital: an addendum to Mernell Thompson's paper] (1971).
21. "The New Emanuel," TDJ, 17 Nov. 1971, p. 15.
22. *Thompson*, p. 10, citing Board of Directors, Minutes, 25 Nov. 1968.
23. "Emanuel History: the Mental Health Wing," TDJ, 26 Nov. 1971, p. 8.
24. Christoffersen notes to Thompson paper, p. 12.

Chapter XXX – Turlock Wins a College

This chapter is condensed from a longer memoir written by Stanley T. Wilson at the editor's request. Wilson was editor and publisher of the *Turlock Daily Journal* at the time he was appointed to chair the Chamber of Commerce committee on a college site. Copies of the full memoir are available in the SSC Library.

1. California, Liaison Committee of the California State Board of Education and the Regents of the University of California, *A Study of the Need for Additional Centers of Public Higher Education in California* (1957).
2. California, Division of State Colleges and Teacher Education, *Factors in the Selection of a State College Site in Stanislaus County* (1957), *passim*.
3. The Public Works Board at that time was composed of Finance Director John Peirce, Real Estate Commissioner Fred Griesinger, and Director of Public Works Frank Durkee.
4. The Modesto committee at this time consisted of Chairman Hardie, George Smeath, Harold Pederson, Ted Brandt, Fonnie Bartholomew, V. E. Barton, Robert Bomberger, Lorne Campbell, James Corson, Folke Floden, Don Hammond, Roy Hansberry, Hans Hartman, Martin Ray, Thomas Reneau, Lawrence Robinson, Jr., M. M. Shelley, James Smith and Donald West.
5. Robert Lee was asked to head the barbecue committee, and those working with him were Otto Zimmerman, Donald L. Smith, Louis Bates, and Snider.

Chapter XXXI – Stanislaus State College's Crucial Formative Years

Dr. Caswell came to SSC as Chairman of the Division of Social Sciences, served as Dean of Instruction from 1961 to 1963, and writes from his personal knowledge and observation.

1. J. Burton Vasche, "The Role of Stanislaus State College." Address to the faculty at its first meeting, 1 September 1960. Mimeographed. See pp. 4-8 particularly.
2. Enrollment data courtesy of C. W. Quinley, Registrar.
3. "Students spot 'phonies' in communist, nazi speakers," editorial, TDJ, 2 May 1966, p. 6.
4. The studies referred to are:
   a. George R. Strayer and others, *Report of a Survey of the Needs of California in Higher Education* (Sacramento, 1948).
   b. T. R. McConnell and others, *A Restudy of the Needs of California in Higher Education* (Sacramento, 1955).
   c. H. H. Semans and others, *A Study of the Need for Additional Centers of Public Higher Education in California* (Sacramento, 1957). See pp. 46-50, 106.
5. Gerard J. Crowley, interviewed by John E. Caswell, August 1971.

Chapter XXXII – Politics and Planning

1. "Traffic Streams over New $330,000 Overpass," TDJ, 6 April 1940.
2. Various articles from the TDJ, April 1940, in the Turlock Chamber of Commerce Scrapbooks.
3. Turlock, Council, Ordinances, No. 361, 22 Dec. 1941. II, 213-216, and later ordinances.
4. Turlock, Planning Commission, Minutes, 22 January 1941.
5. Turlock, Planning Commission, Minutes, 23 May 1944 and 11 Sept. 1945.
6. Lamar Jackson Memorandum, April 1971.
7. Turlock, Council, Ordinances, No. 398, 18 June 1946. III, 295-296.
8. Harold Markley, Memorandum, June 1971.
9. *Ibid.*, and Turlock, Council, Ordinances, No. 401, 17 Sept. 1946. III, 305-306.
10. "Fire Chief tells how City's insurance rates can be cut," TDJ, 24 February 1949.
11. John J. Viarengo became Chief of Police 1 April 1952 and was still serving in that post in 1972. The material on the period 1948-1950 was taken from Lamar Jackson, Memorandum, April 1971, with exceptions as noted. The post of Chief Administrative Officer was created by Ordinance No. 438 of 5 July 1949, III, 23-25.
12. Turlock Elementary School Board, Minutes, Sept. 12, 23; Oct. 10; Nov. 9, 14, 22; Dec. 14, 1949.
13. Turlock Chamber of Commerce, Board of Directors, Minutes, 10 Jan. 1950.
14. *Ibid.*
15. John Beatty, "Address for Turlock P.T.A., Jan. 24, 1950." Beatty private files.
16. Paid political advertisement, TDJ, 18 May 1950.
17. Frank V. Mayo to W. F. Garlough, 11 Oct. 1950. Copy in Beatty file.
18. "Parents Refuse to Send Son to 'Unsafe' School," TDJ, 11 Sept. 1957, pp. 1-2.
19. Contemporary memorandum by John Beatty. Beatty files.
20. Letter to John Beatty, 20 Sept. 1957. Beatty files.
21. Memorandum, 29 Sept. 1957. Beatty files.
22. Mrs. Paul J. Carey, letter to State Fire Marshal J. R. Yonkers, 25 Sept. 1957. Beatty files.
23. Portions of letter from C. F. Richter to John H. Beatty, 14 Oct. 1957. Beatty files.
24. Superintendent Robert Lee wrote Dunsmuir for details and received an answer, copies of which are in the Beatty files.
25. Frank V. Mayo, letter to Beatty, 11 Oct. 1957. Beatty files.
26. "Trustees will be Asked to Call Vote on School Units," *Modesto Bee*, 17 Sept. 1957. See also TDJ, same date, p. 1.
27. For detailed quotations, see "Turlock News," *Modesto Bee*, 20 Dec. 1957.
28. "3-2 Board Vote Closes Lowell, Hawthorne Schools," TDJ, 28 Dec. 1957, p. 1.
29. "Young Mother of 4 Manages Time for School Campaign," TDJ, 19 April 1958, p. 10.
30. Channing Freeway Memorandum (1971). Other committee members were: Emory Bonander, L. V. Etnyre, Ray Vandeford, John Guy, Creighton Geer for the Chamber of Commerce; Ed Cobeen, J. F. Osborn for the Merchants Division, Chamber of Commerce; Richard Ward, R. V. Meikle, Planning Commission; Don J. Smith, Richard Weaver, 20-30 Club; Ellis Delbon, R. E. Boesch, Lions Club; W. W. Ferguson, Jack Rickenbacher, Rotary Club; Dr. O. D. Ellefson, Arthur G. Crowell, Exchange Club; Ruth H. Farmer, Soroptimists. Freeway Highway Committee of Turlock, Minutes, 25 Oct. 1954. W. W. Ferguson, Secretary. Turlock City Archives.
31. Ray Carter, "Statement to the Press" (1957), p. 1. Turlock City Archives.
32. Freeway Committee Minutes, 25 Oct. 1954. City Archives.
33. Harold F. Wise Associates, "Consideration of Alternate Routes for the Construction of U.S. Route 99 Freeway at Turlock, California, November 11, 1954." City of Turlock Archives.
34. Freeway Committee, Minutes, 12 November 1954; and Carter, "Statement to the Press," p. 2.
35. "Turlock's Convenience also Must Be Considered in Freeway," TDJ ed., 16 Nov. 1954, p. 6.
36. "Freeway Committee asks State to offer two or more Routes," TDJ, 4 March 1955, p. 1. *See also* Freeway Committee Minutes, 3 March 1955.
37. "City will Oppose Overpass Idea for Freeway," *Modesto Bee*, 18 January 1956. For Brown's offer, see Carter, "Statement to the Press," p. 3.
38. Channing Freeway Memorandum.
39. "Ex-councilman raps 'Pitifully silly' Officials on 99 Route," *Modesto Bee*, 23 June 1956, p. 21.
40. "Committee Rejects Closer By-pass of Turlock Freeway," TDJ, 28 June 1956, p. 1. Also Carter, "Statement to the Press," p. 3.
41. "Group is Forming to Oppose By-pass Route of Freeway," TDJ, 29 June 1956, p. 1.
42. California, Division of Highways, "Freeway Presentation, 18 July 1956. File X-STA-4-A. *Also* its "Public Hearings on Alternate Proposals...July 18, 1956." Verbatim Transcript. Pp. 38-40, *passim.*
43. Carter, "Statement to the Press," p. 3. Freeway Committee Minutes, 2 August 1956.
44. Carter, "Statement to the Press," p. 3. Freeway Committee Minutes, 22 August. R. E. Boesch, Letter to Division of Highways, Stockton, 8 November 1956. City Archives.
45. "Freeway Subcommittee Views Plans for 'Route K,'" TDJ, 22 February 1957. Carter, "Statement to the Press," p. 4.
46. "Freeway Committee Goes for Route Paralleling SP," *Modesto Bee*, 19 March 1957.

47. Freeway Committee to City Council, 19 March 1957. *Also* R. M. Carter, Chairman, to City Council, 19 March 1957.
48. Carter, "Statement to the Press," p. 5.
49. Channing Memorandum.
50. California, Highway Commission, "Hearing on the Turlock Freeway..., Turlock, 1 Dec. 1959," *Passim.*
51. Jack Bliler, "Route G Freeway Chosen," TDJ, 17 Dec. 1959, p. 1.
52. Enoch S. Christoffersen, "Report." [Prepared for use in this volume.] Pp. 2-3.
53. For the recommendation to purchase, see Turlock, Planning Commission, Minutes, 12 April 1956.
54. Turlock, Planning Commission, Minutes, 14 June 1956. *Also* statement of Planning Director Dan Avila to JEC, 1971.
55. "New Business: What to Allow Stirs Debate," *Modesto Bee*, 12 Oct. 1962, p. B-3.
56. A copy of the brochure is in the FORWARD TURLOCK Minutes, Chamber of Commerce Archives.
57. FORWARD TURLOCK, Minutes, 14 November 1961.
58. "Downtown Turlock—Some Years Away," *Modesto Bee*, 12 Oct. 1962, p. B-3. *See also* article in TDJ, 23 Oct. 1962, and *Modesto Bee* for a drawing and more on the plan, 9 Nov. 1962.
59. "City Council Takes a Look at FTI Plan, Stalls Action," TDJ, 5 Dec. 1962, p. 1.
60. "Some FTI Items Listed in City's Tentative Plans," TDJ, 14 Dec. 1962, p. 1.
61. "Mayor will Push Meeting of Downtown Study Panel," TDJ, 27 Dec. 1962, p. 1.
62. Turlock Chamber of Commerce, Minutes, 8 July 1968.

SELECT LIST OF SOURCES

This list acknowledges various institutions and scores of individuals who have furnished information for this volume. It will also furnish residents of the Turlock region a convenient checklist of individuals consulted. For printed materials, readers are invited to check the appropriate chapter footnotes.

ARCHIVES

California State Archives.
Chamber of Commerce of Turlock.
Fin de Siecle Company.
Stanislaus County. Clerk-Recorder.
Stanislaus State College. Library.

Turlock. City Clerk.
Turlock Elementary School Board.
Turlock Irrigation District.
University of California. Bancroft Library.

INTERVIEWS

The following interviews range from those which have been taped and transcribed to informal conversations. The earliest were made about 1921, the latest in 1972. The principal interviewers are mentioned by surname only. They are Helen Hohenthal, Sarah Sergis Jackson, Tony Kocolas, Ramon Desagun, Geraldine Johnson, Carolyn Larson, Howard Whipple, Victoria Yonan, and John E. Caswell.

Abraham, Bob. Yonan, April 1962; Jackson, 1971.
Adams, Albert J. Jackson, 1971.
Adams, Isaac, M.D. Hohenthal, 1930.
Adams, Mrs. Sarah. Jackson, 1971.
Adams, W. D. Whipple, 8 Aug. 1921.
Ahlberg, Levi. Larson, 1958.
Alexander, Cyrus. Yonan, 1961–1962.
Ahlem, Clarence. Johnson, 17 Nov. 1968; Desagun, 30 July 1970, 29 Aug. 1970; Larson, Nov. 1971; Caswell, 30 Dec. 1971.
Ahlem, William. Caswell, 8 Dec. 1971.
Aibara, Nisaburo. J. Carlyle Parker and Esther Noda, Mr. and Mrs. Emory Fleming, Jr., translators, 22 May 1971.
Alvernaz, Father Manuel V. Caswell, 25 Aug. 1971.
Andrino, Elizabeth (Mrs. Steve). Hohenthal, 1972.
Arakelian, George. Hohenthal, July 1971.
Bache, Dallas C., Sr. Kocolas, 18 May and 3 June 1971; Caswell, 27 July 1971.
Badal, Rev. A. B. Jackson, 1971.
Baddell, Mr. and Mrs. Jerry. Jackson, 1971.
Badell, Sam. Yonan, April 1962.
Balswick, Jerry. Caswell, 11 Oct. 1971.
Benjamin, Mrs. Mary Adams. Jackson, 1971.
Bettencourt, A. T. "Tony." Doran Kopp, 30 April and 2 June 1969.
Bianchini, Carl. Doran Kopp, 30 April 1969.
Bill, Mr. and Mrs. George. Jacqueline Harris, 6 June 1971.
Bishop, C. S. Hohenthal, April 1930.
Bodén, Rev. J. O. Whipple, 1921(?).
Bradley, Earl. Hohenthal, Nov. 1971.
Bussinger, Marjorie Carlson. Hohenthal, 25 Feb. 1972.
Carlson, Carl C. Whipple, 27 July 1921.
Carpenter, Hazel Ornberg. Hohenthal, Nov. 1971.
Carrington, Rev. Robert. Ron Harrelson, 9 May 1969; Caswell, 28 July 1971.
Caswell, Earl W. Caswell, 1965; 23 Jan. 1972.
Channing, Harry D., D.D.S. Larson, 22 Oct. 1971; Caswell, 1971–72.
Chapman, Jeff. Caswell, July 1971.
Christoffersen, Enoch S. Caswell, 25 June, 26 Sept., 8 Oct. 1971; 4 and 6 Jan. 1972.

Crane, Horace S. Hohenthal, 1930; Whipple, 26 July 1921.
Crane, Mrs. Horace. Yonan, July 1962.
Crane, Mrs. Stephen. Whipple, 4 Aug. 1921.
Crawford, Mrs. Gene. Hohenthal, 15 Feb. 1972.
Crouch, Mrs. Roy. Mrs. Christine Chance.
Crowell, Esther Hall (Mrs. Arthur G.). Larson, 28 Oct. 1965; Johnson, 26 Oct. 1968.
David, Dr. and Mrs. Elisha. Jackson, 1971.
De Kelaita, Joash J. Jackson, 1971.
De La Mater, Leslie. Mrs. Christine Chance, 1971; Abe Rojas, 1971.
Detling, Mrs. Artie Varner. Hohenthal, Nov. 1971.
Devitt, Weva Wakefield. Hohenthal, Sept. 1971.
Divanian, Kalem. George Arakelian, 18 April 1971.
Dixon, Ted. Caswell, 28 Dec. 1971.
Domecq, Mr. and Mrs. Joe. Caswell, 2 July 1971.
Eashu, John. Jackson, 1971.
Espinola, Joe. Doran Kopp, 6 May 1969.
Essa, Mrs. Florence Adams. Jackson, 1971.
Fernandes, Mrs. Clara Rogers. Hohenthal, Oct. 1971.
Fernandes, J. C. Hohenthal, 1930.
Fernandes, William R. Hohenthal, 1971.
Feuerstein, Berne W. Caswell, 11 March 1972.
Forsmark, Ernest. Hohenthal, 1930.
Fowler, Mrs. Caryl. Caswell, 21 Feb. 1972.
Fox, Mr. and Mrs. Walter. Caswell, 27 July 1971.
Fredine, W. F. "Fred." Caswell, 11 Oct. 1971.
Freeman, Effie (Mrs. Ernest). Jacqueline Harris, 1 June 1971.
Frost, Mrs. Molly. Ron Harrelson, 20 May 1969.
Fulkerth, Mrs. Abigail. Whipple, 29 July 1921; Hohenthal, 1930.
Fulkerth, Loren. Hohenthal, 1930.
Gaddis, Tom. Whipple, 26 July 1921.
Geiger, Rev. Oren H. Caswell, 28 July 1971.
Giddings, Ralph. Whipple, n.d.
Hagstrom, Rev. Lloyd E. Caswell, 26 Aug. 1971; Larson, 22 Oct. 1971.
Haldeman, Glenn M. Caswell, 22 Dec. 1971.
Hall, Don. Caswell, 2 July 1971.
Harmon, M. L. "Jack." Caswell, 23 Jan. 1972.
Heans, Robert. Mrs. Christine Chance, 1971.

Hersh, Rev. Robert. Caswell, 26 Aug. 1971.
Hill, Mrs. Sybil. Caswell, 27 July 1971.
Hocking, T. C. Hohenthal, 12 June 1930.
Hoobyar, Arby, Sr. Yonan, April 1962.
Hoobyar, Sargis. Yonan, April 1962.
Hood, Bruce. Caswell, 19 Feb. 1972.
Hultberg, Nels O. Whipple, 12 Aug. 1921.
Hupp, Lincoln A. Caswell, 1972.
Ishihara, Matsunosuke. Mrs. Esther Noda, 27 May 1971.
Isaac, Mrs. Mae. Jackson, 1971.
Jackson, Lamar. Caswell, 19 Feb. 1972.
Jacobs, Mr. and Mrs. Alex. Jackson, 1971.
Jessup, Theodore. Mrs. Christine Chance, 1931.
Johnson, Harry. Desagun, 31 July 1970.
Johnson, Irene (Mrs. P. W.). Caswell, 24 Mar. 1972.
Johnson, Pete. Whipple, 6 Aug. 1921.
Johnson, Swan. Larson, 12 April 1931.
Jorgensen, Mr. and Mrs. Homer. Caswell, 21 Feb. 1972.
Kisling, Helen. Caswell, 24 Feb. 1972.
Lamsa, George. Yonan, Feb. 1962.
Larson, Mr. and Mrs. Carl. Caswell, 11 Dec. 1971.
Lazar, Mr. and Mrs. Harvey. Jackson, 1971.
Le Cussan, Bernard. Whipple, 19 Aug. 1921.
Lee, Raymond R. Caswell, 26 Dec. 1971.
Lindgren, Esther Hallner (Mrs. Magnus). Johnson, 24 Oct. 1968.
Lindskoog, Wallace N. Caswell, 25 Sept. 1971.
Long, Florence Lowe (Mrs. James). Hohenthal, 14 Feb. 1972.
Lucas, Mr. and Mrs. Grant T. Caswell, 21 Feb. 1972.
Lundell, M. J. Larson, 5 Apr. 1931.
Mar Shimun, Gen. David d'Beth. Yonan, Feb. 1962.
Mar Shimun, Lady Surma. Yonan, Feb. 1962.
Mar Shimun, Theodore d'Beth. Yonan, Feb. 1962.
McCauley, Jack. Mrs. Christine Chance, 1971.
McGill, A. L. Whipple, 17 Aug. 1921.
Markley, William H. Caswell, 26 Sept. 1971.
Moline, Helen. Johnson, 6 Nov. 1968; Larson, 22 Oct. 1971.
Moody, Gilbert. Caswell, 14 Sept. 1971.
Moosekian, Betty Azhderian (Mrs. Shawn). George Arakelian, 15 Apr. 1971; Hohenthal, Nov. 1971.
Morrison, Opal Wilson. Hohenthal, 1971.
Moyle, J. Mark. Hohenthal, June 1930.
Muller, Mr. and Mrs. Carl W. Caswell, 2 July 1971.
Nelson, Eva. Mernell Thompson, 16 Apr. 1971.
Nelson, Miss Jean. Hohenthal, 1971.
Noda, T. Hohenthal through Mary Noda, 1930.
Odishoo, Louis. Yonan, March 1962.
Osborn, Belle (Mrs. Henry). Hohenthal, 1929.
Osborn, E. B. Whipple, 4 Aug. 1921.
Osborn, Will H. Whipple, 5 Aug. 1921.
Oshana, Rev. Manno. Yonan, 1961–1962.
Paul, Joash. Jackson, 1971.
Paul, Nicholas. Jackson, 1971.
Perrine, George L. Caswell, 20 Nov. 1971.

Perry, Stella. Mrs. Christine Chance, 1971.
Peters, George. Yonan, Dec. 1960; Jackson, 1971.
Phillips, Mrs. Alice. Caswell, 27 Dec. 1971.
Phillips, Jack. Caswell, 31 Dec. 1971.
Porter, Florence Lander. Whipple, 1921.
Powell, Eben. Hohenthal, 10 Jan. 1972.
Rapp, A. C. "Pat." Caswell, 6 Oct. 1971.
Rasmussen, Rev. Gordon F. Caswell, Aug. 1971.
Richard, Marion (Mrs. Arnold). Caswell, 28 Dec. 1971.
Rojas, Abe. Caswell, 11 Oct. 1971, 27 Dec. 1971.
Ross, Norman. Caswell, 25 Jan. 1972.
Rude, Everett. Hohenthal, 19 Feb. 1972.
Santos, John A. Hohenthal, June 1930.
Sargis, William. Jackson, 1971.
Sateren, Sylvia (Mrs. Don). Caswell, 18 Feb. 1962.
Schmidt, William H. Hohenthal, Feb. 1972.
Seibel, Pastor Marvin. Caswell, 29 Dec. 1971.
Sekine, Mura. Mrs. Esther Noda, 20 May 1971.
Service, Estella Updike. Hohenthal, June 1930.
Silva, Irene Cole. Hohenthal, 14 Feb. 1972.
Smith, J. Winter. J. Carlyle Parker, 25 Feb. 1971.
Smith, Rose (Mrs. J. H.). Doran Kopp, 22 May 1969; Hohenthal, 20 Feb. 1972.
Smith, Valesca (Mrs. J. E.). Johnson, 14 Nov. 1968.
Sorenson, Mrs. Anna. Hohenthal, Aug. 1929, June 1930.
Sperry, Fyrne Brier. Hohenthal, Dec. 1971.
Spielman, Mrs. Lillian Shimmon. Jackson, Oct. 1971.
Stevenson, E. E. "Gene." Caswell, 2 July 1971.
Strange, Roger. Caswell, 21 Feb. 1972.
Strauss, Sam. Whipple, 1921(?); Hohenthal, Apr., May 1930.
Swanson, Warner. Johnson, 7 Nov. 1968.
Tamimi, Fred. Caswell, 1971; Jackson, 1971.
Tharp, Mrs. Maude Varner. Hohenthal, Nov. 1971.
Thompson, W. O. "Ted," Jr. Caswell, 31 Dec. 1971.
Tillner, Reynold. Hohenthal, 1971.
Torosian, Rudy. Hohenthal, Nov. 1971.
Turner, Alvin, Jr. Jacqueline Harris, 19 May 1971.
Turner, Fletcher. Hohenthal, 14 Feb. 1972.
Valle, Raul. Caswell, 1 Nov. 1971.
Voight, George G. Caswell, Oct. 1971.
Waite, Bert. Hohenthal, Feb. 1972.
Ward, William. Whipple, 1920.
Weaver, Bernice (Mrs. Roy). Caswell, 21 July 1971.
Weaver, Roy. Caswell, Jan. 1972.
Whitmore, Charles N. Caswell, 13 Sept. 1971; 4 Jan. 1972.
Wing, John G. Caswell, 28 Dec. 1971.
Wood, Col. E. Hohenthal, June 1930.
Yomiye, Hobuo. Mrs. Esther Noda, 1971.
Yonan, Joe K. Jackson, 1971.
Yonan, Keena. Yonan, April 1962; Jackson, 1971.
Yosiph, Mrs. Shaul. Jackson, 1971.
Youngdale, Esther (Mrs. Frank, Sr.). Johnson, 8 Nov. 1968.
Zierenberg, Mrs. Ruth. Caswell, 27 July 1971.

MANUSCRIPTS AND EPHEMERA

(A line preceding a title refers to the author listed above.)

Armour News. Memorandum prepared by editorial office for Caswell. Oct. 1971. Courtesy Harold Lovell.

Arakelian, George. Notes. 15 April 1971.
Azhderian, Beatrice. My Trip from Egypt. 1930.

Azhderian, Mihran. Questionnaire Notes for Hohenthal, recorded by Beatrice Azhderian. 1930.

Bache, Naomi. Letter to other former settlers of Delhi. 30 Jan. 1970.

Bartlett, Leonard. Memorandum on Memorial Hospital. To Caswell. Nov. 1971.

Berg, Hazel. Memory Book. [Assembled for her father, M.M. Berg.]

Beulah Covenant Church. *History Horizons, 1902-1962.* 1962. Pamphlet.

Boehme, Douglas. Notes on Hilmar Schools. To Hohenthal. 1971.

Bollakis, Andrew. Questionnaire Notes. 1971.

Bolter, Mrs. Alfred H. Information on Keyes Grange.

Bratten, Kennard C. Notes to Christine Chance and John E. Caswell. 1971.

Brooks, Marjorie. Hughson High School's Learning Activity Package. To Hohenthal. 1971.

Broughton, J. R. Letter to Hohenthal. 5 June 1930.

Brown, Crystal Klein (Mrs. Walter M.). "Historical Sketch [of First United Presbyterian Church]." *Church Directory, 1961.*
_____. Letter to Hohenthal. 1930.

Brown, Walter. Letter and Notes to Hohenthal. 1930.

Channing, Harry D., D.D.S. Stanislaus County Fair. 1971. MS.
_____. Freeway Fight. 1971. MS.

Christoffersen, Enoch S. Notes on Emanuel Hospital: an addendum to Mernell Thompson's thesis. 1971.

Collins, Chrissie (Mrs. Marion C.). History of the Lillian Collins Hospital. 1971.
_____. History of the Medic Alert Foundation. 1971.

Commons, Walter F. History of Turlock Senior Center: Turlock, the City that Cares. 3 pp, processed, n.d.

Crowell, Esther Hall (Mrs. Arthur G.). Notebooks on the early Swedish settlers and the Hultberg Land Office.

Debely, Joseph S. THS Adult Education and Continuation Classes. To Hohenthal. 1971.

Eddy, Arthur J. Letters and Notes to Hohenthal on Early Turlock and Denair. 1930.

Fernandes, Ida Vincent (Mrs. Wm. R.). Notes to Hohenthal. Dec. 1971.
_____. Letter to Caswell. 7 May 1971.

Fernandes, Wm. R. Questionnaire Notes. Nov. 1971.
_____. Notes to Hohenthal. 7 Feb. 1972.

Ferreira, Anthony. Questionnaire Notes. Apr. 1972.

Flesoras, John. Questionnaire Notes. 1971.

Fluhr, C. G. Letters to Hohenthal. 16 and 21 June 1930.

Frodelius, Rose Luis. Notes to Hohenthal. Apr. 1972.

Fulkerth, Mrs. Abby. Diary; Notes to Hohenthal, 1921.

Haas, Fleming. Notes to Hohenthal. 1971.

Haldeman, Glenn M. Memoranda. 5 unnumbered leaves. 1971(?).

Harmon, Margaret. Notes to Hohenthal. 1971.

Harrelson, Ron. Why Turlock's Many Churches? Graduate Seminar paper, Department of History, SSC. 1969.

Harris, Jacqueline. The History of the Turlock Grange. Senior thesis, Department of History, SSC. 1971.

Hedden, Thomas N. Memorandum to Hohenthal. 25 Feb. 1972.

Hohenthal, Helen. History of the Turlock District. M.A. thesis, Department of History, University of California. 1930.
_____. Memorandum on Turlock's Hospitals. To Caswell. Oct. 1971.

Hultberg, Nels O. Letters and Notes to Hohenthal. 1929-1930.

Hurd, William. Notes on early Hughson schools. To Hohenthal. 1971.

Iwata, Buddy T. Commencement Address, Stanislaus State College. 13 June 1970.
_____. Note to Esther Noda. 7 June 1971.

Johnson, Helen Goodrich. Letters, historical papers, and pictures of Lander family.

Julien, Gertrude (Mrs. Albert). Letter to Caswell. 17 July 1971.

Julien, Mabel (Mrs. Eric). Some Doctors Having Practiced in Turlock since 1900.

Kelly, R. E. Letter to Hohenthal. May 1930.

Kocolas, Tony. California's Experiment at Delhi: Evaluation of the Delhi Land Settlement Project, 1920-1931. Graduate paper, Department of History, SSC. 1971.

Kopp, Doran. A Brief History of the Turlock Melon Industry. Senior seminar paper, Department of History, SSC. June 1969.

Lane, David F. Letter to Hohenthal. 18 June 1930.

Larson, Dean W. Bureau of Dairy Service and Bureau of Milk Stabilization. Term paper, SSC. Fall 1961.

McMahon, Henrietta Gomez. Notes to Hohenthal. Dec. 1971.

McVey, June Jane Ripley. Notes. Nov. 1971.

Marvin, John G. Scrapbook, 1851-52. Now lost, it contained clippings on the Indian Commission and the Mariposa Indian War, which he probably wrote for the *Daily Alta California.*

Masuda, Kazuo. Notes on Yamato Colony at Livingston, CA. 18 June 1971.

Mendonsa, Frank S. Questionnaire Notes. Dec. 1971.

Mendonsa, Iria, Tony, Jr., and Jim. Notes to Christine Chance. Jan. 1972.

Menzies, Mrs. Tom. Letter to Hohenthal. June 1930.

Miguel, Helen Manha. Biography of Matthew Manha. Nov. 1971.
_____. Notes on the Lewis brothers. 1972.

Miles, Nolan. A Brief History of the California Wine Industry. Senior thesis, Department of History, SSC. June 1971.

Morchino, Belle Santos. Notes on the Jesse Santos Family. Nov. 1971.

Nelson, Eva, R.N. A Short History of Emanuel Hospital. 1947.

Nelson, Fridolph E. Letter to Hohenthal. 4 Feb. 1972.

[Nevils], Victoria Yonan. A History of the Assyrian People in the Turlock Community. Graduate paper, Division of Social Sciences, SSC. 1962. MS. 71 pp.

Pallios, Mrs. Athena. Questionnaire notes. 1971.

Pantazopulos, Mary. Questionnaire notes. 1971.

Pedras, Frank. Notes, deeds. Hohenthal. March 1972.

Pitman, John H. Over the Years: Memorandum on THS. To Hohenthal. 1971.

Porter, Florence Lander. Papers.

Pritchard, Richard. Notes on Chatom Union School District. To Hohenthal. 1971.

Puccinelli, Mrs. R. L. Letter to Hohenthal. 14 Aug. 1971.

Ream, Pearl. Notes on Chatom Union School District. To Hohenthal. 1971.

Root, Mrs. John W. Clipping books.

Shireman, Terrance. Tidewater Interurban: a Short History of Electric Interurban Service between Modesto and Stockton. Senior thesis, Department of History, SSC. 1970.

Smith, Valesca Ferguson. Turlock History Memoirs. 1971.

Souza, John J., Sr. Questionnaire and Notes. April 1972.

Stanislaus County. Agricultural Extension Service. Total Acreage of Principal Fruit and Nut Crops, 1939-1969. [Compiled for use in this volume.]

Stanislaus County Dairy Herd Improvement Association. *Annual Report, 48th.*

Tavernas, George Steve, children of. Questionnaire notes. 1971.

Thompson, Mrs. Mernell. History of the Emanuel Hospital. Senior thesis, Department of History, SSC. June 1971.

Thornburg, Helen (Mrs. Vernon). Notes for a talk on History of Tuesday Reading Club. Sept. 24, 1963. [Based on the Club's archives.]

Tillner, Reynold. Notes for Hohenthal. 22 Feb. 1972.

Turlock Junior College. *Circular of Information.* 1920–21.

Turlock Woman's Club. *Yearbooks.* SSC Archives, courtesy of Mrs. Alice Phillips.

University of California. Agricultural Extension Service. *Brief of Land Use Survey of Stanislaus County. . .Stanislaus County Land Use Committee, Modesto, 1940(?). 100 pp.

Vasche, J. Burton. The Role of Stanislaus State College. Address to the faculty at its first meeting, 1 Sept. 1960. Processed.

Walsh, Mrs. F. L. Letter to Howard Whipple. 21 Aug. 1921.

Warren, Anne. Letter to George H. Nunes. 1971.

Wilson, Stanley T. How a College was Won. 1971. 149 leaves.

Winning, Rev. E. B. Letter to Hohenthal. 10 April 1930.

Yokoi, Yae. Questionnaire notes. 18 June 1971.

Yonan, Victoria. *See* Nevils, Victoria Yonan.

Yoshida, Yonezo. Address at Japanese American Citizens League dinner honoring Issei, Nov. 1969. [Tape at SSC Library.]

Zimmerman, Otto F. History of Turlock Exchange Club.

INDEX

338

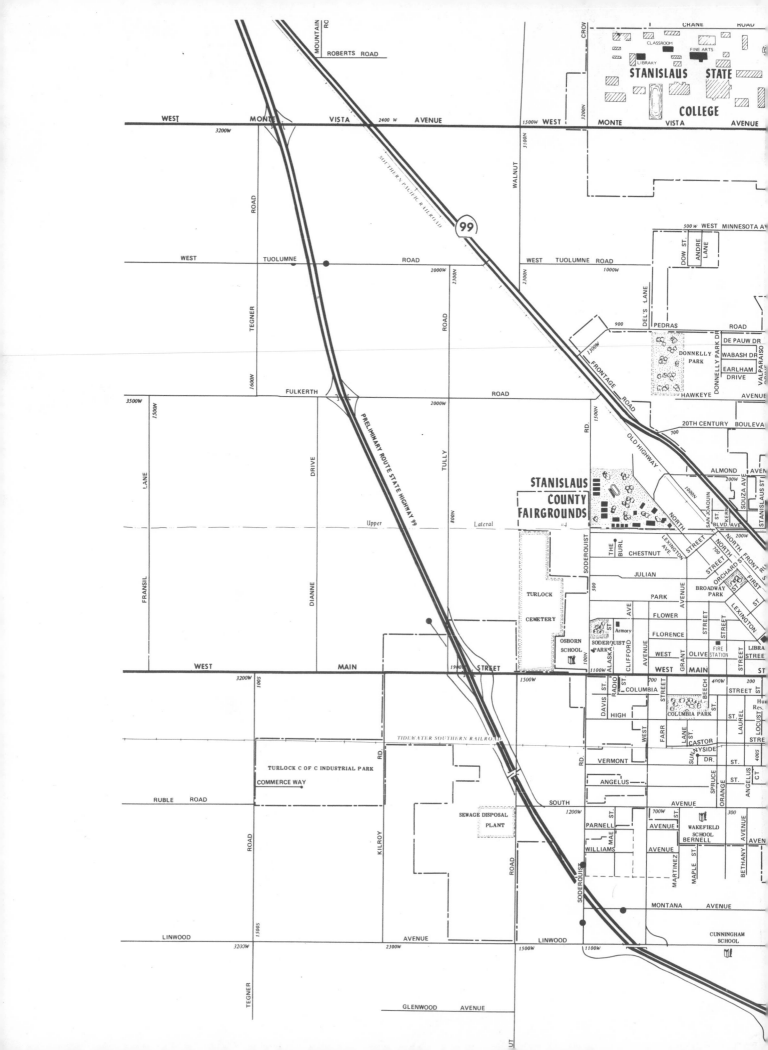